ALL TI
Aire
FRANCE

CW01218457

Freedom of France

French Aires symbolise the freedom of motorhoming because Aires enable motorhomers to travel all year without constraint. France has over 2000 municipally provided motorhome parking areas. This means you can tour France in a camper van with minimal planning nevertheless stopover at official overnight parking every night. French Aires range from small grassy car parks located in remote mountain villages to large motorhome only parking areas at popular tourist destinations. With so many Aires in France to choose from it is good to know that you can make informed choices.

Inspections

Half of the Aires featured in this edition were inspected during 2012 by Meli and Chris, the editors of the guide. This included every Aire listed in the following regions; Normandy, Northern France, Burgundy and Centre. They also drove all over the rest of France inspecting new Aires or those that had closed, moved, or changed in some way. The remainder of the Aires were inspected in the second half of 2010 either by the editors or Keith and Sue Lawrence who undertook inspections in The Mediterranean, Midi Pyrénées, Rhone Alps, Atlantic and Poitou. Research and customer submissions confirmed that the information gained in 2010 was still correct, making this guide the most up-to-date, comprehensive and accurate of its kind. Special thanks to Total who provided their LPG destination list.

Front cover main image: Bogny sur Meuse, Champagne, page 194.

First published in Great Britain by Vicarious Books LLP, 2007. This edition published for 2013.

ISBN: 978-0-9566781-3-3

Editorial Team, Vicarious Books, 62 Tontine Street, Folkestone, Kent, CT20 1JP. www.VicariousBooks.co.uk 0131 2083333
Chief Editor: Meli George
Editor: Chris Doree
Copy editor: Pami Hoggatt
Editorial assistants: Caroline Stacey and Sarah Davis
Design and Artwork: Chris Gladman Design Tel: 07745 856652

MAPS

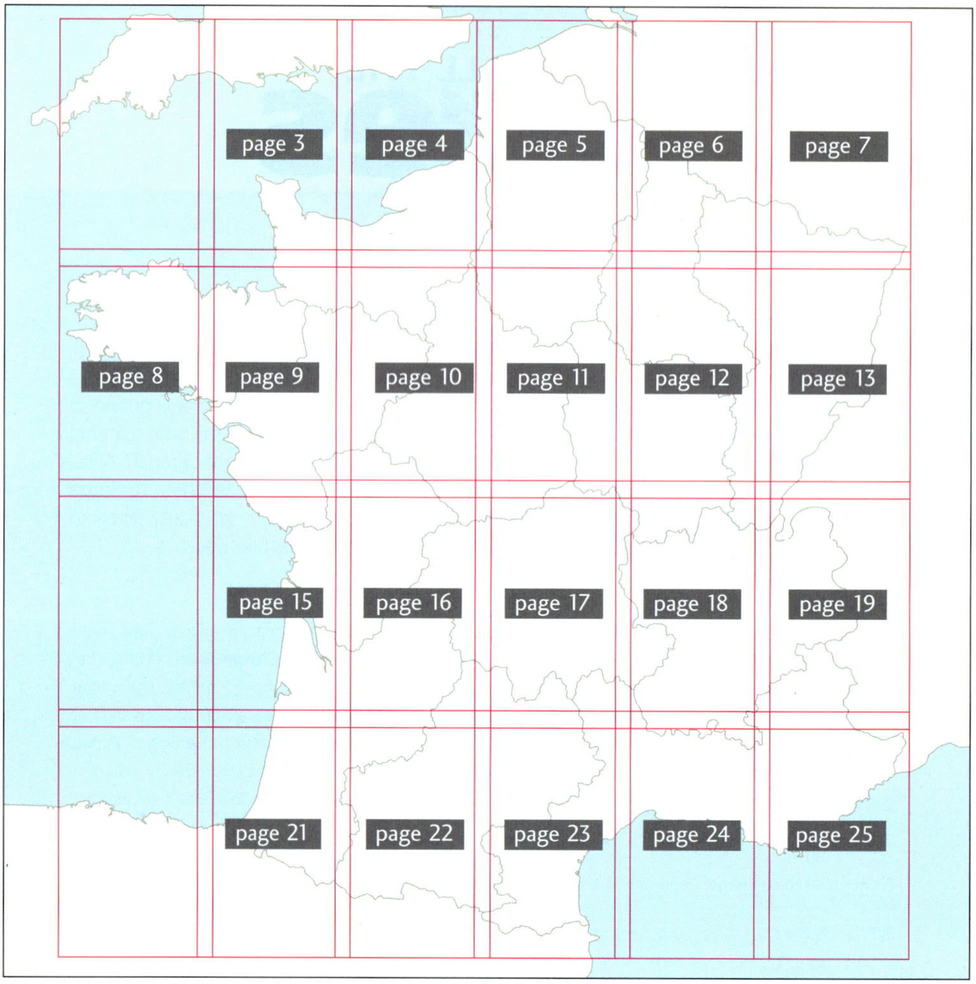

Atlantic Page 41
Brittany Page 89
Burgundy Page 143
Centre Page 163
Champagne Page 193
Eastern France Page 205
Limosusin & Auvergne Page 233
Mediterranean Page 287
Midi-Pyrenees Page 337
Normandy Page 383
Northern France Page 421
Pays de Loire Page 439
Poitou Page 493
Rhone-Alps Page 533
X Closed Aires

Regional borders

Toll motorways and payment points

Non toll motorways

Main dual carriageways

21 pages of maps show the approximate locations of the Aires. For your convenience, a sheet map is available from Vicarious Books. All the regions are colour-coded. For example, Normandy has numbered navy blue boxes as can be seen on the adjacent map and the banner of the example entry below. All regions start at map reference 1 on both the maps and in their corresponding section. For example, Normandy 1 is located at the beginning of the Normandy section and 101 is in the middle. The maps have grid lines and references. Grid references are quoted on the top bar of each Aire listing. Normandy 101 is located at grid reference C3.

AUDERVILLE	↘	101	C3	N49°42.858' W001°56.096'	50440

C
D
E
1
2
3
4
A303
A303
A35
A31
M3
A3
M27
A3(M)
SOUTHAMPTON
Portsmouth
Poole
Bournemouth
Weymouth
Isle of Wight
St Malo
Cherbourg
Caen
St Malo
Bilbao
Santander
Cherbourg
4
4
Guernsey
Sark
Jersey
NORMANDY
101
100
99
98
Tourlaville
94
St-Pierre-Église
Barfleur
CHERBOURG-OCTEVILLE
97
96
95
92
91
St-Vaast-la-Hougue
102
103
88
Valognes
89
90
105
les Pieux
Montebourg
93
104
87
83
84
85
St-Sauveur-le-Vicomte
106
81
82
75
76
73
Barneville-Carteret
107
86
Ste-Mère-Église
79
78
Arromanches-les-Bains
108
la Haye-du-Puits
80
77
109
Isigny-sur-Mer
BAYEUX
N13-E46
Carentan
74
111
Lessay
110
112
Périers
E3-N174
118
119
117
ST-LÔ
64
Balleroy
113
Marigny
114
120
116
Torigni-sur-Vire
121
126
122
62
COUTANCES
115
Tessy-sur-Vire
Villers-Bocage
Montmartin-sur-Mer
123
Gavray
Percy
A84-E401
9

E
F
G
1
2
3
4
M2
Deal
M23
M20
A2
M23
Folkstone
Dover
Dunkirk
Calais
A3
Eurotunnel
A23
A27
Cap Blanc-Nez
Brighton
Newhaven
Hastings
Caen
St Malo
Dieppe
BOULOGNE-SUR-MER
la Touquet-Paris-Plage
Berck
St-Valery-sur-Somme
Ault
le Tréport
Moyenne
NORMANDY
DIEPPE
Blangy-sur-Bresle
St-Valery-en-Caux
Offranville
Londinières
Fécamp
Étretat
Cany-Barville
Doudeville
N27
Neufchâtel-en-Bray
A29-E44
Fauville-en-Caux
Yerville
Tôtes
St-Saëns
Goderville
Criquetot-l'Esneval
A29-E44
D6015
Yvetot
Pavilly
Buchy
Forges-les-Eaux
Lillebonne
A28-E402
LE HAVRE
Quillebeuf-sur-Seine
Duclair
N31-E46
Gournay-en-Bray
Arromanches-les-Bains
A131-E5
Honfleur
Deauville
Routot
Seine
ROUEN
Lyons-la-Forêt
Courseulles-sur-Mer
Oustreham
Pont-Audemer
Fleury-sur-Andelle
N13-E46
A13-E46
Bourgtheroulde-Infreville
Pont-de-l'Arche
D6014
Dozulé
les Andelys
A84-E401-E3
Troarn
LISIEUX
Brionne
A28-E402
Gaillon
CAEN
D613
le Neubourg
Évrecy
N158
St-Pierre-sur-Dives
Touques
Thiberville
D613
N154
Vernon
Villers-Bocage
Dives
Orbec
BERNAY
Beaumont-le-Roger
EVREUX
Livarot
N13
Beaumesnil
Pacy-sur-Eure
A13-E5
10

G
H
I
1
2
3
4
6
6
11
Dunkirk
Calais
DUNKERQUE
Gravelines
CALAIS
Blanc-Nez
Bergues
A16-E40
A25-E42
Wormhout
Steenvoorde
Ardres
Marquise
A26-E15
ST-OMER
D642
Hazebrouck
Kortrijk
Tourcoing
LILLE
Roubaix
Armentières
N42
Lumbres
Desvres
Samer
A16-E402
D901
Fauquembergues
Lillers
N41
Étaples
MONTREUIL
Fruges
BÉTHUNE
Cambrin
Carvin
A23
Pont-à-Marcq
Orchies
Condé-sur-l'Escaut
LENS
Marchiennes
VALENCIENNES
Campagne-les-Hesdin
Hesdin
D939
St-Pol-sur-Ternoise
le Parcq
Vimy
DOUAI
Fort-Mahon-Plage
Crécy-en-Ponthieu
Canche
Avesnes-le-Comte
ARRAS
Denain
Bavay
A2-E19
Le Quesnoy
Auxi-le Château
N25
Beaumetz-lès-Loges
Croisilles
CAMBRAI
Solesmes
Nouvion
St-Riquier
Doullens
D930
D643
St-Valery-sur-Somme
ABBEVILLE
Ailly-le-Ht-Clocher
Bapaume
Landrecies
le Cateau-Cambrésis
Moyenneville
NORTHERN FRANCE
N25
A28-E402
Somme
A16
Villers-Bocage
Albert
A1-E15
A2-E19
Combles
A26-E17
le Catelet
Bohain-en-Vermandois
Oisemont
Corbie
PERONNE
D1029-E44
AMIENS
D1029
Vermand
ST-QUENTIN
VERVINS
A29-E44
Boves
Chaulnes
A29-E44
Aumale
D1029
Poix-de-Picardie
Moreuil
D934
Ham
Nesle
Crécy-sur-Serre
Marle
A29-E44
D1001
Roye
Guiscard
N2
Grandvilliers
Breteuil
Formerie
MONTDIDIER
Lassigny
A1-E15-E19
Chauny
LAON
Forges-les-Eaux
Songeons
Noyon
A16
St-Just-en-Chaussée
D1017
Gournay-en-Bray
N2
Craonne
BEAUVAIS
COMPIÈGNE
SOISSONS
N31-E46
N31-E46
CLERMONT
N31-E46
Aisne
Lyons-la-Forêt
Braine
Auneuil
N2
Fismes
Étrépagny
Noailles
Crépy-en-Valois
Fère-en-Tardenois
D6014
Chaumont-en-Vexin
A4-E50
Villers-Cotterêts
Chantilly
SENLIS
A16
NORTHERN FRANCE
Nanteuil-le-Haudouin
A1-E15-E19
D14
PONTOISE
A4-E50
Giverny
N2
Dormans
Limay
CHÂTEAU-THIERRY
N3
MEAUX
la Ferté-
Montmort-Lucy
1
2
3
4
5
6 7 8
9
10 11
12
13
14
15
16
17
18
19
20
23
24
25
27
30
31
35
39
40
41
42
43 44 45
46
54 55
56
57
58
59
60
63
64
65
66
67
68
69
70
71
72
73
74
75
76
77
78
79
80
81
82
83
84
85
A
X
9
10
10
11
12

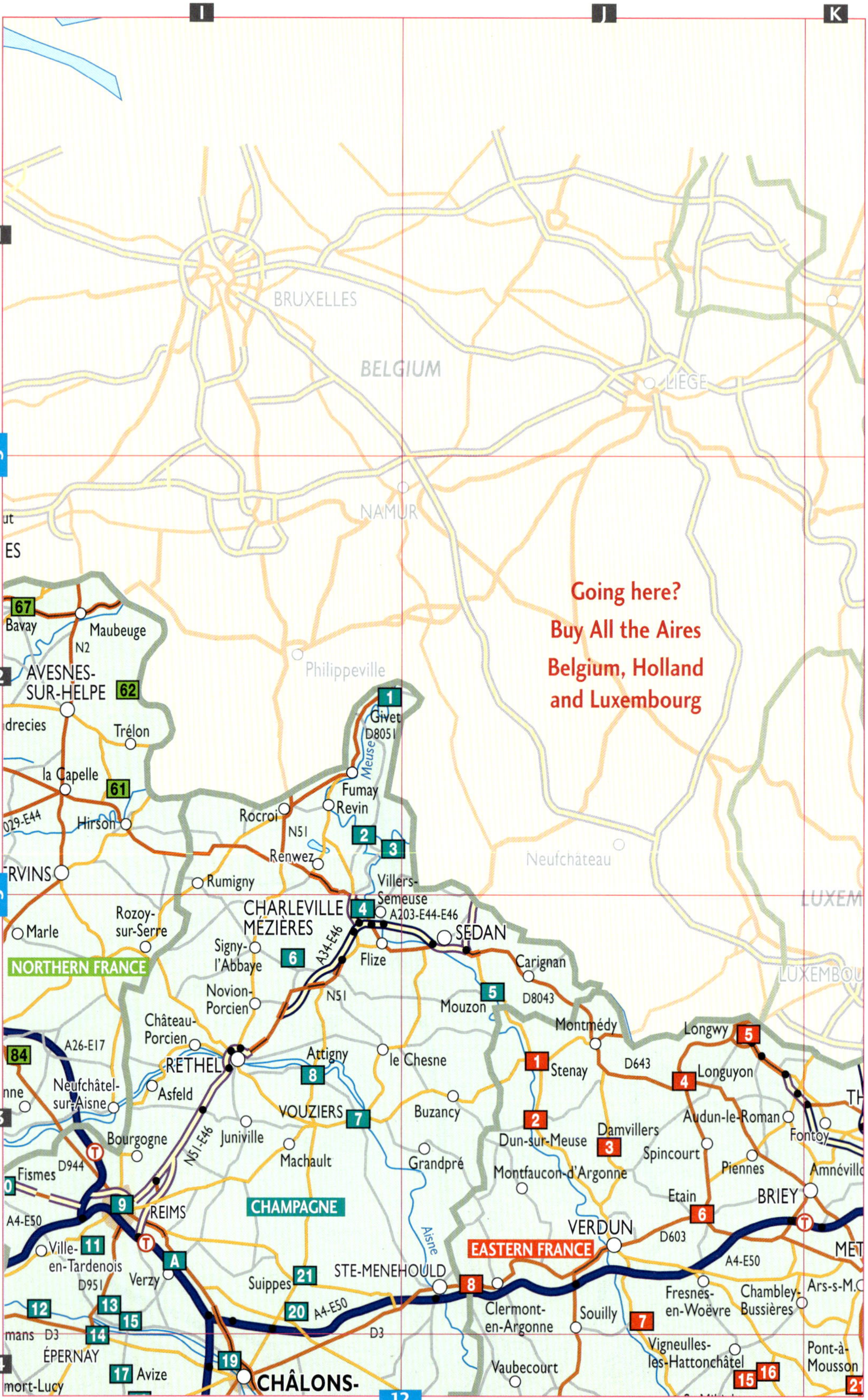

BRUXELLES
BELGIUM
LIÈGE
NAMUR
Philippeville
Neufchâteau
LUXEMBOURG
Going here?
Buy All the Aires
Belgium, Holland
and Luxembourg
Bavay
Maubeuge
AVESNES-SUR-HELPE
Trélon
la Capelle
Hirson
Givet
Fumay
Revin
Rocroi
Renwez
Rumigny
Villers-Semeuse
CHARLEVILLE MÉZIÈRES
SEDAN
Marle
Rozoy-sur-Serre
Signy-l'Abbaye
Flize
Carignan
NORTHERN FRANCE
Novion-Porcien
Mouzon
Montmédy
Longwy
Château-Porcien
RETHEL
Attigny
le Chesne
Stenay
Longuyon
Neufchâtel-sur-Aisne
Asfeld
VOUZIERS
Buzancy
Dun-sur-Meuse
Damvillers
Audun-le-Roman
Fontoy
Bourgogne
Juniville
Machault
Grandpré
Montfaucon-d'Argonne
Spincourt
Piennes
Amnéville
Fismes
REIMS
CHAMPAGNE
Etain
BRIEY
VERDUN
EASTERN FRANCE
Ville-en-Tardenois
Verzy
Suippes
STE-MENEHOULD
Clermont-en-Argonne
Souilly
Fresnes-en-Woëvre
Chambley-Bussières
Ars-s-M.
ÉPERNAY
Avize
CHÂLONS-
Vaubecourt
Vigneulles-les-Hattonchâtel
Pont-à-Mousson
Meuse
Aisne
N2
N51
D8051
A203-E44-E46
A34-E46
D8043
D643
A26-E17
N51-E46
D944
A4-E50
D951
D3
D603

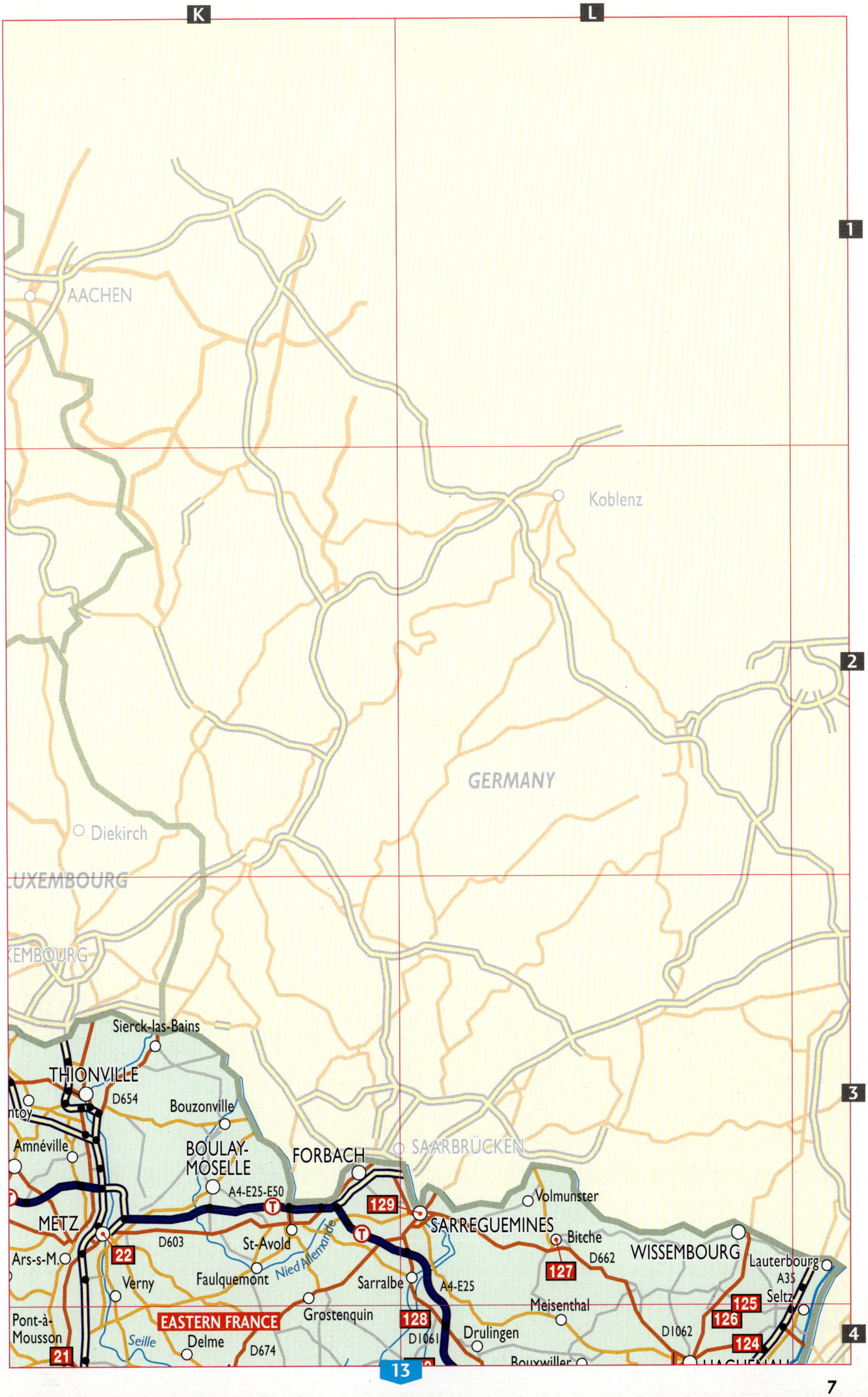
K
L
1
2
3
4
AACHEN
Koblenz
GERMANY
Diekirch
LUXEMBOURG
Sierck-las-Bains
THIONVILLE
D654
Bouzonville
Amnéville
BOULAY-MOSELLE
FORBACH
SAARBRÜCKEN
A4-E25-E50
129
SARREGUEMINES
Volmunster
Bitche
METZ
D603
22
St-Avold
Nied Allemande
Ars-s-M.
Verny
Faulquemont
Sarralbe
A4-E25
127
D662
WISSEMBOURG
Lauterbourg
A35
Seltz
125
126
124
D1062
Meisenthal
Grostenquin
128
EASTERN FRANCE
Pont-à-Mousson
21
Seille
Delme
D674
D1061
Drulingen
Bouxwiller
13

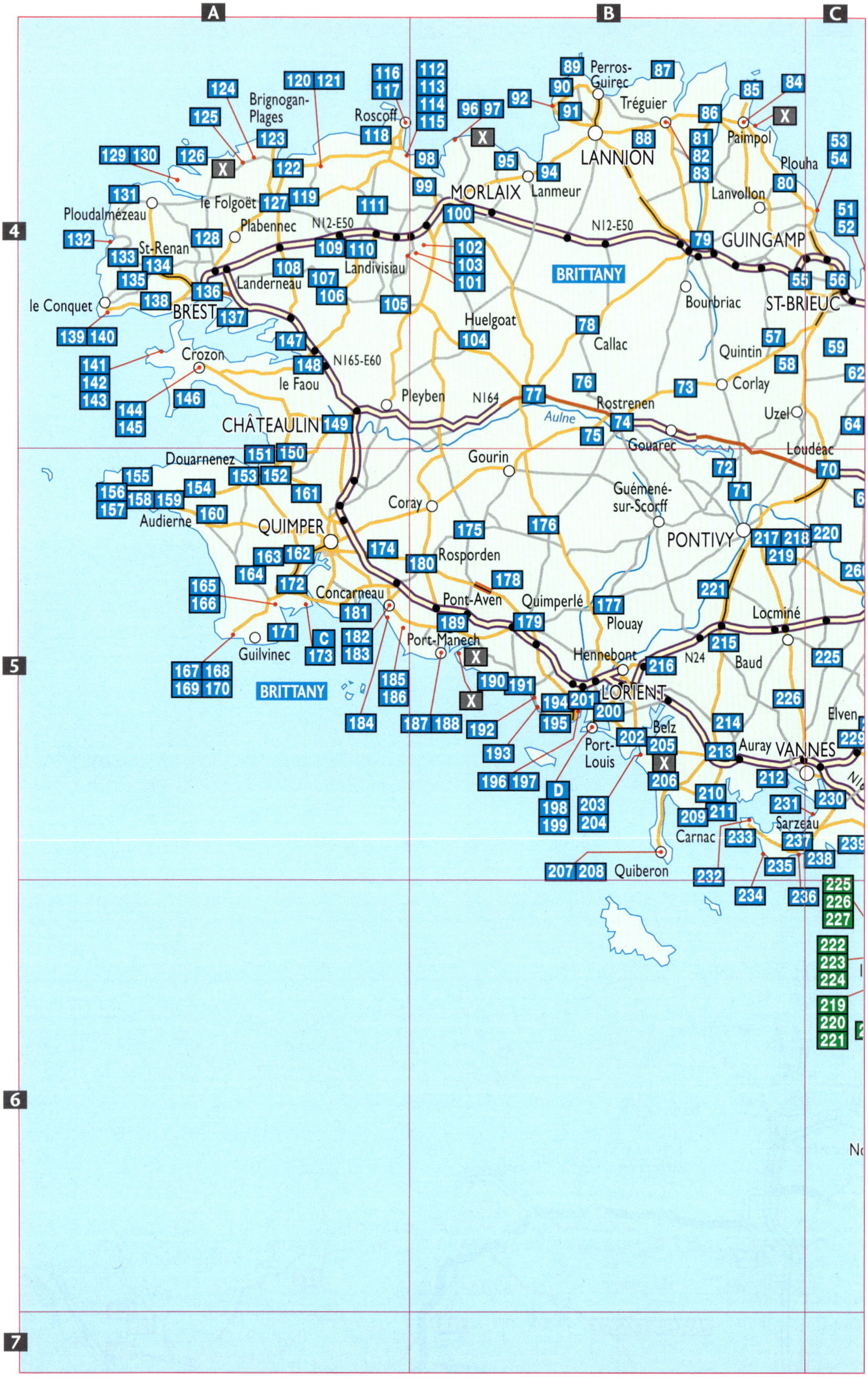

A
B
C
4
5
6
7
Perros-Guirec
Tréguier
Brignogan-Plages
Roscoff
Paimpol
LANNION
Plouha
Ploudalmézeau
le Folgoët
Plabennec
MORLAIX
Lanmeur
Lanvollon
St-Renan
N12-E50
GUINGAMP
Landivisiau
BRITTANY
Landerneau
le Conquet
BREST
Bourbriac
ST-BRIEUC
Huelgoat
Callac
Crozon
N165-E60
Quintin
le Faou
Corlay
Pleyben
N164
Rostrenen
Uzel
Aulne
CHÂTEAULIN
Gouarec
Loudéac
Douarnenez
Gourin
Guémené-sur-Scorff
Coray
Audierne
QUIMPER
PONTIVY
Rosporden
Concarneau
Pont-Aven
Quimperlé
Plouay
Locminé
Port-Manech
Guilvinec
Hennebont
N24
Baud
BRITTANY
LORIENT
Elven
Port-Louis
Belz
Auray
VANNES
Carnac
Sarzeau
Quiberon

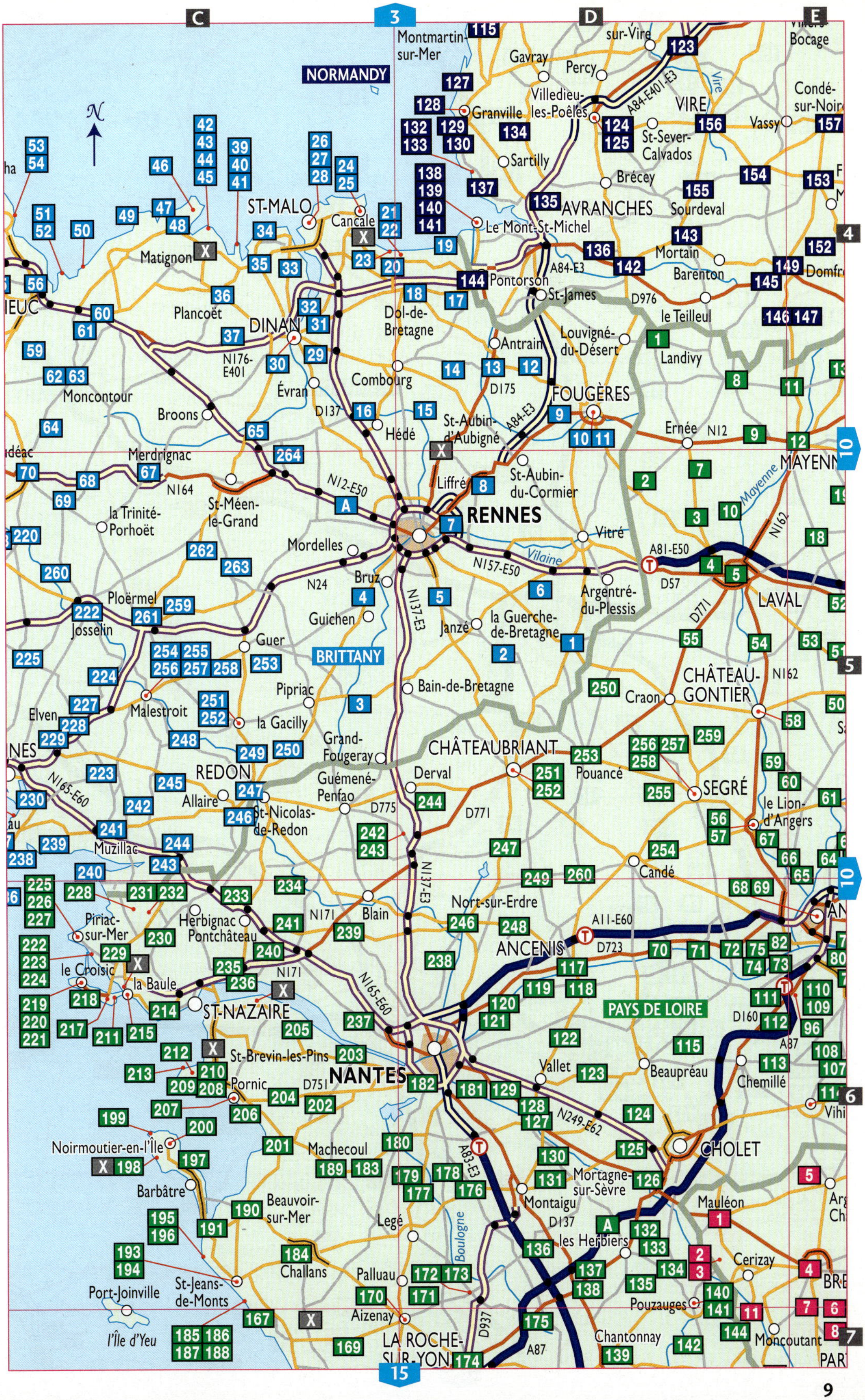

C
3
D
E
NORMANDY
BRITTANY
PAYS DE LOIRE
Montmartin-sur-Mer
Gavray
Percy
sur-Vire
Bocage
Villedieu-les-Poêles
Granville
VIRE
Vassy
Condé-sur-Noireau
St-Sever-Calvados
Sartilly
Brécey
AVRANCHES
Sourdeval
Mortain
Barenton
Domfront
Le Mont-St-Michel
Pontorson
St-James
le Teilleul
Landivy
Louvigné-du-Désert
Antrain
FOUGÈRES
Ernée
MAYENNE
St-Aubin-d'Aubigné
St-Aubin-du-Cormier
Liffré
RENNES
Vitré
Argentré-du-Plessis
LAVAL
ST-MALO
Cancale
Matignon
Plancoët
DINAN
Dol-de-Bretagne
Combourg
Évran
Hédé
Moncontour
Broons
Merdrignac
la Trinité-Porhoët
St-Méen-le-Grand
Mordelles
Bruz
Guichen
Janzé
la Guerche-de-Bretagne
Ploërmel
Josselin
Guer
Malestroit
Elven
Pipriac
la Gacilly
Bain-de-Bretagne
Grand-Fougeray
CHÂTEAUBRIANT
Derval
Pouancé
Craon
CHÂTEAU-GONTIER
SEGRÉ
le Lion-d'Angers
REDON
Allaire
St-Nicolas-de-Redon
Guémené-Penfao
Muzillac
Candé
Blain
Nort-sur-Erdre
ANCENIS
Herbignac
Pontchâteau
Piriac-sur-Mer
le Croisic
la Baule
ST-NAZAIRE
St-Brevin-les-Pins
NANTES
Pornic
Vallet
Beaupréau
Chemillé
Machecoul
CHOLET
Noirmoutier-en-l'Île
Barbâtre
Beauvoir-sur-Mer
Mortagne-sur-Sèvre
Montaigu
Mauléon
Legé
les Herbiers
Challans
Cerizay
Palluau
Pouzauges
St-Jean-de-Monts
Port-Joinville
l'Île d'Yeu
Aizenay
LA ROCHE-SUR-YON
Chantonnay
Moncoutant
A84-E401-E3
A84-E3
D976
D175
N12
N176-E401
D137
N164
N12-E50
N157-E50
N24
N137-E3
A81-E50
D57
D771
N162
N165-E60
D775
N171
A11-E60
D723
D751
N249-E62
D160
A87
A83-E3
D137
D937
Vilaine
Mayenne
Boulogne
Vire
4
5
6
7
10
15

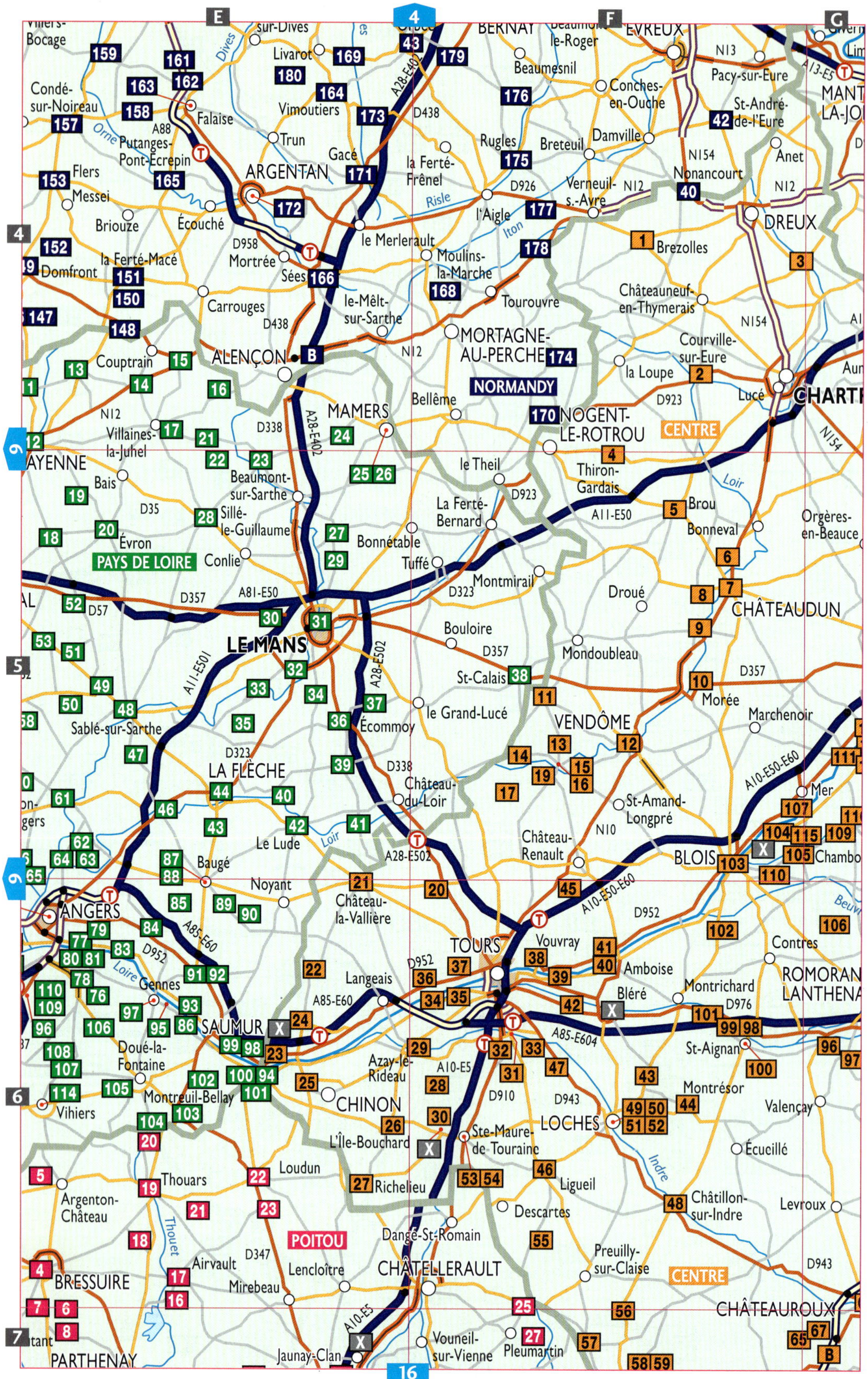
E
4
F
G
Villers-Bocage
Condé-sur-Noireau
Putanges-Pont-Écrepin
Falaise
Livarot
Vimoutiers
Trun
Gacé
BERNAY
Beaumont-le-Roger
Beaumesnil
ÉVREUX
Conches-en-Ouche
Pacy-sur-Eure
St-André-de-l'Eure
MANTES-LA-JOLIE
Rugles
la Ferté-Frênel
Breteuil
Damville
Anet
Nonancourt
Verneuil-s.-Avre
l'Aigle
DREUX
Brezolles
Flers
Messei
Briouze
Écouché
ARGENTAN
le Merlerault
Moulins-la-Marche
Tourouvre
Domfront
la Ferté-Macé
Mortrée
Sées
Carrouges
le Mêlt-sur-Sarthe
MORTAGNE-AU-PERCHE
Châteauneuf-en-Thymerais
Courville-sur-Eure
la Loupe
Lucé
CHARTRES
Couptrain
ALENÇON
NORMANDY
Villaines-la-Juhel
MAMERS
Bellême
NOGENT-LE-ROTROU
CENTRE
MAYENNE
Bais
Beaumont-sur-Sarthe
le Theil
Thiron-Gardais
Brou
Bonneval
Orgères-en-Beauce
Sillé-le-Guillaume
Évron
La Ferté-Bernard
Bonnétable
Tuffé
PAYS DE LOIRE
Conlie
Montmirail
Droué
CHÂTEAUDUN
LE MANS
Bouloire
Mondoubleau
St-Calais
Morée
Marchenoir
Sablé-sur-Sarthe
Écommoy
le Grand-Lucé
VENDÔME
LA FLÈCHE
Château-du-Loir
Mer
St-Amand-Longpré
Le Lude
Château-Renault
BLOIS
Chambord
Baugé
Noyant
Château-la-Vallière
ANGERS
TOURS
Vouvray
Contres
Amboise
ROMORANTIN-LANTHENAY
Gennes
Langeais
Bléré
Montrichard
SAUMUR
St-Aignan
Doué-la-Fontaine
Azay-le-Rideau
Montrésor
Valençay
Vihiers
Montreuil-Bellay
CHINON
LOCHES
L'Île-Bouchard
Ste-Maure-de-Touraine
Écueillé
Thouars
Loudun
Richelieu
Ligueil
Argenton-Château
Descartes
Châtillon-sur-Indre
Levroux
Dangé-St-Romain
POITOU
Airvault
Preuilly-sur-Claise
BRESSUIRE
Mirebeau
Lencloître
CHÂTELLERAULT
CENTRE
CHÂTEAUROUX
Vouneil-sur-Vienne
Pleumartin
Jaunay-Clan
PARTHENAY
A28-E402
A11-E50
A81-E50
A11-E501
A28-E502
A10-E50-E60
A85-E60
A85-E604
A10-E5
N12
N13
N154
N10
D957
D357
D338
D323
D952
D910
D943
D976
D347
D35
D438
D926
D923
D958
Loir
Loire
Indre
Thouet
Risle
Iton
Orne
Dives
16
9
5
6
7

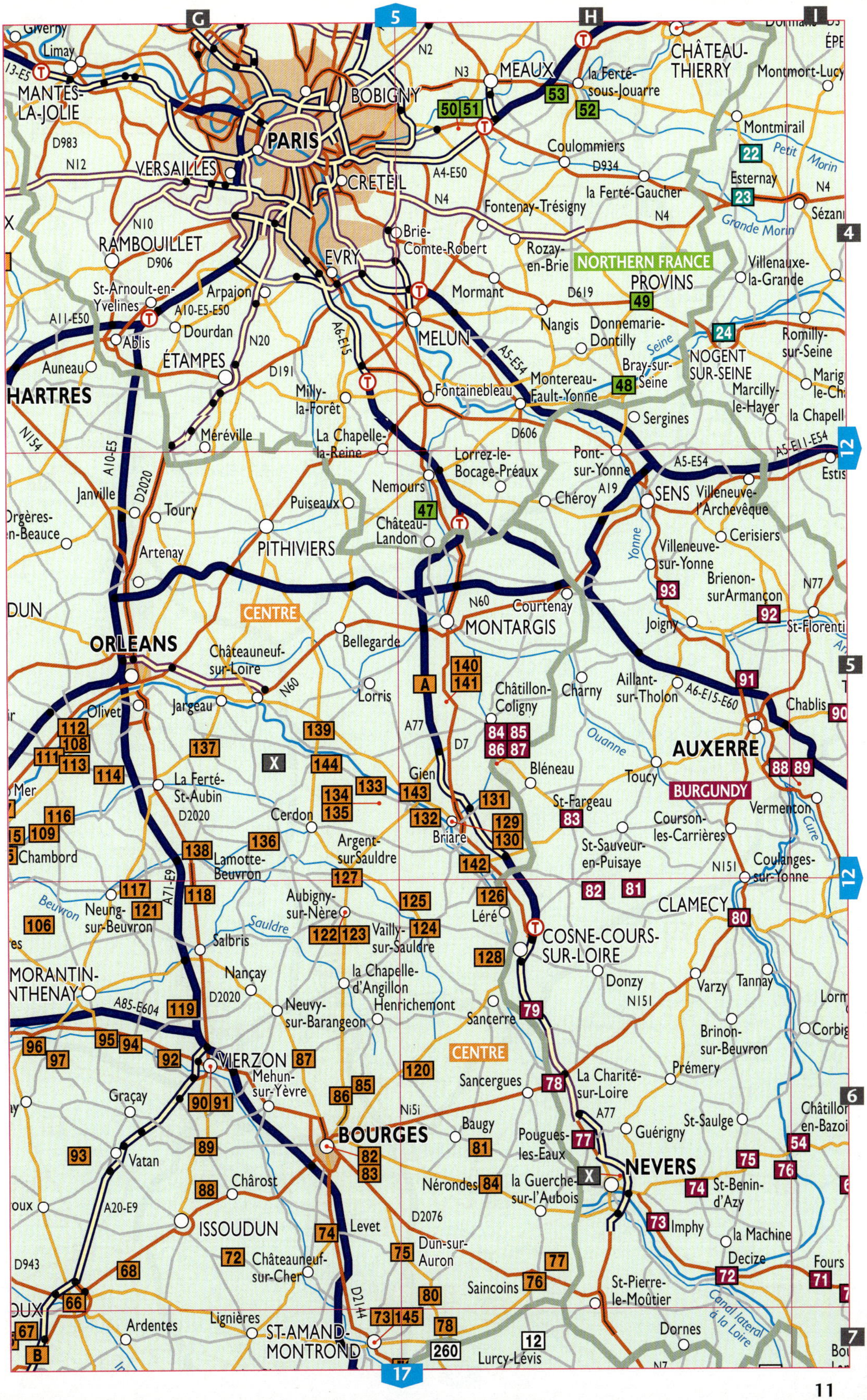

G
5
H
I
PARIS
BOBIGNY
VERSAILLES
CRETEIL
MANTES-LA-JOLIE
Limay
RAMBOUILLET
St-Arnoult-en-Yvelines
Ablis
Arpajon
Dourdan
ÉTAMPES
EVRY
Brie-Comte-Robert
MELUN
Fontainebleau
Milly-la-Forêt
Méréville
MEAUX
la Ferté-sous-Jouarre
CHÂTEAU-THIERRY
Montmort-Lucy
Montmirail
Coulommiers
la Ferté-Gaucher
Esternay
Sézanne
Fontenay-Trésigny
Rozay-en-Brie
Mormant
Nangis
PROVINS
Donnemarie-Dontilly
Bray-sur-Seine
NOGENT SUR-SEINE
Villenauxe-la-Grande
Romilly-sur-Seine
Marcilly-le-Hayer
Montereau-Fault-Yonne
Sergines
NORTHERN FRANCE
Grande Morin
Petit Morin
Seine
CHARTRES
Auneau
Janville
Toury
Artenay
Orgères-en-Beauce
PITHIVIERS
Puiseaux
La Chapelle-la-Reine
Nemours
Château-Landon
Lorrez-le-Bocage-Préaux
Pont-sur-Yonne
Chéroy
SENS
Villeneuve-l'Archevêque
Cerisiers
Villeneuve-sur-Yonne
Brienon-surArmançon
St-Florentin
Joigny
Courtenay
MONTARGIS
ORLEANS
Olivet
Châteauneuf-sur-Loire
Jargeau
Bellegarde
Lorris
CENTRE
Châtillon-Coligny
Charny
Aillant-sur-Tholon
AUXERRE
Chablis
Toucy
Bléneau
Gien
Briare
St-Fargeau
St-Sauveur-en-Puisaye
Courson-les-Carrières
Vermenton
Coulanges-sur-Yonne
BURGUNDY
CLAMECY
La Ferté-St-Aubin
Cerdon
Argent-surSauldre
Lamotte-Beuvron
Chambord
Neung-sur-Beuvron
Aubigny-sur-Nère
Vailly-sur-Sauldre
Léré
COSNE-COURS-SUR-LOIRE
Donzy
Varzy
Tannay
Salbris
Nançay
ROMORANTIN-LANTHENAY
Neuvy-sur-Barangeon
la Chapelle-d'Angillon
Henrichemont
Sancerre
Brinon-sur-Beuvron
Corbigny
VIERZON
Mehun-sur-Yèvre
Sancergues
La Charité-sur-Loire
Prémery
Graçay
Vatan
BOURGES
Baugy
Pougues-les-Eaux
Guérigny
St-Saulge
Châtillon-en-Bazois
NEVERS
St-Benin-d'Azy
Chârost
Nérondes
la Guerche-sur-l'Aubois
ISSOUDUN
Levet
Dun-sur-Auron
Imphy
la Machine
Decize
Fours
Châteauneuf-sur-Cher
Saincoins
St-Pierre-le-Moûtier
Ardentes
Lignières
ST-AMAND MONTROND
Lurcy-Lévis
Dornes
Canal latéral à la Loire
Ouanne
Yonne
Cure
Beuvron
Sauldre
17
12

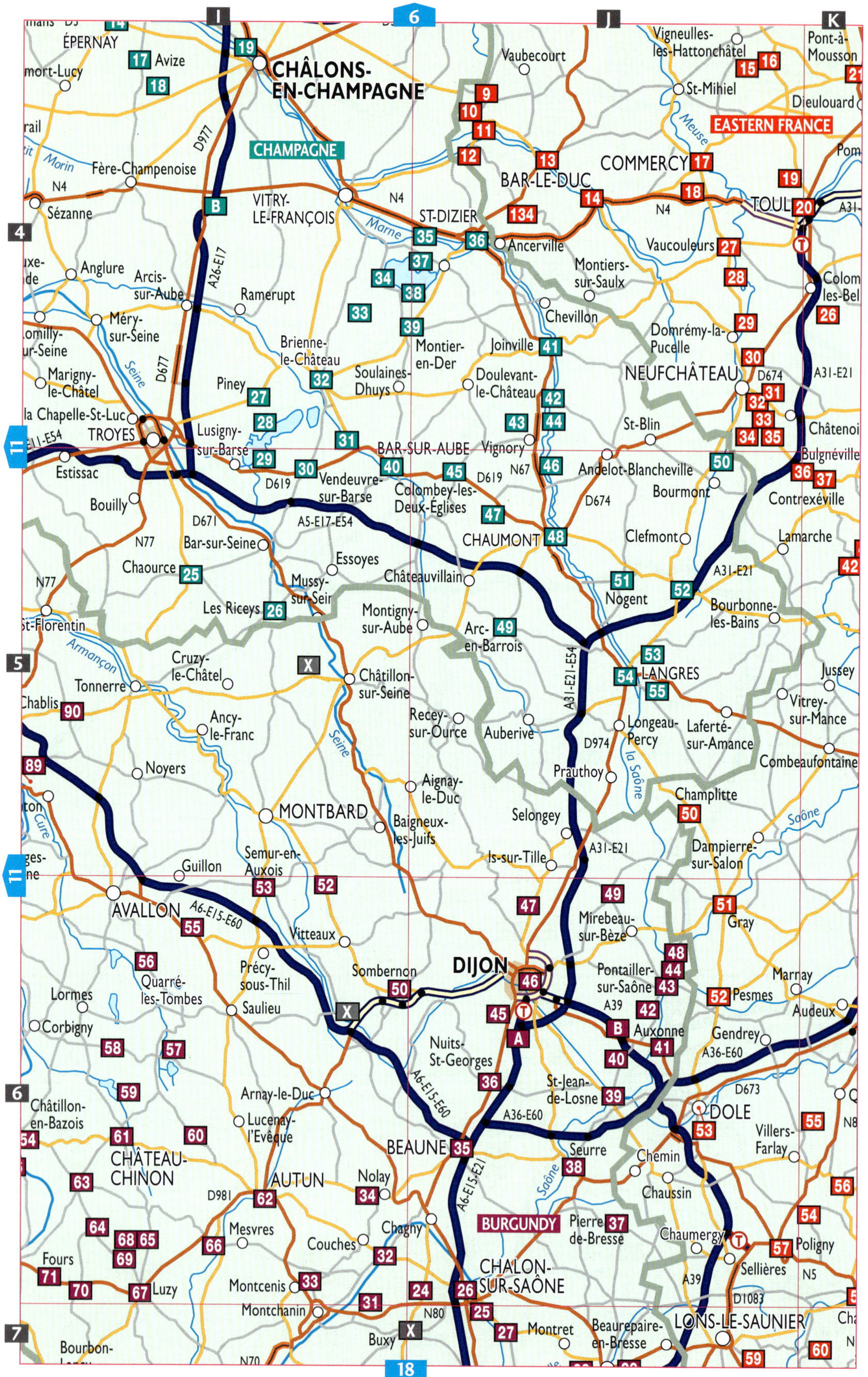
ÉPERNAY
Avize
CHÂLONS-EN-CHAMPAGNE
CHAMPAGNE
Vaubecourt
Vigneulles-lès-Hattonchâtel
Pont-à-Mousson
St-Mihiel
Dieulouard
EASTERN FRANCE
Meuse
Fère-Champenoise
Morin
Sézanne
VITRY-LE-FRANÇOIS
N4
BAR-LE-DUC
COMMERCY
TOUL
ST-DIZIER
Marne
Anceville
Vaucouleurs
Montiers-sur-Saulx
Anglure
Arcis-sur-Aube
A26-E17
D977
Ramerupt
Méry-sur-Seine
Chevillon
Domrémy-la-Pucelle
Brienne-le-Château
Montier-en-Der
Joinville
Marigny-le-Châtel
Seine
D677
Piney
Soulaines-Dhuys
Doulevant-le-Château
NEUFCHÂTEAU
D674
A31-E21
la Chapelle-St-Luc
TROYES
Lusigny-sur-Barse
BAR-SUR-AUBE
Vignory
St-Blin
Châtenois
Estissac
E11-E54
D619
Vendeuvre-sur-Barse
Colombey-les-Deux-Églises
N67
Andelot-Blancheville
Bulgnéville
Bourmont
Contrexéville
Bouilly
D671
A5-E17-E54
CHAUMONT
Clefmont
Lamarche
N77
Bar-sur-Seine
Essoyes
Chaource
Mussy-sur-Seine
Châteauvillain
Nogent
Bourbonne-les-Bains
St-Florentin
Les Riceys
Montigny-sur-Aube
Arc-en-Barrois
Armançon
Cruzy-le-Châtel
Châtillon-sur-Seine
LANGRES
Jussey
Tonnerre
A31-E21-E54
Vitrey-sur-Mance
Chablis
Recey-sur-Ource
Auberive
Longeau-Percy
Laferté-sur-Amance
Ancy-le-Franc
D974
Combeaufontaine
Noyers
Aignay-le-Duc
Prauthoy
la Saône
Champlitte
MONTBARD
Baigneux-les-Juifs
Selongey
Saône
Cure
Semur-en-Auxois
Guillon
Is-sur-Tille
Dampierre-sur-Salon
AVALLON
A6-E15-E60
Mirebeau-sur-Bèze
Gray
Vitteaux
Précy-sous-Thil
Quarré-les-Tombes
Sombernon
DIJON
Pontailler-sur-Saône
Marnay
Lormes
Saulieu
A39
Pesmes
Audeux
Corbigny
Nuits-St-Georges
Auxonne
Gendrey
A36-E60
Arnay-le-Duc
St-Jean-de-Losne
D673
Châtillon-en-Bazois
Lucenay-l'Évêque
DOLE
Villers-Farlay
CHÂTEAU-CHINON
BEAUNE
Seurre
Chemin
Chaussin
AUTUN
Nolay
A6-E15-E21
D981
Mesvres
Chagny
BURGUNDY
Pierre-de-Bresse
Chaumergy
Poligny
Fours
Couches
Sellières
N5
Luzy
Montcenis
CHALON-SUR-SAÔNE
D1083
Montchanin
N80
Montret
Beaurepaire-en-Bresse
LONS-LE-SAUNIER
Bourbon-Lancy
Buxy
N70
I
J
K
6
18
11
4
5
6
7

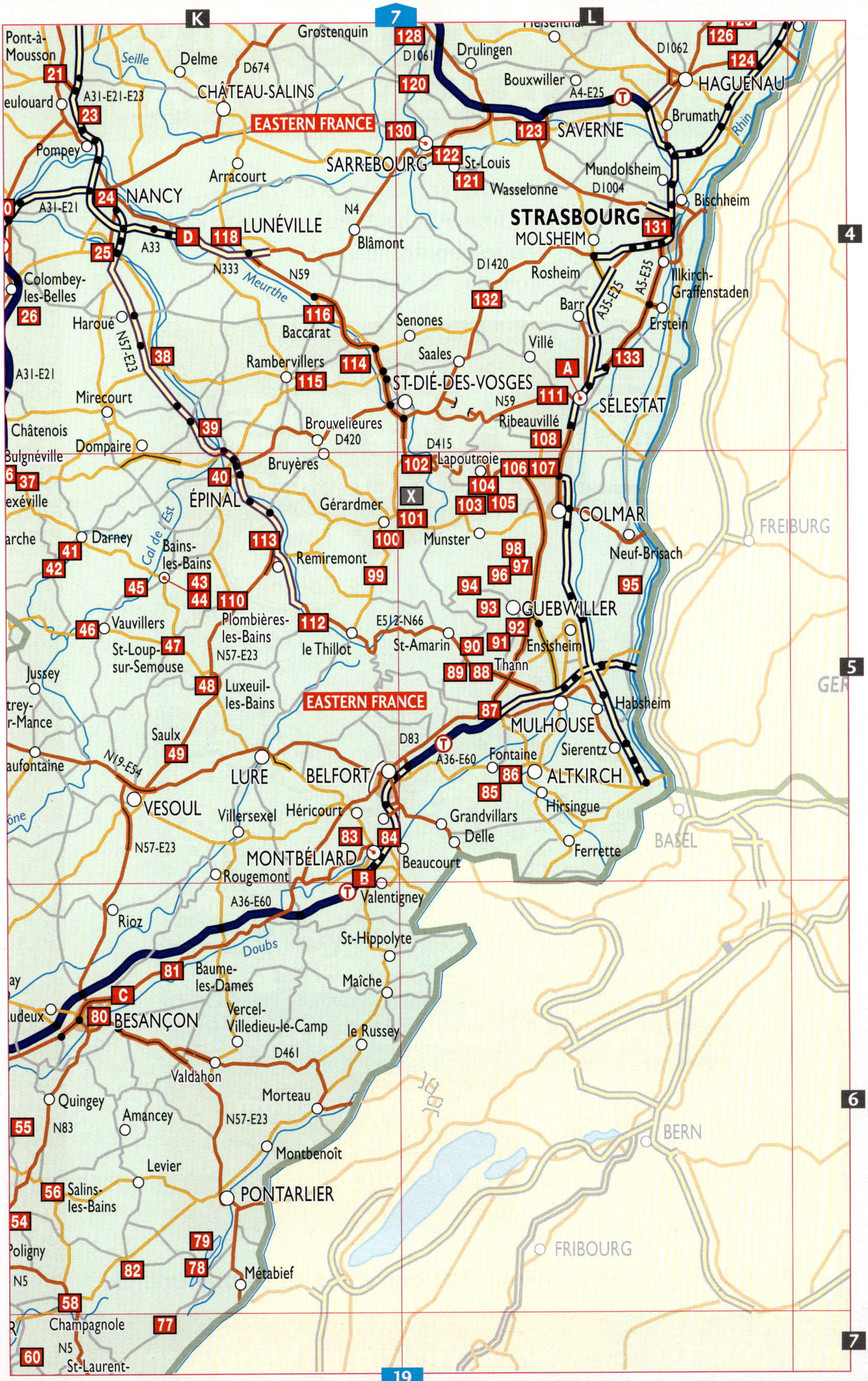

K
7
L
Pont-à-Mousson
Seille
Delme
Grostenquin
Drulingen
D1062
HAGUENAU
D674
D1061
Bouxwiller
A4-E25
CHÂTEAU-SALINS
A31-E21-E23
EASTERN FRANCE
SAVERNE
Brumath
Rhin
Pompey
Arracourt
SARREBOURG
St-Louis
Wasselonne
Mundolsheim
D1004
Bischheim
NANCY
A31-E21
LUNÉVILLE
N4
STRASBOURG
MOLSHEIM
A33
N333
Blâmont
Meurthe
N59
D1420
Rosheim
Illkirch-Graffenstaden
Colombey-les-Belles
A35-E25
A5-E35
Haroué
Baccarat
Senones
Barr
Erstein
N57-E23
Villé
Rambervillers
Saales
A31-E21
ST-DIÉ-DES-VOSGES
SÉLESTAT
Mirecourt
N59
Ribeauvillé
Châtenois
Brouvelieures
D420
Dompaire
D415
Lapoutroie
Bulgnéville
Bruyères
ÉPINAL
Gérardmer
COLMAR
FREIBURG
Darney
Munster
Neuf-Brisach
Canal de l'Est
Bains-les-Bains
Remiremont
GUEBWILLER
Vauvillers
Plombières-les-Bains
E512-N66
Ensisheim
le Thillot
St-Amarin
St-Loup-sur-Semouse
N57-E23
Thann
Jussey
Luxeuil-les-Bains
EASTERN FRANCE
Habsheim
MULHOUSE
Saulx
D83
N19-E54
A36-E60
Fontaine
Sierentz
LURE
BELFORT
ALTKIRCH
VESOUL
Héricourt
Hirsingue
Villersexel
Grandvillars
Delle
N57-E23
BASEL
MONTBÉLIARD
Beaucourt
Ferrette
Rougemont
Valentigney
A36-E60
Rioz
St-Hippolyte
Doubs
Baume-les-Dames
Maîche
BESANÇON
Vercel-Villedieu-le-Camp
le Russey
D461
Valdahon
Morteau
Quingey
Amancey
N57-E23
N83
BERN
Montbenoît
Levier
Salins-les-Bains
PONTARLIER
FRIBOURG
Poligny
Métabief
N5
Champagnole
N5
St-Laurent-
19
4
5
6
7

ATLANTIC
OCEAN
l'Île d'Yeu
Aizenay
LA ROCHE-SUR-YON
Chantonnay
Moncoutant
la Châtaigneraie
Secondigny
Mareuil-sur-Lay-Dissais
Ste-Hermine
Talmont-St-Hilaire
LES SABLES-D'OLONNE
Coulonges-sur-l'Autize
Luçon
FONTENAY-LE-COMTE
Chaillé-les-Marais
Maillezais
PAYS DE LOIRE
la Tranche-sur-mer
NIORT
Ars-en-Ré
Île de Ré
LA ROCHELLE
Courçon
POITOU
Surgères
St Denis-d'Oléran
Tonnay-Boutonne
Fouras
ROCHEFORT
St-Jean-d'Angély
le Château-d'Oléron
Marennes
St-Porchaire
SAINTES
COGNAC
Royan
Cozes
Gémozac
Pons
Archiac
le Verdon-sur-Mer
Soulac-sur-Mer
St-Vivien-de-Médoc
Gironde
LESPARRE-MÉDOC
Mirambeau
Hourtin-Plage
St-Laurent-Médoc
BLAYE
Carcans-Plage
ATLANTIC
Castelnau-de-Médoc
Lacanau-Océan
Lacanau
Ste-Hélène
Carbon-Blanc
BORDEAUX
Floirac
Arès
Gradignan
Cap-Ferret
Arcachon
Audenge
La Brède
la Teste-de-Buch
LANGON
Sanguinet
Belin-Béliet
Villandraut
Biscarrosse
A87
A83
A10-E5
A63-E5-E70
A62-E72
A660
N150
N89
D137
D949
D160
D148
D733
D1215
D6
D106
D1010
D937

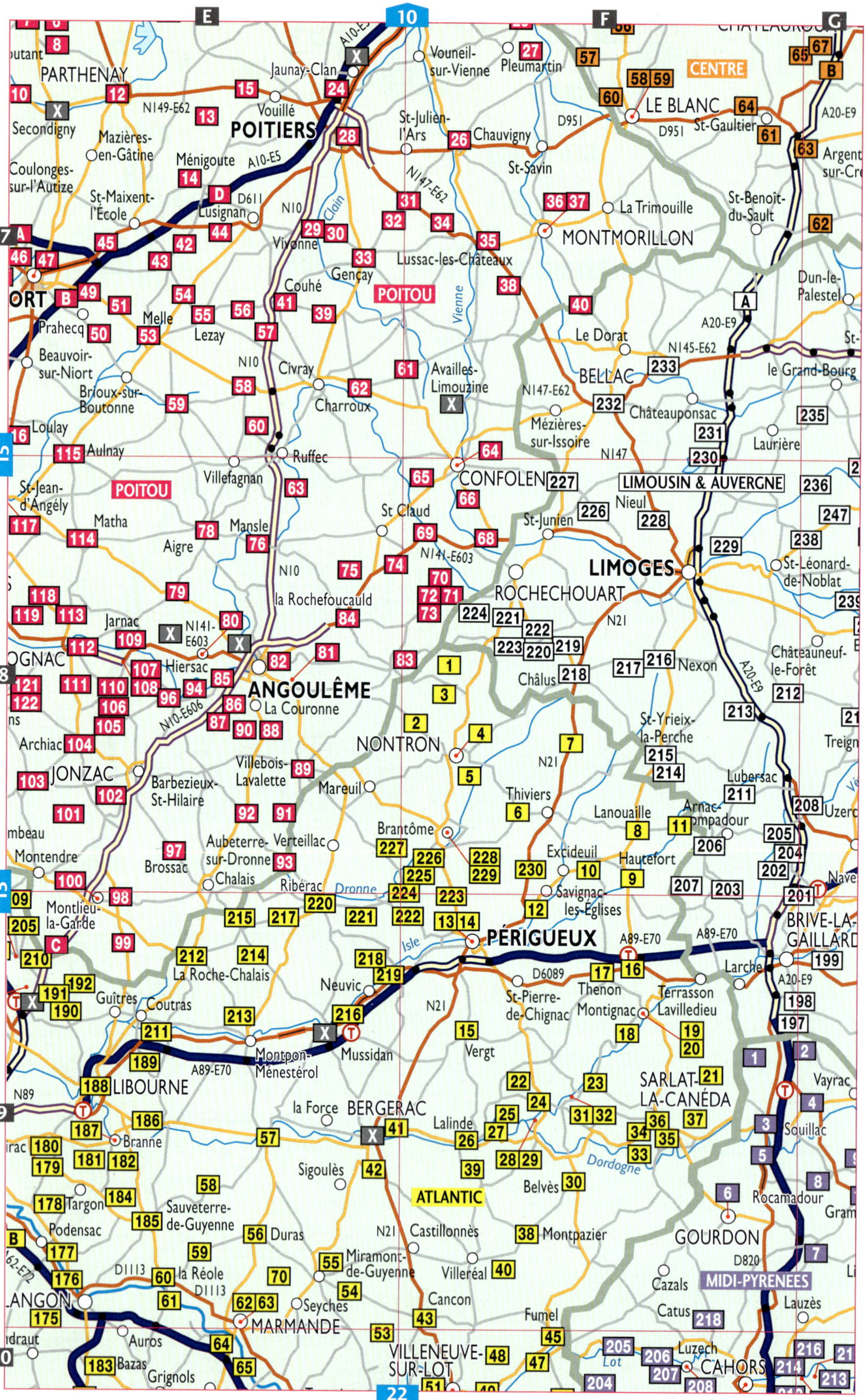
E
F
G
10
15
22
7
8
9
10
PARTHENAY
POITIERS
Jaunay-Clan
Vouillé
Vouneil-sur-Vienne
Pleumartin
CENTRE
LE BLANC
St-Gaultier
Argenton-sur-Creuse
Secondigny
Mazières-en-Gâtine
Ménigoute
St-Julien-l'Ars
Chauvigny
St-Savin
Coulonges-sur-l'Autize
St-Maixent-l'École
Lusignan
Vivonne
Clain
La Trimouille
MONTMORILLON
St-Benoît-du-Sault
Gençay
Lussac-les-Châteaux
POITOU
Vienne
Couhé
Dun-le-Palestel
Prahecq
Melle
Lezay
Le Dorat
Beauvoir-sur-Niort
Brioux-sur-Boutonne
Civray
Charroux
Availles-Limouzine
BELLAC
Châteauponsac
le Grand-Bourg
Mézières-sur-Issoire
Laurière
Loulay
Aulnay
Ruffec
Villefagnan
CONFOLENS
LIMOUSIN & AUVERGNE
St-Jean-d'Angély
Matha
Aigre
Mansle
St Claud
St-Junien
Nieul
LIMOGES
St-Léonard-de-Noblat
ROCHECHOUART
la Rochefoucauld
Jarnac
Hiersac
ANGOULÊME
La Couronne
Châlus
Nexon
Châteauneuf-la-Forêt
Archiac
JONZAC
Barbezieux-St-Hilaire
NONTRON
St-Yrieix-la-Perche
Villebois-Lavalette
Mareuil
Thiviers
Lubersac
Treignac
Montendre
Brossac
Aubeterre-sur-Dronne
Verteillac
Brantôme
Lanouaille
Arnac-Pompadour
Uzerche
Chalais
Ribérac
Dronne
Excideuil
Hautefort
Savignac-les-Églises
Montlieu-la-Garde
PÉRIGUEUX
BRIVE-LA-GAILLARDE
Isle
La Roche-Chalais
Neuvic
St-Pierre-de-Chignac
Thenon
Terrasson Lavilledieu
Larche
Guîtres
Coutras
Montignac
Montpon-Ménestérol
Mussidan
Vergt
LIBOURNE
SARLAT-LA-CANÉDA
Vayrac
la Force
BERGERAC
Lalinde
Souillac
Branne
Sigoulès
Dordogne
Belvès
Rocamadour
ATLANTIC
Targon
Sauveterre-de-Guyenne
Podensac
Duras
Castillonnès
Montpazier
GOURDON
Miramont-de-Guyenne
Villeréal
Cazals
MIDI-PYRENEES
La Réole
LANGON
Seyches
Cancon
Catus
Lauzès
MARMANDE
Fumel
Auros
Bazas
Grignols
VILLENEUVE-SUR-LOT
Luzech
CAHORS
Lot
A10-E5
N149-E62
D611
N10
N147-E62
D951
A20-E9
N145-E62
N147
N141-E603
N141-E603
N10-E606
N21
A89-E70
D6089
N89
D1113
D820
N21

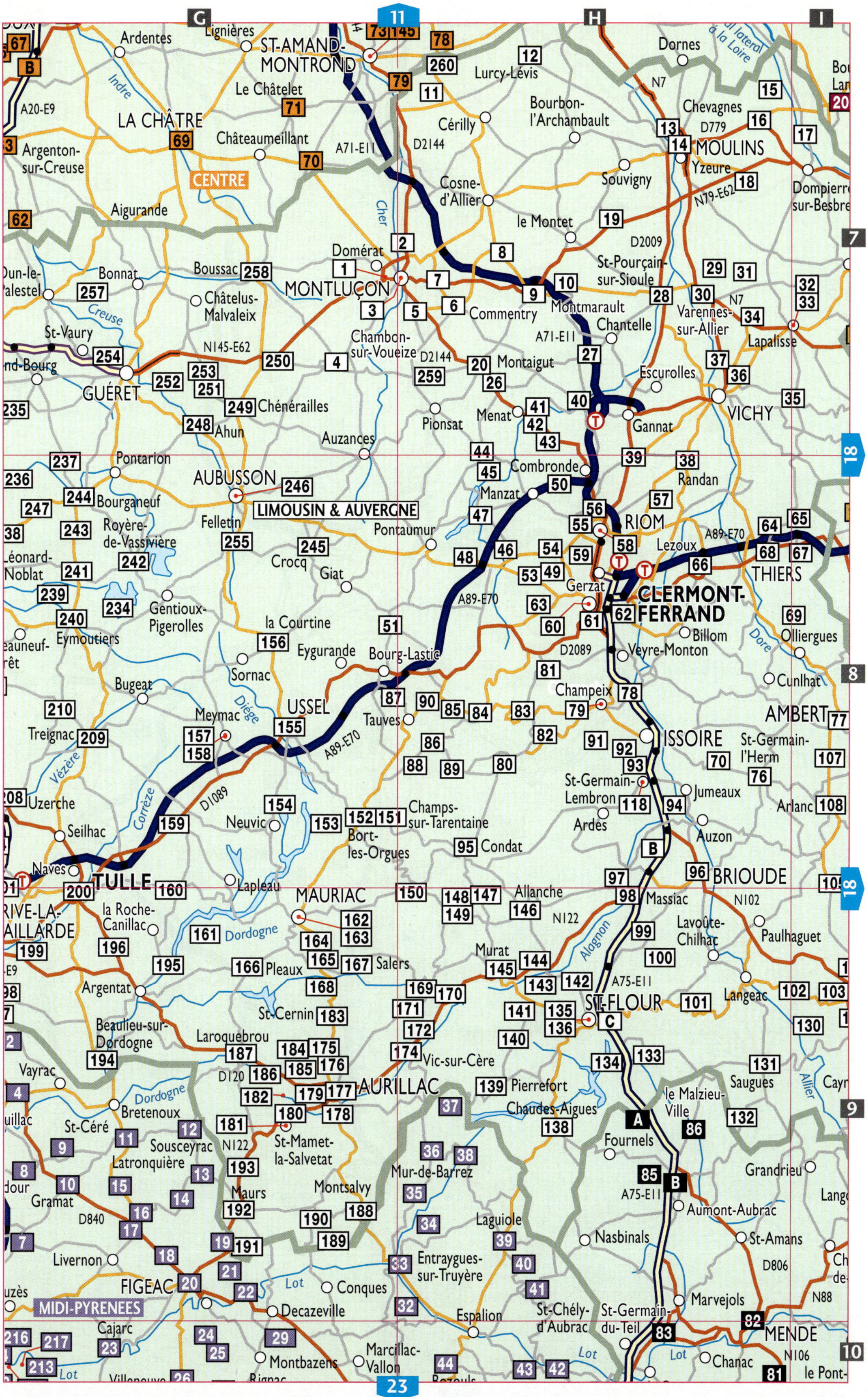

G
11
H
I
Ardentes
Lignières
ST-AMAND-MONTROND
Lurcy-Lévis
Dornes
Indre
A20-E9
Le Châtelet
Cérilly
Bourbon-l'Archambault
Chevagnes
LA CHÂTRE
Châteaumeillant
A71-E11
D2144
MOULINS
Yzeure
Argenton-sur-Creuse
CENTRE
Cosne-d'Allier
Souvigny
Dompierre-sur-Besbre
Aigurande
Cher
le Montet
St-Pourçain-sur-Sioule
Domérat
Bonnat
Boussac
Dun-le-Palestel
Châtelus-Malvaleix
MONTLUÇON
Commentry
Montmarault
Chantelle
Varennes-sur-Allier
Lapalisse
Creuse
St-Vaury
Chambon-sur-Voueize
N145-E62
Montaigut
Escurolles
GUÉRET
Chénérailles
Pionsat
Menat
VICHY
Ahun
Auzances
Gannat
Pontarion
Combronde
Randan
AUBUSSON
Manzat
Bourganeuf
RIOM
Royère-de-Vassivière
Felletin
LIMOUSIN & AUVERGNE
Pontaumur
Lezoux
A89-E70
Crocq
Giat
THIERS
Gerzat
CLERMONT-FERRAND
Gentioux-Pigerolles
Eymoutiers
Billom
la Courtine
Olliergues
Dore
Eygurande
Bourg-Lastic
Veyre-Monton
D2089
Sornac
Cunlhat
Bugeat
Champeix
Meymac
USSEL
Tauves
AMBERT
Diège
Treignac
ISSOIRE
St-Germain-l'Herm
Vézère
Uzerche
St-Germain-Lembron
Jumeaux
D1089
Arlanc
Neuvic
Champs-sur-Tarentaine
Ardes
Seilhac
Bort-les-Orgues
Condat
Auzon
Corrèze
Naves
TULLE
Lapleau
MAURIAC
Allanche
BRIOUDE
BRIVE-LA-GAILLARDE
la Roche-Canillac
N122
Massiac
N102
Dordogne
Lavoûte-Chilhac
Paulhaguet
Alagnon
Murat
Salers
Pleaux
Langeac
Argentat
A75-E11
ST-FLOUR
St-Cernin
Beaulieu-sur-Dordogne
Laroquebrou
Vic-sur-Cère
Vayrac
D120
AURILLAC
Pierrefort
Saugues
Allier
Chaudes-Aigues
le Malzieu-Ville
Bretenoux
St-Céré
St-Mamet-la-Salvetat
Sousceyrac
N122
Fournels
Latronquière
Mur-de-Barrez
Grandrieu
Gramat
Maurs
Montsalvy
Aumont-Aubrac
D840
Laguiole
Nasbinals
St-Amans
Livernon
Entraygues-sur-Truyère
D806
FIGEAC
Lot
Conques
Marvejols
MIDI-PYRENEES
Decazeville
Espalion
St-Chély-d'Aubrac
St-Germain-du-Teil
N88
Cajarc
MENDE
Marcillac-Vallon
Lot
Chanac
N106
Montbazens
le Pont-
7
8
9
10
18
23

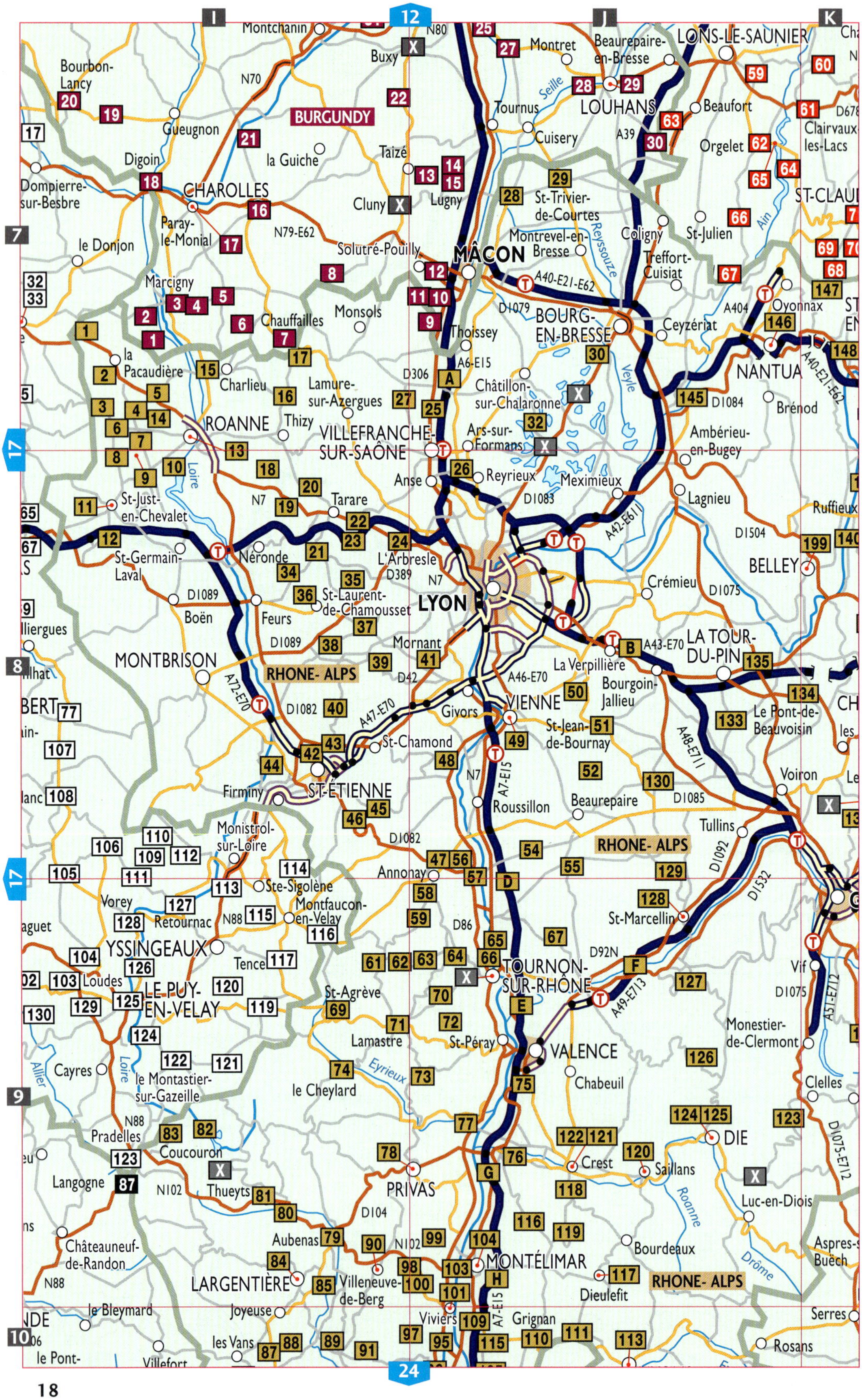

I
12
J
K
BURGUNDY
Montchanin
Buxy
Bourbon-Lancy
Gueugnon
Digoin
Dompierre-sur-Besbre
CHAROLLES
Paray-le-Monial
le Donjon
Marcigny
Chauffailles
la Guiche
Taizé
Cluny
Lugny
Solutré-Pouilly
MÂCON
Monsols
Tournus
Cuisery
Montret
Beaurepaire-en-Bresse
LOUHANS
LONS-LE-SAUNIER
Beaufort
Orgelet
Clairvaux-les-Lacs
ST-CLAUDE
St-Trivier-de-Courtes
Montrevel-en-Bresse
Coligny
St-Julien
Treffort-Cuisiat
Oyonnax
BOURG-EN-BRESSE
Ceyzériat
Thoissey
NANTUA
Brénod
Châtillon-sur-Chalaronne
Ars-sur-Formans
Ambérieu-en-Bugey
la Pacaudière
Charlieu
Lamure-sur-Azergues
ROANNE
Thizy
VILLEFRANCHE-SUR-SAÔNE
Anse
Reyrieux
Meximieux
Lagnieu
St-Just-en-Chevalet
Tarare
St-Germain-Laval
Néronde
L'Arbresle
LYON
BELLEY
Crémieu
Boën
Feurs
St-Laurent-de-Chamousset
MONTBRISON
RHONE- ALPS
Mornant
La Verpillière
LA TOUR-DU-PIN
Bourgoin-Jallieu
VIENNE
Givors
St-Chamond
St-Jean-de-Bournay
Le Pont-de-Beauvoisin
ST-ETIENNE
Firminy
Roussillon
Beaurepaire
Voiron
Tullins
Monistrol-sur-Loire
Annonay
Ste-Sigolène
Montfaucon-en-Velay
Vorey
Retournac
YSSINGEAUX
St-Marcellin
Tence
Loudes
LE PUY-EN-VELAY
TOURNON-SUR-RHÔNE
St-Agrève
Lamastre
St-Péray
VALENCE
Chabeuil
Monestier-de-Clermont
Cayres
le Montastier-sur-Gazeille
le Cheylard
Clelles
Pradelles
Coucouron
Langogne
Thueyts
PRIVAS
Crest
Saillans
DIE
Luc-en-Diois
Châteauneuf-de-Randon
Aubenas
MONTÉLIMAR
Bourdeaux
Aspres-sur-Buëch
LARGENTIÈRE
Villeneuve-de-Berg
Dieulefit
le Bleymard
Joyeuse
Viviers
Grignan
Serres
les Vans
Villefort
Rosans
le Pont-
24

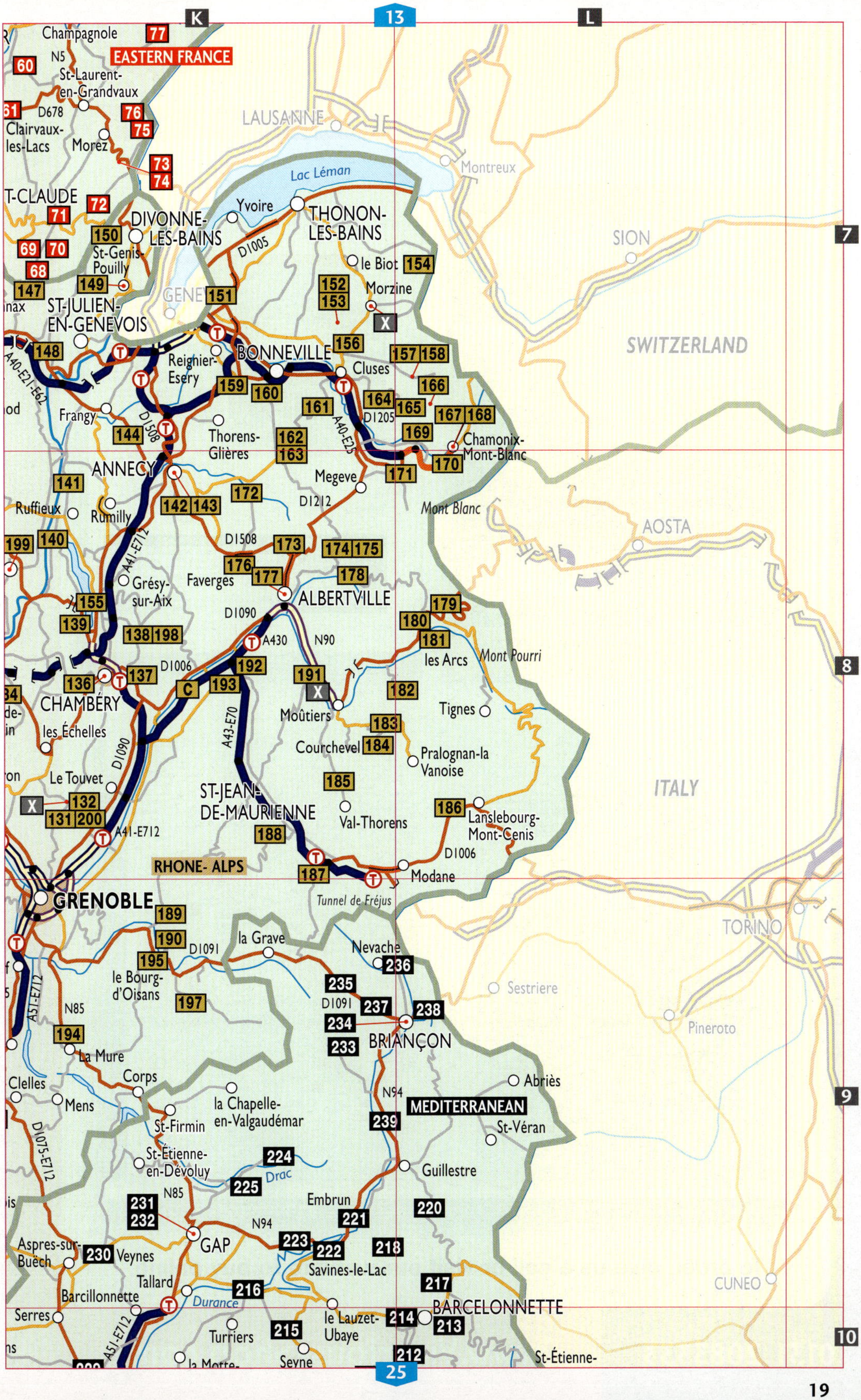
K
13
L
Champagnole
77
EASTERN FRANCE
N5
60
St-Laurent-en-Grandvaux
61
D678
Clairvaux-les-Lacs
Morez
76
75
73
74
LAUSANNE
Lac Léman
Montreux
T-CLAUDE
72
71
DIVONNE-LES-BAINS
Yvoire
THONON-LES-BAINS
SION
7
150
69
70
68
St-Genis-Pouilly
149
147
D1005
le Biot
154
152
153
Morzine
X
ST-JULIEN-EN-GENEVOIS
151
148
A40-E21-E62
Reignier-Esery
BONNEVILLE
156
Cluses
157
158
SWITZERLAND
Frangy
159
160
161
164
166
165
D1205
A40-E25
167
168
D1508
144
Thorens-Glières
162
163
169
Chamonix-Mont-Blanc
ANNECY
170
171
Megeve
141
142
143
172
D1212
Mont Blanc
Ruffieux
Rumilly
AOSTA
140
199
A41-E712
D1508
173
174
175
176
177
Faverges
Grésy-sur-Aix
178
ALBERTVILLE
155
D1090
179
180
139
138
198
A430
N90
181
les Arcs
Mont Pourri
8
D1006
192
191
136
137
C
193
X
182
CHAMBÉRY
A43-E70
Moûtiers
Tignes
183
les Échelles
Courchevel
184
Pralognan-la Vanoise
D1090
Le Touvet
ITALY
X
132
131
200
ST-JEAN-DE-MAURIENNE
185
Val-Thorens
186
Lanslebourg-Mont-Cenis
A41-E712
188
D1006
RHONE-ALPS
187
Modane
GRENOBLE
Tunnel de Fréjus
189
190
la Grave
Nevache
TORINO
D1091
236
195
le Bourg-d'Oisans
235
Sestriere
D1091
237
238
A51-E712
N85
197
234
Pinerolo
BRIANÇON
194
233
La Mure
Corps
Clelles
Mens
Abriès
N94
MEDITERRANEAN
9
la Chapelle-en-Valgaudémar
239
St-Firmin
St-Véran
D1075-E712
St-Étienne-en-Dévoluy
224
Guillestre
Drac
225
N85
231
232
Embrun
220
221
N94
Aspres-sur-Buëch
GAP
223
222
218
230
Veynes
Savines-le-Lac
Tallard
217
CUNEO
216
Barcillonnette
Durance
BARCELONNETTE
Serres
A51-E712
le Lauzet-Ubaye
214
213
215
Turriers
10
212
St-Étienne-
la Motte-
Seyne
25

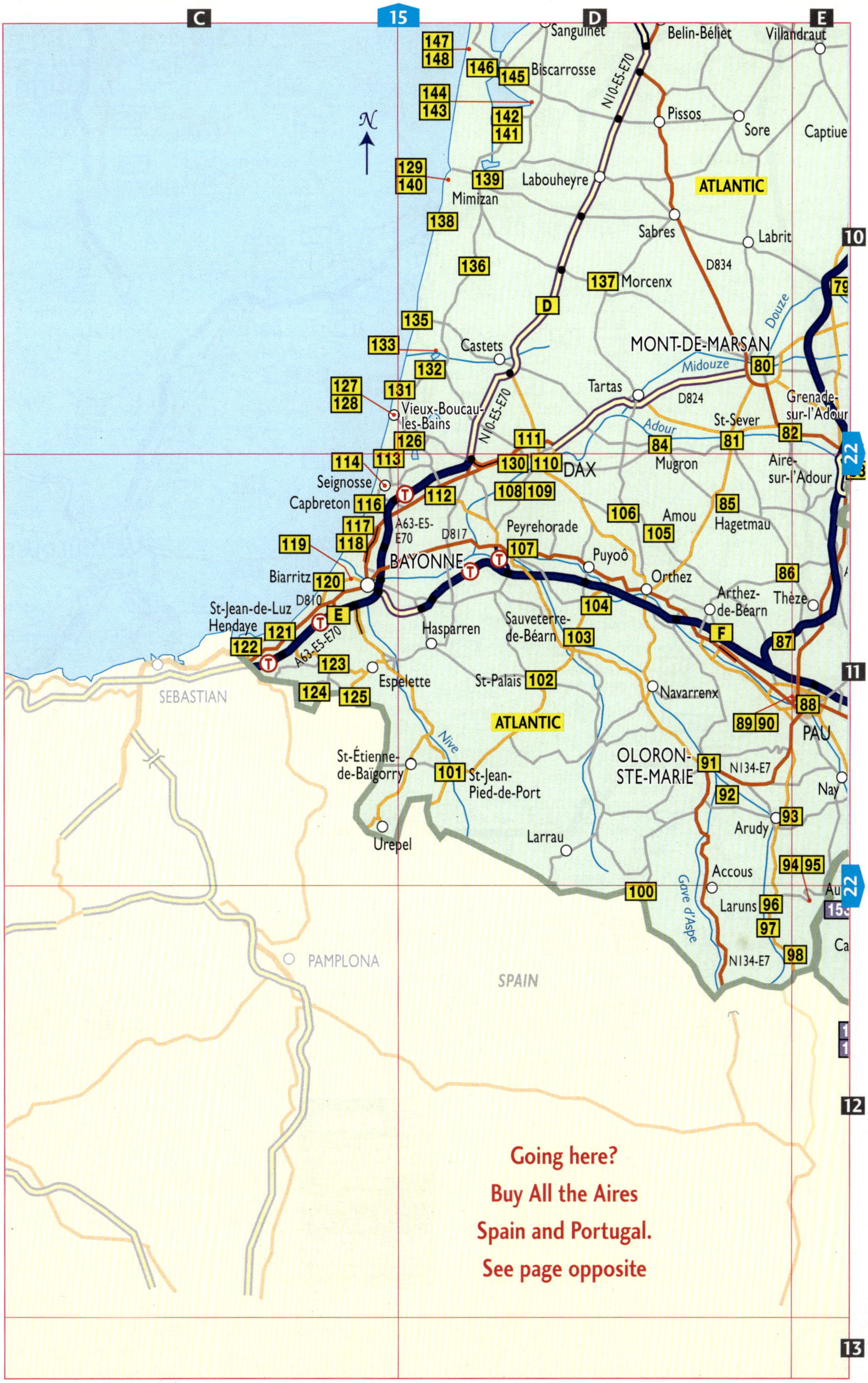
C
15
D
E
Sanguinet
Belin-Béliet
Villandraut
147
148
146
145
Biscarrosse
144
143
142
141
N10-E5-E70
Pissos
Sore
Captieux
129
140
139
Labouheyre
ATLANTIC
Mimizan
138
Sabres
Labrit
10
136
D834
137
Morcenx
79
D
135
Douze
133
Castets
MONT-DE-MARSAN
132
Midouze
80
127
128
131
Tartas
Grenade-sur-l'Adour
Vieux-Boucau-les-Bains
D824
N10-E5-E70
Adour
St-Sever
126
111
84
81
82
22
114
113
130
110
DAX
Mugron
Aire-sur-l'Adour
Seignosse
Capbreton
116
112
108
109
106
Amou
85
Hagetmau
117
A63-E5-E70
D817
Peyrehorade
105
119
118
107
Puyoô
BAYONNE
86
Biarritz
120
Orthez
Arthez-de-Béarn
Thèze
D810
St-Jean-de-Luz
E
104
Hendaye
121
Hasparren
Sauveterre-de-Béarn
F
122
A63-E5-E70
103
87
123
11
Espelette
St-Palais
102
Navarrenx
SEBASTIAN
124
125
88
89
90
ATLANTIC
PAU
Nive
OLORON-STE-MARIE
St-Étienne-de-Baïgorry
101
St-Jean-Pied-de-Port
91
N134-E7
Nay
92
93
Urepel
Arudy
Larrau
Accous
94
95
100
Gave d'Aspe
Laruns
96
22
97
PAMPLONA
N134-E7
98
SPAIN
12
Going here?
Buy All the Aires
Spain and Portugal.
See page opposite
13

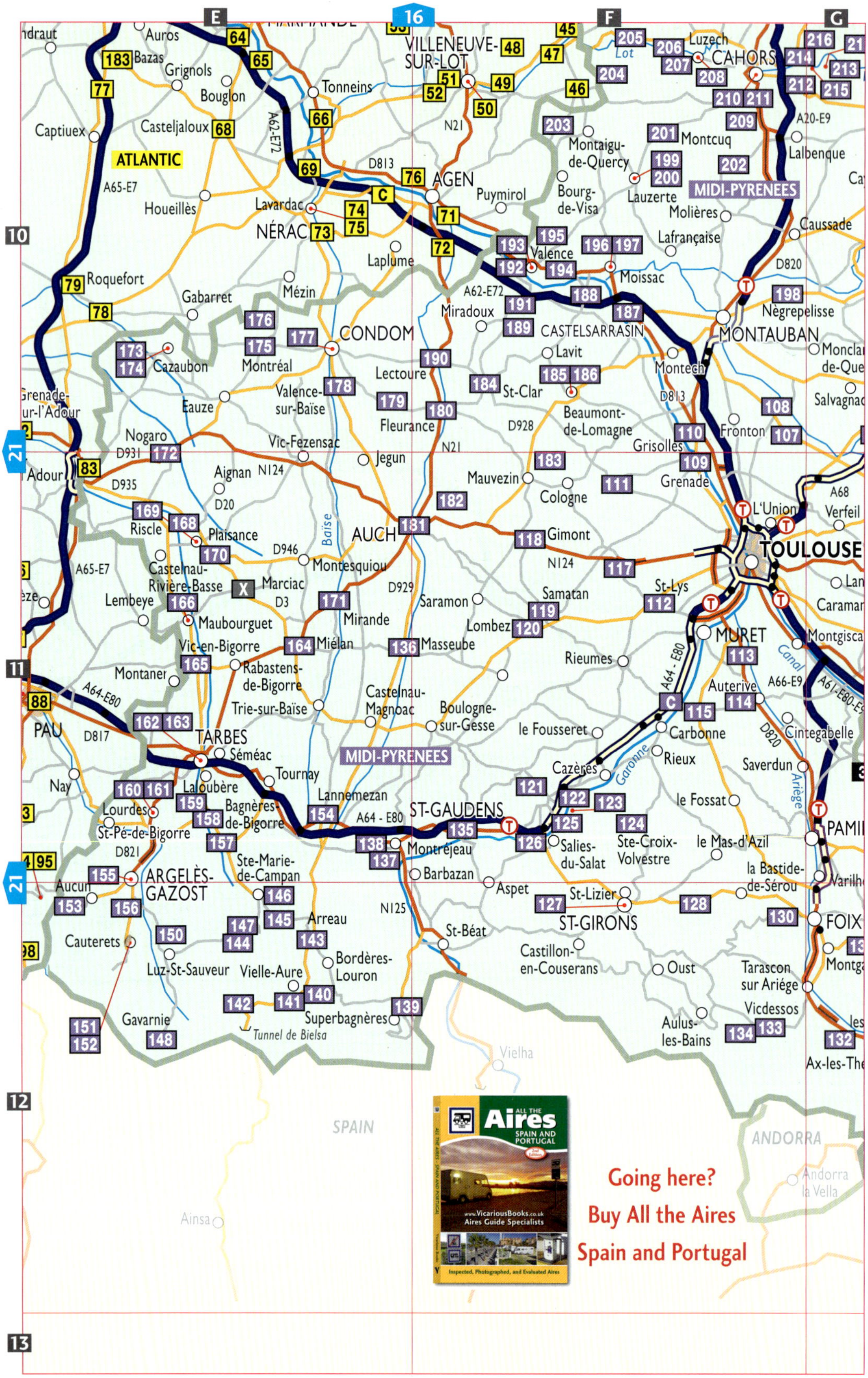

Going here?
Buy All the Aires
Spain and Portugal

G
17
H
I
MENDE
Cajarc
Villeneuve
Montbazens
Marcillac-Vallon
Bozouls
Rignac
VILLEFRANCHE-DE-ROUERGUE
Aveyron
RODEZ
Laissac
Campagnac
la Canourgue
Chanac
Ste-Enimie
Florac
le Pont-de-Mon
Lot
Caylus
Najac
Rieupeyroux
la Salvetat-Peyralès
Pont-de-Salars
Vézins-de-Lévézou
Peyreleau
Meyrueis
Cassagnes-Bégonhès
Salles-Curan
MILLAU
Trèves
Nant
LE VIGAN
Carmaux
Réquista
Valderiès
Roquefort-sur-Soulzon
Monclar-de-Quercy
Gaillac
Salvagnac
ALBI
Cadalen
MIDI-PYRENEES
Alban
St-Sernin-sur-Rance
Camarès
Cornus
le Caylar
A75-E11
Réalmont
Graulhet
Lavaur
Lautrec
Agout
Verfeil
Roquecourbe
Vabre
Lacaune
Murat-sur-Vèbre
LODÈVE
Bédarieux
St-Paul-Cap-de-Joux
Brassac
CASTRES
la Salvetat-sur-Agout
Clermont-l'Hérault
A750-E11
LOUSE
Lanta
Caraman
Cuq-Toulza
Anglès
Labruguière
Mazamet
Olargues
Roujan
Montagnac
Pézenas
Revel
Dourgne
St-Amans-Soult
St-Chinian
Montgiscard
Saissac
Mas-Cabardès
MEDITERRANEAN
BÉZIERS
Agde
Castelnaudary
Conques-sur-Orbiel
le Cap-d'
Midi
CARCASSONNE
Capendu
NARBONNE
Valras-Plage
Belpech
Montréal
Fanjeaux
Narbonne-Plage
A61-E80
A9-E15-E80
PAMIERS
Alaigne
LIMOUX
Gruissan
Mirepoix
Sigean
Port-la-Nouvelle
Varilhes
Chalabre
FOIX
Couiza
Mouthoumet
Montgaillard
Lavelanet
Tuchan
A9-E15
Quillan
Axat
Aude
les Cabannes
St-Laurent-de-la-Salanque
Ax-les-Thermes
PERPIGNAN
Quérigut
MEDITERRANEAN
Millas
Vinça
Têt
Canet-en-Roussillon
Elne
Argelès-sur-Mer
PRADES
Mont-Louis
CÉRET
Port-Vendres
Arles-sur-Tech
Cerbère
Saillagouse
Tech
Prats-de-Mollo-la-Preste
Andorra la Vella
24
10
11
12
13

I
18
J
K
10
11
12
13
23
NDE
le Bleymard
Joyeuse
les Vans
Villefort
le Pont-de-Montvert
Génolhac
N106
Bessèges
St-Ambroix
Barjac
Bourg-St-Andéol
Pont-St-Esprit
Viviers
Grignan
NYONS
Rosans
Eygues
RHONE- ALPS
Vaison-la-Romaine
Séderon
Gardon
le Grand-Combe
ALÈS
Lussan
Bagnols-sur-Cèze
Orange
Malaucène
Sault
St-André-de-Valborgne
Lasalle
Sumène
Uzès
Remoulins
A9-E15
AVIGNON
CARPENTRAS
Banon
Lédignan
D6110
Gard
Sauve
Quissac
Gordes
APT
Reillanne
D900
MEDITERRANEAN
NÎMES
Bouillargues
Tarascon
D570N
D7N
St-Rémy-de-Provence
A9-E15-E80
N113
Sommières
les Matelles
Vauvert
Salon-de-Provence
A7-E714
Pertuis
A51-E712
Lambesc
MONTPELLIER
Lunel
St-Gilles
ARLES
N113-E80
A54-E80
N568
A8-E80
AIX-EN-PROVENCE
750-E11
Aigues-Mortes
ISTRES
Berre-l'Étang
le Grau-du-Roi
Frontignan
Sète
Stes-Maries-de-la-Mer
Martigues
A55
Allauch
Carro
MARSEILLE
le Cap-d'Agde
Cassis
MEDITERRANEAN SEA

K
19
L
Serres
Turriers
215
le Lauzet-Ubaye
214
BARCELONNETTE
213
229
la Motte-du-Caire
Seyne
212
St-Étienne-de-Tinée
Orpierre
211
210
Auron
Tinée
Ribiers
227
228
Sisteron
DIGNE-LES-BAINS
la Javie
209
St-Sauveur-sur-Tinée
Tende
Verdon
207
D6204
N85
208
MEDITERRANEAN
Var
Lantosque
10
226
Peyruis
Bléone
Annot
206
D6202
Breil-sur-Roya
Banon
les Mées
Mézel
205
Entrevaux
FORCALQUIER
Durance
Barrême
Roquesteron
Sospel
147
150
203
204
Reillanne
148
151
CASTELLANE
202
Menton
Riez
153
Manosque
152
D6085
Vence
Monte-Carlo
D996
157
154
201
156
200
NICE
MONACO
146
155
GRASSE
158
197
198
163
A51-E712
Aups
Mougins
Antibes
Rians
Tavernes
DRAGUIGNAN
Vallauris
A8-E80
AIX-EN-PROVENCE
Barjols
159
X
192
Cannes
Cotignac
le Muy
DN7
199
191
190
D559
K
161
M
St-Raphaël
MEDITERRANEAN
L
A8-E80
St-Maximin-la Ste-Baume
164
160
195
196
165
166
D560
BRIGNOLES
189
193
194
11
167
169
175
D97
A57
188
St-Tropez
Cuers
181
168
176
Solliès-Pont
D98
X
186
187
A50
TOULON
Hyères
182
X
183
184
185
La Ciotat
177
le Lavandou
170
173
174
178
179 180
171
172
St-Mandrier-sur-Mer
Giens
12
13

HOW TO USE THIS GUIDE

Page 30. Useful information.

Before you depart read the useful information at the rear.

Introduction L'introduction fournit tout que vous devez savoir.

Einleitung Die Einleitung vermittelt allgemeine Informationen.

Introduzione L'introduzione fornisce tutto che dobbiate sapere.

Introducción La introducción proporciona todo lo que usted necesita.

Cover flaps.
Key to symbols.

l'explication des symbols.

Erklärung der Symbole.

Spiegazione dei simboli.

Explicación de los símbolos.

Inside cover. Colour coded regional overview map with page numbers.

Intérieur de la couverture. Carte avec couleurs codées **régions et numéros de page.**

Innere umschlagseite. Karte mit farbcodierten Regionen und Seitenzahlen.

Interno copertina. Mappa con colori codificati regioni e numeri di pagina.

Interior de la portada. Mapa con códigos de color de las regiones y números de página.

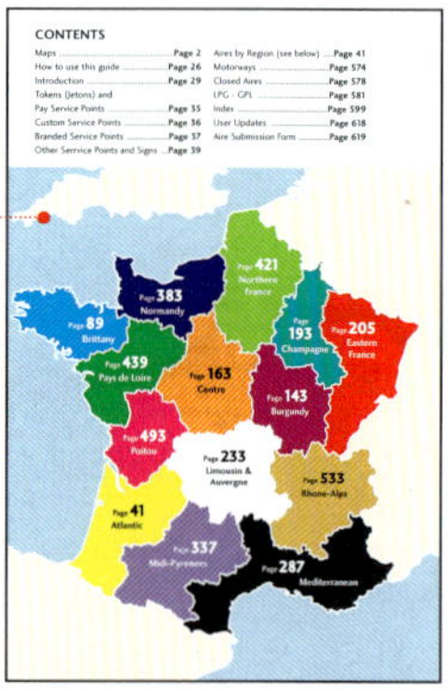

Step by step

Page 2. Overview map.

Carte synoptique.

Übersichtskarten.

Carta panoramica.

Vista general del mapa.

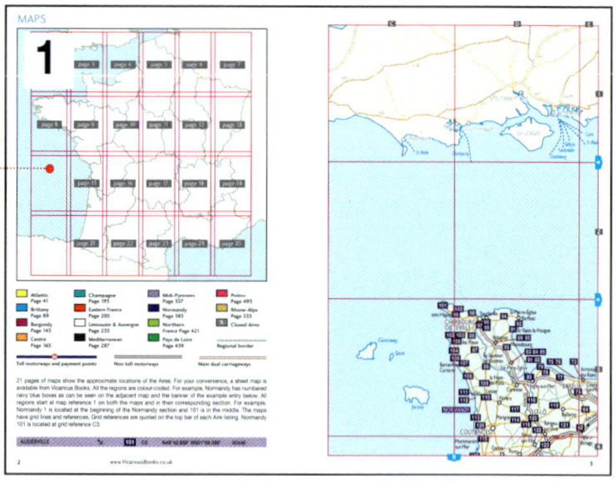

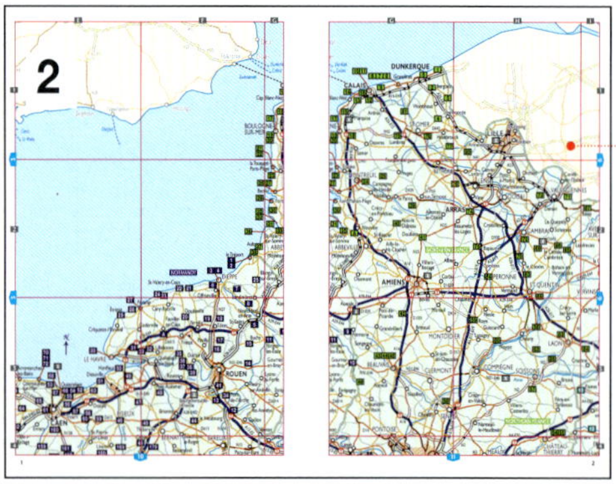

Page 2–25. Maps colour coded by region. All Aires numbered 1-2-3... in each region.

Cartes codées par couleur selon la région. Toutes les aire de service numérotées 1-2-3... dans chaque région.

Karten farblich nach Regionen codiert. Alle stellplätze nummeriert 1-2-3... in jeder Region.

Mappe a colori di un codice regionale. Tutti le aree di sosta numerati 1-2-3... in ciascuna regione.

Mapas codificados por color según la región. Todos área de servicio numerados 1-2-3... en cada región.

Page 41-573. Colour coded chapters by region. All regions use map numbers 1-2-3...

Code couleur chapitres par région. Toutes les régions utilisent des numéros de carte 1- Farbcodierte

Kapiteln nach Region. Alle Regionen verwenden map Zahlen 1-2-3...

Codice colore capitoli per regione. Tutte le regioni usare i numeri 1-2-3...

Código de colores capítulos según la región. Todas las regiones utilizar los números del mapa 1-2-3...

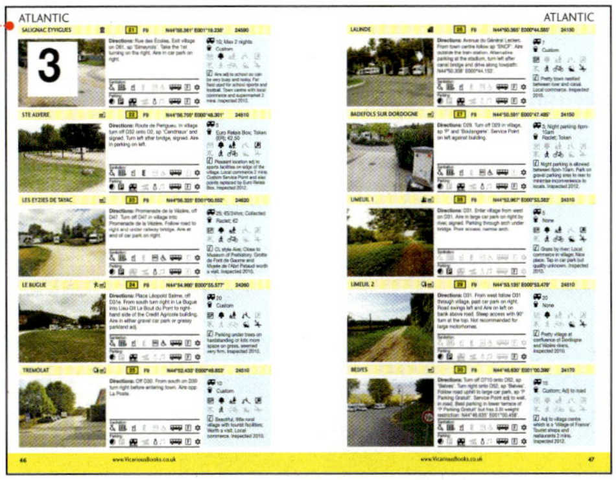

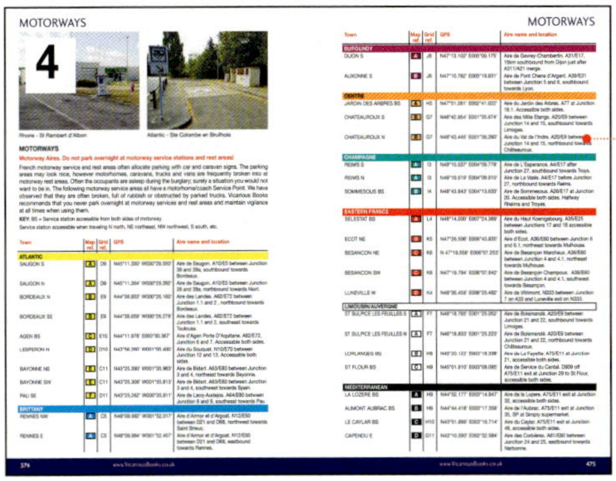

Page 574-577. Autoroute Aires with motorhome Service Points.

Autoroute aires de services avec borne camping car.

Autoroute Service-Bereich mit Wohnmobil Abwasserentsorgung.

Autoroute area di servizio con servizi igienico-sanitari per camper.

Autoroute área de servicio con saneamiento de autocaravanas.

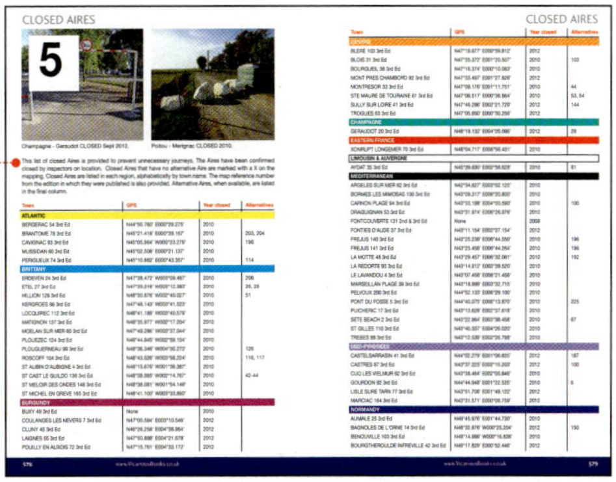

Page 578-580. Closed Aires.

Aires de services fermé.

Whonmobilstellplätze geschlossen.

Aree di sosta chiuso.

Area para autocaravan cerrado.

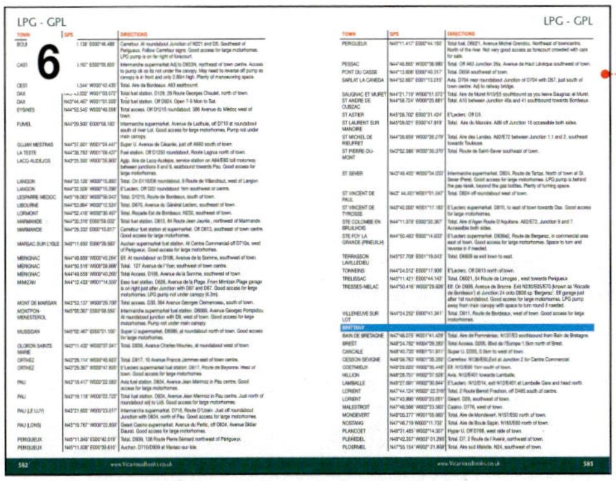

Page 581-598. Fuel stations with LPG by region.

Stations d'essence au GPL par region.

Tankstellen mit Flüssiggas nach Region.

Stazioni di servizio con GPL per regione.

Estaciones de combustible con GLP por región.

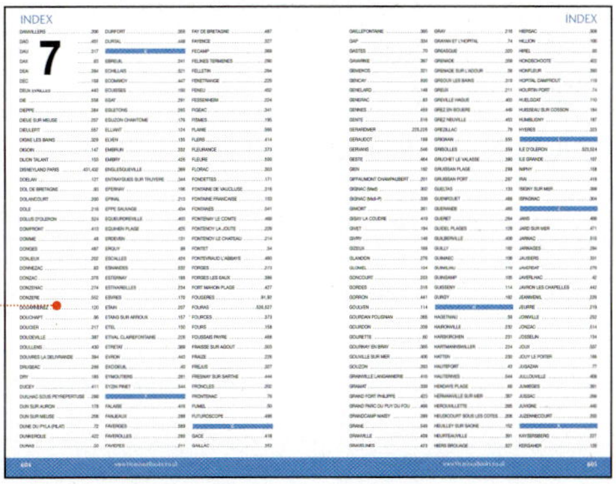

Page 599-617. Alphabetical index by town name.

Index alphabétique par nom de ville.

Alphabetischer Index nach Ort Name.

Indice alfabetico per nome paese.

Indice alfabético por nombre de ciudad.

Explanation of an entry

1 2 3 4 5 6

VALANJOU * | 113 | D6 | N47°12.996' W000°36.199' | 49670

Directions: D84. Signed off D84 on west side of village as exit towards Chemillé, sp 'Camping Cars' and 'Pique-nique'. Aire has narrow entrance.

Sanitation:

Parking:

5

Custom; 1 unmetered Cont elec socket

River views; River walk to village with ruined abbey 2 mins; Exercise trail through park; Lovely spot.

7 8 9 10 11 12 13 14

Note: *Grey symbols = unavailable*

1 Town Name.

* The inspectors have star rated the Aire or location. Often the view or surrounding area is of interest.

2 Surroundings. Key on cover flaps.

3 Map reference number.

4 Map grid reference.

5 GPS coordinates. Further information page 31.

6 Post code. Further information page 31.

7 Photograph of Aire.

8 Directions, Further information page 31

9 Service Point details. Key on cover flaps.

10 Parking details. Key on cover flaps.

11 Number of parking spaces; Cost per night; Time limit

12 Service Point details: Service Point type; Payment type if not cash; Cost.

13 Local amenities. Key on cover flaps.

14 Description.

Abbreviations and Glossary of terms

5 mins	Estimated walking times	**Signed**	Aire signed with symbol or text
Adj	Adjacent	**Sp**	Signposted
CC	Credit card	**'text'**	Extracts from signs
CL style	Small grass parking area	**TO**	Tourist Office
inc	Included in cost	**Tolerated**	Unofficial motorhome parking.
Opp	Opposite	**Inspected**	Vicarious Books staff
Poss	Possible	**Visited**	Customer submission
PP	Per person		

This edition features 30 per cent more Aires than the previous edition.
Vicarious Books inspected 2100 Aires during the second half of 2010 for the third edition of All the Aires France. This is the first time that every Aire in France had been professionally inspected. For this edition Chris and Meli, the editors of this guide, inspected over 1000 Aires including every Aire in Normandy, Northern France, Burgundy and Centre. They also drove all over France inspecting new Aires or those that had closed, moved, or changed in some way. Consequently, this is the most comprehensive and accurate guide of its kind.

Easy come, easy go
Aires provide motorhome travellers with the freedom to come and go as they please. Aires do not have a reception so you cannot reserve a space and there is no booking in. Most Aires should be considered a convenient en-route stopover rather than a holiday destination. This does not mean to say that you cannot have a motorhome holiday when stopping at Aires, just that you should be motorhoming from place to place.

What are Aires and what does Aire mean?
The English translation of 'Aire' is 'area', and many French facilities have 'Aire' in their name. The full title for French motorhome Aires is 'Aire de service/stationment pour camping car', which translates to 'Service area/parking for motorhomes' and are referred to as Aires in this publication. Aires are commonly marked with a sign displaying a motorhome emptying wastewater. Facilities differ significantly but normally include a Service Point for water collection and disposal of waste fluids. Often there is no instruction about overnight parking but it is assumed that 48hrs parking is tolerated. 48hrs is a national standard unless local signs or Mairie regulations are posted.

Motorway Aires. Do not park overnight at motorway service stations and rest areas!
French motorway services are also named "Aire 'something or other'". Motorhomes, trucks and cars are frequently broken into at motorway rest areas. Often the occupants of motorhomes are asleep during the burglary; surely a situation you would not want to be in. For completeness a list of motorway services with Service Points is provided at the back of the guide.

Who can use Aires?
French traffic law forbids caravans and tents from using the Aires in this guide. The law permits motorhome users to park; cook, eat and sleep within the confines of their vehicle. This law actually enabled Aires to develop in the first place. French law does not permit camping activities at Aires, such as winding out awnings or putting out tables and chairs. We see countless examples of the rules being broken, often by French nationals, many of whom seem completely unaware of the written rules and unwritten etiquette. Thus following their example may be unwise. Camping is permitted at all 10,500 French campsites.

Operation evasion

Over the past 10 years there has been a rapid increase in the number of motorhomes on French roads and 95 per cent of them are local camping cars. We have observed that motorhomers like birds of a feather flock together. For example French motorhomers rarely venture off the main trunking routes. Consequently overcrowding can occur at any Aire that is a short distance from a main road and likely when located in a quiet or pleasant location. Motorhomers from all nations appear compelled to drive to the coast and the sheer number of motorhomes has forced coastal authorities to manage parking. Motorhome parking is often controlled at well-known tourist attractions, lakes, rivers and canals. With control comes cost so expect to pay if you want to stopover at popular areas. Freedom seekers should plan to end their day off the beaten trail. We recommend that you travel with regional guidebooks, such as the Michelin green guides, in order to make the most of your visits to the lesser-known tourist attractions and villages.

Offsite parking

Some of the Aires in this guide are Service Points only without any parking. These are provided so that motorhomers can discharge waste responsibly. Motorhoming changed in France during 2012; this was not due to a change in the law but a change in attitude. As explained above, French law permits offsite parking and French motorhomers embraced this freedom. However, we noticed this year that most French motorhomers were parking overnight at official places. Presumably they have realised that because they congregate on-mass they were spoiling it for themselves. We believe that you should continue to enjoy offsite parking but make sure you are away from the popular motorhome destinations. The irony is that if you stopover at Aires away from the popular destinations you are likely to park alone.

Vicarious Books champions responsible tourism

Motorhoming is booming in France and many new Aires have opened. Some act as a control measure but many more were paid for by the local community in the hope that extra tourism would help to keep the local shops, restaurants or fuel stations open. Over the past ten years motorhomes have become much bigger, typically occupying 50 per cent more space. Bear this in mind when you park during siesta in a sleepy town square or in an empty Aire, because you are unlikely to remain alone. When parking somewhere for free you should at least try to spend what you are saving in camping fees. We would all like to see the Aires network continue to grow and this will happen if motorhomers are perceived as valuable visitors.

We can all be valued visitors if we are RESPONSIBLE and:

R espect the environment
E lect to use un-crowded Aires
S pend locally
P ark sensibly
O rganise you recycling
N o camping
S ave water
I mpeccable behaviour
B e quiet
L eave before you outstay your welcome
E valuate your impact

Finding Aires

Forward planning is advised, especially if you intend to drive late into the night. Select an area where there are two or more Aires nearby because Aires can be full, occupied by the funfair, or simply closed for maintenance. Vicarious Books is not responsible for any Aires. This book is a guide only, that was correct at the time of going to press. Should you have any complaints about an Aire or wish to know why an Aire has closed, please speak to the local Mairie. Remember to let us know.

Directions: The directions are written to assist you with map navigation. As far as is practical, the simplest route, that is free of height and weight restrictions, has been selected. Where possible, you should follow signs and be aware of any obstacles or diversions.

GPS navigation: The GPS coordinates provided in this guide were taken onsite and it should be possible to drive to the spot where they were taken. This does not mean to say that your navigator will get you there. Check the directions against your printed map and look at the suggested route on your navigator. Should you not be able to use the coordinates be aware that French postcodes cover at least a 10km radius; therefore you will need to input the town, and street, too.

Signs: When provided, it is advisable to follow the motorhome symbols to the Aire. Signs and symbols differ widely so you will need to look carefully. Unfortunately, campsites have taken to displaying motorhome Aire symbols on their direction and advertising signs. Often there is no indication that the signs are referring to campsite facilities. It is safe to assume that all campsites have sanitary facilities and this deception is unwelcome. Please do not submit campsite details to us unless the service point is in an accessible location outside of the campsite.

Parking

Aires operate on a first come, first served basis. Generally they are unsupervised thus it is not possible to reserve a space. The available parking may be impractical for many reasons and parking your motorhome may make the situation worse, so always consider others first. Use bays when provided. In unmarked parking areas it is normal to park close to your neighbour when necessary, so try to leave enough space for another motorhome to slot in if the need arises. Everybody enjoys a view so share them as much as possible. Never park overnight on the Service Point or obstruct roadways.

Large motorhomes (RVs) >7.5m: Many Aires have been designed to accommodate motorhomes up to 7m long. The highlighted coach symbols identify Aires where the inspectors believe it should be possible for motorhomes over 7.5m to access the parking. In many cases, parking large motorhomes is only possible when there are few or no other motorhomes. Remember to put your responsible tourist hat on when you are making parking decisions. During busy periods Service Point access may not be possible. There are very few Service Points suitable for emptying fixed tank toilet systems. We strongly recommend you have a macerator fitted and travel with a long length of pipe.

Using Aires all year: Aires make suitable night stops all year round and, unlike campsites, few close for the winter. Most Aires have a hard surface. Grass covered parking areas often have compacted gravel underneath. The 'open all year' symbol is not highlighted on grass parking but the Aire is unlikely to be closed. Drinking water is frequently turned off during the winter to prevent frost damage; 'Hors Gel' signs indicate this whereas 'Hors Service' indicates out of order. Flot Bleu, Euro, and Pacific, Service Points normally stay in service all year because they are heated and insulated. Many of the Aires in this guide have been inspected during the winter and the water was found to be on. There is no guarantee that water will be on so plan to visit several Service Points.

Time limits: Known time restrictions are provided in the listings. Many Aires restrict use to 48hrs, which is logical because it should be enough time to visit the local attractions. Aires not displaying time limits should be assumed to be 48hrs.

Service Points

There are several professionally manufactured Service Point brands, the most common are Euro Relais (Raclet) and Aire Services, followed by Flot Bleu, see page 37. Approximately half the Service Points in France are custom made, see page 36. Service Points normally facilitate three vital functions:

Drinking water: French tap water is very palatable, and consistent countrywide. Thoughtless users are known to contaminate taps when rinsing toilet cassettes. Using disinfectant wipes or spray before drawing water will improve hygiene. Taps are normally threaded to assist connection of hoses. Flot Bleu, Euro and Pacific, Service Points have all the facilities located in one enclosed space increasing the risk of cross contamination. In addition, we have found the drinking water hose down the toilet emptying point on several occasions, so consider disinfection essential.

Wastewater: Drive-over drains differ widely in construction. Typically a metal grid is set in concrete near to the Service Point. Some drains are so badly designed or located it is necessary to use a length of flexible pipe to direct wastewater accurately. Some service points do not have a drain but it is often possible to direct a pipe to the toilet emptying point. Flot Bleu, Euro, and Pacific, Service Points often have a short flexible pipe instead of a drive over drain.

Toilet cassette emptying: Cassette emptying points differ so widely you may have to think about it before you work out the correct place. It may be necessary to remove a grid. Some drains are too small, notably Aire Services, so do not rush this operation as spillage will occur. Often two taps are provided; as a general rule toilet rinsing taps are unthreaded. Euro Relais Service Points often have a toilet rinsing tap that will flow even if tokens are required for other services. We often see small amounts of toilet contents on grids. This is not deliberate but as a result of rinsing and assuming that the cassette has liquids only. Flot Bleu, Euro and Pacific, Service Points have to be un-locked before the toilet emptying point is accessible.

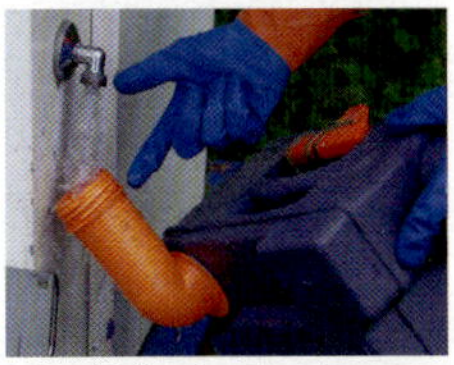

Left: Maintain a hygiene gap.

Electricity

Approximately half of the Service Points in France provide electricity, but unlimited (unmetered) electricity is uncommon at Aires. We have highlighted the electricity symbol **E** for every Aire that has an electricity supply, regardless of cost or duration. No further information is provided if the electricity supply is less than one hour. Aires that offer unlimited or practical electricity supplies have the details written in the further information of either the Service Point or the Parking section.

Flot Bleu Electric

Branded Service Points that charge for use such as Aire Services or Euro Relais normally have one or two electricity points. 55/60 minutes of electricity and 100 litres or 10 minutes of water is distributed upon payment, typically charging €2-3. Flot Bleu Service Points normally provide 20 minutes of 'environ', access to water and electricity. The least we have seen is 12 minutes supply. In addition some brands produce electricity distribution bollards. Flot Bleu, electricity bollards normally provide 4hrs of electricity per token and up to 12 hours of electricity can be paid for in one go. Token costs differ from Aire to Aire.

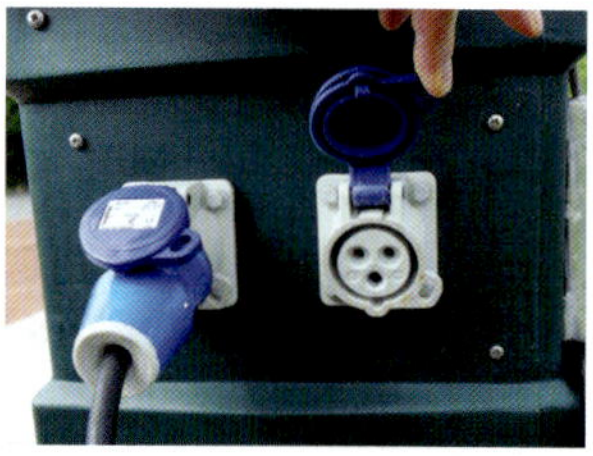

Should you be lucky enough to stay at an Aire with free electricity you will be expected to share it with several motorhomers.

In recent years, there has been a growth in what we have named 'commercial Aires'. These Aires often include electricity in their nightly charge. Be aware that there may not be enough electricity points for the number of motorhomes staying. Approximately half the plug sockets we have tested have reverse polarity and an alarming amount had no earth. Our recommendation is if you must have electricity, then you should book into a campsite.

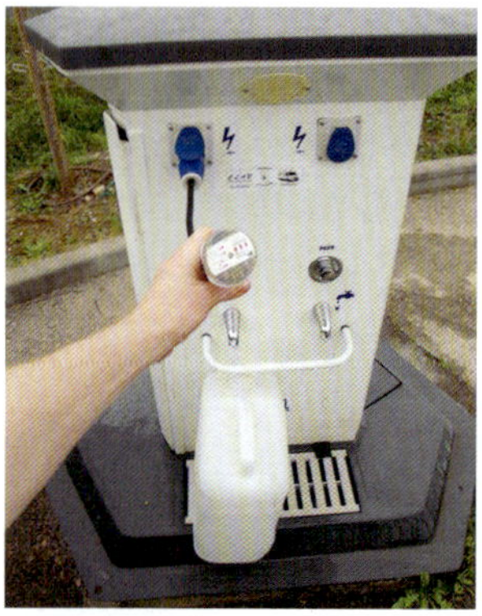

TOKENS (JETONS) AND PAY SERVICE POINTS

Tokens are called 'Jetons' in French. Less than one quarter of French Service Points require tokens. There are less Service Points that require credit cards but they are now the preferred choice when a new pay Service Point is installed. Typically Service Points requiring tokens, coins or credit cards dispense 10 minutes or about 100 litres of drinking water. When provided, electricity is normally available for one hour. Tokens are normally available from local shops, especially boulangeries (bakers), bar tabac's, tourist offices, the Mairie (town hall) and campsites if adjacent. Tokens may be free, but typically cost €2-3. Information panels or signs fixed to the Service Point normally indicate where tokens are available.

Unusually expensive card payment.

The main types of token are:

The front of the Flot Bleu token is branded. It is the size of a £1 coin, but not as thick.

The Aire Services 3/3 token is the same both sides with 3 grooves on each. It is the same size as a 10p piece.

The front of the Euro Relais (ER) token is branded. It is slightly bigger than a 10p piece.

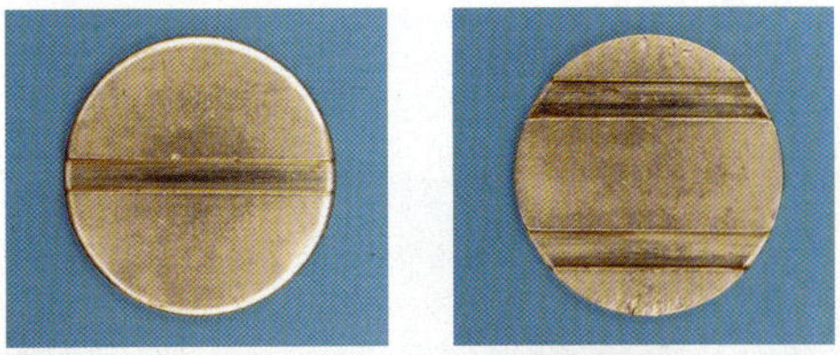

The 2/1 token has one groove on the front and 2 on the back. It is the size of a 2p piece.

Techno Money (TM) has a distinctive pattern on the front. It is the same size as a 10p piece.

CUSTOM SERVICE POINTS

Half of the Service Points in France have been custom-built by local craftsmen with inevitable differences in design and construction. Most are simple but durable and electricity is rarely provided. This has several benefits; they are rarely broken, they normally have a ground level drain, they don't require tokens and are normally free to use all year round. Sometimes the layout of a Service Point is confusing or a facility is a little way from where you expect it to be. Occasionally instructions state that cassettes should be emptied in the adjacent public toilet. However we have seen more signs stating that cassettes must not be emptied in public toilets.

Euro Relais and Raclet - Euro Relais and Raclet are the same. All Raclet units are at least 10 years old. Euro Relais has manufactured various sizes, but they are all basically the same. In general they are easy to use, but are often in a bad state of repair. Intentional damage is common on unsupervised units that take tokens or coins. Often there are two water taps. The one for toilet rinsing normally works without payment. The toilet tap is usually marked 'Eau non potable' for hygiene reasons, but it is in fact plumbed to the same supply. When tokens or payment is required, 100 litres of water and one hour of electricity is dispensed. A lift up cover at the base enables access to the toilet emptying chamber. The hole is big enough to lose the cap from your Thetford cassette.

Mini

Junior stainless steel

Maxi

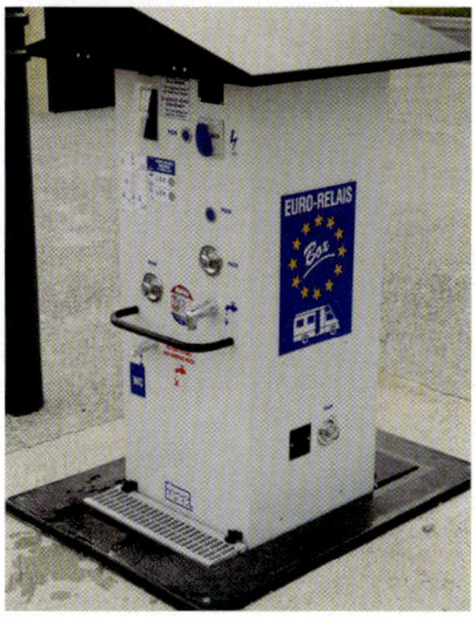

Box

Stainless steel

White plastic

Aire Services - The Aire Services brand of Service Point functions in much the same way as Euro Relais units but is a little more confusing due to the press button operation. The robust stainless steel units are common and normally charge a fee. Credit card payment is the norm for new units. The plastic units are generally free so are less likely to be damaged. Pay units generally have one or two CEE electricity points, all have freshwater and toilet rinsing taps. A small WC disposal drain is located at the front. Water is normally distributed for 10 minutes and electricity for 55 minutes. Waste water is usually disposed of in a separate drain.

Concrete

Electricity

BRANDED SERVICE POINTS

Urba Flux - Urba Flux Tall are becoming more common each year, especially for barrier entry or parking ticket payment. The Service Points are simple and robust units that distribute water and electricity. Toilet and wastewater is usually disposed of in drains at the base.

Urba Flux

Tall

Barrier

Tall

Euro, Pacific, Station Sanitaire

Flot Bleu inside

Electricity

Fontaine, Océane, Marine

Flot Bleu - There are several models in the range but only two designs. Mostly they are blue but can also be green, white or burgundy. Fontaine, Océane and Marine units have all the services fitted to the outside of the casing. Fontaine units are free the others take payment by coin or token.

Euro, Pacific, and Station Sanitare have services located behind a narrow door on the left hand side of the cabinet. These units are rarely free but are very robust and are likely to be in service during winter. Euro units always take bank card payment the others will be coin or token. These cabinets are also used to distribute tokens and operate barrier systems.

Point Belle Eau

SOS

Bollard. These are old.

Signs

There are numerous signs that apply to motorhomes that should be adhered to.

Motorhomes are not allowed.

Designated parking, no unpacking.

Clearway except motorhomes.

La Bastide d'Armagnac

ATLANTIC

Monbahus

BUSSEROLLES

1 F8 N45°40.616' E000°38.562' 24360

Directions: D90. Just off D90 in centre of village, signed. Narrow access.

Sanitation:

Parking:

5

Euro Relais Junior; Token (2/1)

SP

In village centre near bar; Nice woody, hilly region. Inspected 2010.

JAVERLHAC

2 F8 N45°34.060' E000°33.730' 24300

Directions: D75. From Nontron take D75 north. Aire is on right adj to the Total fuel station and repair garage in village.

Sanitation:

Parking:

5

Custom; 5 unmetered elec points

SP

Each bay has elec point. Inspected 2010.

ST ESTEPHE

3 F8 N45°35.368' E000°40.480' 24360

Directions: C201. In St Estèphe turn off D88 onto C201, sp 'Augignac' and 'Le Grand Etang'. Follow road to lake. Service Point in 2nd car parking bay, signed. Motorhome parking: N45°35.684' E000°40.447' off C201, sp 'Stade'. Follow road past campsite to parking on right.

Sanitation:

Parking:

7; Motorhomes banned 8pm-8am

Custom

Service Point only adj to large leisure lake. Inspected 2012.

NONTRON

4 F8 N45°32.167' E000°40.000' 24300

Directions: Ave Jules Ferry, off D675. From D675 turn onto Ave Jules Ferry and follow to Super U. Service Point in car park facing the shop front in the middle of the car park.

Sanitation:

Parking:

Poss

Euro Relais Junior; €2

Supermarket adj; Self service laundry open every day. Inspected 2010.

ST FRONT LA RIVIERE

5 F8 N45°27.983' E000°43.450' 24300

Directions: D83. From south on D83 Aire is approx 500m past Le Caneau going towards Saint Front la Rivière on left at picnic area.

Sanitation:

Parking:

10

Euro Relais Junior; 2 unmetered CEE elec points

Pleasant place overlooking grassy picnic area. Inspected 2010.

ST JEAN DE COLE

6 F8 N 45°25.185' E000°50.433' 24800

Info/Photo: John Cox

Directions: Le Bourg. Turn off the D707 south of the village by the Mairie, sp 'St Martin de Fressengeas'. Turn left in 20m just past tennis courts, signed.

Sanitation:

Parking:

5

Euro Relais Junior; €2

Pretty village with local commerce 2 mins. Visited 2012.

LA COQUILLE

7 F8 N45°32.562' E000°58.689' 24450

Directions: Place St. Jacques de Compostelle. From south on N21 turn 1st right after traffic lights into Place St. Jacques de Compostelle. Drive past front of church and Service Point on right hand side at bottom of car park.

Sanitation:

Parking:

4

Euro Relais Mini

Village 100m. Inspected 2010.

LANOUAILLE

8 F8 N45°23.533' E001°08.417' 24270

Directions: D75/Place de la Bascule, on Rue du Pont Lasveyras. Exit village on D75 towards Payzac. Aire 100m from centre before cemetery. Adj to fire station.

Sanitation:

Parking:

5; Max 48hrs

Euro Relais Junior; 2 unmetered CEE elec sockets; 2 drive over drains

Well maintained Aire with tarmac parking near town. Inspected 2010.

HAUTEFORT

9 F8 N45°15.607' E001°08.937' 24390

Directions: Allées du Avril 1944, off D72. Drive into Hautefort on D62. At square with TO, just past château, turn onto D72, sp 'Flot Bleu'. Aire on left.

Sanitation:

Parking:

5

Flot Bleu Pacific; Out of service

Daytime parking at beautiful hilltop town dominated by impressive château. Worth a visit. Inspected 2010.

EXCIDEUIL

10 F8 N45°20.157' E001°03.157' 24160

Directions: Allée André Maurois, off D705/Rue Léon Barreau. From southwest on D705 take 1st exit (not 'Centre Ville') at roundabout to continue around bypass on Rue Léon Bareau. Turn left into Allée André Mourois at statue. Aire in car park immediately on right.

Sanitation:

Parking:

4

Custom; Elec €3/day with €20 deposit

In village with impressive château. Inspected 2010.

PAYZAC

11 F8 N45°24.004' E001°13.171' 24270

Photo/Info: Mary Preston

Directions: Rue du Parc. Turn off D75 in the centre of village opp the Credit Agricole bank. The Aire is located behind the Hôtel de ville, no signs.

Sanitation:

Parking:

5

Euro Relais Junior; 2 unmetered CEE elec

SP

Local commerce 100m. Childrens play area close by. Large leisure lake, with swimming and watersports 5km. Visited 2012.

SARLIAC SUR L'ISLE

12 F9 N45°14.155' E000°52.448' 24420

Directions: N21 and D705, at roundabout junction to south of town. Turn off roundabout, sp 'Aire de Repos'.

Sanitation:

Parking:

10

Custom; Lift up drain for toilet waste

SP

Large football pitches adj. Town 2 mins. Inspected 2010.

PERIGUEUX 1

13 F9 N45°10.875' E000°43.360' 24000

Directions: Rue de l'Ancienne Préfecture. From south on D2, turn onto D6089 at roundabout, sp 'Centre Ville'. Follow road straight on and after crossing river bridge turn 2nd right into car park. Service Point in 50m on left, signed.

Sanitation:

Parking:

None; See 14

Custom; Obstructed by parked cars

SP

Service Point only. Inspected 2012.

PERIGUEUX 2

14 F9 N45°11.260' E000°43.864' 24000

Directions: Rue des Prés. From south on N21 cross A89/E70 and continue to Périgueux on D6021. At 2nd roundabout turn left onto D6089. Cross river and turn right onto D6021. At traffic lights turn right and cross river, signed. At roundabout take 4th exit, Rue Aubaréde, signed. Turn next left into Rue de la Riviére. At end turn right into Rue des Prés. Aire on right in 400m.

Sanitation:

Parking:

41; €5/night; Max 4 nights; 7m bays

Aire Services

SP

New Aire by river but no views. Adj to flats. Cycle track along river. 20 mins to town. Sat and Wed am market in town. Inspected 2010.

VERGT

15 F9 N45°01.350' E000°42.634' 24380

Directions: D8. From centre exit on D8, sp 'Bergerac'. Turn off D8 just before Intermarché supermarket entrance. Service Point on left adj to supermarket car park, signed.

Sanitation:

Parking:

Poss

Urba Flux Tall; €2

SP

Supermarket adj. Inspected 2012.

AZERAT | 16 | F9 | N45°08.970' E001°07.512' | 24210

Directions: Turn off D6089 in Azerat towards the church, signed. Follow road around church and turn left past Mairie, signed. Aire in car park beside/behind Mairie.

Sanitation:

Parking:

10; €2/night; Honesty box

Custom; €3; Honesty box

Aire located in a small, pleasant village away from main road noise. Views over tennis courts and swimming pool. Inspected 2012.

THENON | 17 | F9 | N45°08.459' E001°04.063' | 24210

Directions: D6089. Service Point at the Carrefour supermarked adj to D6089. Parking on opp side of road behind the Credit Agricole bank: N45°08.491' E001°04.114'.

Sanitation:

Parking:

10; sheltered from road noise

Euro Relais Box; Token (ER)

Supermarket and local commerce adj. The parking is just off D6089 but the buildings screen the road noise. Rural views. Inspected 2012.

ST LEON SUR VEZERE | 18 | F9 | N45°00.730' E001°05.369' | 24290

Directions: Le Bourg. From D706 take D66 into St Leon sur Vézère. Turn right at chapel. Aire adj to village off C201.

Sanitation:

Parking:

5

Euro Relais Mini; Token; €2

Beautiful village with river. Good facilities and restaurants. Inspected 2010.

MONTIGNAC 1 | 19 | F9 | N45°03.668' E001°09.548' | 24290

Directions: Avenue Aristide Briand/D65, on south bank of river la Vézère. After crossing river turn right by Mairie and Aire on right opp stadium. Further parking on other side of stadium.

Sanitation:

Parking:

15

Custom

Alongside river Vézère; 500m to town commerce. Market Wed am. Outdoor swimming pool adj. Inspected 2010.

MONTIGNAC 2 | 20 | F9 | N45°04.067' E001°09.883' | 24290

Directions: Rue des Sagnes, off D704. From south on D704 enter town and turn right at one way system onto D704e2. Cross river and turn left at traffic lights back onto D704/Rue de Juillet. Turn right, sp 'P Vieux Quartiers', 'Marché', and '300 Places'. Parking at end of road in gravel area on left.

Sanitation:

Parking:

20

None; See 19

Town 100m with local commerce. Canoe hire by river 200m. Market Wed. Inspected 2010.

SALIGNAC EYVIGUES

21 F9 N44°58.361' E001°19.238' 24590

Directions: Rue des Écoles. Exit village on D61, sp 'Simeyrols'. Take the 1st turning on the right. Aire in car park on right.

Sanitation:

Parking:

10; Max 2 nights

Custom

SP

Aire adj to school so can be very busy and noisy. Far field used for school sports and football. Town centre with local commerce and supermarket 2 mins. Inspected 2012.

STE ALVERE

22 F9 N44°56.705' E000°48.301' 24510

Directions: Route de Perigueu. In village turn off D32 onto D2, sp 'Cendrieux' and signed. Turn left after bridge, signed. Aire in parking on left.

Sanitation:

E

Parking:

5

Euro Relais Box; Token (ER); €2.50

SP

Pleasant location adj to sports facilities on edge of the village. Local commerce 2 mins. Custom Service Point and elec points replaced by Euro Relais Box. Inspected 2012.

LES EYZIES DE TAYAC

23 F9 N44°56.325' E001°00.552' 24620

Directions: Promenade de la Vézère, off D47. Turn off D47 in village into Promenade de la Vézère. Follow road to right and under railway bridge. Aire at end of car park on right.

Sanitation:

WC

Parking:

25; €5/24hrs; Collected

Raclet; €2

SP

CL style Aire; Close to Museum of Prehistory. Grotte de Font de Gaume and Musée de l'Abri Pataud worth a visit. Inspected 2010.

LE BUGUE

24 F9 N44°54.980' E000°55.577' 24260

Directions: Place Léopold Salme, off D31e. From south turn right in Le Bugue into Lieu-Dit Le Bout du Pont to right-hand side of the Credit Agricole building. Aire in either gravel car park or grassy parkland adj.

Sanitation:

WC F

Parking:

F

20

Custom

SP

Parking under trees on hardstanding or lots more space on grass, seemed very firm. Inspected 2010.

TREMOLAT

25 F9 N44°52.433' E000°49.853' 24510

Directions: Off D30. From south on D30 turn right before entering town. Aire opp La Poste.

Sanitation:

F

Parking:

F

10

Custom

SP

Beautiful, little rural village with tourist facilities; Worth a visit. Local commerce. Inspected 2010.

LALINDE

26 F9 N44°50.365' E000°44.585' 24150

Directions: Avenue du Général Leclerc. From town centre follow sp 'SNCF'. Aire outside the train station. Alternative parking at the stadium, turn left after canal bridge and drive along towpath: N44°50.308' E000°44.153'.

Sanitation:

Parking:

7

Custom

Pretty town nestled between river and canal. Local commerce. Inspected 2010.

BADEFOLS SUR DORDOGNE

27 F9 N44°50.591' E000°47.485' 24150

Directions: D29. Turn off D29 in village, sp 'P' and 'Boulangerie'. Service Point on left against building.

Sanitation:

Parking:

3; Night parking 6pm-10am

Raclet; Token

Night parking is allowed between 6pm-10am. Park on gravel parking area to rear to minimise inconvenience to locals. Inspected 2012.

LIMEUIL 1

28 F9 N44°52.967' E000°53.383' 24510

Directions: D31. Enter village from west on D31. Aire in large car park on right by river, signed. Parking through arch under bridge. Poor access; narrow arch.

Sanitation:

Parking:

5

None

Grass by river; Local commerce in village; Nice place. Tap in car park but quality unknown. Inspected 2010.

LIMEUIL 2

29 F9 N44°53.135' E000°53.479' 24510

Directions: D31. From west follow D31 through village, past car park on right. Road swings left and Aire on left on bank above road. Steep access with 90° turn at the top. Not recommended for large motorhomes.

Sanitation:

Parking:

20

None

Pretty village at confluence of Dordogne and Vézère rivers. Inspected 2010.

BELVES

30 F9 N44°46.630' E001°00.399' 24170

Directions: Turn off D710 onto D52, sp 'Belves'. Turn right onto D52, sp 'Belves'. Follow road uphill to large car park, sp 'P Parking Gratuit'. Service Point adj to wall, in road. Best parking in lower terrace of 'P Parking Gratuit' but has 3.5t weight restriction: N44°46.635' E001°00.458'.

Sanitation:

Parking:

15

Custom; Adj to road

Adj to village centre which is a 'Village of France'. Tourist shops and restaurants 2 mins. Inspected 2012.

ST CYPRIEN 1

31 F9 **N44°52.102' E001°02.663'** **24220**

Directions: Rue du Priolat. Follow sp 'P Centre Ville' through town. Aire just off D703e, main route.

Sanitation:

Parking:

8; €5/24hrs

Euro Relais Mini; Token (ER); 8 elec points; 1 Token/12hrs elec

SP

Town 1 min. Inspected 2010.

ST CYPRIEN 2

32 F9 **N44°51.789' E001°02.430'** **24220**

Directions: D703/Voie de Vallee, at Carrefour supermarket just southwest of town. Follow D703 southwest out of town and Aire at Carrefour supermarket just past railway station.

Sanitation:

Parking:

Poss

Flot Bleu Marine; €2; No drive over drain or toilet emptying

SP

Laundry; Pizza Kiosk. Free WiFi. Inspected 2010.

LA ROQUE GAGEAC

33 F9 **N44°49.500' E001°11.017'** **24250**

Photo: John Barry

Directions: Parking Place Publique, off D703. Aire in large car park at eastern end of village centre, adj to river.

Sanitation:

Parking:

20; €5/7pm-12pm; 10m max

Raclet; €2

SP

Aire 50m from Dordogne. Boat trips and Kayak hire avail. Views of cliffs with Troglodyte Fort. Busy Aire, arrive early. Inspected 2010.

MONTFORT VITRAC

34 F9 **N44°50.125' E001°14.912'** **24200**

Directions: D703. Turn off D703 on west side of village, sp 'Aire Camping-Car'. Follow road and Aire on right in 200m.

Sanitation:

Parking:

15

Euro Relais Junior; Token (ER)

SP

Shaded parking adj to village with imposing château. Touristy area and poss to hire canoes in season in Beynac-et-Cazenac. Inspected 2012.

DOMME

35 F9 **N44°48.050' E001°13.300'** **24250**

Directions: Le Pradal, off D46e. Turn off D46 in Cenac et St Julien onto D50, sp 'Domme'. Immediately keep left on D50 following blue coach and motorhome signs (do not take right hand fork, D49) Follow signs on D50, then D46e for 8km, to avoid the narrow streets and gateways of the hilltop town.

Sanitation:

Parking:

20; €5; Open Apr-Nov

Euro Relais Junior; €2

SP

Rural views; 500m from centre of hilltop town. Inspected 2010.

SARLAT LA CANEDA | 36 | F9 | N44°53.747' E001°12.747' | 24200

Directions: Place Flandres Dunkerque 1940, on D704. From north on D704 go right at roundabout as enter town and Aire by large car park on right. Entry via credit card barrier.

Sanitation:

Parking:

20; €5/24hrs; €12/48hrs; CC

Euro Relais Junior; €2

Town 15 mins. Busy Aire, best to arrive early. Boulangerie adj. Inspected 2010.

STE NATHALENE | 37 | F9 | N44°54.788' E001°15.902' | 24200

Directions: From St Nathalene follow sp 'Camping Maillac' through the lanes. Aire at campsite.

Sanitation:

Parking:

4; €12/night June-Sept; €10 rest of year

Euro Relais Mini; €5

Aire at campsite entrance. Shop and swimming pool adj. Campsite in a very rural location. Inspected 2012.

MONPAZIER | 38 | F9 | N44°41.107' E000°53.619' | 24540

Directions: Off D660, at rear of fire station. Aire near La Poste and Sapeurs Pompiers (Fire station), sp 'Salle des Fêtes' and signed from D660. 3.5t weight restriction on access road.

Sanitation:

Parking:

5

Custom

Bastide village 500m. Inspected 2010.

BEAUMONT DE PERIGORD | 39 | F9 | N44°46.479' E000°45.937' | 24440

Directions: D660. Approach on D660 from north. Turn left as enter Beaumont du Perigord, sp 'Salle des Fêtes' and signed. Aire behind Salle des Fêtes building.

Sanitation:

Parking:

10

Flot Bleu Fontaine

This is a large parking area located just off a main trunking route but is always likely to have space. Inspected 2012.

BIRON | 40 | F9 | N44°37.843' E000°52.247' | 24540

Directions: C203. In village turn off D53 onto C203. Aire adj to road as exit village, by information panel. Service Point reported as non-operational in May 2011.

Sanitation:

Parking:

10

Flot Bleu Pacific; €2

Rural views and views of château; Pleasant. Town 5 mins; Market Wednesday am. Inspected 2010.

ST SAUVEUR DE BERGERAC | 41 | F9 | N44°52.112' E000°35.289' | 24520

Directions: Route de la Rafraigne. Turn off D21, main route through, into car park past Mairie, signed.

Sanitation:

Parking:

3; 7m bays

Custom

Located in a small sloping car park in the village centre. Limited local commerce 1 min. Dordogne river nearby. Inspected 2012.

MONBAZILLAC | 42 | E9 | N44°47.321' E000°29.751' | 24240

Directions: D13. In town turn south onto D13 towards Ribagnac. Aire in 700m on right at vineyard, sp 'Domaine de la Lande'.

Sanitation:

Parking:

5

Custom

Views across vines. Wine tasting on site. Walks around vineyards. Inspected 2010.

CANCON | 43 | F9 | N44°32.192' E000°37.530' | 47290

Directions: Rue des Ecoles. From N21 follow sp 'Office de Tourisme' and 'D124'. Turning next to Mairie (town hall) into car park, facilities against barn wall. Town sq adj.

Sanitation:

Parking:

10

Custom; 1 Cont unmetered elec point

Very quiet night stop. 2 mins from shops. Possibility of cattle market. Inspected 2010.

HAVE YOU VISITED AN AIRE?

GPS co-ordinates in this guide are protected by copyright law

Take at least 5 digital photos showing
• Signs
• Service Point
• Parking
• Overview
• Amenities

Visit www.all-the-aires.co.uk/submissions.shtml to upload your updates and photos.

Sanitation:

Aire Details:

Submit updates

- Amendments
- New Aires
- Not changed

FUMEL | 45 | F10 | N44°29.928' E000°58.316' | 47500

Directions: Place du Saulou off D911. Enter Fumel on D911 from east. Aire is on right after bend as enter town, signed.

Sanitation:

Parking:

10

Custom

Adj to town. Difficult to access Service Point if car park busy. Inspected 2010.

TOURNON D'AGENAIS | 46 | F10 | N44°24.283' E000°59.829' | 47370

Directions: D102. Exit D102 to north and entrance to Aire on right 350m from large roundabout, sp 'Base de Loisirs du Camp Beau' and signed.

Sanitation:

Parking:

10

Custom

Views over Tournon d'Agenais; Hilltop Aire. Small lake; Camping chalets in summer; Restaurants. Inspected 2010.

ST GEORGES | 47 | F10 | N44°26.492' E000°56.251' | 47370

Directions: Ave St Georges de France. Turn off D102 onto C1-515, sp 'St Georges'. At end of road turn left, then turn right, sp 'St Georges'. Aire on right opp Proxi convenience store.

Sanitation:

Parking:

5; By Proxi convenience store

Custom; Lift grid before emptying toilet

In small, rural village adj to new convenience store and restaurant. It is understood that the three cont elec sockets at the back of the store are not for motorhome use. Inspected 2012.

MONFLANQUIN | 48 | F10 | N44°31.484' E000°45.382' | 47150

Directions: Approach Monflanquin on D124 from Cancon. At roundabout turn right, sp 'Centre d'Activities de Mondesir'. Take the 1st right and Aire 100m on right, signed.

Sanitation:

Parking:

2

Custom

Service Point located in an out of town industrial park. Poss to park overnight, but undesirable. Casseneuil is a better option. Inspected 2012.

ST SYLVESTRE SUR LOT | 49 | F10 | N44°23.765' E000°48.281' | 47140

Directions: Rue Jean Moulin. Access from D103 or D911. Aire behind Intermarché, adj to river. Service Point by fuel station at: N44°23.733' E000°48.333'.

Sanitation:

Parking:

10

Custom

Intermarché adj. Town 2 mins. Nice deep spaces for big motorhomes. River Lot 100m. Riverside walking path. Market Wed am. Inspected 2010.

VILLENEUVE SUR LOT | 50 | F10 | N44°24.511' E000°44.062' | 47300

Directions: D911. Enter town on D911 from Fumel. Service Point in E' Leclerc fuel station in retail park on right. Drive through 24/24 fuel pumps to access.

Sanitation:

Parking:

Poss

Aire Services

Supermarket and commerce adj. Inspected 2012.

CASSENEUIL

51 F10 N44°26.791' E000°37.136' 47440

Directions: Place St Pierre. Exit town on D133, sp 'Cancon' and signed. At roundabout take D225, sp 'P Tourisme'. Aire immediately on left in P Tourisme car park, opp cemetery before village exit, signed.

Sanitation:

Parking:

15

Custom

Pleasant parking on edge of town overlooking river. Town centre with local commerce 2 mins across river. Inspected 2012.

STE LIVRADE SUR LOT

52 F10 N44°23.760' E000°35.490' 47110

Directions: Place du Lieutenant Colonel Jean-François Calas. From south on D113 turn at roundabout with Casino supermarket down road lined with plane trees, sp 'Trésor Public' and signed. Aire at end of road past 'Terres du Sud', also sp 'Sapeurs Pompiers' (fire station).

Sanitation:

Parking:

5

Custom

2 mins to town. Aire backs onto old railway station building. Inspected 2010.

MONBAHUS

53 E10 N44°32.825' E000°32.101' 47290

Directions: Rue du Château d'Eau. Turn off D124 in village centre to view point, signed. Drive up very steep, single lane hill. Aire in car park just past footpath to view point. There is very little space to turn around at top so diff for large motorhomes.

Sanitation:

E

Parking:

2

Custom; 2 unmetered CEE elec points not working at time of inspection

Superb 360° view point with interpretation boards 1min uphill via footpath. Village with minimal local commerce 2 mins downhill. Inspected 2012.

LAUZUN

54 E9 N44°37.658' E000°27.589' 47410

Directions: Rue St Colomb. Turn off D1 at village boundry, sp 'Camping'. Follow road around past sports facilities and campsite and take the 1st turning on the left. Parking on left just before village, signed.

Sanitation:

Parking:

2; 7m bays

Custom; Limited water tap and toilets only

Adj to village lake and recreational area. Village centre 1min, dominated by château, with local commerce and restaurants. Inspected 2012.

ST PARDOUX ISAAC

55 E9 N44°36.816' E000°21.585' 47800

Directions: Off D933, at Intermarché. Exit Miramont-de-Guyenne to north on D933 and turn off towards ZAC du Rebequet, sp 'Intermarché'.

Sanitation:

Parking:

Poss

Custom

15 mins to town. Supermarket adj. Fuel Station. 24hr laundry. Inspected 2010.

DURAS — 56 — E9 — N44°40.678' E000°10.639' — 47120

Directions: From south on D708 follow road around village, passing château. Turn next left into C6 and follow road downhill. After 150m fork left sp, 'Aire de Camping-Car' and 'Camping Municipal'. Aire before campsite entrance.

Sanitation: E

Parking:

9; Pay May-Aug

Custom; Only when campsite open

SP

Campsite open May–Aug, no services or toilets rest of year. 12 elec points. Château adj. Inspected 2012.

PORT STE FOY ET PONCHAPT — 57 — E9 — N44°50.532' E000°12.547' — 33220

Directions: From west on D936 at roundabout go straight on following signs for Port Ste Foy et Ponchapt onto D936e2. Cross railway and at 2nd roundabout go straight over onto D708, signed. Take 2nd right and follow signs to Service Point or Aire (opp church).

Sanitation:

Parking:

4

Custom

Nice village; Ste-Foy 5 mins over river bridge with commerce; TO and walks along river Dordogne. Inspected 2010.

PELLEGRUE — 58 — E9 — N44°44.694' E000°04.483' — 33790

Directions: D16e/Rue du Lavoir. Clearly signed at the D15/D16 crossroads north of town. Signed from all directions.

Sanitation: E

Parking:

4

Raclet; 2 unmetered CEE elec points

Aire in small lay-by adj to old wash house and quiet village road. Town 5 mins. Inspected 2012.

MONSEGUR — 59 — E9 — N44°39.056' E000°05.038' — 33580

Directions: Ave Porte des Tours, off D668. From east on D668, as road bears left, carry on straight onto Ave Porte des Tours, sp 'Centre Ville'. Aire on left opp park. Do not enter from other directions.

Sanitation:

Parking:

5; Max 48hrs

Custom

SP

Park with view over town; Interesting covered market. Town 2 mins. Inspected 2010.

LA REOLE — 60 — E9 — N44°34.847' W000°01.815' — 33190

Directions: D1113. From town centre head east on D1113. Aire by small, round tower on right between Ave du Mahon and Rue des Moulins.

Sanitation:

Parking:

10; €4/night Apr-Sept; Grass parking

Custom

SP

Town 10 mins with local shops. Views over river. Some road noise. Inspected 2010.

FONTET

61 E9 N44°33.721' W000°01.406' 33190

Directions: Le Bourg Nord. Follow sp 'Aire de Camping Car' and 'Base de Loisirs Halte Nautique' from entrance of village. May have to phone Mairie to get in.

Sanitation:

Parking:

10; €7/24hrs; Daytime parking outside gate €5; Collected am and pm

Custom; inc elec

Directly adj to canal basin at marina. Restaurant adj; Pretty village; Views of boats. Showers €1. Inspected 2010.

MARMANDE 1

62 E9 N44°29.904' E000°09.626' 47200

Directions: Place du Moulin. From south on D933 cross river and turn right opp Saab/Suzuki garage into Rue de la Cale, signed. Continue into Blvd Richard Coeur de Lion. After 225m turn left into Quai des Capucins. Service Point immediately on right. Turn right into Place du Moulin for parking.

Sanitation:

Parking:

3; Max 48hrs

Custom

Town 2 mins. Canal adj. Inspected 2010.

MARMANDE 2

63 E9 N44°29.696' E000°09.769' 47200

Directions: From south on D933 cross river and turn right opp Saab/Suzuki garage into Rue de la Cale, signed. After 330m turn right (signed) and pass through Parking Filhole, signed. At roundabout turn right into Route de la Filhole, sp 'Aire Camping Car Filhole'. Aire at end of road on left just before barrier.

Sanitation:

Parking:

40; €6; Open May-Sept

Custom; inc

Aire on old campsite in pleasant woodland setting. Pony rides and cycle hire avail on site. 5 mins to town. Inspected 2010.

PONT DES SABLES

64 E10 N44°27.657' E000°08.334' 47200

Directions: D933, at Emeraude Navigation. From Marmande drive south on D933 and Aire on left in 3.5km at 'Emeraude Navigation' immediately, over canal bridge.

Sanitation:

Parking:

2

Custom

Right beside canal but lots of road noise. Bike and canoe hire adj. Inspected 2010.

CAUMONT SUR GARONNE *

65 E10 N44°26.506' E000°10.781' 47430

Directions: D143. On right by canal as enter the village from north on D143. Access made difficult by canal bridge and tree stumps.

Sanitation:

Parking:

18

Custom; €1; 6 elec points; €1/2hrs elec

Beautiful location worth the effort. Overlooking canal. Village adj. Inspected 2010.

VILLETON

66 E10 N44°21.844' E000°16.376' 47400

Directions: D120, by river bridge. Aire located behind Mairie at small marina, sp 'Musée de la Mémoire Paysanne', 'Aire Camping Car', and 'Restaurant la Fluviale'.

Sanitation:

Parking:

4

Flot Bleu Fontaine; €2; 4 elec points

Canal adj, no views. Pizza and museum adj. Very pleasant spot. Pay shower. Inspected 2010.

GPS Co-ordinates for SatNav

The GPS Co-ordinates published in this guide were taken onsite by our inspectors. We consider them a valuable and unique asset and at the time of publishing have decided not to publish them as electronic files for use on navigation devices. You have permission to type in the co-ordinates of an Aire you intend to visit but not to store or share them. For the security of our copyright:

- **Do not compile them into lists**
- **Do not publish, share or reproduce them anywhere in any format**

CASTELJALOUX

68 E10 N44°18.657' E000°04.760' 47700

Directions: Junction of D291/Rue de St Michel and Impasse de la Fôret. From south on D933 turn left onto D291 before entering town by the former railway line, signed. Aire 120m on left.

Sanitation:

Parking:

4; Max 48hrs

Custom

10 mins to town centre. LPG at Intermarché (D933 North). Inspected 2010.

BUZET SUR BAISE

69 E10 N44°15.473' E000°18.329' 47160

Directions: D12, at Port de Buzet. From D8 turn onto D642, sp 'Buzet sur Baise'. In village turn left/straight on onto D12. Aire on right in 180m at Port de Buzet. Not signed. Parking with permission, call at office. Parking on grass or car park.

Sanitation:

Parking:

15; With permission

No waste facilities; Elec €2; Showers €2

Lovely spot on Canal de Garonne and river Baïse. Poss water - ask at office for all services. Inspected 2010.

MONTETON

70 E9 N44°37.377' E000°15.407' 47120

Directions: D423. Aire just off D423 as enter village from north, signed. Service Point past recycling bins.

Sanitation:

Parking:

5; Grass parking

Raclet; 1 unmetered CEE elec point not working at time of inspection

Adj to pleasant hilltop village. No designated parking but motorhomes parked on grass at time of inspection. Inspected 2012.

CASTELCULIER

71 F10 N44°10.488' E000°41.680' 47240

Directions: Rue du Champ de Baze. From N113 turn onto D215. Take 4th left and then 1st right to Aire, signed. 3.5t weight limit on access road and Aire.

Sanitation:

Parking:

Poss

Custom; Token; €2

Service Point only. Inspected 2010.

LAYRAC

72 F10 N44°07.938' E000°39.573' 47390

Directions: Rue du 19 Mars 1962, off N21. Turn off N21 beside war memorial (rusty metal cross) opp D17 junction, signed. Then turn right, signed. Aire on left.

Sanitation:

Parking:

5; Max 3 days; 6-8m bays

Custom

Very basic and small. Inspected 2010.

NERAC

73 E10 N44°08.040' E000°20.134' 47600

Directions: Boulevard Jean Darlan. Turn off D930 in town centre at traffic lights onto D656, sp 'Mezin'. At next traffic lights turn left, sp 'P du Foirail (Gratuit)'. Aire on far side of barns, on left, signed.

Sanitation:

Parking:

5

Custom

Large car park/exhibition area, used for boot fair at time of inspection. Supermarket adj and small town commerce 2 mins. Inspected 2012.

LAVARDAC 1

74 E10 N44°10.235' E000°17.595' 47230

Info/Photo: John Watts

Directions: D408. Turn off the D930 onto D408, sp 'Mezin'. Turn right into Super U supermarket car park and the Service Point is located between the fuel station and carwash, signed.

Sanitation:

Parking:

Poss

Euro Relais Junior; €2

Supermarket and fuel station with car wash for high vehicles. Visited 2012.

LAVARDAC 2

75 E10 N44°10.734' E000°17.954' 47230

Info/Photo: John Watts

Directions: Rue de la Victoire. Turn off D930, main road through, onto D258, sp 'Stade-Tennis', 'Salle Polyvalente' and signed. The Aire is 200m on the left, signed. Lack of space may make it difficult to manoeuvre large motorhomes into Service Point.

Sanitation:

Parking:

3; 6m bays and obstructed by tree

Custom

Parking available further along Rue de la Victoire about 300m from the aire: N44°10.635' E000°18.167'. Local commerce 1 min. Visited 2012.

ST HILAIRE DE LUSIGNAN

76 E10 N44°13.495' E000°30.814' 47450

Photo/Info: Janet and John Watts

Directions: D813. Located between Porte Ste Marie and Agen on D813. Service Point adj to D183 and river at the southern edge of St Hilaire-de-Lusignan.

Sanitation:

Parking:

16

Custom

Service Point under construction in Oct 2012. There appeared to be no parking provision, but there is parking nearby. Visited 2012.

BERNOS BEAULAC

77 E10 N44°22.181' W000°14.556' 33430

Directions: N524 at Halte Nautique. From Bazas take N524 south and the Aire is just south of village on left of main road.

Sanitation:

Parking:

5

Custom

Convenience store nearby. BBQ. Benches. Small lake adj. Kayak course. Gorges du Ciron adj. Inspected 2010.

LABASTIDE D'ARMAGNAC

78 E10 N43°58.321' W000°11.159' 40240

Directions: D11. Turn off D626 in the village onto D11, sp 'Betbezer d Arc' and signed. In 400m turn left into Aire, signed.

Sanitation:

Parking:

30; Grass/sand parking

Custom

Pleasant, large, open, grass/sand parking. 1 min from village centre with local commerce. Voie Verte cycle route through village. Inspected 2012.

ROQUEFORT

79 E10 N44°02.850' W000°19.321' 40120

Directions: Allée de Nauton. Exit village on D932, sp 'Bordeaux'. Turn left, sp 'Camping' and signed. Aire 50m on right past campsite, signed.

Sanitation:

Parking:

10; Grass/sand parking; Max 48hrs

Custom; Lift grid before toilet emptying

Aire adj to municipal campsite in small residential area. Local commerce 4 mins down D932. Inspected 2012.

MONT DE MARSAN

80 D10 N43°54.146' W000°31.186' 40000

Directions: Ave de Sabre/D932. On D932 as exit town to north, sp 'Aire du Rond' and signed.

Sanitation:

Parking:

2

Raclet Maxi; 3 unmetered CEE elec points

Overlooking small pond; Bus stop; Town 20 mins. Inspected 2010.

ST SEVER | 81 | D10 | N43°45.544' W000°34.547' | 40500

Directions: In St Sever centre turn off D32 opp church and next to TO into Allée des Anciens Combattants. Turn left between long school building and war memorial. Aire on gravel car park outside school building. Access can be difficult due to parked cars.

Sanitation:

Parking:

5

Custom

Small town commerce adj. Casino minimart. Jacobean history. Inspected 2010.

GRENADE SUR L'ADOUR | 82 | D10 | N43°46.483' W000°26.100' | 40270

Directions: Place 19 Mars 1962, off D824. From town centre take D824 north towards Mont de Marsan. Turn left before small Carrefour supermarket into Rue des Marronniers, sp 'Parking Rugby'. At end of road turn right, then immediately left and Aire adj to cemetery.

Sanitation:

Parking:

30; Max 24hrs

Custom

Mini supermarket adj; Town 5 mins with restaurants, cafés and shops. Inspected 2010.

AIRE SUR L'ADOUR | 83 | E11 | N43°42.162' W000°15.323' | 40800

Directions: Place 19 Mars 1962. Follow main route through town towards river. On south bank of river turn right before bridge onto Rue des Arènes and bear left onto Rue des Graviers following sp 'Camping les Ombrages de l'Adour'. Aire 500m beyond campsite on left.

Sanitation:

Parking:

24; €3/night; Max 72hrs

Urba Flux; €1

10 mins to town centre. May be closed for 'Fête' third weekend in June. Inspected 2010.

MUGRON | 84 | D10 | N43°44.892' W000°45.047' | 40250

Directions: D32. Approach from Montfort on D32. Turn off D32 as enter village, sp 'Voie Verte de Chalosse' and signed. Service Point on right.

Sanitation:

Parking:

4

Aire Services; 4 unmetered 16amp CEE electric points

Adj to designated cycle path to St Sever (17.9km) and Dax (31.6km). Picnic area adj. Town with local commerce 400m. Inspected 2012.

HAGETMAU | 85 | D11 | N43°39.247' W000°35.898' | 40700

Directions: Rue de Piquette. Turn off D933s bypass, sp 'ZI de Piquette' and signed. Follow road and turn 1st right into Rue de Piquette. Aire in car park on right, signed. Note: very complicated one-way system through town and limited parking.

Sanitation:

Parking:

15

Custom

Located in industrial area, most of which is not in use. Adj to river limited views but good for fishing. Town centre, 4 mins, has numerous restaurants. Market Wednesday. Inspected 2012.

ARZACQ ARRAZIGUET

86 D11 N43°32.094' W000°24.624' 64410

Directions: Place du Marcadieu. Aire on corner of junction of D32 and D944.

Sanitation:

Parking:

20

Custom

Sports centre 400m. Town 100m. Large parking area in bastide town. Adj to covered market building. Inspected 2010.

SAUVAGNON

87 D11 N43°24.233' W000°23.176' 64230

Directions: D216, near junction with D616. From south on D216 drive through town and Aire in car park on right before you reach D616. Service Point behind Centre Festif.

Sanitation:

Parking:

5

Custom

Small town commerce adj. Centre has many events, but Aire quiet afterwards. Good view of the Pyrénées. Inspected 2010.

PAU

88 E11 N43°17.951' W000°22.581' 64000

Directions: Place de Verdun. Exit A64/E80 at Junction 10 and travel 4km crossing over 4 roundabouts and following sp 'Centre Ville', 'Château', and 'Les Halles'. Turn right onto Rue d'Orleans, sp 'OT'. Follow road to end and Aire at large parking area.

Sanitation:

Parking:

100

None

Blue spaces 2hrs, other parking unrestricted. Interesting historic town. Shaded seating; Château. Inspected 2010.

LESCAR 1

89 D11 N43°19.537' W000°26.550' 64230

Directions: Ave du Vert Galant. From west on D817/Blvd de l'Europe take 1st exit at roundabout onto D501/Ave du Vert Galant. Pass ALDI and turn right into Impasse du Vert Galant (GPS is at this turning for clarity). Service Point on right of turning circle, signed.

Sanitation:

Parking:

None; See 90

Custom

Interesting medieval city 1.7km. Inspected 2010.

LESCAR 2

90 D11 N43°20.025' W000°25.806' 64230

Directions: Rue du Vallon. From north on D945. At roundabout by Gendarmerie turn left into Avenue de Plaisance. Continue across roundabout by Pharmacy. Turn right opp end of parade of shops into Rue du Vallon, sp 'Cimetière'. Go straight across mini roundabout and Aire on right in cemetery car park.

Sanitation:

Parking:

5

None; See 89

Car park outside cemetery. Interesting medieval city. Footpath to historic town centre (15 mins). Inspected 2010.

OLORON STE MARIE

91 D11 N43°11.032' W000°36.511' 64400

Directions: Rue Adoue. From Asasp Arros in south on N134 take 2nd exit at roundabout onto Rte du Somport. At next roundabout take 2nd exit into Ave d'Espagne. Aire 600m on right. Gateway may be too narrow to turn into for longer vehicles.

Sanitation:

Parking:

7; Max 48hrs

Aire Services; Token; €4; 8 elec sockets

SP

Pleasant parking. Token from TO, 800m. River adj, but no views. Inspected 2010.

OGEU LES BAINS

92 D11 N43°09.210' W000°30.130' 64680

Directions: D416. From east on D920 turn right in Ogeu les Bains onto D416, sp 'Aire Camping Cars'. Cross railway and Aire on right outside stadium.

Sanitation:

Parking:

6

Custom; Token

SP

Village centre 800m with local commerce. Small Supermarket 650m from Aire on D920 towards Oloron. Inspected 2010.

SEVIGNACQ MEYRACQ

93 D11 N43°06.430' W000°24.962' 64260

Directions: Aire du Gave D'Ossau. From Pau on D934 continue through Sevignacq. Just past picnic spot on right, turn very sharp right at dangerous junction into minor road which turns back north (long motorhomes should approach from Laruns). Do not take road over bridge for Arudy but follow sp 'Camping Car' past marble works to site.

Sanitation:

Parking:

20; €7; Feb-Nov

Custom; €2.50; Elec €1.50

SP

CL style Commercial Aire. Onsite laundry €6. Regional products for sale. Close to small town of Arudy. Inspected 2010.

GOURETTE 1

SKI

94 E12 N42°57.784' W000°20.352' 64440

Directions: Parking de Ley, D918. Outside campsite in large car park on D918. Entrance is on outside of wide hairpin bend. Service Point is at far end of furthest car park.

Sanitation:

Parking:

50

Euro Relais Junior Token (ER); €5

SP

This Aire is situated at the bottom of the Gondola station. Inspected 2010.

GOURETTE 2

SKI

95 E12 N42°57.445' W000°19.837' 64440

Directions: Parking du Cardet. In Gourette turn off D918 by the roundabout on hairpin bend, sp 'Aire de Camping Car'. Drive under a bridge between two blocks of flats and the Aire is straight ahead, signed.

Sanitation:

Parking:

30; Max 7 days

None; See 94

SP

Parking in town at bottom of ski slopes. Inspected 2010.

LARUNS | 96 | D12 | N42°59.300' W000°25.500' | 64440

Directions: D934/Avenue de la Gare. Aire in town centre next to car park off D934. At rear of car park.

Sanitation:

Parking:

22

Euro Relais Junior; Token; €3.50

Waste drain awkward if car park is full; Market day Saturday am. Inspected 2010.

LES EAUX CHAUDES | 97 | D12 | N42°57.117' W000°26.417' | 64440

Directions: D934. In small lay-by beside main road from Spain via Col de Pourtalet.

Sanitation:

Parking:

None

Euro Relais Junior; Token; €3.50

Tokens from Larun or Fabrèges TO. For parking see Laruns 96 or Artouste Fabrèges 98. Inspected 2010.

ARTOUSTE FABREGES SKI | 98 | D12 | N42°52.817' W000°23.917' | 64440

Directions: D431. From south on D934 turn left onto D431, sp 'Artouste Fabréges'. Cross bridge and follow road to left for 1.5km; stay to left for Aire.

Sanitation:

Parking:

40; €3.50

Euro Relais Junior; Token (2/1)

Gravel areas and tarmac car park overlooking lake. Parking must not obstruct residents. Ski resort adj. Mini mountain railway in summer. Inspected 2010.

HAVE YOU VISITED AN AIRE? | GPS co-ordinates in this guide are protected by copyright law

Take at least 5 digital photos showing
• Signs
• Service Point
• Parking
• Overview
• Amenities

Visit www.all-the-aires.co.uk/submissions.shtml to upload your updates and photos.

Sanitation:

Aire Details:

Submit updates

- Amendments
- New Aires
- Not changed

ARETTE PIERRE ST MARTIN SKI | 100 | D12 | N42°58.733' W000°44.883' | 64570

Directions: Braca de Guilhers, off D132 at ski station. Turn off D132 and follow to ski station, sp 'Station de Ski Pierre St Martin'. Pass through large car park and turn right at 1st roundabout into Aire.

Sanitation:

Parking:

40; €7; inc unmetered elec

Custom; inc; 44 elec points

Ski station adj. Adj to ski lift. Free WiFi at TO. Inspected 2010.

ST JEAN PIED DE PORT

101 D11 N43°09.923' W001°13.948' 64220

Directions: Ave Jai Alai. In car park Jai Alai close to Carrefour supermarket and the sports facilities. Turn off D933 at the roundabout, sp 'P Jai Alai'. Aire is at the end of this road.

Sanitation:

Parking:

40; €5.50

Custom; inc

This is the only car park in town that allows motorhomes. Toilets in sports hall. Inspected 2010.

ST PALAIS

102 D11 N43°19.733' W001°01.933' 64120

Directions: Place Sante-Elisabeth, off Rue Theodore D'Arthez. Turn off D11 ring road, sp 'Peyrehorade'. After 400m turn right into the parking area.

Sanitation:

Parking:

5; No parking Thurs pm-Fri am - market

Custom

Covered animal market adj; Busy town car park. Inspected 2010.

SAUVETERRE DE BEARN

103 D11 N43°24.073' W000°56.343' 64390

Directions: Sauterisse. From D933 turn off at roundabout by ZAC Oriete towards town centre. Turn left at town centre onto Ave des Salies and take 2nd right onto Sauterisse.

Sanitation:

Parking:

5

Custom

Quiet village; Riverside walks; Church. Boulangerie 100m. Inspected 2010.

SALIES DE BEARN

104 D11 N43°28.393' W000°56.033' 64270

Info/Photo: John Dunn

Directions: Lieu-Dit Herre. In the centre of town, turn off the D17 at the roundabout, sp 'Office Notarial'. Pass Casino Hotel front entrance. Turn right at next roundabout, sp 'Office Notarial' and signed. Turn left after Office Notorial, sp 'Aire Camping-Cars'. Turn left in 100m into Aire, signed.

Sanitation:

Parking:

25; €6 inc elec; CC

Custom; €2; CC

Commercial Aire located on the outskirts of the small town. Very low amp elec suitable for battery charging only. Pleasant medieval town 10 mins. Visited 2012.

AMOU

105 D11 N43°35.350' W000°44.583' 40330

Directions: Ave de la Digue. From roundabout junction of D13 and D15 turn onto Promenade pour Piétons. Follow road to Ave de la Digue. Service Point at unmanned municipal campsite.

Sanitation:

Parking:

None

Custom; Open Apr-Oct

Campsite in pleasant woodland setting, opp stadium. Guardian calls. Inspected 2010.

POMAREZ 106 D11 N43°37.697' W000°49.700' 40360

Directions: From south on D7 Aire on left on central gravel parking area in front of bullring.

Sanitation:

Parking:

6; Max 72hrs

Custom, 12 unmetered elec points

SP

It may be poss to park at the sports centre. Aire closed when bullring in use (approx 20 days per year). Inspected 2010.

PEYREHORADE 107 D11 N43°32.584' W001°05.996' 40300

Directions: D817/Quai du Sablot, near Carrefour supermarket. From A641 take Exit 6 and follow sp 'Peyrehorade'. Cross river bridge and turn right. Aire on left, signed.

Sanitation:

Parking:

10; Parking on fine gravel with some soft patches

Custom

SP

Carrefour supermarket adj; On busy main route only 5 mins from motorway. Inspected 2010.

POUILLON 1 108 D11 N43°36.595' W000°59.514' 40350

Directions: Blvd des Sports/D322. Service Point outside municipal campsite, opp large 'Maisadour' building.

Sanitation:

Parking:

None; See 109

Custom

SP

Campsite closed at time of inspection (Sept) but Service Point still operational. Inspected 2010.

POUILLON 2 109 D11 N43°35.639' W001°00.942' 40350

Directions: Route du Lac. Follow D61 southwest through Pouillon village. At junction with D22 turn left onto D22, then immediately right into Route du Lac. After 900m turn left into large lower car park. Also parking in smaller, higher car park nearer lake.

Sanitation:

Parking:

6

Tap only; See 108

SP

Pretty lake (no views from parking); Walking; BBQ; Restaurant with lake views; Swimming not allowed. Inspected 2010.

DAX 110 D11 N43°42.833' W001°02.950' 40100

Directions: Boulevard Albert Camus. From D824 take D947 south through St-Paul-les-Dax. Take 1st left across river bridge then turn left again at roundabout into Blvd Albert Camus. Aire immediately on left.

Sanitation:

Parking:

7; Max 72hrs

Custom

SP

Floating restaurant 180m. Town centre 450m. Inspected 2010.

ST PAUL LES DAX

111 D10 N43°44.052' W001°04.604' 40990

Directions: Travel on D524 through town. Once past lake turn right at roundabout onto Allée du Plumet. Follow to Aire entrance at end of road.

Sanitation:

Parking:

8; Max 48hrs

Custom

Woodland setting at the end of the lake road. Lovely lake walks. No lake parking 10pm- 6am. Inspected 2010.

ST VINCENT DE TYROSSE

112 D11 N43°40.113' W001°16.888' 40230

Directions: D810, at Netto supermarket. Entrance in front of McDonalds at the E'Leclerc supermarket roundabout.

Sanitation:

Parking:

None

Custom; Token (2/2)

Service Point only. Self service laundry. Inspected 2012.

SOUSTONS PLAGE

113 D11 N43°46.518' W001°24.628' 40140

Directions: Ave de la Petre. From D652 turn at roundabout sp 'Soustons Plage', 'Port de Albert Sud' and signed. Follow road to end, signed. Entrance through barrier.

Sanitation:

Parking:

50; €11/night inc elec May-Sept; €6/night inc elec Oct-Apr; Pay at machine

Euro Relais Junior; inc

Commercial Aire; Views over tidal lake; Beach through trees. Inspected 2010.

SEIGNOSSE

114 C11 N43°41.447' W001°25.536' 40510

Directions: D79. Adj to D79 coast road, signed. Pay at ticket machine and enter through bollards.

Sanitation:

Parking:

30; €8/night; CC; Grass parking

Custom

Commercial Aire located between noisy D79 coast road and a large campsite. Grass parking under evergreen trees. Inspected 2012.

HAVE YOU VISITED AN AIRE? GPS co-ordinates in this guide are protected by copyright law

Take at least 5 digital photos showing
- Signs
- Service Point
- Parking
- Overview
- Amenities

Visit www.all-the-aires.co.uk/submissions.shtml to upload your updates and photos.

Sanitation:

Aire Details:

Submit updates
- Amendments
- New Aires
- Not changed

CAPBRETON

116 C11 N43°38.143' W001°26.809' 40130

Directions: Allée des Ortolans, at beach. From town centre head southeast towards beach on Ave Georges Clemenceau. Go over 1st roundabout, then left at the next onto Ave des Alouettes and follow to Allée des Ortolans. Aire on right. Follow sp 'Aire Camping Car' through town.

Sanitation:

Parking:

200; €6 low season; €8.50 mid season; €10 high season

Custom; inc elec

Sand dune beach; Sea and surfing adj. No shade. Inspected 2010.

LABENNE OCEAN

117 C11 N43°35.685' W001°27.278' 40530

Directions: D126. From D810 at Labenne take D126 sp 'Labenne-Ocean'. Aire on right as enter Labenne-Ocean sp 'Parc Aquatique'.

Sanitation:

Parking:

70; €6.50 15/6-15/9; Collected early am; Parking between trees on soft sand and grass

Custom

Adventure park adj with waterslide. Washing up sinks. Inspected 2010.

ONDRES PLAGE

118 C11 N43°34.589' W001°29.215' 40440

Directions: D26/Ave de la Plage. From Ondres follow D26, sp 'Ondres Plage'. At end of road, in car parks, drive to far end then turn left and Aire in 'Parking 3'.

Sanitation:

Parking:

41; €7/night; €9/night Jul-Aug; Max 48hrs

Customised Flot Bleu Pacific; 2 unmetered elec points

Sandy surfing beach 2 mins; Restaurant. Inspected 2010.

ANGLET

119 C11 N43°30.427' W001°32.059' 64600

Directions: Parking des Corsaires, off D405/Blvd des Plages. Aire in large car park off D405 adj to beach, sp 'Anglet-Océan' and 'La Barre'.

Sanitation:

Parking:

60; €6 Jul-Aug only; Max 48hrs

Euro Relais Junior

Beach 5 mins downhill; Surfing beach. Long motorhomes may need to manoeuvre to use Service Point. Inspected 2010.

BIARRITZ

120 C11 N43°27.990' W001°34.302' 64200

Directions: Avenue de la Milady. Enter from south on D911. Aire at bottom of hill past golf course. Entrance on right.

Sanitation:

Parking:

50; €10; Max 48hrs; Collected by police 7-8pm

Custom (x2); 24 elec points on 6 bollards

Very busy all year. Beach and supermarket 5 mins; Biarritz centre 20 mins. Inspected 2010.

ST JEAN DE LUZ

121 C11 N43°23.112' W001°39.780' 64500

Directions: Pont Charles de Gaulle, on D810. From south on D810 cross river bridge and Aire immediately on right, adj to marina.

Sanitation:

Parking:

20; Max 48hrs

Raclet; 2 unmetered CEE elec points

Always busy, can be noisy. Between railway line and main road; Unpleasant. Inspected 2010.

HENDAYE PLAGE

122 C11 N43°22.213' W001°45.887' 64700

Directions: Rue d'Ansoenia. Enter town from south on D912. Turn right onto Rue des Rosiers and follow to end. Turn right again and left at roundabout. Aire is on left by train station.

Sanitation:

Parking:

15; Max 24hrs

Custom

Town 10 mins; Popular, arrive early. Nicer stop than St Jean de Luz 121. Inspected 2012.

ST PEE SUR NIVELLE

123 C11 N43°20.983' W001°31.283' 64310

Directions: Promenade du Parlement de Navarre. Large Aire by lake and leisure park about 4km from town. Access via barrier raised by inserting credit card.

Sanitation:

Parking:

62; €8.50/24hrs; 8m bays

Flot Bleu Euro; Token; CC; €2; 12 elec points; 1 Token/4hrs elec

Pleasant lake walk. Swimming; Pedalos. Services outside parking area but elec inside parking. Inspected 2010.

SARE

124 C11 N43°18.794' W001°34.621' 64310

Directions: L'Eglise, at Salle Polyvalente (community centre/village hall). From the east edge of village turn off D4, sp 'Sare' and signed. Aire is on left in car park before the village.

Sanitation:

Parking:

15; €6; Max 48hrs; Pay at machine

Custom

Picturesque Basque village. Inspected 2010.

COL D'IBARDIN

125 C11 N43°18.583' W001°41.133' 64122

Directions: D404, Ibardin, on the border of France and Spain. From Urrugne take D4 to Col d'Ibardin and follow signs to the border at the summit of the hill. Parking on the right adj to road to shops.

Sanitation:

Parking:

20

None

Parking for motorhomes on Spanish border. Ideal for buying cheap goods. Inspected 2010.

SOUSTONS
126 D11 N43°44.798' W001°19.291' 40140

Directions: Avenue de Cramat. From D810 or A63/E70 turn onto D17, sp 'Soustons'. After 8.5km, at start of town, turn left off D17 into Avenue de Cramat. Service Point on left in 200m, in car park of Netto supermarket.

Sanitation:

Parking:

Poss

Custom; Token (2/2); No toilet disposal

Service Point in supermarket car park. Inspected 2010.

VIEUX BOUCAU LES BAINS 1
127 C11 N43°46.815' W001°24.071' 40480

Directions: Avenue des Pêcheurs. From south on D652 turn left at large roundabout, sp 'Port d'Albret entrée Nord' and 'Aire de Camping Car'. Aire 350m on right. Security barrier; pay on exit.

Sanitation:

Parking:

120; €11/night inc elec May-Sept; €5/night inc elec Oct-Apr; Max 48hrs

Custom; inc

SP

Beach 5 mins; Shops, golf course adj; Wind and kite surfing on lake. Inspected 2010.

VIEUX BOUCAU LES BAINS 2
128 C11 N43°47.675' W001°24.322' 40480

Directions: Boulevard du Marensin, near the Plage (beach) des Sablères. North of town. Follow sp 'Municipal Camping des Sableres'. Go past the entrance to small parking area. Take ticket, pay on exit.

Sanitation:

Parking:

35; €11 Summer; €5 Winter; Max 48hrs

Custom; inc; Elec available but most not working

Campsite adj. Inspected 2010.

MIZIMAN PLAGE
129 D10 N44°12.839' W001°16.938' 40200

Photo/Info: Liam Madden

Directions: D626. From Mimizan turn right, as enter Mimizan Plage, at roundabout sp 'Plage du Courant'. Entrance to Aire 230m on right.

Sanitation:

Parking:

50; €6/night; pay at machine

Flot Bleu Pacific; €3

SP

1.5km from Mimizan Plage, 6 mins to estuary. Adj to D626. Visited 2012.

ST PAUL LES DAX
130 D11 N43°43.653' W001°03.650' 40990

Directions: Rue Rene Loustalot. Turn off D824 onto D947 and follow sp 'St Paul les Dax'. At roundabout take the 1st exit, sp 'Lac de Christus' and 'Casino'. Follow sp 'Lac de Christus' and 'Casino' and at the end of road turn right, then immediately left, signed. Service Point on left.

Sanitation:

Parking:

4; No parking Mon-Fri

Custom

Service Point only except Fri and Sat nights. Parking is reserved for municipal staff who arrive early weekday mornings. Inspected 2012.

MOLIETS PLAGE — 131 — C10 — N43°51.040' W001°22.952' — 40660

Photo/Info: D Cox

Directions: Rue du Tuc. Exit Moliets-et-Maa to west on D117/Avenue de L'Ocean, sp 'Plages' and signed. Turn left into Rue du Tuc and Aire immediately on right through barrier, signed.

Sanitation:

Parking:

40; €11/24hrs April-Sept; €5/24hrs Oct-Mar

Custom

SP

Sea 5 mins; Restaurants and bars at sea; Golf adj. Low trees. Inspected 2010.

LEON — 132 — D10 — N43°53.037' W001°19.086' — 40550

Directions: D409/Route de Puntaou. At roundabout in Léon turn onto D409, sp 'Le Lac'. At lake turn left and follow road. Parking area signed 250m from lake.

Sanitation:

Parking:

50; €8; Pay at machine

Custom

SP

Large parking area amongst pine trees; Pleasant; Swimming. Inspected 2010.

LAC DE VIELLE ST GIRONS — 133 — D10 — N43°54.178' W001°18.572' — 40560

Directions: At the lake, opp campsite 'Le Col Vert'. Enter town from east on D652. Pass campsite on left and at next junction turn left, sp 'Camping Car'. Follow road for 400m and bear right, then left in 200m. Follow for 1km more and bear left to Aire.

Sanitation:

E

Parking:

20; €11/24hrs Jul-Aug €8/24hrs Sept-Jun; Max 48hrs; Tax €0.61pp

Custom; inc; Showers; Elec €4.40

SP

Lake 2 mins, Rural views; Mini golf; Bar/restaurant; Beach. Inspected 2010.

GPS Co-ordinates for SatNav

The GPS Co-ordinates published in this guide were taken onsite by our inspectors. We consider them a valuable and unique asset and at the time of publishing have decided not to publish them as electronic files for use on navigation devices. You have permission to type in the co-ordinates of an Aire you intend to visit but not to store or share them. For the security of our copyright:

- **Do not compile them into lists**
- **Do not publish, share or reproduce them anywhere in any format**

VIELLE ST GIRONS — 135 — D10 — N43°57.185' W001°21.478' — 40560

Directions: D42/Aire Camping-Car Les Tourterelles. Turn off D652 onto D42, sp 'St Girons-Plage'. Follow road towards sea then turn right at roundabout, signed. Turn right again to Aire, signed. Entrance to Aire through barrier.

Sanitation:

Parking:

48; €9.30/night May, June, Sept, €13.90/night July, €14.10/night Aug

Aire Services Box; Token (3/3)

SP

Commercial Aire 2 mins from sandy beach. Inspected 2012.

ST JULIEN EN BORN

136 D10 N44°04.248' W001°13.814' 40170

Directions: D652. At small supermarket adj to D652.

Sanitation:

Parking:

Poss

Raclet; €2

Supermarket adj; Fuel. Inspected 2010.

MORCENX

137 D10 N44°02.321' W000°54.576' 40110

Directions: Chemin de L'Abattoir. From town follow D77 towards Sabres. In 200m turn right, signed. Follow road to end and the Service Point on left.

Sanitation:

Parking:

5; Grass/sand parking

Custom

Service Point behind sports facilities and adj to noisy mainline train track. Town centre with small town commerce, 3 mins. Inspected 2012.

CONTIS PLAGE

138 D10 N44°05.600' W001°19.117' 40170

Directions: Ave du Phare. Enter on D41 and turn right, sp 'Le Phare'. Drive down road until houses end then turn left. Aire at end of road.

Sanitation:

Parking:

30; €8/night Jun-Sept; CC; Max 48hrs

Raclet; €2

Showers. 4 mins from beach over dune (uphill); Town commerce 5 mins. Inspected 2010.

MIMIZAN

139 D10 N44°13.178' W001°13.786' 40200

Directions: D87. Adj to D87 as exit town to north, at municipal campsite.

Sanitation:

Parking:

20; €8.40 €13.10 inc 10amp elec

Flot Bleu Pacific; €2

Isolated; Commercial Aire. BBQs in campsite. Inspected 2010.

MIMIZAN PLAGE

140 D10 N44°12.291' W001°17.829' 40200

Directions: Rue des Gourbets. From Mimizan follow sp 'Plage', then turn left, sp 'Mimizan Plage'. Then follow sp 'Station Camping Car'. Aire in large car park adj to beach. Entrance through Flot Bleu Park barrier.

Sanitation:

Parking:

80; €12; Flot Bleu Park

Flot Bleu Pacific; Elec inc

Sand dune adj; Sandy beach 2 mins; Seaside resort with cafés/restaurant; Surfing beach. Inspected 2010.

STE EULALIE EN BORN

141 D10 N44°18.362' W001°10.915' 40200

Directions: Route du Lac, off D652. Turn off D652 onto Route du Lac, sp 'Camping Municipal', and follow for 1.9km to Aire at end of road on left. Park on left-hand side among trees and pay at campsite reception opp.

Sanitation:

Parking:

40; €4/night Apr and Oct; €6.50/night May-Sept; Free Nov-Mar

Custom

SP

Overlooking marina; Parking on left, do not park on right. Café in season. No services when free. Inspected 2010.

GASTES

142 D10 N44°19.714' W001°09.057' 40160

Directions: Ave du Lac. From Gastes head north and turn at roundabout, sp 'Le Lac'. At end of road turn left. Parking on grass, sp 'Aire Naturelle Camping Car'. Bollarded entry/exit, credit card system.

Sanitation:

Parking:

50; €2 16/11-15/3; €4.50 16/3-15/5, 16/9-15/11; €7 16/5-15/9

Custom; CC; inc

SP

Small town with local commerce. Aire overlooking boats adj to lake. Sandy beach. Inspected 2010.

PARENTIS EN BORN 1

143 D10 N44°20.920' W001°03.950' 40160

Directions: D43, at the Super U. Adj to car wash in car park.

Sanitation:

E

Parking:

Poss

Raclet; €2; No drive over drain

SP

Supermarket adj. Inspected 2010.

PARENTIS EN BORN 2

144 D10 N44°20.653' W001°05.907' 40160

Directions: Route des Campings. From centre follow sp 'Le Lac'. Just before lake turn right, sp 'La Paillotte et Le Pipiou'. Aire 100m on right. Entrance bollarded, entry by CC.

Sanitation:

E

Parking:

20; €6/night May-Sept; €5/night Oct-Apr

Euro Relais Junior; inc; 6 elec points

SP

Lake 2 mins; Marina and restaurants adj. Inspected 2010.

BISCARROSSE

145 D10 N44°24.636' W001°10.065' 40600

Directions: D146/Ave de Laouadie, at the E'Leclerc supermarket. From west on D146 cross over river and Aire on right opp McDonalds at large roundabout junction.

Sanitation:

Parking:

Poss

Euro Relais Mini

SP

Supermarket adj; McDonalds. Inspected 2010.

NAVARROSSE

146 D10 N44°25.920' W001°09.958' 40600

Directions: Base de Loisirs, off Chemin de Navarrosse. From east on D305/Rte des Lacs turn right onto Chemin de Navarrosse. Take 2nd right and 2nd right again following sp 'P Camping Car'. Aire at end of road.

Sanitation:

Parking:

15; €7

Euro Relais Junior

SP

Overlooking small marina; Shop in summer. Some hardstanding; Some very soft, deep sand. Inspected 2010.

BISCARROSSE PLAGE 1

147 D10 N44°27.422' W001°14.449' 40600

Directions: Rue du Tit. From Biscarrosse take D146 northwest towards Biscarrosse Plage for approx 7.5km. Cross over 3 roundabouts. At 4th roundabout turn left onto Rue des Alouettes. Turn right at roundabout and Aire in 400m.

Sanitation:

Parking:

80; €7

Raclet

SP

Walk to beach; Beach and sand dunes adj. Parking amongst trees. Inspected 2010.

BISCARROSSE PLAGE 2

148 D10 N44°26.391' W001°14.883' 40600

Directions: Impasse des Pluviers. From Biscarrosse take D146 northwest towards Biscarrosse Plage for approx 7.5km. At roundabout turn left and left again onto Rue des Bécasse. Drive past campsite and Service Point on left in lay-by with recycling bins.

Sanitation:

E

Parking:

None

Euro Relais Junior

SP

Service Point only. Inspected 2010.

SANGUINET 1

149 D10 N44°29.160' W001°05.049' 40460

Directions: Ave de Losa at lake. Follow sp from centre to 'Le Lac'. Turn left and drive around lake road. Turn off 1st turning to left by the Pavillion restaurant, sp 'Parking'.

Sanitation:

Parking:

10; €7; Grass parking

None

SP

Lake and beach adj; Restaurant; Town 5 mins; Boats. Some soft ground. Inspected 2010.

SANGUINET 2

150 D10 N44°29.037' W001°05.495' 40460

Directions: Aire des Bardets, on Ave de Losa at lake. As previous except follow road around past campsite and turn left, sp 'Camping Car'.

Sanitation:

Parking:

10; €7; Grass parking

Custom

SP

Sailing school adj; Campsite adj; Lake adj; Ground soft if wet. Inspected 2010.

DUNE DU PYLA (PILAT)

151 D9 N44°35.833' W001°11.900' 33115

Directions: Access via entry barrier, pay on exit. Motorhome parking area in main car park.

Sanitation:

Parking:

Daytime only; €8/4hrs; €10/10hrs

None

SP

Largest sand dune in Europe accessible at all times; Many gift shops but pleasant in evening. Inspected 2010.

LE TEICH

152 D9 N44°37.984' W001°01.585' 33470

Directions: Rue de l'industrie. Exit A660 at Junction 3. Go straight over roundabout onto D650E1 sp, 'Gare S.N.C.F' and 'Centre ville'. Cross the level crossing and turn immediate left. Follow the railway track on left and cross mini roundabout. The Aire is on the left past the station building at the end of the car park, signed.

Sanitation:

Parking:

5

Urba Flux; €1

SP

Adj to railway so noise from relatively quiet electric trains. Frequent trains to beach resort at Arcachon. Parc Ornithologique at Le Teich is worth a visit. Visited 2012.

AUDENGE

153 D9 N44°41.066' W001°00.293' 33980

Directions: D5e5, in municipal campsite car park. From D3 turn onto D5e5, sp 'Camping Municipal' and 'Camping Cars'. At roundabout turn 1st right. Campsite adj to roundabout.

Sanitation:

Parking:

None

Euro Relais Junior; Token; €4

SP

5 mins from town. Tokens available from TO or campsite. Inspected 2010.

ARCACHON

154 D9 N44°39.096' W001°08.893' 33120

Directions: D650. On entering town Aire is opp Citroën/Total garage next to LIDL, outside stadium.

Sanitation:

Parking:

5

Raclet

SP

Not ideal, on busy main road. Noisy; No views. Inspected 2010.

ANDERNOS LES BAINS

155 D9 N44°44.652' W001°06.516' 33510

Directions: Ave du Commandant Allègre. Turn off D3, main route, following sp 'Port', then 'Aire de Camping Car'. Parking 100m past Service Point under pine trees.

Sanitation:

Parking:

40; €7.50; Max 48hrs

Raclet; Token (ER); €2.10

SP

Oysters for sale. Seafront 5 mins. TO. Inspected 2010.

TAUSSAT — 156 — D9 — N44°43.035' W001°04.180' — 33138

Directions: Avenue Albert Pitres. From south on D3 exit Le Renet and travel 900m. Turn left onto Rue Dominique. At end of road turn right onto Blvd de la Plage and take next right onto Ave Albert Pitres. Aire on right.

Sanitation: E WC F

Parking: P F

4

WC only

SP

Next to small tidal fishing harbour; Beach 50m; Village 300m. Inspected 2010.

ARES — 157 — D9 — N44°46.181' W001°06.707' — 33740

Directions: D106. Service Point at the Hyper U supermarket.

Sanitation: E WC F

Parking: P F

Poss

Flot Bleu Pacific; €2

SP

Supermarket adj. Inspected 2012.

LE PORGE — 158 — D9 — N44°52.362' W001°05.578' — 33680

Directions: Place Saint Seurin, off D3. From south on D3 at roundabout in town turn in front of church into Place St. Seurin. Aire in parking area along roadside between TO and church.

Sanitation: E WC F

Parking: P F

5; Small bays with overhang; No Parking market day Thur 6am-2pm

Tap only

SP

In village. Pleasant stop. WiFi at TO 50m. Inspected 2010.

HAVE YOU VISITED AN AIRE?

GPS co-ordinates in this guide are protected by copyright law

Take at least 5 digital photos showing
• Signs
• Service Point
• Parking
• Overview
• Amenities

Visit www.all-the-aires.co.uk/submissions.shtml to upload your updates and photos.

Sanitation: E WC F

Aire Details: P F

Submit updates

- Amendments
- New Aires
- Not changed

LE MOUTCHIC — 160 — D9 — N44°59.934' W001°08.431' — 33680

Directions: Off Avenue de la Grande Escoure. On D6e4 head south out of Le Moutchic towards Carreyre. D6e4 bends to right, but turn left onto Ave de la Grande Escoure following sp 'Carreyre' and 'Camping le Tedey'. In 300m turn right by memorial into gateway of dilapidated château.

Sanitation: E WC F

Parking: P F

10; €10 inc elec; Summer only

Custom; 16 elec points

SP

Adj to lake; Dilapidated buildings onsite. Village with restaurant 2 mins. Surrounded by wood. Inspected 2010.

LE HUGA

161 D9 N45°00.365' W001°09.925' 33680

Directions: Allée de Sauviels, off D6. From west on D6 as enter le Huga Aire is on both sides of road with Service Points at each. Entrance through barrier.

Sanitation:

Parking:

150; €13/24hrs inc elec; CC

Custom

Large landscaped Commercial Aire. Inspected 2010.

CARCANS

162 D9 N45°05.106' W001°08.904' 33121

Directions: Route de Bombannes. Exit D207 at roundabout onto Rte de Bombannes. Travel approx 1.5km to Aire on left.

Sanitation:

Parking:

30; €5.50; Open Jun-Sept

Flot Bleu Fontaine

Lovely wooded area near lake. Inspected 2010.

HOURTIN PORT

163 D9 N45°10.841' W001°04.885' 33990

Directions: Avenue du Lac. From south on D3 turn left in Hourtin onto D4/Avenue du Lac, sp 'Hourtin Port'. Continue over roundabout and follow road for 1.5km. 500m after Camping les Ormes, turn left at small crossroads. Aire on right.

Sanitation:

Parking:

30; €8/night; CC

Flot Bleu Fontaine; €2

Beach and marina adj. Individual pitches. Pay at cycle hire adj to mini golf. Inspected 2010.

GRAYAN ET L'HOPITAL

164 D8 N45°25.995' W001°08.625' 33590

Info/Photo: Martin & Gail Boizot

Directions: Route de l'Ocean. In Les Eyres turn off the D101 onto C202 sp, 'Le Gurp' and 'Camping Municipal du Gurp'. Follow C202 all the way towards sea, going straight over roundabout and the Service Point is on the right adj to Camping Municipal du Gurp.

Sanitation:

Parking:

12; Max 48hrs

Euro Relais Junior; Token ER; €3.50

700m from a vast sandy beach. Parking on a large, level grassy verge alongside road to coast. Small convenience store, beach shops and restaurants 450m.

MONTALIVET LES BAINS 1

165 D8 N45°22.120' W001°08.657' 33930

Directions: Aire 'La Foret', Avenue de L'Europe. Turn left off D102 onto Ave de l'Europe as enter town from east. Follow road for 900m and Aire just past Camping Municipal de Montalivet.

Sanitation:

Parking:

20; €4/night July/Aug; €2/night May/June/Sept; Free Oct-Apr

Custom

Small woodland Aire. Inspected 2010.

MONTALIVET LES BAINS 2 — 166 — D8 — N45°22.230' W001°08.658' — 33930

Directions: Ave de l'Europe. Enter town from east on D102. Turn left onto Ave de l'Europe before roundabout. Aire in 700m, outside municipal campsite Camping de Montalivet.

Sanitation:

Parking:

20; €8/night Jul-Aug; €4/night May, Jun and Sept

Custom; inc elec

Only open May–Sept. Inspected 2010.

MONTALIVET LES BAINS 3 — 167 — D8 — N45°22.535' W001°09.431' — 33930

Directions: Aire 'Plage Sud', Blvd de Lattre de Tassigny. Enter town from east on D102/Ave de l'Océan and follow to beach. At end of road turn left and follow to end of that road, turning left again onto Blvd de Lattre de Tassigny. Aire next to surf school, sp 'Camping Cars No 3'.

Sanitation:

Parking:

60; €5 Jul-Aug; €3 May, Jun and Sept

Customised Flot Bleu; €2

Beach adj. 1 min to town. Very nice Aire adj to beach and dunes. Sunday market in town. Inspected 2010.

SOULAC SUR MER — 168 — D8 — N45°30.001' W001°08.325' — 33780

Photo/Info: Martin Boizot

Directions: Blvd de l'Amelie. From south on D101 take the 2nd left turn sp 'L'Amelie'. At end of road turn left sp 'L'Amelie'. Turn left onto D101E2, sp 'Camping Les Sables'. Aire on right adjacent to and sp 'Camping les Sables d'Argent'.

Sanitation:

Parking:

45; €8/24hrs June-Sept; €4/24hrs rest of year

Euro Relais Junior; Token; €3.50

This Aire has moved location. Direct access to beach and town accessible via cycle path. Visited 2011

HAVE YOU VISITED AN AIRE? — GPS co-ordinates in this guide are protected by copyright law

Take at least 5 digital photos showing
• Signs
• Service Point
• Parking
• Overview
• Amenities

Visit www.all-the-aires.co.uk/submissions.shtml to upload your updates and photos.

Sanitation:

Aire Details:

Submit updates

- Amendments
- New Aires
- Not changed

LE VERDON SUR MER — 170 — D8 — N45°32.722' W001°03.263' — 33123

Info/Photo: Sally Dingle

Directions: Allée des Baines/D1e4. From south on D1215 turn right onto D1e4, sp 'Le Verdon sur Mer'. Follow road to end (later part on cobbles). Service Point and parking on left. Further motorhome area around corner to left in Avenue de la Plage. Entrance through barrier.

Sanitation:

Parking:

56; €5/night Oct-May, €8/night June-Sept; CC; Max 72hrs

Urba Flux Tall; €2; CC

Some shade; Local commerce 1 min. TO. Handy for ferry and Royan. Inspected 2010.

LESPARRE MEDOC

171 D8 N45°18.769' W000°56.733' 33340

Directions: D1215/Route de Lesparre. Follow D1215 west out of town. After roundabout travel 700m and Service Point at Netto supermarket on left.

Sanitation:

Parking:

3; Max 24hrs

Custom; Token (2/2); €3; No toilet emptying

SP

Small car park but could overhang gravel area at end. Free token when spending €50 in Netto; Ask for key to drain cover. Inspected 2010.

ST ESTEPHE

172 D8 N45°15.850' W000°45.483' 33180

Directions: D2e2. From Lesparre-Medoc take D204. Turn left onto D2, sp 'St Estephe', and follow road through village to estuary. Aire on left of road on grassy area overlooking Gironde Estuary.

Sanitation:

Parking:

20

Euro Relais Junior; Token (ER); Free from local bar

SP

Lovely parking area with 180° views along Gironde Estuary. Noise from road and bar. Village 1.9km. Inspected 2010.

MACAU

173 D9 N45°00.433' W000°36.767' 33460

Directions: Chemin du Mahoura. From D2 turn into Macau at the roundabout and follow the road straight on. At the crossroads, almost in the centre turn right twice and then take the next left. The Aire is on the left.

Sanitation:

Parking:

8; 6m bays

Flot Bleu Océane; Token required for elec only

SP

Small car park with small bays - not ideal. Inspected 2010.

ST JEAN D'ILLAC

174 D9 N44°48.615' W000°46.495' 33127

Directions: Allée J.J. Rousseau off D106 roundabout at the Casino supermarket. Near the LIDL, signed.

Sanitation:

Parking:

4

Flot Bleu Euro; CC; €2

SP

LIDL and supermarket adj. No parking at sports centre. Inspected 2010.

SAUTERNES

175 E9 N44°32.050' W000°20.617' 33210

Directions: D125e1. From Langon take D8 south. Turn right onto D125 sp 'Sauternes'. At village square/one way system continue into village on D125e1. Aire on right immediately past church.

Sanitation:

Parking:

5

Custom

SP

Local shop, TO, wine shops in village. Visited 2011.

PREIGNAC

176 E9 N44°35.125' W000°17.731' 33210

Directions: On D1113. Signed off D1113, main route through. Drive through square with Mairie (town hall) and past trees. Aire before sports ground. Parking area away from road noise.

Sanitation:

Parking:

8

Custom

Nice views of rooftops/church from Aire. Town adj. Inspected 2010.

CADILLAC

177 E9 N44°38.319' W000°19.011' 33410

Directions: Allée du Parc. Follow signs from roundabout junction of D10 and D11. Aire located in the 2nd car park on one-way street.

Sanitation:

Parking:

8; Max 3 nights

Custom; 4 5amp elec points; €2/3hrs

Cadillac is a beautiful walled town, surrounded by vines, 2 mins. Inspected 2010.

CAPIAN

178 E9 N44°42.769' W000°19.775' 33550

Directions: Lavergne Nord, off D13. From Créon take D13, sp 'Cadillac' and 'Capian'. Turn left just before church as enter village into Chemin de Lavergne, signed. Aire on left between boules pitches and walled cemetery, signed.

Sanitation:

Parking:

10

None; Tap in cemetery

Newly made Aire. No services apparent but may be added in future. Overlooking vines. Village 2 mins. Inspected 2010.

CREON

179 E9 N44°46.578' W000°20.920' 33670

Directions: Blvd Victor Hugo. From Bordeaux take D936 then D671, sp 'Créon'. At Créon turn left onto D121e5 ring road. After 150m turn left into car park. Aire at far end of car park. May be barriered to keep cars out - replace barrier after entry.

Sanitation:

Parking:

5; Max 5 days

Flot Bleu Océane; Token for elec only

Boulangerie adj; Town 2 mins. Next village, La Sauve, has ruined abbey. Inspected 2010.

JUGAZAN

180 E9 N44°46.914' W000°08.576' 33420

Directions: D128. Follow D128 east from town for 3km and Aire just after junction with D119 in lay-by on D128 at Librie, small hamlet adj to Jagazan.

Sanitation:

Parking:

4

None; See 187

Parking in lay-by on D128 in Labrie Hamlet next to Jugazan. For services see 187. Better parking at 181. Inspected 2010.

GREZILLAC

181 | E9 | N44°49.034' W000°12.989' | 33420

Directions: Le Bourg, off D11. Turn off D936 onto D11, sp 'Grézillac'. In village turn 2nd left into Le Bourg, signed. Aire in gravel parking area on left opp Foyer Rural and Mairie, signed.

Sanitation:

Parking:

10

None; See 187

SP

Pleasant parking overlooking vines and open countryside. Inspected 2010.

NAUJAN ET POSTIAC

182 | E9 | N44°47.223' W000°10.755' | 33420

Directions: Off D128. From Branne follow D19 south for 4.5km. Turn left onto D128, sp 'Naujan et Postiac'. Drive through village and turn right, sp 'Stade' and signed. Aire in small gravel parking area on left adj to stadium and grass area, opp vines.

Sanitation:

Parking:

3

None; See 187

SP

Cycle track from Bordeaux to Sauvetere de Guyenne signed in village. Stadium adj. Roadside parking but very quiet village road surrounded by vines. Inspected 2010.

BAZAS

183 | E10 | N44°26.022' W000°12.912' | 33430

Directions: D655e1/Cours Gambetta. From south on N524 turn right onto D932e9, sp 'Bazas'. In town follow one way system for 300m. Aire on left of Cours Gambetta in car park between Rue de L'Eyrevieille and Rue du 11 Novembre 1918.

Sanitation:

Parking:

10

Euro Relais Mini

SP

Aire in town centre car park. Inspected 2010.

FRONTENAC

184 | E9 | N44°44.225' W000°09.772' | 33760

Directions: D231. In centre of village, turn opp church and next to Mairie. Aire behind Mairie, signed. Drive to end of road.

Sanitation:

Parking:

10

Custom

SP

Beautiful communal area in centre of village. Toilet block with outdoor sinks avail in summer. Inspected 2010.

SAUVETERRE DE GUYENNE

185 | E9 | N44°41.400' W000°05.183' | 33540

Directions: Rue de la Gare, off D670. On south side of D670 ring road turn right onto Rue de la Gare. Aire on right next to Cave Co-operative. 3.5t weight limit on Aire.

Sanitation:

Parking:

5

Custom; Token; €1.50

SP

Tokens from Casino 'Maison de la Presse'. Cycle path to Créon. Inspected 2010.

ST PEY D'ARMENS — 186 — E9 — N44°51.176' W000°06.406' — 33330

Directions: Château Gerbaud, off D936e7. From Libourne take D670, sp 'Castillon la Bataille'. Turn left onto D936, sp 'Bergerac'. At St Pey D'Armens turn right onto D936e7, sp 'Château Gerbaud' and signed. Follow signs to Aire at château. Well signed.

Sanitation:

Parking:

20; €5; Max 48hrs; Grass parking

Custom; inc

Near St Emillion wine area, tasting onsite. Very pretty town. Some electric facility. Inspected 2010.

BRANNE — 187 — E9 — N44°49.920' W000°11.070' — 33420

Directions: Rue Emmanuel Roy. From west on D936 follow main road through Branne and turn right onto D18 immediately before river bridge, signed. Aire on left in 150m along bank of Dordogne, signed.

Sanitation:

Parking:

5; Roadside

Euro Relais Junior; Token (ER); €2

On bank of Dordogne on edge of town. Inspected 2010.

LIBOURNE — 188 — E9 — N44°54.393' W000°14.032' — 33500

Directions: Off D670. At the Intermarché supermarket.

Sanitation:

Parking:

Poss

Flot Bleu Pacific; €2

Supermarket adj. Inspected 2012.

LUSSAC — 189 — E9 — N44°56.777' W000°05.703' — 33570

Directions: Lieu-Dit la Grange. Enter on D17 from south. Take the 2nd turning on the left, sp 'Aire Touristique'. Follow road and Aire on left, signed.

Sanitation:

Parking:

3; Very sloping, small parking area

Flot Bleu Fontaine; 2 unmetered CEE elec points other side of wooden shed

Aire located overlooking vines 3 mins from local commerce and wineries. Inspected 2012.

MARCENAIS — 190 — E9 — N45°03.484' W000°20.317' — 33620

Directions: Le Bourg. Turn off D18 into Marcenais, signed. Follow the road as it bends right and continue through village. Aire on left behind Salle des Fêtes. Well signed through village and from D18.

Sanitation:

Parking:

10; Max 48hrs

Custom; Tap at WC

Pleasant, rural location on edge of small village. Open views of countryside. Inspected 2010.

MARSAS

191 E9 N45°04.057' W000°23.055' 33620

Directions: D142/Rue Etienne Chaignaud. Exit N10 onto D142, sp 'Marsas'. Follow road into village and parking area on right, opp church and cemetery.

Sanitation:

Parking:

10; Max 48hrs

None; See **204**

Large car park opp church. Inspected 2010.

LARUSCADE

192 E9 N45°06.409' W000°20.692' 33620

Directions: Lac des Vergnes. Exit N10 onto D22 sp 'Laruscade'. In village centre turn right through car park, sp 'Lac des Vergnes' and signed. After 250m parking spaces on left just before lake.

Sanitation:

Parking:

5; Max 48hrs

None; See **204**

Shady parking adj to lake on egde of village. Market days Thurs and Sat. Supermarket on D22 at east of village. Inspected 2010.

ST MARIENS

193 E9 N45°06.915' W000°23.947' 33620

Directions: D22, just off D18/D22 roundabout. Aire on outskirts of St Mariens, sp 'Aire des Lagunes' and signed off D18.

Sanitation:

Parking:

2, Max 48hrs

Custom

In residential area, ideal for night stop. Inspected 2010.

CUBNEZAIS

194 E9 N45°04.507' W000°24.529' 33620

Directions: D248. Exit N10/E606 onto D248e2, sp 'Cubnezais'. At T-junction turn right and follow D248e2/D248e3 into village centre. Turn right/straight ahead onto D248. Aire on left in 100m, signed.

Sanitation:

Parking:

2; Max 48hrs

Tap in WC; See **204**

Small designated area but more space available across road adj to recycling with views of vines. Bus stop adj. Inspected 2010.

CEZAC

195 E9 N45°05.475' W000°25.201' 33620

Directions: Exit N10/E606 onto D18, sp 'Cavignac'. At 1st roundabout take 4th exit onto D249e1, sp 'Cézac'. At T-junction with D249 turn left, sp 'Cézac'. In Cézac centre turn right at traffic lights onto D248, sp 'St Mariens'. Turn next left and Aire on right in 100m, next to Bibliotheque.

Sanitation:

Parking:

2; Max 48hrs

None; See **204**

Parking adj to bibliothèque overlooking football pitch. Inspected 2010.

CAVIGNAC

196 E9 N45°06.009' W000°23.507' 33620

Directions: Rue de la Paix, off D18. Exit N10 onto D18, sp 'Cavignac'. Follow road into town and turn left into Rue de la Paix next to La Poste, sp 'Eglise' and signed. Aire on left in 150m behind 'Maison de la Petite Enfance', signed.

Sanitation:

Parking:

12; Max 48hrs

None; See **204**

Parking next to cemetery overlooking vines. LIDL at north end of town. Super U south of town. Inspected 2010.

CIVRAC DE BLAYE

197 E9 N45°06.717' W000°26.400' 33920

Directions: D135. From St. Mariens take D135 west. On entry to Civrac de Blaye parking at stadium on right. 1 extra designated parking place at Mairie - continue through village on D135 and 'Parc de Mairie' signed on right at N45°06.700' W000°26.683'.

Sanitation:

Parking:

1 at Mairie; 2 at stadium; Max 48hrs

None; See **204**; Tap at stadium

Football pitches and tennis courts adj. Poss up to 10 spaces at stadium. Inspected 2010.

ST VIVIEN DE BLAYE

198 D9 N45°05.900' W000°31.050' 33920

Directions: D132. From St Christoly follow D132 south, sp 'St Vivien de Blaye'. At end of road turn right onto D135. At church turn left onto D132. Aire next to church.

Sanitation:

Parking:

5; Max 48hrs

None; See **204**

Gravel area by church. Pond adj, no fishing. TO at St Savin, 9km. Inspected 2010.

BOURG

199 D9 N45°02.323' W000°33.606' 33710

Info/Photo: John Watts

Directions: Turn off D669, sp 'le Port' and 'Halte Nautique' and follow road downhill. Turn right at the crossroads, sp 'Camping' and follow road to end. Service Point adj to campsite. Unofficial parking available. Go straight on at cross roads at bottom of hill to large open area alongside river, N45°02.279' W000°33.456'.

Sanitation:

Parking:

Tolerated

Raclet; Token (ER); €2

Lively market on Sunday mornings in town square. Panoramic views of river Dordogne from elevated town walls. Steep climb from parking area to commerce in town. Visited 2012.

ST CHRISTOLY DE BLAYE 1

200 D9 N45°07.783' W000°30.467' 33920

Directions: Le Bourg, off D22. From St Savin follow D22 west, sp 'St Christoly'. Turn left in town, sp 'Stade' and signed. Follow road to the right and the Service Point and parking are by entrance to stadium, opp Mairie.

Sanitation:

Parking:

5; Max 48hrs; No parking Sunday am for market.

Custom

Adj to stadium in village centre. Inspected 2010.

ST CHRISTOLY DE BLAYE 2 — 201 — D9 — N45°09.117' W000°28.550' — 33920

Directions: Moulin Blanc, at Lac Baron Desqueyroux . From St Christoly de Blaye follow signs to 'Lacs de Moulin Blanc'. Parking at 'Restaurant de Lac'. Could access from St Savin via D18 to avoid 3.5t weight limit on access road crossing motorway.

Sanitation:

Parking:

5; Max 48hrs

Custom

Lovely woodland area by lakes. Swimming lake with beach. Fishing in smaller lake. No views of lake. Inspected 2010.

ST GIRONS D'AIGUEVIVES — 202 — D9 — N45°08.383' W000°32.567' — 33920

Directions: D134e4, Place du 19 Mars 1962. Follow D134e4 from north or south into town. Aire on bend in D134e4 at war memorial, opposite church and adj to large grassy area.

Sanitation:

Parking:

10; Max 48hrs

None; See 204

Lovely quiet Aire overlooking grassy area. Inspected 2010.

SAUGON — 203 — D9 — N45°10.678' W000°30.281' — 33920

Directions: D252. From St. Savin take D18 north sp 'Saugon, Generac'. As enter village turn right onto D132. In centre of village turn left onto D252. Aire on left in parking area behind mairie and adj to tennis courts.

Sanitation:

Parking:

2; Max 48hrs

Custom

TO at St Savin. Football pitch adj. Inspected 2010.

ST SAVIN 1 — 204 — D9 — N45°08.396' W000°26.516' — 33920

Directions: Rue des Vignes, off D23e2. Exit N10/E606 onto D250, sp 'St Savin'. At roundabout in St Savin take 1st exit onto D23e2. Aire on left behind TO, signed.

Sanitation:

Parking:

2; Max 48hrs

Custom

TO adj has free internet connection, must take own computer. Intermarché 250m. Inspected 2010.

ST SAVIN 2 — 205 — D9 — N45°08.277' W000°26.804' — 33920

Directions: Rue de la Cure, off D18. Exit N10/E606 onto D250, sp 'St Savin'. At roundabout in St Savin take 2nd exit onto D18, signed. After 400m turn left into Rue de la Cure, signed. Aire on left, signed.

Sanitation:

Parking:

2; Max 48hrs

None; See 204

Boulangerie 50m. TO has free internet connection, must take own computer. Intermarché 350m. Inspected 2010.

GENERAC | 206 | D9 | N45°10.822' W000°32.898' | 33920

Directions: D137e4. From Etauliers take D18 south for 5km. Turn right onto D137e4, sp 'Générac'. Aire on left on entry to village, below church.

Sanitation:

Parking:

4; Max 48hrs

None; See 204

Pleasant rural Aire on edge of village overlooking vines and countryside. Inspected 2010.

ST PAUL | 207 | D9 | N45°08.875' W000°36.289' | 33390

Photo/Info: Janet and John Watts

Directions: Place du Souvenir Francais. Drive to crossroads on D737. The Aire is signed from this junction and is located in the car park behind the 1914-1918 war memorial.

Sanitation:

Parking:

10

Aire Services; Token (3/3)

Local commerce in village. St Paul is about 5km east of Blaye which has very popular, large, tolerated parking area used by motorhomers. Visited 2012.

ST CAPRAIS DE BLAYE | 208 | D8 | N45°17.470' W000°34.146' | 33820

Directions: D137. At junction of D137 and D23, north of town. Adj to exercise track.

Sanitation:

Parking:

8; Max 48hrs

Custom

Shop and resturant on site. Village 5 mins, no shops. TO adj, open weekdays only. Inspected 2010.

DONNEZAC | 209 | E9 | N45°14.934' W000°26.583' | 33860

Directions: Le Bourg, near junction of D136 and D115. From St Savin (south) follow D115, sp 'Donnezac'. In Donnezac at junction of D136 and D115 turn right, then immediately left, signed. Pass church and Aire at front of Salle des Fêtes.

Sanitation:

Parking:

2; Max 48hrs

None; See 204

Lots of green space; Services at 204. Inspected 2010.

ST YZAN DE SOUDIAC | 210 | E9 | N45°08.408' W000°24.597' | 33920

Directions: D250/Ave du Général de Gaulle. From St Savin take D250 east, sp 'St Yzan de Soudiac'. Aire on left in village centre in park, opp school and next to Mairie.

Sanitation:

Parking:

2; Max 48hrs

None; See 204

Market day Wed am. Nice rural village. Inspected 2010.

ST MEDARD DE GUIZIERES

211 E9 N45°00.925' W000°03.472' 33230

Directions: D1089/Rue de la République. From Libourne follow D1089 east. At St Medard de Guizieres pass church and turn right opp junction with D21. Aire in small car park, signed.

Sanitation:

Parking:

2

Custom

Just off main shopping area; Church adj. Inspected 2010.

LA ROCHE CHALAIS

212 E9 N45°08.788' E000°00.340' 24490

Directions: D674. Turn off D674 in town into the Intermarché supermarket. The Service Point is adj to the car wash. Access is difficult.

Sanitation:

Parking:

Poss

Euro Relais Junior; €2; Drive over drain in car wash

Supermarket adj; Self-service laundry. Inspected 2012.

MONTPON MENESTEROL

213 E9 N45°01.253' E000°09.601' 24700

Directions: From Montpon Menesterol take D708 north. Cross river then turn left onto D730. Aire 900m on left, signed.

Sanitation:

Parking:

5; €10 inc elec

Aire Services; Token (3/3)

Small amount of regional products for sale. Water not potable from other machines, only Aire Services. Inspected 2010.

ST VINCENT JALMOUTIERS

214 E9 N45°12.022' E000°11.440' 24410

Directions: Moulin de Rafalie. Turn off D44 in village, sp 'Village Vacances' and signed. Cross river bridge and immediately turn right into Aire.

Sanitation:

Parking:

15

Custom; 2 unmetered cont elec sockets under shed roof

Pleasant, peaceful Aire adj to shallow river and grassland. Village centre 2 mins with limited local commerce. Inspected 2012.

ST ANTOINE CUMOND

215 E9 N45°15.350' E000°12.031' 24410

Directions: D43. Adj to D43 to the rear of the village car park.

Sanitation:

Parking:

5

Custom

In village centre. Inspected 2012.

SOURZAC 216 E9 N45º03.097' E000º23.715' 24400

Directions: Ave du 11 Juin 1944, at junction of D6089 and D3e. Aire adj to church and river bridge. Near A89/E70; ideal stopover.

Sanitation:

Parking:

10; Max 24hrs

Euro Relais Junior: Token (ER); 6 5amp elec points; Free

SP

Views of either church or across river and surrounding countryside. Inspected 2010.

VANXAINS 217 E9 N45°12.710 E000°17.036 24600

Info/Photo: Vera Ward

Directions: D708. Exit Vanxains on the D708 to south. In 450m turn right, signed. Aire on right, signed.

Sanitation:

Parking:

3

Euro Relais Junior; 1 unmetered CEE elec

SP

Adj to a newly built residential area and recycling point. Local commerce 8 mins. Visited 2012.

ST AQUILIN 218 E9 N45°11.154' E000°29.315' 24110

Directions: D43. Turn left as exit village on D43 to west, sp 'P'. Aire 20m on right at municipal service building.

Sanitation:

Parking:

5

Custom, on right side of building

SP

A forgotten Aire at a municipal works building in a remote village. Service Point dilapidated. May fall out of use. Local commerce 2 mins. Inspected 2012.

ST LEON SUR L'ISLE 219 E9 N45°06.904' E000°30.029' 24110

Directions: Route de la Lande. Turn off D3 onto D41e2, sp 'St Leon s Isle'. Turn right after crossing river bridge into parking adj to river: N45°07.202' E000°29.781'. For Service Point follow road through village and Service Point is adj to Maison des Associations, signed.

Sanitation:

Parking:

5; Also 15 adj to river

Custom

SP

Located in quiet village with some local commerce. Fishable river adj to parking north of village. Skateboard park adj. Inspected 2012.

RIBERAC 220 E9 N45°15.416' E000°20.545' 24600

Directions: Aux Deux Ponts Ouest, off D708 outside municipal campsite. Follow D708 north out of Ribérac crossing river Dronne. Then turn left onto Aux Deaux Ponts Ouest and Aire on left.

Sanitation:

Parking:

10

Custom

SP

River adj; Kayak hire adj. Some bays have views of river. Inspected 2010.

DOUCHAPT 221 E9 N45°15.083' E000°26.600' 24350

Directions: C1/Beauclair, off D710. From Ribérac take D710 east for 8km, sp 'Périgueux'. After passing through village of St Méard de Drône turn left, sp 'Village de Beauclair' and signed. Road bends left and Aire on right through gates, signed.

Sanitation:

Parking:

5; €5

Euro Relais Junior; Token; €2

Swimming lake in grounds of holiday village; Washing machine available. Go to the Accueill (bar) on arrival. Good sized bays. Inspected 2010.

MENSIGNAC 222 F9 N45°13.378' E000°33.931' 24350

Directions: Rue du Stade, off D710. From Périgueux take D710 towards Ribérac. At entry to Mensignac turn left, sp 'Aire de Service'. Aire straight ahead, adj to stadium.

Sanitation:

Parking:

3

Flot Bleu Fontaine; €2

SP

3 10m concrete patches in shade of trees surrounded by grass. Inspected 2010.

CHATEAU L'EVEQUE 223 F9 N45°14.667' E000°41.233' 24460

Directions: Place du Jardin Public. Turn off D393 at the southern roundabout into the village. The parking is on the right just past the railway line.

Sanitation:

Parking:

10; No parking Sunday am - market

Raclet; Token; €2

Pleasant place alongside gardens. Some train noise. Inspected 2010.

TOCANE ST APRE 224 F8 N45°15.417' E000°29.650' 24350

Directions: D103/Rte de Montagrier, adj to stadium. Turn off D710 onto D103 in village. After 260m Aire on right through gate in large conifer hedge. Aire adj to stadium and campsite. Not signed.

Sanitation:

Parking:

10

Euro Relais Junior; Token (ER); €2

SP

Campsite open 15 Jun-31 Aug. Token from campsite and village shops. River Dronne 2 mins. Inspected 2010.

LISLE 225 F8 N45°16.877' E000°32.402' 24350

Directions: Les Sonneries, off D1. Exit town north on D78 then turn left onto D1. In 300m turn right onto Les Sonneries and the Service Point is on left outside municipal campsite.

Sanitation:

Parking:

Poss when campsite closed

Euro Relais Junior; Token (ER)

Token from campsite, Service Point inoperable when campsite closed. Inspected 2010.

BOURDEILLES 226 F8 N45°19.383' E000°35.000' 24310

Directions: D106. From Brantôme take D78/D106e2 to Bourdeilles. In village continue on D106 and turn left, sp 'Plaine des Loisirs'. Follow signs around football pitch to grass parking by river on edge of village.

Sanitation:

Parking:

50; €2; Grass parking

Euro Relais Mini; Token

Football pitches and tennis courts adj. River adj. Some hard standing near Service Point. Inspected 2010.

PAUSSAC ST VIVIEN 227 F8 N45°20.865' E000°32.309' 24310

Directions: Le Bourg, at Maison de l'Escalade in the village centre. From south on D93 turn right onto Le Bourg before exiting town. Aire 100m.

Sanitation:

Parking:

3; Free 1st 24hrs; then €3.70/24hrs plus €1.60/adult, €1.20/child

Euro Relais Junior; Token; €2; 4 unmetered elec points

Small Aire. Feels like it's in a back garden. Inspected 2010.

BRANTOME 1 228 F8 N45°22.700' E000°38.733' 24310

Directions: Font-Vendôme. From south on D939 follow Brantôme bypass north. At roundabout take 2nd exit onto D675, signed. Turn 1st right onto D675e2, signed. Aire on right next to motorhome dealer.

Sanitation:

Parking:

4; €2

Custom; 4 elec points; €1 Honesty Box

Landscaped Aire. Motorhome dealer adj. Washroom. Inspected 2010.

BRANTOME 2 229 F8 N45°21.641' E000°38.883' 24310

Directions: Chemin du Vert Galant. From south turn right at roundabout on D939. Follow road and turn left by car parks onto Chemin du Vert Galant. Aire on right after car parks in large grass area by river.

Sanitation:

Parking:

100; €3; Collected; Grass parking

Custom; €2

Walk into town through park 400m. Market Fridays. Inspected 2010.

SORGES 230 F8 N45°18.332' E000°52.371' 24420

Directions: N21, as exit town to south. Aire opp truffle museum, 'Maison de la Truffe', in car and coach park, sp 'Parking Bus'. Service Point in adj lay-by.

Sanitation:

Parking:

5

Euro Relais Junior

Village 2 mins. Also coach parking. Inspected 2010.

Kerlouan Neis Vran

BRITTANY

Kerlouan Neis Vran

LA GUERCHE DE BRETAGNE

1 D5 N47°56.556' W001°14.013' 35130

Directions: Off D463/Rue de Rennes. In car park adj to D463/D178 roundabout on main route, signed.

Sanitation:

Parking:

2; 7m bays

Raclet; 2 unmetered elec points

Town centre car park; Commerce adj. Car park used for market Tuesday 7am-2pm. Inspected 2010.

RETIERS

2 D5 N47°54.696' W001°22.766' 35240

Directions: D107/Rue du Maréchal Leclerc. From town centre follow D107 one-way system to south. Aire in car park adj to D107, signed. Service Point in far corner of car park.

Sanitation:

Parking:

4

Custom; Tap by toilet

Town centre car park; Commerce adj. Inspected 2010.

MESSAC

3 C5 N47°49.536' W001°48.852' 35480

Directions: Rue de la Résistance. From west on D772 cross river la Vilaine and turn left onto Rue de la Résistance, following sp 'Port de Plaisance'. Parking is situated at the Port de Plaisance, at rear of railway station.

Sanitation:

Parking:

10; Parking banned on waters edge

Custom

A very pleasant spot by the marina; Trains quiet at night; Town 5 mins. Inspected 2010.

PONT REAN

4 C5 N48°00.133' W001°46.502' 35580

Directions: D577. Adj to D577 in the large car park adj to southbank of the river, signed.

Sanitation:

Parking:

10; Max 24hrs

Unknown

Large car park under renovation, it is understood it will still provide an Aire and the location overlooking the river means it could be lovely. Inspected 2010.

VERN SUR SEICHE

5 D5 N48°03.803' W001°37.452' 35770

Directions: D163, at E'Leclerc. From south on D163 turn off at E'Leclerc, clearly signed next to McDonalds. Service Point in E'Leclerc car park next to the fuel station.

Sanitation:

Parking:

Poss

Euro Relais Junior; 1 unmetered elec point

Supermarket adj; McDonalds adj. Inspected 2010.

AVAILLES SUR SEICHE

6 | D5 | N47°57.751' W001°11.963' | 35130

Directions: D106. Turn off D178 onto D106 north of town. Aire on right before entering town.

Sanitation:

Parking:

Height barriered some of the time

Flot Bleu Fontaine

Service Point only, parking in village for small motorhomes. Riverside walks. Inspected 2010.

CESSON SEVIGNE

7 | D5 | N48°06.773' W001°35.380' | 35510

Directions: D32/Rte de Domloup, at Carrefour supermarket. Exit E50/N136 at Junction 2, sp 'Cesson', and turn left onto D32. At large roundabout turn left into Carrefour supermarket.

Sanitation:

Parking:

Poss

Euro Relais Mini; Token; €1

In out of town retail industrial park. Tokens available from fuel station. LPG available. Inspected 2010.

LIFFRE

8 | D5 | N48°13.495' W001°30.153' | 35340

Directions: D92, at Intermarché. Exit A84/E03 at Junction 27 and turn northwest onto D92. Aire on right before Parc d'Activités Beaugé 2. Service Point in fuel station.

Sanitation:

Parking:

Only when Intermarché closed

Euro Relais Junior; 1 unmetered elec point; No drive over drain

Diesel pump suitable for large vehicles; McDonalds; Parking has 3m height barrier. Inspected 2010.

ROMAGNE

9 | D4 | N48°20.652' W001°16.453' | 35133

Directions: Allée des Prunus, off D812. As enter town on D812 towards Fougères Aire in picnic area on edge of town. Turning opp La Poste. Service Point by toilet block.

Sanitation:

Parking:

5

Custom

Village with local commerce 2 mins. Aire in roadside lay-by. Inspected 2010.

FOUGERES 1

T

10 | D4 | N48°21.313' W001°12.666' | 35300

Info: Andy & Tracey Holmes

Directions: Boulevard De Renes. From west on N12 at the E'Leclerc roundabout drive toward Forgeres. Pass E'Leclerc supermarket on right and cross 2 roundabouts. At the Château roundabout turn left sp, 'P Château', into parking for the Château. Service Point on right as enter parking, signed.

Sanitation:

Parking:

17

Custom

At imposing tourist Château on the edge of a medieval town. TO and commerce 2 mins. Walks around water filled quarry behind Aire. Visited 2012.

FOUGERES 2

11 D4 N48°21.357' W001°12.159' 35300

Directions: Allee des Fetes. From west on N12 at the E'Leclerc roundabout drive toward Forgeres. Pass E'Leclerc supermarket on right and cross 2 roundabouts. At the Château roundabout go straight over. At next roundabout go straight over, sp 'P du Nancon' Service Point adj to toilets in 200m.

Sanitation:

Parking:

10; Height barriers can be lifted

Custom

Fougeres 1 is more popular with motorhomes as there is less noise but this Aire is closer to town. Inspected 2010.

ST BRICE EN COGLES

12 D4 N48°24.684' W001°21.730' 35460

Directions: Rue de Normandie/D102. Follow D102 north out of village, sp 'Gendarmerie' and signed. Turning adj to Gendarmerie, signed.

Sanitation:

Parking:

8; 8m bays

Custom; €2

2 mins from town with commerce; Backs onto cemetery. Inspected 2010.

TREMBLAY

13 D4 N48°25.390' W001°28.247' 35460

Directions: Route de Fougères, off D796 outside the cemetery. From south on D175 take 1st turning to Tremblay. Aire is on left in 600m.

Sanitation:

Parking:

5

Aire Services; €2

On edge of village with local commerce and convenience store. Inspected 2010.

BAZOUGES LA PEROUSE

14 D4 N48°25.452' W001°34.445' 35560

Directions: Blvd Marie Castel, between D796 and D90. Follow D796 through village. Turn off in village centre, sp 'Aire Camping Car'. Aire in car park on right, signed. Aire signed in village.

Sanitation:

Parking:

7; 7m bays

Aire Services

Aire set in very picturesque village with a pleasant surrounding. Commerce in village. Inspected 2010.

MONTREUIL SUR ILLE

15 D4 N48°18.015' W001°40.449' 35440

Directions: Rue de Coubry. At junction by railroad track turn off D221, past the boulangerie, into Rue des Usines, signed. The Aire is on the right when the road meets the canal.

Sanitation:

Parking:

6; Max 48hrs; 5m bays

Custom; Aire Services for boats

Very short bays backing onto road; Aire overlooking canal between two locks. Inspected 2010.

TINTENIAC

16 C4 N48°19.937' W001°50.003' 35190

Directions: Off D20, alongside canal. Turn off D20 in the village centre by the canal bridge, sp 'Musée de Outil et des Metiers'. The Aire is 100m on the right overlooking the canal.

Sanitation:

Parking:

10; Gravel or grass parking

Aire Services

Canal views from one side, open fields from the other; Village 2 mins. Inspected 2010.

SAINS

17 D4 N48°33.184' W001°35.149' 35610

Photo: Don Madge

Directions: D89, opp Mairie. Signed in village.

Sanitation:

E

Parking:

6; €5/night

Raclet; 1 unmetered elec point

SP

A very pleasant Aire in a small village with local commerce. Inspected 2010.

DOL DE BRETAGNE

18 D4 N48°32.902' W001°45.288' 35120

Directions: D155. Exit N176/E401 onto D155 to west of town. Follow D155 through town, past church. Aire in large car park on left at bottom of high street near swimming pool, signed.

Sanitation:

E

Parking:

20

Aire Services; €2

Away from road noise in town centre; Town 2 mins. Inspected 2010.

CHERRUEIX

19 D4 N48°36.306' W001°42.479' 35120

Directions: Rue Théphile Blin, off D82. From church drive past Mairie and the Service Point is on the right in 100m, outside the campsite 'Le Tenzor de la Baie', signed.

Sanitation:

Parking:

None

Custom; Token; €2

Service Point only. Inspected 2010.

HIREL

20 C4 N48°36.478' W001°49.212' 35120

Directions: D155. Just off coast road D155 between St Benoît des Ondes and Hirel. Approaching from west turn off to Aire is on right.

Sanitation:

E

Parking:

50; €6/night 7pm-9am; Grass parking

Aire Services; €2

Town centre 5 mins; Tidal beach across road. 21 has sea view. All parking in this area €5/night. Inspected 2010.

LE VIVIER SUR MER 1

21 C4 N48°36.238' W001°46.785' 35960

Directions: D155. On side of road as exit village towards Hirel, signed

Sanitation:

Parking:

12; €5/7pm-9am

Euro Relais Junior; Token (ER); €2

Views of grass and tidal beach; Village with commerce 2 mins. All parking in this area is €5/night. Inspected 2010.

LE VIVIER SUR MER 2

22 D4 N48°36.324' W001°47.253' 35960

Directions: D155 coastal road, next to cemetery. Follow D155 west towards Hirel past Le Vivier Sur Mer 1 and Aire on left, adj to cemetery.

Sanitation:

Parking:

20; €5/7pm-9am; Pay 15 Mar-15 Nov

None; See 21

Parking only, all parking in area €5/night minimum. Inspected 2010.

ST BENOIT DES ONDES

23 C4 N48°36.992' W001°50.874' 35114

Directions: Off D155. As exit village on D155 heading south. Turning between Virgin Mary statue and round tower, signed.

Sanitation:

Parking:

12; €5/night

Urba Flux; €3

Town close by; Pleasant walks round small lake. Very close to road. Inspected 2010.

CANCALE 1

24 C4 N48°40.735' W001°51.911' 35260

Directions: Avenue du Général de Gaulle/D355, at Super U. As exit town to west on D355 Aire on left in Super U car park, diagonal from ZA les Quatre Vais.

Sanitation:

Parking:

18; 7m bays

Custom; Token (ER); €2.50

Supermarket car park; Self-service laundry. Inspected 2010.

CANCALE 2

25 C4 N48°40.198' W001°51.930' 35260

Directions: Rue des Français Libres. Signed off D76 as you approach Cancale. After picnic spot take next left and the Aire is 200m on left. No trailers.

Sanitation:

Parking:

144; €6/24hrs; Max 3 days

Aire Services; €2.75

15 mins from town; Hilltop location; Commercial Aire; Lacks charm. Inspected 2010.

ST MALO 1

26 C4 N48°38.939' W002°01.064' 35400

Directions: D1/Avenue Louis Martin. Drive towards St Malo centre on D1/Avenue Louis Martin. The parking runs parallel to the road and is before the marina. Narrow access, use entrance half way between roundabouts.

Sanitation:

Parking:

10

None

2 mins from port; Walled city; Edge of busy road, backs onto park. Inspected 2010.

ST MALO 2

27 C4 N48°38.618' W001°59.618' 35400

Directions: Rue Paul Féval. From south on D301 exit to right, then turn left at large bridge junction onto Rue de Triquerville. At next roundabout turn right onto Rue Paul Féval and Aire on right.

Sanitation:

Parking:

50; €7.50/night

Aire Services; €2

Large motorhome commercial Aire. 20 mins from town. Free bus to town. Inspected 2010.

ST MALO 3

28 C4 N48°36.933' W002°00.705' 35400

Directions: La Briantais. Signed off D168 en route to Dinard, just past Dinard sign and sp 'La Briantais'. If heading into St Malo on D168 can go under underpass and then rejoin the D168 towards Dinard.

Sanitation:

Parking:

10; Max 24hrs

None

Reasonably remote and rural. Narrow entrance and exit. Country park nearby. Inspected 2010.

LANVALLAY

29 C4 N48°27.262' W002°01.793' 22100

Directions: Rue du Terrain des Sports. Approaching from the south on D2 turn left at the traffic lighted junction after the Intermarché supermarket, signed. The Aire is located at the sports facilities at the other end of this one-way road, signed.

Sanitation:

Parking:

5; 9m bays

Euro Relais Junior; Token (ER); €2

Adj to the sports facilities overlooking playing fields. Inspected 2010.

LE PORT DE DINAN *

30 C4 N48°27.252' W002°02.309' 22100

Directions: Sous le Viaduc. At the bottom of viaduct (the large bridge spanning river) on edge of river, 2 mins from beautiful river quayside.

Sanitation:

Parking:

30; 8m bays; Free 7pm-8am; €4 during day charged by 30 mins

None

Steps up to hilltop town. Riverside walk; Inspected 2010.

PLESLIN TRIGAVOU

31 C4 N48°32.198' W002°03.018' 22490

Directions: D366/D28. Exit the village on D366/D28, sp 'Plouer' and 'D366'. The Aire is on the left in 700m adj to D366/D28 junction, signed.

Sanitation: E WC F

Parking: P F

10

Custom

SP

Pleasant Aire providing an ideal get away from the hustle and bustle of the seaside. Inspected 2010.

TADEN

32 C4 N48°28.321' W002°01.345' 22100

Directions: Rue de la Robardais, off D12. Aire outside campsite 'La Hallerais', signed from roundabout on D12. 3.5t weight restriction in village.

Sanitation: E WC F

Parking: P F

7

Flot Bleu Fontaine; €2; Flexi hose for waste water

SP

Pretty village. Day parking by river; Other parking behind Salle Neuvilte. Inspected 2010.

PLEURTUIT

33 C4 N48°35.085' W002°03.745' 35730

Directions: D64. At Super U supermarket to the north of the town, adj to D64.

Sanitation: E WC F

Parking: P F

3

Aire Services; €2

SP

Supermarket adj; Self service laundry adj. Inspected 2010.

LANCIEUX

34 C4 N48°36.461' W002°08.995' 22770

Directions: Rue de l'Eglise. Enter town on D786. At roundabout go straight onto Rue de l'Eglise and Aire is on right alongside church.

Sanitation: E WC F

Parking: P F

5

Custom; Drain in ground in front of toilets; Tap by toilet

SP

Coastal village with local commerce. Inspected 2010.

PLOUBALAY

35 C5 N48°34.829' W002°08.708' 22650

Directions: Square Edouard Durst. Enter town on D768 and take third exit onto Square Edouard Durst. Aire on left near cemetery.

Sanitation: E WC F

Parking: P F

None

Custom

SP

Local commerce in village. Inspected 2010.

PLANCOET | 36 | C4 | N48°31.485' W002°14.357' | 22130

RACLET

Directions: Rue Dr Calmette, off D768 at Super U. As exit town to west on D768 turn right onto Rue Dr Calmette or on next road opp cemetery. Aire at Super U adj to small roundabout in car park.

Sanitation:

Parking:

Poss

Raclet; €2

Pretty town around a river weir. Supermarket. Inspected 2010.

PLELAN LE PETIT | 37 | C4 | N48°25.961' W002°13.084' | 22980

Directions: D19/Rue des Rouairies. Aire is in the Intermarché car park on right when heading south on D19. The Service Point is located at the rear of the store.

Sanitation:

Parking:

Poss

Custom

Supermarket adj. Lift grid for WC; No water when inspected in Oct. Inspected 2010.

HAVE YOU VISITED AN AIRE? | GPS co-ordinates in this guide are protected by copyright law

Take at least 5 digital photos showing
• Signs
• Service Point
• Parking
• Overview
• Amenities

Visit www.all-the-aires.co.uk/submissions.shtml to upload your updates and photos.

Sanitation:

Aire Details:

Submit updates

- Amendments
- New Aires
- Not changed

ST JACUT DE LA MER 1 | 39 | C4 | N48°36.337' W002°11.337' | 22750

Directions: Blvd du Rougeret. On entering town on either D26 or D62 both roads converge onto Rue Grande. At junction, the 1st turning on the right is Boulevard Du Rougeret. The parking area is at the end of this road.

Sanitation:

Parking:

7; 8pm-11am only

None: See 40

2 mins from beach; Nice location on edge of village; Pleasant sea view. Inspected 2010.

ST JACUT DE LA MER 2 | 40 | C4 | N48°35.228' W002°11.396' | 22750

Directions: D26. Turn off D26 in Bîord. Aire on right, sp 'Tennis', 'Mini Golf' and signed. Located by community rubbish area.

Sanitation:

Parking:

None

Euro Relais Junior; €2

Service Point only in undesirable area. New motorhome parking being installed, see 41. Inspected 2010.

ST JACUT DE LA MER 3

41 | C4 | N48°35.386' W002°11.422' | 22750

Directions: Off D26/Rue de Dinan. Follow D26 south out of town for 1km past Mairie and turn left. Aire in 100m.

Sanitation:

Parking:

30; €3/night; Max 48hrs; Pay at machine

300m; See 40

New Aire being constructed in a flat area with no views. Inspected 2010.

ST CAST LE GUIDO 1

42 | C4 | N48°36.651' W002°16.098' | 22380

Directions: Follow D13 south out of town. Turn off and follow road at rear of Intermaché which runs parallel to D13. Aire signed off rural road.

Sanitation:

Parking:

20; Max 1 night

None; See 43

SP

Remote and unlit. Inspected 2010.

ST CAST LE GUILDO 2

43 | C4 | N48°37.738' W002°15.219' | 22380

Directions: Rue de La Bataille. Turn off D19 at roundabout towards sea onto Rue Yves Dumanoir, then take next left and the Service Point is on the left opp Piscine Municipal Eau du Mer.

Sanitation:

WC F

Parking:

P F

10

Euro Relais Junior

2 mins from sea; Large golden sandy beach and seafront promenade to town. Inspected 2010

ST CAST LE GUILDO 3

44 | C4 | N48°36.499' W002°13.802' | 22380

Directions: Rue de la Pointe Du Bay. From town follow D19 south for 3km. Turn right onto D114/Route de la Pointe Du Bay. Follow this road to the end of the peninsula. Signed from D19.

Sanitation:

Parking:

P F

20; Banned 10pm-6am

None; See 43

High above bay with excellent views. Overnight parking is banned in the whole town and this Aire from 6pm-9am. Inspected 2010.

ST CAST LE GUILDO 4

45 | C4 | N48°38.054' W002°15.494' | 22380

Directions: Rue Duguay-Trouin, off one-way D19 ring road. Aire on east side of D19 ring road, close to coast. Parking signed.

Sanitation:

Parking:

F

5; 6m Max

None; See 43

Motorhomes are allowed to park in small car park at far end of beach, 1 block back. Far from ideal. Inspected 2010.

PLEVENON

46 C4 N48°39.307' W002°19.939' 22240

Directions: Rue de la Ville Hingant. Aire in village opp Mairie and TO. Signed on D16 at junction with C3.

Sanitation:

Parking:

2

Euro Relais Junior; Token (ER); From Mairie; Open office hrs only

SP

Village centre; Near church; No views, but pleasant. Inspected 2010.

PLEHEREL PLAGE

47 C4 N48°38.982' W002°20.950' 22240

Directions: D34e, outside campsite. Aire on D34e outside campsite between Pléhérel Plage and Plévenon.

Sanitation:

Parking:

30; Pay in summer

Aire Services; €2.50

SP

An isolated Aire redeveloped as commercial Aire. No trailers allowed. Inspected 2010.

PLURIEN

48 C4 N48°37.132' W002°25.407' 22240

Directions: D786, at the Total garage/car wash. Between Erquy and Plurien on D786.

Sanitation:

Parking:

None

Euro Relais Junior; €2

SP

Service Point only. Inspected 2010.

ERQUY

49 C4 N48°37.297' W002°28.389' 22430

Directions: Rue des Sternes. Exit town west on D786 and follow along coast. Turn right off D786 onto Rue des Sternes and Aire on left behind large car park in 450m.

Sanitation:

Parking:

40; €6/24hrs; Pay at machine

Custom; €2

SP

Baker calls 8am; View over hedge to sea; Large sandy beach across road; Sun trap. Inspected 2010.

PLENEUF VAL ANDRE

50 C4 N48°34.523' W002°34.000' 22370

Directions: Chemin du Bignon, at marina. From D786 in Dahouët follow west to Etang du Guebriand. Then turn off D786, sp 'Yacht Club Beureur de Port' and signed. Parking on far side of marina. Pay at Bureau de Port. Registration numbers recorded by port staff.

Sanitation:

Parking:

50; €3.50 + €0.20pp

Euro Relais Junior; €3

SP

On edge of marina; Views across masts to town. Nice location close to water; Pleasant views. Inspected 2010.

HILLION

51 C4 N48°31.040' W002°40.101' 22120

Directions: Rue O. Provost. Turn off D34 in town onto Rue O. Provost to exit Hillion towards Lermot. Aire on left, signed.

Sanitation:

Parking:

7; Max 48hrs

Custom; No water

SP

Aire in front of 'Terraine d'accueil des Gens du Voyage', a gypsy site. Also see Lermot 52. Inspected 2010.

LERMOT

52 C4 N48°31.821' W002°39.859' 22120

Directions: From Hillion follow sp 'Lermot' and 'Lermot Plages'. Parking at end of road on cliff top, signed. Parking up hill on other side of road: N48°31.868' W002°39.831'

Sanitation:

Parking:

5

Custom; No water

SP

Car park overlooking beach downhill 1 min. Amazing views. Cliff path. Inspected 2010.

BINIC 1

53 C4 N48°36.771' W002°49.843' 22520

Directions: Off D786, at the Super U. Signed in fuel station. Accessible via D21.

Sanitation:

Parking:

Poss

Aire Services; Token; €2

SP

Supermarket adj; Motorhomes banned from all waterside parking. Inspected 2010.

BINIC 2

54 C4 N48°36.027' W002°50.104' 22520

Directions: Rue de l'Ic. Turn off D786 in the town centre opp the port, sp 'Complexe Sportif' and signed. Take the next right, signed. The Aire is located down this road on the right.

Sanitation:

Parking:

40

Custom

SP

Large car park in isolated spot; 5 mins to town on footpath; All waterside parking in this town bans motorhomes. Inspected 2010.

TREMUSON

55 B4 N48°31.367' W002°51.153' 22440

Directions: D712. Turn off roundabout opp Intermarché fuel station, signed.

Sanitation:

Parking:

7

Euro Relais Junior

SP

2 mins from village; Just off main road. Use adj car park for view over duck pond and to get away from road noise. Inspected 2010.

PORT PLERIN | 56 | C4 | N48°31.865' W002°43.486' | 22190

Directions: Rue de la Tour. From Plérin take D786 towards St Brieuc. Before crossing the river turn onto D24 following sp 'St Laurant' on the northern side of the river. Follow this road towards the sea for 3.5km and the Aire is on the right, signed.

Sanitation:

Parking:

10

Custom

Views over hedge to large tidal creek. Inspected 2010.

QUINTIN | 57 | B4 | N48°24.039' W002°54.308' | 22800

Directions: Chemin des Côtes, off D7. From D790/D7 roundabout south of town turn onto D7, sp 'Quentin Centre Ville'. Cross over next roundabout and turn left onto Rue de la Fosse Malard. Aire on right at rear of Salle des Fêtes, signed.

Sanitation:

Parking:

5

Custom

Large village with many old buildings and local commerce. Inspected 2010.

LANFAINS/LE PAS | 58 | B4 | N48°21.812' W002°52.740' | 22150

Directions: 'Aire de l'Etang du Pas', off D7 by lake. Turn off D7, sp 'Lanfains', 'Le Pass' and signed. The Aire is situated beside lake in a beautiful setting at the hamlet of Le Pas in picnic area.

Sanitation:

Parking:

15; Grass parking

Custom

Pleasant Aire overlooking lake. Inspected 2010.

ST CARREUC | 59 | C4 | N48°24.133' W002°44.345' | 22150

Directions: D27/Rue de la Lande. Aire signed on right on entering village from north.

Sanitation:

Parking:

5

Aire Services; CC; €2

Aire is in a lakeside setting but with no view and adj to main road; Marked walks. Inspected 2010.

LAMBALLE | 60 | C4 | N48°27.705' W002°30.841' | 22400

Directions: Off D14/Rue Mouexigné, at E'Leclerc supermarket. Exit N12/E401 onto D14 into Lamballe, sp 'Lamballe Gare'. The E'Leclerc supermarket is 600m on the left. Aire in supermarket car park, opp fuel station.

Sanitation:

Parking:

4; Max 24hrs

Aire Services; €2

Supermarket adj. Inspected 2010.

MESLIN

61 C4 N48°26.619' W002°34.164' 22400

Directions: D28. Aire signed in village, situated next to school.

Sanitation:

Parking:

2

Custom

A small village. Inspected 2010.

PLOEUC SUR LIE

62 C4 N48°20.834' W002°45.296' 22150

Directions: Off D22/Rue des Ecoles. Follow D44 to Ploeuc-sur-Lié, road turns to D22 in middle of village then back to D44 at exit of village. Aire signed in village behind church. Difficult access, avoid if possible.

Sanitation:

Parking:

None

Custom

Small village with local commerce. Inspected 2010.

MONCONTOUR

63 C4 N48°21.119' W002°38.248' 22510

Directions: Adj to Camping Tourelle, off D768. From Moncontour follow sp 'Camping Tourelle'. Aire situated next to the campsite to south of Moncontour and east of La Gare.

Sanitation:

Parking:

3; €2; Max 48hrs

Aire Services; CC; €2

Service Point and limited bayed parking outside campsite. Inspected 2010.

PLOUGUENAST

64 C4 N48°16.401' W002°41.771' 22150

Directions: By river, 900m from town. Follow sp 'Guette-es-Lievres' out of the village to a rural, riverside location. The Aire is by the river bridge in the car park with toilets.

Sanitation:

Parking:

5

Custom

Isolated location but lots of green open space and a river walk. Inspected 2010.

CAULNES

65 C4 N48°17.192' W002°09.332' 22350

Directions: Rue Fontaine, off D766. Turn off D766 main route, sp 'Lavoir Fontaine'. Aire is set in the centre of the village next to the fountain and old washing pool.

Sanitation:

Parking:

5

Flot Bleu Océane; €2; Flexi hose for waste water

In a green park area. Inspected 2010.

HAVE YOU VISITED AN AIRE? **GPS co-ordinates in this guide are protected by copyright law**

Take at least 5 digital photos showing
- Signs
- Service Point
- Parking
- Overview
- Amenities

Visit www.all-the-aires.co.uk/submissions.shtml to upload your updates and photos.

Sanitation:

Aire Details:

Submit updates
- Amendments
- New Aires
- Not changed

MERDRIGNAC 67 C5 N48°11.835' W002°24.934' 22230

Directions: Rue du Gué Plat. From north on D6 enter town and turn left onto Rue du Gué Plat, following sp 'Camping Lanarouet'. Aire near campsite after road bends right.

Sanitation:

Parking:

None

Custom

SP

Service Point in bad state; Avoid if possible. Inspected 2010.

PLEMET 68 C5 N48°10.747' W002°35.334' 22210

Directions: Rue de l'Etang. Exit Plemet on D16, sp 'Laurenen'. Turn left in 200m, sp 'Espace de Loisirs' and signed. The Aire is 200m on the right at the lake.

Sanitation:

Parking:

5

SEIFEL; Token

Parking overlooking swimming lake in a pleasant location. Inspected 2010.

LA CHEZE 69 C5 N48°08.030' W002°39.477' 22210

Directions: Chemin de Aliénor. From north on D778/D14 turn left as enter town, sp 'Aire de Service'. Turn right at bottom of road and Aire is adj to the water in 100m.

Sanitation:

Parking:

6

Custom; 6 unmetered elec points

A very tranquil spot between a fishing lake and a river. Day fishing permits available from tabac, 2 mins. Inspected 2010.

LOUDEAC 70 C5 N48°10.817' W002°45.750' 22600

Directions: Blvd de la Gare. From the south follow D41 through town following sp 'Gare'. At the T-junction turn right and after crossing the railway line turn left at the roundabout. The Aire is on the left in 200m to the right of the train station.

Sanitation:

Parking:

3; Max 48hrs

Urba Flux

In a pleasant location adj to a quiet railway station; Town commerce 2 mins. Inspected 2010.

NEULLIAC

71 B5 N48°07.692' W002°59.133' 56300

Directions: Les Deux Croix, off D767. Enter town on D767 and turn onto Les Deux Croix opp Rue de la Mairie, signed.

Sanitation:

Parking:

None

Flot Bleu Fontaine; €2; Flexi hose for waste water

Service Point only. Inspected 2010.

ST AIGNAN

72 B5 N48°10.979' W003°00.813' 56480

Directions: D31. From D18 turn onto D31 into St Aignan. Aire is situated behind the church. Difficult turn into entrance.

Sanitation:

Parking:

10; Max 6m

Custom; Out of service

A small village with pleasant walks in a rural location. Inspected 2010.

ST NICOLAS DU PELEM

73 B4 N48°18.352' W003°09.799' 22480

Directions: D790, at Super U. Service Point on D790 at fuel station.

Sanitation:

Parking:

Poss

Euro Relais Mini; Token (ER); €2; No drive over drain

Large supermarket adj. Inspected 2010.

ROSTRENEN

74 B4 N48°13.995' W003°19.202' 22110

Directions: D23/Rue P. Le Balpe. Follow D23 south out of town, sp 'Plouray' and 'Aire de Camping Car'. Aire on right adj to D23, past large sports stadium.

Sanitation:

Parking:

6; 7m bays

Euro Relais Junior; Token (ER)

Short walk to town; Main road noise; No views; Inspected 2010.

GLOMEL

75 B4 N48°13.228' W003°23.370' 22110

Directions: Etang du Corong, off D3. In village follow sp 'Etang du Corong'. Aire on left up slope before lake.

Sanitation:

Parking:

10; €5

Aire Services; CC; €2

A very pleasant Aire 1 min from lake and swimming beach. Approx 5 mins to village. Inspected 2010.

MAEL CARHAIX — 76 — B4 — N48°17.010' W003°25.269' — 22340

Directions: Place de l'Ecole. Exit the village south on D23, sp 'Rostrenen'. The Aire is adj to the road by a right angle bend, signed.

Sanitation:

Parking:

5

Custom; Token (2/1); €2

SP

Adj to fire station; Village centre 1 min has local commerce. Inspected 2010.

CARHAIX PLOUGUER — 77 — B4 — N48°16.700' W003°34.326' — 29270

Directions: Rue de Bazeilles, off D54 roundabout. From north on D54 turn left at roundabout onto Rue de Bazeilles. Aire on right in small car park near Casino supermarket.

Sanitation:

Parking:

5

Custom; 2 unmetered elec points in corner

SP

On busy road, but good access to town and supermarket. Difficult to find. Inspected 2010.

CALLAC — 78 — B4 — N48°24.125' W003°26.237' — 22160

Directions: Ave Ernest Renan. Turn off D787 at roundabout onto D11 into town. In town follow sp 'Camping Municipal'. Turn left onto D28 and follow west. After 600m turn left onto Ave Ernest Renan and follow to Aire on right near Lac Verte Vallée, next to the municipal campsite.

Sanitation:

Parking:

None

Raclet; €2

SP

Service Point only. Inspected 2010.

GUINGAMP — 79 — B4 — N48°33.576' W003°08.964' — 22200

Directions: Place du Vally, Rue du 19 Mars 1962. In the town centre at D8/D5/D9 junction. Follow sp 'Camping Car' and signed. The Service Point is behind the building.

Sanitation:

Parking:

5

Custom

SP

Car park located adj to fortified town; Large town centre adj. Inspected 2010.

LE PALUS PLAGE * — 80 — B4 — N48°40.554' W002°53.107' — 22580

Directions: Off D32/Rte du Palus. Follow D30 east to sea. Turn right at end of road and Aire in 100m, adj to beach.

Sanitation:

Parking:

20

Euro Relais Junior; €2

SP

Stone beach; Cliff top paths; Restaurants; Very pleasant; Volleyball court. Inspected 2010.

TREGUIER 1 *

81 B4 N48°47.402' W003°13.863' 22220

Directions: Blvd Anatole Le Braz/D70 ring road. Just off D8 as it crosses river into town. Service Point just off road at bridge. Drive past Service Point down slope to Aire. Signed through town.

Sanitation:

Parking:

30

Custom; No water

SP

View of river; Partly shaded; Parkland with walks behind, 5-10 mins from town. Inspected 2010.

TREGUIER 2

82 B4 N48°46.538' W003°14.750' 22220

Directions: D786, at the Intermarché. On D786 south of town, near car wash.

Sanitation:

Parking:

Poss; See 81

Aire Services; €2

SP

Supermarket and car wash adj. Inspected 2010.

TREGUIER 3

83 B4 N48°46.723' W003°13.991' 22220

Directions: Adj to D8/D786 roundabout, at the Super U. On D786 south of town, to rear of petrol station.

Sanitation:

Parking:

Poss

Aire Services; €1

SP

Supermarket adj. Inspected 2010

PAIMPOL

84 B4 N48°47.003' W003°02.821' 22500

Directions: Rue Pierre Loti, Parking Champ de Foire. Aire in wooded area just off large D789 roundabout. From roundabout exit onto Rue Pierre Loti and Aire on right, signed. Further parking at end of road in car park on left.

Sanitation:

Parking:

13; 15 spaces in sunshine further down road

Aire Services; CC; €3

SP

A compact, level site 50m from beach and coastal path. Attractive wooded location. Inspected 2010.

PLOUBAZLANEC

85 B4 N48°49.269' W003°01.023' 22620

Directions: D789. From Ploubazlanec travel to coast on D789 following sp 'Dir Île de Bréhat'. Aire on left before ferry terminal. Free parking signed; Unsigned day parking on upper level. Steep entrance and even steeper exit. 6km from Paimpol.

Sanitation:

Parking:

20; Day parking only

None

SP

Restaurants nearby; Boat trips to Île de Bréhat. Toilets at ferry terminal 100m. Inspected 2010.

LEZARDRIEUX | 86 | B4 | N48°46.813' W003°06.870' | 22740

Directions: Off D787/Rue de Kermarquer. From west enter town on D786. At roundabout junction with D787 turn right onto D787/Rue du Priory following sp 'Camping Municipal'. Turn left after 450m and Service Point outside campsite.

Sanitation: E F

Parking: P F

None

Aire Services; CC; €3

SP

Service Point only. Inspected 2010.

LARMOR PLEUBIAN | 87 | B4 | N48°51.820' W003°05.221' | 22610

Directions: D33/Rue de Lanéros. Take D20 to Larmor Plage, road becomes D33. Service Point signed on the left in the one-way system. Parking at end of road overlooking sea, signed: N48° 51.472' W003°04.737'.

Sanitation: E WC F

Parking: P F

4; Max 24hrs

Raclet Mini

SP

Parking with sea views overlooking pleasure boats. Celtic Whiskey Co adj. Inspected 2010.

LA ROCHE DERRIEN | 88 | B4 | N48°44.791' W003°15.581' | 22450

Directions: D33/Rue du Jouet. From south follow D33 to La Roche-Derrien. Aire signed in village centre. Park in far car park. Don't park in front of houses opp Service Point.

Sanitation: E WC F

Parking: P F

8; €2/night inc elec; Pay Mairie

Custom; Token; €2; 6 elec points inc

SP

Old village with local commerce 1 min. Inspected 2010.

TREGASTEL | 89 | B4 | N48°49.464' W003°29.881' | 22730

Directions: Rue de Poul Palud/D788. From town follow D11 north towards Trégastel-Plage. Then turn right onto D788 and Aire is 900m on left, opp Super U and ZAC Poul Palud, signed.

Sanitation: E WC F

Parking: P F

50; €7/24hrs; CC; Pay at barrier machine

Custom; inc

SP

Just off main route; Other parking bans motorhomes. 2 mins from town, beach and port; Opp supermarket. Inspected 2010.

ILE GRANDE | 90 | B4 | N48°47.942' W003°35.016' | 22560

Directions: On west side of island just before Camping Municipal Ile Grande, signed.

Sanitation: E WC F

Parking: P F

10; €5/24hrs

Custom

SP

Adj to beach; Small, private Aire; Also Raclet outside campsite €2. Inspected 2010.

PLEUMEUR BODOU

91 B4 N48°46.989' W003°31.553' 22560

Directions: Off Route du Radome, at Planetarium de Bretagne. From town follow D21 north for 1km. Turn off D21 onto Rte du Radome, following sp 'Cosmopolis'. After 300m turn left and follow road to planetarium. Planetarium and satellite dishes visible from some distance.

Sanitation:

Parking:

5

Raclet; €2

SP

Crêperie. Planetarium; Viking Museum; Museum of Telecommunication. Most level parking opp Viking museum. Inspected 2010.

TREBEURDEN

92 B4 N48°46.944' W003°34.617' 22560

Directions: D788. From town take D788 northwest towards coast and Trébeurden. Follow for 2km and parking on right, adj to beach. Service Point may have moved to D65 towards Lanon: N48°46.030' W003°33.073'

Sanitation:

E

Parking:

P

15; €5/7pm-9am

Urba Flux Box; €2

SP

Stunning coarse sand beach on opp side of road; 15 mins to town; Bakers van in 9-9:30am. Inspected 2010.

HAVE YOU VISITED AN AIRE?

GPS co-ordinates in this guide are protected by copyright law

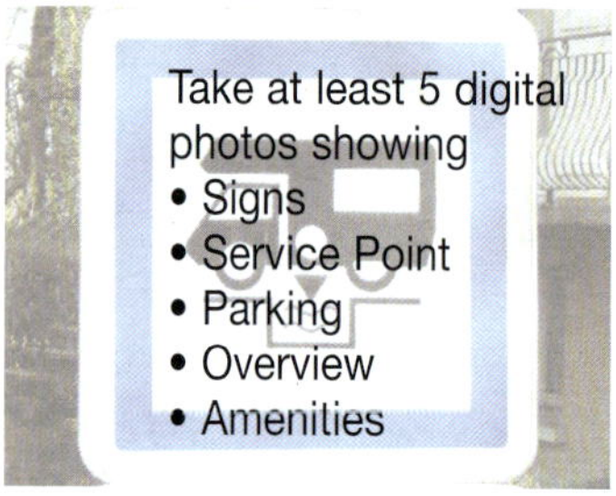
Take at least 5 digital photos showing
• Signs
• Service Point
• Parking
• Overview
• Amenities

Visit www.all-the-aires.co.uk/submissions.shtml to upload your updates and photos.

Sanitation:

Aire Details:

Submit updates

- Amendments
- New Aires
- Not changed

PLESTIN LES GREVES

94 B4 N48°39.741' W003°37.528' 22310

Directions: Rte de Guergay, off D786. Turn off D786 at the LIDL supermarket and drive past the supermarket. The Service Point is at the car wash.

Sanitation:

E

Parking:

None

Euro Relais Junior; €2

SP

LIDL adj. Inspected 2010.

GUIMAEC

95 B4 N48°40.178' W003°42.820' 29620

Directions: At stadium. From Guimaëc turn off D64 and exit town to west. Follow road for 300m and bear right. Aire on right at stadium in 100m.

Sanitation:

Parking:

F

2

Euro Relais Box; €2

SP

Aire is situated on the outskirts of the village by the stadium. Inspected 2010.

PLOUGASNOU 1

96 B4 N48°41.641' W003°47.539' 29630

Directions: Rue Charles de Gaulle. Approach Plougasnou from the south. After the D46/D78 roundabout take the 4th exit at the next roundabout. The Aire is in 450m on the right in the large car park.

Sanitation:

Parking:

8; Max 48hrs

Raclet; €2

Opp sports facilities; Night halt if cannot stay at 94. Inspected 2010.

PLOUGASNOU 2 *

97 B4 N48°42.477' W003°49.646' 29630

Directions: Rue des Forces Française Libres, off D46a2. From town follow D46, then D46a2 to Le Diben port. Turn off onto Rue des Forces Française Libres and Aire at end of road on quay.

Sanitation:

Parking:

7; Max 48hrs; 6m bays

Raclet; €2

Good views over fishing boats; Village 2 mins uphill. Inspected 2010.

CARANTEC

98 B4 N48°39.564' W003°54.861' 29660

Directions: Route de Kerrot and Rue de Castel An Dour, off D73 main road. Through town follow sp 'Tennis Club' and 'Complexe Sportif'. Aire backs onto tennis courts and football pitches. Service Point at base of water tower, signed.

Sanitation:

Parking:

Poss

Euro Relais Junior; Token

5-10 mins from town; 10-20 mins from beach (down hill); No views. Inspected 2010.

PENZE

99 B4 N48°35.916' W003°56.036' 29670

Directions: Rue du Dossen, in the centre of the village. Service Point is adj to the creekside car park.

Sanitation:

Parking:

5

Euro Relais Junior; €2

Several car parks overlooking tidal creek; Pleasant. Inspected 2010.

MORLAIX

100 B4 N48°34.447' W003°49.891' 29600

Directions: D712/Rue de Brest. From south on D712 Aire in car park of Ecomarché as approach town, sp 'P Rue de Brest' and signed.

Sanitation:

Parking:

5; €1/1.5hrs

Raclet

Town 2 mins; Adj supermarket car park. Inspected 2010.

LAMPAUL GUIMILIAU — 101 B4 N48°29.623' W004°02.310' 29400

Directions: From town follow sp 'Aire de Camping Cars'. Aire near the church and cemetery.

Sanitation:

Parking:

30

Custom

Village 2 mins; Pleasant. Inspected 2010.

ST THEGONNEC — 102 B4 N48°31.346' W003°56.741' 29410

Directions: Off D712. Aire opposite the lorry parking just off D712. In large parking area, sp 'Parking Salle des Fêtes' and signed.

Sanitation:

Parking:

15

Euro Relais Junior; Token; Free

On main road 2 mins from town; Nicely presented; Views of town. Inspected 2010.

GUIMILIAU — 103 B4 N48°29.199' W003°59.811' 29400

Directions: Rue des Bruyères. Follow signs to 'Salle Polyvalente' on edge of village, just off D31.

Sanitation:

Parking:

20

Custom

Edge of village; Quiet road; 2 mins to village. Inspected 2010.

HUELGOAT — 104 B4 N48°21.738' W003°45.158' 29690

Photo: Barry and Muriel Crawshaw

Directions: Allée du Lac. Enter town on D14, then turn west onto D769a. Next to 'Camping du Lac', signed.

Sanitation:

Parking:

10; €5

Aire Services; €3.20

Lakeside village with local commerce 3 mins. Inspected 2010.

COMMANA — 105 A4 N48°24.977' W003°57.685' 29450

Directions: Off D11. From town follow sp 'Salle des Sports'. Aire is close to the village recycling point.

Sanitation:

Parking:

5

Custom

Sports facilities adj; Village with local commerce 2 mins; Countryside views. Inspected 2010.

SIZUN

106 A4 N48°24.018' W004°04.739' 29450

Directions: Rue de Cornouaille, off D18. Turn off D18/D30 roundabout, sp 'Camping' and 'Piscine'. Aire 100m on right.

Sanitation:

Parking:

5

Euro Relais Junior; €2

5 mins walk uphill to town. By noisy roundabout; Sports facilities and outdoor pool adj. Inspected 2010.

LA MARTYRE

107 A4 N48°26.949' W004°09.381' 29800

Directions: D35. Aire on right as you exit the village towards Ploudiry, by Maison du Plateau.

Sanitation:

Parking:

20

Euro Relais Junior

SP

Woody location; 2 mins from village with local commerce. Inspected 2010.

LANDERNEAU

108 A4 N48°26.784' W004°15.489' 29800

Directions: Rue de Calvaire. From town turn off D712 onto D29/Route du Quimper, signed. Cross river and turn right towards Quimper, signed. Take the 1st turning on right, signed. Aire is 200m on right, signed.

Sanitation:

Parking:

40; €5/24hrs inc elec; Pay at meter

Euro Relais Junior; €2

On riverside but no views; Town 2 mins; Located on old campsite grounds adj to numerous sports facilities. Inspected 2010.

ST SERVAIS

109 A4 N48°30.633' W004°09.307' 29400

Directions: Off main route through town. Turn off D32 towards St Servais. Aire in village after passing church, all car parks then on right.

Sanitation:

Parking:

2

Raclet; €2

Aire is set in a peaceful location. Inspected 2010.

LANDIVISIAU

110 A4 N48°30.607' W004°04.566' 29400

Directions: Rue Pierre Loti, off D32 roundabout. At D32 roundabout west of town centre turn north onto one-way system and Aire between two roundabouts before Super U.

Sanitation:

Parking:

30

Custom

2 mins to large, pedestrianised town centre via busy main road. Inspected 2010.

BRITTANY

PLOUVORN — 111 — A4 — N48°34.662' W004°01.815' — 29420

Directions: Off D19, at reservoir. Turn off D19, sp 'Plan d'Eau' and 'De Lanorgant'. Aire is in the parking area to the right before you reach reservoir.

Sanitation:

Parking:

20

Euro Relais Junior; On 15 min timer

Parkland with walks, facilities, lake. Skateboard park. Inspected 2010.

ST POL DE LEON 1 * — 112 — A4 — N48°40.805' W003°58.150' — 29250

Directions: Quai de Pempoul. From town centre follow sp 'Port'. Travel on Rue du Port to coast and then turn right onto Quai de Pempoul. Follow to bend in road and Aire on left. Avoid centre on Tuesday due to market.

Sanitation:

Parking:

15

None; See 113

Partial view of harbour; Away from road noise, 2 mins to harbour; 5 mins to town. Inspected 2010.

ST POL DE LEON 2 * — 113 — A4 — N48°40.976' W003°58.249' — 29250

Directions: Ave de la Mer. From town follow Rue de la Rive to coast, then turn right onto Ave de la Mer and Aire on left adj to beach. 2 mins from St Pol de Léon 2.

Sanitation:

Parking:

30; €4/24hrs; May-Sept

Euro Relais Box; €2

Restaurants; 5 mins walk to town; Nice walk along waterfront. Beautiful setting; Views across to Rocher Ste Anne. Inspected 2010.

ST POL DE LEON 3 — 114 — A4 — N48°40.740' W003°59.859' — 29250

Directions: Rue Hervé Mesguen, at E'Leclerc supermarket. From train station follow D788/Rue de Brest west. Turn right at supermarket and Aire in back of car park.

Sanitation:

Parking:

20

Aire Services; CC; €2

Commercial area between garage and supermarket. Truck fuelling at E'Leclerc. Inspected 2010.

ST POL DE LEON 4 — 115 — A4 — N48°40.853' W003°59.018' — 29250

Directions: D769/Rue de Morlax. Follow D75 south out of town. Turn left onto D769 and at roundabout turn right to stay on D769. Aire on right opp cemetery.

Sanitation:

Parking:

5; See 112, 113 and 114.

None

Town centre 2 mins. Inspected 2010.

ROSCOFF 1 *

116 A4 N48°42.707' W004°00.004' 29680

Directions: Route du Laber. Exit Roscoff on D769 south. Just before exiting village turn right on Rue de la Baie. Follow to coast where road bends left and becomes Route du Laber. Follow for 1km along coast and Aire on left.

Sanitation: E WC F

Parking: P F

20

Aire Services; Poss removed

SP

Sea views; Nice location. By beach; Swimming; Bird life. Stroll down beach to town 30 mins. Inspected 2010.

ROSCOFF 2

117 A4 N48°43.135' W003°58.264' 29680

Directions: Off D58, at ferry port. Follow D58 to port and Aire in large parking area at port before ticket office.

Sanitation: E WC F

Parking: P F

40

None

SP

Ferry port adj. No Service Point. Inspected 2010.

SANTEC

118 A4 N48°42.082' W004°02.343' 29250

Directions: Rue du Staol, by Le Bistrot à Crêpes. Follow signs from Santec to Méchouroux. Turn off in Méchouroux onto Rue du Staol and Aire on right by crêperie. 5km from Saint Pol de Léon.

Sanitation: E WC F

Parking: P F

10; Free 1st night

SOS; Token; €2

SP

100m from beach; Restaurant/crêperie adj; Free WiFi. Inspected 2010.

LESNEVEN

119 A4 N48°34.531' W004°19.040' 29260

Directions: Adj to D110/D125 roundabout northeast of town. Aire at the Hyper Casino, by fuel station.

Sanitation: E WC F

Parking: P F

Poss

Flot Bleu Euro; CC

SP

Supermarket adj. Inspected 2010.

PLOUESCAT 1

120 A4 N48°39.072' W004°11.027' 29430

Directions: D10/Blvd de l'Europe. Aire on south side of D10 ring road at Intermarché supermarket. Service Point behind car wash. Parking bays clearly marked.

Sanitation: E WC F

Parking: P F

6

Euro Relais Junior; €2

SP

Supermarket adj. Inspected 2010.

PLOUESCAT 2 * | 121 | A4 | N48°39.540' W004°13.134' | 29430

Directions: Rue de Pen An Théven. Follow signs to 'Camping de la Baie du Kemic'. Aire slightly down road past campsite. Service Point located inside campsite: N48°39.562' W004°13.078'.

Sanitation:

Parking:

5

Unknown; Token

Beautiful location; Ideal for beach holiday/swimming. Located on sand duned spit. Aire very small but in a fantastic, very desirable area. Inspected 2010.

GOULVEN | 122 | A4 | N48°37.865' W004°18.500' | 29890

Directions: Off D10. Approach Goulven from the west on D10. Turn off D10 after roundabout junction with D125, sp 'Aire Naturelle'. Aire 150m on left.

Sanitation:

Parking:

20; €5/night Jun-Sept

Custom; No water or elec in winter

Aire Naturelle for motorhomes and tents only. Open access all year. Inspected 2010.

KERLOUAN 1 | 123 | A4 | N48°40.139' W004°21.713' | 29890

Directions: From Kerlouan follow Rue del'Avoir north 2.5km to Cronzou then to Lézeride. In Lézeride main road bends right, but carry on straight for another 450m then turn left following sp 'Camping Bendin'. Travel approx 500m and turn right. Aire adj to beach outside Camping Bendin.

Sanitation:

Parking:

2

Aire Services; Token; €2

Coastal Aire within walking distance of the beach. Inspected 2010.

KERLOUAN 2 | 124 | A4 | N48°38.681' W004°22.069' | 29890

Directions: D10. In village centre outside Mairie, adj to D10. There are 4 other parking areas close to the beach: **(1)** On coastal road 500m east of La Digue, signed: N48°39.717' W004°22.727'. **(2)** Coast road 1km west of La Digue: N48°39.389' W004°23.635'. **(3)** Follow coastal road 700m along coast from La Digue: N48°39.233' W004°24.175'.

Sanitation:

Parking:

5; Designated bays

None; See 123

(4) Follow road from Lanhir to Neis Vran on coast: N48°39.023' W004°25.933'. Inspected 2010.

GUISSENY | 125 | A4 | N48°37.981' W004°24.698' | 29880

Directions: D10/Rue de Plouguerneau. Outside Mairie on west side of village, adj to main route.

Sanitation:

Parking:

5

Urba Flux Tall; Token

Adj to main road; Road noise. Village 1 min. Inspected 2010.

PLOUGUERNEAU | 126 | A4 | N48°37.037' W004°33.202' | 29880

Directions: D71. From Plouguerneau head to Lilia on D71. Aire on left adj to D71 as enter town, near cemetery.

Sanitation:

Parking:

10

Aire Services; CC; €4

Uninspiring Aire at seaside village. Suggest Kerlouan 124 for better experience. Inspected 2010.

LE FOLGOET | 127 | A4 | N48°33.631' W004°20.081' | 29260

Directions: Route de Gorrekéar, behind church. From D788 drive towards church through green. Entrance is on right by bishop's statue, signed. Also sp 'Omnisports'.

Sanitation:

Parking:

50

Euro Relais Junior

View of church; Green area on edge of village. Away from main road. Inspected 2010.

BOURG BLANC | 128 | A4 | N48°29.497' W004°30.195' | 29860

Directions: Approach on D13 from Brest. At the roundabout turn left, sp 'Bourg Blanc'. Then turn immediately left into car park. Follow gravel track on right to lake, signed.

Sanitation:

Parking:

6; 6m bays

Custom; At building

Pleasant spot adj to Plan d'Eau; One bay has views. Inspected 2010.

LANNILIS 1 | 129 | A4 | N48°33.420' W004°30.383' | 29870

Directions: Adj to D13. Follow D13 south from town. Cross over 1st roundabout. At 2nd roundabout turn right and then left at next roundabout. Follow road 400m to Aire on left. Adj to D13, but not directly accessible from D13.

Sanitation:

Parking:

5

Flot Bleu Fontaine

On side of busy road; Very noisy. Inspected 2010.

LANNILIS 2 | 130 | A4 | N48°34.283' W004°31.300' | 29870

Directions: Rue de la Haie Blanche. Turn off the D13 onto D28. Turn off D28, sp 'Aire de Camping Cars'. Go straight across the roundabout then turn left, sp 'P Poste' and 'Aire de Camping Cars'. Aire on left opp cemetery, sp 'P 100 Places'.

Sanitation:

Parking:

5

Custom; To the side of the white building

Town with commerce 100m via footpath. Inspected 2010.

PLOUDALMEZEAU PORTSALL

131 A4 N48°33.961' W004°41.918' 29830

Directions: Rue de Porsguen. Follow D26 out of Ploudalmézeau towards Portsall. After road bends left follow for 700m, cross roundabout, and turn right onto Rue de Porsguen. Aire on right in 450m. Signed entire route with small green signs.

Sanitation:

Parking:

50

Aire Services; CC; €2

2 mins to sand dunes and beach; Similar to CL/campsite field. Inspected 2010.

LAMPAUL PLOUARZEL

132 A4 N48°26.837' W004°46.587' 29810

Directions: Rue de Beg Ar Vir, off D5. Follow D5 to Lampaul-Plouarzel, then follow signs for 'Aire de Camping Car'. Aire near coast.

Sanitation:

Parking:

20; €3.50/24hrs in Jul/Aug

Aire Services; €2

In a very quiet location; Sea views from top terrace; Shower/washing machine available in Jul and Aug. Inspected 2010.

TREZIEN

133 A4 N48°25.329' W004°47.083' 29810

Directions: Rue du Stiff. From Plouarzel follow D28 east to Trézien. Turn off Route de Ruscumunoc onto Rue du Stiff 1km past Trézien, following sp 'Aire de Camping Car'. Aire straight ahead.

Sanitation:

Parking:

30; €3.50/24hrs; May-Sept

Aire Services; CC; €2;

Landscaped Aire set in quiet location close to the coast. Inspected 2010.

ST RENAN

134 A4 N48°26.318' W004°37.841' 29290

Directions: Off D27/Route de l'Aber, between Lac de la Laverie and Lac de la Camiren. From town follow D27 north. Turn right after passing Lac de la Camiren before roundabout following sp 'Camping Lokournan'. Aire is beside campsite.

Sanitation:

Parking:

12; Max 24hrs

Aire Services; CC; €2

Aire set beside a lake but no views. Outside a campsite. Inspected 2010.

PLOUMOGUER

135 A4 N48°24.313' W004°43.424' 29810

Directions: D28. Exit the village north on D28, sp 'Plouarzel'. Follow sp 'Aire de Camping'. Aire is set next to the sports complex. Reports suggest it is not possible to park at weekends when stadium in use.

Sanitation:

Parking:

30; €3/night; Jul-Aug

Bollard; €2; July-Aug

Landscaped Aire. Local commerce 200m. Inspected 2010.

BREST

136 A4 N48°23.339' W004°26.126' 29200

Directions: Off Rue Alain Colais. From town follow signs for Océanopolis. Parking is situated in the Océanopolis car park P1.

Sanitation:

Parking:

10; Barriers open 10am-8.30pm

None

SP

Limited view over boats; Océanopolis adj. www.oceanopolis.com. Inspected 2010.

PLOUGASTEL DAOULAS

137 A4 N48°22.311' W004°21.860' 29470

Directions: Off D329/Rue de la Fontaine Blanche. From town centre follow D329 500m south. Turn left, sp 'Espace Avel Vor'. Aire at the sports facilities, Halle des Sports, before roundabout, sp 'Salle Jean Joseph Le Gall' and signed.

Sanitation:

Parking:

5

Custom; Difficult

SP

Sports facilities adj; Skateboarding; Town 2 mins uphill. Inspected 2010.

LOCMARIA PLOUZANE

138 A4 N48°22.402' W004°38.582' 29280

Directions: Rue de la Fontaine. From main route through town turn onto Rue de la Fontaine by Mairie. Aire on left.

Sanitation:

Parking:

6; 8m bays

Euro Relais Maxi

SP

Pleasant, nicely landscaped Aire set in village with local walks. Inspected 2010.

PLOUGONVELIN 1

139 A4 N48°20.238' W004°42.369' 29217

Directions: Enter town on D85 then follow sp 'Aire de Camping Car' and 'Fort de Bertheaume'. Aire set on outskirts of village close to coast.

Sanitation:

Parking:

€6/24hrs inc unmetered elec; Price may vary; Pay at machine

None; See 140

SP

Commercial Aire. High on cliff top with great views of sea. Inspected 2010.

PLOUGONVELIN 2

140 A4 N48°20.526' W004°43.380' 29217

Directions: Rue du Stade/D85, at the Intermarché. As enter town from west on D85 turn left when opp one way road. Aire on right at Intermarché. Well signed in town.

Sanitation:

Parking:

None; But can purchase ticket for 139

Aire Services; CC; €2

SP

Supermarket adj, Self-service laundry adj. Inspected 2010.

CAMARET SUR MER 1 — 141 — A4 — N48°16.418' W004°35.693' — 29570

Directions: Rue de la Gare. From D8 turn onto Rue de la Gare. The Aire is signed from both directions. Located on the same street as train station. Road overlooks the Super U.

Sanitation: E WC F

Parking: P F

20

Euro Relais Junior; €2

SP

2 mins from harbour; Parking directly on road. Inspected 2010.

CAMARET SUR MER 2 * — 142 — A4 — N48°16.442' W004°36.525' — 29570

Photo: Carol and Duncan Weaver

Directions: Rue Georges Ancey, off D8a. Aire is at top of hill by stone circle, near Pointe de Penhir. Well signed through town.

Sanitation: E WC F

Parking: P F

75; €4/24hrs; Apr-Oct; Pay at machine

Euro Relais Maxi; Token; €2

SP

On hilltop with stone circle adj; Town 10 mins; Sandy beach 10 mins. Inspected 2010.

CAMARET SUR MER 3 — 143 — A4 — N48°16.644' W004°36.306' — 29570

Directions: Rue du Grouanoch, off D8a. Turn off D8a 600m past turn for Camaret Sur Mer 2. Aire on right in 200m.

Sanitation: E WC F

Parking: P F

None; See 141 or 142

Euro Relais Junior; €2

SP

Service Point only. Inspected 2010.

CROZON 1 — 144 — A4 — N48°15.098' W004°28.434' — 29160

Directions: Blvd Pierre Mendès France/D887. From town centre follow D887 east out of town. At large roundabout turn left and then left again at next roundabout. Aire at Hyper E'Leclerc supermarket.

Sanitation: E WC F

Parking: P F

289; Shared with cars

None; See 145

SP

Supermarket adj; It may not be possible to stay overnight. Inspected 2010.

CROZON 2 — 145 — A4 — N48°14.854' W004°29.614' — 29160

Directions: Blvd de Pralognan/D8/D887. Just off north side of main ring road by TO.

Sanitation: E WC F

Parking: P F

20

Urba Flux Tall; CC; €2

SP

By noisy road; 20 mins from sea; 5-10 mins to town. Motorhomes banned from marina. TO adj. Inspected 2010.

MORGAT — 146 — A4 — N48°13.511' W004°30.476' — 29160

Directions: D255/Rue De L'Atlantique. From north on D887 turn right in Morgat onto D255/Rue De L'Atlantique. Aire on right after the pharmacy, signed.

Sanitation:

Parking:

40

Aire Services; CC; €2;

Convenient for the beach, Port de Plaisance and town, all 2 mins. Inspected 2010.

HOPITAL CAMFROUT — 147 — A4 — N48°19.730' W004°14.684' — 29460

Directions: Enter town on D770. Turn off beside riverbank, sp 'Complexe Sportif'. Parking alongside river bank; Service Point is behind gymnasium.

Sanitation:

Parking:

2

Euro Relais Junior

Sports facilities adj; Town and tidal creek 2 mins. Inspected 2010.

LE FAOU — 148 — A4 — N48°17.692' W004°11.089' — 29590

Directions: Rue de la Grève. Exit N165 onto D42 into Le Faou. Turn right onto D770 in town centre, following sp 'Aire Naturelle de Camping'. Turn left onto Rue de la Grève before river and Aire is situated outside the municipal campsite on the riverbank.

Sanitation:

Parking:

6

Aire Services

Tidal creek adj but no views; Pleasant green space. Inspected 2010.

CHATEAULIN — 149 — A4 — N48°11.787' W004°05.146' — 29150

Directions: Grand'Rue, at Intermarché supermarket. Enter town on D887 by crossing canal bridge. At roundabout carry on straight onto Grand'Rue (one way). Aire on right at supermarket, signed. Some difficult, narrow turns through town.

Sanitation:

Parking:

6

Flot Bleu Pacific; €2

Near busy road; Noisy but only 2 mins down hill to town. Difficult to find. Inspected 2010.

PLONEVEZ PORZAY — 150 — A5 — N48°07.497' W004°13.455' — 29550

Directions: Venelle de Pen ar Prat. From D63/D107 crossroads take D107 towards Douamenez. Take the 2nd turning on the right and then turn left. The Aire is on the right next to the sports field.

Sanitation:

Parking:

15

Aire Services; €2

Pleasant parking area by the sports facilities; Village 2 mins. Inspected 2010.

PLONEVEZ PORZAY PLAGE KERVEL | 151 | A5 | N48°06.940' W004°16.821' | 29550

Directions: Kervel Plage. From Plonevez-Porzay follow sp 'Kervel Plage'. Aire adj to the beach, signed.

Sanitation:

Parking:

6; Max 48hrs; Grass parking

None; See 150

SP

100m from sandy cove popular with kite surfers; Views obstructed by hedge; Stunning cliff top walks. Inspected 2010.

LOCRONAN | 152 | A5 | N48°05.876' W004°12.720' | 29180

Directions: Rue du Prieuré. Approach from south on D63. Turn right into town at large roundabout and the Aire is on the left, signed.

Sanitation:

Parking:

20; €5/24hrs May-Oct; Free Nov-Apr

Aire Services

SP

In pretty historic village with usual tourist facilities; Pedestrian centre adj. Inspected 2010.

DOUARNENEZ | 153 | A5 | N48°04.534' W004°18.349' | 29100

Directions: At the Intermarché supermarket off D765 at Centre Commercial Drève 3. Service Point at fuel station.

Sanitation:

Parking:

Poss

Aire Services; €2

SP

Supermarket adj. Inspected 2010.

PONT CROIX | 154 | A5 | N48°02.506' W004°29.153' | 29790

Directions: Place de la Métairie. Follow D765 to Pont-Croix. Turn off, sp 'Station des Eaux de Kermaria'. Then turn right, signed. Aire in car park on left, signed.

Sanitation:

Parking:

5

Aire Services; €2

SP

Very old town with commerce; Basketball court adj. Inspected 2010.

CLEDEN CAP SIZUN | 155 | A5 | N48°02.915' W004°39.030' | 29770

Directions: D43. Drive through village and Aire opp cemetery, signed.

Sanitation:

Parking:

20

Aire Services; €2

SP

Remote village 2 mins; Boulangerie; Likely to be quiet in summer. Inspected 2010.

PLOGOFF 1 | 156 | A5 | N48°02.238' W004°39.916' | 29770

Directions: D43. Head northeast out of town on D43. Aire is near the church before exiting town, signed.

Sanitation:

Parking:

None; See 157

Aire Services; €2

Service Point only. Inspected 2010.

PLOGOFF 2 | 157 | A5 | N48°01.965' W004°39.737' | 29770

Directions: Rue du Stade. Head east out of town on D784. Turn right beside boulangerie to stadium, signed. The Aire is signed on the left at the stadium.

Sanitation:

Parking:

50

None; See 156

Grass or gravel terraced area; Partial sea views; On edge of village, ideal to escape the crowds. Inspected 2010.

PRIMELIN | 158 | A5 | N48°01.526' W004°37.101' | 29770

Directions: Off Route de la Plage, outside campsite. From town follow sp 'Camping Municipal de Kermalero'. Aire 700m west of town on Route de la Plage, parallel to D784, signed.

Sanitation:

Parking:

10; Low season only

Aire Services; €2

Outside campsite, 2 mins from beach. Inspected 2010.

AUDIERNE | 159 | A5 | N48°01.637' W004°32.233' | 29770

Directions: Rue Lamaritine/D765. Just off D765 near river bridge, signed. Follow sp 'Aquashow'.

Sanitation:

Parking:

20

Aire Services; CC; €2

Views over estuary and boats; Aqua Park adj; Town 2 mins. Inspected 2010.

PLOUHINEC | 160 | A5 | N48°00.963' W004°30.085' | 29780

Directions: D784. Follow sp to Carrefour hypermarket. Aire at Zone Commerciale Ty Frapp.

Sanitation:

Parking:

Poss

Flot Bleu Euro; CC; €2

Supermarket; Near main road. Inspected 2010.

PLOGONNEC

161 A5 N48°04.337' W004°11.237' 29180

Directions: Off D63. Adj to D63 towards Quimper south of the town at the Super U. The Service Point is near the car wash.

Sanitation:

Parking:

Poss

Aire Services; Token; €2

Supermarket adj. Inspected 2010.

PLOMELIN

162 A5 N47°56.037' W004°09.093' 29700

Directions: Hent Keramer. From central square head south, sp 'Complexe Sportif'. Turning left at the stadium, signed.

Sanitation:

Parking:

4; 6m bays

Euro Relais Junior; €2

At sports complex; Mini market and shops 1 min. Inspected 2010.

LANDUDEC

163 A5 N48°00.049' W004°20.286' 29710

Directions: Place des Ecoles, at Super U off D784 in town. As enter from west on D784, Aire on left at Super U near fuel station.

Sanitation:

Parking:

3; 7m bays

Aire Services; €2 or 2 x Token

Supermarket adj; Village 2 mins. Inspected 2010.

PLONEOUR LANVERN

164 A5 N47°54.209' W004°16.763' 29720

Directions: D156/Rue des Alliés. From centre of town near church take D156, sp 'Quimper'. In 400m turn right into car park, signed.

Sanitation:

Parking:

50

Raclet; €2; Token (3/3)

2 mins from town but off main route. Local commerce in small town square. Inspected 2010.

PONT L'ABBE 1

165 A5 N47°51.849' W004°14.152' 29120

Directions: Rte de Saint Jean Trolimon, at E'Leclerc supermarket. Follow signs in town to E'Leclerc. From D2 roundabout to west of town centre, continue west bearing right onto Rue Jean Moulin. Cross over 3 roundabouts and Aire on right in parking area, signed.

Sanitation:

Parking:

5

Aire Services; €2; €2/7 hours elec at rear 4 allotted bays

5-10 mins walk to town. Inspected 2010.

PONT L'ABBE 2 — 166 — A5 — N47°52.217' W004°13.467' — 29120

Directions: Rue de la Gare. From northeast turn off D2/D785 roundabout onto D2 and follow into town. Turn right onto Rue de la Gare before crossing canal and follow as road bends right. Aire is on the left, adj to the Saupers Pompiers.

Sanitation:

Parking:

5; 10m bays

Raclet; Working but in poor condition

By fire station; Commerce 2 mins. Inspected 2010.

ST GUENOLE 1 — 167 — A5 — N47°49.441' W004°22.259' — 29760

Directions: Rue de la Plage. From east take D785 to Penmarch, then D53 to St-Guénolé. After 3km on D53 turn right onto Rue Jean Jaurés. Follow this road for 1km and Aire on right.

Sanitation:

Parking:

20; Poss pay

None; See 168

Aire overlooking sea. Exposed spot in bad weather, sun trap in good. Inspected 2010.

ST GUENOLE 2 — 168 — A5 — N47°48.833' W004°21.640' — 29760

Directions: Rue du Pont Nevez. From east take D785 to Penmarch, then D53 to St-Guénolé. Turn right off D53 onto Rue Leuker Kerameil, signed. Service Point on left in 400m, at water treatment works, signed.

Sanitation:

Parking:

None; See 167, 169 and 170

Aire Services; €2

Service Point only. Inspected 2010.

ST GUENOLE 3 — 169 — A5 — N47°49.055' W004°22.595' — 29760

Directions: Rue L Le Lay, off D80 and D53. Parking opp harbour by cannery, signed. Adj to main road and port.

Sanitation:

Parking:

50; No parking Thursday or Friday night

None; See 168

Views over boats in working harbour. Inspected 2010.

ST GUENOLE 4 — 170 — A5 — N47°47.989' W004°20.855' — 29760

Directions: Follow coastal road past Pointe de Penmarc'h to Kérity. Parking as exit Kérity on Rue Victor Hugo, signed on right.

Sanitation:

Parking:

30; Grass parking; Pay

None; See 168

All other beach side parking banned at night. Grass parking against dunes; No sea view. Inspected 2010.

PALUE DU COSQUER

171 A5 N47°47.928' W004°11.842' 29750

Directions: Rue du Beau Rivage. Aire 4km south of Loctudy. Follow sp 'Palue du Cosquer'. Aire on coast to southwest of village.

Sanitation:

Parking:

8

Service Point removed

Bottom of dunes; Long sandy beach 2 min. Walks along top of dunes. Inspected 2010.

COMBRIT

172 A5 N47°53.248' W004°09.292' 29120

Directions: Place du 19 Mars 1962. Turn off D44 into Combrit and Aire is signed in village in car park just off roundabout by Mairie.

Sanitation:

Parking:

15

Raclet; Token (ER); €2; 4 unmetered elec points; Reported broken

Village with commerce. Church bells from 6am. Inspected 2010.

MOUSTELIN PLAGE

173 A5 N47°51.095' W004°02.762' 29170

Photo/Info: Graham Hay

Directions: D145. From Fouesnant follow D145 towards Benodet. Go straight over a roundabout towards Moustelin, signed. In 200m take the right fork. Take the first exit at the roundabout. Go straight on towards beach and the Aire is on left just before the beach.

Sanitation:

Parking:

20; Max 48hrs

None

Beach 50m but no view. 10 mins walk to nice restaurant and snack bars. Visited 2012.

ELLIANT

174 A5 N47°59.787' W003°53.403' 29370

Directions: Rue St Gilles, off D28/Rue Maurice Bon. Signed 'Salle Polyvalente' through town. Aire by cemetery. Difficult access for large motorhomes.

Sanitation:

Parking:

20

Aire Services; Token (3/3)

Dead quiet; Close to village centre; Overlooking cemetery. Local commerce 2 mins. Inspected 2010.

SCAER

175 B5 N48°01.664' W003°41.695' 29390

Directions: Off D6, outside Camping Municipal Kérisole. Follow sp 'Camping Municipal' through town. Aire outside camping municipal but in a separate designated area.

Sanitation:

Parking:

100; Max 72hrs

Custom; 2 1320w elec points

Wooded area, cool in summer; 2 mins from town. Walking trails. Always likely to have space. Inspected 2010.

LE FAOUET | 176 | B5 | N48°01.841' W003°29.379' | 56320

Directions: Rue des Ecoles, off D782 behind Mairie. Follow sp 'Salle des Fêtes' through town.

Sanitation:

Parking:

5

Flot Bleu Pacific; €2; Out of service

5 mins from local commerce. This Service Point has been out of service for some time, it is unlikely it will be replaced. Inspected 2010.

PLOUAY | 177 | B5 | N47°55.024' W003°20.177' | 56240

Directions: Rue Hélène Châton. Turn off D2 onto D769bis, sp 'Le Faouet'. Then turn left into Rue Hélène Châton. The Aire is on the right in 300m.

Sanitation:

Parking:

10

Aire Services; CC; €2

The Aire is in an urban area of a large village with local commerce. Inspected 2010.

LE TREVOUX | 178 | B5 | N47°53.796' W003°38.513' | 29380

Directions: Rue des Sports. Aire is signed from D22/D106 roundabout by Mairie. Just off D106 as enter/exit town in north, sp 'Stade Municipal' and 'Camping Cars'.

Sanitation:

Parking:

5

Euro Relais Junior

Surrounded by sports facilities. No real reason to stop, but pleasant rural village. Inspected 2010.

QUIMPERLE | 179 | B5 | N47°51.967' W003°32.614' | 29300

Directions: D49/Rue de viaduct. From south on D16 follow into town crossing over 1st roundabout. At fork turn right onto Blvd de la Gare and follow around town. At river turn sharp right onto D49/Rue du Viaduc. Aire on right.

Sanitation:

Parking:

5

Euro Relais Junior

2 mins from river and fairly large town centre. By stream but scrappy. Inspected 2010.

ROSPORDEN | 180 | B5 | N47°57.897' W003°51.176' | 29140

Directions: D765, at Super U. As enter town on D765 from west Service Point and parking near fuel station on left.

Sanitation:

Parking:

5

Aire Services; €2; No drive over drain

Out of town retail area. Inspected 2010.

BEG MEIL

181 A5 N47°51.281' W003°59.573' 29170

Directions: Chemin de Kerlosquen, off D45. From Fouesnant follow sp 'Pointe de Beg Meil' south on D45. Then turn right onto Chemin de Kerlosquen, following sp 'Aire de Stationment' to beachside car park. Well signed.

Sanitation:

Parking:

30; Max 48hrs; Report suggests this may be closed

None

SP

Sandy beach adj but no views; Nice walks. Inspected 2010.

CONCARNEAU 1

182 A5 N47°52.739' W003°55.225' 29900

Directions: Avenue de la Gare. Follow D783/Rue du Quimper, main road, into town, signed. Just off Rue de Quimper on right at the train station.

Sanitation:

E WC

Parking:

P

39; €2/night

Aire Services; €4; CC

SP

Fortified town with commerce, marina and working shipyard. Pedestrian access to town. Train station adj. Inspected 2010.

CONCARNEAU 2

183 A5 N47°51.796' W003°54.309' 29900

Directions: Allée Jean Bouin. On D322 from north follow sp 'Hôpital'. Turn right just past hospital, signed. Aire beside college and sports ground.

Sanitation:

E WC

Parking:

P

20; €2/night

Aire Services; €4

SP

Views and walks through wood along sea. Inspected 2010.

PENDRUC

184 A5 N47°49.782' W003°53.239' 29910

Directions: C2. From D783 in Tregunc take C2 to Pendruc. At roundabout take 3rd exit. After driving along the seafront the Aire is on left as road turns inland.

Sanitation:

Parking:

P F

6; Max 24hrs

None

SP

Isolated parking area overlooking sea; Beach 50m; No other amenities. Inspected 2010.

TREGUNC 1

185 A5 N47°51.250' W003°51.078' 29910

Directions: Off D783. At church square roundabout turn off at Office Notarial, sp 'Parking 200 places'. Aire in car park, signed.

Sanitation:

E WC

Parking:

P F

2

Aire Services; CC; €3

SP

In nice town centre but away from road noise. Inspected 2010.

TREGUNC 2

186 A5 N47°51.366' W003°51.408' 29910

Directions: D783, at the Hyper Casino by fuel station. From west on D783 Aire on right at supermarket, adj to large roundabout.

Sanitation:

Parking:

4; 6m bays

Flot Bleu Euro; CC; €2

Supermarket adj. Inspected 2010.

NEVEZ

187 B5 N47°48.953' W003°47.362' 29920

Directions: Impasse du Stade, off D77/Rue de Port Manec'h. Follow signs to Port Manec'h beside sports ground (might need to follow 'Toutes Directions' and 'Autres Directions' around one way system). Also sp 'Salle Omnisports'. Easiest to approach Aire from south on D77.

Sanitation:

Parking:

20; Max 24hrs

Euro Relais Junior; €2

Clean and tidy; Ideal night halt; Village 1 min; Sports facilities adj inc bmx and skateboard ramps. Inspected 2010.

PORT MANECH

188 B5 N47°48.283' W003°44.600' 29920

Directions: Off Rue de la Plage. From Nevez follow D77 to Port Manec'h and then follow sp 'Plage' down road with 3.5t weight restriction. Parking is on the left and the beach to the right. Likely to be very busy with traffic in summer; arrive early/late or avoid altogether.

Sanitation:

Parking:

5

Public toilets by the beach 150m

Restaurant/bar. Probably very busy at peak times. Very nice beach. Inspected 2010.

PONT AVEN

189 B5 N47°51.236' W003°44.618' 29930

Directions: Rue du Bourgneuf. Signed off D783. Turn at junction with Rue Louis Lomenech. Follow route to Quimperlé up hill. Turn right, sp 'Stade' and signed. Turn right again, signed, and the Aire is 400m on the left.

Sanitation:

Parking:

20; 9m bays

Custom; €2.40

5 mins down hill to town. Town has tourist shops and restaurants. Inspected 2010.

DOELAN

190 B5 N47°46.334' W003°36.453' 29360

Directions: Rue de Keruster, at green lighthouse. Exit Doëlan to north on D316, then turn onto D16. After crossing bay turn right and follow road along coast for 650m. Turn left into Rue de Keruster and Aire on left.

Sanitation:

Parking:

5; Day only

None

Doëlan is a pleasant fishing village. Restaurants. Inspected 2010.

CLOHARS CARNOET

191 B5 N47°47.887' W003°35.113' 29360

Directions: D16/Rue de Quimperlé. Exit town on D16, sp 'Quimperlé'. Aire on left next to 'Salle Omnisports'.

Sanitation:

Parking:

3

Aire Services; €2

2 mins from town; Market on Saturday. Inspected 2010.

GUIDEL PLAGES

192 B5 N47°45.963' W003°31.512' 56520

Directions: Off D152. Follow D152 along coast to south of town. Turn off, sp 'Ecole de Voile'. Ignore the car park in front of building and drive behind building, signed.

Sanitation:

Parking:

8; Max 24hrs

None

Views of sand dunes and sea; Directly on beach. Beside skateboard park; Windsurfing. Inspected 2010.

KERGAHER

193 B5 N47°45.021' W003°30.344' 56520

Directions: Résidence le Maeva. Signed off D152 between Fort Bloqué and Guidel-Plages.

Sanitation:

Parking:

20; Max 24hrs

None

A simple coastal Aire with sea views; Within walking distance of the beach. Inspected 2010.

PLOEMEUR

194 B5 N47°44.278' W003°25.865' 56270

Directions: Rue Louis Lessard/D162. From the church in the town centre turn off D162, sp 'P 85 places' and signed. Aire in 300m adj to cemetery car park, just past 'P 85 places'.

Sanitation:

Parking:

Poss

Raclet

Adj to cemetery in busy, impractical car park. Drive over drain impossible to use. Inspected 2010.

LARMOR PLAGE

195 B5 N47°42.216' W003°23.105' 56260

Directions: Blvd de Port Marie, Camping Les Algues. Take D29 into town and follow sp 'Camping Les Algues'. Service Point outside campsite.

Sanitation:

Parking:

7; €10 May-Sept, €5 rest of year; inc unmetered elec

Custom

Large seaside resort. Aire adj to beach but no views. Inspected 2010.

LE POULDU 1

196 B5 N47°46.084' W003°33.144' 29360

Directions: Rue Anne de Bretagne. Take D24 then D124 from Clohars-Carnoët following sp 'Le Pouldu' and 'Le Pouldu-Plages'. At the end of the one-way system turn right and Aire on left at tennis courts, signed.

Sanitation:

Parking:

10; May-Sept; 10pm-9am; Pay

None

Seaside town; Busy in Summer; Beach 200m with restaurants and mini golf; TO 2 mins. Inspected 2010.

LORIENT

197 B5 N47°43.938' W003°22.780' 56100

Directions: D29. From Lorient centre follow D29 to coast. Aire on east side of D29 bridge near the tidal estuary in the industrial area at the Elephant Bleu, signed.

Sanitation:

Parking:

None

Aire Services; €2

In industrial area adj. Inspected 2010.

PORT LOUIS 1 *

198 B5 N47°42.531' W003°20.607' 56290

Directions: D781/Ave de la Côte Rouge. Approach Port Louis on D781 from Riantec. Aire is on right as enter town, signed.

Sanitation:

Parking:

20; €10 Apr-Oct; €5 Nov-Mar; Pay at machine; CC

Aire Services; 3 unmetered elec points

On edge of town; Views onto beach and sea. Town 2 mins. Popular even in winter. Only downside is D781. Inspected 2010.

PORT LOUIS 2

199 B5 N47°42.294' W003°21.351' 56290

Photo/Info: Mr. G. Myatt

Directions: From 198 go straight over roundabout following coast road. At the T-junction turn left onto Rue De Locmalo sp, 'Port Locmato'. Pass the port and take the left fork around ramparts until you reach La Parc A Boulets, the Aire situated within the 'Espace Sportive des Remparts' about 30m on the right.

Sanitation:

Parking:

20; €10/night June-Sept, €7/night rest of year

Custom

Situated within a walled area, no sea views. Pay at machine. Visited 2012.

RIANTEC

200 B5 N47°42.698' W003°17.921' 56670

Directions: D781. Off roundabout by fishing boat named 'Riantec'. Signed. 1km from junction with D111.

Sanitation:

Parking:

5

Aire Services; €2

Water feature/bathing pool; Pond; Pleasant; Beach/town 5-10 mins. Inspected 2010.

LE POULDU

201 B5 N47°46.084' W003°33.144' 29360

Directions: Off Rue Anne de Bretagne. Turn off in Le Pouldu, sp 'Pouldu' and 'Plages'. At end turn right and Aire on left outside tennis courts, opp 'Club Nautique', signed.

Sanitation:

Parking:

10; 10pm-9am; May-Sept; Pay; 9m bays

None

Large sandy beach 200m. Inspected 2010.

KERVRAN

202 B5 N47°40.854' W003°14.066' 56680

Directions: Between Plouhinec and Kergouric turn off D781 onto D158, sp 'Camping Municipal' and signed. Follow signs. Aire outside municipal campsite 'Camping Municipal de Kerabus', entrance through barrier.

Sanitation:

Parking:

45; €8/24hrs; €15/48hrs; Must display ticket

Aire Services; 16 unmetered elec points

CC required for access code; Isolated spot. Inspected 2010.

ETEL 1

203 B5 N47°38.962' W003°12.102' 56410

Directions: Rue de la Barre. Follow signs to 'Camping de la Barre' from D105 in town. Aire at fenced and barriered entrance past campsite entrance, signed.

Sanitation:

Parking:

15; €6.50 inc unmetered elec

Custom; inc

Fenced area; Outside campsite; Adj to road and dunes. Inspected 2010.

ETEL 2

204 B5 N47°39.532' W003°11.438' 56410

Directions: D16/Rue Victor Hugo. Just off D16 as enter town from northeast, at lavage (car wash) with dolphin sign. Signed.

Sanitation:

Parking:

None

Aire Services; €2

At car wash; Out of service at time of inspection, not sure if it will be fixed. Inspected 2010.

BELZ

205 B5 N47°40.166' W003°10.627' 56550

Directions: Parc de Loisirs on D16. From roundabout junction with D781 turn or stay on D16. Turning on left in 300m, signed.

Sanitation:

Parking:

10

None

Sports facilities adj; Pleasant; Intended as night halt. Inspected 2010.

ERDEVEN — 206 B5 — N47°38.240' W003°09.095' — 56410

Directions: D781. Adj to D781 on right as enter from south. 400m from standing stones. Narrow turn to access.

Sanitation:

Parking:

5; €5/night

Euro Relais Junior; Token (ER); €3

Adj to a hotel. Village 3 mins down main road. Standing stones 400m. Inspected 2010.

QUIBERON — 207 B5 — N47°29.500' W003°08.334' — 56170

Directions: Rue de Port Kerné, off D186a in Parking de Kerné. Turn off D186a on west side of island onto Rue de Port Kerné. Aire on right in 200m. Barriered entrance.

Sanitation:

Parking:

40; €6/24hrs; Pay at machine; Max 72hrs

Custom; €2

Views across to sea; Beach 1 min. Ideal for surfing, kite surfing. Fantastic location with plenty to do but exposed. Inspected 2010.

ST PIERRE QUIBERON — 208 B5 — N47°30.694' W003°08.337' — 56510

Directions: Rue du Stade, off D186a. Follow sp 'Salle Omnisports' through town. From the north as enter St Pierre turn right at the traffic lights after passing the double roundabout with the boat. Well signed from D768.

Sanitation:

Parking:

10; €7/24hrs; Max 48hrs

Aire Services; €5 If don't stay

Next to sports centre, less exposed than 207. Inspected 2010.

CARNAC — 209 B5 — N47°35.103' W003°04.939' — 56340

Directions: D781. On D781 as you enter town, just past LIDL. Aire opp Office Notarial and adj to Gendarmerie Nationale.

Sanitation:

Parking:

10

Raclet; €2

Town adj; 10 mins to large collection of standing stones, from Aire follow sp to 'Auray'. Parking available at stones. Inspected 2010.

CRACH — 210 B5 — N47°36.246' W002°59.789' — 56950

Directions: D28. At the Intermarché supermarket adj to D28, 1km south of Crac'h.

Sanitation:

Parking:

8; 7m bays

Aire Services; €2; No drive over drain

Supermarket adj; Retail park adj. Inspected 2010.

LOCMARIAQUER

211 B5 N47°33.355' W002°56.368' 56740

Photo: Colin Salter

Directions: Route des Plages. Take D781 into town then follow sp 'Aire Camping Car' and 'Camping La Falaise'. Service Point at entrance to Camping Falaise on south coast. Parking beyond Service Point, signed.

Sanitation:

Parking:

10

Euro Relais Junior; €2

Beachside parking, could feel isolated if alone. Visited 2012.

ARRADON

212 B5 N47°37.474' W002°49.503' 56610

Photo: Don Madge

Directions: Rue de la Mairie. From D101 follow sp 'Arradon', then sp 'Camping Municipal'. Service Point is situated outside the municipal campsite.

Sanitation:

Parking:

None

Raclet; €2

At time of inspection the campsite was allowing motorhomes to use the grass pitches, but this is subject to time of year and weather. Inspected 2010.

AURAY

213 B5 N47°39.936' W002°59.411' 56400

Directions: Entering from south on D768 follow sp 'Centre Ville'. Turn right onto Rue Henri Dunant, sp 'Piscine' and 'Centre Culturel Athéna'. The Aire is next left, signed.

Sanitation:

Parking:

3; Very sloping

Flot Bleu Fontaine

Not worth driving to unless really want to visit town; Town 2 mins; Difficult Service Point. Inspected 2010.

BRECH

214 B5 N47°43.162' W003°00.087' 56400

Directions: Rue du Pont Douar, off D19. In town turn off D19 to southwest and follow road towards D786. Aire on left as exiting village, signed.

Sanitation:

Parking:

5; Grass parking

Custom; Token

Service Point at edge of village. Grass parking weather permitted up drop kerb. Inspected 2010.

BAUD

215 B5 N47°52.553' W003°01.528' 56150

Directions: Rue de Pont Augan, off D3. Turn off D724 onto D3 in village, signed. Heading north on D3 towads Bubry, turn right onto Rue de Pont Augan. Parking is further down road in car park behind La Poste: N47°52.581' W003°01.372'.

Sanitation:

Parking:

5

Custom

2 mins from town with commerce. Inspected 2010.

LANGUIDIC — 216 — B5 — N47°50.214' W003°09.705' — 56440

Directions: N24. From east exit N24, sp 'Languidic'. Exit roundabout, sp 'Languidic'. The Aire is on left immediately after crossing bridge, signed.

Sanitation:

Parking:

3

Custom

Very unattractive urban area. Aire being used to store gravel! Inspected 2010.

ROHAN — 217 — B5 — N48°04.310' W002°45.311' — 56580

Directions: D125/Rue de Saint-Gouvry, Port de Plaisance at the marina. Turn off D11/D2, main route, sp 'Port de Rohan'. Aire behind camping municipal in car park by marina and alongside canal.

Sanitation:

Parking:

6; Tolerated

None

Overlooking small marina in a very pleasant spot. Inspected 2010.

GUELTAS — 218 — B5 — N48°05.813' W002°48.080' — 56920

Directions: Just off D125 on edge of village by sports centre. Signed through village.

Sanitation:

Parking:

20

Custom

5 mins to village. Beware of ditch when entering grass parking. Inspected 2010.

BREHAN — 219 — B5 — N48°03.646' W002°41.405' — 56580

Directions: D2/Rue Châteaubriant, at Super U express. Enter village on D2 and Aire in centre of village. Service Point in fuel station.

Sanitation:

Parking:

Poss

Euro Relais Mini; €2

Supermarket and fuel station adj. Inspected 2010.

ST BARNABE — 220 — C5 — N48°08.202' W002°42.082' — 22600

Directions: Rue Pierre Loti. From village centre by church follow road to the left of Mairie. Turn left and the Aire is on the right, signed.

Sanitation:

Parking:

7

Custom

Most village commerce appears to have closed. Inspected 2010.

ST NICOLAS DES EAUX | 221 | B5 | N47°58.996' W003°02.466' | 56930

Directions: Allée du Vieux Blavet. Enter town on D1. At the river bridge turn, sp 'Base Canoe-Kayak'. Follow this road along the river, following the road to the left under the 3m high bridge, signed. Follow road behind buildings and the Service Point is on the left.

Sanitation:

Parking:

5

Custom

Pleasant village with riverside cafés. Inspected 2010.

JOSSELIN | 222 | C5 | N47°57.383' W002°32.961' | 56120

Directions: Rue Saint Martin. From N24 turn south into town towards hospital. Follow signs for Place St Martin. Located in P1 car park in town centre.

Sanitation:

Parking:

20

Aire Services; CC; €2.05

Lovely old town with plenty to visit. Aire in centre by St Martins church. Inspected 2010.

SULNIAC | 223 | D4 | N47°40.647' W002°33.979' | 56250

Directions: Off D183. From north on D183 instead of turning right at roundabout to enter town, carry on straight for 200m and turn left into Aire.

Sanitation:

Parking:

30

Custom

Plenty of space, very peaceful. Gravelled walk into village; Rural views. Inspected 2010.

SERENT | 224 | C5 | N47°49.498' W002°30.105' | 56460

Directions: Rue du Général de Gaulle. From D10 follow sp 'Camping' to Aire. Aire outside campsite.

Sanitation:

Parking:

9

Custom

Small town. Municipal campsite adj. None of the elec points working at time of inspection. Night stop only. Inspected 2010.

ST JEAN BREVELAY | 225 | C5 | N47°50.709' W002°43.490' | 56660

Directions: Place de la Croix des Victimes, off D1. From north on D1 follow sp 'Centre Ville' into town. Where D1 bends left, carry on straight and Aire on left. Aire signed in town centre.

Sanitation:

Parking:

5

Custom

Small town with parking in town centre car park. Intermarché supermarket 1 min. Inspected 2010.

LOCQUELTAS 226 B5 N47°45.497' W002°46.146' 56390

Directions: D133/Rue de la Fontaine. From D767 turn onto D133. Aire on left as enter village. Report to Mairie for key.

Sanitation:

Parking:

4

Custom; Elec €3.05/day; Key from Mairie

SP

Reports suggest Aire being revamped in 2012. Inspected 2010.

ST GUYOMARD 227 C5 N47°46.903' W002°30.737' 56460

Directions: Off D112. Turning next to church in village, signed. Aire is behind the church.

Sanitation:

Parking:

5

Custom; 1 unmetered Cont elec point

SP

Boulangerie; Views over countryside. Inspected 2010.

ELVEN 228 C5 N47°44.308' W002°34.843' 56250

Directions: Ave des Martyrs de la Résistance/D766. From N166 exit onto D1 and follow into town. When D1 bends left, continue straight onto D766/Ave des Martyrs de la Résistance. Cross over 1st roundabout and Aire on left in 500m, opp sports ground.

Sanitation:

Parking:

5

Flot Bleu Pacific; €2; Flot Bleu elec; €0.50/hr

SP

Very pleasant wooded area with adj open access Aire Natural Camping; 5-10 mins to village. Inspected 2010.

ST NOLFF 229 C5 N47°42.192' W002°39.551' 56250

Directions: D135. From west on D775 turn left onto D135 and follow into St Nolff. Aire on left beside railway line before entering town. Well signed through village.

Sanitation:

Parking:

5

Custom

SP

Aire is by a picturesque village in a rural location; Village 4 mins on footpaths. Inspected 2010.

THEIX 230 C5 N47°37.637' W002°39.698' 56450

Directions: Off D7, at ZA de Brestivan. Parking at back of sports complex parking, opp garages.

Sanitation:

Parking:

4

Custom

SP

10-20 mins to town. Sports facilities; Views over open countryside. Inspected 2010.

ST COLOMBIER

231 C5 N47°32.807' W002°43.295' 56370

Directions: Rue du Stang, off D780. From north on D780 turn off in Saint Colombier, signed. There are two possible turnings from D780 to Rue du Stang. Aire by TO, signed.

Sanitation:

Parking:

5; €5/6pm-10am; Max 48hrs

Aire Services; 1 unmetered elec point on 55 min timer

Very close to main road. The worst Aire in the area, avoid if poss. Inspected 2010.

KERNERS

232 B5 N47°33.181' W002°52.970' 56640

Directions: Rue de Bilouris, off D198. From Arzon follow D198 towards Kerners. Turn off D198, sp 'Camping du Tindio'. Service Point outside campsite.

Sanitation:

Parking:

None

Urba Flux; CC; €2

Service Point only. Inspected 2010.

ARZON

233 B5 N47°32.340' W002°52.839' 56640

Directions: Avenue de Kerlun. From the Super U roundabout, Rond-Point du Crouesty, on D780 take C201, sp 'Kerners'. Gated entry requires pin code. Service Point accessible from the road above Aire.

Sanitation:

Parking:

47; €6.70/24hrs; inc water and unmetered elec; CC; Max 72hrs

Euro Relais Junior; Pin code required

Commercial Aire; Not enough elec points for 47. Narrow entrance; Beach 2 mins. Inspected 2010.

ST GILDAS DE RHUYS

234 B5 N47°31.433' W002°51.450' 56730

Directions: Turn off D780 at roundabout onto D198, sp 'Saline'. Turn right off D198 towards La Saline. Drive through town and follow road to end. Then turn left onto Chemin du Kervert and follow to Aire outside Camping Le Kervert. Other parking at: N47°31.347'W002°51.469'.

Sanitation:

Parking:

Poss; May be pay May-Sept

Euro Relais Junior; May-Sept; €2

Campsite adj; Large sandy beach adj. Inspected 2010.

PTE DE ST JACQUES

235 B5 N47°29.378' W002°47.564' 56370

Directions: Rue du Port Saint Jacques. Follow sp 'St Jacques' from D780. The Aire is well signed and near beach.

Sanitation:

Parking:

15; €5/6pm-10am; Jun-Sept; Max 48hrs

Raclet; 1 unmetered elec point

Sheltered location just off beach. 2 mins from marina; No views. Inspected 2010.

LE ROHALIGUEN 236 B5 N47°29.873' W002°46.018' 56370

Directions: Rue du Raker. Signed parking area adj to beach. Follow coast road from St Jacques to La Rohaliguen. Aire is adj to beach.

Sanitation:

Parking:

10; €5/6pm-10am; Max 48hrs

Aire Services

Adj to large sandy beach with sea views adj to small community. Can promenade to St Jacques. Inspected 2010.

SARZEAU 237 B5 N47°31.795' W002°45.577' 56370

Directions: Rue Claude de Brénudel. Turn off D780 onto D198, sp 'Office Notarial'. Turn sharp right onto Rue Claude de Brénudel before roundabout in town. Aire on left in 400m outside school, Ecole Sainte Anne.

Sanitation:

Parking:

20; €5/6pm-10am

Raclet; 1 unmetered elec point

No parking during school terms. Inspected 2010.

BANASTERE 238 C5 N47°30.877' W002°40.043' 56370

Directions: Rue des Chardons Bleus, signed. From D199/C2/D324 roundabout turn onto D324, sp 'Banastère'. Follow road and turn right onto C114, then follow signs.

Sanitation:

Parking:

10; Max 48hrs; €5/6pm-10am

Aire Services; 1 unmetered elec point

Sandy beach adj; Views out to sea. Good walks along seafront. Popular. Inspected 2010.

DAMGAN 239 C5 N47°30.876' W002°33.623' 56570

Directions: D140a. Follow D140a along coast from Damgan towards Kervoyal. Aire is on the left at entrance to Kervoyal, on coastal road near Etang de Pen Mur.

Sanitation:

Parking:

75; €6/night; Max 7 nights

Custom

Coastal Aire in a very popular area. Sandy beach opp road, no views. Inspected 2010.

PENESTIN 240 C5 N47°28.850' W002°28.408' 56760

Directions: Off D34. Follow sp 'Office de Tourisme' in town. Service Point and some parking at TO. Additional parking areas are on the coast road at Plage la Source: N47°28.893' W002°29.403' and at Plage du Loguy: N47°29.393' W002°29.614'.

Sanitation:

Parking:

20; €5.60; Max 48hrs; Pay at TO

Euro Relais Junior; Token (ER)

Parking areas on coast are isolated and without sea views; Parking at TO is adj to main road. Inspected 2010.

MUZILLAC

241 C5 N47°33.538' W002°30.711' 56190

Directions: Super U, at D20/N165 roundabout.

Sanitation:

Parking:

Poss

Euro Relais Junior

Supermarket adj. Inspected 2010.

LE GUERNO

242 C5 N47°35.004' W002°24.384' 56190

Directions: Off D139a. Parking behind church in village centre, sp 'P50 spaces' and signed. The Service Point is outside the municipal campsite to west of town: N47°35.023' W002°24.923'.

Sanitation:

Parking:

10; 3.5t weight restriction

Custom; Diff access

Small pleasant village. Inspected 2010.

LA ROCHE BERNARD

243 C5 N47°31.155' W002°18.321' 56130

Directions: Chemin du Pâtis. From D765 in town follow sp 'Camping' and 'Port'. Service Point is outside campsite. Motorhomes are banned from all car parks 6pm-8am. Campsite offers 6pm-12pm motorhome rates.

Sanitation:

Parking:

18; €9.15 Apr-Jun; €10.65 Jul-Aug; €5 Oct; Elec €4

Aire Services; €2

Parking overlooks port area with restaurants, in a very picturesque setting. Inspected 2010.

MARZAN

244 C5 N47°32.414' W002°19.424' 56130

Directions: D148. Adj to the main road through the village, signed.

Sanitation:

Parking:

10; 12m bays

Custom

Village 2 mins; Convenience store opp. Inspected 2010.

MALANSAC

245 C5 N47°40.694' W002°17.969' 56220

Directions: Rue Saint Fiacre, off D21. Enter the village on D21 from Rochefort-en-Terre. Aire is signed on right off D21. Follow road for 100m and the Aire is on left in car park.

Sanitation:

Parking:

5

Custom

Large village with commerce. Inspected 2010.

RIEUX | 246 | C5 | N47°35.888' W002°06.015' | 56350

Directions: Rue du Château. Turn off D114 onto Rue du Château, sp 'Municipal'. Follow road to end and Service Point is right of toilets outside the municipal campsite.

Sanitation:

Parking:

None

Euro Relais Junior; Token (2/1)

Lovely riverside day parking. Inspected 2010.

REDON | 247 | C5 | N47°38.704' W002°05.383' | 35600

Directions: Quai Surcouf/D775, on canal by lock and marina. At D775/D775b roundabout turn onto D775 into town, sp 'Redon'. Follow this road into town and the Aire is on right in front of marina.

Sanitation:

Parking:

10

Custom

On edge of canal lock and marina; Town 1 min. Poss to walk down canal path. Excellent town Aire. Very popular. Inspected 2010.

ROCHEFORT EN TERRE | 248 | C5 | N47°41.979' W002°19.998' | 56220

Directions: D21. Enter the village on D21 and the Aire is in the car park to the right. Motorhome parking is on the bottom terrace.

Sanitation:

Parking:

10

None

Pretty tourist village with tourist shops 2 mins uphill. Inspected 2010.

BAINS SUR OUST | 249 | C5 | N47°42.325' W002°04.174' | 35600

Directions: Rue du Stade. Turn off D260/D60 onto Rue du Stade. Aire on C3/Rue du Stade between church and football stadium in large gravel parking area just off main square with church. Service Point hidden behind toilet block.

Sanitation:

Parking:

30

Custom

1 min to village centre with commerce inc convenience store. Inspected 2010.

ST JUST | 250 | C5 | N47°45.779' W001°58.014' | 35550

Directions: Les Landes de Cojoux. From D54 in town follow sp 'Camping' out of village on Route de l'Abbé Corbe. Then turn left onto Les Landes de Cojoux. Service Point in sports complex. Parking at megalithic site. Turn left as exit sports complex. Take the next right and parking on right, signed: N47°46.010' W001°58.233'.

Sanitation:

Parking:

5; Grass parking

Custom

Rural parking area 3 mins from megalithic stones, worth a wander. Inspected 2010.

LA GACILLY 1

251 C5 N47°45.791' W002°07.565' 56200

Photo: Rita Renninghoff

Directions: D777. Exit the town on D777 towards Sixt sur Aff. The Service Point is on the left before the municipal campsite. The parking is adj to river on Rue de l'A.F.F. before crossing bridge to D777, signed: N47°45.560' W002°07.835'.

Sanitation:

Parking:

5; Also see 252

Raclet; €2; New Service Point being built

SP

Pretty riverside town; Riverside parking has no views. Inspected 2010.

LA GACILLY 2

252 C5 N47°45.419' W002°09.535' 56200

Directions: D777. Follow D777 west of town to Etang de Beauche, signed.

Sanitation:

Parking:

3

None; See 251

SP

Remote parking on edge of large lake. Inspected 2010.

COMBLESSAC

253 C5 N47°52.633' W002°04.747' 35330

Directions: D48. At Stade Georges Roger as enter town from east on D48, signed. From other directions follow sp 'Complexe Sportif'.

Sanitation:

Parking:

5

Custom

SP

Aire in village beside sports complex. Inspected 2010.

MALESTROIT 1

254 C5 N47°48.566' W002°23.583' 56140

Directions: D776. Behind the gas bottles at the fuel station below the Casino supermarket, on the edge of Malestroit.

Sanitation:

Parking:

Poss

Flot Bleu Pacific; Token; €2

SP

Free Service Point at 255; Parking see 257 and 258 Inspected 2010.

MALESTROIT 2

255 C5 N47°48.548' W002°22.577' 56140

Directions: Rue Narvick/Centre de Secoures. Exit town on D776 towards Redon. Turn off D776 onto D146, sp 'St Laurent'. Then turn right into Rue Narvick and into small industrial estate. Service Point on left beside football field.

Sanitation:

Parking:

None; See 257 and 258

Custom

SP

Service Point only. Inspected 2010.

MALESTROIT 3 | 256 | C5 | N47°48.614' W002°22.728' | 56140

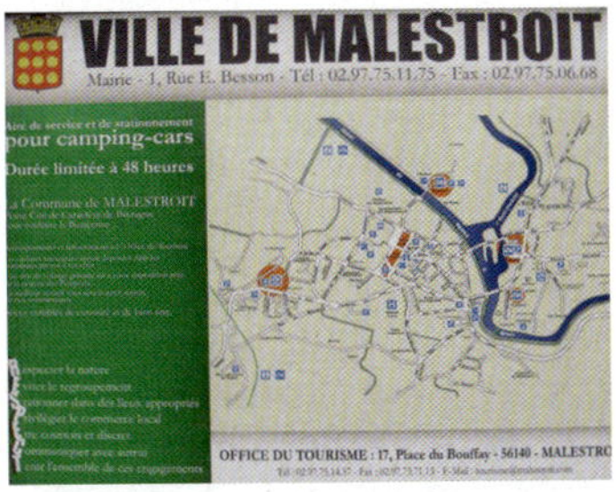

Directions: Off Rue Notre Dame. From east on D776 enter town and cross river on Rue Notre Dame and turn into car park.

Sanitation:

Parking:

4; Max 48hrs

None; See 255

Very popular car park with no designated parking. See 257 or 258 instead. Inspected 2010.

MALESTROIT 4 | 257 | C5 | N47°48.747' W002°22.939' | 56140

Directions: Chemin de l'Ecluse. From town centre follow D10 northwest. Turn off D10, sp 'P L'Ecluse'. Follow this road straight on to the Aire, crossing small bridge on river not suitable for large motorhomes.

Sanitation:

Parking:

12; Max 48hrs

None; See 255

By small river and canal lock; Views over open countryside. Town 2 mins. This is the best parking in town. Inspected 2010.

MALESTROIT 5 | 258 | C5 | N47°48.483' W002°22.741' | 56140

Directions: Chemin des Tanneurs. Turn off D776, sp 'Camping' and signed. The Aire is adj to the sports facility before the campsite, signed.

Sanitation:

Parking:

12; Max 48hrs

None; See 255

Good town Aire ideal for shopping; Sun trap. Inspected 2010.

CAMPENEAC | 259 | C5 | N47°57.408' W002°17.623' | 56800

Directions: Rue de la Fontaine. Service Point signed off D134 and D724, adj to church and Mairie. Parking on Rue des Ecoles. Follow sp 'Salle Polyvalente', 'Ecole Notre-Dame' or 'Plan d'Eau' from N24. Parking overlooking lake: N47°57.461'W002°17.319'

Sanitation:

Parking:

15

Custom; Token (ER)

Village commerce. Gravel parking opposite lake/river outside school; Pleasant. Inspected 2010.

LES FORGES | 260 | C5 | N48°00.911' W002°39.151' | 56120

Directions: Off D117. Take D117 south from Les Forges. Before the road bends left turn right and cross river. Turn into the parking area next to the church, sp 'Aire de Repos'. The Service Point is by the statue of Mary.

Sanitation:

Parking:

2

Custom; 2 unmetered elec points

Very old Service Point against wall. Small village near Canal des Forges. Inspected 2010.

PLOERMEL

261 C5 N47°55.991' W002°23.740' 56800

Directions: Blvd Laennec. Aire has moved to a new car park, it is signed but impossible to find without sat nav. Service Point in Rue Mistringue in car park directly above Aire, signed: N47°55.995' W002°23.884'.

Sanitation:

Parking:

4; Max 7 days; 7m bays

Custom; Up hill; Euro Relais Elec; Token (ER); €3/6hrs elec; At parking

Town commerce 2 mins uphill. Market on Friday morning. Inspected 2010.

MAURON

262 C5 N48°05.080' W002°16.968' 56430

Directions: Place Henri Thébault, off D766bis. In town centre turn off D2 onto D766bis/Rue de la Libération, sp 'Centre Culturel'. Follow the road behind the Mairie and the Aire is opp the cemetery.

Sanitation:

Parking:

2; Max 24hrs

Custom

Village has local commerce. Inspected 2010.

PAIMPONT

263 C5 N48°01.377' W002°10.270' 35380

Directions: Rue de l'Enchanteur Merlin/D71. Signed from the D773. Aire near north side of lake by football pitch.

Sanitation:

Parking:

10

Aire Services; Token (3/3)

On edge of village by sports facilities; Lake and large leisure wood adj. Inspected 2010.

MEDREAC

264 C5 N48°16.207' W002°03.261' 35360

Directions: D220/Rue de la Libération. Follow D220 into Médréac and Aire is on left as enter town, sp 'Camping' and signed.

Sanitation:

Parking:

5

Raclet; Token; €3

Aire is set beside a lake with marked walks, but no views. Small municipal campsite adj. Inspected 2010.

HAVE YOU VISITED AN AIRE?

GPS co-ordinates in this guide are protected by copyright law

Take at least 5 digital photos showing
• Signs
• Service Point
• Parking
• Overview
• Amenities

Visit www.all-the-aires.co.uk/submissions.shtml to upload your updates and photos.

Sanitation:

Aire Details:

Submit updates

- Amendments
- New Aires
- Not changed

Beaune

BURGUNDY

Gurgy

MELAY

1 | I7 | N46°13.298' E004°01.414' | 71340

Directions: D122, adj to canal. Exit Melay towards Artaix on D122, Aire on right before bridge at Halte Nautique. Service Point opp Mairie: N46°12.753' E004°01.132'.

Sanitation:

Parking:

15

Custom

Some road noise. Adj to canal with views. Washing sinks. Village 5 mins. Inspected 2012.

ARTAIX

2 | I7 | N46°15.171' E004°00.640' | 71110

Directions: D122. Turn off D122 at bridge in Artaix. Cross canal bridge and turn right, sp 'Aire Naturelle'. 5t weight limit on bridge.

Sanitation:

Parking:

5; Grass parking; Open Jun-Sept

Custom; At WC; 3 CEE unmetered elec points

SP

Tranquil spot in wooded area beside canal basin; Table tennis. Shower; Washing sinks. Access could be difficult if wet. Inspected 2012.

MARCIGNY

3 | I7 | N46°16.580' E004°02.317' | 71110

Directions: Hôpital Local Marcigny, D989. From town centre turn onto D989, sp 'Roanne' and 'P Place Popard'. Aire in right corner of P Place Popard car park, in front of hospital.

Sanitation:

E

Parking:

10

Euro Relais Junior; Token (ER); €2

Town centre with numerous commerce 2 mins. Voie Vert cycle route through town. Inspected 2012.

SEMUR EN BRIONNAIS

4 | I7 | N46°15.896' E004°05.420' | 71110

Directions: C5. From D989, main route through, turn onto C5, signed. Aire on right, signed. Can also park at sports ground: N46°16.341' E004°06.032'. Follow sp 'Stade'.

Sanitation:

Parking:

10; Max 24hrs

Custom

Elevated, terrace parking overlooking town. Local commerce 2 mins. Inspected 2012.

ST CHRISTOPHE EN BRIONNAIS

5 | I7 | N46°17.077' E004°10.800' | 71800

Directions: C54. Turn off D989 onto C54, sp 'Sernier' and 'Loury'. Aire 300m on right, signed.

Sanitation:

E

Parking:

6

Custom; 4 unmetered elec points

Set in quiet location on hillside. Inspected 2012.

CHATEAUNEUF | 6 | I7 | N46°12.840' E004°15.302' | 71740

Directions: D8. As enter village from Chauffailles follow D8 and the Aire is on left just before the river bridge, signed.

Sanitation:

Parking:

10

Custom

Adj to river; Restaurant 2 mins; Village centre 5 mins. Outdoor sink. Inspected 2012.

CHAUFFAILLES | 7 | I7 | N46°12.096' E004°20.104' | 71170

Directions: Chemin du Tour du Bois. Turn off D985, sp 'Aire de Camping Car' and 'Complexe Sportif' or 'Espace Sports-Loisirs'. Follow signs past ponds and Parc des Sports and Aire is 400m on right, signed.

Sanitation:

Parking:

15

Custom

Football; Basketball; Town 5 mins; Open air swimming pool adj; Fishing €5 per day. Inspected 2012.

MATOUR | 8 | I7 | N46°18.172' E004°28.924' | 71520

Directions: D211. In village centre turn onto D211, sp 'St Pierre le Vieux'. Aire on right at village boundary, signed.

Sanitation:

Parking:

10

Custom

Peaceful rural location 3 mins from village with local commerce. Inspected 2012.

LA CHAPELLE DE GUINCHAY | 9 | J7 | N46°12.618' E004°46.033' | 71570

Directions: Maison de Pays. Turn off N6 onto D95, sp 'St Amour', 'Centre Bourg' and 'Maison de Pays'. Turn right, sp 'Mason de Pays' and signed. The Service Point is in the car park of Maison de Pays.

Sanitation:

Parking:

Poss

Custom

TO and shop selling local products adj. Train noise. Local area produces Beaujolais wine. Inspected 2012.

VINZELLES | 10 | J7 | N46°16.301' E004°46.187' | 71680

Directions: D169E. In village centre turn onto D169E at rear of church, sp 'P 50m'. Aire on left in 50m.

Sanitation:

Parking:

20

Custom; At toilet

In Beaujolais wine village. Vines adj to Aire. Local commerce 2 mins. Inspected 2012.

PRUZILLY | 11 | J7 | N46°15.442' E004°41.874' | 71570

Directions: In the centre of the tiny village. Follow signs 'Aire Camping-Cars' in front of church and parking is on the left.

Sanitation:

Parking:

6; Donation

None

Wonderful views of the Beaujolais vines. Drive to Aire is very scenic. Inspected 2012.

PRISSE | 12 | J7 | N46°19.334' E004°45.177' | 71960

Directions: Rue de l'Ancienne Gare. From village centre turn off, sp 'Chai de Prisse', opp pharmacy. Follow sp 'Chai de Prisse' to Aire at Chai de Prisse wine shop. Parking signed on right and left. Service Point at other end of building. Village has 8m length restrictions.

Sanitation:

Parking:

5; Max 8m

Custom

Wine shop with reasonably priced local wine. To taste, select bottles and take to central counter. Inspected 2012.

ST GENGOUX DE SCISSE | 13 | J7 | N46°27.652' E004°46.510' | 71260

Directions: Off D82. From south enter village and take first right turn, sp 'Cimetière'. Follow road to right and Aire located on right opp cemetery.

Sanitation:

Parking:

10; Max 48hrs

Custom; 4 CEE unmetered elec points

Aire situated among vineyards; View over countryside; Very quiet; Walking distance to town. Inspected 2012.

LUGNY PARKING | 14 | J7 | N46°28.723' E004°48.594' | 71260

Directions: Rue de St Pierre. Turn off D56 at entrance to village, sp 'Stade', 'Camping' and 'Aire de Stationnement'. Follow these signs up steep hill. Watch for a few low branches. Aire on right, signed.

Sanitation:

Parking:

20

None; See 15

Views across Chardonnay Valley. Village downhill with chardonnay wine cellars. Restaurant. Inspected 2012.

LUGNY SERVICE | 15 | J7 | N46°28.269' E004°48.705' | 71260

Directions: Rue du Moulin. Follow D56, sp 'Centre Ville'. Turn onto D103, sp 'La Poste'. Follow road to left onto D355, sp 'Aire de Service'. Turn right before the Poste, signed. Service Point on right before incline, signed.

Sanitation:

Parking:

None; See 14

Custom

Difficult Service Point to use. Large vehicles will have to block road. Inspected 2012.

CHAROLLES

16 I7 N46°26.385' E004°16.922' 71120

Directions: D33/Route de Viry. Aire outside campsite. From D979 follow sp 'Camping' and turn onto D33, sp 'Viry' and 'Camping'. Parking 2 compound on left, signed. Service Point and further parking by campsite entrance.

Sanitation:

Parking:

30; €3/24hrs; Open Apr-Oct; Max 48hrs

Raclet; Token (2/1); €3

Outside campsite; Swimming pool 1 min; Rural views; Noise from main road; Town 7 mins. Inspected 2012.

PARAY LE MONIAL

17 I7 N46°26.893' E004°07.205' 71600

Directions: Boulevard du Dauphin Louis. Exit N79 onto D979, sp 'Parney Sud'. Turn off D979, sp 'Basilique' and follow these signs. Aire to rear of car park adj to coach parking, signed.

Sanitation:

Parking:

7; Max 48hrs

Urba Flux Tall; Token; €4

Adj to large riverside town with numerous shops. Voie Vert cycle route along river. Inspected 2012.

DIGOIN

18 I7 N46°28.855' E003°58.294' 71160

Directions: Place de la Grève, off D979. Aire to west of Digoin off D979 before bridge over river Loire. Follow sp 'Camping' and 'Pont Canal'. Aire opp campsite in large lay-by, sp 'Aire de Repos' and signed.

Sanitation:

Parking:

20

Euro Relais Maxi; 4 unmetered CEE elec points

Popular Aire adj to attractive riverside park; river views from Aire. Riverside walk to town 5 mins. Inspected 2012.

NEUVY GRANDCHAMP

19 I7 N46°35.432' E003°56.158' 71130

Directions: Musée Charolais du Machinisme Agricole. In the village centre turn onto D242, sp 'Salle Communale'. Aire on right outside the museum, signed. Service Point to rear of museum.

Sanitation:

Parking:

5; Max 24hrs

Custom; Closed Monday

Service Point at back of museum of agricultural machinery. Level parking alongside building. Museum entry: adults €4. Inspected 2012.

BOURBON LANCY

20 I7 N46°37.167' E003°45.213' 71140

Directions: Turn off D973 in town, sp 'Plan d'Eau' and 'Camping'. The Aire is outside the campsite. Park at the far end to prevent obstruction.

Sanitation:

Parking:

7

Raclet; €2

Large leisure lake with swimming beach adj. Voie Vert cycle route adj. Very good activity area. Inspected 2012.

GENELARD

21 I7 N46°34.643' E004°14.106' 71420

Directions: D985. Turn off D985 onto D974, sp 'Party le Monial'. Service Point in car park immediately on left adj to canal. The TO would prefer motorhomes (max 2.3m wide) to park opp on level canal side parking.

Sanitation:

Parking:

Poss; Max 2-3m wide

Euro Relais Mini

Busy town centre car park. Parking overlooking canal basin and lock opp. Inspected 2012.

ST GENGOUX LE NATIONAL

22 I7 N46°36.268' E004°40.081' 71460

Directions: l'Espace d'Acceuil Voie Verte. From south on D981 turn onto D67, sp 'Voie Verte'. Follow road, turn right before bridge, sp 'Voie Vert' and signed. GPS taken here. Follow road, Service Point on right, parking on left, signed. Popular Aire.

Sanitation:

Parking:

20; Max 72hrs

Aire Services; CC; €3

Adj to 'Voie Verte', excellent to cycle/walk. Restaurant 100m. Commerce easy walking distance. Inspected 2012.

HAVE YOU VISITED AN AIRE?

GPS co-ordinates in this guide are protected by copyright law

Take at least 5 digital photos showing
• Signs
• Service Point
• Parking
• Overview
• Amenities

Visit www.all-the-aires.co.uk/submissions.shtml to upload your updates and photos.

Sanitation:

Aire Details:

Submit updates

- Amendments
- New Aires
- Not changed

GIVRY

24 J6 N46°46.825' E004°44.901' 71640

Directions: Rue de la Gare. Exit town on D69, sp 'Chalon S/S' and 'Voie Verte'. Turn right, sp 'Voie Verte' and signed. Aire off roundabout, Service Point opp.

Sanitation:

Parking:

16

Euro Relais Box; Token (ER); €2

Popular Aire adj to Voie Verte cycle route. Town with commerce 2 mins. Inspected 2012.

LUX

25 J7 N46°45.004' E004°50.978' 71100

Directions: N6 at Loisirs 71. Next to motorhome dealers, adj to N6 northbound. Not signed.

Sanitation:

Parking:

2; Max 12hrs

Euro Relais Junior; No drive over drain

On busy main road. Motorhome dealer with accessory shop adj. Inspected 2012.

CHALON SUR SAONE
26 J6 N46°47.025' E004°51.643' 71100

Directions: Promenade Ste Marie. From N6 follow river dir 'St Marcel' then turn left, away from river, sp 'P Ville Historique'. Aire 400m on right, signed.

Sanitation:

Parking:

None
Raclet

Large car park located near river Saone and the city centre. Popular Aire. Inspected 2012.

OUROUX SUR SAONE
27 J7 N46°43.074' E004°57.238' 71370

Directions: Rue du Pulimot. Turn off D978 onto D38 at traffic lights, sp 'Centre Bourg'. Turn right, sp 'Salle Polyvalente'. Drive past cemetery and Aire is on left of large car park.

Sanitation:

Parking:

10
Custom

In car park of former supermarket. Building being refurbished at time of inspection but Service Point unaffected. Inspected 2012.

SORNAY
28 J7 N46°37.589' E005°10.812' 71500

Directions: D971/Rue de la Mare au Prêtres. Adj to the main road in lay-by, signed. 3.5t weight limit.

Sanitation:

Parking:

5
Flot Bleu Fontaine; 2 unmetered Continental elec points

Adj to main road. Local shops adj. Inspected 2012.

LOUHANS
29 J7 N46°37.777' E005°12.777' 71500

Directions: Rue du Port. Turn off D971 by river bridge, sp 'Aire Camping-Cars'. Follow sp 'Aire Camping-Cars' along river. Service Point by Haulte Nautique, parking 70m, signed.

Sanitation:

Parking:

22; €5 May-Sept + €0.20pp; Pay at Haulte Nautique
Custom

Adj to river; Train station opp; Some noise. Boat moorings and slipway adj. Town 5 mins; Market on Monday. Inspected 2012.

CUISEAUX
30 J7 N46°29.787' E005°23.167' 71480

Directions: Ave de la Madeleine. Turn off D972 by Renault garage at entrance/exit to village, sp 'La Madeleine' and 'Borne Camping Car'. Aire 100m on left against large, white building, signed.

Sanitation:

Parking:

5
Custom; 4 unmetered elec points

By fire station. Village with local shops and a supermarket 2 mins, market on Friday. Inspected 2012.

ECUISSES

31 | I7 | N46°45.605' E004°31.347' | 71210

Directions: Route du Bourg. Exit N80/N70/E607 roundabout onto D974, sp 'Écuisses'. After 3km turn right and cross canal then turn immediately left, both sp 'Eglise'. Follow road to Aire on left, signed.

Sanitation:

Parking:

10

Custom

SP

Adj to water but no views. Canal and towpath 1 min. Aire renovated May 2012. Inspected 2012.

ST LEGER SUR DHEUNE

32 | I6 | N46°50.685' E004°37.958' | 71510

Directions: Port du Canal, adj to the canal. Turn off D978 on the opp side of the canal to D974 into Port du Canal. The Aire is in 500m.

Sanitation:

Parking:

None

Custom; No drive over drain

SP

No parking and an old, inadequate Service Point. Avoid if possible. Inspected 2012.

LE CREUSOT

33 | I6 | N46°48.709' E004°24.842' | 71200

Directions: Parc Touristique des Comes. Follow sp 'Parc Touristique des Combes' through town. Well sp from all directions. Service Point at parking P2.

Sanitation:

Parking:

10

Custom

SP

Theme park. 20 mins downhill or tourist train to large town; Adventure playground in hills around. Inspected 2012.

NOLAY

34 | I6 | N46°56.997' E004°37.707' | 21340

Directions: D33a/Ave de la Liberté. Turn off D973 in front of Mairie onto D33a, sp 'Couches' and 'P des Halles'. Aire on right in 200m, signed.

Sanitation:

Parking:

10

Euro Relais Junior; Token (ER); €3 from TO/bar

SP

Village with local shops 3 mins. Voie Vert cycle route from town to canals. Inspected 2012.

BEAUNE

35 | J6 | N47°01.046' E004°50.191' | 21200

Directions: D970/Ave Charles de Gaulle. From south on D970, cross roundabout and Aire on right, opp BP fuel station, sp 'P Charles de Gaulle'. Alternatively exit central ring road, sp 'Dole'. U-turn at roundabout, signed. Turn right, sp 'P Charles de Gaulle' and signed.

Sanitation:

Parking:

6; Max 8m

Flot Bleu Pacific (Green); Token; €3.60; 4 elec points give 4 hours/token

SP

Fortified town; Famous hospital; Token dispenser onsite takes CC. Inspected 2012.

NUITS ST GEORGES — 36 — J6 — N47°07.907' E004°57.121' — 21700

Directions: Rue de Cussigny. Approach from south following D35, sp 'Beaune' and signed. Aire adj to D35. From N974 follow sp 'Gare SNCF' and signed.

Sanitation:

Parking:

5; Max 8m

Urba Flux

In wine town; Plenty of cellars to visit. Pleasant spot. Town 5 mins. Can be noisy due to agricultural traffic. Inspected 2012.

PIERRE DE BRESSE — 37 — J6 — N46°53.008' E005°16.045' — 71270

Directions: Rue du Stade. Adj to D73 at the base of the water tower opp château.

Sanitation:

Parking:

20

Custom; 1 unmetered elec point

Large car park adj to sports facilities. Château is also museum. Numerous shops. Market Monday. Inspected 2012.

SEURRE — 38 — J6 — N47°00.263' E005°08.609' — 21250

Directions: Rue de la Perche à l'Oiseau. Turn off D976, sp 'Port de Plaisance', 'Camping du Port' or 'Port Capitainerie'. At river turn right and follow road past marina. Aire on right, signed.

Sanitation:

Parking:

10

Flot Bleu Euro; CC; €4

Adj to river and small marina; Partial views; Quiet; rural views; Lock nearby; Promenade along river to town. Inspected 2012.

ST JEAN DE LOSNE — 39 — J6 — N47°06.296' E005°15.762' — 21170

Directions: Promenade du Port Saint-Jean. Turn off at D20 and D968 roundabout into harbour car park, signed. Follow road around harbour and the Service Point is on the left.

Sanitation:

Parking:

None

Flot Bleu Euro; CC; €4

Service Point only. Inspected 2012.

HAVE YOU VISITED AN AIRE? — GPS co-ordinates in this guide are protected by copyright law

Take at least 5 digital photos showing
• Signs
• Service Point
• Parking
• Overview
• Amenities

Visit www.all-the-aires.co.uk/submissions.shtml to upload your updates and photos.

Sanitation:

Aire Details:

Submit updates
- Amendments
- New Aires
- Not changed

AUXONNE T 41 J6 N47°11.541' E005°23.012' 21130

Directions: Place de l'Iliotte. From west enter town on D905 and follow road, sp 'Dole' across river. Service Point 200m on right in lawn before fortress. Not signed.

Sanitation:

Parking:

Poss

Urba Flux; CC; No drive over drain

Parking adj to fortress. Adj to river but no view. Noisy location. Service Point appeared dysfunctional. Inspected 2012.

LAMARCHE SUR SAONE 42 J6 N47°16.374' E005°23.184' 21760

Directions: From D976 turn off by chapel, signed. Aire at end of road.

Sanitation:

Parking:

7

Flot Bleu Pacific; €3/Token/8hrs elec

Pleasant spot; Views of river. Slipway adj. Token machine onsite. Village 3 mins walk. Inspected 2012.

PONTAILLER SUR SAONE 43 J6 N47°18.166' E005°25.093' 21270

Directions: Rue du Port. Follow D959 through town, sp 'Pesmes'. Turn right at bridge, sp 'Saone'. Aire adj to river on left.

Sanitation:

Parking:

5

Flot Bleu Pacific (White); Token; €3

River views, boat moorings and slipway adj. Local commerce 2 mins. Inspected 2012.

HEUILLEY SUR SAONE 44 J6 N47°19.660' E005°27.244' 21270

Directions: Rue du Patis. Turn off D25D by the church, sp 'Camping-Parking'. The Aire is on the right before the river bridge.

Sanitation:

Parking:

5

Flot Bleu Pacific; Token (FB); €3

Near river but no view. Village with local commerce 1 min. Inspected 2012.

MARSANNAY LA COTE 45 J6 N47°16.289' E004°59.506' 21160

Directions: D108/Rue du Rocher. Turn off D974 as exit Dijon onto D108, sp 'Marsannay la Cote' and signed. Service Point on right, signed. Parking prohibited at Service Point so follow sp 'Office de Tourism'. Parking in car park adj to TO: N47°16.203' E004°59.278'.

Sanitation:

Parking:

4; Max 48hrs

Custom

In wine producing village just south of Dijon. Inspected 2012.

DIJON TALANT — 46 — J6 — N47°19.274' E005°00.655' — 21000

Directions: Blvd du Chanoine Kir. Aire adj to Camping du Lac, south of lake before canal bridge. In Talent follow sp 'Camping'. CC operated entrance barrier. Note: 3m height restricted bridge when approach from Dijon.

Sanitation:

Parking:

17; €10/24hrs inc 10amp elec

Aire Services

Adj to campsite (open April-Oct). River with walks and a leisure park with beach adj. Dijon centre 20 mins. Inspected 2012.

SAVIGNY LE SEC — 47 — J6 — N47°26.033' E005°02.767' — 21380

Directions: Chemin de Saussy. In the village centre turn off D903 at the traffic lights onto D107a, sp 'Messigny'. Follow road to right, sp 'P Camping-Car'. Follow sp 'P Camping-Car' and the Aire is to the right by the sports facilities, signed.

Sanitation:

Parking:

10; €3.50/24hrs

Custom; €2

Payment taken through honesty box. Village with local commerce 4 mins. Inspected 2012.

MAXILLY SUR SAONE — 48 — J6 — N47°20.276' E005°25.845' — 21270

Directions: D976. Turn off D976 as exit towards Talmay, sp 'P Voie Verte'. Parking adj to canal lock, opp industrial unit, signed.

Sanitation:

Parking:

4

Elec bollard 16amp; Token (1/1); €3/3hrs

Adj to working canal and lock. Cycle/walking path on tow-path. No Service Point, see 44. Inspected 2012.

FONTAINE FRANCAISE — 49 — J6 — N47°31.485' E005°22.051' — 21610

Directions: Rue Berthaut. From Beze on D960 cross roundabout, signed. Turn right in 200m, signed. Aire on left in 200m. Access possible, but impractical for motorhomes over 7.5m.

Sanitation:

Parking:

4; Difficult access

Urba Flux; €2

A charming but impractical Aire under trees adj to weir pools. Feed the tame fish. Inspected 2012.

SOMBERNON — 50 — I6 — N47°18.791' E004°42.720' — 21540

Directions: D7. Exit the town on D7, sp 'St-Seine-l'Abbaye'. Aire on left before town boundary by the tennis courts, signed.

Sanitation:

Parking:

5

Euro Relais Junior; Token (ER)

Large parking area. Supermarket 2 mins. Town with numerous commerce 10 mins. Inspected 2012.

HAVE YOU VISITED AN AIRE? GPS co-ordinates in this guide are protected by copyright law

Take at least 5 digital photos showing
• Signs
• Service Point
• Parking
• Overview
• Amenities

Visit www.all-the-aires.co.uk/submissions.shtml to upload your updates and photos.

Sanitation:

Aire Details:

Submit updates
- Amendments
- New Aires
- Not changed

VENAREY LES LAUMES | 52 | I6 | N47°32.612' E004°26.911' | 21150

Directions: At Plan d'eau 'Le Nid a la Caille'. Follow D954 towards D905, sp 'Vitteaux'. Turn off D954, sp 'Plan d'eau Le Nid a la Caille'. Follow road to end and the Service Point is on left before height barrier.

Sanitation:

Parking:

5

Euro Relais; Token (2/1); €2

Lake adj but no views. Swimming beach adj. Inspected 2012.

SEMUR EN AUXOIS | 53 | I6 | N47°29.705' E004°20.966' | 21140

Directions: Avenue Pasteur. Enter town on D954 from Villenotte. Take 1st right, sp 'Pouilly en Auxois' and signed. Turn immediately right, sp 'Lantilly'. Parking at sports facilities on right.

Sanitation:

Parking:

8

Custom

Medieval town 10mins. Intermarché supermarket 2 mins. Inspected 2012.

CHATILLON EN BAZOIS | 54 | I6 | N47°03.200' E003°39.260' | 58110

Info/Photo: Brenda & Maurice Cope/Linda Denning

Directions: Place Pierre Saury. Turn off D978 in town centre, sp 'Complex Sportif' and signed. Go straight on for 100m and Aire is on left before campsite by sports facilities.

Sanitation:

Parking:

5

Euro Relais Junior; Token (ER)

In centre of town adj to sports facility. Local commerce 2 mins. Tolerated parking south on D978 at canal basin on Canal du Nivernais: N47°02.897' E003°39.047'.

ROUVRAY | 55 | I6 | N47°25.370' E004°06.266' | 21530

Directions: Rue du Champ de Foire. Exit village, sp 'St Andeux' and signed. Service Point on left, signed. Parking opp.

Sanitation:

Parking:

3; Max 48hrs

Custom

Small Aire in village with local commerce. Inspected 2012.

QUARRE LES TOMBES

56 I6 N47°22.102' E003°59.980' 89630

Directions: D10. Exit village by church on D10, sp 'St Brisson' and 'Lac des Settons'. Aire on left adj to park, sp 'Aire Camping-Car'.

Sanitation:

Parking:

10

Custom

Pleasant Aire adj to park. Bicycle wash on site. Village with local commerce 1 min. Village in Parc Natural Regional Du Morvan. Inspected 2012.

LAC DES SETTONS

57 I6 N47°11.913' E004°03.794' 58230

Directions: Nr Montsauche Les Settons. From D193 follow sp 'Lac des Settons'. Drive around lake, Aire on opp side of road to lake, signed.

Sanitation:

Parking:

12; Max 48hrs: No parking Thurs in July/Aug

Euro Relais Maxi; Token (2/1); Open May-Oct; €3

Large leisure lake with cruises/boat hire. Walking and cycling routes. Numerous restaurants. Inspected 2012.

OUROUX EN MORVAN

58 I6 N47°11.193' E003°57.118' 58230

Directions: Avenue Michel Baroin. Exit village on D12, sp 'Montsauche'. Aire 200m on left opp fishing lake.

Sanitation:

Parking:

4; Max 24hrs

Custom; Tap on outside of toilet

Commerce in village centre, 300m. A pleasant spot in Morvan National Park. Inspected 2012.

CHAUMARD (BLAISY)

59 I6 N47°09.500' E003°53.453' 58120

Directions: D303. Exit Chaumard on D303, sp 'Montigny-en-M'. Follow road around reservoir and Aire in parking area on left.

Sanitation:

Parking:

10

Aire Services; €2

Adj to large reservoir in Park Natural Regional du Moran. Reservoir being developed. Inspected 2012.

ANOST

60 I6 N47°04.640' E004°05.913' 71550

Photo: Don & Maureen Madge

Directions: Place Centrale de la Mairie, off D2. Aire in car park in village centre, signed. Also inferior parking at Vaumignon: N47°03.536' E004°06.938'. Follow sp 'Auton' from village for 3.5km. Parking by old train station opp pottery, signed.

Sanitation:

Parking:

10

Custom

Quiet. Small village with shops and restaurants. Inspected 2012.

BURGUNDY

CHATEAU CHINON — 61 — I6 — N47°03.779' E003°56.167' — 58120

Directions: Rue Jean Sallonnyer. From D978 follow sp 'Infrastructures Routières' and signed through town. Aire in car park, clearly sp 'Infrastructures Routières'.

Sanitation:

Parking:

20

Flot Bleu Fontaine

Town 5 mins with shops and restaurants. Large sloping car park. Inspected 2012.

AUTUN — T — 62 — I6 — N46°57.307' E004°19.043' — 71400

Photo: Don & Maureen Madge

Directions: Parking Plan d'Eau du Vallon, leisure centre car park opp McDonald's and beside N80, near junction with D973. Additional flatter, quieter parking beside cemetery. Follow sp 'P Delestage Camping-Cars': N46°57.048' E004°18.691'.

Sanitation:

Parking:

20

Euro Relais Junior; Token (ER)

Town packed full of open air Roman ruins. Parking 'P Delestage' is 100m from a Roman amphitheatre. Both parking areas adj to leisure lake. Inspected 2012.

MOULINS ENGILBERT — 63 — I6 — N46°59.103' E003°48.552' — 58290

Directions: Ave Perricaudet, off D985. Turn off D985, signed, onto Avenue Perricaudet. Aire on right, outside camping municipal.

Sanitation:

Parking:

None; Local parking available

Custom

Small campsite adj. Town 2 mins with local shops. Inspected 2012.

ST HONORE LES BAINS — 64 — I6 — N46°54.269' E003°50.442' — 58360

Directions: D403. Exit village on D403, sp 'Vandenesse'. Turn left in 100m, sp '8 à Huit' and signed. The Aire is to the left of the supermarket 8 à Huit, signed.

Sanitation:

Parking:

5

Euro Relais Junior; Token (ER)

Mini market (sells tokens) adj; Town 2 mins. Inspected 2012.

LAROCHEMILLAY — 65 — I6 — N46°52.655' E004°00.054' — 58370

Directions: At church in centre of village. Signed off D27. 2.5m width restriction at village entrance.

Sanitation:

Parking:

4; Max 24hrs

Urba Flux; Token

Pleasant village with local shops and restaurants. Signed walks. Free tokens from local commerce. Inspected 2012.

ETANG SUR ARROUX

66 | I6 | N46°51.978' E004°11.352' | 71190

Directions: Signed off D994 and D61. Follow sp 'Salle des Fêtes'. Aire in large village centre car park adj to Salle des Fêtes.

Sanitation:

Parking:

5

Euro Relais Mini

Local commerce adj. Supermarket 1 min. Inspected 2012.

LUZY

67 | I6 | N46°47.412' E003°58.096' | 58170

Directions: Place du Champ de Foire. Adj to D985 through Luzy. In parking area by Centre de Secours and Renault garage, sp 'Champ de Foire' from both sides of town.

Sanitation:

Parking:

20

Urba Flux; Token

Pleasant town with local commerce 2 mins. On main route through. Tokens are free from local shops/cafés. Inspected 2012.

CHIDDES

68 | I6 | N46°51.658' E003°56.457' | 58170

Directions: D124. Adj to main route through, in parking area diagonally opp church adj to water trough feature, signed.

Sanitation:

Parking:

None

Urba Flux; Token; Free

Pleasant village with local commerce. Free token from local commerce. Inspected 2012.

LA CHAUME (CHIDDES)

69 | I6 | N46°52.061' E003°56.557' | 58170

Directions: La Chaume. Exit Chiddes on D227, sp 'La Chaume'. Aire 800m on left, sp 'La Chaume'. Turn right up steep gravel drive and Aire at top.

Sanitation:

Parking:

6; €2.50/night plus €2/pp

Custom; Elec €2.50/night

Commercial Aire at dairy farm. Nicely developed designated area with far reaching rural views. Local products for sale. Inspected 2012.

REMILLY

70 | I6 | N46°49.198' E003°48.707' | 58250

Directions: D3. Exit village on D3, sp 'Semelay'. Cross 1st river bridge and Aire on left before 2nd river bridge, signed.

Sanitation:

Parking:

4; Grass parking

Urba Flux

Located on a grass triangle between two shallow rivers. Fishing poss and river is great for damming. Village with local commerce 2 mins. Inspected 2012.

FOURS

71 I6 N46°48.983' E003°43.100' 58250

Directions: Rue des Écoles. Travelling towards Decize turn left off D981 just past Hôtel de Ville, signed, onto Rue des Écoles. The Aire is 100m on the right, signed.

Sanitation:

Parking:

8

Euro Relais Mini

SP

Adj to houses. Local commerce 2 mins, market Saturday. Inspected 2012.

DECIZE

72 H6 N46°49.914' E003°27.664' 58300

Directions: Allée Marcel Merle. Approach from Nevers and follow sp 'Moulins' and 'Stade Nautique'. Cross river and turn right onto D978a. At roundabout take 1st exit into car park, sp 'Stade Nautique'. Aire in 200m in very large car park next to tennis courts.

Sanitation:

E WC

Parking:

F

50

Flot Bleu Euro; CC; €3

SP

Large car park with uninterrupted views of river Loire. Town with commerce 1 min. No motorhome parking alongside avenue of trees. Inspected 2012.

IMPHY

73 H6 N46°55.333' E003°15.633' 58160

Directions: Rue Courtet. Turn off main route through town, sp 'Espace Aquatique Amphélia' and signed. Follow sp 'Espace Aquatique Amphelia' across the railway, then turn left at roundabout. Follow the road adj to the river, past the swimming pool to Aire on left.

Sanitation:

E

Parking:

P F

12; Max 48hrs

Flot Bleu Pacific; Token; €3.20/20 mins

Near river but no views. Surrounded by park. Inspected 2012.

ST BENIN D'AZY

74 H6 N47°00.067' E003°23.721' 58270

Directions: D9. From D978 turn into town at roundabout onto D9 and Aire is on right, signed.

Sanitation:

E

Parking:

P F

10

Euro Relais Junior; Token (2/1); €2

SP

Pleasant village with local commerce and convenience store. Inspected 2012.

ROUY

75 H6 N47°01.710' E003°32.057' 58110

Directions: D978. Adj to D978 as exit village towards Châtillon-en-Bazois. Aire next to building marked 'Foyer Rural'.

Sanitation:

F

Parking:

P F

3

Point Belle Eau

Road noise. Steeply sloping gravel parking. Village with local commerce 2 mins. Inspected 2012.

ALLUY | 76 | H6 | N47°02.604' E003°38.091' | 58110

Directions: D978. Directly adj to D978 between Châtillon-en-Bazois and Rouy, sp 'Tout Occas au Chalet' and 'Aire de repos Maison du Bazois'.

Sanitation: E WC F

Parking: P F

10

Raclet

SP

Service Point has been dysfunctional for past 4 years. Notice states Maison de Bazois adj may help but they would not help us! Inspected 2012.

POUGUES LES EAUX | 77 | H6 | N47°05.006' E003°05.608' | 58320

Directions: D907. Exit town on D907 travelling north towards A77 Autoroute. Turn off at roundabout, sp 'Camping'. Aire on right, adj to Casino Planetarium, signed.

Sanitation: E WC F

Parking: P F

5

Urba Flux Tall; Token or CC; €2/10 mins water or elec

SP

Campsite adj. Casino Planetarium adj. Inspected 2012.

LA CHARITE SUR LOIRE | 78 | H6 | N47°10.480' E003°00.674' | 58400

Directions: Quai Romain Mollot, off N151. Follow sp 'Bourges' on N151. Cross river bridge and turn left before 2nd river bridge, signed. Aire on Île du Faubourg between eastern and western banks of the river Loire.

Sanitation: E WC F

Parking: P F

10; Max 24hrs

Aire Services; CC; €4

SP

Aire adj to river, but no view, located on small river island. Town with commerce across river, 5 mins. Inspected 2012.

POUILLY SUR LOIRE | 79 | H6 | N47°17.229' E002°56.795' | 58150

Directions: D243. Outside Camping le Malaga. Follow sp 'Camping' through the narrow town. Service Point before entrance to campsite as exit town towards Les Girarmes.

Sanitation: E WC F

Parking: P F

At campsite

Point Belle Eau

SP

Service Point only. Campsite open May-Sept. Inspected 2012.

CLAMECY | 80 | H6 | N47°27.726' E003°31.358' | 58500

Directions: Place de l'Abottoir, off D951/Rue Jean Jaurès. From Vézelay follow D951, sp 'Nevers' and 'Camping'. Turn off D951, sp 'Camping Cars' and 'Parking'. Aire 50m from town centre near river Yonne.

Sanitation: E WC F

Parking: P F

6; Can be obstructed by parked cars

Point Belle Eau

SP

Old buildings and cobbled streets; Historic link with Bethlehem. Inspected 2012.

TREIGNY

81 H6 N47°32.991' E003°10.867' 89520

Directions: Champ de Foire. In village centre, follow signs. Aire adj to cemetery at the Champ de Foire.

Sanitation:

Parking:

8

Custom

Aire located just off village centre, 1 min. Local commerce and convenience store. Inspected 2012.

ST AMAND EN PUISAYE 1

82 H6 N47°31.974' E003°04.398' 58310

Directions: D955, at the municipal campsite. From village centre take D955 towards St-Sauveur-en-Puisaye. Take D955 to the right at the 5–way junction and the Service Point is 100m on left outside the municipal campsite.

Sanitation:

Parking:

None

Euro Relais Mini

Municipal campsite open June-Sept. Unrestricted car park by TO. Plenty of local potters. Inspected 2012.

ST FARGEAU

83 H5 N47°38.380' E003°04.191' 89170

Directions: Le Chenil. In village adj to D18 and D965. In car park by covered market, sp 'Pique-Nique' and signed.

Sanitation:

Parking:

10

Custom

Covered market with picnic tables inside. Pleasant. Can be very noisy. Inspected 2012.

ROGNY LES SEPT ECLUSES 1

84 H5 N47°44.820' E002°52.863' 89220

Directions: Quai Sully. On D90 from Bleneau go past the campsite, over the bridge and turn right, sp 'Mairie' and signed. After crossing bridge turn left, signed. Aire next to canal, signed.

Sanitation:

Parking:

4; Max 24hrs; Grass parking

Custom

Canalside; Very attractive water system with flight of locks no longer in use. Inspected 2012.

ROGNY LES SEPT ECLUSES 2

85 H5 N47°44.555' E002°52.753' 89220

Directions: D14/Rue Hugues Cosnier. Turn off D90 onto D14, sp 'Ouzouer s T' and 'Les 7 Ecluses'. Parking on right before bridge over lock gates. Not signed.

Sanitation:

Parking:

6

None; See 86

Opp a flight of 7 locks, no longer in use. Village with local commerce 1 min. Inspected 2012

ROGNY LES SEPT ECLUSES 3 | 86 | H5 | N47°44.281' E002°53.119' | 89220

Directions: C4. Turn off D90 onto C4, sp 'Breteau'. In 600m turn right, sp 'Stade'. Follow track for 150m to the sports facilities.

Sanitation:

Parking:

5

None; See 86

At abandoned sports facilities with derelict building. Local commerce 600m. Inspected 2012.

ROGNY LES SEPT ECLUSES 4 | 87 | H5 | N47°44.620' E002°53.289' | 89220

Directions: D90/Rue André Henriat. Parking adj to the eastern town boundary. Signed at far end. Designated parking area can be very boggy.

Sanitation:

Parking:

6

None; See 86

Adj to D90 200m from campsite. Campsite marked as 3 on official map offers a cheap rate of €6/night. Inspected 2012.

CRAVANT 1 | 88 | I5 | N47°40.888' E003°41.035' | 89460

Directions: Port du Canal. Exit Cravant on D606 towards Auxerre. After crossing river turn left immediately before canal bridge, sp 'Informations Touristiques'. Parking past the TO.

Sanitation:

Parking:

5

None; See 89

Canal with boat moorings adj so nice spot but some road noise and overnight truck parking behind. Town with local commerce 3 mins. Inspected 2012.

CRAVANT 2 | 89 | I5 | N47°40.867' E003°41.410' | 89460

Directions: Promenade Saint-Jean. Turn off D606 south of village onto D139/Rue du Moulin, sp 'Salle Polyvalente' and 'P tourisme'. Parking on left, signed. Service Point: Signed off D606 at ZI des Bouchots Sud. From parking turn left onto D606 then 1st right, signed: N47°40.696' E003°41.445'

Sanitation:

Parking:

5

Custom

Pleasant, quiet. Old town very narrow, not advised for motorhomes. Inspected 2012.

CHABLIS | 90 | I5 | N47°49.042' E003°47.049' | 89800

Directions: D235. Turn off D965 on the west side of town, sp 'Chablis'. Aire 200m on left, signed.

Sanitation:

Parking:

8

Custom

Noisy location adj to main route. Chablis centre with numerous wine caves 5 mins. D62 a beautiful drive accessible by all motorhomes. Inspected 2012.

GURGY * | 91 | H5 | N47°51.841' E003°33.281' | 89250

Directions: Quai des Fontaines. Adj to and overlooking river. Signed 'Parking Camping-Cars' from village centre.

Sanitation:

Parking:

19

Raclet; Token; €4; No drive over drain

Parking on river bank; Beautiful views of river. Inspected 2012.

BRIENON SUR ARMANCON | 92 | H5 | N47°59.025' E003°36.798' | 89210

Directions: D84. Exit the town to the south on D84, sp 'Auxerre'. The Service Point is adj to D84 outside Camping de L'Île Saint-Martin.

Sanitation:

Parking:

None

Euro Relais Junior; Token (ER); €3

Service Point only. Campsite open May-Oct. Inspected 2012.

ST JULIEN DU SAULT | 93 | H5 | N48°01.742' E003°18.084' | 89330

Directions: Stade Jean Sax. Turn off D3, sp 'Stade Jean Sax' and signed. Turn left and then right following sp 'Stade Jean Sax' and signed. Aire on left.

Sanitation:

Parking:

13

Custom

Town centre with local shops 1 min. Sports fields adj. Inspected 2012.

Rogny les Sept Écluses 1

Barlieu

CENTRE

Sancoins

BREZOLLES — 1 — F4 — N48°41.450' E001°04.183' — 28270

Directions: D939. Adj to D939 on left as enter town on D939 from Verneuil-s-Avre just after junction with D117 and D102.3.

Sanitation:

Parking:

10

Custom

Edge of village with shops; Views of church. Beautiful gardens, small trees and shrubs. Picnic area. Inspected 2012.

COURVILLE SUR EURE — 2 — F4 — N48°26.756' E001°14.506' — 28190

Directions: Rue des Canaux, at campsite. Approach on D920 from Chatres. Turn off onto D114, sp 'Camping'. Service Point and parking in entrance of municipal campsite.

Sanitation:

E

Parking:

6; Max 48hrs; Max 9m

Euro Relais Junior; Token (ER); €2.50

SP

Designated parking adj to campsite. River adj. Walk through adj park. Town Centre 1 min. Inspected 2012.

NOGENT LE ROI — 3 — F4 — N48°39.035' E001°31.710' — 28210

Directions: Rue des Moulins. The Aire is at the sports facilities but currently there are no signs to follow. The parking bays are signed 'Camping-Car'. The town centre is passable but narrow in places with some difficult blind corners.

Sanitation:

Parking:

4; Max 48hrs

Custom; Under construction at time of inspection

Swimming pool and sports facilities adj, but fenced off. Town centre with commerce 2 mins. Inspected 2012.

THIRON GARDAIS — 4 — F4 — N48°18.711' E000°59.773' — 28480

Directions: Ave de la Gare. As enter village on D922 from Chassant. Turn right, sp 'Aire de Camping car'. Aire on right, signed. Some level parking behind Service Point.

Sanitation:

Parking:

5

Custom; Difficult

Indoor swimming pool, sports fields and basketball adj. Local commerce 1 min. Inspected 2012.

BROU — 5 — F5 — N48°12.824' E001°08.808' — 28160

Directions: D955. Exit D955, sp 'Swin', as enter/exit Brou towards/from Nogent le Rotrou. Aire at Madison Cars 28, motorhome dealer.

Sanitation:

E

Parking:

20; €5/night

Custom; €2; 6amp elec €3/night

At motorhome dealers, habitation repairs poss. 18 hole mini golf course and fishing lakes onsite. Laundry 16kg/€9. Restaurant at weekends. Inspected 2012.

MARBOUE

6 F5 N48°06.744' E001°19.722' 28200

Directions: Rue du Croc Marbot, just off N10, signed in village. From Châteaudun turn 1st left at traffic lights as enter town, signed. Aire 300m down one-way lane.

Sanitation:

Parking:

10

Aire Services; €2

SP

Aire next to park adj to river Loir, no views. Local commerce 1 min. Inspected 2012.

CHATEAUDUN

7 F5 N48°04.303' E001°19.453' 28200

Directions: D31. Enter town on N10 from north. Turn off after roundabout onto D10, sp 'Camping Municipal' and 'Aire de Service'. Follow road along river. Aire in car park opp château alongside river, sp 'Aire de Service pour Camping-Car'.

Sanitation:

Parking:

10; Max 48hrs

Urba Flux Tall; €2

SP

At base of château. River views from some parking bays. River walks and boat launch/canoe club adj. Town 2 mins. Inspected 2012.

ST DENIS LES PONTS

8 F5 N48°04.018' E001°17.362' 28200

Directions: Rue Jean Moulin. By bridge over river on D927. Turn off D927, sp 'La Poste' and signed. Service Point in car park opp 'La Poste'. Parking in large car park adj to river 50m further down road on left, signed.

Sanitation:

Parking:

5

Euro Relais Mini; Token (ER); €2

SP

Service Point in busy car park. Village with local commerce 1 min. Bus stop 10m. Inspected 2012.

CLOYES SUR LE LOIR

9 F5 N47°59.512' E001°13.936' 28220

Directions: D35/Route de Vendôme. Exit the town on D35 heading south and the Aire is on the right, signed. Narrow entrance and exit due to fence.

Sanitation:

Parking:

7

Urba Flux; €2/20 mins water and elec

SP

Adj to river and D35. Town centre with local commerce and riverside restaurants 3 mins. Inspected 2012.

MOREE

10 F5 N47°54.231' E001°13.691' 41160

Directions: D19. At the Plan d'eau. Follow sp 'Camping' in town. Aire outside campsite. As exit/enter town on D19, signed.

Sanitation:

Parking:

None; Overnight parking at lake banned

Custom; €3

SP

Campsite adj open May-August €9/night. Inspected 2012.

SAVIGNY SUR BRAYE

11 F5 N47°52.863' E000°48.135' 41360

Directions: D5. Exit town following sp 'St Calais '. Aire on right after crossing traffic lighted bridge, signed.

Sanitation: E WC F

Parking: F

5; Max 48hrs

Euro Relais Junior; 1 unmetered CEE elec point

SP

Aire adj to riverside park with sports facilities. Town centre with local commerce 3 mins. Inspected 2012

VENDOME

12 F5 N47°47.478' E001°04.536' 41100

Directions: Rue Geoffroy Martel. Turn off N10, sp 'Camping'. Follow sp 'Camping' through town. Aire outside campsite.

Sanitation: E WC F

Parking: F

5

Signed but not present!

SP

Outdoor swimming adj; Park/sports adj; Campsite adj; Beautiful town. Inspected 2012.

LES ROCHES L'EVEQUE

13 F5 N47°46.675' E000°53.519' 41800

Directions: D24. From Vendôme take D917 to Les Roches l'Évêque. Turn right in village towards Lunay. Aire adj to D24 next to tabac and restaurant Les Camping.

Sanitation: E WC F

Parking: F

5

Euro Relais Mini; CEE elec points

SP

Aire in lovely municipal area adj to river. Toilets have been out of order for some time and elec points turned off. Inspected 2012.

TROO

14 F5 N47°46.463' E000°47.038' 41800

Directions: Rue de la Plaine. Turn off D917 at village boundary, signed. Turn right up green lane, signed. Parking on gravel area through the gates. Service Point adj to D917: N47°46.532 E000°47.148'.

Sanitation: E WC F

Parking: F

10

Euro Relais Mini

SP

Isolated spot on hill. Local commerce in next village. Inspected 2012.

MONTOIRE SUR LE LOIR 1

15 F5 N47°45.343' E000°51.834' 41800

Directions: D9. From D917 turn onto D9, signed through town. Aire on left, Service Point behind sign. Alternative parking opp Salle des Fêtes: N47°45.107' E000°51.683'. Turn off central square, sp 'Salle des Fêtes', to parking. This is a busy town car park beside river but no views.

Sanitation: E WC F

Parking: F

10

Custom; Press button for water

SP

Busy town with numerous commerce adj. Market in town square Wednesday morning. Inspected 2012.

MONTOIRE SUR LE LOIR 2

16 F5 N47°45.465' E000°52.169' 41800

Directions: Avenue de la République, off D917. Signed off D917 north of town. The Aire is located at the old train station, sp 'Gare Historique'.

Sanitation:

Parking:

10

Euro Relais Junior; 1 unmetered elec point

SP

This is probably the most peaceful stop in town and is the most popular. Town centre with local commerce 5 mins. Inspected 2012.

TERNAY

17 F5 N47°43.867' E000°46.583' 41800

Directions: Rue St Père. Exit on D8, sp 'Villedieu'. Aire on left just past D8 turning to Troo.

Sanitation:

E WC F

Parking:

P F

5

Euro Relais Mini

SP

Parking at entrance of leisure park with pond. Inspected 2012.

HAVE YOU VISITED AN AIRE?

GPS co-ordinates in this guide are protected by copyright law

Take at least 5 digital photos showing
• Signs
• Service Point
• Parking
• Overview
• Amenities

Visit www.all-the-aires.co.uk/submissions.shtml to upload your updates and photos.

Sanitation:

Aire Details:

Submit updates

- Amendments
- New Aires
- Not changed

ST MARTIN DES BOIS

19 F5 N47°43.567' E000°49.550' 41800

Directions: D116.Turn off D116, sp 'Stade' and 'Tennis'. Aire 10m on left adj to lake and tennis courts.

Sanitation:

Parking:

2; Grass parking

Euro Relais Mini

SP

Lakeside parking next to tennis courts. Local commerce 300m. Inspected 2012.

NEUILLE PONT PIERRE 2

20 F6 N47°32.857' E000°33.113' 37360

Directions: D938. At D938/D766 junction sp 'Picnic Area' and signed. Entrance between La Poste and Gendarmerie, signed. 7.5t weight limit.

Sanitation:

Parking:

8

Raclet; 8 unmetered elec points; Not working at time of inspection

SP

Main road with noisy trucks adj. Inspected 2012.

CHATEAU LA VALLIERE | 21 | E6 | N47°32.506' E000°20.191' | 37330

Directions: D959, at the Super U as exit the town to the east on D959. Next to car wash.

Sanitation:

Parking:

Poss

Custom

Supermarket adj. Inspected 2012.

GIZEUX | 22 | E6 | N47°23.540' E000°11.808' | 37340

Directions: D15/Rue de Lavoir, off D749. Aire signed in village centre.

Sanitation:

Parking:

5

Aire Services; Token (3/3)

Beside entrance to regional nature park; Walking trail to Château de Gizeux. Bus stop adj. Inspected 2012.

CHOUZE SUR LOIRE | 23 | E6 | N47°14.277' E000°07.567' | 37140

Directions: Rue de l'Église. From Tours on D952 turn 1st right as enter town, signed. Go straight on at 1st Stop junc then turn right at end of road, both signed. Aire on left, signed.

Sanitation:

Parking:

8; 4 designated bays

Aire Services; Token (3/3)

Mini market opp. Town centre with local commerce and Loire river 2 mins. Inspected 2012.

RESTIGNE | 24 | E6 | N47°16.823' E000°13.572' | 37140

Directions: Rue Basse. Turn off D35 onto D469, sp 'Restigne' and signed. Go straight over next junc, sp 'Centre Bourg'. Follow road to right past church, signed. Aire on left in 100m.

Sanitation:

Parking:

10; Max 48hrs

Aire Services; Token (3/3)

Pleasant village with local commerce, 1 min, surrounded by vines and local wine producers. Church bells ring all night. Inspected 2012

AVOINE | 25 | E6 | N47°12.767' E000°10.624' | 37420

Directions: Ave de la République. From north on D749 go straight over D749/D418 roundabout onto D749, sp 'Avoine'. Then take 2nd left onto C13, signed. Go straight on at Stop junc. At roundabout turn left and Aire is on right, signed. Bollarded entrance, payment by CC.

Sanitation:

Parking:

11; €4/24hrs; CC

Urba Flux Tall; €2; 11 elec points €2/24hrs

Adj to park with large children's play area. Constant noise from power station. Inspected 2012.

L'ILE BOUCHARD | 26 | E6 | N47°07.326' E000°25.723' | 37220

Directions: Rue du Camping. From centre follow D760, sp 'St Maure-de-T'. Turn off at Super U, sp 'Camping'. Turn right, sp 'Camping'. Service Point outside campsite.

Sanitation:

Parking:

None

Euro Relais Junior; 100L/€2

Service Point only. Campsite adj. Service Point at Super U has been removed. Inspected 2012.

RICHELIEU | 27 | E6 | N47°00.449' E000°19.449' | 37120

Directions: D749. Service Point adj D749 outside campsite, signed. Exit town towards Chatellerault following sp 'Camping'. Parking signed at D658/D749 junc adj to town, 400m from campsite adj to water tower: N47°00.652' E000°19.340'.

Sanitation:

Parking:

50

Custom

Beautiful walled town with statues and turrets adj to parking. Fishing ponds adj to campsite. Inspected 2012.

VILLAINES LES ROCHERS | 28 | F6 | N47°13.281' E000°29.723' | 37190

Directions: Rue des Écoles. Just off D57 in the centre of town. Turn by La Poste, sp 'Mairie' and signed. Service Point to left of Mairie. Parking in the square outside Mairie: N47°13.284' E000°29.783'.

Sanitation:

Parking:

7; Max 24hrs

Custom

Troglodyte village; Basket weaving; Cycle route from square. Restaurant. Inspected 2012.

AZAY LE RIDEAU | 29 | F6 | N47°15.555' E000°28.164' | 37190

Directions: Rue du Stade, outside Le Sabot campsite. Turn off D751 north of town at D39/D751 roundabout, sp 'Camping'. Follow sp 'Camping' straight onto the campsite. Other approaches to Aire go through congested town which is narrow but passable.

Sanitation:

Parking:

15; Max 24hrs

Raclet; Token (2/1); €5

Village 5 mins; Internet available and WiFi at Micro Galaxie in town. Aire can be crowded. Inspected 2012.

ST EPAIN | 30 | F6 | N47°08.640' E000°32.338' | 37800

Directions: Alleé des Peupliers. In village follow sp 'Aire de Repos'. At lake turn either by table tennis or by sign saying no double axles. Pay at Mairie.

Sanitation:

Parking:

10; €1.70/night motorhome; €1.70pp/night; Grass parking; Max 8m

Custom; Unmetered elec €1.80/night

Open style community campsite. No services out of season. Pond adj. Fishing €4/day. Inspected 2012.

VEIGNE | 31 | F6 | N47°17.354' E000°44.090' | 37250

Directions: Les Petit Prés, off D50. At river bridge at entrance/exit Veigné, outside campsite.

Sanitation:

Parking:

3; Grass parking

Aire Services; €2

Adj campsite has changed ownership. Canoe/kayaking possible in river. Inspected 2012.

MONTBAZON | 32 | F6 | N47°17.504' E000°43.195' | 37250

Directions: Allée de la Robinetterie. As enter Montbazon from north on D910 turn left by Intermarché. Aire in residential area behind Intermarché.

Sanitation:

Parking:

3

Custom

Intermarché Supermarket adj. Sports facilities 2 mins; Town 10 mins. Inspected 2012.

ESVRES | 33 | F6 | N47°16.972' E000°47.096' | 37320

Directions: Off D17. Turn off D17 at roundabout in village by church, sp 'Salle des Fêtes' and signed. Aire to rear of car park, signed near tennis club.

Sanitation:

Parking:

10

Custom

River adj; No real views. Town adj. Inspected 2012.

VILLANDRY | 34 | F6 | N47°20.483' E000°30.643' | 37510

Directions: D7. Turn off D7 at the D121 junc into the parking area by TO. The Service Point is to the rear of the car park.

Sanitation:

Parking:

50

Urba Flux Tall; CC; €2

Pleasant village adj. Restaurants and TO adj. Large parking/picnic area used by all visitors. Tourist château 2 mins. Inspected 2012.

SAVONNIERES | 35 | F6 | N47°21.000' E000°33.004' | 37510

Directions: D7. Turn off D7 in town, sp 'Camping'. Service Point outside campsite.

Sanitation:

Parking:

None

Urba Flux Tall; Token (2/1)

Service Point only. See 34 for parking. Inspected 2012.

ST ETIENNE DE CHIGNY | 36 | F6 | N47°21.955' E000°30.372' | 37230

Directions: D952. Turn off D952 near St-Étienne-de-Chigny, sp 'il Buda Park de Loisirs'. Service Point adj to D952.

Sanitation:

Parking:

None

Urba Flux Tall; CC

Riverside park being developed at time of inspection. Currently there is no motorhome parking. Inspected 2012.

FONDETTES | 37 | F6 | N47°24.543' E000°37.449' | 37230

Directions: Rue Édouard Branly, opp ZA la Haute Limougère. Aire located in centre of industrial area, 2km east of Fondettes, follow sp 'ZA la Haute Limouge'.

Sanitation:

Parking:

None

Custom; Toilet emptying point in grass, signed, not in water hydrant!

Service Point only in an industrial park. Inspected 2012.

VOUVRAY | 38 | F6 | N47°24.549' E000°47.812' | 37210

Directions: Voie de la Cissé, off D952. From D952/N152 in Vouvray, turn onto Voie de la Cissé at traffic lights, sp 'Camping' and signed. Aire 10m on left.

Sanitation:

Parking:

3; Max 48hrs

Euro Relais Junior; Token (ER); €2

Village with shops 1 min. Market Friday. Inspected 2012.

MONTLOUIS SUR LOIRE | 39 | F6 | N47°23.067' E000°50.467' | 37270

Directions: Avenue Victor Laloux, at Super U. Follow Super U signs from D751. Service Point to rear of the car wash.

Sanitation:

Parking:

Poss

Aire Services; €2

Supermarket adj. Very large car park. Inspected 2012.

AMBOISE 1 | 40 | F6 | N47°24.501' E000°59.421' | 37400

Directions: Avenue Léonard de Vinci. From roundabout, junction of D61 and D31, west of town exit onto Avenue Léonard de Vinci, sp 'P Camping-Cars'. Follow for 2km and Aire signed on right before traffic lights. Well signed through town. Difficult to manoeuvre large motorhomes when Aire busy.

Sanitation:

Parking:

11

None

Bar/Tabac opp; 4 mins from town centre, river and château. Inspected 2012.

AMBOISE 2

41 F6 N47°25.003' E000°59.160' 37400

Directions: Allée de la Chapelle St-Jean. Next to 'Camping l'Ile d'Or' on island in river Loire. Access from bridge spanning river. Follow sp 'Camping'. Access via electronic gate.

Sanitation:

Parking:

30; €10/24hrs inc unmetered elec

Custom; 8 elec points (may need long lead)

Campsite restaurant, café, shop 10m. River views. Short walk into Amboise across bridge. Inspected 2012.

ATHEE SUR CHER

42 F6 N47°18.854' E000°55.064' 37270

Directions: D83/Rue de Cigogne. From D45 turn onto D83, sp 'Cigogné', 'Reignac', and signed. Follow road for 500m, Aire on left, opp sp 'Village le May'.

Sanitation:

Parking:

3; Max 24hrs

Custom

Views onto fields. Village 2 mins with some facilities; Bar. Inspected 2012.

LE LIEGE

43 F6 N47°12.995' E001°06.827' 37460

Directions: La Gallerie. From Le Liège take D764 south towards Loches. Turn left, sp 'Marsin', then turn off right, sp 'La Galarie'. Turn right after 1.6km and Aire at farm on right in 500m. Parking to right, Service Point straight on.

Sanitation:

Parking:

5; €2; Grass parking

Custom; Elec €2

Secluded farm site; Beautiful location; Very quiet. Strong farm smells and primitive facilities. Inspected 2012.

MONTRESOR

T **44** F6 N47°09.464' E001°12.100' 37460

Directions: Rue du 8 Mai. Exit village on D10, sp 'Genille'. Turn right, sp 'Toutes Directions'. At roundabout go straight over, sp 'College'. Aire on left, sp 'Tennis'.

Sanitation:

Parking:

35

Flot Bleu Fontaine

Overlooking the château, church and general view of a Village of France that is worth a visit. Inspected 2012.

VILLEDOMER

45 F6 N47°32.686' E000°53.225' 37110

Directions: Rue du Lavoir. At La Grande Vallée turn off D910 onto D73, sp 'Aire de Loisirs du Lavoir' and 'Villedômer'. Travel 2km and turn right, signed. Aire outside campsite. Camping signed off N10.

Sanitation:

Parking:

15; Free mid Sept-mid Jun; Pay in summer

Euro Relais Junior; Token (ER); €2

Set in a peaceful location next to park and Aire natural campsite. Local commerce and convenience store. Inspected 2012.

LIGUEIL 46 F6 N47°02.688' E000°49.272' 37240

Directions: Rue des Prés Michau. Turn off D31 onto D59, sp 'St Flovier'. Turn right and follow signs, turning into a narrow one-way street next to Centre de Secours. Service Point on left outside campsite. Well signed from village centre.

Sanitation:

Parking:

1; Max 1hr

Custom; 1 unmetered elec point

SP

Service Point only. Inspected 2012.

REIGNAC SUR INDRE 47 F6 N47°13.735' E000°54.927' 37310

Directions: D58. From village centre exit on D58, sp 'Blere'. Aire on left just after river bridge, signed.

Sanitation:

Parking:

15

Aire Services; Token (3/3)

SP

Parking on former tennis court. River adj, but no view. Village with local commerce 2 mins. Inspected 2012

CHATILLON SUR INDRE 48 F6 N46°59.318' E001°10.267' 36700

Directions: D943. Adj to D943 roundabout as exit town towards Loches. At the Champ de Foire by the TO.

Sanitation:

Parking:

None; See info

Point Belle Eau

SP

Parking regulated. If you want to park contact Mairie for permission. Inspected 2012.

LOCHES - Campsite 49 F6 N47°07.345' E001°00.099' 37600

Directions: Ave Aristide Briand. From south on D943 exit 1st roundabout, sp 'Camping'. Turn right, sp 'Camping'. The Service Point is on the right just over the bridge.

Sanitation:

Parking:

Day only; See 50 - 52

Aire Services; 2 CEE elec sockets, push button for 55 mins elec

SP

Service Point only. Inspected 2012.

LOCHES P1 & P2 T 50 F6 N47°08.242' E001°00.066' 37600

Directions: Rue de l'Amiral. Enter Loches from north. At D943/D764 roundabout exit on the D764, sp 'Genille'. Turn immediately right, sp 'Gare S.N.C.F'. Parking P1 adj to road on left in 200m, signed. Parking P2 (pictured) further down road on right, signed: N47°08.000' E001°00.015'.

Sanitation:

Parking:

10; Max 24hrs

None; See 49

SP

Parking P2 overlooks a riverside park and is the nicer of the two parking areas. Both have a train line adj. Town centre and medieval city 3 mins. Inspected 2012.

LOCHES P3 T 51 F6 N47°07.594' E001°00.131' 37600

Directions: Chemin de la Prairi. From south on D943 exit 1st roundabout, sp 'Camping'. Drive past the campsite and turn right, sp 'Complexe Sportif'. The two-way road is narrow in places. Follow road past sports ground to parking on right before 2.6m bridge, signed.

Sanitation:

Parking:

5; Max 24hrs

None; See 49

Footpath to medieval city opp car park entrance. This is the closest parking to the medieval city but has the most difficult access. Inspected 2012.

LOCHES P4 T 52 F6 N47°07.469' E000°59.589' 37600

Directions: Ave des Bas Clos. Enter Loches from north. At D943/D764 roundabout exit onto D764, sp 'Loches'. Follow sp 'Chatillon s Idre' through town onto D31. Turn left past building on left marked 'Espace Agnes Sorel', sp 'P 89 Places'. Parking signed in far corner of car park.

Sanitation:

Parking:

10; Max 24hrs

None; See 49

This parking is the easiest to access and provides the most shade, but is in the noisiest location. Basketball courts adj. Inspected 2012.

STE MAURE DE TOURAINE 1 53 F6 N47°06.608' E000°36.967' 37800

Directions: Rue de Loches. Enter town on D910 from south. Turn right as enter town, sp 'Espace Rosard' and signed. Aire 50m on right. Narrow access and 3.5t weight restriction.

Sanitation:

Parking:

15

Custom; At WC; Tap in parking area

Pleasant spot. In village centre close to shops and restaurants. Market Friday. Inspected 2012.

STE MAURE DE TOURAINE 2 54 F6 N47°05.592' E000°36.774 37800

Directions: Le Bois Chaudron. From Ste Maure de Touraine head south on D910. Turn left down small lane 800m after roundabout with D760. Aire in 300m.

Sanitation:

Parking:

7; €2.50; Grass parking

Custom; Water €1; Grey waste €2; Toilet waste €3; Elec €2/12hrs; 6 elec points

Showers; Free WiFi; Washing machine €4; Dryer €3. Inspected 2012.

LE GRAND PRESSIGNY 55 F6 N46°55.031' E000°48.392' 37350

Directions: D42, adj to campsite. Enter from Preuilly-sur-Claise or on D60 from Paulmy to avoid one-way system through town. Aire outside campsite, signed. Parking has 3.5t weight restriction.

Sanitation:

Parking:

10

Custom; 2 16amp elec points; Showers €0.50

Interesting château/ruin in village. Campsite adj; Village 3 mins with local commerce. Inspected 2012.

MARTIZAY | 56 | F7 | N46°48.330' E001°02.279' | 36220

Directions: Rue des Anciens. Turn off D975 at large junction before Martizay, sp 'D'A.F.N'. Aire 250m on right.

Sanitation:

Parking:

7; Donation

Custom; 4 unmetered elec points

Adj to leisure park. Local commerce 2 mins. Inspected 2012.

TOURNON ST MARTIN | 57 | F7 | N46°43.863' E000°57.121' | 36220

Directions: Rue de Bel-air. Exit town on D950, sp 'Le Blanc'. Turn right past Menagerie, sp 'aire picnique' and signed. Follow road to right and the Service Point is on the right.

Sanitation:

Parking:

10

Euro Relais Junior; Token (ER)

On edge of town adj to pleasant riverside park. Local shops 1 min. River suitable for white water rafting/canoeing. Inspected 2012.

LE BLANC 1 | 58 | F7 | N46°38.448' E001°04.078' | 36300

Directions: Cour de la Gare. Turn off D975 onto D917, sp 'Rosnay'. Aire at Intermarché supermarket opp roundabout. Service Point near fuel station.

Sanitation:

Parking:

Poss

Euro Relais Junior; €2

Supermarket adj. Inspected 2012.

LE BLANC 2 | 59 | F7 | N46°37.890' E001°03.719' | 36300

Directions: Place du Général de Gaulle. Follow sp 'Centre Ville' to river. At river bridge follow sp 'Tournon' and signed. Take next right, signed, into car park. Aire in 2nd section of car park.

Sanitation:

Parking:

20

Euro Relais Junior; Token (ER); €2

The 2nd parking area is level and peaceful but the 1st car park has river views. Town centre with numerous commerce adj. Inspected 2012.

BENAVENT (POULIGNY ST PIERRE) | 60 | F7 | N46°39.359' E001°01.240' | 36300

Directions: Route du Blanc. Follow D950 through village. As exit village towards Le Blanc, Aire on right, signed next to boulangerie (bakery).

Sanitation:

Parking:

15

Euro Relais Junior; Token (ER)

River 1 min, limited views from Aire. Boulangerie (bakery) adj. Plenty of green space, river walks and fishing. Inspected 2012.

THENAY

61 F7 N46°37.916' E001°25.857' 36800

Directions: Place Mis et Thiennot. Exit St Gaultier on D927, sp 'Thenay', and follow sp 'Thenay'. After bend turn left, sp 'Mairie', towards church. Turn left again, signed, and drive past cemetery. Aire at opp end road, signed.

Sanitation:

Parking:

10

Euro Relais Junior; Token (ER)

SP

Adj to cemetery. Village centre 1 min. Inspected 2012.

EGUZON CHANTOME

62 F7 N46°26.333' E001°34.933' 36270

Directions: D913. At the Super U adj to D913 as exit the town towards Crozant. The Service Point is behind fuel station.

Sanitation:

Parking:

Poss

Euro Relais; €2; Out of service at time of inspection

SP

Supermarket adj. Inspected 2012.

ARGENTON SUR CREUSE

63 F7 N46°35.100' E001°31.350' 36200

Directions: Take D48, sp 'La Pechereu', onto 3.5t restricted route. Parking: Turn left in 200m, signed. Follow road under 3.7m bridge and parking is signed on the right, opp Espace Jean Frappat. Service Point: Turn right in 400m at restaurant Champ de Foire. Service Point on right in 100m, signed.

Sanitation:

Parking:

20; N46°35.263' E001°31.479'

Custom

SP

Parking suitable for long, but not heavy, vehicles. Near sports facilities. Inspected 2012.

OULCHES

64 F7 N46°36.780' E001°17.718' 36800

Directions: Impasse de l'Étang. At the church in the village centre turn off, sp 'Salle de Fêtes'. Aire at end of road.

Sanitation:

Parking:

7

Euro Relais Junior; Token (ER)

SP

Village centre adj. Walk to river. Fishing in ponds, €5.50. Boating poss. Inspected 2012.

NEUILLAY LES BOIS

65 F7 N46°46.150' E001°28.400' 36500

Directions: D1. Take D1, sp 'Buzancais' from village. Aire approx 300m on right.

Sanitation:

Parking:

4; Max 24hrs

Flot Bleu Compact; 2 unmetered elec points

SP

Small parking area by small lake; Fishing €7.60 per day. Toilets and sinks. Small shop/bar/restaurant in village. Inspected 2012.

CHATEAUROUX | 66 | G6 | N46°49.401' E001°41.693' | 36000

Directions: Ave Parc des Loisirs, off Ave Daniel Bernadet outside campsite by river. Follow D151 into town. Turn right at roundabout and right again, sp 'Hall des Expositions' and 'Salle des Fêtes'. Aire 600m.

Sanitation:

Parking:

5; Max 48hrs

Euro Relais Junior; Token

SP

Tokens from adj campsite. Exhibition hall adj. Numerous commerce 3 mins. Inspected 2012.

LA PEROUILLE | 67 | G7 | N46°42.349' E001°31.364' | 36350

Directions: La Roche. Turn off D1 at church opp fuel station, signed. Turn left, sp 'La Roche' and signed. Follow lane and Aire on right, signed.

Sanitation:

Parking:

20; Grass parking

Euro Relais Junior; Token (ER)

SP

Grass parking adj to pond, no fishing, swimming or fires. Access may be difficult after rain. Remote rural location. Inspected 2012.

NEUVY PAILLOUX | 68 | G6 | N46°52.975' E001°50.239' | 36100

Directions: N151. Aire de Repos adj to N151 heading towards Issoudun before Neuvy Pailloux. Only accessible from this side of road.

Sanitation:

Parking:

5

Custom

SP

Adj to main route. Inspected 2012.

LA CHATRE | 69 | G7 | N46°34.934' E002°00.087' | 36400

Directions: D943, at Super U. Approx 2km east of city centre on D943 as exit towards Montlucon.

Sanitation:

Parking:

Poss

Flot Bleu Pacific; €2

SP

Supermarket adj. Inspected 2012.

CULAN | 70 | G7 | N46°32.841' E002°20.785' | 18270

Directions: Place de la Poste, off D943. Parking adj to D943 in town centre beside TO. Service Point behind TO. Tourist château 5mins or park in very sloping car park as exit on D943: N46°32.844' E002°21.189'.

Sanitation:

Parking:

5; Max 48hrs

Custom; Token; €1.50; Showers; Token; €1.50

SP

Adj to town centre with local commerce and TO. Château 5 mins. Inspected 2012.

LE CHATELET

71 G7 N46°38.702' E002°16.696' 18170

Directions: Avenue de la Gare. Enter the village from the west on the D951. After the D3 turning on the left take the next left turn, signed. This road has a 3.5t weight restriction. The Aire is in 50m.

Sanitation:

Parking:

5

Euro Relais Junior; Token (ER); No drive over drain

SP

Quiet location on edge of village. Inspected 2012.

MAREUIL SUR ARNON

72 G6 N46°52.818' E002°08.752' 18290

Directions: D14. Follow D14 through town towards Issoudun. Service Point on left adj to D14.

Sanitation:

Parking:

None

Euro Relais Mini; €2

SP

Aire Natural campsite adj: €3.50/motorhomes, €2.50/pp, €2/elec. Overlooking lake. Inspected 2012.

ST AMAND MONTROND 1

73 G7 N46°43.097' E002°30.242' 18200

Directions: Quai Lutin. Approach on D2144 from south. At roundabout over canal turn left, sp 'Camping-Cars'. Aire on right, signed.

Sanitation:

Parking:

10

Custom

SP

Lovely spot adj to canal. Town 5 mins. Large town with cafés, shops and restaurants. Inspected 2012.

LEVET

74 G6 N46°55.427' E002°24.410' 18340

Directions: Parking Salle des Fêtes. From N144 in village turn off by the church, sp 'Salle des Fêtes'. This road has 3.5t weight restriction. Turn left, sp 'Salle des Fêtes' and Aire is on left past height barriered parking.

Sanitation:

Parking:

3; Max 24hrs; Mar-Oct

Custom; closed in winter; 4 unmetered elec points; No water at time of inspection

SP

Pleasant rural location under trees overlooking fields. Inspected 2012.

DUN SUR AURON

75 G6 N46°52.970' E002°34.014' 18130

Directions: D10/Rue des Ponts. Enter on D28 from Levet. Turn left and cross river bridge. Turn next right and Aire on right, signed.

Sanitation:

Parking:

5

Custom

SP

Parking by Canal du Berry is better than it looks. Small town with local shops adj. Inspected 2012.

SANCOINS 76 H6 N46°50.008' E002°54.894' 18600

Directions: Quai du Canal, adj to Canal de Berry. Exit town on D2076/D43, sp 'Bourges'. Aire on left by canal bridge, signed. Ignore 'No Entry' signs on canal as these are for lorries. Parking on both sides of canal but side opp Service Point most popular.

Sanitation:

Parking:

30

Custom

Popular Aire. Carp fishing competitions some weekends (see sign). Local commerce 3 mins. Inspected 2012.

NEUVY LE BARROIS 77 H6 N46°51.662' E003°02.374' 18600

Directions: Escale camping cars 'La Prairie'. From Neuvy-le-Barrois turn off by church, sp 'Mornay-s-Allier', and head south towards St Caprais. The Aire is on the right in 600m. The parking is behind the farm buildings, drive through Service Point to access.

Sanitation:

E

Parking:

6; €6/night; €10 with elec; Apr-Oct

Custom; €5

Commercial Aire on farm, local produce avail. Cycling distance from the pretty village of Apremont. Inspected 2012.

BESSAIS LE FROMENTAL 78 H7 N46°44.099' E002°47.912' 18210

Directions: Etang de Goule. Turn off D951, sp 'Base de Loisirs de Boule', onto D110. Turn left, sp 'Etang de Goule'. Follow road then turn right into Base de Loisirs de Goule. Follow road to Service Point outside campsite, parking 50m opp the Service Point.

Sanitation:

E

Parking:

3

Euro Relais Junior; €2

At leisure/swimming lake with numerous activities and facilities. Inspected 2012.

AINAY LE VIEIL 79 H7 N46°39.673' E002°33.371' 18200

Directions: D118. Exit village on D118, sp 'Le Perche'. Aire on left 200m from village boundary at Stade de la Tuilerie, signed.

Sanitation:

Parking:

6; Bays marked into grass

Custom

At village football pitch, now looking underused. 200m from village. Inspected 2012.

LE PONDY 80 H6 N46°48.355' E002°39.041' 18210

Directions: D953. Adj to canal bridge as enter Le Pondy from Dun sur Auron.

Sanitation:

E

Parking:

5; Grass and gravel parking

Euro Relais Junior; Token (ER); €2

Aire adj to Canal du Berry. Very pleasant area adj to lock and all parking has canal views. Local restaurants opp. Inspected 2012.

VILLEQUIERS

81 H6 N47°05.256' E002°46.402' 18800

Directions: D93/Rte de Gron. Turn onto D93 in Clanay, sp 'Gron', and follow towards Solérieux for approx 2km. The farm is on the left and parking is adj to drive. Aire signed from village.

Sanitation:

Parking:

6; €6

Custom; €3

Commercial Aire in a remote location. Village with local commerce 2km. Inspected 2012.

BOURGES 1

82 G6 N47°04.554' E002°23.948' 18000

Directions: Rue Jean Bouin. Well signed 'P Centre Historique Gratuit' from all directions and through town. Easiest route from east on D976 following sp 'P Centre Historique' in a straight line. When reach P Centre Historique, Aire on terrace below, well signed.

Sanitation:

Parking:

30; Max 48hrs

Raclet; 2 unmetered elec points not working

Nice tree lined green area in city; Opp stadium. Town 2 mins. Ideal city stop. Inspected 2012.

BOURGES 2

83 G6 N47°04.330' E002°23.608' 18000

Directions: Boulevard de l'Industrie. From D2144 at traffic light junction turn right onto Boulevard de l'Industrie. Aire on left just before 'Camping Municipal de Bourges', opp turning sp 'Base de Loisirs'.

Sanitation:

Parking:

3

Raclet; 2 unmetered elec points not working

Not as nice as **82**. Mainly a Service Point. Adj to cycle path. Inspected 2012.

NERONDES

84 H6 N46°59.945' E002°49.029' 18350

Directions: Rue St Joseph. Turn off D976, sp 'P L'Eglise' and signed. Turn left before church, Service Point on left and the parking is on the right.

Sanitation:

Parking:

10, Except 6am-1pm Saturday for market

Custom

Aire adj to church. Local commerce inc convenience store 1 min. Sports ground opp. Inspected 2012.

MENETOU SALON

85 G6 N47°13.917' E002°29.409' 18510

Directions: Rue de la Mairie. In main town square, located just off D25. From D25 turn off before church. Aire on left in 300m.

Sanitation:

Parking:

6

Point Belle Eau

In town square, local commerce 1 min. Tourist château nearby. Inspected 2012.

ST GEORGES SUR MOULON | 86 | G6 | N47°11.138' E002°25.079' | 18110

Directions: Route de la Ville. From D940 south towards Bourges turn off at traffic lights, sp 'Espace Nature'. Turn left at next junction and Aire is on left in 100m.

Sanitation:

Parking:

2

Point Belle Eau; No drive over drain

Football pitches; Large green spaces. Looks like old reservoir. Inspected 2012.

ALLOGNY | 87 | J8 | N47°13.133' E002°19.400' | 18110

Directions: D944. Exit Allogny on D944 heading south. Turn left in 800m into a roadside lay-by, signed.

Sanitation:

Parking:

Poss

Flot Bleu Fontaine

In picnic area adj to D944. Motorhomes banned from lakeside parking. Inspected 2012.

ST GEORGES SUR ARNON | 88 | G6 | N46°59.894' E002°05.958' | 36100

Directions: Rue de la Vallée, by fishing lakes outside the campsite. Follow sp 'Camping' and 'Parcours de Pêche'. 3.5t weight restriction on entrance bridge.

Sanitation:

Parking:

Poss

Custom

Fishing lakes adj; Campsite adj; Village 15 mins. Inspected 2012.

REUILLY | 89 | G6 | N47°05.113' E002°03.039' | 36260

Directions: Rue des Ponts/D28. As enter Reuilly from north on D918 turn right on D918 and then right onto Rue des Ponts, follow sp 'Camping', Aire on right. Service Point outside campsite.

Sanitation:

Parking:

None

Point Belle Eau

Campsite adj. Inspected 2012.

VIERZON 1 | 90 | G6 | N47°14.769' E002°04.012' | 18100

Directions: D926, at Maison du Pays (an old service station). Exit E9/A20 on Junction 5 onto D2020. Go over roundabout under bridge and turn right at roundabout onto D926, sp 'Maison du Pays'.

Sanitation:

Parking:

2; Not recommended

None; See 91

Noisy, sloping and dilapidated parking adj to A71. Service Point in disrepair for many years. Inspected 2012.

VIERZON 2 | 91 | G6 | N47°13.185' E002°03.704' | 18100

Directions: Rue de la Piscine. From north follow N2020 through town, sp 'Châteauroux'. Turn off N2020 when signed and follow signs into Rue de la Piscine. Service Point on right and parking at far end of car park, signed.

Sanitation:

Parking:

20

Urba Flux Tall; €2/10 mins elec and water

Adj to pretty riverside area, but no river view from parking. In town centre with numerous commerce. Inspected 2012.

MERY SUR CHER | 92 | G6 | N47°14.743' E001°59.374' | 18100

Directions: D2076. Adj to D2076 as exit village towards Vierzon. Entrance via barrier.

Sanitation:

Parking:

6; €5; CC

Custom; 7 unmetered elec points

Landscaped Aire adj to busy main road. Entrance by CC. Inspected 2012.

GUILLY | 93 | G6 | N47°04.721' E001°43.169' | 36150

Directions: Le Prieure. Exit Guilly on D34, sp 'Valencay' and signed. Aire on left, sp 'La Prieure'.

Sanitation:

Parking:

5; €8/night inc service and elec; Grass and gravel parking

Custom

Motorhome parking at hotel/B&B (€65/room). Inspected 2012.

MENNETOU SUR CHER | 94 | G6 | N47°16.080' E001°51.834' | 41320

Directions: Rue du Val Rose. Follow sp 'Camping' in town. Service Point between fire station and 'Gamm Vert'. Parking outside monument/memorial before service station, adj to canal.

Sanitation:

Parking:

10

Euro Relais Junior; Token (ER)

Canal du Berry adj, but no view. Lift bridge adj. Restaurants and castle 2 mins across canal. Inspected 2012.

LANGON | 95 | G6 | N47°16.953' E001°49.714' | 41320

Directions: D976. Adj to D976 as enter village from Mennetou-sur-Cher. In lay-by with 4.5t weight restriction.

Sanitation:

Parking:

5

Raclet; Token (2/1)

Village 2 mins; Road noise; Shallow canal. 94 is a more peaceful stop. Inspected 2012.

SELLES SUR CHER | 96 | G6 | N47°16.596' E001°33.550' | 41130

Directions: D956. Exit Selles-sur-Cher on D956. Aire at campsite near river bridge, sp 'Aire de Camping Car'.

Sanitation:

Parking:

15; €5/night Apr-Sept; Pay at campsite reception

Raclet; Token (2/1)

Designated motorhome parking outside campsite. Town 3 mins; No views of river. Inspected 2012.

CHABRIS | 97 | G6 | N47°15.199' E001°39.078' | 36210

Directions: Place du Champ de Foire. Exit town centre on D4 towards Valencay. At roundabout turn right, sp 'Champ de Foire'. Turn 1st right, signed. Turn left, signed, and the Service Point is on the left.

Sanitation:

Parking:

20; Parking around Champ de Foire

Euro Relais Box; Token (ER)

Shaded parking off main route, 1 min from town centre. Market Saturday morning. Inspected 2012.

NOYERS SUR CHER | 98 | F6 | N47°16.520' E001°23.865' | 41140

Directions: Rue du Port. Turn off main route through, sp 'Embarcadere', onto Rue du Camping. Turn right 50m from river bridge into Rue du Port. Aire on left.

Sanitation:

Parking:

10; Grass parking adj to river

Euro Relais Junior; Token (ER); €2

Pleasant area adj to river siding. Boat pontoons, fishing swims and outdoor gym adj. No designated parking. Inspected 2012.

MAREUIL SUR CHER | 99 | F6 | N47°17.506' E001°19.670' | 41110

Directions: Rue du la Brahaudiere. Turn off D17, sp 'Orbigny'. In 100m turn left and the Service Point is on the right opp cemetery.

Sanitation:

Parking:

5

Euro Relais Junior; Token (ER); €2

On edge of village next to cemetery. Shaded and un-shaded parking available. Local commerce 1 min. Inspected 2012.

ST AIGNAN | 100 | F6 | N47°16.345' E001°22.425' | 41140

Directions: Rue Novilliers. Turn off river bridge in middle between two rivers, sp 'Camping-Cars'. Signed parking adj to river, opp piscine (swimming pool).

Sanitation:

Parking:

8; Grass parking

None

Designated parking overlooking river. Riverside park adj. Town with commerce 2 mins over river. Inspected 2012.

ANGE | 101 | F6 | N47°19.958' E001°14.675' | 41400

Directions: Place de la Mairie. Turn off D17 in village by church, sp 'Aire Camping Cars'. Follow road behind church, signed.

Sanitation:

Parking:

15

Euro Relais Junior; Token (ER); €2; 15 unmetered CEE elec points

SP

Rural views; Local shops and bar 1 min. Some but not all elec points working at time of inspection. Inspected 2012.

OUCHAMPS | 102 | F6 | N47°28.762' E001°19.138' | 41120

Directions: Rue Toussaint Galloux, off D7. Exit D7 onto Rue Toussaint Galloux heading east out of Ouchamps, sp 'Plan d'Eau'. Turn left past tennis court, sp 'Seur' and 'Chopier'. Aire on left opp lake.

Sanitation:

Parking:

3

Euro Relais Junior; Token

SP

Small parking area by fishing lake. Inspected 2012.

BLOIS | 103 | F5 | N47°35.197' E001°19.591' | 41000

Directions: Rue Jean Moulin. On D751 from Tours cross river bridge and follow sp 'Gare SNCF' through multiple traffic lights. Pass railway station on left and follow sp 'P bus St Vincent', then 'P bus Jean Moulin 2', then sp 'Camping-Cars'. Aire on the right, signed.

Sanitation:

Parking:

30; €5/24hrs

Custom

SP

The current barrier will be replaced by a CC barrier. Town with numerous commerce 5 mins. Motorhomes are banned from all riverside parking. Inspected 2012.

MONTLIVAULT | 104 | F5 | N47°38.300' E001°26.621' | 41350

Directions: D98. Parking in car park adj to D98 and Mairie, signed at rear.

Sanitation:

Parking:

4; Max 48hrs

None

SP

Parking in village centre, may be best to park on unsurfaced area. Local commerce 1 min. Inspected 2012.

HUISSEAU SUR COSSON | 105 | F5 | N47°35.628' E001°27.597' | 41350

Directions: D33. Service Point adj to D33, signed. Parking area 50m on left, signed: N47°35.583' E001°27.414'.

Sanitation:

Parking:

4; Max 48hrs

Euro Relais Junior; Token (ER); €2

SP

Parking adj to cemetery. Village with local commerce 1 min. Château in national forest nearby. Inspected 2012.

VERNOU EN SOLOGNE

106 G6 N47°30.218' E001°40.750' 41230

Directions: D13. Adj to D13 as enter village from north, signed.

Sanitation:

Parking:

10

Euro Relais Junior; Token; €2

Pleasant village Aire adj to small river. Village with local commerce 1 min. Inspected 2012.

ST DYE SUR LOIRE

107 G5 N47°39.282' E001°28.739' 41500

Directions: D951. Approach town from Blois and turn off, sp 'Base Canoe Kayak'. Parking in car park adj to the river, signed.

Sanitation:

Parking:

4; Max 48hrs; Grass parking within flood plain

None

Parking only adj and overlooking river Loire. Inspected 2012.

DRY

108 G5 N47°47.896' E001°42.857' 45370

Directions: Turn off D951 onto D718, sp 'Dry' and signed. Follow road past village church, sp 'Meung sur Loire' and signed. The Aire is on the left, signed.

Sanitation:

Parking:

10

Euro Relais Junior; Token (ER)

Parking in village centre. Village park and leisure space adj. Local commerce 1 min. Inspected 2012.

CROUY SUR COSSON

109 G5 N47°38.865' E001°36.626' 41220

Directions: D33. In town turn off D103, sp 'Thoury'. After river bridge turn left, sp 'Camping'. Service Point outside the campsite.

Sanitation:

Parking:

None

Euro Relais Junior; Token (ER); €2

Service Point only. Inspected 2012.

TOUR EN SOLOGNE

110 F5 N47°32.260' E001°29.967' 41250

Directions: D102. Adj to D102 as exit village towards 'Cheverny' on right at picnic area. Also parking at Neuvy: In central square: N47°33.811' E001°36.188', Bauzy: Exit village, sp 'Neuvy', and parking adj to village pond: N47°32.249' E001°36.612', Fontaines-en-Sologne: Turn off D120 in village, sp 'Toilets': N47°30.627' E001°33.041'.

Sanitation:

Parking:

4; Max 48hrs

Euro Relais Junior; Token

Small parking area in small village adj to Fôret de Boulogne with walking and cycling trails. Inspected 2012.

BEAUGENCY

111 G5 N47°46.765' E001°38.231' 45190

Directions: D952/Quai Dunois. From N152 turn onto D925, sp 'Le Pont', 'Camping', and signed. Follow road to river, Aire on left 300m from bridge, signed.

Sanitation:

Parking:

20

Urba Flux; CC

SP

Close to river; Walk along river; Can be crowded. Market on Sundays. Inspected 2012.

MEUNG SUR LOIRE

112 G5 N47°49.401' E001°41.877' 45130

Directions: Chemin des Grèves. Approach from south and turn left after crossing river bridge. Turn left again and the Aire is on the right, signed.

Sanitation:

Parking:

9; Max 8m

Euro Relais Maxi; CC or Token (ER); €2

SP

Adj to riverside park, but no views. Sports facilities and town centre with numerous commerce adj. Inspected 2012.

LAILLY EN VAL

113 G5 N47°46.233' E001°41.100' 45740

Directions: Rue du Bourg. From D19 turn left into Rue du Bourg. Take 3rd right and follow road behind church to parking area. Or from D951 turn off as enter from Blois onto Allee du Petit Bois, sp 'Stade' and 'Mairie'. Follow road to church, then follow road to left behind church.

Sanitation:

Parking:

30

Point Belle Eau

SP

Near large lake and village leisure facilities. Bell rings every hour. Inspected 2012.

JOUY LE POTIER

114 G5 N47°44.886' E001°48.598' 45370

Directions: D15. Turn off D15 opp church, signed. This is a narrow turn. Aire on right in 50m, signed.

Sanitation:

Parking:

5

Euro Relais Junior; Token (ER)

SP

Parking in village centre. Village park and leisure space adj. Local shops 1 min. Inspected 2012.

CHAMBORD

T

115 G5 N47°36.926' E001°30.583' 41250

Directions: In Chambord follow sp 'P Chateau' then 'Parking P1'. Motorhomes can park in P1, signed.

Sanitation:

Parking:

100; €6/day; €20/overnight

None

SP

Visitors parking at very attractive tourist château that is worth a visit, €9.50/adult, www.chambord.org. Inspected 2012.

LA FERTE ST CYR

116 G5 N47°39.407' E001°40.294' 41220

Directions: D925. Turn off D925 in town by river bridge, sp 'Salle Polyvalente'. Service Point to left by tennis court. Parking area straight on beside river.

Sanitation:

Parking:

4; Max 48hrs

Euro Relais Junior; Token (ER); €2

Large parking area adj to river in pleasant town. Local commerce 1 min. Inspected 2012.

LA FERTE BEAUHARNAIS

117 G6 N47°32.655' E001°50.937' 41210

Directions: D922. By the village pond and river bridge off D922, signed. Parking has 3.5t weight restriction.

Sanitation:

Parking:

10

Aire Services; Token (3/3)

Walk around lake; Village with restaurant 2 mins. Inspected 2012.

NOUAN LE FUZELIER

118 G6 N47°31.988' E002°02.020' 41600

Photo: Don & Maureen Madge

Directions: Adj to N2020. Service Point beside tabac at the train station, signed: N47°32.019' E002°01.998'. Access may be difficult as car park busy. Parking opp side of road, signed.

Sanitation:

Parking:

5

Custom

Swimming pool; Bandstand; Train station. Inspected 2012.

THEILLAY

119 G6 N47°19.112' E002°02.263' 41300

Directions: Chemin du Rouaire. Exit Theillay on D60, sp 'La Ferté-Imbault'. Turn right, sp 'Stade'. Aire on right just past fire station, opp cemetery.

Sanitation:

Parking:

10

Custom; Closed Nov-Mar

Access could be difficult in wet conditions. Village centre 4 mins. Inspected 2012.

HUMBLIGNY

120 H6 N47°15.267' E002°39.533' 18250

Directions: From D955 turn onto D44, sp 'Humbligny'. Follow D44 through village and Aire is on left as you exit village.

Sanitation:

Parking:

15

Euro Relais Mini; Token (ER); €2; No drive over drain

Fantastic views of surrounding hills. D923 and D955 nice drive, scenic route. Inspected 2012.

ST VIATRE

121 G6 N47°31.168' E001°56.084' 41210

Directions: Rue du Petit Bois. From village centre follow sp 'Camping'. Aire at Aire Naturelle campsite. Service Point before campsite field. Access across grass.

Sanitation:

Parking:

50; €1.60 pitch, €1.60pp, €1.60 elec; Pay Mairie; Grass parking

Custom; Before camping field

Basic campsite. The Service Point is on opp side of toilet block. Pond adj. Inspected 2012.

AUBIGNY SUR NERE 1

122 G6 N47°28.921' E002°27.022' 18700

Directions: Route de La Chapelotte. Exit town on D923, sp 'Oizon' and 'Aire Camping Car'. Follow road to right onto D7, sp 'La Chapelotte'. Aire on left in 300m, signed.

Sanitation:

Parking:

10

Custom

Very peaceful spot adj to leisure area about 1km from town centre. Foot/cycling path to town with numerous shops. Inspected 2012.

AUBIGNY SUR NERE 2

123 G6 N47°29.482' E002°26.270' 18700

Directions: Ave Charles Lefèvre, off D940. Follow D940 through town. Turn off D940 adj to ALDI into car park, sp 'Complex Sportif Yves du Manoir' and signed. Service Point on right behind ALDI.

Sanitation:

Parking:

25

Custom

Large town with commerce 2 mins. Popular parking for locals on Saturday morning; Washbasin. Inspected 2012.

VAILLY SUR SAULDRE

124 H6 N47°27.449' E002°38.790' 18260

Directions: D923. On left of D923 as enter town from Aubigny-sur-Nère, sp 'Aire Naturelle'. Service Point adj to road outside campsite.

Sanitation:

Parking:

10; €3.50/night Apr-Oct

Custom; Unmetered elec; €2.50

Showers €0.80. Views of fields; TO adj. Town 2 mins; Market Fridays. Inspected 2012.

BARLIEU

125 H6 N47°28.747' E002°37.891' 18260

Directions: D8. From Vailly-s-Sauldre exit on D8 towards Barlieu. The Aire is on left in approx 2km. Very well signed.

Sanitation:

Parking:

10; €3.50/24hrs

Euro Relais Junior; 2 unmetered CEE elec points

Pleasant spot by leisure lakes. Shallow swimming lake adj. Inspected 2012.

BELLEVILLE SUR LOIRE

126 H6 N47°29.781' E002°51.016' 18240

Directions: Route des Coutures. From Belleville sur Loire head south on D751, sp 'Camping Caravanning'. South of village turn right off D751 opp canal bridge, sp 'Camping Caravanning'. At end of road turn left and Service Point is outside Camping Les Pres de la Fontaine on right.

Sanitation: E WC F

Parking: P F

None; See info

Custom; 1 unmetered elec point

SP

Parking at Maison de Loire opp nuclear power station: N47°30.657' E002°52.066'. Power station tours poss. Inspected 2012.

ARGENT SUR SAULDRE

127 G5 N47°32.951' E002°26.877' 18410

Directions: D940. At Super U as exit town on D940 towards Aubigny-s-Nère. Located by lavage (car wash).

Sanitation: E WC F

Parking: P F

2; 5m bays; Inadequate

Euro Relais Junior; €2

SP

Supermarket adj. Inspected 2012.

BOULLERET

128 H6 N47°25.391' E002°52.354' 18240

Directions: Place des Charmes. From village centre take D153, sp 'Step Gemme-en-S'. Aire 50m from square, signed.

Sanitation: E WC F

Parking: P F

3

Euro Relais Junior; Token (ER); Euro Relais Elec; Token (ER); 6amp/6hrs per token

SP

Adj to village centre with local commerce. Inspected 2012.

BRIARE 1

T **129** H5 N47°38.587' E002°43.366' 45250

Directions: Promenade du Martinet. Turn off D957 at the river bridge, sp 'Camping Le Martinet'. Follow signs to Camping Le Martinet. Aire past campsite, access via Flot Bleu Park CC operated barriers.

Sanitation: E WC F

Parking: P F

12; €7/24hrs; CC; Max 72hrs

Flot Bleu Pacific; inc Flot Bleu Marine; inc

SP

Adj to river but no views. Other interesting canals 1 min. Boat hire and town 3 mins. Pont Canal 5mins. Inspected 2012.

BRIARE 2

T **130** H5 N47°37.899' E002°44.409' 45250

Directions: Rue des Vignes. Turn off D957, sp 'Pont Canal' and 'Port de Commerce'. Follow road for 200m and turn left. Go over 5t weight restricted bridge (views of Pont Canal on right) and Aire on right, signed.

Sanitation: E WC F

Parking: P F

30

Flot Bleu Euro; CC; €2/20 mins

SP

Large, unsurfaced car park. Pont canal adj. Town 10 mins with shops, bars, restaurants. Inspected 2012.

OUZOUER SUR TREZEE

131 H5 N47°40.206' E002°48.550' 45250

Directions: Rue Saint Roch. From D47 turn off onto the D46, sp 'Rogny'. Cross bridge and turn left, sp 'Ecole', and drive through car park. Turn left, sp 'Aire Camping Car'. Service Point against building.

Sanitation:

Parking:

4; Max 48hrs

Custom; Showers; 4 unmetered elec points

Notice suggests Aire may close in summer when campsite N47°40.091' E002°48.336' is open. Inspected 2012.

ST BRISSON SUR LOIRE

132 H5 N47°38.805' E002°40.815' 45500

Directions: Rue de Ruets. From D951 turn onto D52, sp 'St Brisson s Loire'. In the village take 2nd right next to Mairie, sp 'Espace Seguier' and signed, opp house 33. Aire on right in 100m.

Sanitation:

Parking:

6

Euro Relais Junior; Token (2/1); €2

Basketball; Village with local commerce 2 mins. Likely to have space when other Aires full. Inspected 2012.

DAMPIERRE EN BURLY

133 G5 N47°45.749' E002°30.838' 45570

Directions: D952. Approach Dampierre en Burly on D952 from Gien. Turn right just after village at end of lake, sp 'Bois de la Charmille'.

Sanitation:

Parking:

12

Custom; At toilet

Adj to lake with walks. Fishing available €6 per day. Inspected 2012.

ST GONDON 1

134 G5 N47°41.888' E002°32.336' 45500

Directions: D951. Follow D951, main route, through village. Turn off, sp 'Coullons', and Aire is immediately on left adj to village pools. Alternative parking advertised but not possible at 'Sologne Autruches' (Ostrich farm, meat €35.47/kg).

Sanitation:

Parking:

3; Max 48hrs

Custom

Village 2 mins. Small river and pools adj. Commerce in village. Inspected 2012.

ST GONDON 2

135 G5 N47°41.993' E002°32.613' 45500

Directions: Rue de l'Ormet. Turn off in St Gondon, sp 'Paturiau'. Drive past cemetery on the right and the Aire is on left at base of water tower.

Sanitation:

Parking:

10

Custom

In the village centre. Local commerce 1 min. Inspected 2012.

CHAON | 136 | G5 | N47°36.581' E002°09.982' | 41600

Directions: D129. Enter Chaon on D129 from Vouzon. The Aire is on the right before you enter Chaon, sp 'La Maison du Braconnage' and signed.

Sanitation:

Parking:

5

Custom; At far end of parking

Secluded spot on edge of village. Inspected 2012.

MARCILLY EN VILLETTE | 137 | G5 | N47°45.721' E002°01.470' | 45240

Directions: Rue du Lavoir. From west on D921 turn 1st right into Rue de la Fontaine St-Blaise at the edge of town. Follow road to end and turn right. Aire adj to wooded area past tennis courts.

Sanitation:

Parking:

10

Point Belle Eau

Pleasant grassy dell in peaceful riverside park. Inspected 2012.

LAMOTTE BEUVRON | 138 | G5 | N47°35.887' E002°01.513' | 41600

Directions: N20. In parking area adj to river. As exit town on N20 to south turn left after Total fuel station and follow road. Aire on left.

Sanitation:

Parking:

18

Point Belle Eau; No drive over drain

River adj. Very popular Aire at weekends/holidays. Local commerce 3 mins. Inspected 2012.

LES BORDES | 139 | G5 | N47°48.630' E002°24.451' | 45460

Directions: D952. As enter Les Bordes from Gien on D952 Aire is before pond in parking area by what looks like a house, sp 'Aire de Stationnement'.

Sanitation:

Parking:

6

Custom

If barrier closed phone Mairie. River; Woodland walks; Seating. Inspected 2012.

NOGENT SUR VERNISSON 1 | 140 | H5 | N47°50.443' E002°44.434' | 45290

Directions: Rue du Gué Mulet, parking overlooking lake. From village centre turn onto D41 and follow sp 'Le Choux'. Turn left, sp 'Le Choux'. Turn left, sp 'Montbouy' and signed. Go straight on at next junction, signed.

Sanitation:

Parking:

5

None; See 141

Pleasant parking overlooking lake. Fishing €10/day. Numerous walking trails. Inspected 2012.

NOGENT SUR VERNISSON 2

141 H5 N47°51.221' E002°44.406' 45290

Directions: Rue Georges Bannery, off N7. Exit N7 north of town, sp 'Nogent s/ V.' and 'Office de Tourisme'. Service Point 200m on right by tennis courts and football pitches.

Sanitation:

Parking:

None; See 140

Euro Relais Junior; Token (ER); €2

SP

Service Point only. Tokens from TO opp. Inspected 2012.

BONNY SUR LOIRE

142 H5 N47°33.585' E002°50.354' 45420

Info/Photo: Mike Crampton

Directions: Chemin de la Cheuille. Exit the N7 onto the D926 to Bonny sur Loire. In 200m turn left at the crossroads onto the D907 into the village centre. Turn left in 500m into Rue du Docteur Legendre sp 'Camping du Val'. Turn right in 50m towards the church and the Aire is on the left.

Sanitation:

Parking:

5

Urba Flux Tall

SP

New Aire in a peaceful location next to a park. No river views and have to cross N7 to access. Local commerce 5 mins. Visited 2012.

GIEN

143 H5 N47°40.792' E002°38.568' 45500

Directions: D952/Quai de Nice. Enter Gien on D952 from Briare. Go straight across roundabout and Aire 2km on left.

Sanitation:

Parking:

8; Max 48hrs

Urba Flux; Token; €2; No drive over drain

SP

River adj but obscured by conifer trees. Swimming pool adj. River walk to town with numerous shops. Inspected 2012.

SULLY SUR LOIRE

144 G5 N47°46.278' E002°23.069' 45600

Directions: D948. Turn off D948 at river bridge into entrance/car park to château. Continue through parking area and Aire signed in 600m. Difficult entrance for long vehicles due to bollards (these will probably be removed).

Sanitation:

Parking:

26

Custom

SP

Aire beside river, but no view. Tourist Château du Sully 600m; Town centre 5mins. Inspected 2012.

ST AMAND MONTROND 2

145 G7 N46°44.080' E002°29.354' 18200

Info/Photo: John Cox

Directions: D2144. Heading south towards St Amand Montrond on the D2144. Pass Hotel Noirlac and turn right at roundabout sp 'Base de Loisirs Lac Virlay' and signed. Aire 75m on left.

Sanitation:

Parking:

20

Custom

SP

New Aire next to Virlay lake, no views. Intermarche supermarket and McDonalds 100m. St Amand centre 2km. Visited 2012.

Bogny sur Meuse

CHAMPAGNE

Mouzon

GIVET

1 I2 N50°08.600' E004°49.558' 08600

Directions: Rue Ampere. From D8051 at river bridge follow blue sp 'Caravaning Base Nautique' through town, which is narrow in places. Opp ALDI turn right, signed. The Aire is on the left, in the car park before the campsite.

Sanitation:

Parking:

5

Euro Relais Junior; Token (ER); €3

Outside campsite; Pleasant riverside town 10 mins walk. Inspected 2012.

MONTHERME

2 I2 N49°52.881' E004°43.806' 08800

Directions: D1. Adj to D1 alongside river as enter Monthermé from Deville. On left-hand side just past Monthermé sign. Adj to recycling, signed.

Sanitation:

Parking:

2; Max 24hrs

Euro Relais Junior; Token (ER)

Small parking area adj to river. Really just a Service Point. Inspected 2010.

BOGNY SUR MEUSE *

3 I2 N49°51.430' E004°44.472' 08120

Directions: Rue de la Meuse. Turn off D1 at river bridge, sp 'College'. After crossing bridge turn left. Turn left again, sp 'P 50m'. At end of road turn right and follow road along river. Service Point on left, signed. Parking 50m on left, signed.

Sanitation:

Parking:

5

Euro Relais Junior; €2

Aire adj and overlooking Meuse river. Local commerce 2 mins. Inspected 2012.

CHARLEVILLE MEZIERES

4 I3 N49°46.744' E004°43.206' 08000

Directions: Rue des Pâquis. Follow sp 'Montcy-Notre-Dame' and 'Camping Mont Olympe'. Road has 3.5t weight and 3.4m height restriction.

Sanitation:

Parking:

8

Raclet; €2; No drive over drain; Elec €5/24hrs see campsite

River and boat basin with pontoons adj. Town 2 mins across pedestrian bridge. Inspected 2010.

MOUZON

5 J5 N49°36.417' E005°04.610' 08210

Directions: Rue du Moulin Lavigne. Heading south on D964 turn onto D19 as enter town, sp 'Mouzon- Centre'. Turn left and turn left again after monument on left. Aire on right and left adj to river. Access difficult with motorhomes over 8m due to tight turns.

Sanitation:

Parking:

7; €7.50; Pay at adj office

Custom; 7 unmetered elec points

Popular Aire overlooking river. Washing machine inc; Showers. Town 3 mins. Inspected 2012.

LAUNOIS SUR VENCE

6 I3 N49°39.492' E004°32.397' 08430

Directions: D20. Exit town on D3 towards Jandun. Turn left at town boundary onto D20, sp 'La Fosse a l'eau'. Service Point 50m on left.

Sanitation:

Parking:

None

Euro Relais Junior; Token (ER); €2

Service Point only. Inspected 2012.

VOUZIERS

7 I3 N49°23.767' E004°40.973' 08400

Directions: Rue Bournizet. Exit town on D946, sp 'Reims' and 'Rethel'. As exit town turn right at roundabout into industrial area. Service Point at the new E'Leclerc fuel station near car wash.

Sanitation:

Parking:

None

Flot Bleu Pacific; €2 (2x€1)

Fuel station in industrial park. Inspected 2012.

ATTIGNEY

8 I3 N49°29.150' E004°34.846' 08130

Directions: D987. Adj to D987 on the northern boundary of town by the road sign. Near Total fuel station.

Sanitation:

Parking:

4; Difficult

Bollard

Adj to main road; Town 10 mins with local commerce and a canal. Inspected 2010.

REIMS

9 I3 N49°14.936' E004°01.208' 51100

Directions: Enter Reims on D951/N51. At roundabout turn left, sp 'Maison Blanche'. Follow sp 'Maison Blanche' and then 'Reims Centre' for 3.6km. Turn left at large traffic light junction before river bridge. The barriered entrance to Aire is immediately on right. Walk through Service Point to reception building, employee will open barrier.

Sanitation:

Parking:

7; Max 48hrs

Custom

Despite barriered entrance, it is easy to get in and free. Located at youth hostel. Road noise. Park adj; Town centre 5 mins. English spoken. Inspected 2010.

FISMES

10 I3 N49°18.797' E003°40.806' 51170

Photo: Janet and John Watts

Directions: D967. Exit town, sp 'Laon'. Follow road across railway bridge, then a river bridge and turn immediately right before roundabout, signed.

Sanitation:

Parking:

5

Euro Relais Junior; Token (ER)

River adj, limited views. Bakery opp. Town centre 4 mins. Inspected 2012.

CHAMERY

11 | I3 | N49°10.453' E003°57.229' | 51500

Directions: D26/Salle Polyvalente. Just off D26 at edge of village on left towards Ecueil. Signed.

Sanitation:

Parking:

8

Aire Services; €2

In champagne producing village surrounded by grapes; Tasting possible. Inspected 2010.

VILLERS SOUS CHATILLON

12 | I3 | N49°05.787' E003°48.050' | 51700

Directions: Rue du Parc. Signed in village, turn off D501 by church.

Sanitation:

Parking:

5

Euro Relais Junior; Token (3/1); €3

Village surrounded by grapes. Champagne tasting adj. Bar 2 mins; On champagne route. Inspected 2010.

MUTIGNY

13 | I3 | N49°04.113' E004°01.631' | 51160

Directions: At the entrance of the village. Do not turn left into the village but continue towards Montflambert Manor. The Aire is left 200m.

Sanitation:

Parking:

8

Urba Flux; €5

In the heart of the Champagne region with stunning views; Surrounded by grapes. No drive over drain. Inspected 2010.

EPERNAY

14 | I3 | N49°02.166' E003°57.072' | 51200

Directions: Rue Dom Pérignon. From south on D951 follow sp 'Centre Ville'. Turn right just before traffic light junction, sp 'Palais des Fêtes' and 'Piscine'. Aire on left behind church, signed.

Sanitation:

Parking:

2

Euro Relais Junior; Token

In Champagne town with famous brands. Town centre 10 mins. Also Service Point at campsite, approx 3.2km, for €2 N49°03.483' E003°57.013'. Inspected 2010.

MAREUIL SUR AY

15 | I3 | N49°02.721' E004°02.062' | 51160

Photo: Rodney Martin

Directions: Place Charles de Gaulle. From D1, main route through village, turn into tree-lined village square opp Mairie. Aire adj to canal on other side of square.

Sanitation:

Parking:

8; Under trees

Custom; Elec €5/3hrs; WC emptying is lift up drain

Adj to working canal with views. Several champagne producers (châteaux) in village 2 mins. Inspected 2010.

HAVE YOU VISITED AN AIRE? **GPS co-ordinates in this guide are protected by copyright law**

Take at least 5 digital photos showing
• Signs
• Service Point
• Parking
• Overview
• Amenities

Visit www.all-the-aires.co.uk/submissions.shtml to upload your updates and photos.

Sanitation:

Aire Details:

Submit updates
- Amendments
- New Aires
- Not changed

AVIZE | 17 | I4 | N48°58.301' E004°00.593' | 51190

Directions: Rue du Bourg Joli. From D9 turn onto D19, sp 'Avize Centre'. Drive past 1914-1918 memorial on right then take next right. Follow one-way system around block and you will find the Aire in the car park on right, past the Mairie.

Sanitation:

Parking:

10; 7m bays

SOS

In Champagne area. Wine tasting possible. Car park with no outstanding features but ideal if Mareuil-s-Ay 15 is full. Inspected 2010.

CHEVIGNY | 18 | I4 | N48°54.757' E004°03.343' | 51130

Photo: Russ and Mandy Valentine

Directions: Turn off D437 into the village and follow road. Aire clearly signed. Also a France Passion site.

Sanitation:

Parking:

5; €6 inc elec and service

Custom; inc

Champagne tasting. Baker at end of drive about 08:30am, except Mondays. Inspected 2010.

ST MARTIN SUR LE PRE | 19 | I4 | N48°59.450' E004°20.562' | 51520

Directions: N44. Exit N44, sp 'Aire de St Martin s/ Le P'. Aire adj to N44, accessible from both directions.

Sanitation:

Parking:

Not recommended

Flot Bleu (Red); Token

Main road parking area. Inspected 2012.

LA CHEPPE | 20 | I3 | N49°02.918' E004°29.575' | 51600

Directions: Rue du Camp d'Attila. Follow signs to Camp d'Attila in the village. Aire adj to the fortification.

Sanitation:

Parking:

4

Urba Flux; €2

Adj to Camp Attila, an old fortification. Access to fortification free and would take about 1hr to walk around. Inspected 2010.

SUIPPES

21 I3 N49°07.849' E004°32.040' 51600

Directions: Rue de l'Abreuvoir. Approach on D977 from north. Turn left by church before D931 junc, signed. Aire at rear of car park on left.

Sanitation:

Parking:

5

Urba Flux Tall; CC

Aire nearby former WW1 frontline. Local area has numerous military cemeteries and monuments. Inspected 2012.

LE GAULT SOIGNY

22 H4 N48°49.055' E003°35.443' 51210

Directions: D373. Just behind building off D373, main route through village, near traffic lights, signed.

Sanitation:

Parking:

2

Euro Relais Mini

Small area behind building in small village. Inspected 2010.

ESTERNAY

23 H4 N48°43.947' E003°33.409' 51310

Directions: Place des Droits de l'Homme. From N34/N4 follow sp 'Centre Ville'. The Service Point is behind the church. Parking is beside the church, signed.

Sanitation:

Parking:

10

Euro Relais Mini; Token; Open Mar-Nov

In centre of town. Plenty of commerce. Inspected 2010.

NOGENT SUR SEINE

24 H4 N48°30.204' E003°30.504' 10400

Directions: Rue du Camping. Follow sp 'Piscine' and 'Camping', well signed through town. Narrow access.

Sanitation:

Parking:

3; Max 48hrs

Custom; 3hrs only

Outside campsite by sports facilities. Inspected 2010.

CHAOURCE

25 I5 N48°03.583' E004°08.317' 10210

Directions: Chemin de Ronde. Turn off in the village centre, signed. The Service Point is on the left past the Gendarmerie.

Sanitation:

Parking:

6; Grass parking

Euro Relais; Token; €2

Parking on grass area behind Service Point. Pleasant spot in pretty village. Inspected 2010.

LES RICEYS | 26 | I5 | N47°59.533' E004°21.875' | 10340

Directions: In stadium parking area. Turn off at the D452/D70 roundabout, sp 'Salle Polyvalente' and 'Bourne Camping Car'. The Service Point is in the car park at the end of the road.

Sanitation:

Parking:

5

Euro Relais Junior; Token (ER); €2

Pleasant. Adj to sports fields in Champagne producing village. Inspected 2010.

PINEY | 27 | I4 | N48°21.524' E004°20.069' | 10220

Directions: In Piney turn off D960 onto D79, sp 'A5' and signed. Follow road to end. Service Point behind barrier.

Sanitation:

Parking:

None

Euro Relais Junior; Token (ER)

At old train station. Old covered market in village. Inspected 2010.

GERAUDOT | 28 | I4 | N48°18.151' E004°20.247' | 10220

Photo: Ian Cooper

Directions: D43. In Géraudot at roundabout follow D43 sp 'Lac d'Orient'. Turn left sp 'Camping l'Epine aux Moines'. Service Point outside campsite.

Sanitation:

Parking:

None

Euro Relais Junior; Token (ER); €4

Service Point only. All lakeside parking height barriered or restricted. Inspected 2012.

MESNIL ST PERE | 29 | I5 | N48°15.772' E004°20.761' | 10140

Directions: D43. Adj to lake outside Camping Lac d'Orient. Taped up at time of inspection.

Sanitation:

Parking:

None

Euro Relais Junior; Token (ER); €3

Service Point only with day parking allowed in car park of lake. Sandy beach. Inspected 2010.

VENDEUVRE SUR BARSE | 30 | I5 | N48°14.235' E004°28.165' | 10140

Directions: Rue d'Alger. From D619, main route, follow sp 'P Centre Commercial' and signed. Turn left opp ATAC supermarket, signed. Aire 100m on right.

Sanitation:

Parking:

5

Euro Relais Junior; Token (2/1)

Difficult Service Point to use. Parking limited. Town 1 min. Inspected 2010.

DOLANCOURT | 31 | I4 | N48°15.692' E004°36.792' | 10200

Directions: D44. Turn off D44 into Nigloland, sp 'Hôtel des Pirates'. Follow sp 'Hôtel des Pirates'. The Aire is outside the hotel. Go to reception of hotel to pay.

Sanitation:

Parking:

25; €5/24hrs inc elec

Custom

Hotel and restaurant adj. Adj to theme park Nigloland www.nigloland.fr. Inspected 2010.

BRIENNE LE CHATEAU | 32 | I4 | N48°23.766' E004°31.900' | 10500

Directions: Place de la Gare. Follow sp 'Gare SNCF' through town. Aire outside the train station.

Sanitation:

Parking:

4; Shared with trucks

Aire Services; Token; €3

Supermarket 2 mins; Town centre 5 mins; Train station adj. Inspected 2010.

CHAVANGES | 33 | I4 | N48°30.459' E004°34.587' | 10330

Directions: D6. Exit village on D6, sp 'Montmorency-Beaufort'. The Aire is on the right behind the Centre de Secours, signed.

Sanitation:

Parking:

5

Aire Services; Token (3/3)

Table tennis, basketball. Village 2 mins. Inspected 2010.

ARRIGNY PORT DE CHANTECOQ | 34 | I4 | N48°34.143' E004°42.174' | 52100

Directions: D13, at Port de Chantecoq. From Arrigny head south on D13. Turn off into parking area, sp 'Site de Chantecoq'. Service Point and parking to the right.

Sanitation:

Parking:

50

Aire Services; Token; €2.50; Token from TO

Lake adj, no views; Bird watching. 25km cycle around lake. Inspected 2010.

SAPIGNICOURT | 35 | J4 | N48°39.065' E004°48.357' | 52100

Directions: D660/Rue Deperthes à Larzicourt. Exit the village on D660 towards Larzicourt. Turn left up gravel road just past village exit. Aire on right in 10m, signed.

Sanitation:

Parking:

2; Grass parking

Aire Services; Token (3/3); €2

On edge of village. Further parking 50m at sports facilities. Inspected 2012.

ST DIZIER

36 | J4 | N48°38.529' E004°54.725' | 52100

Directions: D221, at motorhome dealers. Exit town on D221 to Villiers-en-Lieu. Dealer on left.

Sanitation: E WC F

Parking: P F

6

Euro Relais Junior

SP

Motorhome dealer with accessory shop open 9-12 and 2-6.30pm. Inspected 2010.

STE MARIE DU LAC NUISEMENT

37 | J4 | N48°36.169' E004°44.941' | 51290

Directions: From Ste-Marie du Lac Nuisement follow D13a towards Arrigny. Turn off, sp 'Plage' and 'Port'. Aire at next roundabout.

Sanitation: E WC F

Parking: P F

6

Aire Services; Token; €2.50; Token from TO

SP

Adj marina; Views of lake. No Shops. Beach/museum close by. Numerous unrestricted parking areas. Inspected 2010.

GIFFAUMONT CHAMPAUBERT

38 | I4 | N48°33.209' E004°46.042' | 51290

Directions: D13. On D13 on west side of Lac du Chantecoq. From D13 turn off, sp 'Station Nautique' and 'Office de Tourisme'. Service Point in main car park, signed.

Sanitation: E WC F

Parking: P F

20; Max 24hrs

Aire Services; Token; €2.50; Token from TO

SP

Adj to holiday village and TO. Lake 100m. Bars in summer. Bird watching. Inspected 2010.

MONTIER EN DER

39 | I4 | N48°28.704' E004°46.120' | 52220

Directions: D384. Follow sp 'Office de Tourisme' in town centre on main route through. Aire next to TO.

Sanitation: E WC F

Parking: P F

10

Aire Services; Token; €2.60

SP

Beer tasting at La Dervois brewery 400m on D384: N48°28.870' E004°46.165'. English spoken. Inspected 2010.

BAR SUR AUBE

40 | I5 | N48°14.090' E004°42.044' | 10200

Directions: Espace Jean Pierre Davot. Exit town, sp 'Troys', on D619. Turn left opp Renault garage, sp 'Salle de Spectacles' and signed. Turn right at end of road, and the Aire is on the right, signed.

Sanitation: E WC F

Parking: P F

1

Euro Relais Maxi; Token (ER); €3.50

SP

Aire adj to large car park with height barriers. Aire has 2 service bays and 1 parking space. Town 3 mins. Inspected 2012.

JOINVILLE

41 J4 N48°26.709' E005°08.946' 52300

Directions: Rue des Jardins. On right as enter town from Thonnance-lès-Joinville on D60, before LIDL supermarket, sp 'Halte Nautique'.

Sanitation:

Parking:

15

Aire Services; €2; CC; 4 elec points

SP

10 mins walk to town. Road and train noise. Working canal adj. Very popular. Inspected 2010.

DONJEUX

42 J4 N48°21.994' E005°08.952' 52300

Directions: D13. Turn off N67, sp 'Donjeux'. Travel under railway bridge and the Aire is in front of you, adj to canal.

Sanitation:

Parking:

4

Custom; 4 unmetered elec points

SP

2 spaces with views over canal; Pleasant; Some road noise. Village 2 mins. Inspected 2012.

CERISIERES

43 J4 N48°17.925' E005°03.789' 52320

Directions: D186. Enter Cerisières from Marseille on D186. The Aire is in the parking area on the right before the village. Signed in entrance.

Sanitation:

Parking:

20

Custom; In far corner

SP

Rural Aire not far from N67 and always likely to have space. Inspected 2012.

FRONCLES *

44 J4 N48°17.964' E005°09.155' 52320

Directions: At Froncles follow sp to 'Doulaincourt', then sp 'Halte Nautique'. Aire is at Halte Nautique.

Sanitation:

Parking:

10; €1.50/night; Elec €1.50/12hrs; Pay at reception

Custom; Water €1.50; Showers €2

SP

Canal adj with views. Very pleasant spot. TO in summer. Village 5 mins. Inspected 2010.

COLOMBEY LES DEUX EGLISES

45 J5 N48°13.374' E004°53.176' 52330

Directions: D23/Rue du Général de Gaulle. From main route turn off, sp 'D23' and 'La Boisserie Cimetière'. Aire before Mairie, signed. Parking on left above tennis courts.

Sanitation:

Parking:

10; Open Apr-Nov

Custom; At toilets

SP

Toilets and toilet disposal by entrance. Charles de Gaulle house, museum and Memorial 800m, adult €14.50. Inspected 2012.

VIEVILLE

46 J5 N48°14.284' E005°07.759' 52310

Directions: D167. Follow sp 'Vraincourt' on D167. Turn left immediately after canal down track with grass in centre. Aire adj to canal in 1st parking area on left.

Sanitation:

Parking:

10; €1.50/night; Attendant calls pm

Custom; Elec €1.50/night

Adj to canal but views obscured by bushes. Distant road noise. Inspected 2010.

JUZENNECOURT

47 J5 N48°11.064' E004°58.742' 52330

Directions: Rue de la Mairie, by church in square. Turn off D619 opp La Poste into Rue de la Mairie.

Sanitation:

Parking:

4

Custom; 4 unmetered elec points

In town square. No toilet disposal. Inspected 2010.

CHAUMONT

48 J5 N48°07.114' E005°09.239' 52000

Directions: Head out of town on D417/D674 towards Biesles. Aire at Halte Nautique near turning to Reclancourt. Look for sp 'Port de la Maladière'. Pay at Captains Office on right when arrive.

Sanitation:

Parking:

6; €3.15 without service; €6.30 with elec plus tax pp €0.40; Open Apr-Oct

Custom; €3

Adj to canal, near busy main road. You must report to Capitainerie. Inspected 2010.

ARC EN BARROIS

49 J5 N47°57.050' E005°00.334' 52210

Photo: Gerald and Lesley Thorne

Directions: Off D3 as exit village to north, signed. By junction with D159.

Sanitation:

Parking:

5; €3/night

Custom; inc

Pleasant village Aire with CL feel. Inspected 2010.

GONCOURT *

50 J5 N48°14.183' E005°36.559' 52150

Directions: Rue du Lavoir. From St-Thiébault turn right off D74 as enter village, by river. Signed.

Sanitation:

Parking:

20; Max 48hrs

Custom; €2 donation

Beautiful river location. Tranquil spot. Inspected 2010.

NOGENT

51 | J5 | N48°01.491' E005°20.856' | 52800

Directions: From Chaumont on D417 turn off towards Nogent at the roundabout onto D1. Follow sp 'Maison de Retraite' and 'Aire de Stationnement Camping-Car' through town. Turn left past ALDI and the Aire is on right, signed.

Sanitation:

Parking:

5; Grass parking

Custom

A pleasant Aire with a view. Shady grass parking. Inspected 2010.

MONTIGNY LE ROI

52 | J5 | N48°00.051' E005°29.802' | 52140

Directions: Rue Hubert Collot. Follow sp 'Camping' in town. Service Point to the left of campsite reception.

Sanitation:

Parking:

None

Euro Relais Junior; €2

Service Point outside campsite. Service Point taped up at time of visit. Inspected 2010.

PEIGNEY

53 | J5 | N47°52.383' E005°22.827' | 52200

Directions: D284. Follow sp 'Lac de la Liez' and 'Camping'. Aire at entrance to Camping Lac de la Liez.

Sanitation:

Parking:

6; €10.50 inc service and 16amp elec

Custom; €6

By lake, no real views; Outside campsite. Inspected 2010.

LANGRES

54 | J5 | N47°51.453' E005°19.795' | 52200

Directions: Ruelle de la Poterine. Signed off N19/Avenue Jean Ernest Darbot as it passes through town.

Sanitation:

Parking:

12

Custom

Interesting town with 3.5km of 14th century ramparts which make a nice walk. Inspected 2010.

CORGIRNON

55 | J5 | N47°48.421' E005°30.178' | 52500

Directions: Allée du Paré. Follow sp 'Camping' through village. As enter woods Aire is immediately on right.

Sanitation:

Parking:

6; €3; Attendant may call at 7pm

Custom; Unmetered elec

Landscaped Aire with each bay having electric. Inspected 2010.

Fontenoy la Joute

Etival Clairefontaine

EASTERN FRANCE

Hatten

STENAY *

1 J3 N49°29.451' E005°11.016' 55700

Directions: Rue du Port. Just off D947 towards Buzancy and Reims. Follow sp 'Port de Plaisance' through town. Service Point by building, signed. Parking on both sides of river, some parking barriered. Call at Capitainerie if barrier down.

Sanitation:

Parking:

30; €7/day inc unmetered elec

Custom; €2

Overlooking river. Laundry, showers, restaurant/bar 1 min; Town centre 3 mins. Attendant calls in evening. Inspected 2010.

DUN SUR MEUSE *

2 J3 N49°23.296' E005°10.712' 55110

Directions: Rue du Vieux Port. From D964 turn off in Dun-Sur-Meuse, sp 'Port de Plaisance'. Follow road along river, Aire on right.

Sanitation:

Parking:

20; €4/24hrs

Urba Flux; Token

River adj, all spaces with views. Boat jetty. Reception has shower and washing machine. Inspected 2010.

DAMVILLERS

3 J3 N49°20.281' E005°23.862' 55150

Directions: Rue de l'Isle d'Envie. Follow D905, main route through town, and turn off, sp 'Gendarmerie'. At base of watertower by Gendarmerie, signed. Other parking: N49°20.996' E005°24.035' on right as exit towards Montmedy, signed, adj to lake.

Sanitation:

Parking:

3

Euro Relais Junior; €2

Limited parking; Main road adj. Other parking has obscured lake views. Inspected 2012.

LONGUYON

4 J3 N49°26.869' E005°36.005' 54260

Directions: D618. From north follow D618 into Longuyon. Follow road under railway bridge, sp 'Toutes Directions'. Turn left and the Aire is in the car park of the TO, signed.

Sanitation:

Parking:

2

Urba Flux; CC

Adj to TO in town centre. Local commerce adj. River adj, no view. Inspected 2012.

LONGWY

5 J3 N49°31.592' E005°45.909' 54400

Directions: Ave du 8 Mai 1945. Follow D918, sp 'Logwy-Haut'. Turn left, sp 'Maison de Sante' and signed. Aire on right.

Sanitation:

Parking:

6

Flot Bleu Pacific; Token (FB); €2.50; Flot Bleu Elec; 1 token/4hrs

Adj to sports facilities, residential flats and main road. Local commerce 3 mins down hill. Large fortification down hill past shops. Inspected 2012.

ETAIN

6 J3 N49°12.562' E005°38.270' 55400

Directions: Allée du Champ de Foire. Exit town on 3.5t weight restricted route to Metz. Aire on left, sp 'Codecom' and signed. If approaching from Longuyon follow sp 'Warcq'.

Sanitation:

Parking:

10

Water at toilets

Town adj; Sports facilities at end of road. Convenience store opp. Inspected 2010.

DIEUE SUR MEUSE

7 J3 N49°04.235' E005°25.601' 55320

Directions: Port de Plaisance, off Rte des Dames. Turn off D964 at roundabout in village, sp 'Ancemont'. Turn left into large car park just before canal. Aire is adj to canal and the WC emptying point is at end of car park behind building: N49°04.174' E005°25.645'.

Sanitation:

Parking:

5; Tolerated

Custom

Canal moorings adj. Tolerated parking popular with motorhomes. Village centre 5 mins on other side of canal. Inspected 2010.

LES ISLETTES

8 J3 N49°07.286' E005°02.268' 55120

Directions: Route de Locheres. Turn off D603 to east of Les Islettes onto D2e, sp 'C.S.A' and signed. In 100m turn right towards Locheres and follow road into forest and Aire is on left.

Sanitation:

Parking:

10; €5/24hrs inc service and elec

Custom

Pleasant parking in woodland. Pay in office by Service Point; Shower at office; Area dominated by WW1 graves and memorials. Inspected 2010.

LAHEYCOURT

9 J4 N48°53.332' E005°01.339' 55800

Directions: D20. Enter Laheycourt on D20 from Revigny sur Ornain. The Aire is on right before river bridge.

Sanitation:

Parking:

10

None; See 11

Beautiful, grassy area adj to river. Very pleasant. Inspected 2010.

NETTANCOURT

10 J4 N48°52.667' E004°56.434' 55800

Directions: D994. Adj to D994 in village by gates, signed.

Sanitation:

Parking:

5

None; See 11

Grass parking by recycling. Inspected 2010.

REVIGNY SUR ORNAIN

11 J4 N48°49.576' E004°59.019' 55800

Directions: Rue du Stade, off D995. Follow sp 'Camping'. Aire outside campsite.

Sanitation:

Parking:

2

Euro Relais Junior

TO adj; Municipal campsite; Sports stadium; Town 4 mins. Inspected 2010.

CONTRISSON

12 J4 N48°48.287' E004°56.790' 55800

Directions: In the village follow sp 'Aire de Liberté Camping-Car'. Before crossing canal bridge turn left and the Aire is in 100m, signed.

Sanitation:

Parking:

10

None

Pleasant spot beside Plan d'Eau. Village 5 mins. BBQs allowed. Good for swimming. Large fish. Inspected 2010.

BAR LE DUC

13 J4 N48°46.533' E005°09.964' 55000

Directions: Rue du Débarcadère. Follow main route D694 alongside canal. At north edge as exit town towards Revigny turn back into town at small roundabout, signed. Then immediately left before railway bridge, signed.

Sanitation:

Parking:

8

Euro Relais Junior; Token (ER)

Located between D694, the canal and the railway; Difficult Service Point. Inspected 2010.

LIGNY EN BARROIS

14 J4 N48°41.266' E005°19.156' 55500

Directions: N135. From N4 exit, sp 'Ligny-en-Barrois'. At roundabout follow truck route into Ligny-en-Barrois, signed. Then follow sp 'Relais Camping Car'.

Sanitation:

Parking:

6

Aire Services; €2

Overlooking canal basin. Slipway adj. Town 2 mins. Inspected 2010.

HEUDICOURT SOUS LES COTES

15 J4 N48°56.100' E005°42.924' 55210

Directions: D133. From Heudicourt head east following sp 'Lac de Madine'. Turn off D133, sp 'Lac de Madine 2-3'. Drive past campsite, behind sports field and Aire is grass and gravel parking adj to lake. Service Point is near building Madine 3.

Sanitation:

Parking:

50; €8 inc elec/€5 without elec

Custom; inc

Aire adj to lake, ideal for fishermen and great for families. Toilet block with showers by Service Point. Inspected 2010.

NONSARD LAMARCHE | 16 | J4 | N48°55.672' E005°45.541' | 55210

Directions: Lac de Madine. From the village head west to the lake. Parking is adj to the lake. Access to Aire through barrier. See campsite reception for access. There are numerous places to park, reception will advise.

Sanitation:

Parking:

50; €5; Apr–Oct

Flot Bleu Euro; Token; CC; €3; Located inside barrier

SP

Large holiday complex with marina, campsite, restaurant and leisure facilities adj to lake. Inspected 2010.

COMMERCY | 17 | J4 | N48°45.851' E005°35.764' | 55200

Directions: Rue du Docteur Boyer. Turn off D958, sp 'Vélodrome'. Well signed through town.

Sanitation:

Parking:

4

Flot Bleu Pacific; Token; €2; Flot Bleu elec; 1 token/4hrs elec

SP

Busy town with numerous commerce 2 mins; River, park and vélodrome adj. Pleasant. Inspected 2010.

VOID VACON | 18 | J4 | N48°40.955' E005°37.149' | 55190

Directions: D10. Turn off D964 onto D10 as you enter the town from Vaucouleurs, signed. Turn left and Aire is at the old railway station, signed.

Sanitation:

Parking:

10

Flot Bleu Océane; Token; €2

SP

Sports facilities adj; Convenient if using N4. Steps to canal. Inspected 2010.

BRULEY | 19 | J4 | N48°42.384' E005°51.332' | 54200

Directions: D118a. Turn off D908 onto D118a and follow into the village. The Aire is adj to D118a on corner of Rue St Martin and Rte de Voisel, signed.

Sanitation:

Parking:

10

Aire Services; Token; €3; Provides 8hrs elec

SP

Aire located in attractive, wine producing village. Inspected 2010.

TOUL | 20 | J4 | N48°40.750' E005°53.305' | 54200

Directions: Avenue du Colonel Péchot, outside police station. From D400 in north turn off opp train station, sp 'Police', as enter town.

Sanitation:

Parking:

9; €5 inc elec; Max 48hrs

Custom; 8 elec points

SP

Almost overlooking river and lock. Fortified town 7 mins walk. Noisy road adj. Access to canal. Inspected 2010.

PONT A MOUSSON

21 K4 N48°54.131' E006°03.677' 54700

Directions: D120/Avenue des Etats Unis. Adj to river at Port de Plaisance as exit towards A31. Well signed through town. Barrier opened remotely on arrival 8-12 noon and 3-8pm. Otherwise phone number on barrier or see warden on barge.

Sanitation:
E WC F

Parking:
P F

30; €7/24hrs inc unmetered elec; Max 15 days

Custom; inc elec

SP

Marina and river adj. Inspected 2010.

METZ

22 K3 N49°07.423' E006°10.134' 57000

Directions: Allée de Metz Plage. In town centre at the municipal campsite adj to the Moselle river. Follow sp 'Camping'. Busy town car park popular with motorhomes.

Sanitation:
E WC F

Parking:
P F

8

Urba Flux

SP

Adj to river with views. In centre of Metz outside municipal campsite. Metz worth a visit. Inspected 2010.

MILLERY

23 K4 N48°48.931' E006°07.641' 54670

Directions: D40/Avenue de la Moselle. Just off main road adj to river Moselle, signed.

Sanitation:
E WC F

Parking:
P F

3

Custom

SP

Small parking area; River views. Base Nautique - canoeing adj. Inspected 2010.

NANCY

24 K4 N48°41.526' E006°11.608' 54000

Directions: N57. Adj to N57 in the centre of town in the car park adj to the marina. See Capitainerie at rear of Aire for access. Would not recommend as difficult to access and parking not ideal (double parking).

Sanitation:
E WC F

Parking:
P F

6; €10; Max 48hrs

Custom

SP

Adj to marina in centre of Nancy. Bike hire adj. Inspected 2010.

RICHARDMENIL

25 K4 N48°35.691' E006°09.670' 54630

Directions: Rue du Lac. Turn off D570 in the village centre, signed. Follow Rue du Lac towards the canal and D115. Aire is on the left before bridge to D115, not accessible from D115.

Sanitation:
E WC F

Parking:
P F

6

Custom; 4 unmetered elec points

SP

Pleasant Aire adj to woods. 2 canals and a river within 5 mins, ideal for fishermen. Village 5 mins uphill. Inspected 2010.

FAVIERES 26 K4 N48°27.990' E005°57.683' 54115

Directions: Base de Loisirs. Follow sp 'Base de Loisirs' through the village. The Aire is located at the Base de Loisirs on Rte de Gélaucourt.

Sanitation:

Parking:

5; Max 48hrs

Aire Services; CC; €4

SP

Pleasant parking; 2 mins to village. Sports field and lake adj. Inspected 2010.

VAUCOULEURS 27 J4 N48°36.117' E005°40.023' 55140

Directions: Rue du Cardinal Lépicier, in right-hand corner of large car park in centre of town. Enter town from east on D960. Go over roundabout, take 1st left and 1st right, signed. 3.5t weight restriction.

Sanitation:

Parking:

3; Max 24hrs

Urba Flux; Token

SP

Culvert adj. Town centre adj with local commerce. Pleasant town. Inspected 2010.

MAXEY SUR MEUSE 28 J4 N48°26.900' E005°41.706' 88630

Directions: D19. Enter village from Greux then turn right, signed. At sports facilities.

Sanitation:

Parking:

2

Water tap on side of building

SP

Football pitch, table tennis. Situated at old railway station. Road was track. Inspected 2010.

GREUX 29 J4 N48°26.997' E005°40.585' 88630

Directions: D164. Just off D164 adj to church in village centre, signed.

Sanitation:

Parking:

5

Water tap only

SP

Local commerce adj. Clock chimes 6am- 9pm. Inspected 2010.

ST ELOPHE 30 J4 N48°24.559' E005°44.359' 88630

Directions: Rue du Stade. At the Mairie and sports field, near the church, signed.

Sanitation:

Parking:

5

Custom; €2; Honesty box

SP

Small village. Rural views. Football pitches adj. The water tap is inside the buiding. Inspected 2012.

ROLLAINVILLE

31 J4 N48°21.717' E005°44.321' 88300

Directions: Rue de la Cure, next to Mairie. Enter village on D77. At T-junction turn left then immediately right. Aire in car park next to Mairie. Only suitable for small panel van motorhomes.

Sanitation:

Parking:

1; 6m max

Custom

Only suitable for small campers. Narrow access and difficult to find. Inspected 2010.

REBEUVILLE

32 J4 N48°20.120' E005°42.070' 88300

Directions: Rue du Cougnot. Enter village from D164. At T-junction turn left and follow road to end, keeping to left.

Sanitation:

Parking:

6

Custom; 6 unmetered elec points

Adj with views over river; Main road and railway provide some noise but very pleasant spot. Horse riding adj. Inspected 2010.

TILLEUX

33 J4 N48°17.972' E005°43.583' 88300

Directions: Grande Rue. Parking at the church. Turn off D164 at Tilleux, signed. Follow road to church. Parking at church very sloping.

Sanitation:

Parking:

2

Water only

Small village offering a night stop. Pleasant rural views. Better stop and facilities at Rebeuville 32 5 mins. Inspected 2010.

POMPIERRE

34 J4 N48°15.431' E005°40.374' 88300

Directions: Off D1. Turn off D1, main route through village, when signed. Aire on left adj to barn, signed.

Sanitation:

Parking:

2

Custom; 2 Cont unmetered elec points

Rural location off main village road. Inspected 2010.

CERTILLEUX

35 J4 N48°18.720' E005°43.622' 88300

Directions: Signed from D164. Turn off D164 to village and drive towards church. Aire near church, signed.

Sanitation:

Parking:

8

Water only

Flat parking with stunning views. Inspected 2010.

BULGNEVILLE

36 | J5 | N48°12.442' E005°50.296' | 88140

Directions: Rue des Recollets. Turn off in the village centre by the church, sp 'Aire de Févry'. Follow sp 'Aire de Févry' to Aire. Adj to sports fields and pond.

Sanitation:

Parking:

10; €3

Custom

Adj to and views of lake. Pleasant village with local commerce 3 mins. Football pitch adj. Inspected 2010.

CONTREXEVILLE

37 | K5 | N48°11.267' E005°52.800' | 88140

Directions: Rue des Magnolias. Off D429 towards Bulgnéville in 'Zone d'Activitiés' situated behind E'Leclerc supermarket, signed.

Sanitation:

Parking:

None

Custom; Dilapidated

Pleasant spa town with thermal bathing. Very dilapidated Service Point in industrial zone. Inspected 2010.

CHARMES *

38 | K4 | N48°22.387' E006°17.739' | 88130

Directions: Port de Plaisance. At the bridge crossing river Moselle follow sp 'Port de Plaisance'. Aire adj to canal.

Sanitation:

Parking:

20; €6/night

Custom

Laundry. Showers. Views over canal. Town 2 mins up steps. Pleasant. Inspected 2010.

THAON LES VOSGES *

39 | K4 | N48°15.005' E006°25.521' | 88150

Directions: Rue du Coignot. From D157, main route through town, follow sp 'Aire du Coignot', signed.

Sanitation:

Parking:

10

Custom

Adj to working canal with views. Table tennis adj; Lock 500m. Town commerce 5 mins. Very pleasant spot. Inspected 2010.

EPINAL

40 | K5 | N48°10.723' E006°28.133' | 88000

Directions: Chemin du Petit Chaperon Rouge. Turn off N57, sp 'C3' and 'Razimont'. Follow road towards Epinal and turn left, sp 'Camping Park du Château' and signed. The Aire is on the left next to the stadium and before the campsite.

Sanitation:

Parking:

5

Flot Bleu Pacific; Token

Football pitches adj; Some parking with rural views; Town a long walk away. Inspected 2010.

ATTIGNY

41 K5 N48°03.533' E006°00.460' 88260

Directions: D460. Sp 'Miel Antoine' on roof of house.

Sanitation:

Parking:

5; Grass parking

Custom

Honey farm. Parking near main road under trees, free to France Passion. Non-members may need to buy honey. No English spoken. Inspected 2010.

MONTHUREUX SUR SAONE

42 K5 N48°01.892' E005°58.421' 88140

Directions: D460. Adj to D460 and the river in the village as exit towards Affigney, signed.

Sanitation:

Parking:

8

Custom

Very pleasant spot; Village 2 mins up steps; Pay WiFi. Inspected 2010.

BAINS LES BAINS 1

43 K5 N47°59.968' E006°15.714' 88240

Directions: D434. From centre follow D434, sp 'Fontenoy le Ch'. Aire just off town centre in large car park. Service Point to rear of car park.

Sanitation:

Parking:

None; See 44

Custom

Service Point only. May be obstructed by market on Friday mornings. Inspected 2012.

BAINS LES BAINS 2

44 K5 N47°59.944' E006°15.872' 88240

Directions: D434. From centre follow D434, sp 'St Loup'. Aire just off town centre, follow signs ' P Camping-Cars' down back streets.

Sanitation:

E

Parking:

12; Max 24hrs

Custom; Report to TO for elec

Town centre with 2 mins. Supermarkets on outskirts. Market Fri morning. Toilet emptying at 43. Inspected 2012.

FONTENOY LE CHATEAU

45 K5 N47°58.625' E006°12.342' 88240

Directions: D434. Aire on left adj to D434 as exit village towards Bains les Bains, signed.

Sanitation:

Parking:

5

Custom

Pretty village with canal and river. Restaurant adj; Village adj: Nice walks. Inspected 2010.

CORRE | 46 | K5 | N47°54.820' E005°59.605' | 70500

Directions: Off D44. Turn off D417 onto D44, sp 'Aisey' and signed. Turn left, signed. Aire at marina.

Sanitation:

Parking:

14; €7/24hrs inc unmetered elec

Custom

Commercial Aire adj to marina/boat yard; Canal adj but no views; Café; Walk along canal to village 5 mins; Inspected 2010.

ST LOUP SUR SEMOUSE | 47 | K5 | N47°53.178' E006°16.215' | 70800

Directions: Rue des Jardins. Follow main route through town and turn off by church, sp 'Aire Camping Car'. Aire on right, signed.

Sanitation:

Parking:

2

Euro Relais; Token (ER)

Town 2 mins with local commerce. Inspected 2010.

LUXEUIL LES BAINS | 48 | K5 | N47°49.036' E006°23.202' | 70300

Directions: Rue Gambetta. Turn off N57 onto D6 to Luxeuil-les-Bains. Past the ALDI turn right, sp 'Centre'. Turn right again, sp 'P des Thermes', then left, sp 'Aire de Vidange'. Aire on right adj to pond.

Sanitation:

Parking:

30; Max 72hrs

Euro Relais Junior; Token

Pleasant spot; Stroll around pond; No fishing. Town 5 mins. Inspected 2010.

SAULX | 49 | K5 | N47°41.803' E006°16.795' | 70240

Directions: Place de l'Eglise. Turn off at church, drive past church and car park and then turn left, signed. Service Point behind church, by fire station.

Sanitation:

Parking:

5

Euro Relais Junior; €2

Village with local commerce 100m. Inspected 2010.

CHAMPLITTE | 50 | J5 | N47°36.985' E005°31.104' | 70600

Directions: D17. In Champlitte take D17 off D460/Rue Pasteur, sp 'Champlitte-la-Ville' and signed. Aire at wine producer 'Vin des Coteaux de Champlitte', signed. Parking through arch into small courtyard.

Sanitation:

Parking:

3; Max 6m

Custom

Wine cellar for Pinot Noir and Chardonnay. Local produce. Not open Sunday. Inspected 2010.

GRAY — 51 — J6 — N47°27.152' E005°36.111' — 70100

Directions: Rue de la Plage. Follow sp 'Camping', 'Plage' and signed. Outside the campsite.

Sanitation:

Parking:

7; May be pay in season

Custom; Token (2/1)

River 100m; Activities adj; Bar/restaurant in season (take away). Town 10 mins. Inspected 2010.

PESMES — 52 — J6 — N47°16.600' E005°33.989' — 70140

Directions: Off D475. Exit town towards Dole. The Service Point is at the campsite just over the river bridge. Drive into entrance and the Service Point is just past reception.

Sanitation:

Parking:

None

Flot Bleu Pacific (Green); Token; €2

Service Point only. Inspected 2010.

DOLE — 53 — J6 — N47°04.405' E005°29.201' — 39100

Photo/Info: Janet & John Watts

Directions: Aquaparc ISIS. From south on D405. At roundabout turn left, sp 'Dijon' and 'Zone Portuaire'. Straight over next roundabout, then right at next, sp 'Aquaparc ISIS'. Service Point in Aquaparc parking; riverside parking possible. Town parking adj to river N47°05.389' E005°29.791': Follow sp 'Stades-Camping'. Parking in 'P La Commanderie', signed.

Sanitation:

Parking:

20

Euro Relais Box

Service Point at water park. Parking located on island adj to sports ground and campsite. Town centre commerce across river. Visited 2011.

MESNAY — 54 — K6 — N46°53.871' E005°48.054' — 39600

Photo/Info: J Leach

Directions: D217. Exit village on the D217, sp 'Les Planches'. Aire on right in front of Ecomusee du Carton, adj to D217 as exit village.

Sanitation:

Parking:

20

Aire Services; €2; CC

Plenty of parking around the museum. Opening hours April-June + Sept-Oct, 14-18.00hrs, Mon-Sat. July-Aug, 10-12 & 14-18.00hrs, all days. Entry €5.50. Visited 2012.

ARC ET SENANS — 55 — K6 — N47°02.002' E005°46.831' — 25610

Directions: D17. 100m from the Royal Saltworks, sp off D17.

Sanitation:

Parking:

5

Custom; Token (2/2); €1

Fire station adj; The Royal Saltworks, a UNESCO World Heritage Site, 2 mins walk. Inspected 2010.

SALINS LES BAINS | 56 | K6 | N46°55.940' E005°52.749' | 39110

Directions: D472. Just off D472 main route through town, by turning to Bracon, sp 'Fort Saint André' and 'P'.

Sanitation:

Parking:

3

Urba Flux

In thermal town adj to main road. Town centre 3 mins. Inspected 2010.

POLIGNY | 57 | J6 | N46°50.062' E005°41.894' | 39600

Directions: N83. Follow sp 'Camping'. Service Point to left of campsite entrance.

Sanitation:

Parking:

1; Max 2hrs

Custom

Service Point only. Inspected 2010.

CHAMPAGNOLE | 58 | K6 | N46°44.794' E005°53.935' | 39300

Directions: Rue des Tennis. Follow sp 'Camping'. The Aire is outside Camping de Boyse.

Sanitation:

Parking:

4; €5/night; Max 1 night; Jun-mid Sept

Aire Services; Token (3/3); €3.50

SP

Outside campsite; Town 7 mins. Inspected 2010.

CONLIEGE | 59 | J7 | N46°39.162' E005°35.989' | 39570

Directions: Just off D678, main route through village, as exit towards Revigny.

Sanitation:

Parking:

1; 7m bay

Flot Bleu Fontaine

Village with local commerce 100m. Inspected 2010.

DOUCIER | 60 | K7 | N46°39.846' E005°48.691' | 39130

Directions: Route de Chalain. From D27 turn onto Rte de Chalain and follow sp 'Camping Domaine de Chalain' for 3.2km. Service Point against building on left as enter parking.

Sanitation:

Parking:

Banned 10pm-8am

Custom

Motorhomes banned from car park from 10pm-8am. Campsite open May-Sept. Holiday place with limited access to lake. Inspected 2010.

CLAIRVAUX LES LACS

61 K7 N46°34.879' E005°44.838' 39130

Directions: D678. Exit town towards 'Lons Le Saunier'. Aire just past the ATAC supermarket opp Gendarmerie, signed.

Sanitation:

Parking:

4; 8m bays

Flot Bleu Fontaine; No drive over drain

SP

15 mins from town; Adj to busy main road. Inspected 2010.

ORGELET

62 J7 N46°31.351' E005°36.491' 39270

Directions: D2. Exit Orgelet on D2 to Beffia. Aire on right as exit town, signed.

Sanitation:

WC F

Parking:

F

4

Custom

SP

Village 3 mins with local commerce. Inspected 2010.

COUSANCE

63 J7 N46°31.777' E005°23.491' 39190

Directions: Grande Rue/D178. Aire on left as exit village towards Cuiseaux, by boule courts and Gizia turning. Service Point in bottom corner over old boules court.

Sanitation:

WC F

Parking:

P F

4

Custom

SP

Village centre 1 min. Inspected 2012.

LA MERCANTINE

64 J7 N46°27.900' E005°41.323' 39260

Photo: Phyl Leslie

Directions: From D301, lake road, follow sp 'Plage de la Mercantine'. The Aire is the woods, signed.

Sanitation:

Parking:

P

10; €9

Custom; €4

Aire has been relocated and no longer has lake views. Parking under trees. Inspected 2010.

LA TOUR DU MEIX

65 J7 N46°31.257' E005°40.263' 39270

Directions: Off D470. From Orgalet turn off D470 before bridge, sp 'Camping de Surchauffant'. Turn 1st left for Service Point.

Sanitation:

F

Parking:

None

Custom

Service Point only. Motorhomes are banned from all parking. Inspected 2010.

ARINTHOD 66 J7 N46°23.783' E005°34.200' 39240

Directions: D80/Rue de la Prélette. Adj to D80 as exit village, sp 'Fetigny'. Aire next to cemetery, signed.

Sanitation:

Parking:

6; €6 inc unmetered elec

Custom

SP

2 mins to pleasant village. Overlooking and adj to sports fields. Inspected 2010.

THOIRETTE 67 J7 N46°16.157' E005°32.109' 39240

Directions: D936. Adj to D936 between the supermarket 8 à Huit and the river bridge, signed.

Sanitation:

Parking:

5; €6 inc unmetered elec

Custom

SP

Supermarket adj. Village 2 mins. Inspected 2010.

LA PESSE SKI 68 K7 N46°17.024' E005°50.898' 39370

Directions: Next to the boulangerie in the tiny village, signed.

Sanitation:

Parking:

5

Flot Bleu Pacific; Token; €2

SP

In village centre; Some local commerce; Walking and cross country skiing adj. Inspected 2010.

LES MOUSSIERES SKI 69 K7 N46°19.267' E005°53.867' 39310

Directions: Exit the village on D292 towards Lajoux. Turn off D292, sp 'Tele Ski' and signed. The Aire is on the right in 400m.

Sanitation:

Parking:

5

Flot Bleu Pacific; Token; €2

SP

Next to smelly sewerage works. Very small ski resort 100m. Tokens from the cheesemakers. Inspected 2010.

JEURRE 70 K7 N46°21.940' E005°42.347' 39360

Directions: D27. Turn off D436 onto D27 towards Jeurre, signed. Turn 1st right into Jeurre, signed. Parking on left, signed.

Sanitation:

Parking:

10; €4/24hr; Grass parking; May-Oct subject to weather

Custom; €2; Elec €2; 15amp

SP

Commercial Aire on edge of village - CL feel. Inspected 2010.

ST CLAUDE 71 K7 N46°22.817' E005°51.117' 39200

Directions: D436/Ave de la Libération. Approach St Claude from the west and the Aire is on the right adj to D436, signed.

Sanitation:

Parking:

3; 8m bays

Euro Relais Junior

Adj to noisy, busy truck route. St Claude is famous for smokers' pipes, but is too far to walk. Inspected 2010.

LAMOURA PORTE DE LA SARRA SKI 72 K7 N46°24.642' E005°59.652' 39310

Directions: D25. On D25 between Lamoura and Les Rousses, sp 'P Porte de la Sarra' and signed. Service Point on D25 towards Lamoura, signed. N46°24.069' E005°59.153'.

Sanitation:

Parking:

20; May be pay in ski season

Euro Relais Mini

Local commerce and ski facilities; Hotel. At base of ski lift. Inspected 2010.

LES ROUSSES 1 73 K7 N46°29.283' E006°04.000' 39220

Directions: Route du Lac. Turn right off D29e when entering town. Aire on right next to football pitch. Also signed from town centre.

Sanitation:

Parking:

20

Euro Relais Junior; Token; €3.60

On edge of Ski resort - ski bus stop adj. Town centre and TO 2 mins. Inspected 2010.

LES ROUSSES 2 SKI 74 K7 N46°26.926' E006°04.515' 39220

Directions: D1005. At 'Le Balancier' ski station south of Les Rousses at the bottom of the chair lift.

Sanitation:

Parking:

20

Flot Bleu Euro; CC; €3

Ski lift adj; Ski jump 400m; Restaurant in season. Inspected 2010.

BOIS D'AMONT 75 K7 N46°32.262' E006°08.360' 39220

Directions: Outside 'Museum Boisellerie'. Turn off D415 into village. Follow sp 'Museum Boisellerie' in village.

Sanitation:

Parking:

10

Raclet; Token (2/1)

Numerous walks, mountain bike trails and cross country skiing. Inspected 2010.

CHAPELLE DES BOIS — SKI — 76 — K7 — N46°36.157' E006°06.769' — 25240

Directions: Route des Paturages, at the ski station to the north of the village. Turn off, sp 'SKI VVT', at large multiple sign. Service Point in shed on left near recycling containers.

Sanitation:

Parking:

20

Aire Services (in shed); Token; €3

SP

Small cross country ski resort close to the Swiss border. Many signed walks. Inspected 2010.

MOUTHE — 77 — K7 — N46°42.616' E006°11.711' — 25240

Directions: Rue de la Source du Doubs. Turn off D437 in Mouthe onto D433, sp 'Centre de Secours', 'Camping', and signed. The Aire is near the church.

Sanitation:

Parking:

20

Aire Service; Token (3/3); €3.50

SP

Mountain biking routes; Local ski resort; Fire station adj. Inspected 2010.

LABERGEMENT STE MARIE — 78 — K6 — N46°46.288' E006°16.644' — 25160

Photo: Paul Taylor

Directions: Rue du Lac, off D437. Turn off D437 onto Rue de Lac, sp 'Camping du Lac' and 'Aire de Camping-Car'. The Aire is on the left before the campsite and the lake car park.

Sanitation:

Parking:

8; Max 48hrs

Aire Services; €2

SP

Likely to be crowded. Motorhomes banned from lakeside car park May- Oct. Inspected 2010.

ST POINT LAC — 79 — K6 — N46°48.761' E006°18.225' — 25160

Directions: Rue du Lac, off D129. Turn off D129 in village, sp 'Camping', 'La Plage' and 'La Port'. Aire on left opp campsite adj to lake, signed.

Sanitation:

Parking:

30; €7.50/night Apr-Nov

SOS

SP

Adj beach complex with swimming, boating and windsurfing (crowded at weekend). Parking fee collected in evening by attendant. Inspected 2010.

BESANCON — 80 — K6 — N47°14.221' E006°00.999' — 25000

Directions: Quai Veil Picard. Cross the river from south on D683 and turn immediately right, sp 'Aire Accueil en Camping-Car'. Turn left into Aire, signed. 7m max.

Sanitation:

Parking:

12; €5; 7m max

Aire Services

SP

Town centre 2 mins; Hilltop fort on outskirts; Access difficult if busy. Inspected 2010.

BAUME LES DAMES

81 K6 N47°20.403' E006°21.436' 25110

Directions: D277. South side of town just off D50 by bridge over canal. Follow sp 'Port' and 'Aire de Stationnement' through town. This site is busy every evening and often full by 4pm. Arrive early to avoid disappointment.

Sanitation:

Parking:

38; €7 inc unmetered elec

Custom; €2 service only

Commercial Aire. Some pitches with canal views; Showers €1.20. Inspected 2010.

NOZEROY

82 K6 N46°46.349' E006°02.139' 39250

Photo/Info: Janet & John Watts

Directions: Rue des Ramparts. Turn off D119 towards city wall clock tower, sp Toutes Commerces'. Turn left in front of clock tower into Rue des Ramparts. Follow road to roundabout and turn left. Aire 100m on right, signed.

Sanitation:

Parking:

10; €6/night inc elec; Grass parking

Custom; No waste water or toilet emptying point

Historic village with local commerce 2 mins. Arrive with empty toilet tank as there is no toilet emptying point. Visited 2011.

MONTBELIARD

83 K5 N47°30.407' E006°47.482' 25200

Directions: Rue du Champ de Foire. From Junction 8 on A35/E60 follow sp 'Montbéliard Centre', then sp 'Champ de Foire'. Aire to left of large, unrestricted car park by river and canal.

Sanitation:

Parking:

2

Raclet; Token

500m town centre. Main road adj; Canal adj; No views. Small Aire with difficult access. Inspected 2010.

BROGNARD

84 K5 N47°31.697' E006°51.383' 25600

Directions: Heading southbound on A36 exit at Junction 10, sp 'Grand Charmont'. At the roundabout take the 1st exit and then turn right. The Aire is near the lake at the Base de Loisirs, sp 'Bus et Camping car'.

Sanitation:

Parking:

3; Max 48hrs

Custom

Leisure lakes adj. Inspected 2010.

MONTREUX CHATEAU

85 L5 N47°36.124' E007°00.108' 90130

Directions: D11. Adj to D11 by canal bridge, opp 'Communante de Communes du Bassin de la Bourbeuse', signed. Service Point outside barrier. Parking inside barrier.

Sanitation:

Parking:

7

Flot Bleu Euro; Token; €5/24hrs elec and water

Canalside near lock. Pleasant location with cycling and walking. Inspected 2010.

CHAVANNES SUR L'ETANG | 86 | L5 | N47°37.987' E007°01.148' | 68210

Directions: D419. Adj to D419 at the information point at the edge of village heading towards Foussemange, signed.

Sanitation:

Parking:

10; €5/6pm-9am

Flot Bleu Fontaine; Multiple unmetered elec points

SP

Pleasant area adj to fields; Free day parking. Inspected 2010.

BURNHAUPT LE HAUT | 87 | L5 | N47°44.456' E007°08.851' | 68520

Directions: D26/Rue du Pont d'Aspach. Turn off D483 at large roundabout with D466, sp 'Burnhaupt le Haut'. At next roundabout turn off, sp 'Zone Commerciale'. Aire on right, signed.

Sanitation:

E

Parking:

3

Aire Services; €3

SP

Super U and boulangerie adj. Inspected 2010.

THANN | 88 | L5 | N47°48.650' E007°06.296' | 68800

Directions: Rue Anatole Jacquot. Follow sp 'Centre Ville'. Aire in large car park, signed.

Sanitation:

Parking:

10

Custom; Inaccessible Saturday morning

SP

Pleasant spot adj to river; Small town commerce 2 mins, market Saturday. Inspected 2010.

BOURBACH LE HAUT | 89 | L5 | N47°47.678' E007°01.721' | 68290

Directions: D146biv. Narrow winding roads to village. Next to picnic area, nursery school and village recycling bins. Small asphalt parking area with views.

Sanitation:

E

Parking:

2; €5; Mar-Nov

Flot Bleu Fontaine

SP

Good views across Vosges wooded hills to Alps in distance. Inspected 2010.

WILLER SUR THUR | 90 | L5 | N47°50.590' E007°04.357' | 68760

Directions: Rue du Maréchal Foch. Turn off N66, sp 'D13bis' and 'Goldbach-Altenbach'. The Aire is on the left outside the church.

Sanitation:

E

Parking:

1; 6m max

Flot Bleu Pacific; 1 unmetered elec point

SP

Village adj. Parking in church car park not ideal. Parked cars obstruct access. Inspected 2010.

HARTMANNSWILLER | 91 | L5 | N47°51.796' E007°12.842' | 68500

Directions: From Soultz turn off D5, sp 'Hartmannswiller', onto D44. Follow road for 450m and turn right opp Bois de Chauffage, sp 'Salle Polyvalente' from opp direction. Narrow roads through village.

Sanitation:

Parking:

5; 7m bays

Flot Bleu Euro; CC; €4.10

SP

Village 2 mins; Always likely to have space. Inspected 2010.

SOULTZ HAUT RHIN | 92 | L5 | N47°53.305' E007°13.885' | 68360

Directions: Rue de la Marne. From Bollwiller on D83 turn onto D429 to Soultz. Turn right off D429 at roundabout onto Rue de la Marne. The Service Point is visible from the road in large car park on right.

Sanitation:

E

Parking:

F

5

Flot Bleu Euro; CC; €4.10

SP

Outside factory outlet jean shop and 2 schools. Town 2 mins. Inspected 2010.

MURBACH | 93 | L5 | N47°55.392' E007°09.632' | 68530

Directions: D4011/Rue de Guebwiller. On the main road through the village, clearly signed, at the village car park. On the left before the abbey.

Sanitation:

E

Parking:

F

5

Flot Bleu Euro; CC; €4.10

SP

Abbey adj open to public; Restaurant adj. Inspected 2010.

LINTHAL | 94 | L5 | N47°56.692' E007°07.647' | 68610

Directions: D430. Adj to D430 as exit village towards Le Markstein.

Sanitation:

Parking:

P

F

5

Flot Bleu Euro; CC; €4.10

SP

Village 2 mins; Road noise from D430; Green space adj. Inspected 2010.

FESSENHEIM | 95 | L5 | N47°55.100' E007°31.895' | 68740

Directions: D3bis. 100m from the Super U on D3bis. In village turn off D468, sp 'Super U' and 'Aire de Service', onto D3bis. Aire on right at Complex Sportif before Super U.

Sanitation:

Parking:

P

F

10

Flot Bleu Pacific; Token; €1.50

SP

Tokens from Super U or swimming pool adj. Amenities include sports centre/swimming pool. Main village 2 mins. Inspected 2010.

ORSCHWIHR * 96 L5 N47°56.231' E007°13.872' 68500

Directions: Rue de la Source. Just off D5, main road, signed.

Sanitation:

Parking:

4

Flot Bleu Euro; CC; €4.10

Wine tasting - you could drink yourself silly here! Rural views of grapes; Village adj. Inspected 2010.

ROUFFACH 97 L5 N47°57.325' E007°17.737' 68250

Directions: Place des Sports. From D83 exit, sp 'Rouffach', onto D18bis. At end of road turn right onto D18bis, sp 'Centre Ville' and signed after turn. This road has a 3.5t weight restriction. After 550m turn right, sp 'Camping Municipal'. Travel 100m and turn left, Aire on left in 100m.

Sanitation:

Parking:

10

SOS; Token; €3

Swimming pool/sports facility adj. Germanic style town with some interesting architecture. Very short bays. Inspected 2010.

WESTHALTEN SOULTZMATT 98 L5 N47°57.376' E007°15.078' 68250

Directions: D18bis. Adj to D18bis, main road from south as you drive past Westhalten. Just before you enter Soultzmatt.

Sanitation:

Parking:

3

Euro Relais; €2

Additional parking for large vehicles 200m; Brewery adj; Wine caves in the small, pretty village. Inspected 2010.

LA BRESSE 99 K5 N47°59.679' E006°51.307' 88250

Directions: Route de Niachamp. On D486 as enter La Bresse from Le Thillot. Turn left at first roundabout, sp 'Z.I. Niachamp' and signed. Follow road and Service Point is on left, signed.

Sanitation:

Parking:

Poss

Urba Flux; €2

Service Point only, however adj parking (barriered off and filled with gravel) has two Service Points. Local campsite offers discounts to motorhomers. Inspected 2012.

GERARDMER STATION DU SKI SKI 100 K5 N48°03.536' E006°53.425' 88400

Directions: Chemin du Rond Faing, at base of ski station. From Gérardmer follow sp 'Domaine Skiable Alpin'.

Sanitation:

Parking:

50; €4; Pay at machine

None; See 101

Ski slopes and ski shops adj. Views. Inspected 2010.

GERARDMER | 101 | L5 | N48°04.350' E006°52.488' | 88400

Directions: Boulevard d'Alsace. Follow D417/Blvd d'Alsace through town, following sp 'Tourist Office' and 'Centre'. Aire past ALDI supermarket car park. Service Point opp, signed.

Sanitation:

Parking:

80; €4; Pay at machine

Flot Bleu Euro; CC; €3

Town 2 mins; Lake with pedaloes, waterslides and swimming 5 mins. Inspected 2010.

FRAIZE | 102 | L5 | N48°10.928' E007°00.220' | 88230

Directions: Adj to N415 in village centre by TO and Ed supermarket, sp 'Office de Tourisme' and signed.

Sanitation:

Parking:

6

Euro Relais Mini; Token (2/1)

Ed supermarket adj; TO adj; Builders yard adj. Inspected 2010.

COL DE LA SCHLUCHT | SKI | 103 | L5 | N48°03.836' E007°01.349' | 88230

Directions: Off D417, at Col de la Schlucht car park.

Sanitation:

Parking:

50; Tolerated

None

Alt 1139m. Spectacular alpine views; Ski lift 100m. Restaurant adj. Toboggan run. Inspected 2012.

ORBEY | SKI | 104 | L5 | N48°08.124' E007°05.494' | 68370

Directions: D48. From Orbey follow sp 'Lac Blanc'. The Aire is at the restaurant Les Terrasses du Lac Blanc adj to D48, signed.

Sanitation:

Parking:

7; €5

Custom; Elec €2.50

Walking distance to 3 man chair lift. Popular mountain biking area. Inspected 2010.

LES TROIS EPIS | 105 | L5 | N48°06.050' E007°13.767' | 68410

Directions: Long winding climb up D11 from Turckheim. Turn right in front of church, then left into car park. Aire adj to car park behind church and fire station. Not signed from main road.

Sanitation:

Parking:

8

Raclet; €2

Up steep winding road. Village adj. Parking on lower terrace. Inspected 2010.

KAYSERSBERG — 106 — L5 — N48°08.148' E007°15.740' — 68240

Directions: Just off D415 in Kayserberg. Follow sp 'P1' and signed.

Sanitation:

Parking:

80; €6/24hrs; Pay at machine

Custom

On Alsace wine route, plenty of wine caves. Aire complete suntrap. Town 2 mins; Very popular. Inspected 2010.

RIQUEWIHR — 107 — L5 — N48°09.980' E007°18.122' — 68340

Directions: D3, off D1b. As you enter town on D3/D3.ii, parking on right-hand side after roundabout, signed. This is a tourist town and the Aire is in a busy car park, so exercise caution.

Sanitation:

Parking:

5; €6/24hrs; Pay at machine

Euro Relais; €2

Attractive but touristy half-timbered town. On Route du Vin. Inspected 2010.

RIBEAUVILLE — 108 — L4 — N48°11.531' E007°19.719' — 68150

Directions: Route de Guemar/D106. Enter town from east on D106. Aire is on left as you approach town centre. Signed.

Sanitation:

Parking:

17; €5/24hrs; Pay at machine

Custom; €2

At start of Route du Vin, which is very beautiful. Popular Aire, arrive early; Town 2 mins. Inspected 2010.

HAVE YOU VISITED AN AIRE? — GPS co-ordinates in this guide are protected by copyright law

Take at least 5 digital photos showing
• Signs
• Service Point
• Parking
• Overview
• Amenities

Visit www.all-the-aires.co.uk/submissions.shtml to upload your updates and photos.

Sanitation:

Aire Details:

Submit updates

- Amendments
- New Aires
- Not changed

PLOMBIERES LES BAINS — 110 — K5 — N47°57.735' E006°27.235' — 88370

Photo/Info: Alan Hoida

Directions: D157b. From centre follow sp 'St-Loup', 'Zone de Loisirs' and signs onto D157 the right hand fork. Follow road down hill past Le Prestige Imperial hotel and Thermes Napoleon to Aire on right, signed.

Sanitation:

Parking:

5; €8/24hrs; April-Oct pay at machine

Custom; 2 unmetered elec

Interesting town with many thermal baths. Town commerce 5 mins. Just across the D157b there is woodland with marked trails. Visited 2012.

CHATENOIS

111 | L4 | N48°16.484' E007°23.912' | 67730

Directions: Allee des Bains. Enter Chatenois on N59 from Ste-Marie-aux-Mines. Turn right onto D35 at roundabout as enter town, sp 'Kintzheim'. In 100m turn right, sp 'State Badbronn' and signed. Aire on left, signed.

Sanitation:

Parking:

7; Max 24hrs

Custom; €2

SP

Commerce 1 min. Nothalten: N48°21.270' E007°25.191' and Blienschwiller: N48°20.570' E007°25.338' have wine establishments offering motorhomes parking. Inspected 2012.

RUPT SUR MOSELLE

112 | K5 | N47°55.247' E006°39.717' | 88360

Directions: Rue D'Alsace. Turn off D466, main route through town, opp the Total fuel station, signed.

The 4 official motorhome bays in the large car park are too far away for most elec cables.

Sanitation:

E

Parking:

4

Urba Flux Tall; Token; 1 Token = Elec 3hrs/water 10mins

SP

Although there are 4 elec points these are located in the coach parking. Local commerce 3 mins. Inspected 2012.

ST NABORD

113 | K5 | N48°02.698' E006°34.918' | 88200

Directions: Rue de la Croix St Jacques. From Epinal exit N57, sp 'St Nabord Centre'. Go straight over 1st junction, then turn left at next junction, signed. Cross the railway track and the Aire is on the right.

Sanitation:

E

Parking:

2

Flot Bleu; Token; €3

SP

Boulangerie 100m across railway track with large parking area. Constant road noise. Inspected 2010.

ETIVAL CLAIREFONTAINE

114 | K4 | N48°21.805' E006°51.885' | 88480

Directions: Rue du General Nicholas Haxo. From N59 enter town on D424. Turn right, sp 'Rambersville'. Cross railway line and follow road for 400m. Turn left beside church onto D65, sp 'Nompatelize'. Turn right just past La Poste, signed. Aire 10m in car park.

Sanitation:

Parking:

20

Custom

SP

Peaceful residential location adj to shallow river. Local commerce 3 mins. Inspected 2012.

JEANMENIL

115 | K4 | N48°20.098' E006°41.195' | 88700

Directions: Rue des Ecoles. Turn off D32 by the church, sp 'Autrey'. The Aire is in the car park directly behind church.

Sanitation:

E

Parking:

30; Max 48hrs

Urba Flux; €2

SP

Pleasant car park, unlikely to be busy. Noisy church bells. Inspected 2010.

BACCARAT

116 K4 N48°26.851' E006°44.381' 54120

Directions: Place du Général Leclerc. Follow D935 sp 'Rambervillers', signed. Cross river bridge and turn left at roundabout. By Hôtel de Ville and unusual concrete church. Aire in car park on left.

Sanitation:

Parking:

11; €4/7pm-7am; CC

Urba Flux Tall; €2/90 mins elec

Views of river; Town 5 mins across bridge. Very noisy bells through night. Inspected 2012.

FONTENOY LA JOUTE

117 K4 N48°27.381' E006°39.916' 54122

Directions: D22F. Exit village on D22F, sp 'Glonville'. The Aire is in the car park on the right just before the village boundary, signed.

Sanitation:

Parking:

20

Euro Relais Mini; Token (ER)

Peaceful location in large grass and gravel parking area. Village with local commerce 3 mins. Inspected 2012.

LUNEVILLE

118 K4 N48°35.875' E006°29.844' 54300

Directions: Turn off N59 to Lunéville. Follow sp 'Lunéville', then 'Centre Ville'. At roundabout turn left, sp 'Centre Ville', then immediately right. Turn right at end of road, then left at roundabout. Turn left at end of road and take 2nd exit at next roundabout. Aire on left adj to river.

Sanitation:

Parking:

6

Custom; Token (2/1)

River adj; Town 5 mins; Château 5 mins; Inspected 2012.

GPS Co-ordinates for SatNav

The GPS Co-ordinates published in this guide were taken onsite by our inspectors. We consider them a valuable and unique asset and at the time of publishing have decided not to publish them as electronic files for use on navigation devices. You have permission to type in the co-ordinates of an Aire you intend to visit but not to store or share them. For the security of our copyright:

- **Do not compile them into lists**
- **Do not publish, share or reproduce them anywhere in any format**

FENETRANGE

120 L4 N48°51.219' E007°01.634' 57930

Directions: D43. Signed off D43 to the north of the village. At Wally Services and G20 supermarket.

Sanitation:

Parking:

5; Max 48hrs

Raclet; €2

Car wash; G20 supermarket with fuel; Fénétrange is a fortified town. Inspected 2010.

ABRESCHVILLER | 121 | L4 | N48°38.136' E007°05.589' | 57560

Directions: Place Norbert Prevot. Follow D44 through village towards Lorquin. Turn off D44 opp church, sp 'Plan d'Eau' and 'Camping'. Service Point on right outside campsite.

Sanitation:

Parking:

None

Euro Relais Maxi; Token (ER)

Service Point only. Camping €9. Adj swimming lake open July/Aug until water temperature falls below 18°C. Inspected 2012.

NIDERVILLER | 122 | L4 | N48°43.033' E007°05.900' | 57565

Directions: Rue de Lorraine/D45. Exit the village to the north on D45. The Aire is adj to D45 on the left before the canal bridge. At the marina, signed.

Sanitation:

Parking:

6; €10; Mar-Nov

Custom; Water €0.50 Elec €0.50/kwh

Adj to marina, canal and marine shop. Inspected 2010.

SAVERNE | 123 | L4 | N48°43.879' E007°21.302' | 67700

Directions: Rue Jean de Manderscheid, outside municipal campsite. Turn off D1004, sp 'Camping ***', 'Club Hippique', and 'C.E.S. Sources', into Rue du Grottenhouse. Follow road to end and the Service Point is to the left of the campsite entrance.

Sanitation:

Parking:

None

Custom

Service Point only. Inspected 2010.

SOUFFLENHEIM | 124 | L4 | N48°49.777' E007°57.298' | 67620

Directions: Rue des Fleurs. Take D1063 from Haguenau. Turn onto D2063 at the roundabout, sp 'Soufflenheim'. 200m after entering town, turn right onto 3.5t weight restricted road, signed. Aire at rear of car park on right.

Sanitation:

Parking:

2

Euro Relais Mini; 2 CEE unmetered elec points

Town centre with local commerce 3 mins. Inspected 2012.

HATTEN | T | 125 | L3 | N48°53.957' E007°58.159' | 67690

Directions: Musée de l'Abri. Turn off D28 in Hatten, sp 'Musée de l'Abri'. Follow sp 'Musée de l'Abri' and the Aire is outside the museum. Service Point outside museum entrance, signed.

Sanitation:

Parking:

20

Euro Relais Mini

Adj to WW2 bunker and collection of military vehicles. Site open to public May-Sept, €5/pp. Inspected 2012.

BETSCHDORF

126 L3 N48°53.681' E007°54.657' 67660

Directions: Rue de l'Avenir. Turn off D243 onto D344, sp 'Soufflenheim'. Turn right, sp 'Piscine'. Go straight over the 1st roundabout and turn left at the 2nd roundabout, signed. Aire on left.

Sanitation:

Parking:

10

Euro Relais Mini; No drive over drain

SP

Parking under deciduous trees adj to the sports facilities. Town centre 5 mins. Inspected 2012.

BITCHE

T

127 L3 N49°03.270' E007°26.069' 57230

Directions: Bitche Citadelle. Follow sp 'Citadelle' in Bitche. Aire to the right of car park.

Sanitation:

E

Parking:

5; Plenty of overflow parking

Aire Services; €2

SP

Parking adj to citadel. Town centre 5 mins down hill. Inspected 2012.

HARSKIRCHEN

128 L4 N48°56.348' E007°01.707' 67260

Directions: Port de Plaisance. Exit town to west on D23. Cross canal and turn immediately right onto D423, sp 'Bissert' and signed. Aire 200m in parking on right, signed.

Sanitation:

E

Parking:

3; €6; Open Mar-Nov

Custom; Water €1/5mins; Elec €1/12hrs

SP

Adj to river and boat moorings. Tow-path for walking and cycling. Village 5 mins. Parking in Keskastel refers to a campsite. Inspected 2012.

SARREGUEMINES

129 L3 N49°06.133' E007°04.600' 57200

Directions: Rue de Steinbach. Enter Sarreguemines from south on D919. Follow D919 under bridge and left alongside river. The Aire is 500m on the right before the flyover at Base Nautique, signed.

Sanitation:

E

Parking:

14; €5/12pm-12pm

Custom; Water €1/100l; Elec €0.50kwh

SP

The motorhome parking is in a fenced compound adj to a busy main road and industrial units. Inspected 2012.

SARREBOURG

130 L4 N48°43.361' E007°02.239' 57400

Directions: Rue de la Piscine. From N44 turn off, sp 'D44'. Turn into town at the first roundabout, sp 'Zone de Loisirs'. At next roundabout turn left, sp 'La Sarre Ouest'. Drive through retail park to end of road and turn left, sp 'Imling'. Turn right immediately after bridge and follow road to end. Turn left and Aire on left, signed.

Sanitation:

E

Parking:

10; Unlevel roadside parking

Flot Bleu Fontaine; No drive over drain

SP

Adj to swimming pool in pleasant landscaped park. Inspected 2012.

STRASBOURG — 131 — L4 — N48°33.993' E007°48.012' — 67000

Directions: Parking de l'Auberge de Jeunesse des Deux Rives. Follow sp 'Kehl' through town, then sp 'Jardin des Deux Rives'. Aire signed in park. For ease enter Strasbourg from Kehl, Germany.

Sanitation:

Parking:

10; Max 7 days

Euro Relais Junior; CC or Token (ER); €2.50; No drive over drain

SP

Pleasant park adj to river on German border. Inspected 2010.

ROTHAU — 132 — L4 — N48°27.240' E007°12.120' — 67570

Directions: Aire outside municipal campsite. Turn off D1420 in Rothau, sp 'Camping Municipal' and signed. Coordinates take you to small bridge which you cross and turn immediately left. Aire 200m.

Sanitation:

Parking:

8; €6 inc unmetered elec May-Sept; Free rest of year

Flot Bleu Euro; €2.50

SP

Near Le Struthof WW2 concentration camp (museum). Inspected 2010.

BENFELD — 133 — L4 — N48°22.657' E007°35.861' — 67230

Directions: D1083, at motorhome dealer CLC Alsace. Adj to D1083 on local service road, accessible from southbound lane. Turn off D1083 after passing dealer and follow sp 'CLC Alsace'.

Sanitation:

Parking:

None

Euro Relais Junior

SP

At motorhome dealer with reasonable accessory shop. Inspected 2010.

HAIRONVILLE — 134 — L4 — N48°41.065' E005°05.173' — 55000

Info/Photo: Rod and Liz Sleigh

Directions: D4, Rue Charles Collet. From D635 take D4 south, sp 'Haironville'. From N4 turn north, sp 'Haironville'. Aire south side of pretty river bridge, behind village hall.

Sanitation:

Parking:

6

Aire Services; 3/3 Token €2

SP

Pleasant and peaceful riverside location. Local commerce inc convenience store 4 mins. Visited 2012.

Lac de Madine, *Photo: Rita Renninghoff*

Champagnac

LIMOUSIN & AUVERGNE

Lurcy Levis

PREMILHAT

1 | H7 | N46°20.081' E002°33.518' | 03410

Directions: Route de l'Etang de Sault. Exit Montlucon following sp 'Limoges' and 'Gueret'. After passing retail park with large Auchan supermarket, turn left at roundabout onto D605, sp 'Premilhat'. Follow road and Aire is on left opp lake, signed.

Sanitation:

Parking:

8; Max 72hrs

Euro Relais Maxi; Water €5/150l; CC; Euro Relais elec; €2.50/10hrs

Landscaped Aire with partial lake views over road and through willows. Pleasant lakeside park and swimming beach opp. Inspected 2012.

ESTIVAREILLES

2 | H7 | N46°25.499' E002°36.933' | 03190

Directions: Off D3. From D2144 turn onto D3 at Estivareilles, sp 'Herisson'. The Aire is 100m on left, sp 'Salle Polyvalente' and signed.

Sanitation:

Parking:

20

Custom; Near entrance

Large, uninspiring car park; Village with local commerce 2 mins. Inspected 2010.

MONTLUCON

3 | G7 | N46°21.301' E002°35.188' | 03100

Directions: Place de la Fraternité. Enter town on D943. Just off D943 in large square, signed. Just before D916/D301 junction if coming from north.

Sanitation:

Parking:

50; No parking on market day Thursday 6am-3pm

Euro Relais Mini

Elec bollards throughout car park; Town centre 20 mins; Small park adj. Inspected 2010.

CHAMBON SUR VOUEIZE

4 | G7 | N46°11.170' E002°26.035' | 23170

Photo: Vicky and Nick Church

Directions: Rue du Stade, off D915. Exit village on D915, sp 'Evaux les B' and 'Camping Municipal'. Turn off at Intermarché supermarket, signed. Service Point in 200m on left at entrance to the campsite.

Sanitation:

Parking:

5

Euro Relais Junior; €2

Service Point outside campsite. Nice village with 2 rivers and local commerce. Inspected 2010.

NERIS LES BAINS

5 | H7 | N46°17.207' E002°39.137' | 03310

Directions: D155, at Camping du Lac. Follow sp 'Camping du Lac' through town. Located directly on D155 on west side of town.

Sanitation:

Parking:

6; €7 inc 10amp elec and showers; Pay at campsite

Raclet; Token (2/1); €2.50

In thermal spa town. Beautiful town centre 10 mins, worth a visit. Parking available when campsite open. Inspected 2010.

COMMENTRY | 6 | H7 | N46°17.383' E002°45.634' | 03600

Directions: Rue des Platanes, off D69. Turn off D998 at the roundabout onto D69, sp 'Moilins'. In 300m take road on right and Aire on left in 50m.

Sanitation:

Parking:

10

Euro Relais Junior

Adj to D69; Green space opp; Night halt or service only. Inspected 2010.

CHAMBLET | 7 | H7 | N46°20.018' E002°42.150' | 03170

Directions: Rue St Maurice. Turn off D2371 at traffic-lighted crossroads, sp 'P Mairie' and signed. Turn right in 50m, sp 'P Mairie' and signed. Turn right again in 20m opp church, signed. Service Point immediately on right, signed.

Sanitation:

Parking:

5

Custom; No drive over drain; 4 CEE elec points not working

Aire located in village centre adj to D2371 which may be noisy. Local commerces 1 min. Inspected 2012.

VILLEFRANCHE D'ALLIER | 8 | H7 | N46°23.736' E002°51.431' | 03430

Directions: D16. From D16/D33 traffic lighted junction in town centre exit to south on D16, sp 'Bezenet'. Aire is on left in 50m, signed.

Sanitation:

Parking:

4

Urba Flux; Token; 1 Token/2hrs elec

Sports facilities adj; Centre with local commerce 1 min. Inspected 2010.

MONTMARAULT | 9 | H7 | N46°19.087' E002°57.309' | 03390

Directions: Rue de Turenne. Enter town on N79 from Le Montet. At roundabout turn left onto D204, sp 'Blomard'. Turn right onto D68, sp 'Centre Ville', and in 20m turn left into large car park. In 30m turn right into Aire, signed.

Sanitation:

Parking:

5

Euro Relais Junior; €2; Token (ER); 5 CEE elec bollard points; Token; No drive over drain

Small, landscaped Aire. 2 mins from town centre with small town commerce. Adj parking holds market 6am-3pm on Weds. Inspected 2012.

ST MARCEL EN MURAT | 10 | H7 | N46°19.304' E003°00.462' | 03390

Directions: D429. Approach on D429 from the west. The Aire is on the left on entering the village, opposite the Mairie, signed.

Sanitation:

Parking:

10

Euro Relais Junior; Token (ER); €2

Very pleasant rural location with farmland views. Only a restaurant in the village. Tokens available from Mairie and restaurant. Visited 2012.

ST BONNET TRONCAIS | 11 | H7 | N46°39.609' E002°41.824' | 03360

Directions: D39. Enter village from south on D39. Service Point is on left at sports ground. Parking on grass behind the car park in the village, opp TO: N46°39.530' E002°41.538'.

Sanitation:

Parking:

10; Max 48hrs; Grass parking

Custom; Token; €1.50/50L water; 1 Continental unmetered elec point

In Tronçais forest, a large forest with marked trails. Inspected 2010.

LURCY LEVIS * | 12 | H7 | N46°44.293' E002°56.336' | 03320

Directions: Plan d'Eau des Sezeaux, Rue du Fontgroix. Turn onto Rue du Fontgroix at junction of D1 and D144, sp 'Plan d'Eau des Sezeaux' and signed. Follow to lake.

Sanitation:

Parking:

6; 7m bays

Aire Services; Token (3/3)

Small town close to Nevers and Loire river. 5 mins from town centre. Inspected 2012.

AVERMES | 13 | H7 | N46°35.218' E003°18.907' | 03000

Directions: Rue Alphonse Daudet off D707, at the E'Leclerc fuel station. Well signed from town centre. Follow sp 'Nevers' from south.

Sanitation:

Parking:

Poss

Flot Bleu Euro; CC; €2

Supermarket; LPG at fuel station. Inspected 2010.

MOULINS | 14 | H7 | N46°33.506' E003°19.506' | 03000

Directions: Chemin de Halage. Approach Moulins on D13 from Montilly. At roundabout go straight over, sp 'Montlucon' and signed. In 100m turn left, signed. Turn left again, signed, and follow road to Aire. Service Point on right. Parking accessed through Flot Bleu Park barrier.

Sanitation:

Parking:

30; €2.40/24hrs; CC; Pay at Flot Bleu Park; Grass parking

Flot Bleu Pacific; Token (FB); €2; CC; 4hrs elec or 20 mins servicing

Former municipal campsite turned commercial Aire. Town centre 5 mins across river bridge. Inspected 2012.

PARAY LE FRESIL | 15 | H7 | N46°39.282' E003°36.775' | 03220

Directions: D238, adj to roundabout by church. From Chevanges take D238 to Paray-le-Fresil. At Paray-le-Fresil follow sp 'St Martin des Lais' around church. Aire located off roundabout opp church, signed.

Sanitation:

Parking:

3

Aire Services Box; €2/55 mins CEE elec or 10 mins water; CC

Located adj to church, with daytime bells, in a small rural village. Inspected 2012.

CHEVAGNES 16 H7 N46°36.598' E003°33.125' 03230

Directions: Rue de l'Ancienne Poste. Exit village on D779 towards Bourbon-Lancy and turn off just after Mairie and La Poste, signed. Aire in far right corner, signed.

Sanitation:

Parking:

4

Aire Services Box; €2/55mins CEE elec or 10 mins water; CC

Located behind Mairie which obscures main road. Village with local commerce 1 min. Inspected 2012.

BEAULON 17 H7 N46°36.219' E003°39.490' 03230

Directions: Base Nautique. Turn off D15 at roundabout onto D298, sp 'Chevagnes', 'Base Nautique' and signed. Follow D298 across canal bridge and Aire is on left, signed.

Sanitation:

Parking:

5

Aire Services

This Aire is in a rural location adj to canal but with no view. Canal walks/cycle path with picnic area opp. Inspected 2012.

THIEL SUR ACOLIN 18 H7 N46°31.330' E003°35.242' 03230

Directions: Route de Dompierre. Exit village on D12 towards Dompierre-sur-Besbre. Turn left immediately before cemetery. Aire on left in 10m.

Sanitation:

Parking:

11

Aire Services

New Aire under constructed at time of inspection, expected to open in 2013. Local commerce 2 mins. Inspected Sept 2012.

CRESSANGES 19 H7 N46°26.816' E003°09.641' 03240

Directions: Grand Rue. Exit N79 to Cressanges. In Cressanges follow D18, sp 'Service Station'. Turn right onto D137, sp 'Moulins'. Aire on left in 20m, signed.

Sanitation:

Parking:

4

Euro Relais Box; €2

Adj to town square with rural views from the four marked bays. Village with local commerce 2 mins. Inspected 2012.

MONTAIGUT 20 H7 N46°10.624' E002°48.376' 63700

Directions: Off D988. In town turn south onto D988 at traffic light junction, sp 'Pionsat' and to truck parking. Turn left as exit town, sp 'Tennis'. Aire adj to tennis courts.

Sanitation:

Parking:

5

Flot Bleu Pacific; Token; €2

On edge of village; Sport facilities adj; Town centre 3 mins. Inspected 2010.

ST ELOY LES MINES | 26 | H7 | N46°09.337' E002°50.152' | 63700

Directions: D2144. Adj to D2144 as enter from south, signed. Parking overlooking large lake.

Sanitation:

Parking:

20; Max 48hrs

Euro Relais Junior; €2

Views over lake possible; Town centre 5 mins. Swimming, boating, fishing adj. Inspected 2010.

BELLENAVES | 27 | H7 | N46°12.325' E003°04.666' | 03330

Directions: D68. Exit Bellenaves on D68, sp 'Louroux de Bouble' and 'Vernusse'. Service Point adj to D68 on left outside campsite.

Sanitation:

Parking:

None

Aire Services; €2

Service Point only. Adj campsite charges €6.40 inc 2 adults. Inspected 2012.

ST POURCAIN SUR SIOULE * | 28 | H7 | N46°18.715' E003°17.708' | 03500

Photo: CM Nash

Directions: Rue des Béthères. Turn into Rue de la Moutte at La Poste. Turn right at the end of the road into Rue des Béthères. Well signed.

Sanitation:

Parking:

58

Flot Bleu Pacific/Elec; €2; 8 elec points; Elec €2/4hrs

Some pitches have river views; Town 5 mins; Showers. Inspected 2010.

MONTOLDRE | 29 | H7 | N46°19.962' E003°26.831' | 03150

Directions: D268. In village centre opp Mairie, signed. Turn off D21 into village and follow D268 as bends south.

Sanitation:

Parking:

3

Euro Relais Mini; €2

Village with bar/restaurant. Inspected 2010.

VARENNES SUR ALLIER | 30 | H7 | N46°18.777' E003°24.272' | 03150

Directions: Rue de Beaupuy. On N7 from south follow sp 'Centre Ville'. Aire in town centre car park to right of Hôtel de Ville. 3.5t weight restriction in car park.

Sanitation:

Parking:

20; No parking 6am-1pm Monday

Raclet; Token (ER); €2

In tree-lined sq; Adj to town centre. Inspected 2010.

TRETEAU

31 H7 N46°22.086' E003°31.048' 03220

Directions: Chemin du Vieux Moulin. From D21 turn onto D463 in town, signed. Take 1st right turn, signed. At end of road turn right again and follow road to Service Point.

Sanitation:

Parking:

5; €3/night Mar-Oct

Euro Relais Junior; €2

Overlooking village pond; Pleasant; Village centre 5 mins. Inspected 2010.

LAPALISSE 1

32 I7 N46°14.956' E003°38.407' 03120

Directions: Off D990a. Turn off the roundabout by the river bridge onto D990a, sp 'Bert' and 'Château Lapalisse'. Follow the road up hill and turn beside church. Parking is behind church.

Sanitation:

Parking:

10; Max 12hrs

None; See 33

SP

Ideal if 33 closed; Château and church adj; Town 2 mins down hill. Inspected 2010.

LAPALISSE 2

33 I7 N46°15.000' E003°38.133' 03120

Directions: Place Jean Moulin. From west on D707 turn left in town centre near river bridge, sp 'P 200 Places' and signed. In 300m turn right, signed. Aire at end of road.

Sanitation:

Parking:

10

Euro Relais Juior; Token (ER); €2

By shallow river; Town 2 mins; Impressive château 5 mins up hill. Inspected 2010.

PERIGNY

34 H7 N46°15.122' E003°33.237' 03120

Directions: Rue de l'Eglise. Turn off N7 in Perigny, sp 'D472' and 'Servilly'. Turn 1st left and the Aire is 100m on the left.

Sanitation:

Parking:

8

Custom

Located in a semi-rural location 100m from the N7, but the road is still audible. Local commerce adj to N7 1 min. Inspected 2012.

LE MAYET DE MONTAGNE

35 H7 N46°04.321' E003°39.983' 03250

Directions: Avenue de la Libération. Enter town on D7 from north. Turn off D7 at 2nd right after the church into Avenue de la Libération, sp 'Le Pré Colombier' and 'Centre Social'. The Aire is in the large car park on the right.

Sanitation:

Parking:

10

Raclet; €2

Village 1 min with local commerce; D7 very scenic drive. Inspected 2010.

CREUZIER LE VIEUX	36	H7	N46°09.270' E003°25.879'	03300

Directions: D258. Exit village on D558, sp 'Vichy', then turn left onto D258, sp 'Vichy'. The Service Point is 400m on left, signed. There is a small car park directly behind the Service Point and one 100m further back from the road: N46°09.259' E003°25.925'. Turn left after Service Point and the parking is on the left, signed.

Sanitation:

Parking:

5

Euro Relais Junior; €2; Token (ER)

This Aire is 3km north of Vichy centre. Local commerce adj. Inspected 2012.

BILLY	37	H7	N46°14.159' E003°25.833'	03260

Directions: Place de l'Ancien Marché, off N209. The Service Point is behind a bus stop in the village centre, adj to N209, signed. For parking take the 1st right on the one-way system, signed.

Sanitation:

Parking:

3; Max 48hrs; Apr-Oct weekends and school holidays only

Custom; Lift covers

Inadequate parking; Village has castle to explore; Local commerce. Inspected 2010.

RANDAN	38	H8	N46°00.973' E003°21.070'	63310

Directions: D59/Rue du Puy de Dôme. From centre turn onto D59, sp 'Riom'. Aire on left in 200m, signed.

Sanitation:

Parking:

5

Euro Relais Junior; Token (ER)

Town 3 mins; Intermarché supermarket 2 mins. Inspected 2010.

AIGUEPERSE	39	H8	N46°01.561' E003°12.192'	63260

Directions: From Grande Rue/D2009 turn onto D984 at roundabout. Turn right at next roundabout and take 2nd left into Rue de la Porte aux Boeufs. Aire situated at junction with Boulevard Charles de Gaulle.

Sanitation:

Parking:

10

Raclet; €2

Town 2 mins. Inspected 2010.

EBREUIL	40	H7	N46°06.656' E003°04.855'	03450

Directions: Chemin du Vieux Bard. From D998 through town follow sp 'Camping Municipal'. Service Point outside camping municipal. For parking continue 300m past the Service Point and at the end of the road turn left, then right into parking for the playing fields: N46°06.590' E003°04.537'.

Sanitation:

Parking:

20; At sports stadium

Euro Relais Junior

Tourist village. Playing fields adj. Inspected 2010.

POUZOL | 41 | H7 | N46°06.189' E002°55.854' | 63440

Directions: Le Pont de Menat. Turn off D2144 near Pouzol, sp 'La Passerelle' and signed. The entrance is quite steep. Drive through the gates into Le Pont de Menat. Take the 1st turning on the left, signed, and follow the road to the right, signed.

Sanitation:

Parking:

8; May-Oct

Flot Bleu Pacific; €2/20mins

SP

Aire in a pleasant rural location adj to the Gorges de la Sioule and Gorges de la Chouvigny. Distant road noise. Inspected 2012.

ST REMY DE BLOT | 42 | H7 | N46°04.624' E002°55.894' | 63440

Directions: D99. From D2144 in north turn onto D109, sp 'St-Rémy-de-Blot' and signed. From D109 turn left onto D99, sp 'St-Rémy-de-Blot' and signed. Aire adj to D99 on left, by Mairie.

Sanitation: E WC F

Parking: P F

5

Flot Bleu Pacific; Customised

Isolated village with restaurant/local produce. Challenging drive on D109 through Gorges de la Sioule. Canoeing at D109 turning. Inspected 2010.

ST PARDOUX * | 43 | H7 | N46°03.624' E002°59.710' | 63440

Directions: D2144. Enter village on D2144 from St Eloy. Turn right, sp 'Accueil Camping-Car'. Drive 1.5km and turn left onto track, sp 'Etang des Cayers' and 'Accueil Camping-Car'. Follow track down hill and around lake. GPS at turn onto track for clarity.

Sanitation: E

Parking: P F

4

Euro Relais Junior; Token (ER)

A remote, rural location. Not suitable for RVs. Beautiful area. Inspected 2010.

ST GERVAIS D'AUVERGNE | 44 | H8 | N46°02.203' E002°49.107' | 63390

Directions: Follow sp 'Base de Loisirs - Etang Philippe' through town. The Service Point is at Base de Loisirs - Etang Philippe. Parking is off D534 in the car park opp the Carrefour supermarket and Sapeurs Pompiers (fire station) in the village centre: N46°01.845' E002°49.249'.

Sanitation: E WC

Parking: F

15; In village centre

Euro Relais Junior; €2

Service Point at very pleasant leisure lake; Campsite open Apr-Sept. Parking in very ordinary town centre car park. Inspected 2010.

SAURET BESSERVE | 45 | H8 | N45°59.544' E002°48.441' | 63390

Directions: D523. Near the church, adj to D523 in tiny village.

Sanitation: F

Parking: F

5

Euro Relais Junior

Tiny village near Gorges de la Sioule. Inspected 2010.

CHARBONNIERES LES VARENNES | 46 | H8 | N45°53.076' E002°58.814' | 63410

Directions: D90. Turn off D943 west of Volvic onto D16, sp 'Paugnat' and signed. Follow road for 4km to roundabout taking 2nd exit onto D90. In 500m turn left, signed.

Sanitation:

Parking:

4, between trees

Aire Services; €2; Token (3/3)

Although close to habitation the Aire is shielded by trees and feels remote. In national park famous for springs, inc Volvic mineral water. Inspected 2012.

ST GEORGES DE MONS | 47 | H8 | N45°56.393' E002°50.573' | 63780

Directions: Place des Anciens Combattants. Turn off D19 onto D19 ring road. Turn off before town centre, sp 'Camping'. Service Point directly outside camping municipal.

Sanitation:

Parking:

Poss when campsite closed; Oct onwards

Euro Relais Junior; €2

Town centre adj. Adj to large car park. Inspected 2010.

BROMONT LAMOTHE | 48 | H8 | N45°50.394' E002°48.821' | 63230

Directions: Off D941. Turn off D941 to west of village, sp 'Camping' and signed. The Service Point is outside the campsite.

Sanitation:

Parking:

None

Raclet; Token (2/1); €3

Service Point only outside campsite. Inspected 2010.

ORCINES | 49 | H8 | N45°47.271' E003°00.578' | 63870

Directions: D941. The Service Point is located adj to D941 as exit the town towards Pontgibaud. Service Point near electricity pylon beside road.

Sanitation:

Parking:

None

Euro Relais Junior; €2

Service Point only outside campsite. Inspected 2012.

MANZAT | 50 | H8 | N45°57.724' E002°56.296' | 63410

Directions: D148. Turn off D19/D227, onto D418, sp 'Pulverieres' and signed. Aire 50m on right, signed.

Sanitation:

Parking:

20

Custom

Large gravel car park; Town centre and local commerce 2 mins. Inspected 2010.

ST GERMAIN PRES HERMENT | 51 | G8 | N45°43.716' E002°32.711' | 63470

Photo/Info: Carol Weaver

Directions: D98. Visible and signed off D98 between Lastic and Verneugheol on one of two roads to the lake etang. Service Point 30m on left.

Sanitation:

Parking:

5

Flot Bleu Pacific; €2

Lake 100m and restaurant perhaps open in season. Very nice place off beaten track. May feel isolated out of season. Visited 2012.

HAVE YOU VISITED AN AIRE? **GPS co-ordinates in this guide are protected by copyright law**

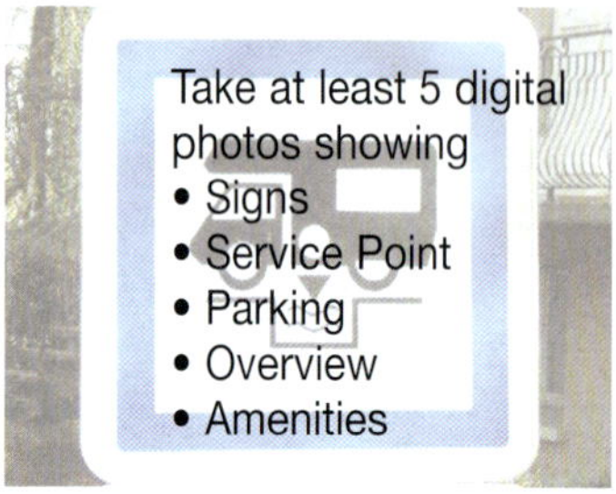
Take at least 5 digital photos showing
• Signs
• Service Point
• Parking
• Overview
• Amenities

Visit www.all-the-aires.co.uk/submissions.shtml to upload your updates and photos.

Sanitation:

Aire Details:

Submit updates

- Amendments
- New Aires
- Not changed

VULCANIA | 53 | H8 | N45°48.967' E002°56.691' | 63230

Directions: D941. Turn off D941, sp 'Vulcania'. Designated motorhome parking in car park. Near roundabout junction with D559.

Sanitation:

Parking:

20

None

Vulcania country park adj; Entry €21pp; www.volcania.com; Parking is free. Inspected 2010.

VOLVIC | 54 | H8 | N45°52.355' E003°02.813' | 63530

Directions: Rue de Chancelas. Turn off D986, sp 'Camping'. Aire is outside the campsite.

Sanitation:

Parking:

5; Max 6m

Aire Services; €2

Designated parking located directly outside campsite; €10.50/2 people. Volvic has walking trails. Inspected 2012.

CHATEL GUYON | 55 | H8 | N45°55.394' E003°03.962' | 63140

Directions: Avenue du Général de Gaulle. Located just off D15 on town ring road in car park with plane trees. Sp 'Centre Ville' through town. Also parking at Parking des Roches and Parking Dupré Morand.

Sanitation:

Parking:

7; €5; Pay police municipal

Flot Bleu Pacific; Token

In thermal town. Town 2 mins with plenty of commerce. Inspected 2010.

ST BONNET PRES RIOM | 56 | H8 | N45°55.635' E003°06.832' | 63200

Directions: Place de la Liberté, off D2144. Turn off D2144 at church into Place de la Liberté and stay to right at fork (higher road). Aire between church and Salle Municipal.

Sanitation:

Parking:

5; Max 24hrs

Custom

Town adj with local commerce. Views of countryside. Inspected 2010.

LE CHEIX | 57 | H8 | N45°57.088' E003°10.695' | 63200

Directions: D425/Rue du Faubourg. From D2009 in village turn onto Rue du Stade. At end of road turn right onto D425/Rue du Faubourg towards Varennes sur Morge. Aire immediately on right. Well signed.

Sanitation:

Parking:

6

Custom

Countryside setting within walking distance of village. Beautiful spot. Inspected 2010.

RIOM | 58 | H8 | N45°53.680' E003°07.497' | 63200

Directions: Route d'Ennazat. From Volvic approach on D986 and follow sp 'Riom', then turn left at traffic lights, sp 'Riom-Centre'. Follow sp 'Ennazat', 'A71' and signed. Cross railway bridge and the Aire is directly across the roundabout, signed.

Sanitation:

Parking:

4

Urba Flux; €2/15 mins elec and water

Adj to road which can be noisy during the day. Old town centre 8mins. Inspected 2012.

CHATEAUGAY | 59 | H8 | N45°50.964' E003°05.077' | 63119

Directions: Place Charles de Gaulle. Turn off D402, main route through, opp La Poste into car park just before exit village towards Volvic, sp 'Ecole Maternelle'. Service Point in far right corner, signed.

Sanitation:

Parking:

Poss, car park by school, busy during school run.

Aire Services; €2

Adj to school, no designated parking but should be poss out of school hrs and at weekends. Inspected 2012.

CLERMONT FERREND | 60 | H8 | N45°47.884' E003°06.794' | 63100

Directions: P+R Les Pistes. Approach Clermont Ferrand from north on D2009. At traffic-lighted roundabout go straight on, sp 'Le Mont Dore' and 'P+R Les Pistes'. Turn 1st right and cross tramway, sp 'P+R Les Pistes' and signed. Aire 2nd entrance on right through barrier, signed.

Sanitation:

Parking:

7; €5; See Accueil, 20m, for access 6.30am-8.30pm Mon-Sat

Euro Relais Mini; Water turned on at 'Accueil' building

Barrier lifts automatically on exit. Adj tram stop direct to town (€2.60 return). Inspected 2012.

PERIGNAT LES SARLIEVE | 61 | H8 | N45°44.214' E003°08.310' | 63170

Directions: Rue Marcel Margard. Turn off D978 north edge of village, sp 'Ateliers Municipaux' and signed. Follow road to left and turn left, then turn immediately right, all signed.

Sanitation: E

Parking:

6; 8m bays

Euro Relais Junior; Token (ER)

Village location. Walk through adj park to reach local commerce. Convenient stop near A75 motorway. Clermont Ferrand has reasonably priced fuel. Inspected 2012.

COURNON D'AUVERGNE | 62 | H8 | N45°44.397' E003°13.366' | 63800

Directions: Rue des Laveuses, at the campsite. Follow D52 around town following sp 'Camping' and 'Zone de Loisirs'. The Aire is outside the campsite.

Sanitation: E

Parking:

15; €4.50/24hrs; Max 24hrs

Flot Bleu Pacific; Token

All other parking restricted 8pm-8am; Leisure lake and river adj. Inspected 2010.

ORCINES - LE PUY DE DOME T | 63 | H8 | N45°46.176' E002°59.081' | 63870

Directions: Panoramique des Domes. Follow sp 'Le Puy de Dome' onto D68. Turn off, sp 'P Panoramique des Domes', and follow road around parking area to designated coach and motorhome parking, signed.

Sanitation:

Parking:

20

Custom

Adj to Le Puy du Dome visitor centre and tourist train to summit. Numerous walking and cycling trails. Popular tourist attraction. Inspected 2012.

ST REMY SUR DUROLLE | 64 | H8 | N45°53.718' E003°35.838' | 63550

Directions: At Lac des Moines, off D201. Exit town to north on D201. Turn off to Lac des Moines by the Elan garage, sp 'Plan d'Eau'. Drive down to the lake and follow sp 'Village Vacannes' and signed.

Sanitation:

Parking:

5

Custom

Large leisure lake/resevoir; Swimming; Walking; Restaurants. Inspected 2010.

PALLADUC | 65 | I8 | N45°54.284' E003°37.802' | 63550

Directions: D201. Adj to D201 as exit village to northeast, sp 'P Camping Cars'. Near D201/D64 junction.

Sanitation:

Parking:

2

None

Sports facilities adj. Mountain village; Remote. Inspected 2010.

LEZOUX	66	H8	N45°49.630' E003°23.141'	63190

Directions: Musee de Ceramique. Follow brown sp 'Musée de Céramique' through town. The Aire is in the free visitors parking for the ceramic museum, signed.

Sanitation:

Parking:

5

Custom

Ceramic museum adj. The town was a major ceramics producer since Roman times and is famous for Samian ware pottery. Visited 2012.

LA MONNERIE LE MONTEL	67	I8	N45°52.174' E003°36.393'	63650

Directions: D2089. Adj to and signed off D2089. Parking located between main road and railway line.

Sanitation:

Parking:

10; No parking Sat 5am-1pm - market

Campsite bollard, dilapidated

Service Point in disrepair, but working; Town centre with commerce adj. Inspected 2010.

THIERS	68	H8	N45°52.255' E003°29.057'	63300

Directions: D44, at the Base de Loisirs ILOA. Turn off D906 onto D44 at roundabout junction near A72/E70, sp 'Dorat'. Follow D44 for 1.8km and turn left, sp 'Base de Loisirs ILOA'. The Service Point is in 200m on left, signed.

Sanitation:

Parking:

Poss

Custom (in yellow box); In disrepair

Activity centre; Kart track; Archery; Lake; Campsite. Inspected 2010.

LAC D'AUBUSSON	69	H8	N45°45.248' E003°36.902'	63120

Directions: On connecting road between D41 and D45, by reservoir and Base de Loisirs. 5km north of Augerolles on D45, signed.

Sanitation:

Parking:

20; €6

Custom

Near reservoir with bathing beach. Inspected 2010.

VERNET LA VARENNE	70	H8	N45°28.406' E003°26.933'	63580

Directions: D999. Aire in large car park adj to D999 in village, signed.

Sanitation:

Parking:

15

Raclet; €2

Alt 800m. Leisure/swimming lake adj; In small village with château. Inspected 2010.

ST GERMAIN L'HERM | 76 | H8 | N45°27.602' E003°32.631' | 63630

Directions: D37. Adj to D37 at junction with D999 to east of town, signed.

Sanitation:

Parking:

20

Euro Relais Junior

Village with local commerce 2 mins. Inspected 2010.

AMBERT | 77 | I8 | N45°32.369' E003°43.724' | 63600

Directions: D906. Service Point located outside 'Camping Les 3 Chênes' south of Ambert, adj to D906.

Sanitation:

Parking:

None

Euro Relais Junior; €2

Service Point only open May-Sept. Inspected 2010.

MONTPEYROUX | T | 78 | H8 | N45°37.489' E003°12.041' | 63114

Directions: Parking Obligatoire. Exit A75 at Junction 7 and follow sp 'Montpeyroux'. Turn left before village, sp 'Parking Obligatoire', and park in the furthest section. Just off A75 in an elevated position adj to petting farm.

Sanitation:

Parking:

10; Large motorhomes poss if not busy

Aire Services; Token (3/3)

Montpeyroux is a 'Village of France' and the narrow streets are just 3 mins away. Distant road noise from the A75 300m. May feel isolated at night and suffers cold winds. Inspected 2012.

CHAMPEIX | 79 | H8 | N45°35.293' E003°06.886' | 63320

Directions: D996. Exit Champeix towards Le Mont-Dore. Turn left across bridge over stream then turn right, signed.

Sanitation:

Parking:

10

Raclet; Token (2/1)

Town 3 mins; Tokens from fuel station. Service Point is fenced and closed in winter, parking is always available. Inspected 2010.

SUPER BESSE | SKI | 80 | H8 | N45°30.219' E002°51.294' | 63610

Photo: Mike and Jenny Woodthorpe

Directions: D149. Adj to D149 as exit resort to west. Aire in car park P6 and P7 south of Lac des Hermines, signed. Pay with credit card at entrance barrier.

Sanitation:

Parking:

200; €5.40/24hrs; decreasing to €4.40/24hrs

Flot Bleu Euro; Free; Flot Bleu Elec; 1 Token/4hrs

Alt 1276m. Ski resort; Ski lifts 3 mins; Ski bus stop adj; Restaurants and shops in resort. Cheaper for longer stays. Inspected 2010.

AYDAT

81 H8 N45°39.630' E002°58.628' 63970

Directions: Rue du Stade, off D90. Turn behind the church and entrance 150m, signed. Entry system involving lots of instructions and two raising bollards. Aire within former municipal campsite. The Aire is signed from Ponteix on D213.

Sanitation:

Parking:

30; €7 inc unmetered elec; CC; Pay on entry; Grass parking

Euro Relais Junior; €2

SP

2 mins from large leisure lake; All parking around lake bans motorhomes from 8pm-8am. Inspected 2010.

CHAMBON SUR LAC

82 H8 N45°34.209' E002°54.285' 63790

Directions: Off D996. In Chambon sur Lac turn off D996, main route, sp 'Camping les Bombes' and signed. Service Point directly adj to campsite entrance. Designated parking is 100m on left, signed.

Sanitation:

Parking:

50; €6

Flot Bleu Fontaine; Token; €3

SP

5 mins to lake; No views of lake; All lakeside parking bans motorhomes. Inspected 2010.

MUROL

83 H8 N45°34.372' E002°56.480' 63790

Directions: D5. Car park opp junction with D168, by TO.

Sanitation:

Parking:

10; No parking 15th Jun-31st Aug

None

SP

Village centre with small park adj. Ski hire shop opp. Inspected 2010.

LE MONT DORE

SKI 84 H8 N45°34.637' E002°48.263' 63240

Directions: Ave des Crouzets, off D130. Approach on D130 from La Bourboule. Aire outside camping 'Les Crouzets', signed. Drive towards campsite barrier and Service Point on right, signed.

Sanitation:

Parking:

None

Flot Bleu Pacific; €2

SP

Ski resort; Campsite adj with hard standing pitches. Inspected 2010.

LA BOURBOULE

SKI 85 H8 N45°35.391' E002°45.016' 63150

Photo: Alan and Jane Fletcher

Directions: D130/Ave d'Alsace-Lorraine. Follow sp 'Le Mont-Dore' in town. The Aire is signed on right, at the football stadium. Report suggests this may have closed.

Sanitation:

Parking:

10

Euro Relais Mini; €2; Closed in winter

SP

It may be poss to park at Intermarché supermarket adj D996: N45°35.652' E002°45.708'. Inspected 2010.

LA TOUR D'AUVERGNE SKI | 86 | H8 | N45°31.969' E002°41.216' | 63680

Directions: D203. Parking only in car park overlooking lake. Follow sp 'D203'. Aire by D203/D47 junction.

Sanitation:

Parking:

20

None; See 89

Very pleasant spot overlooking lake in mountain village. D129 a pleasant drive. Local cross country skiing routes nearby. Inspected 2010.

LES GANNES (MESSEIX) | 87 | G8 | N45°36.935' E002°33.389' | 63750

Directions: Place des Pins. Turn off D987 at Les Gannes onto D73c, sp 'Messeix' and signed. Aire in car park 200m on left, signed.

Sanitation:

Parking:

7

Aire Services; Token (3/3)

Located in a small hamlet adj to a small park, no dogs, and bar/tabac. Inspected 2012.

BAGNOLS | 88 | H8 | N45°29.844' E002°38.093' | 63810

Directions: Outside Camping Municipal. Turn off D47, main route, at church, sp 'Camping' and signed. Follow road for 400m then turn right, sp 'Camping' and signed. Service Point to right of campsite entrance, signed.

Sanitation:

Parking:

None

Custom; Apr-Oct

Service Point only. Inspected 2012.

CHASTREIX SKI | 89 | H8 | N45°30.744' E002°44.083' | 63680

Directions: Off D615, behind the church in the centre of small village. Local ski resort also offers motorhome parking: N45°32.125' E002°46.610'.

Sanitation:

Parking:

5

Custom

Alt 1064m. Very small parking area La Tour d'Auvergne 86 has better parking; Local ski resort. Inspected 2010.

MURAT LE QUAIRE | 90 | H8 | N45°36.174' E002°44.251' | 63150

Photo/Info: John Cox

Directions: Route de la Banne d'Ordanche. Turn off D219 opposite church in centre of Murat le Quaire. Follow road and Aire is on right before the lake. Enter through Urba Flux popup barrier.

Sanitation:

Parking:

37; €8/night

Urba Flux tall; 10min water or 2hrs elec €1

Near lake up in the hills. Shower and toilet block onsite; shower €1 for 10 mins. Local commerce 12 mins. Visited 2012.

TOURZEL RONZIERES *

91 | H8 | N45°31.701' E003°08.038' | 63320

Directions: D23/Rue du Dauphiné D'Auvergne. As enter village on D23 from southwest Aire on left, signed. Steep initial acess. GPS given at entrance to avoid confusion.

Sanitation:

Parking:

15

Custom; 1 unmetered elec point

SP

Awesome 180° views of countryside; Pleasant but exposed. Inspected 2010.

SOLIGNAT

92 | H8 | N45°31.026' E003°10.245' | 63500

Directions: Route de Florat, off D32. Follow signs in village from D32, main road through. Do not follow GPS. Aire adj to cemetery.

Sanitation:

Parking:

15; Grass parking

Raclet; €2

SP

Views; Local commerce. Very pleasant, untouristy area; Good views. Inspected 2010.

LE BREUIL SUR COUZE

93 | H8 | N45°28.142' E003°15.663' | 63340

Directions: Allée des Treize Vents, just past railway station. Turn right off D726a after crossing train tracks, sp 'Mairie' and signed. Follow road past train station and Aire on right.

Sanitation:

Parking:

5

Custom

SP

Village with local commerce 5 mins. Inspected 2010.

BRASSAC LES MINES

94 | H8 | N45°24.811' E003°20.118' | 63570

Directions: Place du Musée, by D34/D34a junction. Follow sp 'Jumeaux' and signed as exit town to east on D34. Service Point on right.

Sanitation:

Parking:

None

Flot Bleu Pacific (Green); €2

SP

Service Point adj to main road. Inspected 2010.

CONDAT

95 | H8 | N45°20.335' E002°45.766' | 15190

Directions: D678. Adj to D678 just beside roundabout junction with D679, by river bridge. The Service Point is visible from roundabout.

Sanitation:

Parking:

5

Flot Bleu Pacific; Token

SP

Sign suggests for your security you should stay in campsite but does not ban motorhomes. Inspected 2010.

BRIOUDE | 96 | H8 | N45°17.679' E003°23.256' | 43100

Directions: D588. From N102 enter Brioude on D588 from roundabout. Go under 4m bridge following sp 'Centre Ville', then turn right, sp 'P Centre Historique' and signed. Service Point 50m on right. Parking adj. Sp 'P Centre Historique' throughout town.

Sanitation:

Parking:

20

Flot Bleu Pacific (Burgundy); Token

SP

Adj to city wall; Town 3 mins uphill or via lift. Inspected 2010.

LE BABORY DE BLESLE | 97 | H8 | N45°18.747' E003°11.211' | 43450

Directions: D909, at Hotel Scorpion. Adj to D909 as exit town to north, signed.

Sanitation:

E WC

Parking:

P

25; €10/24hrs; Grass parking

Custom

SP

Pleasant, riverside Commercial Aire; Shower; Dutch owned; English spoken. Inspected 2010.

MASSIAC | 98 | H9 | N45°15.178' E003°11.794' | 15500

Photo: John McMahon

Directions: Rue de l'Allagnon, at the train station. Turn off A75/E11 at Junction 23. Follow sp 'Centre Ville' on N122. Turn right at roundabout with Spar supermarket, sp 'P' and signed. Aire is at far end of car park, sp 'Gare SNCF'.

Sanitation:

E WC F

Parking:

F

10

Custom; Elec €2; May have relocated

SP

Town 2 mins with local commerce. Train station adj. Inspected 2010.

LA CHAPELLE LAURENT | 99 | H9 | N45°10.830' E003°14.635' | 15500

Directions: D10. On D10 as exit town towards St-Laurent-Chabreuges. 20 mins from Junction 25 on A75.

Sanitation:

Parking:

F

10; Grass parking

Custom; €1; Turned off in winter

BBQ; Football pitches. Plenty of local commerce in town. Inspected 2010.

ALLY | 100 | H9 | N45°09.661' E003°18.796' | 43380

Directions: Off D22. In the village follow sp 'Moulin Panoramique'. The Aire is to north of village just before the road to Moulin Panoramique (windmill), behind the buildings.

Sanitation:

E WC

Parking:

F

5

Euro Relais Junior; €2

Alt 1000m. Small windmill adj; Service Point virtually impossible to use due to raised platform. Inspected 2010.

PINOLS | 101 | H9 | N45°03.175' E003°24.760' | 43300

Directions: Off D590. Signs through town. Access narrow in places, do not try any other route. Alternative roads EXTREMELY narrow. Due to difficult access and inadequate facilities we do not advise motorhomes visit here.

Sanitation:

Parking:

5; Max 6m due to access; Grass parking

Custom; €2; Inadequate

Alt 1000m. Next to sports hall, tennis court and playing field. Toilets at sports hall. Inspected 2010.

SIAUGUES ST ROMAIN | 102 | H9 | N45°05.572' E003°37.660' | 43300

Directions: D590. On left adj to D590 as exit village to west.

Sanitation:

Parking:

5

Euro Relais Junior; €2

Centre of mountain bike area. Village adj with small selection of shops; Very small campsite 100m. Inspected 2010.

LOUDES AERODROME | 103 | I9 | N45°04.488' E003°45.671' | 43320

Directions: D906, at Aérodrome. Turn off D906, sp 'Loudes Airport' or follow sp 'Aérodrome de Loudes'. Aire at picnic area on left.

Sanitation:

Parking:

5

Euro Relais Mini; Token (ER)

Overlooking airfield; Parachuting poss. Inspected 2010.

ST PAULIEN | 104 | I9 | N45°07.223' E003°47.607' | 43350

Directions: D25. Turn off D906 in St Paulien by the church onto D13, sp 'Allegre'. Turn left onto D25, sp 'Loudes' and 'Camping'. Service Point on left outside campsite entrance.

Sanitation:

Parking:

None

Urba Flux Tall; €3

Service Point only. Inspected 2012.

CHOMELIX | 105 | I8 | N45°15.707' E003°49.544' | 43500

Directions: D135. Turn off D1 in village centre onto D135, sp 'Estables'. In 10m turn left, sp 'Multi Activities'. Service Point immediately on left. Parking 10m on right.

Sanitation:

Parking:

10

Euro Relais Junior; Token (2/1)

Located adj to sports facilities, 1 min from village centre and commerce. Inspected 2012.

CRAPONNE SUR ARZON	106	I8	N45°20.034' E003°51.043'	43500

Directions: Place de la Gare, D498. Follow D498 out of town to the northeast. The Service Point is adj to D498 at old train station, signed.

Sanitation:

Parking:

None

Euro Relais Junior; €2; Closed in winter

Town 1 min down hill; Adj to old train station in semi industrial area. Inspected 2010.

MARSAC EN LIVRADOIS	107	I8	N45°28.800' E003°43.855'	63940

Directions: D252, outside campsite. Follow D252 east out of town towards river and Aire adj to D252, sp 'Gandrif' and 'Camping de la Graviere'.

Sanitation:

Parking:

None

Aire Services; €2

Service Point only. Inspected 2010.

ARLANC	108	I8	N45°24.718' E003°43.102'	63220

Directions: D300. Exit town to west on D300, sp 'St Bonnet'. Aire is adj to the sports pitch, signed.

Sanitation:

Parking:

5

Euro Relais Junior; Closed in winter

Nice parking under trees in picnic area; Outdoor swimming pool and swimming river; Sports facilities adj. Inspected 2010.

TIRANGES	109	I8	N45°18.421' E003°59.457'	43530

Directions: Heading north on the D24. Turn right in the village centre, sp 'Eco Point' and signed. Aire on right in 400m.

Sanitation:

Parking:

6

Euro Relais Junior; €2

Located on edge of small hamlet 2 mins from centre. Park opp. Inspected 2012.

VALPRIVAS	110	I8	N45°18.627' E004°02.697'	43210

Directions: Rue du Lavoir. Turn off D42 onto D44, sp 'Valprivas'. Turn right in 100m, sp 'Valprivas'. Follow road and the Aire is on the right as enter village.

Sanitation:

Parking:

5

Euro Relais Junior; €2

Located on edge of village 2 mins from centre with bar. Inspected 2012.

ST ANDRE DE CHALENCON | 111 | I8 | N45°16.357' E003°58.215' | 43130

Directions: In village centre turn opp church, the Aire is visible at this point. Aire is 10m on right, signed.

Sanitation:

Parking:

4; Residents use car park

Euro Relais Junior; €2

Sweeping views from parking, but access may be obstructed by local vehicles. Bar 1 min. Inspected 2012.

BAS EN BASSET | 112 | I8 | N45°18.454' E004°07.097' | 43210

Directions: Camping La Garenne. Turn off D42 onto D12 to Bas-en-Basset. At the roundabout turn right, sp 'La Garenne'. Service Point on right outside Camping La Garenne.

Sanitation:

Parking:

5

Euro Relais Junior; €2

Adj to campsite entrance and overlooking carp fishing lake. Campsite €16/night. Reception confirmed that it was OK to stay overnight at the Aire. Town 4 mins walk. Inspected 2012.

BEAUZAC | 113 | I9 | N45°15.717' E004°06.115' | 43590

Directions: D42. Turn off D42 at north side of village, sp 'Espace la Doriliere'. Follow road straight on and the Aire on the lower terrace, signed.

Sanitation:

Parking:

15

Euro Relais Mini

Adj to function hall. Slightly protected from road noise due to high banks. Local commerce 2mins adj to main route and in citadel. Market 8am-12 noon Sun. Inspected 2012.

ST ROMAIN LACHALM | 114 | I8 | N45°15.849' E004°20.149' | 43620

Directions: From the large D45/D23 roundabout take the D25, sp 'St Romain Lachalm' and signed. Follow road to right and turn right in 200m, before La Poste, signed. Exit town and Aire 100m on left, signed.

Sanitation:

Parking:

4

Flot Bleu Pacific; Token; Flot Bleu Electric; 1 Token/4hrs

Landscaped Aire on edge of town with rural views. Local commerce 2 mins. Inspected 2012.

RAUCOULES | 115 | I9 | N45°11.178' E004°17.862' | 43290

Directions: Turn off D61 onto D66, sp 'Raucoules' and signed. Follow road and turn left immediately after cemetery, signed. Aire on right in 20m, signed.

Sanitation:

Parking:

4

Flot Bleu Pacific; Token; Flot Bleu Electric; 1 token/4hrs

Landscaped Aire on edge of town with rural views. Butcher opp, local commerce 2 mins. Inspected 2012.

ST BONNET LE FROID | 116 | I9 | N45°08.481' E004°26.064' | 43290

Directions: Lotissement Herbier des Boenes. Approach on D105 from Montfaucon-en-Velay. In village turn right, signed, and drive up hill into residential area. At top of hill turn left. In 200m turn left again at end of garages, signed.

Sanitation:

Parking:

6; €4/night inc elec

Custom; Water in wooden bin box; 16amp elec in lockable box

Landscaped Aire overlooking town square. Key for elec and Service Point from local commerce (Bar les Genets d'Or/Boucherie Chatelard) on receipt of payment. Inspected 2012.

TENCE | 117 | I9 | N45°06.943' E004°17.549' | 43190

Directions: Off D18. Follow D18 one-way system through town. Turn off D18 down a narrow road which quickly widens, sp 'Parking le Fieu' and 'Maison de Retraite'. Aire in car park on left.

Sanitation:

Parking:

10

Raclet; 2 unmetered elec points

Large car park at rear of town; Service Point turned off in winter, but elec points working when inspected in Nov. Inspected 2010.

ST GERMAIN LEMBRON | 118 | I9 | N45°27.331' E003°14.208' | 63340

Info: Brenda and Maurice Cope

Directions: Rue de la Ronzière. Exit town on D214, sp 'Ardes s/C' and signed. Turn left in 200m, sp 'Salle Polyvalente' and signed. Service Point on left adj to the Salle Polyvalente, signed.

Sanitation:

Parking:

None

Custom

Service Point only. Inspected 2012.

MAZET ST VOY | 119 | I9 | N45°03.246' E004°15.261' | 43520

Photo: Andy and Sue Glasgow

Directions: Off D7. From town centre follow sp 'Camping' east on D7 out of town. Take 2nd left turn. At end of road turn left and follow to campsite. Aire outside Camping Surnette.

Sanitation:

Parking:

None

Raclet; €7.50; Closed in winter

Service Point only. Inspected 2010.

ST JULIEN CHAPTEUIL | 120 | I9 | N45°02.347' E004°03.713' | 43260

Directions: D28/Route de l'Holme. Exit town to north on D28, sp 'Yssingeaux'. Aire adj to the municipal campsite. Entrance by sports field, signed.

Sanitation:

Parking:

None

Custom

Service Point only. Inspected 2010.

LES ESTABLES

121 I9 N44°54.155' E004°09.427' 43150

Directions: D36. Situated in the village centre at fuel station, signed.

Sanitation:

Parking:

10

Custom; Free if buy fuel

Alt 1343m. Small village with lots of parking. Inspected 2010.

LE MONASTIER SUR GAZEILLE

122 I9 N44°56.228' E003°59.584' 43150

Directions: Rue Augustin Ollier. Follow D38, main route, through village and turn beside church, sp 'Camping'. The parking area is the 2nd turning on the right by the sports facilities, signed. For the Service Point do not take the 2nd right but carry straight on. It is outside the campsite, signed: N44°56.207' E003°59.155'. Be careful exiting town as it is narrow in places.

Sanitation:

Parking:

15

Custom

Aire at the sports facilities. Town 2 mins uphill with local commerce. Parking has rural view. Inspected 2010.

PRADELLES

123 I9 N44°46.537' E003°53.244' 43420

Directions: N88. On N88 to north of town at local produce shop 'Saveurs des Montagnes', next to the football pitch. Opp side of road to boucherie and charcuterie 'Saveurs des Montaunes'.

Sanitation:

Parking:

20; Max 48hrs; Grass parking

Custom; Elec avail; Pay at shop

Alt 1200m. Aire/France Passion at local produce shop; English spoken. Inspected 2010.

COUBON

124 I9 N44°59.836' E003°55.006' 43700

Photo: Andy and Sue Glasgow

Directions: D37/Route du Plan d'Eau. In Coubon centre by the river bridge at the village car park, beside the church and cemetery.

Sanitation:

Parking:

10; 6m max

Custom; €2.50; Open Mar-Nov

Village centre adj; Very busy car park with local cars; 5m bays, max 6m motorhomes; Inspected 2010.

LE PUY EN VELAY

125 I9 N45°02.979' E003°53.394' 43000

Directions: D13/Boulevard de Cluny. From D91 exit, sp 'Vichy'. Service Point in 200m on right before the Super U fuel station, signed.

Sanitation:

Parking:

None; See **124**

Euro Relais Junior; Token (ER)

Service Point only. Inspected 2010.

BEAULIEU | 126 | I9 | N45°07.554' E003°56.833' | 43800

Directions: Tir Sportif. Turn off D103 at traffic lights in Lavoute-sur-Loire onto D7, sp 'Beaulieu'. In Beaulieu turn right at Elan fuel station, sp 'Tir Sportif' and signed. Take the next left, signed, and the Aire is 200m on right, signed.

Sanitation:

Parking:

6

Custom; 4 unmetered CEE elec points

Aire with rural views adj to sports facilities. Village centre with local commerce 4 mins. Inspected 2012.

RETOURNAC | 127 | I9 | N45°12.259' E004°02.712' | 43130

Directions: Rue de l'Industrie. Turn off D9 at river bridge, sp 'Aire de Pique Nique' and signed. Follow sp 'Aire de Pique Nique' and the Aire is adj to the picnic area, signed. Service Point 100m by toilets.

Sanitation:

Parking:

6

Custom; Push down red tops for water

A popular Aire adj to river suitable for fishing, but no view. Riverside park with picnic tables adj. Town centre and commerce 4 mins. Inspected 2012.

VOREY | 128 | I9 | N45°11.200' E003°54.283' | 43800

Directions: Chemin des Félines, next to Camping les Moulettes. Turn off D103 north of the river, signed. Pass the campsite and Aire is alongside the river.

Sanitation:

Parking:

3

Custom; Token; €3

Adj to river overlooking sports field; Town centre 2 mins. Inspected 2010.

ST CHRISTOPHE SUR DOLAISON | 129 | I9 | N44°59.881' E003°49.293' | 43370

Directions: D31. Turn off D906 onto D31 in St Christophe sur Dolaison. Drive through village and Service Point is situated against a building behind Mairie, signed.

Sanitation:

Parking:

5

Euro Relais Mini; Token (ER)

Pleasant village with local commerce. Inspected 2010.

LE VERNET | 130 | I9 | N45°02.117' E003°40.193' | 43320

Directions: D48. Aire located on right as exit village on D40 towards St Berain, signed.

Sanitation:

Parking:

40; €2 inc service; Collected

Custom; €2; CEE elec; Collected

Large parking area adj to wood with adventure activities, maps from TO 150m. Village and bar adj. Inspected 2012.

SAUGUES | 131 | H9 | N44°57.587' E003°32.641' | 43170

Directions: Place du Breuil. Exit town centre, sp 'Langeac'. Turn left and left again both, sp 'Centre Culturel - Aire Camping-Car'. Aire on left in large car park, signed.

Sanitation:

Parking:

20

Euro Relais Mini

Aire in large car park. Small town commerce, tourist/walking shops and restaurants 1 min. Inspected 2012.

CHANALEILLES | 132 | H9 | N44°51.567' E003°29.431' | 43170

Directions: D587. Enter village from Sauges and the Aire on left adj to D587, signed.

Sanitation:

Parking:

5

Custom; Not finished, cost unknown

Landscaped Aire on edge of village adj to stream and has rural views. Gîte adj. Inspected 2012.

RUYNES EN MARGERIDE | 133 | H9 | N45°00.075' E003°13.437' | 15320

Directions: D4. Turn off D4 as exit village towards Paulhav, signed. Service Point in corner on left beside trees, opp houses.

Sanitation:

Parking:

20; Plenty of parking space

Aire Services; €2

Small park adj. Village with local commerce and convenience store 1 min. Inspected 2012.

FAVEROLLES | 134 | H9 | N44°56.339' E003°08.858' | 15320

Directions: D248. Turn off D13 onto D248, sp 'St Marc'. Aire on left in 200m, signed.

Sanitation:

Parking:

5

Aire Services; €2

In town square adj to Mairie. Local commerce adj. Château, 4 mins, open 2-6pm. Viaduc de Garabit 5km north, goes over D909 and was designed by Eifel, of Eifel tower. Inspected 2012.

ST FLOUR 1 | 135 | H9 | N45°02.157' E003°05.905' | 03100

Directions: Rue Marie-Aimee Maraville. Exit at Junction 28 on A75, sp 'St Flour'. At roundabout follow sp 'St Flour'. Follow road until enter town (at bottom of hill). Turn right, signed. Follow road, turning left across bridge, and Aire is then on right.

Sanitation:

Parking:

10

Euro Relais Maxi; €2

Views of hilltop town. Thermal water. Shops and lower town centre 2 mins. Inspected 2012.

ST FLOUR 2

136 | H9 | N45°02.053' E003°05.250' | 15100

Directions: Cours Chazerat. Take D926 up hill, sp 'Haute Ville'. At top of hill go straight on at roundabout and through car park. Turn left at roundabout and then next left into Cours Chazerat. Service Point in Cours Chazerat.

Sanitation:

E

Parking:

50

Euro Relais Maxi; €2

SP

Hilltop town; Bandstand; Town 2 mins. Inspected 2012.

HAVE YOU VISITED AN AIRE? **GPS co-ordinates in this guide are protected by copyright law**

Take at least 5 digital photos showing
• Signs
• Service Point
• Parking
• Overview
• Amenities

Visit www.all-the-aires.co.uk/submissions.shtml to upload your updates and photos.

Sanitation:

E

Aire Details:

Submit updates
- Amendments
- New Aires
- Not changed

CHAUDES AIGUES

138 | H9 | N44°50.986' E003°00.182' | 15110

Directions: Off D981. Turn off D921 onto D989 in town, signed. Do not cross river bridge, but drive straight on through gap into large car park behind.

Sanitation:

E

Parking:

20

Raclet; €2

SP

Town 2 mins; Natural spring water 87°F. Aire in unglamorous, but well located car park. Inspected 2010.

PIERREFORT

139 | H9 | N44°55.331' E002°50.494' | 15230

Directions: Côte de Chabridet, off D990. Turn off D990 in the town onto Côte de Chabridet, signed. Aire is on right in 300m next to Centre Medico-Social.

Sanitation:

E

Parking:

3

Euro Relais Tall; CC or Token; €2

SP

Residential street. Just uphill from town centre. Board indicates other villages that allow motorhome parking. Inspected 2010.

PAULHAC

SKI | 140 | H9 | N45°00.387' E002°54.246' | 15430

Directions: D44. Exit village northwest on D44 towards Plomb du Cantal. Service Point adj to end of Mairie, signed.

Sanitation:

E

Parking:

None at Service Point; Limited village parking

Custom; 1 unmetered elec point; No drive over drain

SP

Service Point turned off in winter; Local cross country skiing. Inspected 2010.

VALUEJOLS | 141 | H9 | N45°03.216' E002°55.782' | 15300

Directions: Place du 19 Mars 1962, off D134. Turn off D34 onto D134 in the village, sp 'Centre d'Accueil'. Aire is at the Centre d'Accueil, next to the cemetery.

Sanitation:

Parking:

15; €3; Collected

Euro Relais Mini; €2; Honesty box

SP

Cross country skiing; Walking in summer. Inspected 2010.

TALIZAT | 142 | H9 | N45°06.846' E003°02.754' | 15170

Directions: D679. Clearly signed off D679 in village. From west Aire on right, opp Mairie.

Sanitation:

E

Parking:

F

2

Raclet; Token (ER); No drive over drain

SP

Small village adj. Inspected 2010.

COLTINES | 143 | H9 | N45°05.754' E002°59.142' | 15170

Directions: D40. Exit the village to north towards Celles and the Aire is adj to the sports facilities, signed.

Sanitation:

E

Parking:

P

F

5

Euro Relais Junior; Token (ER)

SP

Exposed rural Aire with far reaching views. Inspected 2010.

NEUSSARGUES MOISSAC | 144 | H9 | N45°08.065' E002°58.881' | 15170

Directions: N122/D679 junction. Turn off N122 to Neussargues-Moissac and Aire is on the right, signed.

Sanitation:

E WC

Parking:

P

F

5

Euro Relais Tall; CC/Token (ER)

SP

On edge of village near main road. Inspected 2010.

MURAT | 145 | H9 | N45°06.563' E002°52.147' | 15300

Directions: N122. From south on D926 turn left onto N122 immediately after crossing train tracks, sp 'Aurillac'. Service Point at far side of train station car park in 200m. Parking: Stade, opp train track: N45°06.531' E002°52.240'. Swimming pool: N45°06.503' E002°51.713' or Car park at D3 roundabout: N45°06.859' E002°51.747'.

Sanitation:

E WC

Parking:

F

3 parking areas in town

Raclet; €2

SP

Large town ideal for servicing motorhome and stocking up before visiting Le Loiren Ski resort. Inspected 2012.

ALLANCHE | 146 | H9 | N45°13.788' E002°55.892' | 15160

Photo: Rita Renninghoff

Directions: Chemin de la Roche Marchal. Exit town to north on D9, sp 'Vernols'. Aire 300m from centre of town, adj to D9 at old train station (La Gare), signed.

Sanitation:

Parking:

25

Bollard; Token (2/1); €2

TO adj; Railway track now a Vélo-Rail; Small town commerce 4 mins. Inspected 2010.

ST SATURNIN | 147 | H9 | N45°15.520' E002°48.143' | 15190

Directions: D21A. Follow sp 'Camping' from town. Service Point is in the entrance to the municipal campsite.

Sanitation:

Parking:

20; Pay in high season; Open May-Sept

Euro Relais Mini

Service Point in entrance of very basic municipal campsite. Bar and lake opp. Village centre 2 mins. Inspected 2012.

SEGUR LES VILLAS | 148 | H9 | N45°13.390' E002°49.111' | 15300

Directions: Turn off D3 into Segur-les-Villas. Turn off main route through at Vival convenience store and drive along side of store, signed. In 250m turn right, signed.

Sanitation:

Parking:

8; Grass parking

Euro Relais Junior; Token (ER)

Alt 1200. Aire located adj to sports pitch in an isolated mountain village with local commerce. Inspected 2012.

ROIM ES MONTAGNES | 149 | H9 | N45°17.059' E002°39.263' | 15400

Directions: Between D3 and Rue du Champ de Foire. Turn off D49 at roundabout by old train station, signed. Cross the tracks and turn immediately right, signed. Service Point on right, opp cattle market.

Sanitation:

Parking:

Local parking

Flot Bleu Pacific; €2; No drive over drain

Service Point only but there is lots of local unrestricted parking. Inspected 2010.

VALETTE | 150 | H9 | N45°16.198' E002°36.135' | 15400

Directions: Off D678. Turn off D678 in village, signed. Aire in 100m in new housing development.

Sanitation:

Parking:

5; 8m bays

Euro Relais Junior; €2

Landscaped Aire in rural location; On cheese route. Inspected 2010.

CHAMPS SUR TARENTAINE MARCHAL | 151 | G8 | N45°23.672' E002°33.486' | 15270

Directions: D679. Adj to D679 through gate to house 16, signed. Nearly opp Elan garage, specializing as HGV mechanic.

Sanitation:

Parking:

1 hard surface; Additional grass parking

Euro Relais Mini

SP

Start of Gorges de la Rhue drive. Village 1 min with local commerce. Inspected 2010.

BORT LES ORGUES | 152 | G8 | N45°23.950' E002°29.833' | 19110

Photo: Rita Renninghoff

Directions: Rue Font Grande. Best access via D979. Turn off D979 into town. Turn right before river bridge by Gendarmerie, sp 'Complex Sportif' and signed. Follow road along river to Aire. Aire is signed on all routes through town. Some routes are narrow with difficult turns.

Sanitation:

Parking:

5

Custom

SP

River views; Town commerce 1 min; Hyper market within walking distance. Inspected 2010.

CHAMPAGNAC | 153 | G8 | N45°21.455' E002°23.956' | 15350

Directions: D12. Turn onto D12 between the church and the war memorial, sp 'St Pierre'. Take next right, signed, and Service Point is on right.

Sanitation:

Parking:

Poss, in village square by church

Euro Relais Mini

SP

In remote village near Dordogne river. There is no designated parking or parking by the Service Point. Inspected 2012.

LAC DE NEUVIC (LIGINIAC) | 154 | G8 | N45°23.460' E002°18.214' | 19160

Directions: Turn off D982 north of Neuvic onto D183, sp 'Yeux'. Follow D183 around lake edge towards Liginiac. Turn off D183, sp 'Le Maury' and follow road downhill. Service Point on left, signed. Unrestricted parking with lake view further down hill.

Sanitation:

Parking:

10

Urba Flux

SP

Adj to reservoir with swimming beach and sports facilities. Parking adj to water does not exclude motorhomes even though there is a campsite nearby. Inspected 2012.

USSEL | 155 | G8 | N45°32.865' E002°17.013' | 19200

Directions: D157/Rte de Ponty. After crossing river take D157 northwest towards Meymac. Aire is at Centre Touristique de Ponty at the lake to the west of Ussel, opp Camping Municipal de Ponty.

Sanitation:

Parking:

None

Raclet; €2

SP

Service Point only. Inspected 2010.

LA COURTINE | 156 | G8 | N45°42.351' E002°15.545' | 23100

Photo/Info: John Cox

Directions: Impasse Jacques Bayle. From La Courtine take the D982 towards Aubusson. Turn right to the side of the Casino convenience store, signed. Follow road for 250m and turn left into Impasse Jacques Bayle and Aire on right, signed.

Sanitation:

Parking:

10; Max 24hrs

Euro Relais Junior; Token; €2

Local commerce 5 mins. Large lake 2 mins.

MEYMAC 2 | 157 | G8 | N45°31.803' E002°08.521' | 19250

Directions: D36, outside Casino supermarket. Adj to roundabout junction of D36/D30.

Sanitation:

Parking:

Poss; Also see 158

Flot Bleu Euro; CC

Adj to supermarket. Inspected 2010.

MEYMAC 1 | 158 | G8 | N45°31.500' E002°07.657' | 19250

Photo: Rita Renninghoff

Directions: Base Nautique de Sèchemaille, at lake off D76. Outside of village at holiday village by Lac de Sèchemailles. Follow sp 'Lac de Sèchemailles' through town.

Sanitation:

Parking:

20

Euro Relais Junior; Token (ER)

Leisure lake with good walks. Likely to be busy July/Aug. Inspected 2010.

EGLETONS | 159 | G8 | N45°24.233' E002°02.850' | 19300

Directions: Parking de l'Espace Ventadour on Rue Henri Dignac, off D1089. Turn off D1089 onto Rue Henri Dignac, signed. Follow road down hill and Service Point at bottom on right, signed.

Sanitation:

Parking:

5

Custom; €2

Village 1 min with local commerce. Inspected 2010.

MARCILLAC LA CROISILLE | 160 | G9 | N45°15.725' E002°00.343' | 19320

Photo: Rita Renninghoff

Directions: At corner of Rte du Puy Nachet and Promenade du Lac. 2km from village at Barrage de la Valette. Follow sp 'Lac du Valette' from village.

Sanitation:

Parking:

20

Raclet; No drive over drain

Parking overlooking large leisure lake with boating and swimming. Inspected 2010.

ST PRIVAT | 161 | G9 | N45°08.406' E002°05.860' | 19220

Directions: Rue des Chanaux, off D13. Follow sp 'Aire Service' through town. Aire on outskirts of village, well signed.

Sanitation:

Parking:

5

Euro Relais Junior; €2

SP

Village with commerce 2 mins; Pleasant location. Inspected 2010.

MAURIAC | 162 | G9 | N45°13.110' E002°19.311' | 15200

Directions: On road to Lac du Barrage D'Enchanet. Follow sp 'Camping' through village. Aire on left as approach campsite and lake, signed.

Sanitation:

Parking:

10

Euro Relais Tall; Token (ER) or CC

SP

Leisure lake with swimming beach, boats and play area 2 mins down hill; Motorhomes banned from all other car parks. Inspected 2010.

MAURIAC 2 | 163 | G9 | N45°12.864' E002°20.801' | 15200

Directions: D922. Exit town on D922 towards Aurillac. Turn off roundabout into Carrefour supermarket and the Aire is located in the car park near the fuel station.

Sanitation:

Parking:

2

Flot Bleu Marine; €2/20 mins; No drive over drain

SP

Supermarket adj. Inspected 2012.

DRUGEAC | 164 | G9 | N45°10.026' E002°23.203' | 15140

Photo: Margaret Dean

Directions: D29. Turn off D922 onto D29, sp 'Drugeac' and signed. Cross the railway track and take the 1st turning on the right onto D29. The Aire is 200m at the old train station.

Sanitation:

Parking:

8

Euro Relais Maxi; €2; Apr-Nov; No drive over drain

SP

Village 2 mins down hill; Waterfall walk on D922 at Salins. Inspected 2010.

SALINS | 165 | G9 | N45°11.492' E002°23.617' | 15200

Directions: D922. Heading south on D922 turn off, sp 'Salins' and signed. Drive down steep hill and turn left in 200m, signed.

Sanitation:

Parking:

3; 7m max

Custom

SP

3 small bays in a small car park with difficult access; Cascade waterfall visible from N922, can be walked to from village. Inspected 2010.

PLEAUX | 166 | G9 | N45°08.141' E002°13.708' | 15700

Directions: Place d'Empeyssine, off D666. Approach from north on D680 and take the 1st left turn, sp 'D666', 'Centre Ville', and signed. The Aire is adj to square, on the left.

Sanitation:

Parking:

5; Parking opposite Service Point

Custom

Small town commerce 1 min. Inspected 2010.

SALERS | 167 | G9 | N45°08.909' E002°29.927' | 15140

Directions: Off D680. Follow sp 'Camping' through village. Service Point is outside Camping Le Mourial, sp 'Camping Municipal'. Parking is adj to campsite and sports facilities, signed. Day parking on D680 ring road to north of town, signed: N45°08.417' E002°29.676'.

Sanitation:

Parking:

10; €3 + €0.50pp tax

Aire Services; Token; €2

Pretty, historic village with cobbled streets. Inspected 2010.

ST MARTIN VALMEROUX | 168 | G9 | N45°06.958' E002°25.231' | 15140

Directions: D37/Rue de Montjoly. Turn off D922 in the village onto D37, sp 'Loupiac' and 'Camping'. The Service Point is in 450m past the campsite, signed. 3.5t weight restriction on car park.

Sanitation:

Parking:

10

Euro Relais Maxi; €2

Adj to pleasant campsite; Town centre 3 mins. Inspected 2010.

MANDAILLES ST JULIEN | 169 | H9 | N45°04.157' E002°39.368' | 15590

Photo: Ruth Grant

Directions: D17/Route des Crêtes. Enter town from south on D17. Cross over bridge and turn left to Aire.

Sanitation:

Parking:

5; Max 24hrs

Euro Relais Junior; Token; €3.50

On road to Puy Mary. Very Scenic drive up to 1500m, closed if it snows. Inspected 2010.

LE LIORAN | SKI | 170 | H9 | N45°05.300' E002°44.300' | 15300

Photo: Rita Renninghoff

Directions: Off D67. Turn off N122 onto D67 at the roundabout before the tunnel. Turn right, then left following sp 'Parking Camping-Car'. Parking 100m in car park.

Sanitation:

Parking:

30

None; See 172

Popular ski area and parking is 2 mins from chair lifts. Local commerce open ski season or high summer 2 mins. Inspected 2010.

VELZIC — 171 — H9 — N45°00.110' E002°32.777' — 15590

Directions: From Aurillac turn left off D17 in Velzic, signed. Drive past Mairie and follow road. The Aire is adj to the river, signed.

Sanitation:

Parking:

6; Max 24hrs

Euro Relais Mini; Token (ER)

Pleasant riverside spot in rural location. Inspected 2010.

THIEZAC — 172 — H9 — N45°00.961' E002°39.762' — 15800

Photo:Rita Renninghoff

Directions: D59. Turn off N122 onto D59 or D759 into Thiézac. Follow road through village and the Aire is by the river bridge, signed.

Sanitation:

Parking:

5; Max 24hrs

Raclet; Token; €3.50

Alt 788m. Local commerce in village. Ski resort Le Lioran nearby. Inspected 2010.

HAVE YOU VISITED AN AIRE?

GPS co-ordinates in this guide are protected by copyright law

Take at least 5 digital photos showing
- Signs
- Service Point
- Parking
- Overview
- Amenities

Visit www.all-the-aires.co.uk/submissions.shtml to upload your updates and photos.

Sanitation:

Aire Details:

Submit updates
- Amendments
- New Aires
- Not changed

VIC SUR CERE — 174 — H9 — N44°58.942' E002°37.891' — 15800

Photo: Rita Renninghoff

Directions: Place de l'Egalité, Avenue des Tilleuls. Turn off N122, sp 'Camping' and 'Aire de Camping-Car'. Turn left in front of cemetery, signed. Follow road past campsite and the Aire is on the right.

Sanitation:

Parking:

10

Euro Relais Junior; Token (ER)

Alt 667m. Ecomarché nearby; 4 mins to local commerce. Inspected 2010.

NAUCELLES — 175 — G9 — N44°57.393' E002°25.044' — 15000

Directions: Rue du Terrou. Turn off D922 onto D253 at roundabout south of Naucelles, sp 'Crandelles'. In 200m turn right, sp 'Mairie'. At the stop junction turn right, signed. Turn right at next junction and Service Point is on left side of car park.

Sanitation:

Parking:

7

Euro Relais Mini; Token (ER)

Located 300m from D922 in centre of village but is surrounded by sports facilities and amenity grass. Local commerce 2 mins. Inspected 2012.

JUSSAC | 176 | G9 | N44°59.327' E002°25.158' | 15250

Directions: Promenade des Sports, off D922. Turn off D922 in Jussac, sp 'Salle Polyvalente'. Aire at sports facilities, signed.

Sanitation:

Parking:

5; Max 24hrs; No parking Jul-Aug

None

SP

Parking only adj to sports facilites. Village with local commerce 2 mins. Inspected 2010.

AURILLAC | 177 | G9 | N44°55.790' E002°26.971' | 15000

Directions: Champ de Foire, off D17. Follow sp 'Puy Mary' through town, then 'Aire de Camping Car'. In town near river, well signed.

Sanitation:

Parking:

10

Euro Relais Junior; Token (ER)

SP

Busy town with commerce 2 mins; River 2 mins. Noisy bar opp. Inspected 2010.

VEZAC | 178 | G9 | N44°53.425' E002°31.073' | 15130

Directions: D206. Turn off the D990 onto D206, sp 'Labrousse', 'Golf', and signed. The Aire is on the left in 600m, signed.

Sanitation:

Parking:

2; Max 24hrs

Euro Relais Mini; Token (ER)

SP

Golf course opp; Restaurant 1 min. Inspected 2010.

LACAPELLE VIESCAMP | 179 | G9 | N44°55.275' E002°15.820' | 15150

Directions: D18. On the outskirts of the village at the entrance of municipal campsite, opp local shop.

Sanitation:

Parking:

None

Euro Relais Junior; Token (ER); €2

SP

Service Point only outside campsite; Large reservoir with some parking. Inspected 2010.

SANSAC DE MARMIESSE | 180 | G9 | N44°53.036' E002°20.805' | 15130

Directions: Rue de la Vidalie, off N122. Adj to N122 at the local shops/retail area, signed.

Sanitation:

Parking:

3; Max 24hrs

Euro Relais Junior; Token (ER)

SP

Local commerce adj; Convenient night halt just off N122. Inspected 2010.

ST MAMET LA SALVETAT

181 | G9 | N44°51.422' E002°18.596' | 15220

Directions: Allée des Coudercs. Turn off N122 onto D32, sp 'St Mamet'. Follow D32 into village. Go straight over roundabout onto D20, signed. Aire on left in 400m.

Sanitation:

Parking:

3

Euro Relais Junior; Token (ER)

Peaceful location on edge of village. Picnic area 100m and local commerce 2 mins. Inspected 2012.

YTRAC

182 | G9 | N44°54.902' E002°21.816' | 15000

Directions: Impasse Jean de la Fontaine, off D18 at Parking Centre Culturel et Sportif. Aire adj to D18, signed as enter village from north. Follow road in front of cultural building and Aire behind building.

Sanitation:

Parking:

4; Max 48hrs

Raclet; Token (ER)

Village adj; Benches; Commerce 2 mins. Inspected 2010.

ST CERNIN

183 | G9 | N45°03.191' E002°25.584' | 15310

Directions: D160. Follow D160 south out of town, staying left when road forks, sp 'Route des Crêtes'. Aire on right.

Sanitation:

Parking:

None

Euro Relais Junior

Service Point only. Inspected 2010.

AYRENS

184 | G9 | N44°59.138' E002°19.627' | 15250

Directions: Off D53c. At D52/D53 junction in village turn onto D53, sp 'Jassac'. Follow road behind church and turn left, sp 'Terrain de Sports'. Aire in 100m.

Sanitation:

Parking:

5

Euro Relais Mini; Token (ER)

Limited parking in tiny village adj to small wood yard. Inspected 2010.

CRANDELLES

185 | G9 | N44°57.529' E002°20.512' | 15250

Directions: Off D59, at Lac des Genevrières. At Crandelles follow sp 'Lac des Genevrières' and signed. Aire overlooking lake.

Sanitation:

Parking:

5; Max 24hrs

Raclet; Token (ER)

Overlooking lake; Village 2 mins; Bar adj. Swimming/activity lake adj; Pleasant. Inspected 2010.

ST PAUL DES LANDES | 186 | G9 | N44°56.562' E002°19.008' | 15250

Directions: D53. Turn off D120 onto D53. Aire signed on right.

Sanitation:

Parking:

5; Max 24hrs

Euro Relais Mini; Token (ER)

SP

Near D120, some road noise; In residential area. Inspected 2010.

LAROQUEBROU | 187 | G9 | N44°57.892' E002°11.803' | 15150

Directions: D653. As enter village from east on D653. Aire opp turning to municipal campsite on east bank of river.

Sanitation:

Parking:

1

Flot Bleu Fontaine; €2

SP

Service Point near pleasant municipal campsite on edge of riverside town. Inspected 2010.

MONTSALVY | 188 | G9 | N44°42.477' E002°29.792' | 15120

Photo: June and Michael Beevers

Directions: Off D19. From north turn off D920 onto D19 into town. Aire 250m on left before Centre de Secours.

Sanitation:

Parking:

8

Raclet; €2

SP

Near village with countryside views. Showers €1. Inspected 2010.

VIEILLEVIE | 189 | G9 | N44°38.662' E002°25.064' | 15120

Directions: D141. Adj to D141 in the centre of the village opp TO, signed. D141 is a narrow, but passable, gorge road.

Sanitation:

Parking:

5

Euro Relais Junior; €2; Closed in winter

SP

Located in centre of village with local and tourist shops and cafés. There is a river 100m across a flood plain that is used as summer car parking. Inspected 2012.

CASSANIOUZE | 190 | G9 | N44°41.629' E002°22.949' | 15340

Directions: Lieu-Dit le Bourg Nord. Turn off D601 in the village, signed. Turn right and right again, signed.

Sanitation:

Parking:

6

Euro Relais Junior; €2; Closed in winter

SP

Aire in very rural village. Calvinet has a municipal campsite masquerading as an Aire but is charging €6.40 per night. Inspected 2012.

MONTMURAT | 191 | G9 | N44°37.685' E002°11.860' | 15600

Directions: D345. From Maurs on D663 turn right onto D45 at St Constant. Turn right onto D345, sp 'Montmurat'. Follow D345 and Aire on left just before village. DO NOT take motorhome into village, very narrow and steep.

Sanitation:

Parking:

5

Flot Bleu Fontaine; €2

Picnic area and viewpoint above Aire with 360° views. Inspected 2010.

MAURS LA JOLIE | 192 | G9 | N44°42.872' E002°11.762' | 15600

Directions: Route de Quezac. Turn off N122 in town, signed. Follow road beside Hotel Bar Le Plaisance and drive for 500m. Aire on left outside cemetery, signed.

Sanitation:

Parking:

6

Euro Relais Junior; Token (ER)

Adj to cemetery. 3 mins from town with local commerce and a bank. Inspected 2012.

CAYROLS | 193 | G9 | N44°49.783' E002°13.967' | 15290

Photo: Rita Renninghoff

Directions: D51, at sports facilities. On main route through village, signed. Parking has 5.5t weight restriction.

Sanitation:

Parking:

10

Euro Relais Junior; Token (2/1)

Pleasant location by community sports facilities; Local commerce in village. Inspected 2010.

BEAULIEU SUR DORDOGNE | 194 | G9 | N44°58.590' E001°50.464' | 19120

Directions: Rue Gontrand Roye. Turn off D940 near TO onto D41, sp 'Astaillac'. Turn left off D41 as exit town, sp 'Du Pont (Municipal)'. Aire 50m.

Sanitation:

Parking:

20; €5/night Sept-June, €10/night July-Aug

Custom; Tap under green cover, hose connection needed; Turned off in Oct

Aire adj to canoe slalom course. Town centre 3 mins bans motorhomes but has town commerce. Inspected 2012.

SERVIERES LE CHATEAU * | 195 | G9 | N45°08.670' E002°02.201' | 19220

Directions: At the northern edge of Lac de Feyt, off D75. Follow D75 to north of village. Follow sp 'Centre Touristique du Lac de Feyt', then sp 'Camping'. At campsite entrance turn left and follow road to end.

Sanitation:

Parking:

15

Euro Relais Junior; €2

Pleasant parking overlooking large leisure lake; Set in woodland; Boating and swimming. Inspected 2010.

FORGES | 196 | G9 | N45°09.205' E001°52.265' | 19380

Directions: Rue Pierre et Marie Curie. Exit D1120, sp 'Camping Municipal'. Aire at entrance of municipal campsite.

Sanitation:

Parking:

5; 2 hardstanding

Euro Relais Junior; €2

Small basic municipal campsite and sports ground adj. Parking is possible on 2 hard standing bays beside the Service Point. Local commerce 1 min. Inspected 2012.

TURENNE | 197 | F9 | N45°03.233' E001°34.837' | 19500

Directions: D8. Turn off D8 in Turenne at TO. Drive behind TO and follow road. Aire on left, signed.

Sanitation:

Parking:

14; Max 48hrs

Euro Relais; Token; €4

Views of town. Quaint hilltop town. Local commerce, TO 2 mins uphill. Inspected 2010.

COLLONGES LA ROUGE | 198 | F9 | N45°03.523' E001°39.551' | 19500

Directions: P Le Marchadial, off D38. Exit town to west towards Meyssac on D38. Take right turn, sp 'Village de Vacances'. Turn right again, sp 'Aire de Service CC'. Aire on left.

Sanitation:

Parking:

40; €5/24hrs

Custom

Pretty tourist village 1km. Rural views. Inspected 2010.

DAMPNIAT | 199 | G9 | N45°09.763' E001°38.258' | 19360

Directions: From church in Dampniat centre follow signs to Aire. Located down narrow lane at sports facilities, 1km from centre.

Sanitation:

Parking:

5

Euro Relais Junior; €2

By sports facilities; Panoramic views. Village with local commerce 1km (hilly). Inspected 2010.

TULLE | 200 | G9 | N45°16.494' E001°46.440' | 19000

Directions: Quai Victor Continsouza. Exit town centre to north on D23, sp 'Correze'. In 200m turn right across river bridge into retail park. Service Point in fuel station of Intermarché supermarket, signed.

Sanitation:

Parking:

Poss

Euro Relais Box; Token (ER) or €2

Supermarket and retail park adj. Inspected 2012.

DONZENAC | 201 | F9 | N45°13.126' E001°31.140' | 19270

Directions: D25. Follow sp 'La Rivière' out of town on D920. At roundabout turn onto D25 and entrance on right. Aire just before campsite barrier on left, signed.

Sanitation:

Parking:

10

Euro Relais Mini; Elec €3.40/night; Not working June 2012

Historic town over 1km up hill; Campsite adj; Showers €2 when campsite open. Inspected 2010.

ALLASSAC | 202 | F8 | N45°15.531' E001°28.410' | 19240

Directions: Ave du Saillant, opp train station. Follow sp 'Gare' in town. 6m bays with no opportunity to overhang.

Sanitation:

Parking:

4; 6m bays; Max 3 days

Euro Relais Junior; 2 unmetered elec points

Town centre 5 mins with local commerce. Train station adj. Pretty town. Inspected 2010.

OBJAT | 203 | F8 | N45°16.267' E001°24.717' | 19130

Photo: Rita Renninghoff

Directions: D148e3/Ave Jules Ferry. From D901 turn onto D148e3 in Objat. Follow road north out of town towards Les Grandes Terres, following sp 'Aire de Camping-Car'. Aire on right, signed. Entry code from TO in village by war memorial: N45°15.869' E001°24.591'.

Sanitation:

Parking:

21; €5/day inc 16amp elec; Max 72hrs

Euro Relais Junior; Token (3/3)

Small lake nearby; TO, open 10am-12 noon and 2pm-6pm daily, has internet access; Showers available by token. Inspected 2010.

SADROC | 204 | F8 | N45°16.983' E001°32.918' | 19270

Directions: D9, in the village centre by the church. Follow sp 'Sadroc' from A20/E9. In Sadroc centre turn right by tabac and right again to Aire.

Sanitation:

Parking:

6; Max 24hrs

Custom

In village centre; Church adj. Inspected 2010.

VIGEOIS - LAC DE PONTCHARAL | 205 | F8 | N45°22.049' E001°32.037' | 19410

Photo/Info: John Cox

Directions: D7. Exit E9/A20 at Junction 45, sp Vigeois and take the D3 to Vigeois. Exit Vigeois on D7 to south, sp 'Lac de Pontcharal'. Aire on left adj to the D7, signed.

Sanitation:

Parking:

10

Euro Relais Junior; Token ER; €2

Located by leisure lake with beach but no views. Lovely area but may feel isolated at night. Visited 2012.

CONCEZE | 206 | F8 | N45°21.267' E001°20.733' | 19350

Directions: D56e, in small village. Turn off D901 onto D56e heading east into town. Turn by church and Aire is 10m on left, signed.

Sanitation:

Parking:

5; Grass parking

Custom

Restaurant/bar; On Limousin Apple Orchard route; Local parking by church or on grass in summer. Inspected 2010.

AYEN | 207 | F8 | N45°14.988' E001°19.410' | 19310

Info/Photo: John and Janet Thay

Directions: Exit village to north on D39 towards St Robert. Turn left by Centre D'incendie et de Secours building on outskirts of village, sp 'Ayen-Bas' and signed. The Aire is behind the Secours building outside the Atelier Municipal, works yard

Sanitation:

Parking:

5

Custom

Small Aire with rural views on edge of small village Visited 2012.

UZERCHE * | 208 | G8 | N45°25.471' E001°33.968' | 19140

Directions: Rue Paul Langevin, at Place de la Petite Gare. Well signed through town. Aire located adj to river, off D3 as exit town to east towards Eyburie.

Sanitation:

Parking:

20

Custom; 40 unmetered elec points

Nice town to wander around. River views; Cannot stay during fair visit; No parking Sat am or 20th of each month. Inspected 2010.

TREIGNAC | 209 | G8 | N45°32.608' E001°47.949' | 19260

Directions: Parking des Rivieres, off D940 in large gravel area by river. Adj to D940 north of Treignac, towards Gueret. At roundabout with industrial park turn off, signed.

Sanitation:

Parking:

50

Custom

Rural location too far to walk to village; Shallow river with canoe club boat launch adj. Inspected 2010.

CHAMBERET | 210 | G8 | N45°34.767' E001°43.236' | 19370

Directions: Route de la Font Blanche. Exit village to west on D3, sp 'Masseret' and 'M.A.S. Stade'. Turn left onto Rte de la Font Blanche, signed. Aire at sports ground, opp cemetery.

Sanitation:

Parking:

4; 12m bays

Custom; Toilet disposal at WC

Overlooking sports field; Village centre with local commerce adj. Inspected 2010.

LUBERSAC	211	F8	N45°26.201' E001°23.803'	19210

Directions: D901, at the Super U. On D901 southbound towards Arnac-Pompadour, by the Super U fuel station.

Sanitation:

Parking:

Poss

Euro Relais Junior

Supermarket adj; LIDL adj; Château in town. Inspected 2010.

ST VITTE SUR BRIANCE	212	F8	N45°37.526' E001°32.762'	87380

Directions: Place de la Mairie, D16. Next to the Mairie in the centre of the village.

Sanitation:

Parking:

1; Small parking area

Custom; 4 unmetered elec points; Honesty box

Inadequate parking so really just a Service Point. Elec requires a really long elec cable. Inspected 2010.

MAGNAC BOURG	213	F8	N45°37.051' E001°26.063'	87380

Directions: Route du Moulin, off D82/Route de la Gare. Exit A20/E09 at Junction 41 and follow D82 into town. In town turn right onto Route du Moulin and Aire on right by pond.

Sanitation:

Parking:

None

Custom

Service Point only. Inspected 2010.

GLANDON	214	F8	N45°28.621' E001°13.718'	87500

Directions: D18. Exit town to south on D18. Aire is adj to D18 just past the sports facilities by the weigh bridge.

Sanitation:

Parking:

2

Euro Relais Mini; Token (2/1); €3.50

Village 2 mins; Local parking available. Inspected 2010.

ST YRIEIX LA PERCHE	215	F8	N45°30.753' E001°12.380'	87500

Directions: D704/Ave Gutenberg. Turn off at the roundabout junction of D704/D901 and the Aire is in the car park on the left, adj to roundabout, signed.

Sanitation:

Parking:

Poss

Euro Relais Mini; Token (2/1); €3.50

Really just a Service Point in a very unlevel town car park; Medieval town 5 mins. Inspected 2010.

NEXON | 216 | F8 | N45°40.255' E001°10.866' | 87800

Directions: D15a1, near Etang de la Lande. Turn off D11 in town onto D15, sp 'Etang de la Lande'. In 1.6km turn left onto D15a1, signed. Follow road towards lake and Aire on left.

Sanitation: E WC F

Parking: P F

3

Custom

SP

Service Point outside campsite near small lake/swimming pond. Less commercial than 217 Inspected 2010.

ST HILAIRE LES PLACES | 217 | F8 | N45°38.053' E001°09.700' | 87800

Directions: At Lac Plaisance. Turn off D11, sp 'Lac Plaisance' and follow sp 'Lac Plaisance'. At campsite entrance keep left through gates. Travel down hill past car park on right and Aire in bottom of car park on left.

Sanitation: E WC F

Parking: P F

10; €1.50pp Jul/Aug; Pay at campsite

Raclet; Token (2/1)

SP

At leisure/swimming lake; Lake views from bottom and top car park. Inspected 2010.

CHALUS | 218 | F8 | N45°39.656' E000°59.286' | 87230

Directions: N21. Exit town on N21 towards Limoges. Aire on right, sp 'Aire des Energies' and signed. Designated parking behind building, signed.

Sanitation: E WC F

Parking: P F

15

Custom; €2; Showers €2

SP

Adj to N21 but sheltered by banks. This is a motorway style fuel station which also appeals to trucks. There is a small shop and café onsite. Inspected 2012.

PAGEAS | 219 | F8 | N45°40.690' E001°00.135' | 87230

Directions: N21. From north on N21 turn right at bottom of hill before village onto D141a, sp 'Pageas'. Aire immediately on right in large, flat grass parking area. Limited hardstanding for winter use.

Sanitation: E WC F

Parking: P F

10; Grass parking

Euro Relais Junior; Token (ER); €2

SP

Lake; Play area in adjoining park. Well kept; Easy walk to village. Restaurant next to Aire. Inspected 2012.

ST LAURENT SUR GORRE | 220 | F8 | N45°45.922' E000°57.390' | 87310

Directions: Allée des Lilas. Exit town on D34, sp 'Vayres' and signed. Turn left in front of Gendarmerie, sp 'La Cote' and signed. After passing the stade municipal turn left and follow road to lake. Aire in former municipal campsite, sp 'Accueil Camping-Cars Les Chenes'.

Sanitation: E WC F

Parking: P F

30; €6/night; Grass parking between trees

Custom; Numerous unmetered continental elec points

SP

Former campsite turned commercial Aire beside small leisure lake and park. Local commerce 7 mins, partially uphill. Inspected 2012.

ST MATHIEU | 221 | F8 | N45°42.912' E000°47.242' | 87440

Directions: C65. Turn off D675 in St Mathieu onto D699, sp 'Limoges'. Turn off D699 onto D127, sp 'Centre Tourisme du Lac'. Turn off D127 onto C65, sp 'Centre Tourisme du Lac'. Turn left into Centre Tourisme du Lac. Aire is on right, signed.

Sanitation:

Parking:

20

Depagne; €2

Aire adj to leisure lake with walks and boat hire. Views of lake from the very uneven parking. Adj campsite open May-Sept. Inspected 2012.

ORADOUR SUR VAYRES | 222 | F8 | N45°43.963' E000°51.942' | 87150

Directions: Rue Jean Giraudoux. Turn off D901 into Rue Jean Giraudoux by the château opp D75 junction, sp 'Relais de la Vaynes' and signed. Service Point 50m on left, undesignated parking opp.

Sanitation:

Parking:

5

Custom

Local commerce 1 min. you can join a Voie Verte cycle/walking route to Chalus from town. Inspected 2012.

CUSSAC | 223 | F8 | N45°42.318' E000°50.957' | 87150

Photo/Info: Pat and Phil Wilde

Directions: Rue de 8 Mai 1945. From Saint Mathieu on the D699 . Turn right alongside the cemetery onto D73 sp, 'Marval'. Turn first left opp the cemetery parking. The Aire is 75m on right, signed.

Sanitation:

Parking:

5

Euro Relais Junior; Token (ER); €2

Close to centre of pleasant village with local commerce. Visited 2012.

LES SALLES LAVAUGUYON | 224 | F8 | N45°44.422' E000°42.056' | 87440

Directions: D33. From southeast take D699 west for 3km. Turn right onto D33. Aire on left 650m before reaching village by two barns in large, grassy area, signed. Parking on terraced, gravel pitches backing onto trees.

Sanitation:

Parking:

6; €4/24hrs; Pay in honesty box

Euro Relais Junior

Idyllic spot; Countryside views; Village with local commerce 10 mins. Inspected 2010.

GPS Co-ordinates for SatNav

The GPS Co-ordinates published in this guide were taken onsite by our inspectors. We consider them a valuable and unique asset and at the time of publishing have decided not to publish them as electronic files for use on navigation devices. You have permission to type in the co-ordinates of an Aire you intend to visit but not to store or share them. For the security of our copyright:

- **Do not compile them into lists**
- **Do not publish, share or reproduce them anywhere in any format**

ORADOUR SUR GLANE | 226 | F8 | N45°56.129' E001°01.531' | 87520

Photo: Barrie Wilson

Directions: Rue du Stade, off D3 at sports ground. Well sp 'Aire de Repos' from D101 and D3.

Sanitation:

Parking:

27

Raclet; €2

Memorial to village destroyed during WW2 10 mins. Busy, arrive by 3.30pm and expect to double up on pitches. Inspected 2010.

JAVERDAT | 227 | F8 | N45°57.145' E000°59.158' | 87520

Directions: C8. Turn off D711 in village centre by church onto C8, signed. Aire on right as exit village, signed.

Sanitation:

Parking:

4; Max 72hrs

Aires Services; Token; Aire Services Electric; Token/55 mins

We recommend a visit to this landscaped Aire in a small village. Onsite toilet block. Local commerce 1 min, tokens free from Auberge bar. Inspected 2012.

NIEUL | 228 | F8 | N45°55.553' E001°10.318' | 87510

Directions: Rue de la Gare. Turn off D28 into car park opp château, signed. Service Point in car park, parking on grass behind car park.

Sanitation:

Parking:

22; Max 72hrs; Grass parking

Custom; Empty toilet down toilet

Pleasant parking area with views of château, which has open access gardens, in one direction and grassland in the other. Local commerce 2 mins. Inspected 2012.

ST PRIEST TAURION | 229 | F8 | N45°53.172' E001°23.785' | 87480

Directions: Stade Municipal. Follow D29 through town towards Royeres. After crossing river bridge turn right in 100m into stade municipal, signed. Drive to the right and the Service Point is close to the river.

Sanitation:

Parking:

17

Custom

Adj to river with limited views but does have interesting water management ruins. Fishing is private. Sports ground adj. Local commerce 1 min on D29. Inspected 2012.

RAZES - Lac de St Pardoux | 230 | F8 | N46°02.050' E001°17.892' | 87640

Photo: Donna Garner

Directions: Lac de St Pardoux. From Razes follow D44, sp 'Lac de St Pardoux'. Turn off D44, sp 'Lac de St Pardoux', and Service Point is in 1st parking area on left.

Sanitation:

Parking:

15; Max 1 night

Aire Services; €3.50; Token (3/3)

Large leisure lake adj and partial views from parking. Swimming beach, boating, walk/cycle around lake 24km (6hrs). Inspected 2012.

BESSINES SUR GARTEMPE | 231 | F7 | N46°06.587' E001°22.205' | 87250

Directions: Parking Champ de Foire, Rue d'Ingolsheim. In village turn beside Mairie, signed. Aire in car park in 100m.

Sanitation:

Parking:

2

Raclet; €2; No drive over drain

Local commerce 2 mins. Inspected 2010.

BELLAC | 232 | F7 | N46°06.956' E001°03.086' | 87300

Directions: Rue des Tanneries. Approach from south on N147. Exit roundabout onto D947, sp 'Bellac'. Turn left onto D3, sp 'Blond' and signed. Turn right, signed. Follow road to Service Point on right, signed. Parking is on left: N46°06.891' E001°03.128'.

Sanitation:

Parking:

3; Max 8.5m

Custom

Beautiful riverside park in tranquil setting. Roman bridge and marked walks adj. Town with commerce 5 mins uphill. Inspected 2012.

RANCON | 233 | F7 | N46°07.653' E001°10.885' | 87290

Directions: D1. Exit village on D1 towards Bellac. Aire on right in lay-by as exit village, signed. Parking is in the stade (sports stadium) through adj gate up steep slope.

Sanitation:

Parking:

5

Custom

The sports facilities include football pitch, play area, outdoor exercise trail, table tennis and basketball. The village is small with limited local commerce, 2 mins. Inspected 2012.

LAC DE VASSIVIERE | 234 | G8 | N45°47.188' E001°52.134' | 87470

Info/Photo: Mr. John Cox

Directions: Traveling east go through Beaumont-du-Lac to north on D43. Turn left in 1km onto D43B sp 'Lac Vassiviere'. At D222 T-junction turn right then in 100m turn left and re-join the D43B both sp 'Peirrefitte' and signed. Follow road straight on, sp 'Plage' and signed to lake, The Service Point is on the left after the campsite.

Sanitation:

Parking:

15

Euro Relais Junior; €2

Peaceful lakeside Aire with views of lake and a swimming beach adj. There is a holiday village behind the Aire but no other commerce. Great area to discover by boat, bike or on foot. Visited 2012.

MARSAC | 235 | G7 | N46°05.995' E001°34.780' | 23210

Directions: Off D42. Follow sp 'Camping' northwest out of village on D42. At campsite entrance take road to right, signed. Service Point 100m on left, signed.

Sanitation:

Parking:

5

Custom; €5

Small parking area at stadium 100m past Service Point. Campsite adj. Inspected 2010.

CHATELUS LE MARCHEIX | 236 | G8 | N45°59.931' E001°36.198' | 23430

Directions: Off D8. Exit the village to the west on D8 towards Villemaumy. Turn off at the edge of the village, sp 'Camping'. The Service Point is in 50m on the left, outside municipal campsite.

Sanitation:

Parking:

5; When campsite closed

Raclet; €2

Lovely rural views. Adj campsite open Jul-Aug €11.50/night. Inspected 2010.

ST DIZIER LEYRENNE | 237 | G8 | N46°01.390' E001°43.032' | 23400

Directions: D912. From south follow D912 to St Dizier Leyrenne. Aire on right adj to D912 when enter village, next to municipal campsite and Etang de la Valodie.

Sanitation:

Parking:

3

Custom

Village 10 mins; Lake walk adj. Inspected 2010.

SAUVIAT SUR VIGE | 238 | G8 | N45°54.559' E001°36.911' | 87400

Directions: N141. Adj to N141 as enter village from northeast, signed. Aire on left in large parking area.

Sanitation:

Parking:

20

Urba Flux; €2; No drive over drain

Town adj. Inspected 2010.

BUJALEUF | 239 | G8 | N45°48.297' E001°38.207' | 87460

Directions: D16. Exit village to northeast on D16, sp 'Cheissoux' and 'Lac de Ste Helene'. Parking adj to Lake Ste Helene 1.5km from the village, signed. Service Point on Rue du Champ du Foire. Turn off D14 as exit village towards Eymoutiers, signed: N45°47.856' E001°37.893'.

Sanitation:

Parking:

5

Custom

Parking adj to large open space and leisure lake/resevoir; Village has local commerce. Inspected 2010.

EYMOUTIERS | 240 | G8 | N45°44.293' E001°44.108' | 87120

Directions: D979. Exit town to west on D979 towards Limoges. The Service Point is located at the Casino supermarket fuel station on the left as exit town.

Sanitation:

Parking:

Poss; No long term parking near Service Point

Flot Bleu Fontaine; 1 unmetered elec point; No drive over drain

Supermarket adj. Inspected 2010.

PEYRAT LE CHATEAU	241	G8	N45°48.881' E001°46.251'	87470

Directions: Place du Pré de l'Age. Turn off D940 main road in town centre opp TO. Aire 100m on left.

Sanitation:

Parking:

10

Custom; Token; €1; Open Nov-Mar

SP

Rural views; Village 1 min with local commerce, museum and lake. Inspected 2010.

ROYERE DE VASSIVIERE	242	G8	N45°50.403' E001°54.668'	23460

Directions: D3. Exit the village to south on D3, sp 'Gentious'. The Aire is adj to D3 in the car park by the Proxi mini market, signed.

Sanitation:

Parking:

5

Euro Relais Mini

SP

Pleasant village with local commerce adj. Inspected 2010.

ST JUNIEN LA BREGERE	243	G8	N45°52.950' E001°45.190'	23400

Directions: D13, off D940. Turn off D940, onto D13 in village. Turn right in 200m, signed.

Sanitation:

Parking:

3

Custom

SP

Rural views; Village 2 mins. Some road noise from D940. Inspected 2010.

BOURGANEUF	244	G8	N45°57.265' E001°45.460'	23400

Directions: D912. Enter town from north on D912. Turn left in front of turreted building, signed. Turn right in car park, signed.

Sanitation:

Parking:

5

Euro Relais Mini

SP

Pleasant town with multiple commerce 200m uphill. Inspected 2010.

CROCQ	245	G8	N45°51.812' E002°22.125'	23260

Directions: Route de la Bourboule. Follow D996, main route, through Crocq towards Giat. The Aire is at the sports facilities adj to D996, signed. Entrance is narrow but passable with care.

Sanitation:

Parking:

6; Grass parking but other hard standing parking poss

Euro Relais Junior; Token (ER)

SP

Located adj to sports facilities and fire station. Local commerce 3 mins. Inspected 2012.

AUBUSSON

246 G8 N45°57.407' E002°10.514' 23200

Directions: Place du Champ de Foire, off D988, signed. Enter town from north on D990. Turn onto D988, sp 'Aubusson D94a'. Follow road past Intermarché and Aire is in car park 100m on left, signed.

Sanitation:

Parking:

20

Euro Relais Junior; €2

Large town 2 mins; Do not attempt to drive through town in anything but van-style motorhome. Inspected 2010.

MONTBOUCHER

247 G8 N45°57.089' E001°40.866' 23400

Directions: Off D36, in village centre. Turn off D941 onto D36, sp 'Montboucher'. Follow signs to Aire. In village centre follow road behind church and to right.

Sanitation:

Parking:

10

Euro Relais Mini

Located in a rural village. Tennis court adj. Inspected 2010.

AHUN

248 G7 N46°04.797' E002°02.648' 23150

Directions: Route de Limoges. Turn off D942 onto D13, sp 'Camping Municipal' and signed. Service Point on left outside municipal campsite, signed.

Sanitation:

Parking:

Poss, when campsite closed

Euro Relais Mini

Service Point outside small, pleasant municipal campsite that charges €6.50 inc 2 people. Village with local commerce 2 mins. Inspected 2012.

CHENERAILLES

249 G7 N46°06.641' E002°10.683' 23130

Directions: D990. Exit town towards Aubusson and the Aire is on the left, signed.

Sanitation:

Parking:

5

Euro Relais Junior; Token (ER)

Next to housing estate; Adj to main road; Village centre 2 mins with local commerce. Inspected 2010.

GOUZON

250 G7 N46°11.486' E002°14.412' 23230

Directions: Place du Champ de Foire, Rue d'Alcantera. Drive out of Gouzon on D997, sp 'Aubusson'. Turn off, sp 'Camping'. Before road splits turn left, sp 'Parking Ombragé: Pique-Nique' and signed.

Sanitation:

Parking:

10

Raclet

Shaded under trees, Town and restaurants 2 mins. Inspected 2010.

CRESSAT | 251 | G7 | N46°08.363' E002°06.610' | 23140

Directions: Off D990. As enter Cressat from Chénérailles, Aire just past lake on left, signed.

Sanitation:

Parking:

5; 8m bays

Raclet; Token (2/1)

SP

Lake adj, but no view; Village 2 mins uphill. Inspected 2010.

ST LAURENT | 252 | G7 | N46°09.983' E001°57.700' | 23000

Directions: D3. Turn onto D3 in village centre at rear of church, sp 'Bourne Camping-Car'. Aire 50m on right in car park, adj to church.

Sanitation:

Parking:

4; 8m bays

Euro Relais Junior; 2 unmetered elec points

SP

Good stopover. Local commerce nearby. Inspected 2010.

JARNAGES | 253 | G7 | N46°11.064' E002°04.870' | 23140

Directions: D65. In Jarnages turn right at La Poste onto D65, sp 'Accueil Camping Car'. Service Point adj to play area and lake.

Sanitation:

Parking:

5

Euro Relais Junior; €2

SP

Lake, mini golf, village/shops 3 mins; Level walk to town. Inspected 2010.

GUERET - AIRE DES MONT DE GUERET | 254 | G7 | N46°10.945' E001°50.918' | 23000

Directions: D942/DN145. Exit N145 at Junction 45, sp 'Gueret Ouest', and follow sp 'Aire des Mont de Gueret'. Aire located at motorway services behind main building, signed.

Sanitation:

Parking:

10; Not Recommended

Euro Relais Junior; €2

SP

Motorway services with shop/café that is technically off the motorway but as with all motorway Aires we advise you not to stay overnight. Inspected 2012.

FELLETIN | 255 | G8 | N45°52.923' E002°10.546' | 23500

Directions: Rue des Fosses. Located off D10 and D982, sp 'Crocq'. Well signed from all directions. Service Point accessible from slope at rear of car park.

Sanitation:

Parking:

5

Euro Relais Mini

SP

Town with commerce 200m. Inspected 2010.

HAVE YOU VISITED AN AIRE? **GPS co-ordinates in this guide are protected by copyright law**

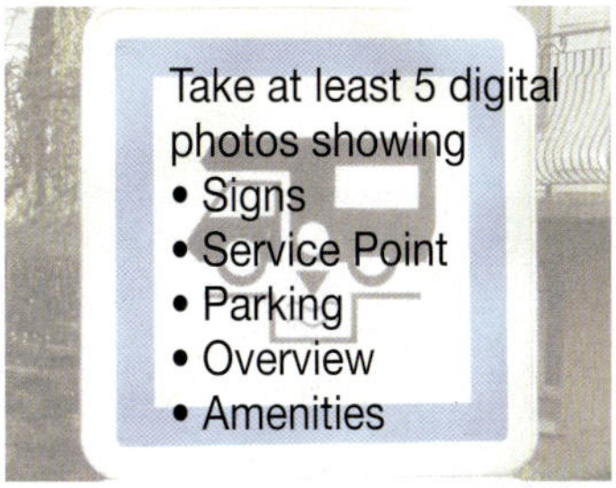
Take at least 5 digital photos showing
• Signs
• Service Point
• Parking
• Overview
• Amenities

Visit www.all-the-aires.co.uk/submissions.shtml to upload your updates and photos.

Sanitation:

Aire Details:

Submit updates
- Amendments
- New Aires
- Not changed

LA CELLE DUNOISE

257 | G7 | N46°18.534' E001°46.459' | 23800

Directions: D48a/Rte du Canard. Exit village to south on D22, sp 'Gueret' and signed. Turn left onto D48a, signed. Service Point is on left outside municipal campsite.

Sanitation:

Parking:

None
Euro Relais Junior; €2

Service Point only. Inspected 2010.

BOUSSAC

258 | G7 | N46°20.867' E002°13.242' | 23600

Directions: D997. Follow D997 through town towards Gueret. Aire on left adj to large car park/livestock market, signed.

Sanitation:

Parking:

10
Euro Relais Box

Adj to livestock market and D997, both of which can be busy and noisy. Small town commerce 1 min. Inspected 2012.

MARCILLAT EN COMBRAILLE

259 | H7 | N46°09.785' E002°38.240' | 03420

Info/Photo: Roy Geddes

Directions: D1089 Rue de Combrailles. In village centre at roundabout take D1089, sp 'Poinsat'. Aire next to Gendarmerie (Police Station) on Rue de l'Économique, Adj to D1089 signed.

Sanitation:

Parking:

18
Custom

A lovely, typical French village with local commerce and convenience store. Visited 2012.

AINAY LE CHATEAU

260 | H7 | N46°42.322' E002°41.654' | 03360

Directions: D953. South of the village adj to D953 at Internarche supermarket. Signed.

Sanitation:

Parking:

Poss
Flot Bleu Ocean; €2

Supermarket adj. Self-service laundry adj €9/18kg, €6/8kg, tumble dryer €1/10mins. Inspected 2012.

Faverolles

Liginiac

Villeneuve

MEDITERRANEAN

La Salvetat sur Agout, *Photo: Rod and Liz Sleigh*

MONTFERRAND

1 G11 N43°21.130' E001°49.442' 11320

Directions: D218/Lieu-Dit Naurouze. From Castelnaudary on D6113 turn left, sp 'P' and 'Obelisque de Riquet' and signed, opp the turning for Montferrand. Parking 350m on left, not signed. 3.5t weight restriction.

Sanitation:

Parking:

15

Bollard; Delapidated

SP

Adj to Canal du Midi, no views. Signed walks along canal and to the obelisk. Inspected 2010.

SALLES SUR L'HERS

2 G11 N43°17.533' E001°47.233' 11410

Directions: Rue des Ecoles. Turn off D625 in village by communal bins, sp 'Borne Camping Car'. Follow road downhill. Aire outside stadium.

Sanitation:

E F

Parking:

P F

10

Custom; Tap requires male hose connector; 2 unmetered elec points

SP

Adj to sports stadium on edge of village. Stream adj and footpaths into open countryside. Very pleasant spot. Inspected 2010.

BELPECH

3 G11 N43°11.915' E001°44.709' 11420

Directions: Rue du Stade. At the stadium. From D502 turn down Rue du Stade opposite the CA bank. Follow road to end.

Sanitation:

E WC F

Parking:

F

5; Grass parking

Bollard; No drive over drain; 2 unmetered elec points

SP

If the barrier is closed see the Mairie; Some hardstanding space avail. Inspected 2010.

FANJEAUX

4 G11 N43°11.154' E002°01.933' 11270

Directions: Chemin des Fontanelles. On D119 from Carcassonne, on entering village pass under a bridge and take 1st right. Follow sp 'Borne Camping Cars' up the hill. Aire 300m on left.

Sanitation:

F

Parking:

P F

15; Max 48hrs

Bollard; No drive over drain

SP

Medieval hilltop village. Bakery, minimart, pharmacy, restaurant, bar/tabac and TO, all within 300m. Inspected 2010.

PEZENS

5 G11 N43°15.329' E002°15.813' 11170

Directions: Place de la Libérty. Heading towards Carcassonne, car park on left just after cross river. Difficult access, reverse in if poss.

Sanitation:

E F

Parking:

F

4

Bollard; No drive over drain; 1 unmetered elec point

SP

Adj shops and restaurants. Noise from road. No river views. Inspected 2012.

CARCASSONNE T 6 G11 N43°12.324' E002°22.362' 11000

Directions: P2. Approach from east on D6113. Exit D6113 sp 'La Cite'. Follow sp 'La Cite' uphill and turn right, sp 'La Cite'. Take 1st right, sp 'P2' and signed. Aire 50m on right through barrier, signed.

Sanitation:

Parking:

50; 1st hr free; 2-6hrs/€5 then €1/hr; 8pm-8am free entry, pay on exit

Custom; Inside barrier

This is a large out of town parking area for buses and motorhomes just 4mins from the fairy tale city of Carcassonne. Inspected 2012.

ROUTIER 7 G11 N43°06.492' E002°07.391' 11240

Directions: Place du Malepere, off Ave de Madailhan. From D623 turn onto D309, sp 'Routier'. Continue through village and turn left into Place du Malepere, sp 'Caravanning'. Follow track to Aire.

Sanitation:

Parking:

5

Bollard; 2 unmetered elec points

Individual bays with nice, far reaching views over countryside. Inspected 2010.

VILLENEUVE MINERVOIS 8 G11 N43°18.900' E002°27.850' 11160

Directions: D111. Turn into the car park in the town centre, opp the Mairie and next to Spar shop.

Sanitation:

Parking:

12; Max 48hrs

Bollard

Small, peaceful village. Sports stadium behind the village hall. Inspected 2010.

LIMOUX 9 G11 N43°03.033' E002°13.117' 11300

Directions: Esplanade François Mitterrand, adj to D118 at town car park. Service Point is visable from road. Enter car park directly from roundabout at junction of D104/D118. Service Point adj to D118.

Sanitation:

Parking:

5

Bollard; Drain in floor lifts up

Town car park adj to college. Road noise. Tap on Service Point not working at time of inspection. Inspected 2010.

LAGRASSE 10 H11 N43°05.563' E002°37.245' 11220

Directions: At 'Parking 2', Avenue des Condamines. Follow sp to 'P2', clearly signed on D3 through village.

Sanitation:

Parking:

15

Custom

Lovely old, sleepy town with abbey. Approach via D212 from south very scenic. Inspected 2010.

VILLEROUGE TERMENES | 11 | H11 | N43°00.287' E002°37.601' | 11330

Photo: Carol Weaver

Directions: D613. Aire adj to D613 at rear of parking for château. Not signed.

Sanitation:

Parking:

5
Custom

Good parking for visiting château. Inspected 2010.

FELINES TERMENES | 12 | G12 | N42°59.225' E002°36.776' | 11330

Photo: Ken and Jean Fowler

Directions: On D613. From St Laurent de la Cabrerisse. Aire on left in village beside the tennis courts.

Sanitation:

Parking:

5
Bollard; No drive over drain

Pleasant with trees. Short walk to village centre. Very old Service Point. Inspected 2010.

QUILLAN | 13 | G12 | N42°52.450' E002°10.950' | 11500

Photo: Rodney Martin

Directions: La Gare, Sq Andre Tricoire on D117. Aire in car park off main road next to railway station and coach park.

Sanitation:

Parking:

5
Custom; Token; €2

Rural views. Inspected 2010.

LAPRADELLE PUILAURENS | 14 | G12 | N42°48.583' E002°18.517' | 11140

Directions: Rue de la Devez, off D117. Turn off D117 at viaduct. Aire between viaduct and fire station.

Sanitation:

Parking:

6
Custom

A beautiful drive to this Aire. Views of mountains and château. Inspected 2010.

DUILHAC SOUS PEYREPERTUSE | 15 | G12 | N42°51.683' E002°33.917' | 11350

Photo: Rita Renninghoff

Directions: D14, at village entrance. From D117 at Maury turn onto D19, sp 'Cucugnan'.

Sanitation:

Parking:

20
Custom; Token; €4

Beautiful views of surrounding mountains and castle above. Village centre 250m. Castle 3.5km by road. Inspected 2010.

PUYVALADOR SKI 16 G12 N42°39.076' E002°04.622' 66210

Directions: Rue des Sources. Turn off D118 onto D32g and follow signs to Puyvalador ski station. Aire on left in 'Parking 3'. Access road in poor condition.

Sanitation:

Parking:

20

Custom

Remote parking at ski station. Service Point in very poor condition and difficult to access due to broken up surface. Tap missing at time of inspection. Inspected 2010.

LES ANGLES PLA DEL MIR SKI 17 G12 N42°33.787' E002°04.008' 66210

Directions: Pla del Mir ski station on road Pla del Mir. Turn off D32 just south of Les Angles and follow sp 'Parking Camping Car'.

Sanitation:

Parking:

40

Custom

This Aire is set in a very scenic location adj to the ski station and animal park. Inspected 2010.

MONT LOUIS 18 G12 N42°30.409' E002°07.345' 66210

Directions: Parking des Remparts. Turn off N116 into car park, sp 'Parking Entrée', on right-hand side of arched entrance into town. Pass through barriers and Aire is at rear of car park. Do not drive through arch into town.

Sanitation:

Parking:

20; €4/4pm-10am; Pay at machine

Custom

Parking adj to impressive walls outside town. Inspected 2010.

THUES ENTRE VALLS 19 G12 N42°31.333' E002°13.283' 66360

Photo: Rita Renninghoff

Directions: N116. Turn at Thuès-entre-Valls for 'Gorges de la Carança' parking. 3.5t weight restriction on approach. Follow signs in car park for motorhome parking. Access roads steep and narrow. Difficult in ice and snow.

Sanitation:

Parking:

10; €4/day

Custom

Yellow train runs past; Lovely spot for walking in gorges. Spectacular drive on N116 from Mont Louis. Inspected 2010.

EGAT 20 G12 N42°29.850' E02°00.800' 66120

Directions: D618, at Super U in Égat. Located at the roundabout junction of D618 and D33f, southwest of Egat. Service Point at the supermarket fuel station.

Sanitation:

Parking:

Poss

Euro Relais Junior; €2; No drive over drain.

Toilets in shop. Free Wifi. Larger parking area to rear of shop. Inspected 2010.

SAILLAGOUSE

21 G12 N42°27.467' E002°02.250' 66800

Directions: Lieu-Dit Village. Aire in small car park off N116, opp Hôtel de Ville in village centre.

Sanitation:

Parking:

5

Flot Bleu Pacific; Token; €3

SP

Amazing statues in town centre. Tokens from TO or Mairie 150m. Inspected 2010.

BOLQUERE PYRENEES 2000 1 SKI

22 G12 N42°30.983' E002°03.533' 66210

Directions: Rue du Belvédère. Turn off D618, Égat to Mont Louis road, at roundabout into Ave du Serrat de l'Ours, sp 'Bolquère Pyrénées 2000'. Take 2nd turning left into Rue du Belvédère. Aire at rear of Pizzeria/Crêperie.

Sanitation:

Parking:

20

See 23

SP

Toilet disposal point only at this location. For full Service Point, see 23. Good skiing area. Inspected 2010.

BOLQUERE PYRENEES 2000 2

23 G12 N42°30.867' E002°03.733' 66210

Directions: D618, at Casino supermarket. Located on D618, Mont Louis to Égat road, north of Bolquère.

Sanitation:

Parking:

None; See 22

Flot Bleu Euro; CC; €2

SP

Service Point only. Inspected 2010.

CASTEIL

24 G12 N42°32.017' E002°23.517' 66820

Photo: Rita Renninghoff

Directions: D116. Small parking area reserved for motorhomes before village.

Sanitation:

Parking:

5

Custom; WC and Tap

SP

Pleasant woodland setting. Tap and toilet up steps in car park but not accessible to motorhomes due to height barrier. Inspected 2010.

HAVE YOU VISITED AN AIRE?

GPS co-ordinates in this guide are protected by copyright law

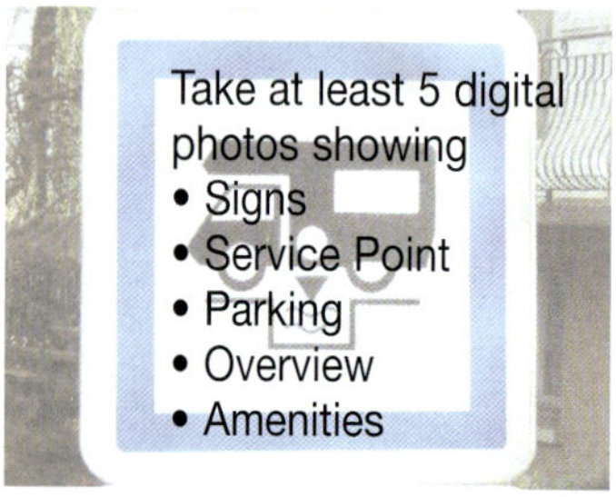
Take at least 5 digital photos showing
• Signs
• Service Point
• Parking
• Overview
• Amenities

Visit www.all-the-aires.co.uk/submissions.shtml to upload your updates and photos.

Sanitation:

Aire Details:

Submit updates

- Amendments
- New Aires
- Not changed

VERNET LES BAINS — 26 — G12 — N42°32.567' E002°23.433' — 66820

Directions: Chemin de la Laiterie. Turn off D116 at roundabout at southern end of village. Cross river bridge and follow sp 'Aire Camping Car' past pink hotel. Follow road to right of car park. Aire at end of road.

Sanitation:

Parking:

20; €10/night

Custom

Parking on 2 levels overlooking thermal spa town. Inspected 2010.

RIGARDA — 27 — H12 — N42°37.562' E002°31.747' — 66320

Directions: Route de Finestret. Very small sign marks gravel path to private Aire off Carrer de l'Era, approx 700m from village; difficult to find. Very narrow roads through villages on approach; only really suitable for panel vans.

Sanitation:

Parking:

5; €5/night; €8/night inc services

Water from tank; Cesspit

A very scruffy, weedy patch of gravel with an equally unkempt owner. The drain was clogged with weeds and almost invisible. Assess before staying. Inspected 2010.

ST MARSAL — 28 — H12 — N42°32.250' E002°37.400' — 66110

Directions: D618. From Amélie-les-Bains-Palalda take D618 to St Marsal. Turn right shortly after enter village, signed. Aire down track by tennis court.

Sanitation:

Parking:

5; €3; Pay at shop

Tap; Also tap in car park above

Village shop; Looks like old campsite. Showers €1. Inspected 2010.

AMELIE LES BAINS — 29 — H12 — N42°28.717' E002°40.433' — 66110

Photo: Rita Renninghoff

Directions: Rue des Lledoners. Turn off D115, sp 'Camping Municipal'. Aire adj to campsite.

Sanitation:

Parking:

5; €5.50; Max 48hrs

Raclet Maxi; Token (ER); €4; No drive over drain

Short walk to pretty town nestled in wooded hills. Inspected 2010.

ST PAUL DE FENOUILLET — 30 — H12 — N42°48.633' E002°30.267' — 66220

Directions: Place St Pierre. Access from D117 in town centre, signed.

Sanitation:

Parking:

Poss; in town car park

Flot Bleu Euro; CC; No drive over drain

Service Point in small town centre car park. Inspected 2010.

LE BOULOU

31 H12 N42°31.636' E002°50.229' 66160

Directions: Chemin du Mouli Nou. Exit Boulou towards Perpignan on D900 and turn right, sp 'P. Cimetière' and signed. Take next turn left, signed. Aire in 50m by the cemetery.

Sanitation:

Parking:

21; Max 24hrs

Euro Relais Junior; €2

SP

Stadium adj; Football pitch. Inspected 2010.

ST ANDRE

32 H12 N42°33.135' E002°58.396' 66690

Directions: Rue de Taxo. Exit N114 at Junction 11, sp 'St André'. Follow sp 'St André' drive behind Intermarché supermarket and turn left, signed. Aire 100m past cemetery, signed.

Sanitation:

E

Parking:

6; €2.30/night; Max 3 nights

Flot Bleu Océane; Token; €2; Flexi hose for grey waste

SP

Town 2 mins; Supermarket adj. Inspected 2010.

COLLIOURE

33 H12 N42°31.517' E003°04.100' 66190

Directions: D86/Route de Madeloc. Turn off D914 at Junction 14, sp 'Collioure'. Follow D86 for 750m. Aire in lower corner of large terraced car park on left-hand side of road, adj to Complexe Sportif.

Sanitation:

E WC

Parking:

12; €10/24hrs inc service and elec

Custom

SP

'Park and Ride' type car park with shuttle bus to village May-Sept. Inspected 2010.

PORT VENDRES

34 H12 N42°31.063' E003°06.815' 66660

Directions: Route de la Jetée. Turn off D914 onto D86b, sp 'Aire Camping Car'. Follow road to port entrance and turn right at roundabout. Aire 100m on right.

Sanitation:

WC

Parking:

40; €5.50; Collected; inc service

Sani Station; inc; Token; €1.10

SP

No views but adj to sea and harbour. Charles Renée Mackintosh has pictures on walks. Town 5 mins round port. Inspected 2010.

HAVE YOU VISITED AN AIRE?

GPS co-ordinates in this guide are protected by copyright law

Take at least 5 digital photos showing
- Signs
- Service Point
- Parking
- Overview
- Amenities

Visit www.all-the-aires.co.uk/submissions.shtml to upload your updates and photos.

Sanitation:

Aire Details:

Submit updates
- Amendments
- New Aires
- Not changed

LATOUR BAS ELNE

36 H12 N42°35.998' E003°00.438' 66200

Directions: Parking Camping Cars Roussillon. Sp 'Latour Bas Elne', 'McDonald's' and signed off D81/Argelès-St-Cyprien/C9 roundabout. Aire approx 1.5km from roundabout.

Sanitation:

Parking:

40; €6/24hrs; Grass parking

Custom; €4; Elec €3

Motorhome dealers, some English spoken. Workshop. Security gates locked at night. Inspected 2010.

CANET EN ROUSSILLON

37 H12 N42°41.967' E003°01.335' 66140

Directions: D617. Turn off the D617 at the roundabout into the Hyper Casino, sp 'Hyper Casino Entree'. The Service Point is adj to the fuel station.

Sanitation:

Parking:

Poss

Euro Relais Junior; €2

Supermarket adj. Visited 2012.

LE BARCARES 1 - PORT

38 H12 N42°48.000' E003°01.883' 66420

Directions: Quai Alain Colas. Exit D83 at Junction 11 and turn into Quai du Grau Saint Ange. Turn into Quai Alain Colas. Aire on quayside, adj to marina.

Sanitation:

Parking:

5; Max 24hrs

None

Large quayside parking area. Views across boats in marina (Bassin de la Tourette). Also see **39** **40** **41** **42** **43**. Inspected 2010.

LE BARCARES 2

39 H12 N42°48.667' E003°02.067' 66420

Directions: Rue André Malraux. From south on D83 exit at Junction 12 and at 1st roundabout take 3rd exit onto Rue Andre Malraux, sp 'La Grande Pinede'. Aire on left adj to pine woodland.

Sanitation:

Parking:

2; Max 24hrs

None

2 dedicated parking spaces adj to pine woodland (La Grande Pinede). Also see **38** **40** **41** **42** **43**. Inspected 2010.

LE BARCARES 3

40 H10 N42°49.450' E003°01.833' 66420

Directions: Avenue de la Coudalère. From north on D83 exit at Junction 13 and at roundabout take 1st exit into Avenue de Coudalère. Aire on right overlooking lake.

Sanitation:

Parking:

3; Max 24hrs

None

Dedicated parking spaces overlooking lake, kite/windsurfers etc. Also see **38** **39** **41** **42** **43**. Inspected 2010.

LE BARCARES 4

41 H12 N42°50.067' E003°02.267' 66420

Directions: Rue des Marines. From south on D83 exit at Junction 14. At roundabout take 3rd exit into Rue de Cerdagne which becomes Rue des Marines and runs parallel to D83. Aire 400m in parking bays on left.

Sanitation:

Parking:

3; Max 24hrs

None

Adj to D83 so some road noise. Cycle track adj. Also see 38 39 40 42 43. Inspected 2010.

LE BARCARES 5

42 H12 N42°47.350' E003°02.033' 66420

Directions: Rue Annibal. Leave D83 at Junction 10, sp 'Village'. Go straight over roundabout and take 2nd right into Rue Annibal. Aire in small car park on right at rear of town hall and La Poste.

Sanitation:

Parking:

2; Max 24hrs

None

In small car park at rear of town hall. Less busy than sea front car park (see 43) and only 600m from beach. Inspected 2010.

LE BARCARES 6

43 H12 N42°47.200' E003°02.283' 66420

Directions: Boulevard de la Côte Vermeille. Exit D81 onto D90, sp 'Le Barcares'. Travel 2.3km following signs for TO to seafront car park. 3 large green painted spaces reserved for motorhomes adj to TO.

Sanitation:

Parking:

3; Max 24hrs; No parking Wed, Fri and Sun 7am-1pm

None

Local commerce nearby. Also see 38 39 40 41 42. Inspected 2010.

LEUCATE PLAGE

44 H12 N42°54.010' E003°03.156' 11370

Directions: From D627 take D327, sp 'Leucate Village', and follow through Leucate, signed. Then turn right, sp 'Camping Sable Mer et Soleil' and signed. Aire past campsite approx 500m. Do not approach from south on Chemin du Centre Ostreicole to avoid height barrier.

Sanitation:

Parking:

200; €7.20/night Apr-Oct; No services Nov-Apr

Flot Bleu Fontaine; €2.50

Adj to Med and salt lake used for oyster production. Direct access to beach, no shade. Barriered entry. Inspected 2010.

LEUCATE

45 H12 N42°54.817' E003°01.200' 11370

Directions: D327. From south exit D627, sp 'Leucate'. Turn right onto D327. Aire on left.

Sanitation:

Parking:

100; €7.20/night

Flot Bleu Fontaine

Terraced and overlooking lake with views of mountains beyond. Town centre 600m. Inspected 2010.

LA FRANQUI PLAGE | 46 | H12 | N42°56.625' E003°01.830' | 11370

Directions: Chemin de las Pitchinos. From D627 turn off, sp 'La Franqui', and follow sp 'Camping Les Cousseles'. Hidden left turn after 700m, sp 'Camping Les Cousseles'. Follow road another 1.8km across bridge onto island.

Sanitation:

Parking:

10

Custom; Token; €2.50

SP

At opening to salt lake on island. Ideal for bird watching. Inspected 2010.

PORT LA NOUVELLE 1 | 47 | H12 | N43°00.890' E003°02.779' | 11210

Directions: Boulevard Francis Vals, outside the municipal campsite. Follow sp 'Camping Municipal' in town. Located in 3.5t weight restricted area.

Sanitation:

E

Parking:

When campsite closed

Flot Bleu Euro; CC

SP

Campsite open Apr-Sept. Inspected 2010.

PORT LA NOUVELLE 2 | 48 | H12 | N43°00.817' E003°02.450' | 11210

Directions: Chemin des Vignes. Off Blvd du Général de Gaulle, sp 'Gare SNCF' and signed. Opp déchetterie (recycling).

Sanitation:

E

Parking:

100

Flot Bleu Euro; CC; €2

SP

3 mins to town centre; Adj to railway and main road so poss noisy. Inspected 2010.

PEYRIAC DE MER | 49 | H11 | N43°05.551' E002°57.749' | 11440

Directions: D105. Turn off D6009, sp 'Peyriac de Mer'. Follow road through village, signed. Exit village on D105, sp 'Bages'. Aire on left, signed.

Sanitation:

Parking:

6; €5/night; Basic municipal campsite adj

Custom; Adj to 1st building

SP

Adj basic campsite being used as overflow out of season. Inland sea and beach opp but no view. Adj to sports ground. Village has local commerce and 30 min motorhome parking is allowed. Inspected 2012.

GRUISSAN PORT | 50 | H11 | N43°06.256' E003°05.983' | 11430

Directions: Quai de la Tramontane. Enter Gruissan from D32. Follow Blvd de la Corderie to left for 750m. Turn left, sp 'Aire 4 Vents' and 'Gendarmerie – Maritime'. Follow road to end, and Aire at marina.

Sanitation:

WC

Parking:

100; €7.50/24hrs from midday; Mar-Nov

Urba Flux; inc

SP

Adj to marina with views across water/boats. Town 5 mins. Showers. Inspected 2010.

GRUISSAN PLAGE — 51 — H11 — N43°05.754' E003°06.591' — 11430

Directions: Ave de la Jetée. Enter Gruissan from D32. Follow Blvd de la Corderie for 1.2km following sp 'Plage de Chalets'. Aire is 1.8km down road on left. Also parking July/Aug D332 - N43°07.223' E003°06.849'

Sanitation:

Parking:

40; €7/24hrs from midday; Mar-Nov

Custom; inc

Commercial Aire; Sandy beach adj; Snack bar adj. Multiple water sports. Inspected 2010.

ARGENS MINERVOIS — 52 — H11 — N43°14.448' E002°45.865' — 11200

Photo: Mike and Jan Green

Directions: D124/Avenue des Platanes. From D611 turn onto D424, sp 'Argens Minervois'. Cross river on metal bridge. At T-junction turn left onto D124 along canal. Parking on right. Not signed.

Sanitation:

Parking:

5; Grass parking

None

Small area of canalside parking adj to height barriers. Inspected 2010.

OUVEILLAN — 53 — H11 — N43°17.533' E002°58.208' — 11590

Directions: Rue de la Cooperative, just off D13. 15km north of Narbonne at the last roundabout going north out of the village next to the cooperative winery. Access is tight and narrow but if negotiated slowly with care most motorhomes should get in.

Sanitation:

Parking:

5

Custom

Local commerce in village. Great area to explore by bike as the Canal du Midi is not far away. Inspected 2010.

NARBONNE 1 — 54 — H11 — N43°10.550' E002°59.656' — 11100

Directions: Ave du Général Leclerc. D6009. At the Casino supermarket. Enter town sp 'Centre Ville' on D6113. Then follow sp 'Perpignan'. Casino on left in 650m by fuel station.

Sanitation:

Parking:

None

Flot Bleu Euro; CC; €2

Supermarket adj; Café; Fuel; Many shops within walking distance. Inspected 2010.

NARBONNE 2 — 55 — H11 — N43°10.834' E003°01.419' — 11100

Directions: Ave de la Mer, at parking 'La Narbonette'. Enter Narbonne from east on D168 (road also goes to Narbonne Plage). Aire opp Parc des Expositions, not signed. Barriered entrance.

Sanitation:

Parking:

34; €9 inc elec; Max 72hrs; Pay on exit

Flot Bleu Euro; CC; €2

Free bus to Narbonne every 15 mins. Cycle hire €15. 5 mins to busy lively town. Inspected 2010.

NARBONNE PLAGE — 56 — H11 — N43°08.828' E003°09.249' — 11100

Photo: Barrie Wilson

Directions: Turn off D332 towards Gruissan. Aire on right, sp 'Aire Camping Car' and 'Aqua jet'. Barrier at entry; warden during day.

Sanitation:

Parking:

100; €7/night

Custom

Commercial Aire. Adj to beach, popular with wind/kite surfers, no views. Swimming pool adj. Inspected 2010.

PORT DE BROSSOLETTE — 57 — H11 — N43°10.281' E003°10.846' — 11100

Directions: Quai Pierre Brossolette. In Narbonne, between Narbonne Plage and St-Pierre-sur-Mer. Adj to marina, signed.

Sanitation:

Parking:

2; Max 24hrs

None

2 car sized bays on side of busy road by marina. Only use if desperate! Inspected 2010.

VINASSAN — 58 — H11 — N43°12.278' E003°04.451' — 11110

Directions: Ave Docteur Etienne Montestruc. Turn off main route through village, signed. Aire 10m on left through Aire Services barrier, signed.

Sanitation:

Parking:

10; €8/24hrs inc elec; CC

Aire Services; 16amp elec inc

Aire located under trees providing deep shade. Village with local commerce 1 min. Inspected 2012.

ST PIERRE LA MER — 59 — H11 — N43°11.388' E003°11.805' — 11560

Directions: Enter town from Narbonne on D1118. Take Blvd des Embruns through town and turn right before the roundabout, sp 'Ecole de Voile'. Follow past municipal campsite 230m, signed.

Sanitation:

Parking:

100; €5/night; CC

Flot Bleu Océane; Token; €2; Elec 1 token/4hrs

Informal feel. Sailing school adj; Sea adj; 5 mins to town. Inspected 2010.

LES CABANES DE FLEURY — 60 — H11 — N43°12.910' E003°14.088' — 11560

Photo: Geoff Swann

Directions: From Fleury or Valras-Plage follow sp 'Les Cabanes de Fleury'. The Aire is on right past new marina.

Sanitation:

Parking:

35; €6

Flot Bleu Océane; Token; €2

Small river port town against Med. Shops. Inspected 2010.

SERIGNAN

61 H11 N43°16.140' E003°17.020' 34410

Directions: D64. Approach from north on D64. At roundabout turn right off D64 towards Super U supermarket. At next roundabout turn left, drive past fuel station, follow road to left, then turn left into fuel station. Service Point on right, signed.

Sanitation:

Parking:

Poss

Aire Services; €2

Supermarket adj; Self-service laundry adj. Inspected 2012.

VILLENEUVE LES BEZIERS

62 H11 N43°18.994' E003°17.076' 34420

Directions: Promenade des Vernets. Adj to canal outside Camping des Berges du Canal. From town centre cross canal and turn immediately right. Service Point 100m on left. Track narrow in places.

Sanitation:

Parking:

Poss

Custom; €2

Boat moorings adj; no restriction on parking visible. Inspected 2010.

VALRAS PLAGE

63 H11 N43°14.600' E003°16.903' 34350

Directions: Boulevard Pierre Giraud. Follow sp 'Casino'. From D19, main route, turn right onto D37 sp 'Casino'. Service Point on right just before road turns towards sea.

Sanitation:

Parking:

None

Aire Services; €2 for 50L water

Parking restrictions in town. Resort along sandy beach with restaurants etc. Inspected 2010.

PORTIRAGNES PLAGE

64 H11 N43°16.527' E003°21.105' 34420

Info/Photo: Liam Madden

Directions: Ave de la Grande Maire. Turn off the D37 at the roundabout north of town, sp 'Plage OUEST'. Turn right sp 'Plage OUEST'. Follow round to left, and then go straight over roundabout sp 'Plage Ouest Parking'. Aire on left, signed.

Sanitation:

Parking:

12; Max 48hrs

None

Large sandy beach 200m. Toilet 150m. Large wetland area with paths adj, no view. Roadside parking banned. Visited 2012.

LE CAP D'AGDE

65 H11 N43°17.148' E003°31.037' 34300

Directions: Parking de la Bavière. As enter Cap d'Agde on D612 turn left at 1st roundabout and right at 2nd roundabout, signed. The Aire is on right, signed. Entry phone at barrier. Pay at 'Camping de la Clape' 100m. Service Point outside barrier.

Sanitation:

Parking:

22; €10/24hrs; Pay at campsite 100m; 7m bays

Flot Bleu Euro; CC

Sea 10 mins walk, no views. Inspected 2010.

AGDE — 66 — H11 — N43°17.954' E003°28.259' — 34300

Directions: Route de Guiraudette. At Hyper U just off N112 towards Le Cap d'Agde.

Sanitation:

Parking:

None

Euro Relais Mini; Token (ER); €2.50

Supermarket; Garden centre, McDonalds. Inspected 2010.

SETE — 67 — I11 — N43°22.019' E003°36.962' — 34200

Directions: N112. From Agde follow N112 beach road for 6km towards Sète. Aire on right off roundabout.

Sanitation:

Parking:

35

Aire Services; €1; CC

Isolated Aire off main road adj to railway; Large sandy beach adj via footpath. Inspected 2012.

MARSEILLAN PLAGE — 68 — I11 — N43°19.149' E003°32.928' — 34340

Directions: Rue des Goelands. From Sete on N112 turn off at roundabout, sp 'Marseillan-Plage'. At next roundabout go straight over, sp 'Plage-Centre'. Turn left in 50m, signed. Aire on left, Service Point past Urba Flux barrier entrance.

Sanitation:

Parking:

€4/24hrs Jan-Mar/Nov-Dec, €6/24hrs Apr-Jun/Sept-Oct, €10 July-Aug; CC

Urba Flux Tall; €2/10mins; CC

Former municipal campsite turned Aire. Town and beach 7 mins. Inspected 2012.

MEZE — 69 — I11 — N43°26.453' E003°35.700' — 34140

Directions: Avenue du Stade. From roundabout on D613 west of village turn onto D158 sp 'Loupian'. Take 3rd right sp 'P Camping car', 'Stade' 'Parc de Sesquier'. This avoids 3.5t weight restriction through Meze on D5.

Sanitation:

Parking:

8

Custom

15 mins from town. Next to sports facilities. Inspected 2010.

BALARUC LES BAINS — 70 — I11 — N43°26.739' E003°40.665' — 34540

Directions: Turn off D2, sp 'Balurac les Bains' and signed. Drive to centre, signed. At roundabout turn left, signed. In 200m turn right, signed. Additional 6 places N43°26.711' E003°40.510', Exit parking and turn right then right at roundabout and right at end of road. Parking 100m on left, signed.

Sanitation:

Parking:

6+6; Max 24hrs

Aire Services; Token (3/3)

Thermal spa adj. Inspected 2012.

MONTAGNAC — 71 — H11 — N43°28.517' E003°29.467' — 34530

Photo: Roy France

Directions: Junction of D613/D5e11. Exit town towards Mèze. Aire on left adj to dual carraigeway. Signed.

Sanitation:

Parking:

5

Custom

Parking area small and there will be some road noise. Inspected 2010.

ANIANE — 72 — I11 — N43°41.183' E003°34.950' — 34150

Directions: D32. In Aniane go past La Poste and take the 2nd road on left and go right to the end to large turning circle.

Sanitation:

Parking:

12

None; See 73

Gravel surface but some soft grass areas between trees. Local commerce 200m. Inspected 2012.

GIGNAC — 73 — H11 — N43°39.716' E003°33.522' — 34150

Directions: Chemin de la Meuse, outside Camping de la Meuse. Exit north of village on D32 to Aniane. Turn left, sp 'Camping Municipal de la Meuse'.

Sanitation:

Parking:

None; See 72

Euro Relais Mini; Token (ER)

Free out of season and working at time of visit. Inspected 2010.

LAC DU SALAGOU — 74 — H11 — N43°38.806' E003°23.373' — 34800

Directions: Outside municipal campsite at Lac du Salagou. From Clermont l'Herault take D908 then D156, sp 'Lac du Salagou'. Also signed off A75 at Junction 55.

Sanitation:

Parking:

6; €5 inc elec

Custom; Token; €2; 4 16amp elec points

Pay at campsite reception. Inspected 2010.

MOUREZE — 75 — H11 — N43°37.040' E003°21.661' — 34800

Directions: D8. Aire in small car park by TO adj to main road, approx 350m east of village. Additional parking alongside the road.

Sanitation:

Parking:

15; €6/24hrs

Toilet only

Lovely area with walks around Cirque de Moureze, but can be busy. Inspected 2010.

FRAISSE SUR AGOUT * 76 H11 N43°36.267' E002°47.750' 34330

Photo: Rita Renninghoff

Directions: From west on D14 turn right just before village into Chemin de la Salvetat à Fraisse/Rue des Jardins, sp 'Ile sur l'Agout' and signed. Aire on right in 180m.

Sanitation:

Parking:

10; €7/24hrs; Collected in evening; Grass parking

Flot Bleu Compact; 2 unmetered elec points

Pleasant Aire by riverside. BBQ point. River can flood. TO and local shops in village. Inspected 2010.

LA SALVETAT SUR AGOUT 77 H11 N43°36.021' E002°40.749' 34330

Info/Photo: Rod & Liz Sleigh

Directions: Sailing Club car park. Turn of D907 South of La Salvetat sur Agout onto D14E1, sp 'Lac de la Raviège' and 'Base Touristique des Bouldouïres'. In 1.5km turn left sp 'Base Touristique des Bouldouïres'. Follow road past the campsite to the sailing school car park adj to lake, Aire in car park.

Sanitation:

Parking:

6; Max 48hrs

Custom

Adj to large leisure lake with sandy beach. Sailing and swimming poss. May feel isolated out of season. Visited 2012.

LUNAS 78 H11 N43°42.351' E003°11.179' 34650

Directions: D35. On right as approach Lunas from Le Bousquet d'Orb.

Sanitation:

Parking:

30

Custom

Pleasant spot with view of small lake and footpath to village. Inspected 2010.

LODEVE 79 H11 N43°44.017' E003°19.083' 34700

Photo: Barrie Wilson

Directions: Blvd du Général Leclerc. From south exit A75 at Junction 53. Follow sp 'Centre Ville'. Cross river, turn right and follow road through town for 1.2km. Aire on right. 3.5t weight restriction in town. Follow lorry route to bridge northeast of town. Turn left and left again at end of road to Aire.

Sanitation:

Parking:

5

None

Busy town centre car park; No services. Advise arrive after 5pm. Inspected 2010.

FLORAC 80 I10 N44°19.528' E003°35.414' 48400

Photo: Carol and Duncan Weaver

Directions: Parking Chatemale, Ave Michel Gillibert. From N106 cross river into town. From Avenue Jean Monestier turn into Avenue Maurice Tour. Turn right into Esplanade Marceau Farelle then continue into Rue du Causse and the Aire is up the hill on right.

Sanitation:

Parking:

20; Max 24hrs

Raclet; €2

Nice spot. Alpine views. Inspected 2010.

ISPAGNAC

81 H10 N44°22.256' E003°32.202' 48320

Directions: Chemin des Plots. On entering village from the north turn right off D907bis (Gorges du Tarn) at the 'Information' sign into the car park, signed. Aire is through car park and on the left just beyond the TO.

Sanitation:

Parking:

5

Custom; Token (2/1); €3.80

SP

Pretty village adj to river tarn. Service Point difficult, care needed. Near Gorges du Tarn. Inspected 2010.

MENDE

82 H10 N44°31.282' E003°29.797' 48000

Photo: John Barry

Directions: Rue du Faubourg Montbel, parking Faubourg Montbel. From N88 at roundabout turn left into Quai de la Petite Roubeyrolle. Follow road along riverside to car park on left. Aire in rear of car park.

Sanitation:

Parking:

24

Bollard

SP

Parking backs onto river with weir under bridge. Inspected 2010.

LE MONASTIER

83 H10 N44°30.534' E003°15.104' 48100

Directions: N9, at the train station. From A75 turn off at junction 39, sp 'Le Monastier' and follow road down hill. At roundabout turn left and Aire is 150m on right at train station, signed.

Sanitation:

Parking:

4

Raclet; Token (ER); €3

SP

At train station. Inspected 2010.

Marseillan Plage

ST CHELY D'APCHER

85 H9 N44°48.050' E003°16.473' 48200

Directions: Avenue de la Gare. Turn off D809/Boulevard Guerin d'Apcher into car park. Service Point on right.

Sanitation:

Parking:

2

Euro Relais Junior; Token (ER)

SP

Small, busy town centre car park. Tokens from TO 200m. Supermarket 400m. Local commerce adj. Inspected 2010.

LE MALZIEU VILLE

86 H9 N44°51.302' E003°20.003' 48140

Directions: Place du Foirail. From D989 follow signs into Rue du Barry. At end of road turn left and the Aire is on right.

Sanitation:

Parking:

6

Custom

Pleasant spot on edge of pretty, medieval walled town adj to river. Inspected 2010.

LANGOGNE

87 I9 N44°44.250' E003°50.050' 48300

Directions: Parking at Lac de Naussac off D26. From Le Puy en Velay take N88 to Langogne. Turn left by the Pharmacie and Cinéma. Follow this road northeast for 2.2km to Aire, sp 'Lac de Naussac' and 'Base Nautique'.

Sanitation:

Parking:

20; €5; Jun-Sept; Max 48hrs

Euro Relais Maxi; Token (ER); €3

Lake views; Lake adj; Hotel; Restaurants; Sailing school. Snack bar adj. Inspected 2010.

VILLEFORT

88 I10 N44°26.033' E003°55.833' 48800

Directions: Rue du 19 Mars 1962. From south on D901 turn left just before village, sp 'Les Sédariès'. Aire on left just past Gendarmerie.

Sanitation:

Parking:

5

Euro Relais Junior; €2

Roadside parking but very quiet road. D901 from south is very scenic. Inspected 2010.

ALES

89 I10 N44°07.208' E004°04.927' 30100

Directions: Ave Jules Guesde. To avoid town approach from south on N106. At roundabout turn left, sp 'Ales-Centre' and 'La Prairie'. After crossing river bridge turn right, sp 'Centre Ville' and 'La Prairie'. Follow road along river edge. Go straight roundabout over, sp 'Le Bresis' and signed. Aire 100m on right, signed.

Sanitation:

Parking:

8; Large motorhomes subject to wheelbase

Custom

5.5m bays but plenty of overhang. Locals also use parking. Adj river is more of a storm drain. Large town commerce 1 min. Inspected 2012.

LES MAGES

90 I10 N44°14.082' E004°10.184' 30960

Directions: Off D904. Travelling south on D904 turn left, sp 'Les-Mages', Aire 220m on left.

Sanitation:

Parking:

10

Custom

Local commerce in village. Inspected 2010.

ST LAURENT DE CARNOLS

91 | I10 | N44°12.612' E004°31.853' | 30200

Directions: D166. Turn off D980 onto D166, sp 'St Laurent de Carnols' and signed. Aire 700m on right, signed.

Sanitation:

Parking:

4; Max 48hrs; Need to reverse out

Urba Flux Tall; €2; Token

Landscaped Aire with 4 bays but no opportunity to turn around. Adj to wine seller. Bar in village 1 min. Inspected 2012.

BARJAC

92 | I10 | N44°18.347' E004°20.634' | 30430

Directions: D901. Enter town from south on D979. At roundabout turn right onto D901, sp 'Bagnols s/c'. Turn left in 50m. Service Point on left against building, parking down slope past Service Point.

Sanitation:

Parking:

10

Aire Services; €3; Token (3/3); 1 CEE elec point

Adj to busy main road. Restaurant adj. Toilets and water fountain adj. Town centre 4 mins uphill. Inspected 2012.

ST JEAN DU GARD

93 | I10 | N44°06.094' E003°53.042' | 30270

Directions: Rue Beaux de Maguielle. Turn off D907 at traffic lights into St Jean du Gard, sp 'Centre Ville' and 'Gare'. Follow road straight on through town and over river where road ends at train station. Aire to left of the station.

Sanitation:

Parking:

10

Raclet

Gard steam train to Anduze - 40 min trip. Town and mini Super U 5 mins. Inspected 2010.

ANDUZE

94 | I10 | N44°02.992' E003°59.070' | 30140

Directions: Place de la Gare. Turn off D907/Avenue du Pasteur Rollin into train station car park. 3.5t weight restriction in town; large vans follow 'lorry route' across low bridge for Nîmes.

Sanitation:

Parking:

20

Euro Relais Junior; €2

Town in lovely setting surrounded by rocky hills. Toilets open only during station hours. Fair in Sept. Busy on Thurs market day. Inspected 2010.

SAUVE

95 | I10 | N43°56.390' E003°57.160' | 30610

Directions: D999. Parking adj to D999. Signed.

Sanitation:

Parking:

20

Custom; Tap missing

Medieval village. Aire shared with cars. Inspected 2010.

ST MAMERT DU GARD — 96 — I10 — N43°53.117' E004°11.450' — 30730

Directions: Rue du Gres. From D22 turn into village on D1/Route du Stade. Take 2nd right into Rue du Gres. Turn left and follow road to parking area on left. Service Point is on Route du Stade behind recycling point, signed: N43°53.084' E004°11.418'.

Sanitation: E WC F

Parking: P F

5

Custom

SP

May need to reverse out, slightly uphill. Inspected 2010.

ST MATHIEU DE TREVIERS — 97 — I10 — N43°45.733' E003°51.634' — 34270

Directions: Chemin de la Ville. From D17 south of village turn west at roundabout, signed. After 200m turn right. Look for elec stands through main gate on right. Gate locked 10pm-8am.

Sanitation: E WC F

Parking: P F

10; €5/24hrs; Collected

SOS; 9 unmetered elec points

SP

Aire adj to sports centre in gravel car park with unmarked bays. Inspected 2010.

SOMMIERES — 98 — I10 — N43°47.183' E004°05.233' — 30250

Directions: Chemin de la Princesse. Directly outside Camping Municipal Le Garanel. Follow sp 'Camping Municipal' in town. The streets are narrow and a one way system operates through town.

Sanitation: E WC F

Parking: P F

5

Euro Relais Mini; Token (ER); €3

SP

Tokens from campsite adj. Inspected 2010.

PALAVAS LES FLOTS — 99 — I11 — N43°31.808' E003°55.471' — 34250

Directions: Rue Frédéric Mistral. On D986 from north go straight over roundabout, sp 'Halte Camping Cars'. Take next left, sp 'Halte Camping Cars', which turns back on itself under 3.7m bridge. GPS taken from top of road. Exact GPS: N43°31.855'E003°55.438'.

Sanitation: E WC F

Parking: P F

120; €8-€12/24hrs; €15/24hrs in Aug

Custom; €3

SP

Adj to port and river, some views. Showers; Commercial Aire can be packed like sardines. Inspected 2010.

CARNON PLAGE — 100 — I11 — N43°33.033' E003°59.633' — 34280

Directions: Rue de l'Aigoual, at Carnon Plage. Follow sp 'Carnon Est' along D59 then turn, sp 'Les Saladelles' and signed. Keypad barrier into Aire.

Sanitation: E WC F

Parking: P F

20; €11/night inc elec; Apr-Sept

Custom

SP

Commercial Aire. BBQ point; 80m from sea. Inspected 2010.

HAVE YOU VISITED AN AIRE? **GPS co-ordinates in this guide are protected by copyright law**

Take at least 5 digital photos showing
• Signs
• Service Point
• Parking
• Overview
• Amenities

Visit www.all-the-aires.co.uk/submissions.shtml to upload your updates and photos.

Sanitation:

Aire Details:

Submit updates
- Amendments
- New Aires
- Not changed

LA GRANDE MOTTE

102 I11 N43°34.033' E004°04.467' 34280

Directions: Ave de la Petite Motte. From D39 follow sp 'Campings'. Aire on right at end of road adj to campsite.

Sanitation:

Parking:

30; €13 May-Sept; €11 Oct-Mar; CC

Custom; Plenty of unmetered elec points

SP

5-10 mins from sea. Showers. Motorhome campsite. Inspected 2010.

LE GRAU DU ROI

103 I11 N43°32.437' E004°08.011' 30240

Directions: D62a. Enter town and follow sp 'Port de Pêche'. Aire just off large roundabout with D62a. Visible from road and signed.

Sanitation:

Parking:

50; Up to €15.50; Pay at machine

Aire Services; €2

SP

Beach adj; Difficult access when full. Water park adj. Inspected 2010.

AIGUES MORTES 1

104 I11 N43°33.950' E004°11.117' 30220

Photo: Phil Peyton

Directions: Rue du Port, parking at port. Enter town from D62 and follow signs.

Sanitation:

Parking:

30; €12; CC barrier; Pay on entry.

Custom; inc

SP

Some river/boat views. Views of ramparts. Town 5 mins walk. Inspected 2010.

AIGUES MORTES 2

105 I11 N43°33.933' E004°11.733' 30220

Directions: Located in car park P4. As enter town follow road alongside city wall to barriered car park P4. Signed.

Sanitation:

Parking:

50; €9.40; CC or cash; Barrier/machine; Pay on exit

None; See **104**

SP

Walled city adj with pristine walls all the way around. Central square with cafés and restaurants. Worth a visit. Inspected 2010.

AIGUES MORTES 3

106 I11 N43°34.650' E004°11.966' 30220

Directions: D979, parking at Intermarché. On northern outskirts of town at roundabout junction of D62/D979/D46. On entering car park turn right and parking signed at rear of Intermarché against grass bank.

Sanitation:

Parking:

10

None; See **104**

Supermarket with LPG in out of town shopping area. Inspected 2010.

LES SAINTES MARIES DE LA MER 1

107 I11 N43°27.326' E004°25.649' 13460

Directions: Rue Crin Blanc. Adj to D570 Avenue d'Arles. At end of pony rides/ranches, go across roundabout and turn left in 20m opp pond.

Sanitation:

Parking:

60; €9.50/night; Max 48hrs; Collected

Custom; inc

Popular; Pony rides; Town centre 3 mins. Service Point open limited hours each day. Inspected 2010.

LES SAINTES MARIES DE LA MER 2

108 I11 N43°27.222' E004°26.231' 13460

Directions: Vallée des Lys. At the end of pony rides turn left at roundabout and follow road straight across. Then turn left onto Ave JY Cousteau. Aire just off roundabout after campsite turning, sp 'Plage Est'.

Sanitation:

Parking:

50; €9.50; Pay attendant at barriered entrance

Custom

Adj to beach and promenade; less busy than **107**. Service Point open limited hours each day. Inspected 2010.

SALIN DE GIRAUD

109 J11 N43°24.739' E004°43.851' 13129

Directions: Rue de la Bouvine. From Arles follow D36. After traffic lights turn right, sp 'Centre Ville' and signed. Turn left at Medi@site, then right just before fire station, signed.

Sanitation:

Parking:

10

Custom

Town 3 mins; sign indicates showers, not open at time of visit. Toilet closed in winter. Chain ferry across Rhone €5. Inspected 2010.

PORT ST LOUIS DU RHONE 1

110 J11 N43°23.006' E004°48.439' 13230

Photo: Peter Gordon

Directions: Quai Bonnardel. Follow main road through town. Road will turn right and left. After bridge Service Point on left. Signed throughout.

Sanitation:

Parking:

None, See **111**

Urba Flux; Token

Service Point only. Inspected 2010.

PORT ST LOUIS DU RHONE 2 — 111 — J11 — N43°23.067' E004°49.162' — 13230

Directions: Avenue de la 1ere D.F.L. Follow signs through town on main road passing service area on right. Cross bridge and at roundabout follow signs into Ave de la 1ere D.F.L. Aire 800m on left.

Sanitation:

Parking:

200; Max 48hrs; €6 inc token; Collected

None; See 110

In old dock area. Some distance from town centre. Inspected 2010.

CARRO — 112 — J11 — N43°19.758' E005°02.416' — 13500

Directions: Quai Jean Vérandy. Turn off D49b into Carro and follow main route through town. Road bends to left and becomes Quai Jean Vérandy. Entrance on right at ticket gate; take ticket on entry.

Sanitation:

Parking:

60; €8/24hrs Jun-Sept; €6/24hrs Oct-May; Max 72hrs

Custom; inc

Views over sea; Beach 2 mins. Harbour and boats adj but no views. Inspected 2010.

SAUSSET LES PINS — 113 — J11 — N43°20.294' E005°06.513' — 13960

Directions: Ave Pierre Matraja, at the stadium Complexe Michel Hidalgo. Enter Sausset les Pins from D5 south. At roundabout turn left, sp 'Le Brûlot'. The Aire is 450m on the left.

Sanitation:

Parking:

20

Euro Relais Junior; Token/coin; €2; No drive over drain

Town and harbour 7 mins downhill. Very unlevel. Inspected 2010.

ST MARTIN DE CRAU — 114 — J11 — N43°38.309' E004°48.823' — 13310

Directions: N1453. Enter from east on D113. At roundabout follow sp 'St Martin de Crau'. Go straight over next roundabout. At traffic lights turn right, sp 'Mouries', then immediately left opp Gendarmerie. Aire in large car park adj to toilets, signed.

Sanitation:

Parking:

3; Max 24hrs

Urba Flux Tall

Despite being a large car park, only 3 bays have been allocated to motorhomes. Town centre, 2 mins, has 3.5t weight restriction. Library opp. Inspected 2012.

SENAS — 115 — J10 — N43°44.644' E005°04.853' — 13560

Directions: Ave des Jardins. From Salon de Provence enter town at 1st turning, sp 'Sénas'. Go straight across 1st roundabout, sp 'La Cappallette' and 'Centre de Secours'. Follow road and the Aire are on left alongside school, signed.

Sanitation:

Parking:

10

Euro Relais Junior; Token (2/1)

Outside school, best avoided during school hrs; Village 4 mins. Inspected 2010.

REDESSAN 116 I10 N43°49.526' E004°29.754' 30129

Directions: D999. Service Point in fuel station of Casino supermarket adj to D999/D3 roundabout, signed.

Sanitation:

Parking:

Poss

Flot Bleu Euro; €2; CC

Supermarket adj. Inspected 2012.

VALLABREGUES 117 J10 N43°51.464' E004°37.586' 30300

Info/Photo: Jean and Ken Fowler

Directions: Route d'Aramon. Exit Vallabregues to the north on D183A, sp 'Avignon'. The Aire is 300m on the left, signed.

Sanitation:

Parking:

7

Euro Relais Junior, Token (ER)

Landscaped Aire with plenty of space adj to road. River Gard nearby but no view. Local commerce and convenience store 11 mins. Visited 2012.

BELLEGARDE 118 I10 N43°44.657' E004°31.135' 30127

Directions: Port de Bellegarde. Approach from south on D6113. At roundabout turn left, then immediately right into Ave Eric Tabarly, both sp 'Port de Plaisance' and signed. Follow road straight on over bridge then turn left in 50m, signed. Follow road to end.

Sanitation:

Parking:

20; Max 48hrs

Euro Relais Maxi; €2; Token (ER)

Parking overlooking pleasure boats just off main road. All other riverside parking is restricted. Village with local commerce 3 mins. Inspected 2012.

ARLES 119 J11 N43°41.026' E004°37.821' 13200

Directions: Exit N113 Junction 7, sp 'Arles – ZI Port'. Turn left, sp 'Arles-Centre'. Drive 1.5km and turn right at traffic lights by city wall, sp 'Gare SNCF'. Go straight over roundabout into car park, signed. Turn right at end of road, and the Service Point is immediately on right, signed. For parking drive 100m along river to lion statues, signed.

Sanitation:

Parking:

5; Waterfront now restricted

Euro Relais Junior; 2 unmetered CEE elec points

Beautiful historic town with Roman amphitheatre, historic monuments, and commerce. Inspected 2012.

COMPS * 120 J10 N43°51.257' E004°36.488' 30300

Directions: Rue St Nicolas. From D986l turn into town, sp 'Comps'. Town narrow. After turning right through bullfighting arena continue straight on for riverside parking or turn 1st right for services and parking within flood barrier, signed. Well signed through town.

Sanitation:

Parking:

50; €4/24hrs

Aire Services; CC; €4

Grass parking under trees at riverside, prone to flooding; If in doubt park on hard standing adj to Service Point behind barrier. Pay attendant at 9am or in village, 2 mins. Inspected 2010.

REMOULINS 121 I10 N43°56.258' E004°33.321' 30210

Directions: D981. Turn off at roundabout with D986l and D6086, signed. Service Point on D981. Parking across bridge on right: N43°56.287' E004°33.521'.

Sanitation:

Parking:

10

Flot Bleu Euro; CC; €5

Parking near town and adj to river but no views. Inspected 2010.

ST ALEXANDRE 122 I10 N44°13.648' E004°37.369' 30130

Directions: Route des Remparts. From Pont St Esprit follow N86 south then take D306 to village. Aire is next to cemetery as enter village, signed.

Sanitation:

Parking:

3

Custom

SP

Views over vines and hills from Aire. This is a rural location and there is a bar/restaurant in village, nearest commerce 3km. Visited 2012.

L'ARDOISE 123 J10 N44°05.717' E004°42.083' 30290

Directions: Place de la Resistance, off N580. From south on N580 turn left into Place de la Resistance. Adj to tennis court, opp Police Municipale and La Poste.

Sanitation:

Parking:

6

Custom

Small town on Rhône. Inspected 2010.

LAUDUN L'ARDOISE 1 124 J10 N44°06.228' E004°39.829' 30290

Directions: Vignerons de Laudun, Avenue du Général de Gaulle. From N580 take D9, sp 'Laudun'. In 2km turn right onto D121/Rte du Général de Gaulle. Aire on right in 1.5km. Well signed.

Sanitation:

Parking:

5; Max 24hrs

Custom

SP

Wine producer on edge of village. Super U 250m. Also France Passion, but non members welcome. Inspected 2010.

LAUDUN L'ARDOISE 2 125 J10 N44°06.470' E004°39.363' 30290

Directions: Place du 19 Mars 1962. From D6086 turn onto D9 at the roundabout sp 'Laudun l'Ardoise'. After 4km turn left, off D9, sp 'Laudun l'Ardoise'. Follow sp 'Parking des Arènes' and signs through town.

Sanitation:

Parking:

3

Customised Flot Bleu; No drive over drain

Basketball courts; 2 mins downhill to pretty town. Côtes du Rhône producing area. Inspected 2010.

BAGNOLS SUR CEZE

126 J10 N44°10.102' E004°37.178' 30200

Directions: Rue du Moulinet. Enter town from north on N86. At roundabout turn left, sp 'Avignon' and signed. Turn right in 100m, signed, then right again, signed. Follow road for 200m to Aire on right, signed.

Sanitation:

Parking:

6; Max 24hrs

Flot Bleu Fontaine

Adj to noisy main road, but it is an acceptable stop close to town. Commerce 4 mins walk. Inspected 2012.

CHUSCLAN

127 J10 N44°08.733' E004°40.644' 30200

Directions: D138. From N580 at roundabout take turning, sp 'Chusclan' and 'D138'. Follow road for 2km and Aire on right by Côtes du Rhône producer.

Sanitation:

Parking:

6

Custom

Côtes du Rhône cellar open 9am-noon and 4-6.30pm all year. Views across vines. Toilet at wine producer. Inspected 2010.

BOLLENE

128 J10 N44°19.317' E004°44.650' 84500

Directions: D26, at E'Leclerc supermarket. Turn off D26 into Centre Commercial north of Bollène. Ignore motorhome sign on entering complex and go straight on at roundabout adj to fuel station. Then drive to left-hand side of big 'E'Leclerc' sign. Better parking here, with space to overhang grass, adj to new Flot Bleu.

Sanitation:

Parking:

20

Flot Bleu Pacific

LPG; Carwash; Hypermarket. Can be noisy until late. Inspected 2010.

ST LAURENT DES ARBRES

129 J10 N44°03.554' E004°42.672' 30120

Directions: D101. Turn off N580 at roundabout north of St Laurent des Arbres onto D101, sp 'Roquemaure'. At next roundabout turn left. Service Point located at the fuel station of the Casino supermarket, signed.

Sanitation:

Parking:

Poss

Flot Bleu Euro; CC; 1 CEE elec point

Supermarket adj. Inspected 2012.

AVIGNON

130 J10 N43°57.111' E004°47.621' 84000

Directions: Park & Ride Ile Poit. From south on D2 follow sp 'Avignon' and 'Centre Ville' to cross river bridge on Pont Edouard Daladier (D900). Take 1st turning right sp 'Park & Ride Ile Poit'. Aire is 1st parking area in P&R. P&R well signed.

Sanitation:

Parking:

13; Max 24hrs

None

Free, frequent shuttle bus to walled city. Tap adj at skate park. Full Service Point inside camping Bagatelle: €3.40: N43°57.175' E004°47.967'. Inspected 2010.

STE CECILE LES VIGNES

131 J10 N44°15.078' E004°53.409' 84290

Directions: D976, Cave des Vignerons Réunis. Adj to D976 as exit town to south.

Sanitation:

Parking:

If purchase wine

Unknown

A large commercial wine producer/factory. Not ideal for overnight stop. Cairanne **132** is a much nicer vineyard Aire, 5km. Inspected 2010.

CAIRANNE

132 J10 N44°13.807' E004°55.721' 84290

Directions: D8. Adj to D8 as exit town towards Ste-Cécile-les-Vignes at Cave de Cairanne, signed. Open 8am-7pm 7 days per week. Motorhomes park behind shop, ask in shop before proceeding.

Sanitation:

Parking:

1

Custom

Wine shop/producer. Parking with security. Signs in English. Inspected 2010.

VAISON LA ROMAINE

133 J10 N44°14.786' E005°04.445' 84110

Directions: Avenue André Coudray. From D975 at roundabout turn into Ave André Coudray. Follow sp 'Stade' and signed. At T-junction at end of road turn left and the Aire is 150m on left.

Sanitation:

Parking:

20; €7; Collected 8pm

Custom

Short walk to village. Inspected 2010.

SABLET

134 J10 N44°11.598' E004°59.695' 84110

Directions: D977. Adj to D977 before entering village. At wine producer Domaine du Parandou clearly signed from road.

Sanitation:

Parking:

2; €1.50

SOS; €3

Côtes du Rhône producer. Free for France Passion. Inspected 2010.

SARRIANS

135 J10 N44°04.776' E004°58.671' 84260

Directions: Off D221. Turn off D950 at southern edge of town onto D221 at the Intermarché roundabout, sp 'Camping Municipal'. Turn left at municipal campsite past entrance into parking area, signed.

Sanitation:

Parking:

5

Euro Relais Junior; Token (3/1); €2

Campsite adj; BMX bike track. Inspected 2010.

MALAUCENE

136 J10 N44°10.652' E005°07.792' 84340

Directions: Ave Charles de Gaulle. From D938 heading south, turn left when signed and the Aire is in 200m. Near the Gendarmerie and the sports facilities.

Sanitation:

Parking:

20

Custom

Market on Wednesday. Inspected 2010.

CARPENTRAS

137 J10 N44°03.366' E005°02.543' 84200

Directions: Cours de la Pyramide. Follow sp to 'Parking de la Port d'Orange' through town, signed. Service Point and one parking space by obelisk. Further parking, inc 3 designated spaces, on lower terrace.

Sanitation:

Parking:

None

Custom

Large walled town; Football pitch; Basketball. Inspected 2010.

PERNES LES FONTAINES

138 J10 N43°59.989' E005°04.097' 84210

Directions: Chemin du Camping, off D28. From D28 in town turn into Chemin du Camping, sp 'Camping Municipal - Le Coucourelle'. Follow road behind sports facilities and Service Point is just prior to municipal campsite.

Sanitation:

Parking:

None

Flot Bleu Fontaine; Open 15 Mar-15 Oct

Parking poss to visit town at P F Mistral. Inspected 2010.

BEDOIN 1

139 J10 N44°07.483' E005°10.333' 84410

Directions: Chemin de Bedoin a Malaucene. From south on D974 turn left at 1st roundabout in town onto D138/Le Cours, sp 'Camping Municipal', 'Piscine', and 'Tennis'. After 200m turn right into Chemin des Sablières. Aire in 400m. Service Point on right before Aire.

Sanitation:

Parking:

40; €3/night; Collected in morning; Max 72hrs

Euro Relais; €2

Outside municipal campsite. Awnings allowed; No BBQ. 2 mins from charming village with local commerce. Inspected 2010.

BEDOIN 2

140 J10 N44°07.927' E005°10.239' 84410

Directions: D19. From Bedoin follow D19 north for 1.3km. Service Point is on left of road outside Camping le Pastory.

Sanitation:

Parking:

None; See **139**

Euro Relais Mini; Token

Service Point only. Inspected 2010.

FONTAINE DE VAUCLUSE

141 | J10 | N43°55.159' E005°07.010' | 84800

Directions: D25. Large riverside car park adj to D25 just prior to village. Barriered entrance.

Sanitation:

Parking:

60; €3.50; Pay on exit

Custom; Lift up cover

SP

Canoe hire; Some Troglodyte evidence. Source of River Sorgue. Spring best time to visit when water high. Inspected 2010.

GORDES 1

142 | J10 | N43°54.961' E005°11.857' | 84220

Photo: Adrian and Rachael Rutter

Directions: D15, on west side of Gordes. From south approx 2km from D15 junction with D2. Aire is at far end of car park, sp 'Bus Parking'. Approaching from other directions requires navigating narrow village roads.

Sanitation:

Parking:

20; €5/24hrs

Aire Services; €2

SP

Beautiful hillside town, well worth a visit. 5 mins walk from village centre and commerce. Inspected 2010.

GORDES 2

143 | J10 | N43°54.067' E005°11.583' | 84220

Directions: D2. From D900 turn onto D2 at Coustellet, sp 'Gordes' from west and 'Musee de la Lavande' from east. Aire on left after 5.6km, just before Village des Bories. Signed.

Sanitation:

Parking:

40

None

SP

Large gravel parking area adj to Village des Bories. 1.5km walk to Gordes village. Well worth a visit. Inspected 2010.

PUYVERT

144 | J10 | N43°44.828' E005°20.247' | 84160

Directions: D973. South of Puyvert on D973. Follow sp 'Super U'. Aire behind car wash and adj to laundry.

Sanitation:

Parking:

Poss

Raclet; 2 unmetered elec points

SP

Supermarket adj. Can be noisy. Self-service laundry adj. Inspected 2010.

PELISSANNE

145 | J11 | N43°37.699' E005°09.225' | 13330

Directions: Chemin de la Prouvenque, adj to D15. From D572 enter town, sp 'Prouvenque' and 'Sapeurs Pompiers'. Aire at the sports facilities.

Sanitation:

Parking:

5

Custom

SP

Town 3 mins; Football; Skate park. Elec decommissioned since 2010. Inspected 2012.

STE TULLE

146 K10 N43°47.073' E005°45.824' 04220

Directions: Parc Municipal des Sports. Enter Ste Tulle on D996 from Miabeau. Turn 1st left on entering town, then turn right at stop junction, sp 'Parc des Sports'. Turn into 1st car park on left. Service Point against building.

Sanitation:

Parking:

10

Custom

Parking under plane trees in municipal sports area. Park, boules court, and other sports facilities adj. Town centre 3 mins. Inspected 2012.

ST MICHEL L'OBSERVATOIRE

147 K10 N43°54.938' E005°42.982' 04870

Photo: motorhomeandaway.co.uk

Directions: D305. From village centre take D305, sp 'Observatoire'. Aire on left in 600m. Ground soft after heavy rain.

Sanitation:

Parking:

12

Custom; Token; €2

Some shade (low trees). Visited 2012.

VILLENEUVE

148 K10 N43°53.773' E005°51.705' 04180

Directions: Cimetière. Turn off D4096 at roundabout, sp 'Villeneuve'. Follow sp 'P Cimetière' and signs up the hill then out of village. Turn right towards cemetery then follow road and signs downhill around the cemetery, signed.

Sanitation:

Parking:

12

Custom; No water Dec-Feb

Parking under trees next to cemetery; dead quiet. Hilly walk to village centre 4 mins which has local commerce and convenience store. Inspected 2012.

SAULT

149 J10 N44°05.718' E005°24.703' 84390

Info/Photo: Jean and Ken Fowler

Directions: D950. Enter town on D950. Go straight over roundabout. Turn left opp Sampiers Pompiers, sp 'P P3' and 'Cimetiere'. Aire in Parking P3, signed.

Sanitation:

Parking:

20

Euro Relais Mini; €2

The Aire is 5 mins walk from the lovely old town with local commerce. Good base for exploring Mont Ventoux and Gorges de Nesque.

DAUPHIN

150 K10 N43°54.034' E005°47.041' 04300

Directions: D316/Route de la Rencontre. From east on D13 turn left onto D513 and follow sp 'Salle des Fêtes'. Not signed.

Sanitation:

Parking:

5

Custom

Small car park adj to village hall. Toilets locked, tap not working, and drive over waste blocked at time of inspection. Inspected 2010.

LA BRILLANNE

151 K10 N43°55.922' E005°53.409' 04700

Directions: D4096. Adj to main route through town at the fuel station of the Carrefour supermarket. 3m height barrier avoidable.

Sanitation:

Parking:

Poss

Flot Bleu Pacific; Token/20 mins

Supermarket adj. Inspected 2012.

RIEZ

152 K10 N43°48.933' E006°05.450' 04500

Directions: Rue Hilarion Bourret/D952. From south on D11 turn left into D592/Rue Hilarion Bourret. After 300m turn right into large car park. Aire in opp corner adj to school and playground. GPS taken at car park entrance for clarity.

Sanitation:

Parking:

7

Custom

Parking in village centre. Inspected 2010.

MOUSTIERS STE MARIE

153 K10 N43°50.617' E006°13.100' 04360

Photo: Daren Fasey

Directions: Off D952. From south on D952 turn left to Aire below village, sp 'Parking 5' and signed. Aire on 2 levels; loose, gravelly slope to lower level.

Sanitation:

Parking:

30; €6/24hrs; Max 48hrs

Urba flux; €2

Walk up into town. Lovely village, 360° views. No shade. Inspected 2010.

TRIGANCE

154 K10 N43°45.611' E006°26.495' 83840

Directions: D90. Turn off D955, onto D90, sp 'Trigance'. The Aire is located just off a hairpin bend on this road.

Sanitation:

Parking:

5; €5 inc elec; Apr-Oct; Max 72hrs

Custom

Pretty village in scenic location with good views from the Aire. Inspected 2010.

COMPS SUR ARTUBY

155 K10 N43°42.375' E006°30.392' 83840

Directions: D955. South of Comps-Sur-Artuby on bend in the D955.

Sanitation:

Parking:

19; Max 24hrs

Custom; Token; €3

Token available from Le Rouable Pizzeria on site, 500m to village. Views over valley. Inspected 2010.

STE CROIX DE VERDON

156 K10 N43°45.651' E006°09.058' 04500

Photo: motorhomeandaway.co.uk

Directions: D111. From Reiz on D11 turn left (straight on at bend) onto D111, sp 'Ste Croix du Verdon'. Follow signs for Camping Municipal and lake, not village centre. Sharp right hand turn into Aire.

Sanitation:

Parking:

16; €6; Max 48hrs
Custom

SP

Near to village with good views over the lake. Fee collected in evening. Inspected 2010.

GREOUX LES BAINS

157 K10 N43°45.336' E005°53.314' 04800

Photo: David Shoesmith

Directions: Chemin de la Barque. From north on D82 continue through town to roundabout with fountain. Take 2nd exit onto D8, sp 'St Julien'. Just before river bridge turn sharp right into Chemin de la Barque. Aire 160m on right behind crèche. Well signed.

Sanitation:

E

Parking:

€7/24hrs; Mar-Nov; Pay at barrier on exit; Max 3.5t and 8m
Custom; Inc

SP

In town 100m from river Verdon. Well organised Aire. No trailers or cars. Inspected 2010.

QUINSON

158 K10 N43°41.881' E006°02.347' 04500

Directions: Allée des Pres du Verdon. From south on D13 turn right into Allée des Pres du Verdon, sp 'Parking du Musée'. Turn left into car park and Aire is just before the height barriers.

Sanitation:

F

Parking:

F

5
Custom

Aire in car park for prehistoric museum. There is a tap but the water is non potable. Inspected 2010.

SILLANS LA CASCADE

159 K11 N43°34.047' E006°10.932' 83690

Photo: Colin and Maggie Fancourt

Directions: D560/Route de Salernes, on main road to south of village. 3.5t weight restriction on Aire.

Sanitation:

E WC

Parking:

F

10; Max 24hrs
Urba flux; Token; €3

SP

Village 2 mins. Direct walk to famous waterfall. Inspected 2010.

BRIGNOLES

160 K11 N43°24.579' E006°03.722' 83170

Directions: D2007. From DN7 at roundabout take D1007 towards town centre. At traffic lights turn right onto D2007 and 1st right into Casino supermarket. Service Point at fuel station.

Sanitation:

E

Parking:

F

Poss
Flot Bleu Pacific; Token

Town centre 2 mins; Supermarket adj. Inspected 2010.

STE MAXIMIN LA STE BAUME — 161 — K11 — N43°27.420' E005°51.196' — 83470

Directions: D560. Follow sp 'Aix en Pce' through town. Service Point adj to D560/DN7 at the Hyper U. To locate Service Point enter supermarket parking and drive beside car wash, then turn right. Service Point on left.

Sanitation:

Parking:

Poss

Flot Bleu Pacific; €2

Supermarket, retail park, McDonalds, and bank adj. Inspected 2012.

ROUSSILLON — 162 — J10 — N43°53.782' E005°17.760' — 84220

Info/Photo: Rod and Liz Sleigh

Directions: D149, Route de Bonnieux A Roussillon. Approaching from the south on D900, take the D149 or D108, sp 'Roussillon'. Drive to village and turn right into car park 30m before roundabout. Take ticket at barrier. Motorhomes banned in Roussillon village.

Sanitation:

Parking:

10; €2 8am-10pm; €5 10pm-8am; Max 48hrs

None

Designated parking for motorhomes at southern edge of village. 5 mins to village with tourist attractions commerce and Ochre dye museum.

ST PAUL LES DURANCE — 163 — K11 — N43°41.241' E005°42.336' — 13115

Directions: Chemin du Retour. From east on D952 cross river on 2nd bridge (signed) onto D11/Grand Rue. Turn 1st left into Chemin du Retour.

Sanitation:

Parking:

6; Max 48hrs

Flot Bleu Fontaine

Small Aire at far end of residential campsite. Shower. Inspected 2010.

GREASQUE — 164 — K11 — N43°25.996' E005°32.044' — 13850

Directions: Route de la Chapelle. Follow sp 'Gardanne', then sp 'Hély d'Oissel' at roundabout, signed. Follow road uphill to mine.

Sanitation:

Parking:

25

Custom

At mining museum; Village 7 mins; BMX trails. Inspected 2010.

LA BOUILLADISSE — 165 — K11 — N43°23.386' E005°35.912' — 13720

Directions: D96, at Casino supermarket. As exit village on D96 towards Aubagne. Service Point at fuel station, has own entrance.

Sanitation:

Parking:

Poss

Flot Bleu Pacific; Token

Supermarket adj. Inspected 2010.

AURIOL — 166 — K11 — N43°22.081' E005°38.483' — 13390

Directions: D560. Exit Auriol towards Péage on D560. At Casino supermarket entrance.

Sanitation:

Parking:

Poss

Flot Bleu Pacific (Green); Token

Supermarket adj. Inspected 2010.

GEMENOS — 167 — K11 — N43°17.877' E005°37.760' — 13420

Directions: Cours Sudre. From D396, main route through town, turn sp 'Vallée de St Pons' and signed. At end of road turn left into car park and Aire is behind La Poste.

Sanitation:

Parking:

3; Max 24hrs

Custom

Village adj with local commerce. Market day Wed. Inspected 2010.

LE BEAUSSET — 168 — K11 — N43°11.900' E005°48.371' — 83330

Directions: DN8. On right at Casino supermarket.

Sanitation:

Parking:

Poss

Flot Bleu Euro; CC; €2

Supermarket adj. Inspected 2010.

CUGES LES PINS * — 169 — K11 — N43°16.868' E005°42.350' — 13780

Directions: From west on D8n turn left in Cuges les Pins, signed. Access road approx 1km, steep and narrow in places; not advised for larger motorhomes. Open gate to enter and see attendant at house on left. No access 9:30pm-7am.

Sanitation:

Parking:

20; €3/24hrs (12-12)

Custom; €1.50

Terraced hillside Commercial Aire. Steep gradient to upper terrace with loose, unmade surface. Elec avail from generator. Village 5 mins downhill. Inspected 2010.

SANARY SUR MER — 170 — K11 — N43°07.467' E005°47.217' — 83110

Directions: Chemin de Beaucours, at Camping Mogador. Exit town towards Bandol on D559. Turn left after Total fuel station, sp 'Camping' 'Beaucours'. Campsite 100m on left.

Sanitation:

Parking:

None

Euro Relais Junior; Token (ER); €5

Available when campsite open; Putting in specialist motorhome parking at time of inspection. Inspected 2010.

SIX FOURS LES PLAGES 1

171 K11 N43°06.752' E005°48.714' 83140

Directions: Sq Hippolyte Cesmat, along seafront of Six-Fours-les-Plages by TO. Difficult to spot; accessible only from behind TO. After using have to reverse out into road.

Sanitation:

Parking:

Pay; Also see **172**

Custom

Adj to beach and promenade with restaurants. Difficult. Inspected 2010.

SIX FOURS LES PLAGES 2

172 K11 N43°04.760'E005°48.587' 83140

Directions: Rue Robert Forrer. From north on D616 follow sp 'Brusc'. After marina go straight on at roundabout and at traffic lights turn left uphill into Rue Robert Forrer (one way), sp 'Les Charmettes'. Aire on left just before end of road. Not signed.

Sanitation:

Parking:

10; Tolerated

None; See **171**

SP

Car park outside old peoples' home (Maison de Retraite Les Charmettes). Inspected 2010.

LA SEYNE SUR MER

173 K11 N43°06.795' E005°51.469' 83500

Directions: Blvd de l'Europe. Adj to D26. Turn off A50 onto D26, sp 'La Seyne Centre'. Turn off, sp 'Centre Commercial'. Entrance on right, signed on fuel price display board. Service Point visible from road in parking on right.

Sanitation:

E

Parking:

Not recommended

Euro Relais Junior; Token (2/1); €4.60

Must exit where enter to avoid 2.5m height restriction. Inspected 2010.

ST MANDRIER SUR MER

174 K11 N43°04.636' E005°54.326' 83430

Directions: Ancienne Route de Saint-Mandrier, off D18. On D18 go past tennis courts and turn right after 220m. Follow road to right, signed. Service Point on right just past football pitches outside tennis club. Parking next right turn: N43°04.661' E005°54.262'.

Sanitation:

Parking:

6; Max 48hrs

SOS

SP

May be pay in season; Very tight, difficult parking, may have to reverse onto road. Inspected 2010.

LA ROQUEBRUSSANNE

175 K11 N43°20.164' E005°58.775' 83136

Directions: Ave St Sébastien. Approach from south on D5. Turn right off D5, as enter village, onto D64, sp 'Neoules'. Turn immediately right and Aire on right, signed.

Sanitation:

E

Parking:

6

Euro Relais Maxi; €2; Token; No drive over drain

SP

Adj to noisy road. Wine seller opp. Village centre, 2 mins, has 3.5t weight restriction and is too narrow for most motorhomes to drive through. Inspected 2012.

SOLLIES PONT | 176 | K11 | N43°12.137' E006°02.813' | 83210

Directions: Ave Jean Brunet. Heading south on A57 exit at Junction 8. At roundabout turn left, sp 'Centre Commercial'. Turn right, then drive through car park and turn left, then right. Service Point adj to Casino fuel station.

Sanitation:

Parking:

Poss but very noisy

Flot Bleu Euro; €2

Supermarket adj. Motorway adj. Inspected 2012.

HYERES | 177 | K11 | N43°06.478' E006°07.710' | 83400

Directions: D559/Ave Geoffroy St Hilaire, at the Casino supermarket. From Toulon go across roundabout on A570 then at traffic lights turn right onto D559. The Aire is down this road on right. Narrow access. Not signed from road.

Sanitation:

Parking:

None

Flot Bleu Euro (Green); CC; €3

Cheap fuel at time of visit. Inspected 2010.

HYERES 'LE MEROU' | 178 | K11 | N43°06.550' E006°10.893' | 83400

Directions: D42. Exit N98 onto D12 sp 'Les Salins'. In Les Salins turn right onto D42 at beach sp 'Le Merou', signed. Service point 200m after river bridge on left by toilets.

Sanitation:

Parking:

None

Flot Bleu Euro; CC

Service Point not working at time of visit. Inspected 2010.

LA LONDE LES MAURES 1 | 179 | K11 | N43°07.905' E006°13.836' | 83250

Directions: Rond Point Ducourneau. Turn off N98, sp 'La Londe Les Maures'. Follow sp 'Centre Ville'. Service Point and parking adj to roundabout 'Ducourneau', by side of main road.

Sanitation:

Parking:

4; Max 24hrs

Flot Bleu Euro; CC

Pleasant; Vines surround village; Local commerce 5 mins. Inspected 2010.

LA LONDE LES MAURES 2 | 180 | K11 | N43°08.303' E006°14.259' | 83250

Directions: D559, at Casino supermarket fuel station as exit town on D559 towards 'Bormes les Mimosas'.

Sanitation:

Parking:

Poss

Flot Bleu Euro (Green); CC

Fuel station; Mini Casino supermarket; Town centre adj. Inspected 2010.

COLLOBRIERES — 181 K11 N43°14.237' E006°18.170' 83610

Directions: D14. Approach from west on D14. At village boundary turn right, sp 'Sampiers Pompiers' and signed. Aire 20m, signed. Do not approach from any other direction unless you are happy to drive along narrow, twisting roads with no barriers!

Sanitation:

Parking:

30

Custom

Pleasant tourist village with restaurants and craft shops 2 mins. Park at Aire and walk in. There is pleasant grass parking at other side of village but we suggest walking to it first. Inspected 2012.

LA FAVIERE — 182 K11 N43°07.494' E006°21.708' 83230

Directions: Blvd du Port. Follow sp 'Port'. At port follow road to 'Le Lavandou' Service Point 100m from port, adj to road and park.

Sanitation:

Parking:

None

Raclet; Token (ER); €2

Raised up; Only enough stopping space for 1 motorhome; Difficult. Inspected 2010.

CAVALIERE — 183 K11 N43°09.124' E006°25.842' 83980

Directions: D559. Adj to main road. When can see sea on right, parking on left as exit to St Tropez. At rear of large gravel car park, entrance sp 'Camping-Car'.

Sanitation:

Parking:

100; €15/24hrs inc service

Custom; Token; €4

Large partially terraced Commercial Aire. Some sea views; Town commerce 1 min. All a bit rough and ready. Inspected 2010.

RAMATUELLE 1 — 184 L11 N43°12.676' E006°39.731' 83350

Directions: Bonne-Terrasse. From D93, St Tropez to La Croix Valmer, turn off, sp 'Déchetterie' and signed. Follow road and Aire entrance is on left 200m past tennis courts, before beach. 5.5t weight restriction on road.

Sanitation:

Parking:

100; €7.30/night; Open Apr-Oct; Max 48hrs; Pay at kiosk by entrance

Custom; Limited hrs

Sandy beach adj; Pay at entry. Inaccessible out of season. Showers. Inspected 2010.

RAMATUELLE 2 — 185 L11 N43°14.341' E006°39.693' 83350

Directions: Route des Tamaris. Turn off D93 between St Tropez and Pampelonne, sp 'Les Tamaris'. Parking on left near end of road.

Sanitation:

Parking:

40; €10 low season; €18 high season; 9am-9am

Custom; Token; €2; Elec available at extra cost

Closed low season, adj car park accessible. Beach adj. Inspected 2010.

ST TROPEZ 1

186 L11 N43°16.180' E006°38.054' 83990

Directions: Parking du Nouveau Port. Parking at the port. Follow sp 'P Port' when enter town. Enter parking through bus barrier.

Sanitation:

Parking:

100; Only between Nov-Mar; €1.10/hr; €14/24hrs

None

SP

At St Tropez yacht marina, ideal for the high life. Sea view. Inspected 2010.

ST TROPEZ 2

187 L11 N43°15.893' E006°40.333' 83990

Directions: Chemin de la Moutte. Through town follow sp 'Centre Ville'. Then follow Route des Salins east. After 2.6km turn left into Chemin de la Fontaine du Pin. Ignore GPS request to turn into turning before, it's a narrow, weak bridge. Take next left. Aire 100m on right, signed.

Sanitation:

Parking:

20; €11/night

Custom; Water €2; Elec €2.50/night

SP

Commercial Aire close to St Tropez. 150m from Cannebiers beach. Walk into St Tropez along coast. Bus nearby. Inspected 2010.

PORT GRIMAUD

188 K11 N43°16.792' E006°34.716' 83310

Directions: N98. On N98 adj, signed after junction with D14 if travelling from St Tropez. There were machines for barriers in place, but no barriers at time of inspection.

Sanitation:

Parking:

10

Euro Relais Maxi; CC

SP

Nearest services to St Tropez; Boulangerie and restaurant adj. Inspected 2010.

LA GARDE FREINET

189 K11 N43°18.865' E006°28.287' 83680

Directions: D75. From south on D558 turn right onto D75 at edge of village. Aire in small car park immediately on left, opp small sports stadium. Not signed.

Sanitation:

Parking:

4; Tolerated

None; Water tap only

SP

Easy walk to local commerce in pretty village. Market Sunday morning, car park busy. Bus to St Tropez. Inspected 2010.

LES ARCS SUR ARGENS

190 K11 N43°27.161' E006°29.463' 83460

Directions: D555. Turn off DN7 onto D555, sp 'Draguignan'. At any of the next three roundabouts turn left into the Hyper U supermarket. The Service Point is to the rear of the fuel station.

Sanitation:

Parking:

Poss

Flot Bleu Euro; CC

SP

Supermarket adj. Inspected 2012.

LES ARCS

191 K11 N43°27.292' E006°28.644' 83460

Directions: Ave des Laurons, at Cellier des Archers. From Draguignan (north) on D555 turn off at roundabout junction with D91, sp 'Gare'. Follow road along train tracks, past station, and across T-Junction, sp 'Cellier des Archers'. Aire in 100m.

Sanitation:

Parking:

50; Private Aire

Custom; Trees overhang drive over drain

Côtes de Provence wine cellar. Restaurants 5 mins. Some train noise. Inspected 2010.

LA MOTTE

192 K11 N43°29.794' E006°31.894' 83920

Directions: D47/Route de Trans. From south on D1555/N555 turn right at roundabout onto D54. Follow motorhome sign and sp 'Domaine de Valbourgès'. Pass Domaine de Valbourgès and cross river, then turn right onto D47, signed. Aire on left after 2.3km. Well signed.

Sanitation:

Parking:

10; Max 24hrs

Urba Flux Tall; €6

New Aire on edge of village. 3.5t weight restriction on Aire. Inspected 2010.

STE MAXIME 1

193 L11 N43°19.025' E006°37.799' 83120

Directions: D25. Just off large D25 roundabout with McDonalds. If approach from St Tropez (south) on N98 follow route sp 'Le Muy' to large roundabout.

Sanitation:

Parking:

25; €10 Apr-Sept; €5 Oct-Mar; Max 48hrs; Pay at machine

Urba Flux; inc

McDonalds; LIDL 3 mins; Town and beach 8 mins. Water taxi from harbour to St Tropez €12 high season. Inspected 2010.

STE MAXIME 2

194 L11 N43°18.474' E006°37.992' 83120

Directions: Ave Théodore Botrel, by drainage ditch. Follow sp 'Le Muy' then cross bridge and turn right, sp 'P145 Places' and 'Espace des Arts'. Narrow gateway and barriered entry.

Sanitation:

Parking:

20; €16/24hrs; Pay by hr

None

Town adj; Beach access. Overlooked by flats. Height barrier may be in place at times. Inspected 2010.

LA GAILLARDE

195 L11 N43°21.934' E006°42.720' 83370

Directions: N98/D1098, Chez Marcel. Signed off N98 - 100m from main road at La Gaillarde. Narrow, not advised for large motorhomes. Terraced with a one way system and a steep ramp between levels; long motorhomes could ground.

Sanitation:

Parking:

30; €10/24hrs inc service

Custom; €4; Elec €3

Commercial Aire; Beach 2 mins. Gated with attendant. Shower €0.50; Washing machine €5. Inspected 2010.

FREJUS — 196 — L11 — N43°26.367' E006°44.671' — 83600

Directions: D100/Ave André Léotard. On D100 towards St-Raphaël, at Casino supermarket. As enter Fréjus on D37 go straight across at roundabout. Supermarket on left. Service Point adj to fuel station.

Sanitation:

Parking:

None

Flot Bleu Euro; CC; €2

Supermarket adj. Overnight parking not permitted. Inspected 2010.

FAYENCE — 197 — L11 — N43°37.380' E006°41.412' — 83440

Directions: D563. Enter town from south on D19 or D563. Turn off roundabout onto D563 towards town, sp 'Mons' and 'Centre Ville'. Turn immediately left, signed. Service Point on left, two designated bays on right, one bay obstructed by tree.

Sanitation:

Parking:

2; Max 48hrs; Max 8m

Urba Flux; €4/15 mins; Diff access

Hilltop town. Parking la Ferrage: N43°37.314' E006°41.589'. Follow road to centre, parking adj to 1st hairpin, signed. Parking P3: N43°37.481' E006°41.802'. Follow D563 through town, then follow sp 'P3' and signed. 3 bays closest to town. Inspected 2012.

CALLIAN — 198 — L11 — N43°36.251' E006°45.290' — 83440

Directions: D562. Turn off D562 east of Callian at roundabout towards McDonalds. Pass McDonalds and turn left at the roundabout. Service Point on left adj to car wash.

Sanitation:

Parking:

None

Urba Flux; €2; Token

Service Point only. Inspected 2012.

CANNES — 199 — L11 — N43°33.002' E006°58.236' — 06150

Directions: D6007. Exit A8 at Junction 41 and follow sp 'Cannes-La Bocca' onto D6207. Under bridge fork left, then go straight across two roundabouts, sp 'Cannes'. Go straight over at traffic lights, sp 'La Bocca'. Service Point by fuel station of Hyper Casino supermarket, 400m on left. Road adj to supermarket being altered at time of inspection so may have to drive to next roundabout and return.

Sanitation:

Parking:

Poss

Flot Bleu Euro; €2

Supermarket adj. Inspected 2012.

ST LAURENT DU VAR — 200 — L10 — N43°41.119' E007°11.116' — 06700

Directions: Route des Pugets. Exit A8 at Junction 49 and follow sp ' St Laurent-Centre'. Go straight on at roundabout, sp 'Cimetière St Marc' and signed. At next roundabout go straight on, sp 'Parc d'Activities'. Turn left at next roundabout, sp 'Cimetière St Marc' and signed. Turn left at roundabout, sp 'Cimetière', then left again, sp 'Cimetière St Marc'. Aire 400m on right, signed.

Sanitation:

Parking:

7; Not suitable for motorhomes with trailers

Custom

Hillside location opp cemetery and overlooking industrial park. Popular Aire with difficult access. Town 4 mins. Inspected 2012.

CAILLE

201 L10 N43°46.733' E006°43.997' 06750

Directions: Junction of Rue St Pons and Rue des Ecuries. Turn of D6085 onto D79, sp 'Caille'. Enter village and follow signs to lower village. Aire on left, signed. Very small Aire, not suitable for large motorhomes.

Sanitation:

Parking:

3

Flot Bleu Pacific; €4; No drive over drain

Ancient village; 2 restaurants; Local commerce. Inspected 2010.

LAC DE THORENC

202 L10 N43°47.967' E006°48.500' 06750

Directions: Lac de Thorenc. Turn off D2 at parking, signed.

Sanitation:

Parking:

20

Custom

Pony rides; Woodland walks around lake; Lovely peaceful spot. Inspected 2010.

CASTELLANE 1

203 K10 N43°50.763' E006°30.950' 04120

Directions: D4085/D952. Aire on right as enter town on D4085 from Grasse, next to river under big rock with chapel on top, sp 'Parking Obligatoire Camping Cars'. Insert payment into machine barrier which lifts to enter; correct Euros needed.

Sanitation:

Parking:

40; €6; Max 48hrs

Custom; inc

Close to town centre with local commerce. Very popular Aire with good facilities. Beneath Notre Dame du Roc. Inspected 2012.

CASTELLANE 2

204 K10 N43°51.150' E006°30.500' 04120

Directions: D955, at Casino supermarket. On northern edge of town at roundabout junction of D955 and D4085. Flot Bleu machine at fuel station.

Sanitation:

Parking:

Poss

Flot Bleu Pacific; Token

Too small for overnight parking. Narrow access. Inspected 2012.

ST ANDRE LES ALPES

205 K10 N43°57.921' E006°30.439' 04170

Directions: D2/Grand Rue. From south on N202 take 2nd exit onto D2, turning back on yourself onto D2/Grand Rue, signed. Aire 120m on left.

Sanitation:

Parking:

20

Flot Bleu Euro; Token or CC; €3

Large tarmac parking area. No shade. Inspected 2010.

ANNOT — 206 — L10 — N43°57.793' E006°39.860' — 04240

Directions: Chemin de la Colle Basse. From south on D908 turn left in village centre, sp 'Aire de Camping Car'. Cross river and follow signs for 300m. Aire on left in woodland area on edge of village.

Sanitation:

Parking:

10

Custom

Lovely woodland setting; Some bays not hardstanding; Washing sink. Inspected 2010.

VALBERG — SKI — 207 — L10 — N44°05.766' E006°56.204' — 06470

Directions: Follow 'Aire Accueil' signs through town. Turn off D28, sp 'Ecole des Neiges'. Go past a tall stone bell tower. Turn right, signed, just before the road widens for parking. Turn immediately right as go around bend, signed. Follow this road and the Aire is on the right, clearly signed.

Sanitation:

Parking:

21; €10 inc services and elec

Custom; 24 elec points

Stunning scenery through Gorges de Daluis on approach via D2202. Lovely alpine views from Aire. Well worth the drive. Inspected 2010.

DIGNE LES BAINS — 208 — K10 — N44°04.796' E006°15.637' — 04000

Directions: Ave des Thermes. In town follow sp 'Les Thermes' and 'Piscine les Eaux Chaudes' onto D20. Pass Intermarché supermarket, drive 1.5km. Aire is on right near Thermal spa, signed. Riverside day parking: N44°05.419' E006°13.718' between the two road bridges on other side of river.

Sanitation:

Parking:

30

Euro Relais Junior; Token (ER); €2.50

Adj to thermal baths. Pleasant 3km walk to town. Inspected 2010.

COLMARS LES ALPES — 209 — L10 — N44°10.761' E006°37.577' — 04370

Directions: Turn off the D908 opp the Garage des Alps, signed. In 50m turn left before the river bridge. The Service Point is on the left. Approach from north via Col d'Allos not advised.

Sanitation:

Parking:

5

Flot Bleu Euro; CC; €3

Interesting, well preserved, walled town, well worth a look. Footpath to Cascade de la Lance. Inspected 2010.

ALLOS — SKI — 210 — L10 — N44°14.583' E006°37.367' — 04260

Directions: Park de Loisirs, off D908. From south on D908 go through town and turn left immediately before river bridge, sp 'Park de Loisirs' and signed. Approach from north via Col d'Allos not advised. Barriered entry; pay on exit, CC only.

Sanitation:

Parking:

20; €5 1st night; €4 subsequent nights; Max 72hrs; CC

Flot Bleu Standard Plus inc; 8 600watt elec points

At base of ski lift. Inspected 2010.

LA FOUX D'ALLOS SKI 211 K10 N44°17.738' E006°34.135' 04260

Directions: D908. From south on D908, the Service Point is on left immediately after exiting the tunnel. Approach from north via Col D'Allos not advised due to 3.5t weight and 7m length restriction for 24km of virtually single track road.

Sanitation:

Parking:

None

Flot Bleu Euro; CC

Flot Bleu behind wooden toilet block, under ski lift. Only really a roadside Service Point, but parking poss if desperate. Inspected 2010.

UVERNET FOURS 212 L10 N44°22.091' E006°37.668' 04400

Directions: D902, Lotissement le Bachelard. From Barcelonnette follow D902 south for 3km. Aire on right before village of Uvernet-Fours.

Sanitation:

Parking:

6; Not in 'storm conditions' due to flooding

Flot Bleu Pacific; €2

SP

Shady Aire among pine trees alongside river. Rural setting with mountain views. Inspected 2010.

BARCELONNETTE 213 L10 N44°22.917' E006°39.483' 04400

Directions: Chemin des Alpages. From west on D900 turn right to cross river on D902. Immediately after crossing river turn left onto Digue de la Gravette. After 600m turn right. Aire on left behind stadium. Well signed from D900.

Sanitation:

Parking:

15

Euro Relais Junior; Token (ER)

SP

Rural location on edge of town. Parking on grass among trees. Token machine onsite. Mountain views. Inspected 2010.

PRA LOUP 1600 SKI 214 L10 N44°22.054' E006°36.367' 04400

Directions: D109. Roadside Aire next to bottom gondola station 'Choupettes'. Good access road, signed.

Sanitation:

Parking:

20

Flot Bleu Standard Plus; €3

Alt 1600m. Ski resort. Free bus/ski lift adj to Aire. Not a pretty resort but good skiing. www.praloup.com Inspected 2010.

SELONNET 215 K10 N44°22.101' E006°18.912' 04140

Directions: From south on D900 turn left onto D900c, sp 'Selonnet'. Turn left onto D1 then left again. Aire 400m on left. Signed from D900.

Sanitation:

Parking:

7

Aire Services; Token (3/3)

Aire on edge of village. Pleasant, rural location adj to river with lovely views of surrounding mountains. Inspected 2010.

LA BREOLE

216 K9 N44°27.466' E006°17.518' 04340

Info/Photo: Kevin Holley

Directions: D707. Traveling east on the D900B turn left onto D707, sp ' La Breole'. Aire 50m on left, signed.

Sanitation:

Parking:

5

Flot Bleu Fontaine

Rural views from Aire. Large reservoir nearby. Local commerce 2 mins. Visited 2012.

JAUSIERS

217 L9 N44°24.712' E006°43.750' 04850

Directions: D900. Aire adj to D900 as enter village from Barcelonnette. If full, further parking over river bridge on right.

Sanitation:

Parking:

4

Flot Bleu Euro; CC; €3

Small rough parking area. Border with Italy via Col de Larche on D900. Inspected 2010.

LES ORRES

SKI

218 K9 N44°29.980' E006°33.435' 05200

Directions: Parking Bas de Champs Lacas, off D40. From Embrun follow D40 approx 16km. Aire in large parking area, sp 'Parking B', below chairlift ticket office. Well signed.

Sanitation:

Parking:

50; Max 15 days

Flot Bleu Pacific; €3; Showers at TO: Pay

Alt 1564m. Ski resort/ summer walking in alps. Inspected 2010.

ARRE

219 K10 N43°58.048' E003°31.293' 30120

Info/Photo: Rod and Liz Sleigh

Directions: D999. Aire adj to D999 at eastern end of the village, 200m from Mairie.

Sanitation:

Parking:

5

Euro Relais Mini; €2

Sports grounds inc football and tennis adj. Village commerce within 500m. Walking and cycling on old railway track. Visited 2012.

VARS LES CLAUX *

SKI

220 L9 N44°34.534' E006°40.675 05560

Directions: D902. Carpark No 5, at top of resort of Vars-les-Claux.

Sanitation:

Parking:

50

Flot Bleu Pacific in building; Elec 15 mins; No drive over drain

Alt 1600m. Free Chairlift adj. Good for walking. Free WiFi at TO. Inspected 2010.

EMBRUN — 221 K9 N44°32.773' E006°28.815' 05200

Directions: N94 at Intermarché supermarket. From Embrun take N94 south. After crossing river turn right at roundabout, sp 'Centre Commercial'. Flot Bleu on left as road bends, outside Intermarché fuel station.

Sanitation:

Parking:

Poss

Flot Bleu Pacific; €2

Laundry at fuel station. Free WiFi at McDonalds. Inspected 2010.

SAVINES LE LAC — 222 K9 N44°31.483' E006°24.033' 05160

Photo: Peter Slade

Directions: D954/Avenue Faubourg. From west on N94, after crossing lake on long bridge, take 1st right onto D954/Avenue Faubourg, sp 'P Camping Cars'. Aire on left in 180m.

Sanitation:

Parking:

17; €7/24hrs (12 noon-12 noon) inc elec

Custom; €2; 14 unmetered elec points

100m from village by lake with beach (water freezing in summer!) and boat trips available. Inspected 2010.

CHORGES — 223 K9 N44°32.750' E006°16.800' 05230

Directions: Chemin la Butte. From southeast on D94 turn right onto Avenue D'Embrun sp 'Chorges'. Signed. After 800m turn right into Place du Champ de Foire. Continue between Gendarmerie and Salle des Fêtes. Aire on right in 150m.

Sanitation:

Parking:

20; Max 12hrs

None

BMX bike park adj. Inspected 2010.

ORCIERES — SKI — 224 K9 N44°41.704' E006°19.562' 05170

Directions: Les Balcons d'Orcieres. From west take D944 to Orcieres then follow D76 up to Orcieres-Merlette ski resort. Follow signs for 'Parking P2'.

Sanitation:

Parking:

24; €12/24hrs inc elec; Pay warden

Raclet

Dramatic top floor car park on top of ski area. Lots of signed walks and stunning mountain views. May be free in summer. Inspected 2010.

PONT DU FOSSE * — 225 K9 N44°40.200' E006°14.317' 05260

Directions: Off D944. From the river bridge in Pont du Fosse follow D944 northeast for 900m. Ignore sign to Aire that crosses 3.5t weight restricted bridge. Continue and take next right turn adj to Toyota garage (The GPS given is at this turning for clarity). Follow road to right and Aire is in 500m.

Sanitation:

Parking:

20

Euro Relais Junior; Token (ER); €2; 8 elec points

Very pleasant Aire in woodland setting. Located adj to river with beautiful mountain views. Inspected 2010.

CHATEAU ARNOUX ST AUBAN — 226 — K10 — N44°05.762' E006°00.603' — 04160

Directions: D4096. Turn off D4096 north of town into car park, sp 'P Resistance' and 'Salle des Fêtes'. Park near the war memorial, Service Point 50m further on, signed.

Sanitation:

Parking:

15

Custom; Push down hard on red tops

SP

Adj to a busy and very noisy road. Small town commerce 2 mins walk through adj park. Inspected 2012.

SISTERON — 227 — K10 — N44°12.000' E005°56.617' — 04200

Directions: D4085/Cours Melchior Donnet. From south follow D4085 through town. Aire in car park on right, below picturesque citadel.

Sanitation:

Parking:

10

Flot Bleu Standard Plus; €2

SP

Castle adj. Close to main road but only a few minutes walk from town and has lovely views at night of floodlit rocks. Inspected 2012.

SISTERON - NORTH — 228 — K10 — N44°14.208' E005°54.701' — 04200

Directions: D4. Exit D4085 at roundabout north of Sisteron onto D4085, sp 'Gap'. At next roundabout turn left, sp 'Zone Commercial'. At next roundabout turn left into Super U. Service Point is near fuel station adj to car wash, signed.

Sanitation:

Parking:

Poss

Flot Bleu Pacific; Token/20 mins

SP

Supermarket adj. Self-service laundry adj, €0.50/kg. 10 mins drive from town. Inspected 2012.

LARAGNE MONTEGLIN — 229 — K10 — N44°18.735' E005°49.559' — 05300

Directions: C12/Chemin des Vergers. From south on D1075/E712 turn left onto C12/Chemin des Vergers at roundabout, sp 'Parking Gratuit'. Aire 200m on right.

Sanitation:

Parking:

20

Custom; 20 mins free elec; No drive over drain

SP

Nice town. Parking for motorhomes and HGVs. Inspected 2010.

VEYNES — 230 — K9 — N44°31.997' E005°49.367' — 05400

Directions: D994, Place du 19 Mars 1962. Enter the town from Gap on D994. Follow D994, sp 'Toutes Directions'. The parking is just past the roundabout with the D48, on left in a small car park adj to road.

Sanitation:

Parking:

5; 6m max

Custom

SP

Small car park; Suitable for small vans only as sign insists 1 vehicle/bay. Inspected 2010.

GAP | 231 | K9 | N44°33.900' E006°05.033' | 05000

Directions: N85, parking Dumont. Follow sp 'Grenoble' on N85. Aire on right, signed. Next to the Intermarche supermarket. 2 spaces for motorhomes in very busy car park with narrow access to bays, signed.

Sanitation:

Parking:

2

Flot Bleu Euro; €2; CC

Service Point not working in June when inspected. Inspected 2010.

LAYE | 232 | K9 | N44°38.422' E006°05.142' | 05000

Directions: Off N85. From Gap follow N85 north for 11km. Ignore the turning for Laye ski station (D88) to the left. Continue on N85 for 800m then turn right, sp 'Monument de la Resistance'. Aire on right in 50m.

Sanitation:

Parking:

10; Max 24hrs

None

Gravel car park adj to small hamlet with restaurant and lovely views of surrounding mountains. Inspected 2010.

PUY SAINT VINCENT STATION 1600 SKI | 233 | K9 | N44°49.187' E006°29.198' | 05290

Directions: D804, Station 1600. From N94 follow D994e, sp 'Puy St Vincent'. After 8.5km at La Casse, turn left onto D4. At Puy St Vincent turn right onto D804 and continue up to 'Station 1600'. Aire is 1st parking on left as enter one way system, signed.

Sanitation:

Parking:

12; €6/day; €35/week; Max 2 weeks

Custom; 10 6amp elec points; inc

Nice ski/summer walking resort in Ecrins Nature park. Inspected 2010.

BRIANCON | 234 | K9 | N44°53.418' E006°37.767' | 05100

Directions: Rue Georges Bermond Gonnet. From south on N94 turn right onto D2/Avenue Maurice Petsche. Turn right at roundabout onto D136, sp 'Park des Sports'. Cross river and turn right into Avenue Jean Moulin. Follow road for 450m and turn left into Rue Georges Bermond Gonnet. Aire on right in 100m.

Sanitation:

Parking:

4; €6/12hrs; €12/24hrs

Euro Relais Maxi; Token or CC; €2

Large car park with 4 designated spaces and 2 Service Points on outskirts of town. Inspected 2010.

LE MONETIER LES BAINS SKI | 235 | K9 | N44°58.285' E006°30.748' | 05220

Directions: From Briancon enter the town on D1091. Just after the town sign turn left sp 'Espace Loisirs'. Follow the lane to parking adj to the river accessed via bridge. Signed.

Sanitation:

Parking:

50; €4.80

Euro Relais Maxi

Pleasant aire in picturesque valley. Very scenic drive over Col du Lautaret (2058m). Inspected 2010.

NEVACHE | 236 | K9 | N45°01.004' E006°38.177' | 05100

Directions: D994g. From Briançon on N94 turn left onto D994g, sp 'La Vachette'. Follow road for 15km. Road very narrow through villages. Service Point is on left on gravel track, opp D1 turning to Col Echelle, signed.

Sanitation:

Parking:

At campsite

Custom

Camping Municipal de la Lame 500m further towards Névache. Camping in low season: Motorhome €3, Adults €1. Inspected 2010.

LA SALLE LES ALPES | SKI | 237 | K9 | N44°56.867' E006°33.333' | 05240

Directions: Chemin des Preras. From south on D1091 turn left into Allée des Peupliers 700m after roundabout, sp 'Plan d'Eau'. Keep left and follow road for 300m. Cross river and turn right at roundabout. Aire immediately on left.

Sanitation:

Parking:

20; €8/24hrs inc elec

Raclet

Adj to ski lift and small swimming lake. Inspected 2010.

MONTGENEVRE | SKI | 238 | K9 | N44°56.074' E006°44.185' | 05100

Directions: Off N94. Large purpose built Aire well signed in town. Italy 1 mile by road. Need snow chains for Col du Lautaret coming from Grenoble. Also access via Fréjus tunnel.

Sanitation:

Parking:

280; €10/day decreases day by day; Pay on exit; 10amp elec inc

Custom; €3; Pay at machine

Summer walking resort. Excellent skiing. 100m to slopes. Free shuttle bus to/from Aire. Inspected 2010.

ST CREPIN | 239 | K9 | N44°42.250' E006°36.055' | 05600

Directions: D138. From south on N94 turn left onto D138, sp 'Aerodrome'. Turn left immediately after river bridge towards aerodrome buildings. Aire on left. Signed on N94 from south, but not from north.

Sanitation:

Parking:

None

Custom

Rural location between river and campsite charging €6/night. Visited 2011.

AVEZE | 240 | K9 | N43°58.545' E003°35.931' | 30120

Info/Photo: Rod and Liz Sleigh

Directions: Lieu Dit le Pouchounet. Turn off D999 onto D48, sp 'Aveze'. Turn right before river bridge, sp 'Salle Polyvalente' and signed. Service Point on approach road, parking at sports facility car park in 250m.

Sanitation:

Parking:

5

Euro Relais Mini

Park adj. River nearby, no views. Visited 2012.

Sete

Saint Genis, *Photo: Rod and Liz Sleigh*

Valance d'Agen

MIDI-PYRENEES

Bouziers

GIGNAC

1 | F9 | N45°00.350' E001°27.400' | 46600

Directions: Place des Troubadours. Turn off D820 onto D34, signed. In village join D87. After 300m turn right into Rue Pierre Cerou, signed. Aire at rear of Salle des Fêtes, signed.

Sanitation:

Parking:

15

Custom

Small village; Interesting metal tree sculpture in town. Inspected 2010.

LES QUATRE ROUTES DU LOT

2 | G9 | N44°59.425' E001°39.139' | 46110

Directions: D32. Turn off D96 by railway track onto D32, sp 'St Denis' and signed. In 400m turn left into campsite entrance, signed. Service Point on right.

Sanitation:

Parking:

None

Custom

Service Point only; Camping €6/night, train track adj. Inspected 2012.

SOUILLAC

3 | F9 | N44°53.497' E001°28.574' | 46200

Directions: Parking at Chemin du Baillot. From D820 turn into D703 in town centre. Turn 2nd left into Rue de la Pomme, signed. Turn 1st right and 1st right again into Parking du Baillot, both signed.

Sanitation:

Parking:

20

Flot Bleu Euro; CC; €3

The Byzantine cathedral is a must see, 5 mins. Aire can be busy. Inspected 2010.

MARTEL

4 | G9 | N44°56.029' E001°36.575' | 46600

Directions: Rue Albert Lachieze. From west on D803 take 1st exit onto D23 at roundabout. After 250m turn left into Rue Albert Lachieze, signed. Aire in station car park. For Service Point: From west on D803 take 1st exit at roundabout in town onto D23. After 140m turn right into Rue du 19 Mars, signed. Service Point immediately on right: N44°56.083' E001°36.367'

Sanitation:

Parking:

10

Custom

Service Point and parking in two separate places. Parking in steam train station car park. Toilet when station open. Inspected 2012.

PINSAC

5 | F9 | N44°51.293' E001°30.719' | 46200

Photo: Rodney Martin

Directions: D43, adj to Salle des Fêtes and Mairie. From north on D820 turn left onto D43 just south of Souillac. After 4km Aire on right at rear of Mairie and Salle des Fêtes. Parking under trees alongside Mairie, opp new toilet block.

Sanitation:

Parking:

Tolerated

Removed

Toilet block under construction. Inspected 2010.

GOURDON

6 F9 N44°44.067' E001°23.116' 46300

Directions: Place du Foirail. Follow one-way system in town towards Figeac/Rodez. From D801/Boulevard Gambetta turn into Avenue Jean Admirat, sp 'Aire du Foirail'. Follow signs past car park to Aire on right.

Sanitation: E WC F

Parking: P F

8

Custom; 8 12amp elec points; €1/3hrs

SP

Pleasant Aire on edge of attractive hilltop town. Town centre 10 mins. Inspected 2010.

LABASTIDE MURAT

7 G9 N44°39.004' E001°34.237' 46240

Directions: D677. Exit town on D677, sp 'Gramat'. Turn left as exit town into Carrefour supermarket car park. Service Point located behind supermarket in what is believed to be municipal space.

Sanitation: E WC F

Parking: P F

5; Closest to Service Point

Custom

SP

This Aire feels different to most supermarket stops because of the views, and rural location. Pleasant town centre with local commerce 2 mins. Inspected 2012.

ROCAMADOUR

8 G9 N44°48.013' E001°36.933' 46500

Directions: Parking Château. From west on D673 turn right onto D200 in L'Hospitalet, sp 'Parking du Château' and 'Remparts'. Parking at coach park in 700m just beyond funicular railway station. Do not attempt to drive through lower Rocamadour village.

Sanitation: E WC F

Parking: P F

25

None

SP

Funicular railway to village adj (€4 return). If Aire is full try parking area on corner of D200/D673: N44°48.254' E001°37.299'. Inspected 2010.

ALVIGNAC

9 G9 N44°49.502' E0001°41.827' 46500

Photo: Carol and Duncan Weaver

Directions: D673/Route de Padirac. From south on D840 turn right onto D673, sp 'Alvignac'. Follow road through village and Aire on right on inside of bend 150m after junction with D20, signed.

Sanitation: E WC F

Parking: P F

8

Raclet

SP

Village adj with local commerce. Inspected 2010.

GRAMAT

10 G9 N44°46.789' E001°43.705' 46500

Directions: Avenue Louis Mazet. From D840 follow sp to 'Gramat Centre'. At roundabout north of town turn left onto D807. At next roundabout by Shopi supermarket turn left, signed. Follow road and Aire on left.

Sanitation: E WC F

Parking: P F

20; Max 48hrs

Euro Relais Junior; 2 unmetered elec points; off at time of inspection

SP

Large town 5 mins. Inspected 2010.

ST CERE

11 G9 N44°51.683' E001°53.183' 46400

Directions: Chemin du Stade, parking at stadium. Turn off D940 into Quai de Trémeille. Follow this road and turn left into Chemin du Stade. Sports stadium on your left.

Sanitation:

Parking:

Spaces: 3

Service Point: Flot Bleu Fontaine; No drive over drain

Interesting old village with view of castle on hill above Aire. Inspected 2010.

SOUSCEYRAC

12 G9 N44°52.361' E002°02.201' 46190

Directions: D653. Adj to D653 in village centre car park facing La Poste and Mairie. Service Point behind toilet block, not visible from road.

Sanitation:

Parking:

Spaces: 10; No parking Sun 8am-2pm - market

Service Point: Euro Relais Junior; 1 unmetered elec point; No drive over drain

Parking and Service Point poss blocked by parked cars. Inspected 2010.

LATRONQUIERE

13 G9 N44°47.951' E002°04.741' 46210

Directions: Place du 19 Mars 1962. From D653 turn onto D31 in village centre. After 230m turn left onto D16 and then next right. Keep left and Service Point next to La Poste with parking adj.

Sanitation:

Parking:

Spaces: 5

Service Point: Euro Relais Junior; No drive over drain

Mini golf adj. Inspected 2010.

LA VITARELLE

14 G9 N44°44.471' E002°01.169' 46210

Directions: D653. From north on D653 the Service Point is on the right between car wash and 24hr fuel station.

Sanitation:

Parking:

Spaces: None

Service Point: Euro Relais Junior

Service Point at fuel station. Inspected 2010.

LEYME

15 G9 N44°47.001' E001°54.044' 46120

Directions: From south on D39 Service Point at 24hr fuel station on right at entry to village, opp church. Parking: Continue towards village for 140m and turn left. 'Parking Tennis' 200m on left: N44°47.042' E001°53.878'. Further parking other side of football pitch in Allées des Platanes: N44°47.127' E001°53.846'.

Sanitation:

Parking:

Spaces: 8 Tennis Courts; 5 Allée des Platanes

Service Point: Aire Services

Parking is roadside but little used roads. Lots of green space adj and around village. Inspected 2010.

LACAPELLE MARIVAL

16 G9 N44°43.685' E001°55.799' 46120

Directions: D653/Place Larroque. From D840 turn onto D940, sp 'Lacapelle Marival'. In town turn right onto D653, sp 'Latronquière'. Follow road to large parking area. Aire on right at rear of car park.

Sanitation:

Parking:

5

Euro Relais Junior; €2

Pretty town 2 mins. 13th century château in centre. Inspected 2010.

THEMINES

17 G9 N44°44.466' E001°49.784' 46120

Directions: D840, outside the church. Turn onto D40 at Thémines, sp 'Halle de Thémines'. Or turn left onto C1, sp 'Albiac', opp boulangerie. Turn left at covered market, opp Mairie. Aire at top of hill.

Sanitation:

Parking:

Poss

Euro Relais Junior; 1 unmetered elec point; No drive over drain

Church adj, Small village with local commerce. Slope too steep to sleep. Inspected 2010.

CARDAILLAC

18 G9 N44°40.755' E001°59.874' 46100

Directions: Off D15, by the church in village centre. Signed from D15 main route through town. Narrow turns to access, max 6m.

Sanitation:

Parking:

10

Euro Relais Junior; 1 unmetered elec point

Pretty village up country lanes. Medieval parts. Inspected 2010.

BAGNAC SUR CELE

19 G9 N44°40.082' E002°09.475' 46270

Directions: Parking Laplanquette. Adj to N122 at junction with D16. Aire in large parking area.

Sanitation:

Parking:

10

Custom

Undesirable stop, road on 3 sides. Inspected 2010.

FIGEAC

20 G9 N44°36.661' E002°02.213' 46100

Directions: From N122 or D13 at roundabout exit onto D19, signed. Service Point is 300m on right in small car park with trees against town wall, signed. For better parking continue across next roundabout into Parking du Foirail: N44°36.721' E002°02.095'.

Sanitation:

Parking:

40

Euro Relais Junior; €2

Service Point difficult to access if car park busy. Large town. Motorhomes can park anywhere. Inspected 2010.

BOUILLAC — 21 — G9 — N44°34.372' E002°09.459' — 12300

Directions: D840. Drive 15km towards Capdenac Gare from Figeac and the Aire is on the right.

Sanitation:

Parking:

10; Max 24hrs

Custom; Token; €3

SP

Picnic area with tables and parking. Renault garage adj. Alongside main road. Inspected 2010.

BOISSE PENCHOT — 22 — G9 — N44°35.517' E002°12.333' — 12300

Photo: Rita Renninghoff

Directions: Off D42. Turn off D840 onto D42, sp 'Boisse Penchot' and signed. After 1.2km turn left, signed, and Aire on right in 125m.

Sanitation:

E

Parking:

P

F

8

Euro Relais Junior; Token (ER); €3

SP

Lovely spot by river Lot. BBQ. Brasserie on corner of D42. Well set out bays with green space. Inspected 2010.

CAJARC — 23 — G10 — N44°29.075' E001°50.744' — 46160

Photo: motorhomeandaway.co.uk

Directions: Avenue de la Gare. Aire situated in front of old railway station in town.

Sanitation:

Parking:

P

F

10

Custom; €1

SP

Adj to road so may be some noise. Tourist train occasionally. Inspected 2010.

NAUSSAC — 24 — G10 — N44°31.293' E002°04.774' — 12700

Directions: Aire de Loisirs de Naussac/Lieu Dit le Causse Naut. From D922 turn onto D88 at Loupiac. Follow road towards Naussac for 5.5km. Turn left off D88 into Lieu Dit le Causse and Aire on right in 400m.

Sanitation:

E

F

Parking:

P

8; €4/night

Custom; 6 unmetered elec points

SP

Nice Aire among trees. Inspected 2010.

PEYRUSSE LE ROC — 25 — G10 — N44°29.683' E002°08.333' — 12220

Photo: Rita Renninghoff

Directions: D87. Steep climb out of village for Aire in direction of Naussac.

Sanitation:

F

Parking:

P

F

7

Custom

SP

Old medieval village; Local commerce in village; Lovely spot with views. Inspected 2010.

VILLENEUVE

26 G10 N44°26.292' E002°01.969' 12260

Directions: Blvd de la Dime/D48, near junction of D48 and D248. Follow sp 'Villeneuve Centre'. Aire in town centre adj to D48. Signed opp La Poste.

Sanitation:

Parking:

13; Day only

Custom; See below

SP

Service Point and overnight parking at campsite; €5, adj to D40: N44°26.506' E002°02.215'. Visited 2012.

VILLEFRANCHE DE ROUERGUE

27 G10 N44°20.545' E002°01.560' 12200

Directions: Camping du Rouergue. Follow sp 'Camping' through town. Drive around the stadium and the Service Point is to the right of the campsite entrance.

Sanitation:

Parking:

None

Custom; €3; Open 8am-11pm mid Mar-Oct; Visit reception to unlock services

SP

Very difficult access when stadium in use. Inspected 2010.

LANUEJOULS

28 G10 N44°25.600' E002°09.670' 12350

Directions: Behind church. Follow D1 through village and turn off by church onto D635, sp 'Pachins' and signed. Aire on left at back of church car park. Barrier opened via card available to purchase from shops in town.

Sanitation:

Parking:

14; €5/night

Custom; inc; 12 unmetered elec points

SP

Showers and dishwashing sinks. Cards difficult to obtain after 6pm, need to phone. Inspected 2010.

CRANSAC LES THERMES

29 G10 N44°31.367' E002°16.433' 12110

Directions: Avenue de la Gare. Turn off D11 in town onto Ave de la Gare. The Aire is before you cross the railway track.

Sanitation:

Parking:

6; €5; Max 48hrs

Custom

SP

6 landscaped bays separated by shrubs. Pleasant Aire in thermal town. Inspected 2010.

RIGNAC

30 G10 N44°24.272' E002°17.379' 12390

Directions: Parc de la Peyrade. From Rodez on D994 take 1st exit at roundabout onto D997, sp 'Rignac'. At next roundabout take 3rd exit into Avenue du Segala. After 650m turn left into Le Hameau du Lac, signed. At end of road turn right and Aire on right in 75m.

Sanitation:

Parking:

10; No parking 10am-7:30pm mid Jun-Aug

Euro Relais Mini

SP

Grassy car park near 'Odalys' hotel. Pleasant parkland setting. Inspected 2010.

BELCASTEL

31 G10 N44°23.131' E002°19.724' 12390

Directions: D285. Exit the town to west along the northern riverbank. The parking is on the left down steep slope with tight bends on loose gravel.

Sanitation:

Parking:

10; Pay; Grass parking

Custom; 4 unmetered elec points

Village car parks don't allow motorhomes. Aire along riverside on grass, can be muddy if wet. Shower in toilet block. Inspected 2010.

CAMPUAC

32 H9 N44°34.091' E002°35.368' 12580

Directions: Off D46. From south on D904 turn right onto D46, sp 'Campuac'. After 3.7km turn right between church and cross. Parking on left at end of road. For Service Point carry on D46. Follow for 225m straight over mini roundabout. Service Point straight ahead: N44°34.200' E002°35.483'

Sanitation:

Parking:

4

Custom

Parking overlooking open countryside. On edge of village. Service Point by toilets, recycling, and sports ground. Inspected 2010.

ENTRAYGUES SUR TRUYERE

33 H9 N44°38.406' E002°34.162' 12140

Directions: D904/Route de Villecomptal. From south on D920 turn left onto D904 across river bridge before town. Immediately after road bends right, turn sharp right and follow road steeply downhill to Aire, large motorhomes not advised. Service Point 380m further towards campsite.

Sanitation:

Parking:

10; Grass parking

Euro Relais Junior; Token (ER)

On bank of river Truyère. Town centre 800m. Service Point 380m from parking area N44°38.557' E002°33.976'. Inspected 2010.

MONTEZIC

34 H9 N44°42.617' E002°38.633' 12460

Directions: From south on D97 turn right onto D504 in village centre. After 300m turn right and follow road through new housing development and Aire 175m on left. Well signed.

Sanitation:

Parking:

8; Max 48hrs

Custom

Small Aire 2 mins from village below stadium. Inspected 2010.

LACROIX BARREZ

35 H9 N44°46.675' E002°37.890' 12600

Directions: Exit the village on D505 towards Murols. Turn right in 200m and Aire on left in 100m.

Sanitation:

Parking:

20; Max 72hrs; Grass parking

Flot Bleu Compact; Free 1/5-10/10; 6 elec points

Lovely Aire with separate grass bays, 5 mins to village. Inspected 2010.

MUR DE BARREZ

36 H9 N44°50.483' E002°39.567' 12600

Directions: Place du Foirail, adj to Parc de la Corette. Enter village from south on D904. Take 1st turning left and follow road north parallel to D904. Turn left to Service Point. Parking 100m further along on left: N44°50.533' E002°39.567'.

Sanitation: E WC F

Parking: P F

5

Euro Relais Junior; Token (ER)

SP

Pleasant parkland setting on edge of village. Tokens free from Mairie or TO. Inspected 2010.

THERONDELS

37 H9 N44°53.900' E002°45.567' 12600

Directions: From Mur de Barrez take D900, sp 'Barrage de Sarrans'. In Brommat turn right onto D18, sp 'Thérondels'. Take the 1st right after D236 and Service Point is 200m on right.

Sanitation: E WC F

Parking: P F

5; Max 24hrs

Flot Bleu Pacific

SP

Grass parking around the Service Point but notice on Service Point also invites parking in village centre. Inspected 2010.

STE GENEVIEVE SUR ARGENCE

38 H9 N44°48.117' E002°45.733' 12420

Directions: Rue de l'Argence. From D900 heading south, or D78 heading east, turn into Rue de l'Argence (which connects the two roads). The parking is adj to the river, signed.

Sanitation: E WC F

Parking: P F

10

Flot Bleu Pacific; Token; €2

SP

Pleasant spot adj to small river; Village 5 mins. Tokens from TO, Mairie, and shops. BBQ point. WiFi at TO. Inspected 2010.

LAGUIOLE

39 H9 N44°40.917' E002°51.250' 12210

Directions: Outside Camping Les Monts D'Aubrac, off D921. From south turn right off D921, signed. Follow road to campsite.

Sanitation: E WC F

Parking: P F

None; See 40

Custom

SP

Service Point only outside entrance to campsite. Inspected 2010.

LAGUIOLE SKI STATION

SKI

40 H9 N44°40.367' E002°55.633' 12210

Directions: Lieu-Dit le Bouyssou, off D15. From Laguiole take D15, sp 'Aubrac' and 'Station de Ski de Laguiole'. Follow road for 9.8km and Aire on right at 'Station de Ski de Laguiole'. Location labelled on map as 'Chalets du Bouyssou', but not on signposts.

Sanitation: E WC F

Parking: P F

20

None; See 39

SP

Alt 1360m. Large parking area at ski station. Lots of summer walks, well marked footpaths. Dog sledge rides all year. Inspected 2010.

AUBRAC

41 H9 N44°37.233' E002°59.200' 12470

Directions: D533. From north on D987 turn left in village centre onto D533, sp 'St Chely D'Aubrac'. Aire on right in 150m on edge of village.

Sanitation:

Parking:

20

Flot Bleu Fontaine

Alt 1345m. Pleasant parking area on the edge of the village. Botanical gardens. Toilets 150m towards village. Inspected 2010.

ST GENIEZ D'OLT

42 H10 N44°28.183' E002°59.000' 12130

Directions: D503/Route de la Cascade. From village centre head northeast on D509/Rte de la Cascade and Service Point is 500m, outside campsite.

Sanitation:

Parking:

None

Aire Services; €1

Service Point only outside entrance to campsite. Campsite open April-Sept. Inspected 2010.

STE EULALIE D'OLT

43 H10 N44°27.883' E002°56.950' 12130

Directions: Rue de la Grave. From east on D988 turn right at start of village onto D597. After 700m turn right into Route de la Passerelle, then right into Rue de la Grave. Aire at end of road outside Camping Municipal La Grave.

Sanitation:

Parking:

13; €8; 15/5-15/9

Custom; inc; 16amp elec inc

Machine outside campsite office gives tokens for entrance barrier (correct money needed). Pretty historic village. Inspected 2010.

BOZOULS

44 G/H10 N44°28.326' E002°43.264' 12340

Directions: Rue Marc André Fabre, off D20. From north on D920 turn right in Bozouls centre onto D20, sp 'Bibliothèque' and 'Mediathèque'. Go straight over roundabout then turn 1st left into Rue Marc André Fabre. Aire immediately on left.

Sanitation:

Parking:

5

Custom

Pleasant Aire. Gorge 100m. Intermarché supermarket 1.6km on D988, has self-service laundry. Inspected 2010.

CAMPAGNAC

45 H10 N44°25.185' E003°05.313' 12560

Directions: Lotissement la Sagne, off D37. Exit A75 at Junction 41 onto D37 towards Campagnac. Follow D37 for 5.5km through village centre as it bends right, then left. Turn right at Gendarmerie and Aire on right at rear, signed.

Sanitation:

Parking:

5; €3/night Jul-Sept; Free Oct-Jun

Custom

Quiet village with local commerce. Inspected 2010.

LAISSAC

46 H10 N44°23.140' E002°49.282' 12310

Directions: From N88 turn onto D28, sp 'Laissac'. Take 1st right, signed. Drive around Intermarché and turn right, signed.

Sanitation:

Parking:

6

Custom

Intermarché supermarket 2 mins; Adj to N88, road noise. Town 5 mins. Livestock market Tues morning in adj parking area. Inspected 2010.

RODEZ

47 G10 N44°21.467' E002°35.647' 12000

Directions: D162, opp ZI Cantaranne. Turn off N88 at roundabout onto D217/Ave de la Roquette. After 2km turn left over level crossing, still on D217. Follow road to end at T-junction with Rue de Salelles. The Aire is straight across the road.

Sanitation:

Parking:

6; Max 72hrs

Custom

In green fields with walk/cycle to Rodez adj. If full car park in town centre (3.2km) allows parking max 24hrs: N44°21.067' E002°34.100'. Inspected 2010.

SEGUR

48 H10 N44°17.441' E002°50.104' 12290

Directions: Rue de la Mairie, off D95. From Rodez take D29 28km to Ségur. In village turn right onto D95 then left into Rue de la Mairie. Service Point signed.

Sanitation:

Parking:

Poss; Max 48hrs

Custom

Parking not designated but poss on grass to right of Service Point or hardstandings past Service Point on left. Showers at Service Point, €2, token. Inspected 2010.

PONT DE SALARS

49 H10 N44°16.688' E002°43.706' 12290

Photo: Carol and Duncan Weaver

Directions: Place de la Rivière, centre of village. In large car park, sp 'Aires'. Near public toilets.

Sanitation:

Parking:

5; May-Oct; Max 72hrs

Custom; Token; €3

River adj; Hotel/restaurant opp. Inspected 2010.

BARAQUEVILLE

50 G10 N44°16.702' E002°25.976' 12160

Photo: Russ Price

Directions: Rue du Val de l'Enne. From N88 towards Albi turn right into town car park just before reaching N88/D911 roundabout. Aire is behind shops, signed from car park.

Sanitation:

Parking:

12

Euro Relais Junior; Token (ER); €3

Pleasant spot overlooking fields with a lake in the distance. Town 1 min. Adj to livestock market. Inspected 2010.

CASTANET

51 G10 N44°16.734' E002°17.365' 12240

Directions: About 4km off D911 as enter village from north. By mini island and village hall in the village centre. Very small village, so unmissable.

Sanitation:

Parking:

4; €5; Honesty box

Custom; Bays with own unmetered elec point and tap

Small village; Pleasant Aire. No commerce in village. Inspected 2010.

SAUVETERRE DE ROUERGUE

52 G10 N44°12.960' E002°19.014' 12800

Photo: Tony Middleton

Directions: D997. On right of D997 as enter town from Naucelle, signed.

Sanitation:

Parking:

11; May-Oct; Grass parking

Custom; Elec €2/24hrs

Shower €1.50. On edge of town, 5 mins. Free municipal campsite. Inspected 2010.

MONTEILS

53 G10 N44°16.021' E001°59.802' 12200

Photo: Richard Taylor

Directions: Off D47 on northwest edge of village.

Sanitation:

Parking:

4

Custom

Adj to a stream and in a small park with trees. Local commerce and convenience store 100m. Pretty, well kept village. Inspected 2010.

CAYLUS

54 G10 N44°14.022' E001°46.282' 82160

Directions: D19. On D19 as exit Caylus towards St Antonin. On left opp Maison du Patrimoine, signed.

Sanitation:

Parking:

20

Custom

Adj to main road; Opp pond; BBQ; Table tennis. Pleasant place. Service Point old with surrounding concrete breaking up. Inspected 2010.

ST ANTONIN NOBLE VAL 1

55 G10 N44°09.144' E001°45.085' 82140

Directions: Chemin de Roumegous. Entering town on D5/D958 from Caussade turn 1st right onto Blvd de la Condamine, sp 'P Gratuit'. Turn right again onto Rte des Fours Á Chaux then left into Chemin de Roumegous. Service Point at entrance to car park.

Sanitation:

Parking:

20

Custom

Town centre 2 mins; Gorges adj. Inspected 2010.

ST ANTONIN NOBLE VAL 2 | 56 | G10 | N44°09.073' E001°45.462' | 82140

Directions: D958. From east on D958 follow road into town and Aire on right 100m past Gendarmerie on inside bend, signed. Follow sp 'Salle Polyvalente', 'Piscine', and 'Parking'.

Sanitation:

Parking:

5

Custom

SP

Tourist village. St Antonin 1 55 nicer. Local commerce and TO nearby. Inspected 2010.

NAJAC | 57 | G10 | N44°13.289' E001°58.041' | 12270

Directions: From Najac follow D39 to Mazerolles, following signs to campsite/Aire. Go past campsite, left over bridge, then left towards swimming pool and tennis courts. Aire on left 400m after bridge.

Sanitation:

E

Parking:

P

10

Euro Relais Junior; Token (ER); €2

SP

Aire by river next to campsite. 1.5km steep climb to castle and church. Beautiful spot. Inspected 2010.

LAGUEPIE | 58 | G10 | N44°08.693' E001°58.317' | 82250

Directions: Quai de la Libération. Turn off D958 just south of river L'Aveyron into Quai de la Libération, signed. Service Point against wall on right.

Sanitation:

F

Parking:

F

Poss

Custom

SP

In small cul de sac above river. Road used as car park so could be difficult to access/turn around. Inspected 2010.

LE SEGUR | 59 | G10 | N44°06.533' E002°03.517' | 81640

Directions: Mairie and Maison du Temps Libre. Just off D27 in small village 6km northwest of Monestiés.

Sanitation:

WC F

Parking:

F

Poss

Custom; Large bore flexi hose for waste water

SP

In tiny village. Inspected 2010.

MIRANDOL BOURGNOUNAC | 60 | G10 | N44°08.513' E002°10.000' | 81190

Directions: Place du Foirail. Turn off D905 in centre of the village, signed. The Aire is in the car park and the Service Point is to the rear of the car park against a building, signed.

Sanitation:

WC F

Parking:

F

5

Custom; Flexi hose for waste water

SP

Car park in village centre. Inspected 2010.

NAUCELLE

61 G10 N44°11.830' E002°20.510' 12800

Directions: Place du Ségala, at back of village square. From D997 turn into square by water fountain, public toilets and La Poste. Aire at rear.

Sanitation:

Parking:

5

Custom

Local commerce adj. Parking not ideal and likely to be busy at times. Inspected 2010.

ST JUST SUR VIAUR

62 G10 N44°07.433' E002°22.533' 12800

Directions: Parking at Place des Fêtes. From N88 take D10 south to Castelpers. Turn right onto D532, sp 'St Just'. Aire on left in 2km.

Sanitation:

Parking:

5; Max 48hrs

Euro Relais Junior; 2 unmetered elec points

Pleasant rural location with BBQ site. On the Gorges du Viaur road and close to the Viaduc du Viaur. Inspected 2010.

TANUS

63 G10 N44°06.150' E002°19.006' 81190

Directions: Rue de Tanus le Vieux. The Aire is by the cattle market as you exit the village on D688. Turn off N88 after dual carriageway/bridge, sp 'Tanus'. Follow the main route D688 and turn left by church and cattle market.

Sanitation:

Parking:

10

Custom

Might be busy when cattle market on. Local commerce. Inspected 2010.

PAMPELONNE

64 G10 N44°07.334' E002°14.651' 81190

Directions: Place du Foirail. Follow D78 through village and turn onto D53, sp 'Tanus'. The Aire is on right at edge of village green, with weighbridge and public toilets.

Sanitation:

Parking:

5

Custom; Large bore flex hose for waste water

Pleasant; restaurant adj. Inspected 2010.

CARMAUX 1

65 G10 N44°00.824' E002°08.286' 81400

Directions: Off D25. At theme park south of Carmaux. Follow sp 'Cap Decouverte'.

Sanitation:

Parking:

20; €8 inc unmetered elec

Campsite Bollard

Good for a visit to theme park but outlook and Service Point poorly kept. Inspected 2010.

CARMAUX 2

66 G10 N44°03.021' E002°09.879' 81400

Directions: Turn off N88 onto D91 and follow sp 'Carmaux'. Follow rd to right, then turn right into Rue Gambetta. Drive around main square to opp side and turn off, sp 'Aire Camping-Car'. Follow road to right, sp 'Rosieres'. As road bends to left, go straight on and Aire is immediately on left, signed.

Sanitation:

Parking:

20

Custom

SP

The Aire is located adj to sports facilities, 2 mins from town centre commerce. Market Friday morning. Some noise from local industry during day. Inspected 2012.

CORDES SUR CIEL

67 G10 N44°03.855' E001°57.474' 81170

Directions: Parking les Tuileries, off D8. From D600 turn off in village onto D8, sp 'Parkings 1 and 2' and 'Bournazel'. Turn 1st right, signed. Aire is 400m on right in Parking les Tuileries.

Sanitation:

Parking:

40; €5; Mar-Nov

Custom; Token inc; 6 16amp elec points

SP

Town centre 5 mins uphill; Payment collected. Inspected 2010.

VALDERIES

68 G10 N44°00.725' E002°14.014' 81350

Directions: D91. Follow road through town and Aire is the large car park opp Mairie, by La Poste and taxi parking.

Sanitation:

Parking:

10

Custom; Large bore flex hose for waste water

SP

Small town commerce adj. Inspected 2010.

ST JUERY

69 G10 N43°57.043' E002°12.597' 81160

Directions: D100. Service Point in the fuel station of the Carrefour supermarket, adj to D100 main through route.

Sanitation:

Parking:

Poss; 3.5t weight restriction on parking

Euro Relais Mini; Token (2/1); 3.5t weight restriction

SP

Supermarket adj. Token available 8.30am-7pm Mon-Sat from supermarket. Inspected 2012.

MONESTIES

70 G10 N44°04.269' E002°05.628' 81640

Directions: From Carmaux take D91, sp 'Monestiès'. Follow road through Monestiès centre. Turn left, sp 'Maison de Retraite' and 'Stade'. At end of road turn left into Route des Ecoles then left, sp 'Camping Municipal'. Aire on right outside Camping Municipal les Prunettes.

Sanitation:

Parking:

4; Parking only when campsite closed 13/9-11/6

Custom; Flexi hose for waste water

SP

Pretty town. Day parking in village centre. Inspected 2010.

CAHUZAC SUR VERE — 71 — G10 — N43°58.923' E001°54.667' — 81140

Directions: Place du Mercadial. From south on D922 turn right into Chemin de L'Escalfadou. At end of road turn left into Route des Tres Cantous, signed. At junction continue straight into Place du Mercadial. Parking along fence on right. Service Point adj to toilet in 'tower' on corner.

Sanitation:

Parking:

2; Roadside

Custom

Boules pitch opp is not parking area. Small town with municipal campsite and local commerce. Inspected 2010.

CASTELNAU DE MONTMIRAL — 72 — G10 — N43°58.007' E001°48.163' — 81140

Directions: Aire privée Les Miquels. Off D964 between Castelnau de Montmiral and Puycelci. Very clearly sp 'Les Miquels' from both directions.

Sanitation:

Parking:

6; €9.50 summer; €8 winter

Custom; inc unmetered elec

Commercial Aire with English speaking owners. Use of swimming pool inc. Inspected 2010.

GAILLAC — 73 — G10 — N43°53.977' E001°53.696' — 81600

Directions: Parking Rives Thomas in Rue des Silos. From south on D964 follow road into town. At square turn left onto D988, sp 'P Centre Ville'. Go straight over roundabout, signed, and turn left in 350m, signed. Follow road to Aire. 3.5t weight restriction in town centre.

Sanitation:

Parking:

20

Custom

Pleasant town and commerce 2 mins up short slope. Inspected 2010.

LISLE SUR TARN — 74 — G10 — N43°51.729' E001°49.106' — 81310

Directions: Off D988 at roundabout as you enter town from Gaillac. Turn left at roundabout before lake, sp 'Office de Tourisme' and 'Camping Car'. Aire on southeast corner of lake by small pond.

Sanitation:

Parking:

15

Custom

Adj pond, no views; BBQ. Town 7 mins; Local commerce. Inspected 2010.

HAVE YOU VISITED AN AIRE?

GPS co-ordinates in this guide are protected by copyright law

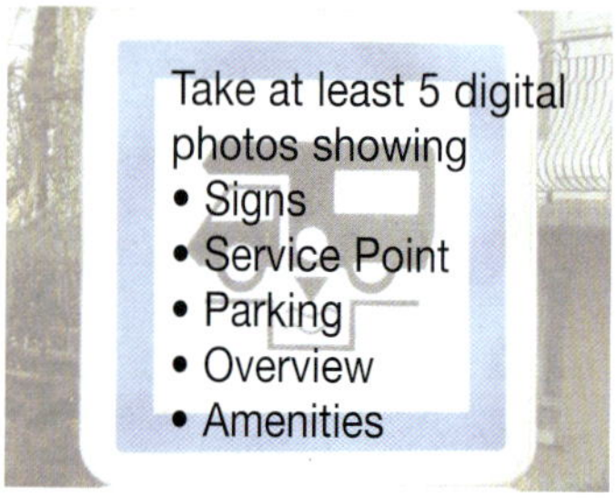
Take at least 5 digital photos showing
• Signs
• Service Point
• Parking
• Overview
• Amenities

Visit www.all-the-aires.co.uk/submissions.shtml to upload your updates and photos.

Sanitation:

Aire Details:

Submit updates

- Amendments
- New Aires
- Not changed

ALBI 1

76 | G10 | N43°56.761' E002°09.071' | 81000

Directions: Avenue Albert Thomas. From north on N88 turn onto D988 at roundabout in Saint-Michel, sp 'Centre Ville'. The Service Point is on right in 600m, signed.

Sanitation:

Parking:

None; See 77

Custom; Toilet waste disposal at waist height

Road parking available but real parking at cathedral. Inspected 2010.

ALBI 2

77 | G10 | N43°55.630' E002°08.458' | 81000

Directions: Blvd du Général Sibille, Parking Bondidou. From Albi 1 63 follow sp 'Centre Ville'. After crossing bridge take 2nd right, sp 'Coeur Historique' and 'Centre Hospitalier'. When road opens to square follow sp 'Cathédrale'. At end of road enter car park and follow down hill to Aire on left, signed.

Sanitation:

Parking:

9; Max 48hrs; Max 7m

None; See 76

Over 7m cannot negotiate car park. Views of cathedral. Historic town adj worth a visit. Inspected 2010.

REQUISTA

78 | G10 | N44°02.073' E002°32.163' | 12170

Directions: Place François Fabié. From north on D902 turn left into Place François Fabié opp Renault garage. Aire adj to Salle des Fêtes.

Sanitation:

Parking:

6

Custom

Individual bays separated by hedges; Adj to large open area in front of Salle des Fêtes. Inspected 2010.

ARVIEU

79 | H10 | N44°11.526' E002°39.569' | 12120

Directions: D56. Exit Arvieu to the north on D56. Aire on left, near the tennis courts, signed. Access bumpy, may be difficult for motorhomes with long overhang.

Sanitation:

Parking:

12; Max 72hrs

Custom; Token; €2

Large parking area on the edge of the village. Village 2 mins. Inspected 2010.

SALLES CURAN

80 | H10 | N44°11.500' E002°47.175' | 12410

Photo: Mark Hirons

Directions: Off D243. From north on D993 turn right onto D243. After 500m turn sharp left and parking on left along lakeside.

Sanitation:

Parking:

Tolerated; Max 48hrs

None

Tolerated parking area on lakeside. Inspected 2010.

BROQUIES | 81 | H10 | N44°00.294' E002°41.617' | 12480

Directions: From Vabres L'Abbaye follow D25 to Broquiès. In village centre turn left onto D54. Turn next left into Place de la Mairie, then 1st right into Rte de Mazies/D200e. Aire on left in 140m as road bends left.

Sanitation:

Parking:

15

Custom; 1 unmetered elec point

Toilet and shower. Lovely Aire on terrace below village with nice views over wooded hills. Inspected 2010.

ROQUEFORT SUR SOULZON | 82 | H10 | N43°58.867' E002°58.867' | 12250

Directions: D23, at entrance to village next to TO. From Millau take D992/D999 then D23, sp 'Roquefort'. Aire is on left as you enter village.

Sanitation:

Parking:

10

Custom

Short walk uphill to 'Société', Roquefort cheese shop and cave tour. Inspected 2010.

MILLAU 1 | 83 | H10 | N44°05.695' E003°04.944' | 12100

Directions: Parking de la Grave, Rue Cantarane. From south on D992 take 2nd exit at roundabout past Super U onto D809 and cross river. Take 1st slip road on right. Follow under D809 then turn immediately right into Rue Cantarane. Service Point in front of Parking de la Grave on right. Signed.

Sanitation:

Parking:

None; See 84

Aire Services; CC; €6

Service Point only. Inspected 2010.

MILLAU 2 | 84 | H10 | N44°05.750' E003°05.133' | 12100

Directions: Rue de la Saunerie. From south on D992 take 2nd exit at roundabout past Super U onto D809 across river. Take 1st slip road on right. Follow under D809 then turn immediately right into Rue Cantarane. Pass Service Point and turn right at mini roundabout into Rue de la Saunerie. Aire on right.

Sanitation:

Parking:

32

None; See 83

Popular Aire, often full by 5pm. Large wooden bay dividers make it impossible if over 7.5m long. Inspected 2010.

LA COUVERTOIRADE | 85 | H10 | N43°54.776' E003°18.970' | 12230

Directions: Off D55. Enter 1st car park and follow signs to motorhome area.

Sanitation:

Parking:

30; €3; Pay on exit

None

Within 200m walk of large, 12th century, fortified Templar village. Inspected 2010.

ST JEAN ET ST PAUL | 86 | H10 | N43°55.600' E003°00.517' | 12250

Photo: Brian and Heather Mason

Directions: D516. Aire next to cemetery on east/southeast edge of village, signed.

Sanitation:

Parking:

10

Custom

Old fortified Templar village. Roquefort cheese town nearby, see 82. Inspected 2009.

VABRES L'ABBAYE | 87 | H10 | N43°56.728' E002°50.367' | 12400

Directions: Rue de la Vigne. From St Affrique (north) on D999 turn left into Rue du Coustel at village hall and pharmacy, signed. Turn next right into Rue de la Vigne and Aire on right in 60m.

Sanitation:

Parking:

20

Euro Relais Mini; Token (ER); €2

WC at village hall adj. Aire in larger car park at rear of village hall. Inspected 2010.

CAMARES | 88 | H11 | N43°49.017' E002°52.883' | 12360

Directions: Base de Loisirs, Chemin des Zizines. Turn off D902 just south of village, sp 'Plan d'Eau', 'Base de Loisirs', and signed. Cross bridge and turn left into Chemin des Zizines. After 430m turn left and Aire in car park for swimming lake.

Sanitation:

Parking:

25; Max 72hrs

Custom

Aire between river Dourdou and popular swimming lake with 'beach'. Busy on summer weekends, early arrival advised. Inspected 2010.

ST SERNIN SUR RANCE | 89 | H10 | N43°53.205' E002°36.103' | 12380

Directions: From east on D999 pass through village and turn right immediately before high river bridge. Follow road downhill and Aire on right under bridge, signed. Access road steep with a sharp bend at end which could be difficult in icy conditions.

Sanitation:

Parking:

5; Max 72hrs

Custom

Pleasant; 5 mins up the road to village which has local commerce. Inspected 2010.

COUPIAC | 90 | G10 | N43°57.100' E002°35.033' | 12550

Directions: D90, at rear of 'Station Service'. From D999 turn onto D33, sp 'Réquista'. After 12km turn right onto D60, sp 'Coupiac'. Continue through village and following sp 'Station Service'. Turn right onto D90 and right again in 540m. Aire on left immediately behind 24hr service station.

Sanitation:

Parking:

5; Grass parking

Custom

Pleasant Aire on grass between trees. 200m from medieval village and château. Inspected 2010.

ALBAN

91 G10 N43°53.230' E002°27.545' 81250

Directions: Rue Italo Zaccaron. From east on D999 turn left in Alban into Rue Italo Zaccaron, sp 'Complexe Sportif'. Aire at end of road on left at sports stadium. 3.5t weight restriction on Aire.

Sanitation:

Parking:

10

Euro Relais Junior; €2

SP

Aire at stadium. Inspected 2010.

RAYSSAC

92 G10 N43°49.067' E002°24.950' 81330

Directions: From D81 turn onto D59, sp 'Rayssac'. Aire on right on entry to village in small car park adj to Mairie. Approach from north not advised, very narrow roads.

Sanitation:

Parking:

3; Max 24hrs

Flot Bleu Compact; €3.05; Pay Mairie; 2 unmetered elec points

SP

Tiny village. BBQ point. Inspected 2010.

BELMONT SUR RANCE

93 H10 N43°48.979' E002°45.164' 12370

Directions: Adj to D32 in car park, opp Mairie.

Sanitation:

Parking:

3; Max 24hrs

Flot Bleu Fontaine

SP

Popular Aire with lovely garden. No animals in garden. Interesting village with old church. Local commerce adj. Inspected 2010.

LAC DU LAOUZES

94 H11 N43°38.815' E002°46.938' 81320

Directions: D162, on edge of Rieu-Montagne. From northeast on D162 the Aire is on north shore of lake 3km after junction with D162c, signed. If wish to hook-up, consider length of electricity cable before parking.

Sanitation:

Parking:

20; €6.50; €7.50 Jul-Aug

Custom

SP

Bays along shore of lake, some with shade, some with views. Popular spot, busy at weekends. Inspected 2010.

MAZAMET

95 G11 N43°29.450' E002°22.800' 81200

Directions: Parking 'Champ de la Ville', Rue du Champ de la Ville. Turn off D612/N112 at roundabout onto D118/Avenue de la Chevalière. Follow one way system and Aire signs to Parking Champ de la Ville entrance at junction of Rue Galibert Ferret and Rue du Champ de la Ville.

Sanitation:

Parking:

20

Custom

SP

Town centre car park with Service Point on lower parking area. Short walk to town centre, signed. Some shade from large trees. Inspected 2010.

MAZAMET LAC DES MONTAGNES | 96 | G11 | N43°27.733' E002°20.800' | 81200

Directions: Lac des Montagnes. From Mazamet take D118, sp 'Lac des Montagnes'. After 6km turn right, sp 'Lac des Montagnes' and signed. Service Point located at 'Parking 1'. Better parking available at 'Parking 2' further round lake: N43°27.917' E002°20.517'.

Sanitation:

Parking:

10; Max 48hrs

Custom

Swimming lake; Beach; Outdoor showers; Green space; Crazy golf; Lake walks. Parking 2, adj to grassy area. BBQ. Inspected 2010.

LACROUZETTE | 97 | G11 | N43°39.779' E002°20.919' | 81210

Directions: Place du Theron. Approach Lacrouzette from Roquecourbe on D30. Follow road through town, turning right onto one-way system, sp 'Toutes Directions'. Turn left, sp 'Brassac'. Turn next left, sp 'P Place du Theron'. Aire on right behind sculpture.

Sanitation:

Parking:

10

Flot Bleu Océane; €2; Token

Aire in large open car park with plenty of space. Local commerce 1 min. Near national park and gorges. Inspected 2012.

LAUTREC | 98 | G11 | N43°42.239' E002°07.830' | 81440

Directions: Espace Aquatique Base de Loisirs. Approach on D83 toward Castres. Turn off D83 onto D92, sp 'Vielmur', 'Base de Loisirs' and signed. Follow road then turn left, signed. Turn left again and Aire is on right, signed. Town centre has 3.5t weight restriction.

Sanitation:

Parking:

40

Euro Relais Junior; €2; Token (ER)

Aire on outskirts of hilltop town adj to leisure park, lakes (no views) and recreational facilities. Local commerce 10 mins up hill. Inspected 2012.

HAVE YOU VISITED AN AIRE? | GPS co-ordinates in this guide are protected by copyright law

Take at least 5 digital photos showing
• Signs
• Service Point
• Parking
• Overview
• Amenities

Visit www.all-the-aires.co.uk/submissions.shtml to upload your updates and photos.

Sanitation:

Aire Details:

Submit updates

- Amendments
- New Aires
- Not changed

CASTRES | 100 | G11 | N43°35.431' E002°12.398' | 81100

Directions: N126. Approach Castres on N126 from south. Turn left at 2nd roundabout by Dacia showroom. Service Point on right, signed. For night parking exit town on D89. Turn right sp, 'Parc de Gourjade' and follow road to car park.

Sanitation:

Parking:

None

Custom

Service Point only. Restricted overnight parking Max 1 night 5pm-10am only N43°37.225' E002°15.203'. Inspected 2012.

LABRUGUIERE

101 G11 N43°31.883' E002°15.317' 81290

Directions: Parc du Montimont. From central roundabout turn off, sp 'Domaine d'En Laure', down one way street between D621 Toulouse and D621 Mazamet turning. Follow this road until sp 'Domaine d'En Laure' on left. Aire at Domaine d'En Laure.

Sanitation:

Parking:

10

Urba Flux; €2

In a quiet public park with fishing lake and holiday bungalows. BBQ point. Gates locked 8pm-8am. Inspected 2010.

REVEL 1

102 G11 N43°27.262' E002°00.934' 31250

Directions: Chemin de la Pergue, just off D1/D85. Follow sp 'Piscine' and 'Camping'. Aire next to campsite, very well signed.

Sanitation:

Parking:

Some parking available on verges

Raclet; Token (2/1)

Town 1km. Swimming pool opp. Walks along river. Nice holiday feel. Inspected 2010.

REVEL 2

103 G11 N43°27.779' E002°00.318' 31250

Directions: Chemin d'En Besset. At Casino supermarket just off D622, sp in town. Service Point in fuel station by gas bottles.

Sanitation:

Parking:

Poss

Aire Services; Token (3/3); Free from supermarket

5 mins to lovely town with commerce. TO in covered market. Inspected 2010.

PUYLAURENS

104 G11 N43°34.122' E002°00.725' 81700

Directions: Rue Albert Thorel. From N126 turn onto D84, sp 'Puylaurens'. At roundabout take 1st exit to continue on D84 and follow road for 900m. Turn right into Rue Edouard Vairette, signed. Follow road and Aire on left after 300m.

Sanitation:

Parking:

12

Custom

Pleasant Aire on part of an old campsite with some hedged pitches and some shade. Outdoor swimming pool adj. Inspected 2010.

LAVAUR

105 G11 N43°41.177' E001°49.083' 81500

Directions: Chemin d'en Trabouillou. Exit town on D112 towards Castres. Turn off D112 onto D87, sp 'Caraman'. Go straight over roundabout, sp 'Caraman'. In 200m turn left, sp 'Cuisine Centrale' and signed. In 100m turn left, signed.

Sanitation:

Parking:

5

Custom

Parking behind school. Small town commerce 5 mins. Market Saturday mornings. Inspected 2012.

DURFORT

106 G11 N43°26.358' E002°03.909' 81540

Directions: D44. Exit D85 onto D44, sp 'Durfort'. Follow road and as enter village turn right signed, into large car park. Service Point to left.

Sanitation:

Parking:

10

Custom

Aire in large car park close to village centre. Local commerce 1 min. Rural views of surrounding national park. Inspected 2012.

LA MAGDELAINE SUR TARN

107 F10 N43°48.611' E001°32.407' 31340

Directions: Chemin du Lac. Turn off D630 onto D15, sp 'La Magdelaine'. Follow road and at roundabout turn onto D61, sp 'Montjoire'. Follow road around sports facilities then turn right into Chemin du Lac. Follow road and Aire is on left, signed.

Sanitation:

Parking:

2, plus grass parking

Aire Services; €5/30mins; CC

Adj to and overlooking leisure lake. Grass parking when dry. Local commerce 4 mins. Short Voie Verte cycle track from D630. Inspected 2012.

VILLEMUR SUR TARN

108 F10 N43°51.176' E001°29.879' 31340

Directions: Ave du Général Leclerc. Turn off D630 onto D14, sp 'Villemur sur Tarn'. Follow road and Aire adj to D14 before town on right, signed.

Sanitation:

Parking:

3; One bay obstructed by tree

Aire Services; €5/30mins; CC

Adj to main road and sports facilities. Town centre 4 mins. Inspected 2012.

GRENADE

109 F11 N43°46.300' E001°17.817' 31330

Directions: Quai de la Garonne. From D17/D29 roundabout follow D17 towards Ondes, signed. Turn left off D17 at recycling point, signed. Service Point in front of recycling bins.

Sanitation:

Parking:

None

Custom

Saturday morning market can make Service Point access difficult. Inspected 2010.

GRISOLLES

110 F10 N43°49.759' E001°17.884' 82170

Info: John Cox/John and Margaret Leach

Directions: Chemin du Canal. Turn off D820 at roundabout onto D49, sp 'Grisolles' and signed. Cross canal and turn 1st right. Take the 2nd left and Aire is located behind Espace Socioculturel, signed.

Sanitation:

Parking:

10

Custom

Behind social centre. 2 mins to village centre with commerce. Canal 100m for walks and cycling. Visited 2012.

CADOURS — 111 — F11 — N43°43.368' E001°02.916' — 31480

Directions: Chemin d'En Cornac, located at stadium. From town join D24 towards Garac. At roundabout turn left onto Chemin d'En Cornac. Aire 500m.

Sanitation:

Parking:

3

Custom

Town 10 mins. Inspected 2010.

ST LYS — 112 — F11 — N43°30.920' E001°10.553' — 31470

Directions: Route de Saiguede. From town centre turn off by church, sp 'Fontenilles'. Turn left onto D12, sp 'L'Isle Jourdain' truck route and 'Le Moulin'. Service Point is 10m on right, poorly signed and may be obstructed by parked cars. For suitable overnight parking follow road round bend and turn left into car park.

Sanitation:

Parking:

5

Custom; Poss obstructed by cars

Parking adj to boules courts. Town with numerous commerce 2 mins uphill. Service Point is very old and underused. Inspected 2012.

VENERQUE — 113 — F11 — N43°26.010' E001°26.406' — 31810

Directions: Base de Loisirs/Allées du Duc de Ventadour. On D19 follow sp 'Venerque'. Turn off, sp 'Base de Loisirs' and signed. Aire by bridge before church.

Sanitation:

Parking:

4

Custom

Tree lined seating area; Boules. Local commerce 2 mins. Inspected 2010.

AUTERIVE — 114 — F11 — N43°21.100' E001°28.583' — 32550

Directions: Rue des Docteurs Basset. From D820 turn onto D622/Rue Jean Jaurès and cross river. Turn next left into Rue des Docteurs Basset. Parking on left in Place Alfred Melchiori, signed. Service Point across main road in Grande Allée du Ramier: N43°21.011' E001°28.637'.

Sanitation:

Parking:

12

Custom

Pleasant canalside parking. River Ariège across gardens. Town with commerce 2 mins. Inspected 2010.

ST SULPICE SUR LEZE — 115 — F11 — N43°19.812' E001°18.999' — 31410

Directions: D622. Adj to D622 as enter/exit from A64. The Service Point is in the fuel station of the Intermarché supermarket, next to the car wash.

Sanitation:

Parking:

Poss

Euro Relais Junior; €2

Supermarket adj. Inspected 2012.

HAVE YOU VISITED AN AIRE? **GPS co-ordinates in this guide are protected by copyright law**

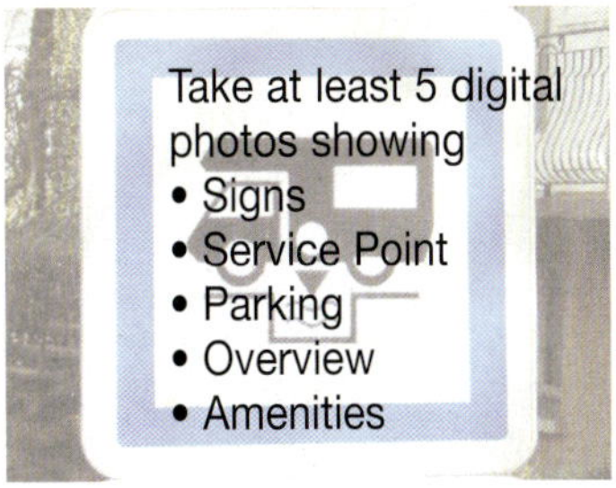
Take at least 5 digital photos showing
• Signs
• Service Point
• Parking
• Overview
• Amenities

Visit www.all-the-aires.co.uk/submissions.shtml to upload your updates and photos.

Sanitation:

Aire Details:

Submit updates
- Amendments
- New Aires
- Not changed

L'ISLE JOURDAIN

117 F11 N43°37.174' E001°04.335' 32600

Directions: Allée du Lac. Exit town to west on D161. Turn right, 500m from town, onto D654, signed. Turn left in front of railway track into Allée du Lac. Service Point immediately on left, signed. Unrestricted parking before Service Point.

Sanitation:

Parking:

5

Custom

At leisure lake with waterskiing, indoor swimming pool and other water related sports. No designated parking but unrestricted parking available. Inspected 2012.

GIMONT

118 F11 N43°37.810' E000°52.187' 32200

Directions: N124, as exit town towards Auch. Just after river bridge on right.

Sanitation:

Parking:

10

Bollard

Overlooking lake; Large town with commerce. Inspected 2010.

SAMATAN

119 F11 N43°29.296' E000°55.628' 32130

Directions: D39. At Les Rivages Vacanciel holiday resort as exit the town on D39 towards Lombez.

Sanitation:

Parking:

10; €3.80/night

Custom; Pay; Water tap in box

Holiday village with lake; Town 5 mins. Sandy beach; Exercise track around lake. Inspected 2010.

LOMBEZ

120 F11 N43°28.485' E000°54.959' 32220

Directions: D632. Enter Lombez on D634 from Samatan. The Aire is in the car park on right just after the D626 junction before the Gendarmerie, signed.

Sanitation:

Parking:

40

Custom

Large gravel car park adj to stadium and Gendarmerie. Inspected 2010.

AUZAS

121 F11 N43°10.200' E000°53.217' 31360

Directions: Off D33. From St Martory on D52 turn left onto D33, sp 'Auzas'. After 900m turn left to lake and Aire in lower car park overlooking lake.

Sanitation:

Parking:

6; €3; Max 15 days

Custom; inc; 8 unmetered elec points inc

Adj to small lake, with children's boats, etc. Service Point in village centre opp church: N43°10.158' E000°53.102'. Inspected 2010.

MARTRES TOLOSANE

122 F11 N43°12.134' E001°00.665' 31220

Directions: From central one-way system turn off, sp 'Cimetière'. The Aire is on right opp cemetery as exit village on D10 to Alan.

Sanitation:

Parking:

2

Bollard

Local commerce 2 mins; Boussens 123 or Mazeres sur Salat 125 both nicer stops. Inspected 2010.

BOUSSENS

123 F11 N43°10.666' E000°58.482' 31360

Directions: Promenade du Lac. From north on D817 turn left at traffic lights into Rue du 11 Nov 1918, sp 'Boussens Village'. At mini roundabout take 1st exit, sp 'Camping'. Follow road to end and turn left into Rue du Port. Aire on left in 500m just before municipal campsite.

Sanitation:

Parking:

3

Custom

Picturesque location overlooking lake. Inspected 2010.

ST CROIX VOLVESTRE

124 F11 N43°07.600' E001°10.250' 09230

Directions: D35. Exit the village on D35 towards Latour. The Aire is at the sports fields. Signed off D35.

Sanitation:

Parking:

7

Custom

Small village with some local commerce 5 mins. Inspected 2010.

MAZERES SUR SALAT

125 F11 N43°08.080' E000°58.579' 31260

Directions: Near Rue du Vieux Ruisseau, off D3. Follow D13 from village centre, sp 'Cassagne'. Turn right off D13 onto Rue du Stade. Turn left just before river bridge and Aire straight ahead.

Sanitation:

Parking:

5

Custom; 1 unmetered elec point

Overlooking river with pretty weir and fish ladder. Commerce in town. Inspected 2010.

ST MARTORY

126 F11 N43°08.507' E000°55.726' 31360

Directions: D52e. In car park adj to D117, by river bridge.

Sanitation:

Parking:

2

Custom

Pleasant; Large motorhomes when empty. Overlooking river. Shops and café. Market Friday. Inspected 2010.

ST GIRONS

127 F12 N42°59.303' E001°08.366' 09200

Directions: D117. Enter from north on D117. Adj to large Renault/Peugeot Garage on right of D117, signed. At rear of old station building.

Sanitation:

Parking:

6

Urba Flux; €2

10 mins to town. Near the medieval city of St Lizier with 2 cathedrals. Inspected 2010.

CASTELNAU DURBAN

128 F12 N42°59.996' E001°20.398' 09420

Directions: D117. In village centre, opp church. Parked cars could make access difficult.

Sanitation:

Parking:

30; Max 48hrs

Urba Flux; €2

Pleasant, shady parking next to main road adj to small river, no view. Inspected 2010.

MIREPOIX

129 G11 N43°05.097' E001°52.453' 09500

Directions: Allée des Soupirs. From D119/D625 roundabout take the turning by the Avia fuel station, sp 'D119' and 'Carcassonne'. Turn left, sp 'Piscine' and signed. The parking is on the left, visible from D119 on the southern edge of the town.

Sanitation:

Parking:

25

Custom

Aire located in small park, 3 mins to beautiful medieval city with original arcaded market square. Super U 150m. Inspected 2010.

SERRES SUR ARGET

130 F12 N42°58.150' E001°31.133' 09000

Directions: D45/D21. Approach from Foix on D17. Turn right onto D21, sp 'Serres sur Arget'. Turn onto D45 at Mairie, sp 'St Martin'. The parking is behind the 'Salle Polyvalente' (village hall): N42°58.167' E001°31.150'. Service Point on D21.

Sanitation:

Parking:

20

Custom; €4; Pay at Mairie

Small lake and park below parking area. Inspected 2010.

MONTFERRIER

131 G12 N42°53.554' E001°47.522' 09300

Info/Photo: Jean and Ken Fowler

Directions: Fount de Sicre. Exit the village on the D9, sp 'Camping'. Turn right off D9 at Camping La Fount de Sicre, signed. Drive between campsite and river to Aire on right, signed.

Sanitation:

Parking:

7; Grass and gravel parking

Custom

Aire in small mountain village on route to mountain passes. Visited 2012.

LES CABANNES

132 G12 N42°47.067' E001°40.967' 09310

Directions: Quartier la Bexane. From E9/N20 take D522, sp 'Les Cabannes'. Follow signs to Aire adj to Gendarmerie. Both well signed.

Sanitation:

Parking:

30; €4/24hrs

Custom; €2

Very scenic location. Inspected 2010.

VICDESSOS

133 F12 N42°46.133' E001°30.150' 09220

Directions: Rue de l'Eglise. Turn off D8 into D708/Rue de l'Eglise, sp 'Parking Camping Cars'. Immediately turn right, passing 8 à Huit supermarket. Aire just beyond the shop.

Sanitation:

Parking:

20; €6; Pay at Mairie

Custom; inc; 12 unmetered elec points

Adj to river on outskirts of village amid beautiful scenery. Inspected 2010.

AUZAT

134 F12 N42°45.867' E001°28.833' 09220

Directions: Rue des Jardins. From Vicdessos follow signs for Auzat. Do not turn off into village, but continue on D8 and Aire signed to right on outskirts.

Sanitation:

Parking:

2

Custom

Very small car park suitable only for small motorhomes, manoeuvring diff. Lovely mountain views. Inspected 2010.

ST GAUDENS

135 F11 N43°06.610' E000°42.493' 31800

Directions: Rue des Chanteurs du Comminges. Exit St Gaudens towards Montréjeau on D817. Turn right at roundabout with D399, sp 'Camping de Belvédère'. Aire in 100m.

Sanitation:

Parking:

None

Custom; Closed Oct-May

Service Point only. Inspected 2010.

MASSEUBE

136 | E11 | N43°26.566' E000°34.687' | 32140

Directions: D929. Exit D929 north of town at roundabout into Super U supermarket car park. Service Point adj to self-service laundry.

Sanitation:

Parking:

Poss

Custom

Supermarket and self-service laundry adj. Inspected 2012.

MONTREJEAU

137 | E11 | N43°05.059' E000°34.306' | 31210

Directions: D817. Just off main road near centre of town at Place de Verdun, around octagonal, covered car park.

Sanitation:

Parking:

5

Toilet only

Small car park at viewing point. WC on site open 8am-7:30pm. Busy on market day, Monday. Inspected 2010.

GOURDAN POLIGNAN

138 | E11 | N43°03.611' E000°35.529' | 31510

Directions: D825. Adj to D825 just befoer roundabout with N125. In Super U fuel station, signed.

Sanitation:

Parking:

Poss

Euro Relais Junior; €2

Supermarket adj. Inspected 2012.

BAGNERES DE LUCHON

139 | E12 | N42°47.706' E000°35.920' | 31110

Directions: Rue Jean Mermoz. Approaching from north on D125 turn left, sp 'D125', 'Espagne', and 'Accueil Camping Car' on very small sign at road level. Take the next left and follow this road. The Aire is on the left, opp the sports ground.

Sanitation:

Parking:

30; €4; 7m bays

Custom; Token; €4

Path to Lac de Badech from Aire. LIDL nearby; Thermal baths. 10 mins to town. Tokens from TO. Inspected 2010.

LOUDENVIELLE

140 | E12 | N42°48.083' E000°24.650' | 65510

Directions: D25/Chemin du Hourgade. From north take D618. Turn off onto D25 and continue south approx 3.5km. Aire adj to lake on right.

Sanitation:

Parking:

20

Euro Relais Junior; Token (ER); €2

Adj to Lac de Genos-Loudenvielle; Thermal baths. Inspected 2010.

ST LARY SOULAN — SKI — 141 — E12 — N42°49.348' E000°19.397' — 65170

Directions: D19, at Parking du Stade. From north on D929 take 1st exit at roundabout as enter town onto D116. At next roundabout turn left onto D19. Aire 100m on right in car park, opp stadium.

Sanitation:

Parking:

34; €6/7pm-8am

Euro Relais Junior; €2

Ski resort with all necessary facilities. Cable car 500m from Aire. Convenient stop en route to Spain via Bielsa Tunnel. Inspected 2010.

PIAU ENGALY — SKI — 142 — E12 — N42°47.150' E000°09.467' — 65170

Directions: D118, Parking 5 at ski station. From north on D929 turn right onto D118 after Aragnouet, sp 'Piau Engaly'. Follow road up to ski station and Aire is in Parking 5 on right, signed.

Sanitation:

Parking:

100; €6 ski season and July/Aug

Custom; €6 for 4amp elec in ski season

Alt 1855m. Stunning views. Parking free in summer but no services. www.piau-engaly.com Inspected 2010.

ARREAU — 143 — E12 — N42°54.437' E000°21.549' — 65240

Directions: Avenue de la Gare. Turn off D929 into Ave de la Gare, sp 'Volerie: Les Aigles d'Aure', and cross river bridge. Aire in car park on left within 150m.

Sanitation:

Parking:

15; €2/night

Custom

Pretty, small village en route to Bielsa Tunnel to Spain. Inspected 2010.

LA MONGIE 1900 STATION — SKI — 144 — E12 — N42°54.750' E000°10.733' — 65200

Directions: Place Pène Nègre. From Ste Marie de Campan follow D918 to La Mongie ski station. Turn sharp right just before 'Le Choucas' restaurant. Follow road uphill for 500m to Place Pène Nègre. May be signed 'Parking 4' in ski season.

Sanitation:

Parking:

20

None

Lovely views and lots of walking. Cable car to Pic du Midi de Bigorre in summer: €30. Inspected 2010.

PAYOLLE — 145 — E12 — N42°56.309' E000°17.498' — 65710

Directions: D113. From east on D918 turn left in Payolle onto D113, sp 'Complexe Touristique du Lac de Payolle'. After 700m fork right, sp 'Hourquette D'Ancizan'. Aire on left adj to stream. Service Point above parking area at fork in road, signed.

Sanitation:

Parking:

15

Custom

Beautiful location alongside mountain stream in area with unfenced livestock. View of Pic du Midi de Bigorre. Inspected 2010.

STE MARIE DE CAMPAN

146 | E12 | N42°58.959' E000°13.692' | 65710

Directions: D918/Rue Emillien Frossard, off D935. Between Bagneres de Bigorre and Col d'Aspin off D935.

Sanitation:

Parking:

5; Max 48hrs

Custom

SP

Aire alongside D918, above small river. Local commerce in village. Inspected 2010.

LA MONGIE

SKI

147 | E12 | N42°55.168' E000°11.403' | 65200

Directions: Just off D918 between Artigues-Campan and La Mongie. Large gravel parking area. May be signed as 'Parking 5' in ski season.

Sanitation:

Parking:

100

None

SP

Alt 1575m. Just below ski resort of La Mongie, with cable car to summit of Pic du Midi de Bigorre with stunning scenery. Inspected 2010.

GAVARNIE

SKI

148 | E12 | N42°44.317' W000°01.167' | 65120

Photo: Motorhomeandaway.co.uk

Directions: D923. From Gavarnie turn onto D923 from D921. Parking on left opp monument in 3km.

Sanitation:

Parking:

50; €4 in season

Custom

SP

Popular walk to Cirque de Gavarnie and waterfalls. Inspected 2009.

HAVE YOU VISITED AN AIRE?

GPS co-ordinates in this guide are protected by copyright law

Take at least 5 digital photos showing
• Signs
• Service Point
• Parking
• Overview
• Amenities

Visit www.all-the-aires.co.uk/submissions.shtml to upload your updates and photos.

Sanitation:

Aire Details:

Submit updates

- Amendments
- New Aires
- Not changed

PIERREFITTE NESTALAS

150 | E12 | N42°57.572' W000°04.608' | 65260

Directions: Rue Victor Hugo. From D921 turn off by the Mairie following signs to 'Aire de Pique-Nique'.

Sanitation:

Parking:

14

Walther; €1

SP

Popular Aire directly adj to foot/cycle path to Cauterets/Lourdes. Inspected 2010.

CAUTERETS 1

SKI | 151 | E12 | N42°53.577' W000°06.769' | 65110

Directions: Place de la Gare/D920a/Route de Pierrefitte. Adj to D920a in car park after campsite, signed.

Sanitation:

Parking:

30; €10 inc elec; CC; Pay at machine

Custom; inc; 4amp elec

Ski area, gondola adj. Pont d'Espagne, Cascades and Lac de Gaube 6km. Lovely walks. Inspected 2010.

CAUTERETS 2

SKI | 152 | E12 | N42°53.183' W000°06.917' | 65110

Directions: Avenue du Docteur Charles Thierry, off D920a. From north on D920a pass through the town following sp 'Pont d'Espagne'. Aire on left at rear of casino just before leaving town.

Sanitation:

Parking:

25; €10/night

Custom; inc; Elec inc

Some shade and quieter than 151. Inspected 2010.

ARRENS MARSOUS

153 | E12 | N42°57.483' W000°12.433' | 65400

Directions: D918. Exit the village on D918 towards Argèles-Gazost. Parking area on right, turn right beside La Balaguere building. Aire is signed with a small sign on road edge. Follow road to parking area.

Sanitation:

Parking:

10

Custom

Pleasant area on edge of village. Small convenience store nearby. Inspected 2010.

LANNEMEZAN

154 | E11 | N43°07.651' E000°22.859' | 65300

Directions: Espace du Nebouzan/Chemin du Carrérot de Blazy. From east on D817 at roundabout turn onto D17, sp 'Centre Ville'. Cross next roundabout then turn right onto D939/Rue Carnot. Pass large car park then turn left into Place du Château. Continue and Aire at end of road on right, signed.

Sanitation:

Parking:

30

Aire Services

Must park in official area Tue night. Market on Wed. Local commerce; Self-service laundry. Inspected 2010.

ARGELES GAZOST

155 | E11 | N43°00.562' W000°05.129' | 65400

Directions: Turn off D821 at roundabout, sp 'Zone Artisanale' and signed. Tirn 1st left and Service Point on right at PIKYCO, signed.

Sanitation:

Parking:

None

Flot Bleu Pacific; €2

Service Point only. Inspected 2012.

SOULOM

156 E11 N42°57.350' W000°04.364' 65260

Directions: D921/Avenue des Deux Ponts. From south on D921 Aire on right 700m after roundabout junction with D13. Large rectangular parking area as enter Soulom.

Sanitation:

Parking:

20

Custom

Pleasant open area with mountain views. Snack bar in corner of car park. Inspected 2010.

CAMPAN

157 E11 N43°01.099' E000°10.687' 65710

Directions: D8. From Bagneres de Bigorre take D8/Route d'Aste and follow road into Campan. Service Point and parking adj to this road by the war memorial metal cross.

Sanitation:

Parking:

5; Max 48hrs

Custom

Quaint village. Lots of 'Moumaques' (Puppet Lignes) in village. Scenic location above small river. Inspected 2010.

BAGNERES DE BIGORRE

158 E11 N43°04.396' E000°09.139' 65200

Directions: Off Rue René Cassin. From north on D935 enter town and turn left at roundabout onto D8/Boulevard de l'Adour by Gendarmerie. After 600m cross river and turn right opp scrap yard into Rue René Cassin. Turn 1st left into industrial area. Aire on right, signed.

Sanitation:

Parking:

20

Euro Relais Mini

Industrial but quiet. Bus to town Mon-Sat. Inspected 2010.

POUZAC

159 E11 N43°04.750' E000°08.482' 65200

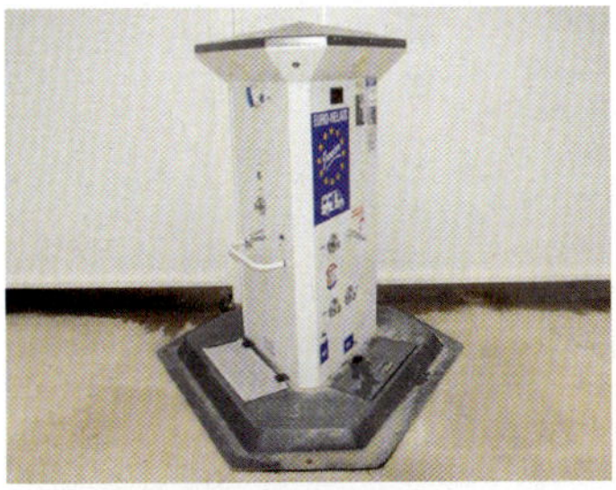

Directions: D935 at Intermarché supermarket. Adj to the D935 on the left as drive toward Bagnères de Bigorre from north. Service point behind fuel station adj to self-service laundry.

Sanitation:

Parking:

Poss

Euro Relais Junior; €2

Supermarket and self-service laundry adj. Inspected 2012.

LOURDES 1

160 E11 N43°05.900' W000°02.517' 65100

Photo: Malcolm and Janet Webb

Directions: D97/Blvd du Lapacca. From north on N21 take 1st exit at roundabout onto D914, sp 'Centre Ville'. At traffic lights by railway bridge continue straight on D914. At roundabout cross straight over, staying on D914. Take 3rd turning left into Blvd du Lapacca. Parking on right in 300m by toilets.

Sanitation:

Parking:

20

Custom; €5

Roadside parking just before coach park. Services from adj toilet block. Arrive early as popular. Inspected 2010.

LOURDES 2 | 161 | E11 | N43°05.296' W000°03.161' | 65100

Directions: Avenue Monseigneur Rodhain. From south on D821 at roundabout take 3rd exit onto D914. Turn 1st left into Boulevard Georges Dupierris, sp 'La Grotte' and 'P Arrouza'. Take 2nd left into Boulevard du Gave. Turn 2nd left into Esplanade du Paradis. Cross river and Aire immediately on left at rear of coach parking.

Sanitation:

Parking:

50; €10/24hrs; €6/12hrs; Pay cash to guardian; Open Easter-Oct

Custom; €5

Park by river. Manned 24hrs. Inspected 2010.

TARBES 1 | 162 | E11 | N43°13.116' E000°04.354' | 65000

Directions: N21. Follow sp 'Toutes Directions'. Just past N21/D935 roundabout opp stadium, sp 'Stade', 'Parc des Expositions', and signed.

Sanitation:

Parking:

None; See 163

Flot Bleu Euro; CC; €3

Large parking other side of stadium. Inspected 2010.

TARBES 2 | 163 | E11 | N43°13.282' E000°04.493' | 65000

Directions: Avenue Pierre de Coubertin. From Lourdes on N21 follow 'Toutes Directions'. Pass stadium on left then at next roundabout turn left into Avenue d'Altenkirchen. Turn left at roundabout into Avenue Pierre de Coubertin.

Sanitation:

Parking:

30

None; See 162

Parking area is under trees between park and stadium. E'Leclerc supermarket 200m. Inspected 2010.

MIELAN | 164 | E11 | N43°25.994' E000°18.519' | 32170

Directions: Rue du Cubet. Approach town on N21 from Mirande. Turn left as enter town, signed. Follow road for 300m and Aire is in car park on left, signed.

Sanitation:

Parking:

6; Additional parking

Custom

Just off N21 but sheltered from road noise. Town with small town commerce and historic covered market 5 mins. Inspected 2012.

VIC EN BIGORRE | 165 | E11 | N43°23.085' E000°02.956' | 65500

Directions: Rue du Stade. From town centre follow sp 'Pau'. After crossing river bridge turn left onto D61, sp 'Montaner' and signed. Turn immediately right, signed, and Aire immediately on right under plane trees, signed.

Sanitation:

Parking:

6; Under trees

Custom

Parking is possible with care under low plane trees that provide excellent shade on hot summer days. Noisy main road adj. Town centre commerce 5 mins. Inspected 2012.

MAUBOURGUET

166 E11 N43°26.584' E000°02.493' 65700

Directions: D935. Turn off D935 south of town to Super U supermarket. Aire adj to fuel station, signed.

Sanitation:

Parking:

6

Flot Bleu Pacific; €2; Flot Bleu Electric; €1/3hrs; 4 CEE elec points

Designated parking at supermarket just off main route. Inspected 2012.

HAVE YOU VISITED AN AIRE? **GPS co-ordinates in this guide are protected by copyright law**

Take at least 5 digital photos showing
• Signs
• Service Point
• Parking
• Overview
• Amenities

Visit www.all-the-aires.co.uk/submissions.shtml to upload your updates and photos.

Sanitation:

Aire Details:

Submit updates

- Amendments
- New Aires
- Not changed

PLAISANCE

168 E11 N43°36.491' E000°02.918' 32160

Directions: Place des Arenes. Turn off D946 by river bridge into car park, signed. Opp outdoor swimming pool. Drive behind bull ring and Service Point is on left, signed.

Sanitation:

Parking:

None; Max parking 4hrs no parking 8pm-6am

Euro Relais Mini

Service Point only. Inspected 2012.

RISCLE

169 E11 N43°39.697' W000°04.737' 32400

Directions: Rue des Loubines. Turn off D935 at river bridge as exit town to north, signed. Follow road and Service Point is on right and parking is beyond.

Sanitation:

Parking:

6; Grass parking

Custom

Part of former campsite with partial views over river. Quiet location that may feel isolated if alone. Town with local commerce 5 mins. Inspected 2012.

BEAUMARCHES

170 E11 N43°35.243' E000°05.536' 32160

Directions: Off D946. Turn off D3 onto D946, sp 'Beaumarchés'. Turn left, sp 'Beaumarchés Plastiques' and signed. Follow road past plastics company and Aire 2nd turning on left. Signed.

Sanitation:

Parking:

5; Grass parking

Custom

Quiet with views over lane to open countryside and vines. 300m to village centre. Inspected 2010.

MIRANDE — 171 — E11 — N43°30.801' E000°24.501' — 32300

Directions: Chemin du Batardeau. Turn off N21, sp 'Chalets L'ile du Pont', and follow sp 'L'ile du Pont'. Service Point to right of campsite entrance.

Sanitation:

Parking:

None
Custom; Token

SP

Campsite adj €15/night. Inspected 2012.

NOGARO — 172 — E11 — N43°45.871' W000°01.995' — 32110

Directions: Avenue des Sports. From D931 from Eauze turn right just past glider Aerodrome down Avenue des Sports, signed.

Sanitation:

Parking:

10
Flot Bleu Euro; CC

SP

Adj to VIP reception for racing circuit. ALDI 2 mins. Outdoor swimming pool opp. Inspected 2010.

BARBOTAN LES THERMES — 173 — E10 — N43°56.967' W000°02.600' — 32150

Directions: Off D656, at the casino. Turn off D656, sp 'Parking Nocturne Payant' and 'Casino'. Bear left and park in front of casino.

Sanitation:

Parking:

20; €6/night (10pm-6am)
None; See 174

SP

Large parking area adj to town centre, ideal night stop. For longer stays see 174 Toilets and free WiFi at TO adj. Inspected 2010.

LAC DE L'UBY (BARBOTAN LES THERMES) — 174 — E10 — N43°56.150' W000°01.950' — 32150

Directions: Lac de l'uby. Must apply for barrier key at TO in Barbotan les Thermes, see 173. From TO turn right onto D656 and continue over roundabout. After 500m turn left, sp 'Lac de l'uby' and signed. After 1.8km turn right onto track to height barriers. Aire in car park beyond.

Sanitation:

Parking:

50; €6
Custom; inc; Elec inc

SP

TO in Barbotan has key to barrier, €60 deposit. Lovely location. Long elec leads needed for some bays. Insufficient elec points for every bay. Inspected 2010.

MONTREAL — 175 — E10 — N43°57.222' E000°11.835' — 32250

Directions: D29, at stadium as exit village. From town centre travel north on D29, sp 'Fources'. Aire on left, signed.

Sanitation:

Parking:

20
Custom

SP

Football; Village 5 mins. Inspected 2010.

FOURCES

176 E10 N43°59.649' E000°13.767' 32250

Directions: D114. Turn off D29 onto D114, sp 'Fources-Village'. Follow road past village green, sp 'Aire de Camping-Car'. In 50m turn right, sp 'P Autos'. Follow road and parking on grass before Service Point.

Sanitation:

Parking:

6; Grass parking, limited hard standing in low season

Custom; Tap removed

Located in pleasant recreation area 1 min from the centre of a 'Village of France'. Restaurants 2 mins. Inspected 2012.

CONDOM

177 E10 N43°56.917' E000°21.821' 32100

Directions: Rue Boileau. Exit town on D931, sp 'Pau'. Turn left, sp 'Camping l'Argente'. Turn left in 50m and drive up slope to Aire.

Sanitation:

Parking:

12

Custom; Water tap badly designed

Former municipal campsite. Outdoor swimming pool with waterslides adj. Town centre commerce 20 mins. Inspected 2012.

VALENCE SUR BAISE

178 E10 N43°52.383' E000°23.267' 32310

Directions: D930. On D930 in lay-by picnic area as enter town from Auch, signed. Further parking on grass behind Service Point.

Sanitation:

Parking:

2

Custom

Adj to main road; Town 7 mins with local commerce. Inspected 2010.

ST PUY

179 E10 N43°52.557' E000°27.742' 32310

Directions: Turn off D654 into St Puy opp D42 turning, signed. The Aire is well signed and outside the building marked Salle des Fêtes.

Sanitation:

Parking:

3

Custom

Small Aire in village centre. Boulangerie adj. Inspected 2010.

FLEURANCE

180 F10 N43°50.842' E000°40.318' 32500

Info/Photo: Mick and Jackie Varney

Directions: D953. From N21 at roundabout take D953, sp 'St Clar'. Turn right immediately after crossing river bridge. Aire on right, signed.

Sanitation:

Parking:

43; Grass; Roadway parking poss

Flot Bleu Océane; Token €2

Aire relocated to former municipal campsite. Adj lake, swimming pools, and tennis accessed over river footbridge. Village centre 10 mins. Market on Tuesdays. Visited 2012.

AUCH

181 E11 N43°38.192' E000°35.325' 32000

Directions: Rue du Général de Gaulle. From north on N21 follow sp 'Tarbes'. In town turn left at traffic lights (by pharmacy) into Rue du Général de Gaulle. Aire on right after 400m just before river bridge, sp 'Camping', and adj to 'Salle de Table Tennis'. Signed

Sanitation:

Parking:

3; €4/night; Pay at campsite

Point Belle Eau

SP

Service Point accessible when campsite closed. Inspected 2010.

PREIGNAN

182 F11 N43°42.748' E000°38.053' 32810

Directions: Rue Emile Zola. When entering from Auch turn right at 1st roundabout, sp 'Municipal Sports'. Follow road for 1.5km and Aire on right, signed.

Sanitation:

Parking:

5

Custom

SP

Parking limited to the 5 marked bays to left of the car park. Service Point opp. Inspected 2010.

SARRANT

183 F11 N43°46.537' E000°55.679' 32120

Directions: D165. From Cologne as enter village on left, signed. In large sloping field.

Sanitation:

Parking:

20; Grass parking

Custom

SP

Small fortified village with basic amenities. Inspected 2010.

ST CLAR

184 F10 N43°53.474' E000°46.375' 32380

Directions: Leave St Clar on D13 towards Gramont. Aire to east of village on left.

Sanitation:

Parking:

10; Max 24hrs

Custom

SP

Very nice Aire spaced out amongst fruit trees with good views. Village approx 5 mins. Showers. Inspected 2010.

BEAUMONT DE LOMAGNE 1

185 F10 N43°52.824' E000°59.452' 82500

Directions: Boulevard Georges Brassens/D3, as enter town on D3 from south. Turn 1st right at roundabout and Aire on right, signed. 3.5t weight restriction on Aire.

Sanitation:

Parking:

10

Custom

SP

Town 2 mins. Inspected 2010.

BEAUMONT DE LOMAGNE 2 — 186 — F10 — N43°53.543' E001°00.695' — 82500

Directions: D928. Adj to D928 as enter town from Larrazet in east. At the car wash in the Casino supermarket car park.

Sanitation:

Parking:

Poss

Flot Bleu Euro; €2/20mins; CC or Token

Supermarket adj. Inspected 2012.

CASTELSARRASIN — 187 — F10 — N44°02.314' E001°06.136' — 82100

Directions: Allee de la Source. Exit E72/A62 Junction 9. Take D813 and follow sp 'Toulouse' onto one way system. Turn right into Rue du Gaz, signed. Take 1st right into Allee de la Source, signed. Aire on left, access via Aire Services barrier.

Sanitation:

Parking:

30; €3/24hrs

Aire Services; €2.50; Aire Services Electric; 16 CEE points €2.50/24hrs

Aire located in residential streets 5 mins from town centre. Inspected 2012.

ST NICOLAS DE LA GRAVE — 188 — F10 — N44°03.828' E001°01.494' — 82210

Directions: Rue Bouchotte, off D26. Enter town on D26, D15, or D67 and follow sp 'Centre Ville'. Drive behind church and follow signs to Aire.

Sanitation:

Parking:

5

Euro Relais Mini

Small town centre 1 min; Some parking with views. Inspected 2010.

ST ANTOINE — 189 — F10 — N44°02.149' E000°50.542' — 32340

Directions: D953. Enter St Antoine from Valence on D953. As enter village turn left, signed. Follow arrows behind stone barns on gravel track and turn right into parking before recycling point.

Sanitation:

Parking:

10

Custom

Rural views; Village 1 min with restaurant; Lots of green open space. Inspected 2010.

LECTOURE — 190 — F10 — N43°56.078' E000°38.030' — 32700

Photo: Janet and John Watts

Directions: Avenue Jacques Descamps. From north on N21 turn right in Lectoure into Avenue Jacques Descamps. Service Point, fuel station, and laundry on left of road, supermarket and main car park on right.

Sanitation:

Parking:

Poss

Euro Relais Box

Laundry (open 24/7) adj to fuel pay kiosk: €8/18kg; €6/8kg inc powder; €1/16kg/12 mins drying. Inspected 2010.

BARDIGUES

191 F10 N44°02.316' E000°53.551' 82340

Directions: Outside cemetery. Between D89 and D11, signed off D11 but more easily accessible from D89 as road doesn't go through village. Exit D89, sp 'Bardigues' from either direction. Aire at top of hill by cemetery.

Sanitation:

Parking:

4

Custom; €2

SP

Gated, not lockable. Village 2 mins uphill. Pleasant. Inspected 2010.

DONZAC

192 F10 N44°06.855' E000°49.239' 82340

Directions: D30, at Lac des Sources. From north on D813 turn right onto D30 at Lamagistère, sp 'Donzac' and signed. Cross river and Aire on right at lake, signed.

Sanitation:

Parking:

10; 9m max

Custom

SP

Views of pond (no fishing); Power station 1.6km away. Pleasant. Village commerce 2 mins. Inspected 2010.

VALENCE D'AGEN

193 F10 N44°06.342' E000°53.168' 82400

Directions: Rue des Tanneries. Turn off D813 to the west of town onto D11E, sp ' Centre Ville' and signed. Drive into town and turn right opp covered market, sp 'Mairie' and 'Port Canal'. Turn left, then right, signed. Cross canal and Aire on right.

Sanitation:

Parking:

20

Aire Services; €4/15mins water and 2hrs elec; Showers April-Oct

SP

Adj to canal but no view. Showers and toilets in former abattoir. Small town commerce 2 mins. Inspected 2012.

MALAUSE

194 F10 N44°05.483' E000°58.402' 82200

Directions: D4. Turn off D813 at the roundabout by the church onto D4, sp 'Boudou'. Turn immediately left into the car park by the church and the Service Point is on the right.

Sanitation:

Parking:

5

Flot Bleu Océane; Token/30mins

SP

Noisy as just off D830 trunking route. Local commerce adj. 193 (10 mins) a quieter stop. Inspected 2012.

MONTJOI

195 F10 N44°11.868' E000°55.347' 82400

Directions: D46. In village just off D46 opp church, signed.

Sanitation:

Parking:

10

Custom

SP

Recommended off the beaten track stop not far from D813. Pleasant and quiet, village Aire with rural views. Good walking. Inspected 2012.

ST BENOIT (MOISSAC) — 196 — F10 — N44°05.776' E001°05.317' — 82200

Directions: Chemin du Moulin de Bidounet. At St-Benoît across the river from Moissac. Take D813 south from Moissac and turn left at roundabout onto D72. Turn left off D72, sp 'Camping de l'Île du Bidounet'.

Sanitation:

Parking:

None

Custom

SP

Just a Service Point. For parking see Moissac 197. Inspected 2010.

MOISSAC — 197 — F10 — N44°05.994' E001°05.087' — 82200

Directions: Promenade Sancert. From south on D813 cross river then turn 1st right into Quai du Vieux Port, sp 'Uvarium', 'P Pont Canal', and 'Espace Nautique'. Follow road for 200m. Parking on right adj to river Tarn and Moulin de Moissac Hotel and Restaurant.

Sanitation:

Parking:

5

Flot Bleu Electric; Token; €2/24hrs elec; 4 elec points

SP

Views of river Tarn. Town centre 5 mins. Main services across river at St Benoît 196. Inspected 2010.

NEGREPELISSE — 198 — F10 — N44°04.442' E001°31.582' — 82800

Info/Photo: Donna Garner

Directions: D958 Avenue Jean Fleury. Approach from east. At the D115/D65/D958 roundabout take the D958 following sp 'Centre Ville' and signed. Turn left at next roundabout continuing on D958, signed. Aire 200m on right, adj to D958 before centre, signed.

Sanitation:

Parking:

6

Custom

SP

Some road noise. Local commerce including laundry 300m in town centre. Visited 2012.

LAUZERTE 1 — 199 — F10 — N44°16.026' E001°08.447' — 82110

Directions: D953. From north on D953 at junction with D2 go straight on into small road Lieu-Dit Vignal. Aire immediately on right.

Sanitation:

Parking:

10

Custom

SP

Shady parking adj to pond/river. BBQs. 1.7km walk to pretty historic village, 'Cite Medieval'. Inspected 2010.

LAUZERTE 2 — 200 — F10 — N44°15.251' E001°08.192' — 82110

Directions: D58e/Route de Moissac. From D953 at roundabout take D58e, sp 'Centre Ville' and 'Aire de Camping Car'. Follow road through village and Aire in small car park on right, signed.

Sanitation:

Parking:

3

Custom

SP

Service Point in small medieval village centre car park. Better, larger parking area outside village, see 199. Inspected 2010.

MONTCUQ — 201 — F10 — N44°20.452' E001°12.151' — 46800

Directions: D653/Ave de St Jean. From Cahors on D653 Aire on right between Shopi supermarket and Total fuel station, signed.

Sanitation:

Parking:

20

Euro Relais Junior; Token (ER); €2

SP

Roadside; Opp campsite. Tokens available from TO or Total station 200m. Inspected 2010.

CASTELNAU MONTRATIER — 202 — F10 — N44°16.473' E001°21.123' — 46170

Directions: Causse du Moulin à Vent. Exit town on D659 towards Lalbenque. At the windmill on the right, turn left and follow the road uphill. Aire on left, signed.

Sanitation:

Parking:

10

Euro Relais Junior; Token (2/1); €2

SP

Adj to a line of windmills. Municipal campsite adj. Village centre with local commerce and convenience store 3 mins downhill. Inspected 2012.

ROQUECOR — 203 — F10 — N44°19.393' E000°56.651' — 82150

Directions: On D656 from Tournon d'Agenais take 1st turning on left by two plane trees, sp 'Roquecor'. Drive into village and Aire on left, signed.

Sanitation:

Parking:

6; 10m bays

Custom

SP

Rural views; Village 2 mins with local commerce and convenience store. Inspected 2010.

MAUROUX — 204 — F10 — N44°27.099' E001°02.870' — 46700

Directions: Aire de Repos 'La Garenne', D5. Approx 180m south of village in woodland, but hardcore roads and parking spots.

Sanitation:

Parking:

10; Apr-Oct

Custom

SP

Local commerce in village. Pleasant woodland Aire. Covered BBQ and kitchen area open Apr-Oct. Inspected 2010.

PUY L'EVEQUE — 205 — F10 — N44°30.406' E001°08.141' — 46700

Directions: Rue Henri Dunant. From Cahors on D911 turn right opp Mairie, sp 'La Poste'. Parking on right opp Gendarmerie, signed.

Sanitation:

Parking:

30

Custom; Tap and drain next to bench

SP

Town 5 mins; Lots of space. Inspected 2010.

PRAYSSAC

206 F10 N44°30.199' E001°11.502' 46220

Directions: D911. Adj to D911 in town, signed.

Sanitation:

Parking:

20

Custom; Water under green cover; Hose/tap adaptor needed

SP

Pleasant; Small town commerce 2 mins. Inspected 2010.

ALBAS

207 F10 N44°28.488' E001°13.965' 46140

Directions: D8. Exit Albas to north on D8. After 800m turn right, sp 'Camping Pech Del Gal'. Aire outside campsite, adj to river. Signed on entry to village from north.

Sanitation:

E

Parking:

10

Custom

SP

Riverside parking area adj to barrage. Inspected 2010.

LUZECH (CAIX)

208 F10 N44°29.431' E001°17.702' 46140

Directions: D9. From Luzech take D9/Quai Lefranc de Pompignan along the river Lot, sp 'Caix' and signed. Turn right after 2km into campsite, visible from road, sp 'Restaurant le Capitaine' as enter Caix. Drive into campsite entrance then turn right into Aire.

Sanitation:

E

Parking:

20; €7.50/night inc elec

Bollard; €2

SP

Commercial Aire adj to campsite; By river, no views. Inspected 2010.

LABASTIDE MARNHAC

209 F10 N44°23.163' E001°23.856' 46090

Directions: D67. Turn off D7 onto D67, sp 'l'Hospitalet' and signed. Turn immediately left, signed, then 1st right. Aire on left.

Sanitation:

E

Parking:

10

Custom

SP

Adj to picnic area and tennis courts. Bar/restaurant adj. On popular GR65 walking route. Inspected 2012.

CAHORS 1

210 F10 N44°26.420' E001°26.468' 46000

Directions: Parking St Georges. Approach Cahors from south on D820. Follow sp 'Centre Ville' and 'Cahours' from south then turn off to P St Georges at roundabout before river bridge. Aire directly adj to river bridge on south side in Parking St Georges.

Sanitation:

E

Parking:

3

Custom

SP

Large historic town with commerce 5 mins. Parking overlooking river. Laundry 50m in Place de la Resistance. Inspected 2010.

CAHORS 2

211 F10 N44°27.689' E001°27.033' 46000

Directions: Avenue Edouard Herriot. From Cahors centre follow D911, sp 'Rodez'. 70m after Total fuel station turn left into Rue Jean Racine. Aire at Intermarché at end of road opp. In 'Terre-Rouge' area, east of main town.

Sanitation:

Parking:

Poss

Custom; Token; €2

SP

Token available from supermarket, free when spending over €20 in shop, not on fuel. Inspected 2010.

ARCAMBAL

212 F10 N44°27.412' E001°30.966' 46090

Directions: D8. At Arcambal centre turn onto D8 at traffic lights, sp 'St Cirq Lapopie'. Aire immediately on right behind Mairie.

Sanitation:

E

Parking:

5; Long bays

Euro Relais Junior; Token (ER); €2

SP

Table tennis; Basketball; Restaurant. Inspected 2010.

ST CIRQ LAPOPIE

213 G10 N44°28.233' E001°40.830' 46330

Directions: Turn off D662 at roundabout in Tour de Faure onto D181/D8 and cross river Lot. After 500m turn right, sp 'Aire de Camping Car'. Aire is in both directions along the river bank.

Sanitation:

E

Parking:

P

50; €7

Raclet; €2

SP

Nice spot on bank of river Lot. Very pretty village of St Cirq Lapopie 1.2km up hill. Showers €2. Inspected 2010.

VERS

214 F10 N44°29.131' E001°33.302' 46090

Photo: Rodney Martin

Directions: Off D662. From east on D662 turn left on entering village, sp 'Aire de Camping Car'. For parking turn immediately right or for services turn immediately left down gravel track: N44°29.175' E001°33.391'.

Sanitation:

WC F

Parking:

P

6; €5/night

Custom

SP

By old station. Shower, toilet, and tap at parking area. Inspected 2010.

ST GERY

215 G10 N44°28.702' E001°34.895' 46330

Directions: D662. Adj to D662 in village centre, signed.

Sanitation:

WC F

Parking:

F

30

Custom

SP

Pleasant location just off village centre with local commerce. Miniature train and museum 2 mins. No river access. Inspected 2012.

CABRERETS

216 G10 N44°30.463' E001°39.736' 46330

Directions: D41. Follow D41 north of the village. Service Point outside Camping Familial Cantal.

Sanitation:

Parking:

None

Custom; April-Oct

Service Point only. Adj to basic riverside campsite set into gorge. €3.50 pitch, €2.80pp, €2.50 elec. Inspected 2012.

BOUZIES

217 G10 N44°28.993' E001°38.716' 46330

Directions: D40. Turn off D662 onto 10t weight and 2.3m (wheelbase) width restricted bridge to D40, sp 'Bouziers'. Turn left and left again. Service Point in car park on left. Overnight car park to right adj to river. To avoid bridge approach from St-Cirq-Lapopie.

Sanitation:

Parking:

15

Custom

Adj to river park. Partial views through trees to river. Canoe hire adj. D662, a pleasant river drive under rocky overhangs and tunnels. Inspected 2012.

CATUS

218 F9 N44°33.346' E001°20.344' 46150

Directions: Off D6. Situated by the river bank, north of the river in the centre of the village. Well signposted.

Sanitation:

Parking:

10

Custom

2 mins from village centre with local commerce; Market on Tuesday. Inspected 2010.

Lacrouzette

St Valery en Caux

NORMANDY

St Nicholas de Bliquetuit

LE TREPORT 1

1 | F2 | N50°03.569' E001°23.352' | 76470

Directions: Zone D'Activité Sainte-Croix, off Rue Pierre Mendès France. Turn off D940/D1915 roundabout onto D1915, sp 'Aire de Camping-Car'. Follow sp past campsite to Aire on right. Enter through barrier.

Sanitation:

Parking:

61; €9.30 inc unmetered elec; Pay on entry

Aire Services

SP

Commercial Aire in pleasant surroundings. Inspected 2012.

LE TREPORT 2 - FUNICULAIRE

2 | F4 | N50°03.463' E001°21.733' | 76470

Directions: D940. Enter Le Treport from south on D940. Turn left, sp 'Funicilaire' and 'Aire de Service du Funiculaire'. Follow road past the funicular and the Aire is on left.

Sanitation:

Parking:

50; €5; Pay at machine; Max 48hrs; Reinforced grass parking

Aire Services; CC; €2

SP

Pleasant Aire on hilltop adj to funicular to Le Treport. Some bays are boggy after rain. Trailers banned. Inspected 2012.

DIEPPE 1

3 | F4 | N49°55.915' E001°05.046' | 76200

Directions: Blvd de Verdun. From Dieppe 1 follow road around harbour to car park on other side, visible from Dieppe 1. Route inaccessible on Saturday due to market.

Sanitation:

Parking:

40; €7 pay at machine; Max 48hrs

None; See Dieppe 1

SP

5 bays with sea view. Very popular parking; Manoeuvring 8m plus motorhomes may be difficult. Commerce adj. Market Saturday. Inspected 2012.

DIEPPE 2

4 | F2 | N49°55.802' E001°05.191' | 76200

Photo: Susan Matthews

Directions: Pollet Quarter, Quai de la Marne. Follow D485 sp 'Car Ferries'. At port entrance take next exit on roundabout and drive past cliff. Go straight over the next roundabout and the Aire is on left.

Sanitation:

Parking:

€7/24hrs; Max 48hrs; Pay at machine

Custom

SP

On quay road. Town centre 5-10 mins; Market Saturday. Inspected 2012.

ST SAIRE

5 | F3 | N49°41.808' E001°29.697' | 76270

Directions: D7. Exit D1314 onto D7, sp 'St Saire'. Aire on left in 50m adj to former train station. Grass parking, not accessible in wet weather.

Sanitation:

Parking:

5; Max 48hrs

Aire Services; Token (3/3)

SP

Avenue Vert cycle/walking path adj which runs from St Aubin le Cauf to Beaubec la Rosière. Inspected 2012.

PETIT APPEVILLE | 6 | F2 | N49°53.790' E001°03.255' | 76550

Directions: D153/Rue de la Gare. Exit Dieppe to west on D925. Turn left at traffic lights onto D153, sp 'Camping la Source'. Service Point adj to D153 in 400m, signed.

Sanitation:

Parking:

None

Custom

Service Point only. Inspected 2012.

ST NICOLAS D'ALIERMONT | 7 | F2 | N49°52.830' E001°13.248' | 76510

Directions: Rue d'Arques, off D256. In town turn off D56 opp church onto D256, sp 'Intraville' and signed. In 100m turn left, sp 'P 100 Places' and signed. Aire on left in 50m by building marked 'JS St-Nicolas'.

Sanitation:

Parking:

3; Past club house

Euro Relais Junior; Token (ER)

Pleasant location. Town with local shops 1 min. Local clock museum advertised. Inspected 2012.

MESNIERES EN BRAY | 8 | F3 | N49°45.987' E001°22.864' | 76270

Directions: D1. Approach on D1 from south. Turn 2nd right in village after Mairie, sp 'Borne de Service'. Not signed if approach from north. Service Point in 1st car park on left may be obstructed by cars. Parking straight on up hill, signed.

Sanitation:

Parking:

10

Aire Services; Token (3/3)

1 min from village centre. Cycle/walking path runs along valley bottom adj to D1. Inspected 2012.

GAILLEFONTAINE | 9 | G3 | N49°39.200' E001°36.879' | 76870

Directions: D135. Aire located in village centre car park opp Esso fuel station, signed.

Sanitation:

Parking:

20; Max 48hrs

Custom

Large roadside car park also used by buses and trucks. Local shops adj. Inspected 2012.

GOURNAY EN BRAY | 10 | G3 | N49°28.823' E001°43.543' | 76220

Directions: Avenue Sadi Carnot. From south on N31/E46 turn left onto D916 at roundabout opp old train station, sp 'Gisors'. After passing LIDL on left take next right, sp 'P Centre Ville' and signed. Aire is on left, signed.

Sanitation:

Parking:

8

Custom

No parking at Aire Tuesday morning due to market. Town centre adj. Park adj. Inspected 2012.

FORGES LES EAUX 11 G3 N49°36.350' E001°32.550' 76440

Directions: D921/Rte d'Argueil. Follow sp 'Camping' from main route through. From south on D921 turn left onto Blvd Nicolas Thiessé and Aire on left at bend in road, opp Camping la Miniere.

Sanitation:

Parking:

24; €6.50 inc unmetered elec; Pay at campsite opp; Max 48hrs

Custom; No water/elec 15 Oct-15 Mar

SP

Spa town with plenty of grand architecture; Aire is in a rural location 5 mins from town centre. Inspected 2012.

LE VAUDREUIL 12 F3 N49°15.486' E001°12.522' 27100

Directions: Place du Vieux Marche. From south drive through town on D6154 and turn right after traffic lights, sp 'Boulodrome'. Turn right at mini roundabout. Turn next left, then immediately left into car park, signed.

Sanitation:

Parking:

2; Max 48hrs

Urba Flux Tall; CC; €2 water; €3 elec

SP

Sports field opp. Pleasant village centre with local commerce. Inspected 2012.

ST PIERRE LES ELBEUF 13 F3 N49°17.270' E001°02.749' 76320

Directions: Rue Aux Thuilliers. Exit D921 at St Pierre lés Elbeuf, sp 'Le Bosc Tard' and signed. At Stop junc turn right and next Stop junc turn right. Aire on left in 50m outside 'Ataliers Municipal' building.

Sanitation:

Parking:

None

Custom

SP

Service Point located in industrial estate. Inspected 2012.

RY 14 F3 N49°28.345' E001°20.667' 76116

Directions: Place Flaubert, off D13. Follow sp 'P Museum Bovary'. Car park by TO. The car park is small and no motorhome parking is signed, although it is identified on the map outside the TO. Ask at TO about parking. Additional parking is available at: N49°28.191' E001°20.444', which has 5.5m bays plus overhang.

Sanitation:

Parking:

5; 5m bays

Water tap on TO

SP

Pretty village. Home of Madame Bovary. On Madame Bovary trail. Inspected 2012.

BUCHY 15 F3 N49°35.167' E001°21.883' 76750

Photo: Carol Weaver

Directions: D919. Adj to D919 by college as exit town to east, sp 'Forges Les E'. Aire on left past Gendarmerie and college, signed.

Sanitation:

Parking:

12

Urba Flux; Token/10 mins elec

SP

Adj to secondary school. Town centre 3 mins. Inspected 2012.

MONTVILLE

16 F3 N49°32.837' E001°04.353' 76710

Directions: Off Rue André Martin/D155. Approach on D44 and turn onto D155, sp 'Malaunay'. In town centre turn into church car park, sp 'Espace Loisirs'. Turn right in front of church and drive through car park to Aire at the rear of the car park adj to sports facilities, signed.

Sanitation:

Parking:

20

Euro Relais Junior; Token

Town 2 mins with amenities, sports centre, and swimming pool. Close to lake. Free WiFi. Inspected 2012.

CLERES

17 F3 N49°36.084' E001°07.025' 76690

Directions: D6/Rue Edmond Spalikowski. Exit Clères to east on D6, sp 'Grugny'. Turn left after the D3 turning up drop curb, signed. Aire adj to the sports facilities.

Sanitation:

Parking:

20; Max 72hrs; Max 8m

Custom; Token (1/1); €3; 10 CEE elec points; Token 6hrs elec or 100L water

10 mins from village; Sports facilities adj. Inspected 2012.

AUFFAY

18 F3 N49°43.050' E001°06.028' 76720

Directions: Place de Bleckede, off D3/Rue Roger Fossé. From D927/N27 exit, sp 'Auffay'. In Auffay turn right opp church tower onto D3, sp 'Mairie'. Turn left into car park opp war memorial. Aire on right at rear of car park.

Sanitation:

Parking:

5

Euro Relais Junior; Token (ER)

Service Point difficult to access; Village centre adj with local commerce. Inspected 2012.

VAL DE SAANE

19 F3 N49°42.237' E000°57.895' 76890

Directions: Rue du Moulin Traversin. Take D25, sp 'Affay', then when facing the church doorway and spire take road to right of church. The Aire is on right in 150m, signed.

Sanitation:

Parking:

6; 7m bays

Euro Relais Junior; Token (ER)

Pleasant; Stream adj. School adj. Inspected 2012.

DOUDEVILLE

20 F3 N49°43.188' E000°47.284' 76560

Directions: Parking du Mont Criquet. Turn off D20 at southern boundary of town, sp 'P Mont Criquet' and 'Stade Vert Galant'. Follow road to right and Aire on left.

Sanitation:

Parking:

15; Max 48hrs

Euro Relais Mini; Token; €3

Aire adj to sports facilities. Convenience store adj. Local shops 1 min. Inspected 2012.

VEULES LES ROSES

21 F2 N49°52.549' E000°48.132' 76980

Directions: Avenue Jean Moulin/D68. Turn off D925 onto D68, sp 'Les Mouettes'. Follow D68 for 400m to village boundary and turn right and immediately right again. Aire directly in front of camping Les Mouettes, access via barrier.

Sanitation:

Parking:

18; €10/24hrs; €17/24hrs July/Aug

Raclet; €3

Report to campsite reception (Open 9am-12 noon and 2-7pm). War memorial nearby. Village 4 mins. Inspected 2012.

ST VALERY EN CAUX

22 F2 N49°52.330' E000°42.560' 76460

Directions: Quai d'Aval. From D20 follow sp 'Port', then sp 'Camping-Car'. After 100m the road to Aire becomes a 3.5t weight limit single carriageway lane with cliffs one side and the quay the other. Falling rocks!

Sanitation:

Parking:

50; €5/night May-Sept and at weekends Mar, Apr, Oct; 8m bays; Max 48hrs

Euro Relais Junior; Token; €3

At port, sea views; Direct access to stony beach; 2 mins to town. Always busy. Inspected 2012.

LES PETITES DALLES

23 F2 N49°48.796' E000°31.969' 76540

Directions: D68. Exit D68 onto C16, sp 'Vinnemerville' and signed. Aire in 10m on left, signed.

Sanitation:

Parking:

3; 9am-8pm only

None

Day parking only. Inspected 2012.

VEULETTES SUR MER

24 F2 N49°51.239' E000°36.308' 76450

Directions: D79. Parking area is adj and parallel with the seafront and clearly visible from the road. Use 2nd entrance; 1st is steep and possibility of grounding. Signed.

Sanitation:

Parking:

50; €4.50/night; Grass parking

Raclet; Token (ER); €3.50

Pleasant undeveloped small seaside resort; Pebble beach opp; Commerce 1 min. Inspected 2012.

NEUFCHATEL EN BRAY

25 E4 N49°44.244' E001°25.761' 76270

Info/Photos: Violette Coombs/Malcolm Webb

Directions: Rue Sainte Claire. Exit A28/E44 at Junction 9. Follow D928 into Neufchâtel-en-Bray. Go over river bridge and turn immediate left sp 'Dieppe' and camping 'st Claire'. Pass ALDI, LIDL and E.Leclerc, the Aire is 200m on left adj to Camping Ste Claire..

Sanitation:

Parking:

15

Not known

This new Aire was publicised to open in March 2013. Adj to voi verte path to Dieppe. Supermarkets 2 mins small town commerce 5 mins. Visited 2012.

GPS Co-ordinates for SatNav

The GPS Co-ordinates published in this guide were taken onsite by our inspectors. We consider them a valuable and unique asset and at the time of publishing have decided not to publish them as electronic files for use on navigation devices. You have permission to type in the co-ordinates of an Aire you intend to visit but not to store or share them. For the security of our copyright:

- **Do not compile them into lists**
- **Do not publish, share or reproduce them anywhere in any format**

FECAMP | 27 | E3 | N49°45.637' E000°22.306' | 76400

Directions: Off D925. Turn off D925 at marina, adj to TO, signed. Additional parking and Service Point in car park opp TO, signed: N49°45.615' E000°22.446'. The additional parking has no marina views but can take any size motorhome.

Sanitation:

Parking:

9

Aire Services; Token (3/3)

Overlooking boats. Popular town 2 mins. Inspected 2012.

YPORT | 28 | E3 | N49°44.249' E000°18.881' | 76111

Directions: D211/Rue Charles de Gaulle. Enter town on D104 and follow one-way system. In 200m turn left, sp 'Camping Car'. The Aire is in the car park straight ahead and to the left, signed.

Sanitation:

Parking:

10; No parking 6am-2pm Wednesday (market)

None

Village 1 min. Inspected 2012.

ETRETAT | 29 | E3 | N49°42.004' E000°12.948' | 76790

Directions: D39. Next to municipal campsite as exit the village on D39 to south towards Criquetot l'Esneval. Enter through coin-operated barrier.

Sanitation:

Parking:

30; €8/24hrs; Max 24hrs

Euro Relais Junior; €2

10 mins to beach; Market day Thurs. Inspected 2012.

LE HAVRE | 30 | E3 | N49°29.078' E000°06.428' | 76600

Directions: Chaussée John Kennedy, adj to harbour. Follow sp 'Car Ferries' then 'Ste Adresse' and 'Port de Plaisance'. Entrance by Maison de Qualité, Sécurité Environnement and Espace des Projets at traffic lights, signed.

Sanitation:

Parking:

19; Max 48hrs; 9m bays

Aire Services; CC; €5

Town adj; Industrial port area but water views from some bays. Inspected 2012.

ST ROMAIN DE COLBOSC — 31 — E3 — N49°31.245' E000°20.821' — 76430

Directions: Turn off D6015 at roundabout with Super U supermarket. Drive past Super U and follow road to roundabout and turn right. Aire immediately on right, signed.

Sanitation:

Parking:

13; Max 48hrs; 9m bays

Custom; 13 unmetered CEE plug sockets

SP

Large bays each with own elec socket. Some road noise. Super U 2 mins; Village centre with local shops 7 mins. Inspected 2012.

ST NICOLAS DE LA TAILLE — 32 — F3 — N49°30.765' E000°28.445' — 76170

Directions: D17/Grand Rue. Parking is opp Mairie, signed. Service Point is adj to the Mairie off main route through, signed: N49°30.771' E000°28.369'.

Sanitation:

E

Parking:

7; Max 6m

Raclet; Token (ER); €3; Max 6m

SP

Service Point is very difficult to access. Small village with local shops. Inspected 2012.

GRUCHET LE VALASSE — 33 — E3 — N49°32.505' E000°29.856' — 76210

Directions: D173. Turn off D487/D173 roundabout, sp 'EANA Parc de Loisirs' and 'Abbaye du Valasse'. Follow sp 'P3' for the Service Point. GPS taken on approach drive to avoid confusion.

Sanitation:

E

Parking:

10; Max 48hrs

Euro Relais Junior; €2

SP

Parking for country park. Abbey with restaurant adj. Some road noise. Inspected 2012.

PONT DE L'ARCHE — 34 — E4 — N49°18.342' E001°09.450' — 27340

Info/Photo: Barrie Avis/R Geddes

Directions: Quai de Verdun. Heading south on D6015 cross over Seine. Immediately turn left at lights towards river. Turn left along river and go under bridge. Parking on right and Service Point 100m in next car park by campsite entrance.

Sanitation:

Parking:

4

Urba Flux Tall; € 2.50; CC

SP

Very pleasant location adj to a tributary of the Seine. Insufficient parking for demand. Some road noise from river bridge. Small town shops 3 mins. Visited 2012.

ST NICOLAS DE BLIQUETUIT — 35 — F3 — N49°31.260' E000°43.621' — 76940

Directions: Route du Bac, on banks of river Seine. In St Nicolas de Bliquetuit turn onto Route du Bac at the D40/D65 junction, sp 'Aire de Camping-Cars'. Follow road to end and Aire on left, signed.

Sanitation:

E

Parking:

12; Max 48hrs

Raclet; Token (ER)

SP

River Seine adj, some bays have river views. No swimming. Long walk to village. Inspected 2012.

LA MAILLERAYE SUR SEINE * | 36 | F3 | N49°29.001' E000°46.443' | 76940

Directions: Quai Paul Girardeau. From D490 at roundabout take D131 into town, sp 'La Mailleraye' and signed. Drive through town to river, then turn left. Service Point 250m at far end of parking. Note: noise comes from sewerage plant behind hedge and no parking in front of chapel.

Sanitation:

Parking:

34; €5; Money collected 6pm-7pm; Grass parking

Raclet; Token (ER); €3

On edge of river Seine, lots of bays with river views and working barges pass frequently. 2 mins from town. Inspected 2012.

HEURTEAUVILLE | 37 | F3 | N49°26.865' E000°48.837' | 76940

Directions: At cherry farm 'Les Cerisiers'. Adj to D65 between Heurteauville and La Mailleraye sur Seine.

Sanitation:

Parking:

12; €5; Open Apr-Sept

Custom; €3; Elec €3

At cherry farm adj to Seine river, 6 bays have river views. Rural CL feel. Inspected 2012.

JUMIEGES | 38 | F3 | N49°25.848' E000°48.884' | 76480

Directions: D143/Rue Alphonse Callais. In town turn off main route at TO, opp abbey, onto D143, sp 'Heurteauville Car Ferry'. Turn right in 100m, signed.

Car ferry has 3.5t weight restriction and does not accept motorhomes due to grounding issues when boarding.

Sanitation:

Parking:

20

Custom; Token; €3; Open Mar-Oct

Ruined abbey worth a visit, 100m. TO, tourist shops and café in town. Inspected 2012.

LE MESNIL SOUS JUMIEGES | 39 | F3 | N49°24.709' E000°50.659' | 76480

Directions: D65/Route du Mesnil, opp golf course on D65 as exit village. Follow sp 'Base de Plein Air'. Service Point outside campsite. Entrance gated, gates open 6am-10pm daily.

Sanitation:

Parking:

None

Raclet; Available when campsite open.

Service Point only outside campsite. Inspected 2012.

NONANCOURT | 40 | F4 | N48°46.351' E001°11.529' | 27320

Directions: Rue Hippolyte Lozier. Turn off D53 west of town centre SP 'Sampier Pompiers' and Signed. Aire down slope to right of Sampler Pompiers, beside Mairie, signed.

Sanitation:

Parking:

6; Max 48hrs

Aire service; One unmetered CEE elec point

Riverside park surrounds Mairie. Town Centre 3 mins. Fire station adj. Inspected 2012

OISSEL | 41 | F3 | N49°20.281' E001°05.515' | 76350

Directions: Quai de Stalingrad. From south cross river on D13 bridge. As enter Oissel turn left at roundabout, last exit before going back over bridge. At end of road turn right and follow road along river. Aire is at other end on left, adj to river.

Sanitation:

Parking:

2; Max 9m; Access/exit difficult

Aire Services; Token (3/3)

Pleasant; Adj to river Seine, partial river views. Inspected 2012.

ST ANDRE DE L'EURE | 42 | F4 | N48°54.398' E001°16.135' | 27220

Directions: C523. Turn off D833 by railway track onto D52, Sp ' Zone Industrielle'. Follow road and turn left, Sp 'Jumelles'. Aire immediately on left.

Sanitation:

Parking:

6; Max 48hrs; Hedged bays

Custom

At edge of Industrial estate overlooking fishing ponds. traffic and industrial noise. inspected 2012.

LA VESPIERE | 43 | E4 | N49°01.642' E000°25.339' | 14290

Directions: D4. Exit La Vespière on D4 towards Brigolie. Aire on left in 200m next to gas tanks, signed.

Sanitation:

Parking:

2

Euro Relais Junior; Token (ER)

Adj to main road. Village 2 mins with Carrefour supermarket and local commerce. Inspected 2012.

LE NEUBOURG | 44 | F3 | N49°08.932' E000°55.101' | 27110

Directions: D840. Near D133/D840 roundabout at the E.Leclerc supermarket. Parking in car park, signed. Service Point at car wash, on opp side to supermarket: N49°08.902' E000°54.988'.

Sanitation:

Parking:

10

Euro Relais Junior; CC Token from machine;

Car wash and car parts shop adj. Supermarket has 2.5m height barrier. Inspected 2012.

THIBERVILLE | 45 | F3 | N49°08.145' E000°27.444' | 27230

Directions: Place de Écoles. Turn off D613 at roundabout onto D28, sp 'Thiberville'. At traffic lights turn left onto D22, sp 'Berney'. At Stop junc turn left, then turn right in 50m. Aire at far end of car park.

Sanitation:

Parking:

2; Max 48hrs

Euro Relais Junior; Token (ER)

2 large hedged bays. Primary school adj. Village centre 1min with local shops and a market Monday mornings. Inspected 2012.

LISIEUX | 46 | E3 | N49°08.553' E000°13.667' | 14100

Directions: D579, Parking Carmel. From south on D576 drive straight into town, sp 'Centre Ville'. Turn left, sp 'Office du Tourisme'. The Service Point is in car park opp TO. Busy car park navigable by max 7m. TO advised parking opp Basilica on D267: N49°08.474' E000°14.062'.

Sanitation:

Parking:

Opp Basilica

Euro Relais; Token; (ER)

SP

Large town with commerce and Basilica adj. Inspected 2012.

CORMEILLES | 47 | E3 | N49°14.948' E000°22.417' | 27260

Directions: D111/Route du Château de Malou. Exit town on D96, sp 'P 150 Places'. Turn right onto D111, sp 'Camping Car'. Aire on right, adj to height barriered parking.

Sanitation:

Parking:

5

Custom

Pleasant town 2 mins with plenty of commerce. Inspected 2012.

CAMPIGNY | 48 | F3 | N49°18.681' E000°33.120' | 27500

Directions: Off D29. By church in village turn towards village green, sp 'Stade'. Then turn left, signed. Drive past boules court and through gate. The Service Point is on the right and parking is on a lawn between Service Point and house.

Sanitation:

Parking:

3; Grass parking

Custom

In small hamlet. Although this is a municipally provided Aire you are effectively in someone's front garden. Inspected 2012.

LA RIVIERE ST SAUVEUR | 49 | E3 | N49°24.517' E000°16.143' | 14600

Directions: A29/E44. Exit A29/E44 at Junction 3 and exit roundabout, sp 'La Rivière St Sauveur' and signed. At end of road turn left under A29/E44, signed. Aire on left as enter village, signed.

Sanitation:

Parking:

15; 8m bays

Custom; Token (3/1)

Nice village adj with local commerce. Inspected 2012.

HONFLEUR | 50 | E3 | N49°25.150' E000°14.586' | 14600

Directions: Bassin Carnot, off D580. From southeast follow D580 into town. At large roundabout by water, turn right over bridge to Aire. Sp 'Parking' and signed.

Sanitation:

Parking:

100; €10/24hrs; Pay at machine

Custom; Numerous CEE 5amp elec points

On edge of waterway. Plenty of elec points. Main town 10 mins; Very pretty, worth a visit. Inspected 2012.

DEAUVILLE — 51 — E3 — N49°21.436' E000°05.044' — 14800

Directions: Boulevard des Sports; enter via D27A. From large D27A/D513 roundabout (Rond-Point des Jumelages) turn onto D27A, sp 'Lisieux'. Drive parallel to sports fields and take 1st turning on right. Aire immediately on left.

Sanitation:

Parking:

7; Max 24hrs; 7m bays

Custom; 6 unmetered elec points

SP

By sports facility, 10 mins from town. Train station across road. Inspected 2012.

CABOURG — 52 — E4 — N49°16.667' W000°08.073' — 14390

Directions: D400A. Service Point at Carrefour supermarket fuel station.

Sanitation:

Parking:

Poss

Euro Relais Junior

Supermarket adj. Inspected 2012.

DOUVRES LA DELIVRANDE — 53 — E3 — N49°18.010' W000°22.822' — 14830

Directions: D7. Turn off D7 at the D7/D35 roundabout to Hyper U supermarket. Service Point in rear car wash bay. Water at air bollard marked 'Gonfleur'.

Sanitation:

Parking:

Poss

Custom; €1

Supermarket adj. Inspected 2012.

MERVILLE FRANCEVILLE PLAGE — 54 — E3 — N49°17.117' W000°12.582' — 14810

Directions: Blvd Wattier. From D514 at roundabout with wooden boat turn in direction of town, sp 'Plage' and 'Centre Ville'. Take 1st left into Ave des Dunes. Follow road to seafront and the Aire is on left, signed.

Sanitation:

Parking:

6; 7m bays; Must park in bays

Aire Services; Token (3/3)

Difficult due to parked cars and narrow entrance. Possible to access in a large motorhome, but exiting may be difficult. Inspected 2012.

SALLENELLES — 55 — E3 — N49°15.891' W000°13.606' — 14121

Directions: Blvd Maritime, alongside D514. From Merville-Franceville as enter village the Aire is on right adj to main road, behind school in 1st visible parking area.

Sanitation:

Parking:

2; Max 48hrs; 6m bays

Aire Services; Token (TM)

Village 2 mins; Can only park in designated bays. Inspected 2012.

HEROUVILLETTE 56 E3 N49°13.196' W000°14.678' 14850

Directions: D37c/Avenue de Caen. Aire on right as exit village, sp 'Ste Honorine' and signed.

Sanitation:

Parking:

6

Euro Relais Junior

SP

Village 2 mins; Pleasant location; Close to amenities. Near Overlord trail. Bus stop adj. Inspected 2012.

TROARN 57 E3 N49°10.695' W000°11.486' 14670

Directions: D675, at Super U supermarket between D225 and D675, signed. Services in fuel station.

Sanitation:

Parking:

Poss

Euro Relais Junior; €2

SP

Supermarket adj. Inspected 2012.

BEUVRON EN AUGE 58 E3 N49°11.178' W000°02.961' 14430

Directions: At the Mairie, off D49. Follow 'P Mairie' from village centre. Pass Mairie and the Service Point is 50m on right, against building. Parking at end of road on left.

Sanitation:

Parking:

20; €6 inc token; Max 24hrs; Pay at Tabac

Euro Relais Mini; Token (ER) inc

SP

1 min to one of the 'Villages of France' with timber framed houses; Cider route. Inspected 2012.

CAMBREMER 59 E3 N49°08.979' E000°02.788' 14340

Directions: Place de l'Europe. From the south exit D50 onto D101 towards Cambremer. The Aire is located on the left as you enter the village.

Sanitation:

Parking:

20

Euro Relais Junior; Token (ER)

SP

2 mins to village. In area famous for cider on cider route. Calvados distillery opp. Inspected 2012.

ARGENCES 60 E3 N49°07.125' W000°10.515' 14370

Directions: D80. At D613/D80 roundabout, at Intermarché supermarket. Service Point near car wash in fuel station.

Sanitation:

Parking:

Poss

Euro Relais Junior; €2; No drive over drain

SP

Supermarket adj. Inspected 2012.

BRETTEVILLE SUR ODON

61 E3 N49°11.073' W000°24.882' 14760

Directions: Ave des Carrières. Turn off D9 at roundabout, sp 'Venoix'. Turn right, sp 'Bretteville s Odon'. Turn left, sp 'Déchèterie'. Aire on right at rear of motorhome dealer.

Sanitation: E WC F

Parking: P F

Poss; Ask at dealer

Custom

SP

Adj to motorhome dealer/repairs. Inspected 2012.

VILLERS BOCAGE

62 E3 N49°04.802' W000°39.640' 14310

Directions: D67, at junction with D675. Follow D675 through town. At end of main street turn right onto D67, signed. Aire on left by tennis courts, signed.

Sanitation: E WC F

Parking: P F

3; 8m bays; Max 48hrs

Aire Services; CC; €2

SP

Town commerce 1 min; Basketball, tennis courts and outdoor gym adj. Inspected 2012.

BREVILLE LES MONTS

63 E3 N49°14.496' W000°13.693' 14860

Directions: Allée des Dentelliéres, off D37B. Turn off D223 onto D37B in the village, sp 'Amfreville'. The Aire is in 150m clearly signed and visible from the road.

Sanitation: E WC F

Parking: P F

5

Aire Services; Token (3/3); €2

SP

Village 3 mins; Pleasant stop not far from coast. On Overlord tour. Inspected 2012.

TILLY SUR SEULLES

64 E3 N49°10.567' W000°37.499' 14250

Directions: D13, near D6/D13 junction. From junction take D13, sp 'Fontenay'. Service Point on right in roadside parking. It is often obstructed by parked cars. No parking Sat pm/Sun am due to market.

Sanitation: E WC F

Parking: P F

15

Euro Relais Junior; €2; No drive over drain

SP

Local commerce and convenience store. Sports facilities down hill. Market Sunday morning. Inspected 2012.

ROTS

65 E3 N49°11.998' W000°27.576' 14980

Directions: Chemin de la Croix Vautier, at Cora supermarket. Turn off N13/E46 onto D220, sp 'Rots' and 'Carpiquet'. Cora supermarket visible from road on right. Follow signs to Cora fuel station. 3.5m height restriction.

Sanitation: E WC F

Parking: P F

Poss

Custom; 2 unmetered elec points

SP

Supermarket; Consistently cheap fuel; Numerous motorhome dealers in area. Inspected 2012.

OUISTREHAM — 66 — E3 — N49°17.258' W000°14.998' — 14150

Directions: Blvd Maritime. Follow sp 'Car Ferry', then sp 'Plage'. When road bends sharp left, Aire straight ahead, signed. Or, on exiting car ferry turn right and follow road alongside port.

Sanitation:

Parking:

30; €8/24hrs; CC

Aire Services; inc; CC

SP

Sandy beach with attractions adj; WW2 D-day landings Sword beach adj; Fish market 2 mins; Noise from ferry when in. Inspected 2012.

COLLEVILLE MONTGOMERY — 67 — E3 — N49°16.266' W000°17.946' — 14880

Directions: D35/Rue de Saint Aubin. Turn onto D35 from D514. Aire adj and signed on D35.

Sanitation:

Parking:

9; €5/24hrs; 5m bays; Grass parking

Raclet

SP

Sports ground adj. Village with bar/Tabac 1 min. Inspected 2012.

HERMANVILLE SUR MER — 68 — E3 — N49°17.169' W000°18.728' — 14880

Directions: Rue Verte, off D60 in town centre, behind La Poste. 100m from church.

Sanitation:

Parking:

6; 5m bays with max 3m overhang

Custom; Lift grid

SP

Small car park; Always likely to have space; Local commerce adj. Inspected 2012.

HAVE YOU VISITED AN AIRE? — GPS co-ordinates in this guide are protected by copyright law

Take at least 5 digital photos showing
• Signs
• Service Point
• Parking
• Overview
• Amenities

Visit www.all-the-aires.co.uk/submissions.shtml to upload your updates and photos.

Sanitation:

Aire Details:

Submit updates

- Amendments
- New Aires
- Not changed

COURSEULLES SUR MER 1 — 70 — E3 — N49°20.229' W000°27.976' — 14470

Directions: Parc Juno Beach, Place du Général de Gaulle off D514. Follow sp ' Centre Juno Beach'. Parking to left of visitor centre by sand dune. DO NOT use coach bays.

Sanitation:

Parking:

20; Day only Apr-Aug; 7m bays; Max 8m

None; See 71 or 72

SP

Beach used in Normandy Beach landings during WW2, information and sights on structured walk. Inspected 2012.

COURSEULLES SUR MER 2

71 E3 N49°20.061' W000°26.733' 14470

Directions: Avenue de la Libération, outside Camping le Champ de Course. Turn off D514 onto Avenue de la Libération on the east edge of town and follow sp 'Camping Le Champ de Course'.

Sanitation:

Parking:

13; €6.20; Pay at adj campsite; 7m bays, some with overhang

Euro Relais Mini; Token (ER); Free water adj

2 mins to beach. Surrounded by flats. Inspected 2012.

COURSEULLES SUR MER 3

72 E3 N49°19.316' W000°27.149' 14470

Directions: Chemin de la Délivrande, parallel to D79. Adj to Carrefour supermarket, well signed in town. Service Point at rear of fuel station in Planet Wash, but must drive around store to access.

Sanitation:

Parking:

Poss

Euro Relais Mini; €2

Supermarket adj. Inspected 2012.

ARROMANCHES LES BAINS

73 E3 N49°20.368' W000°37.504' 14117

Directions: Rue François Carpentier. Enter town from south on D516 and follow road across roundabout where it becomes D514. Carry on straight at next large junction and then road bends right. Aire is signed on the right up a small lane. Signed.

Sanitation:

Parking:

14; 9m narrow bays

Euro Relais Junior; €2; No drive over drain

5 mins to sea with WW2 Normandy landing harbour; Overlord Visitor Centre and view point on cliff top. Inspected 2012.

BAYEUX

74 D3 N49°16.812' W000°42.457' 14400

Directions: Rue de Montfiquet. Turn off D613 ring road near Carrefour supermarket at small traffic lighted junc opp shop 'Picard', sp 'Centre Ville'. Go straight over at Stop junc and turn left at traffic lights. Aire on right opp church. To exit turn right, sp 'Toutes Directions' past church.

Sanitation:

Parking:

50

Euro Relais Junior

1 min from town centre with everything including the Bayeux tapestry depicting the battle of Hastings. Inspected 2012.

PORT EN BESSIN 1

75 D3 N49°20.731' W000°45.490' 14520

Directions: Rue du II Novembre, off D514. Turn off D514 into Rue du II Novembre, sp 'Tennis' and signed. Aire on left, signed.

Sanitation:

Parking:

20; €3.50/24hrs

None; See **76**

Adj to golf course and footpath. Some sea glimpses. Town 5 mins. Inspected 2012.

PORT EN BESSIN 2 | 76 | D3 | N49°20.563' W000°45.128' | 14520

Directions: D6, at the Super U. Service Point at Super U by car wash on D6, near D6/D514 roundabout.

Sanitation:

Parking:

Poss; See 75

Raclet; Token (ER); €3

Supermarket adj. Inspected 2012.

STE HONORINE DES PERTES | 77 | D3 | N49°20.917' W000°48.967' | 14520

Directions: D514/Rte d'Omaha Beach. Adj to D514 as exit Ste Honorine des Pertes towards Grandchamp Maisy, signed.

Sanitation:

Parking:

15; €8/24hrs inc elec; Pay at garage

Euro Relais Junior; Token (ER); €2.50

Fuel station, small motorhome accessories shop (toilet chemicals etc). Part hard standing, part grass. Inspected 2012.

ENGLESQUEVILLE | 78 | D3 | N49°23.211' W000°56.885' | 14710

Directions: D125, off D514. Turn off D514 onto D125 towards Longueville, signed. Follow signs through farm to parking area.

Sanitation:

Parking:

6; €5 inc unmetered elec

Custom; €3

Pleasant, rural farm Aire overlooking pasture beside pretty, well-kept farm house. Inspected 2012.

GRANDCAMP MAISY | 79 | D3 | N49°23.178' W001°02.258' | 14450

Directions: Le Moulin Odo. Signed off D514 next to sports facility, near the fire station.

Sanitation:

Parking:

14; Max 48hrs

Aire Services; Token (3/3); €2.50

10 mins to superb beaches and shops; WW2 museum in town. Inspected 2012.

ISIGNY SUR MER | 80 | D3 | N49°19.289' W001°06.272' | 14230

Directions: Quai Neuf. Turn off D613 at the river bridge, sp 'Port de Plaisance' and signed. The Aire is 300m on the right. This road has a 3.5t weight restriction.

Sanitation:

Parking:

6; 5m bays

Euro Relais Junior; €2

Overlooking tidal creek; Village with local shops. Inspected 2012.

UTAH BEACH 1 — 81 — D3 — N49°25.066' W001°11.198' — 50480

Directions: From seafront at UTAH beach turn off, sp 'Camping d'UTAH Beach' and signed. Follow road past campsite on left and the Service Point is on the right after holiday lodges/caravans.

Sanitation:

Parking:

None; See 82

Euro Relais Junior; Token; €4

Service Point only. Inspected 2012.

UTAH BEACH 2 — 82 — D3 — N49°24.851' W001°10.738' — 50480

Directions: UTAH beach museum. Exit N13, sp 'UTAH beach'. Follow sp 'UTAH beach'. Motorhome parking in 1st car park on right, signed.

Sanitation:

Parking:

10

None; See 81

UTAH beach memorial adj. Inspected 2012.

STE MERE EGLISE 1 — 83 — D3 — N49°24.610' W001°18.619' — 50480

Directions: Rue 505E Airborne. From south on D67 turn right onto D17 in town centre. Drive past the church and the Airborne museum following sp 'Camping'. Service Point is located outside the campsite.

Sanitation:

Parking:

None; See 84

Custom; €1

Service Point only outside campsite. Inspected 2012.

STE MERE EGLISE 2 — 84 — D3 — N49°24.540' W001°18.938' — 50480

Directions: D17/Rue Eisenhower, outside the Musée Airbourne. By the church in car park, signed.

Sanitation:

Parking:

10; €5 8pm-8am; Pay at machine; Free 8am-8pm

None; See 85

Airebourne museum adj; Town centre adj; Noisy church clock. Inspected 2012.

STE MERE EGLISE 3 — 85 — D3 — N49°24.278' W001°19.329' — 50480

Directions: Off D67, at Super U in industrial area. Clearly signed. Service Point in fuel station.

Sanitation:

Parking:

Poss; See 84

Euro Relais Junior; €2

Supermarket adj. Inspected 2012.

ST SAUVEUR LE VICOMTE | 86 | D3 | N49°23.233' W001°31.764' | 50390

Directions: D900. At town square on D900, signed on pavement opp town square. Aire right in town centre. Some parking at adj lake.

Service Point inaccessible and plumbed into by temporary building housing Credit Mutual bank in May 2012. Parking still available.

Sanitation:

Parking:

3

Custom

Opportunity to enjoy French town; City wall at adj château; Weighbridge onsite. Inspected 2012.

BRICQUEBEC | 87 | D3 | N49°28.423' W001°38.789' | 50260

Directions: Route de Cherbourg/D900. Head northwest on D900, sp 'Cherbourg'. Aire is on the left at the far edge of the lake, signed.

Sanitation:

E

Parking:

6

Aire Services; 2 unmetered elec points; Push button every 55 mins

Fishing lake adj; Town 3 mins down hill with numerous commerce. Inspected 2012.

RAUVILLE LA BIGOT | 88 | E4 | N49°30.969' W001°41.020' | 50260

Directions: D900. From Bricquebec on D900 turn left as enter Rauville la Bigot, signed. Aire on right before Residence La Moinerie.

Sanitation:

Parking:

6; Max 48hrs

Euro Relais Mini

Pleasant area with green space adj. Village with local commerce 3mins. Inspected 2012.

VALOGNES 1 | 89 | D3 | N49°30.658' W001°28.641' | 50700

Directions: Blvd Félix Buhot/D974. Just off main road through town, opp LIDL, in car park next to Carrefour supermarket, signed.

Sanitation:

E

Parking:

7

Raclet; €2

5 mins to town; Supermarket adj; Designated corner of large car park behind flats. Inspected 2012.

VALOGNES 2 | 90 | D3 | N49°30.860' W001°30.002' | 50700

Directions: Route de Sottevast, off D62 at the Elephant Bleu. Exit town on D62, sp 'Sottevast'. Follow sp 'Sottevast' until you arrive at the Elephant Bleu on the right.

Sanitation:

E

Parking:

4; €5 inc elec and shower

Raclet; €2; 16 unmetered elec points

Self-service laundry and car wash. Pizza restaurant opp. Inspected 2012.

ST VAAST LA HOUGUE — 91 — D3 — N49°35.036' W001°16.040' — 50550

Directions: Aire de la Gallouette, Rue de la Gallouette off D1, outside the campsite. follow sp 'Camping Gallouette' then 'Aire de Service'. This is a private Aire.

Sanitation:

Parking:

27; €7.50; Collected

Euro Relais Junior; €2

SP

Pleasant seaside town; Market at marina on Saturday; Sea view obstructed by hedge. Inspected 2012.

REVILLE — 92 — D3 — N49°37.546' W001°15.223' — 50760

Directions: D10. Exit Reville on D1, sp 'Barfleur'. Turn off right at D10 junction, signed. Aire is 150m on right, signed.

Sanitation:

Parking:

7; €5 inc elec; Grass parking

Custom; €3

SP

Farm site selling vegetables. CL style. Beach 2km. Inspected 2012.

MONTEBOURG — 93 — D3 — N49°29.137' W001°22.367' — 50310

Directions: At the Louis Le Cacheux stadium, Follow D974 towards Ste Mere Eglise. Turn left 100m south of shops by zebra crossing, signed. Aire on right 100m up hill.

Sanitation:

Parking:

15

Custom

SP

Next to sports facilities; 5 mins from town. BBQ point. Inspected 2012.

ST PIERRE EGLISE — 94 — D3 — N49°40.127' W001°24.181' — 50840

Directions: Rue dy 8 Mai 1945. Well signed in town. Follow D901 to the market square. Aire down road just off market square, near junction of D901 and D26, sp 'College Gilles de Gouberville' and signed. Turn left opp college, signed.

Sanitation:

Parking:

20

Campsite bollard; Token (3/3)

SP

2 mins from town square with local commerce; Very sloping car park. Inspected 2012.

TOURLAVILLE 1 — 95 — D3 — N49°39.251' W001°33.970' — 50110

Directions: Rue des Algues/D116. Outside Camping Collignon. Follow sp 'Espace Loisirs de Collignon'.

Sanitation:

Parking:

When campsite closed Oct - Apr

Euro Relais Mini; Token (ER)

SP

Potential to stay overnight in car park; Swimming pool. Inspected 2012.

TOURLAVILLE 2 | 96 | D3 | N49°38.092' W001°35.455' | 50110

Directions: D901, at E.Leclerc supermarket. Service Point at far end of fuel station, signed. Supermarket, adj to D901.

Sanitation:

Parking:

None

Custom

Service Point only. Fiat main garage opp. Inspected 2012.

LA GLACERIE | 97 | D3 | N49°36.022' W001°35.930' | 50470

Directions: Exit N13 at roundabout onto D352, sp 'La Glacerie'. At next roundabout turn right, sp 'Auchan'. Service Point at Auchan supermarket fuel station.

Sanitation:

Parking:

Poss; 3.5t parking restriction

Euro Relais Junior; €2; No drive over drain

Auchan supermarket adj. Inspected 2012.

EQUEURDREVILLE | 98 | D3 | N49°39.266' W001°39.040' | 50120

Directions: Rue Jean Bart. Service Point adj to D901. Turn off D901 at traffic lights, sp 'La Saline Camping'. Then take the next right. The Service Point is 100m from the campsite.

Sanitation:

Parking:

None

Aire Services; Token (3/3) or CC; €2

Service Point only. Inspected 2012.

BEAUMONT HAGUE | 99 | D3 | N49°39.677' W001°50.105' | 50440

Directions: Turn off D901, sp 'Beaumont Hague'. Turn off main road, sp 'Super U', before entering village centre. Follow road to Super U, Service Point by car wash.

Sanitation:

Parking:

Poss

Custom; €1

Supermarket adj. Inspected 2012.

GREVILLE HAGUE | 100 | D3 | N49°40.533' W001°48.076' | 50440

Directions: D45. From village centre roundabout turn into car park, sp 'Salle des Fêtes'. Service Point on right.

Sanitation:

Parking:

7

Aire Services; €2

In small village with local commerce. Inspected 2012.

AUDERVILLE

101 C3 N49°42.858' W001°56.096' 50440

Directions: North of town on road to Goury. Exit the village on D901 towards Goury. Parking on the left, sp 'Obligatoire Camping-Cars' 700m before height barrier.

Sanitation:

Parking:

20

None

Parking at end of point with sea view; Windswept spot. Inspected 2012.

SIOUVILLE HAGUE

102 C3 N49°33.813' W001°50.663' 50340

Directions: Avenue des Peupliers/ D64e2. Follow road out of town along coast to Siouville Hague. Aire adj to main route through, signed.

Sanitation:

E

Parking:

30; Max 48hrs; Grass parking

Aire Services; €2

Large sandy beach 100m, popular with surfers; Small parade of shops and laundrette 100m. Inspected 2012.

TREAUVILLE

103 D3 N49°32.655' W001°50.130' 50340

Directions: D65. Signed off D23 as head towards Siouville Hague from Les Pieux.

Sanitation:

Parking:

10; €6.50/night inc unmetered elec and services

Custom; €2.50 service only

Commercial Aire in rural Normandy overlooking farmland. Grass/gravel parking area. Inspected 2012.

SCIOTOT

104 C3 N49°30.407' W001°50.870' 50340

Directions: D517. Just off D517 north of Sciotot.

Sanitation:

WC F

Parking:

F

10; Max 24hrs

None; See 105

Views of sea; Slipway; Sandy beach popular with all types of surfers. Inspected 2012.

LES PIEUX

105 D3 N49°31.004' W001°47.905' 50340

Directions: D23, at fuel station. Service Point at Intermarché fuel station off D23/D4 roundabout. 7 designated bays to rear of parking.

Sanitation:

E

Parking:

F

7; At rear of supermarket

Euro Relais Junior; €2; No drive over drain

Supermarket adj. Inspected 2012.

SURTAINVILLE — 106 C3 — N49°27.837' W001°49.672' — 50270

Directions: Route des Laguettes. Follow D66 to Surtainville, then continue to follow D66 north out of town, sp 'Le Rozel' and signed. Turn left before road becomes D517, signed, and follow road towards coast. Turn right, signed, and Aire is next to camping municipal, well signed.

Sanitation:

Parking:

10

Aire Services; Token (3/3); €4.10

Small seaside resort, sandy beach dunes popular with surfers. Inspected 2012.

BARNEVILLE CARTERET — 107 D3 — N49°23.148' W001°45.160' — 50270

Directions: D130. Turn off D650, sp 'Barneville Carteret', onto D130. The Service Point is at the Carrefour supermarket adj to D130, by car wash. Parking on other side of Service Point.

Sanitation:

Parking:

Poss

Euro Relais Junior; €2

Supermarket adj. Inspected 2012.

PORTBAIL — 108 D3 — N49°20.266' W001°41.564' — 50580

Directions: Rue Robert Asselin/D264. Turn off D650 onto D264, sp 'St Marc'. Follow road to the Service Point on the left outside Sapeurs Pompiers. Well signed in town.

Sanitation:

Parking:

5

Aire Services Maxi; CC; €2

Outside Sapeurs Pompiers (fire station) by the old railway station. Parking may be possible at the old railway station (tourist train) opp. Inspected 2012.

LA HAYE DU PUITS — 109 D3 — N49°17.597' W001°32.625' — 50250

Directions: Rue du Champ de Foire. In town turn onto D900El, sp 'Valognes' then turn off D900El, sp 'P Champ de Foire'. The Aire is in the large car park near the cemetery, signed.

Sanitation:

Parking:

20; Max 48hrs

Custom

A space is always likely to be available at this Aire. Green space with old stone tower adj. Town centre with local shops 2 mins. Inspected 2012.

LESSAY — 110 D3 — N49°13.134' W001°32.110' — 50430

Directions: D72. On main route through at edge of town, clearly signed. Do not block residents driveways.

Sanitation:

Parking:

7; 7m max

Custom; 4 unmetered elec points and tap inside bollard

On edge of pleasant village dominated by large church, 2 mins. Launderette 1 min. Inspected 2012.

CREANCES — 111 — D3 — N49°11.926' W001°34.054' — 50710

Directions: Rue du Haut Chemin/D72, at Carrefour supermarket. Follow sp 'Pirou' onto D72. Carrefour 150m on left. Service Point behind the car wash.

Sanitation:

Parking:

2; 6m bays

Euro Relais Junior; Token (ER); €2

Supermarket adj; Local commerce adj. Inspected 2012.

PIROU — 112 — D3 — N49°09.920' W001°35.400' — 50770

Directions: Rue Des Hublots. Turn off D650 at roundabout to Pirou Plage. Turn 1st left, signed, and follow road round to left back towards D650. Aire adj to D650. Well signed.

Sanitation:

Parking:

6

Aire Services; Token (3/3); €2

Adj to D650, therefore noisy, but in residential area. Inspected 2012.

GOUVILLE SUR MER — 113 — D3 — N49°05.978' W001°36.544' — 50560

Directions: Chemin du Beau Rivage. Follow the D268 through the town to the sea. Turn right and the Aire is to the left behind sand dune by toilet, signed.

Sanitation:

Parking:

75; €4.50/7pm-10am; Pay at Service Point; CC

Aire Services; inc

Large Aire adj to large sandy beach but no view; Ideal for beach holiday. Inspected 2012.

MARIGNY — 114 — D3 — N49°05.962' W001°14.846' — 50570

Directions: Rue de St Sauveur Lendelin. Turn off D972 onto D29, sp 'Marigny'. At end of road, opp church, turn left, sp 'D29' and 'St Sauveur Lendelin'. Turn immediately left onto D53, signed. Turn right into residential street, signed. Aire on left in 10m, signed.

Sanitation:

Parking:

20; Max 48hrs

Aire Services; €2

Small pond behind Aire. Village with local commerce 2 mins uphill. German WW2 cemetery nearby. Inspected 2012.

MONTMARTIN SUR MER — 115 — D4 — N48°59.164' W001°30.945' — 50590

Directions: D49/Rue du Clos. Exit town on D49, sp 'Herenguerville'. Aire on left as exit town, adj to Renault garage.

Sanitation:

Parking:

Poss opp

Aire Services; €2

Village 2 mins. Carrefour Contact 1 min. Inspected 2012

CANISY

116 D3 N49°04.557' W001°10.531' 50860

Directions: Impasse des Jouquets. Turn off D38 at roundabout onto D77, sp 'Tessy sur Vire', and turn immediately right between Mairie and Credit Agricole bank, signed. Aire 10m on left.

Sanitation: E WC F

Parking: P F

5; Max 48hrs

Aire Services; Token (3/3)

SP

Village with local commerce adj; Château nearby. Inspected 2012.

REMILLY SUR LOZON

117 D3 N49°10.702' W001°15.284' 50570

Directions: D94/Rue de la Vannerie. Turn off D8 onto D94 into village, signed. Aire on left in 200m, signed.

Sanitation: E WC F

Parking: P F

10

Euro Relais Junior; €2; No drive over drain; Out of service for two years!

SP

Village 2 mins; BMX course adj. Inspected 2012.

ST FROMOND

118 D3 N49°13.321' W001°05.377' 50620

Directions: Off D8. In village square adj to D8, by bridge and roundabout, signed.

Sanitation: E WC F

Parking: P F

15

Euro Relais Junior; €2

SP

Parking overlooking river. Cycle/walking route to St Lo 100m over bridge. Inspected 2012.

CERISY LA FORET

119 D3 N49°11.904' W000°55.939' 50680

Directions: At abbey, off D34. From D34 in Cerisy la Forêt turn into the abbey entrance by sculpture. Drive towards abbey and follow road to left. Opp lake turn left into small picnic area containing sculptures. Possible for large motorhomes if space.

Sanitation: E WC F

Parking: P F

5

Euro Relais Junior; €2; No drive over drain

SP

Sculptures, pond and abbey open to public; 2 mins from town. Inspected 2012.

ST LO

120 D3 N49°06.818' W001°06.181' 50000

Directions: Place de la Vaucelle. Exit N174/E03 at Junction 6 and turn onto D900, sp 'Agneaux'. Then follow sp 'St-Lô' into town. Turn right directly after crossing the river bridge, signed. Aire 200m down this road, signed.

Sanitation: E WC F

Parking: P F

12

Urba Flux Tall; CC; €2

SP

Town 2 mins; Riverside walk, cannot see river from designated places. Inspected 2012.

CAUMONT L'EVENTE

121 D3 N49°05.466' W000°48.958' 14240

Directions: D71. Follow sp 'Le Souterroscope Des Ardoisieres' from the village. Aire in car park adj to the attraction.

Sanitation:

Parking:

3

Aire Services; Token (3/3); €2.70

SP

Village 3 mins; Geological attraction and caves open every month except Jan, Adult €9.75. www.souterroscope-ardoisieres.fr. Inspected 2012.

CONDE SUR VIRE

122 D3 N49°03.558' W001°01.978' 50890

Directions: Route de Herpeur. At roundabout junction of D551 and D286 turn onto D551 north. Aire on left in 200m at Super U. Service Point at Super U fuel station. Super U is well signed in town.

Sanitation:

Parking:

Poss

Euro Relais Mini; Token (ER); No drive over drain

SP

Supermarket adj. Inspected 2012.

GUILBERVILLE

123 D4 N48°59.236' W000°57.032' 50160

Directions: D96. Adj to D96 on right as enter village on D96 from D974, signed.

Sanitation:

Parking:

10; Max 48hrs

Euro Relais Junior; Token (ER)

SP

Adj to recreational area with play area. Road noise from N174. Hymer/Liaka dealer 2 mins. Inspected 2012.

VILLEDIEU LES POELES 1

124 D4 N48°50.502' W001°13.363' 50800

Directions: Place des Quais. Turn off D924, sp 'Garrey' and 'Hôpital'. Turn right at next turning. Aire in 100m on right, opp Hopital Local, signed.

Sanitation:

Parking:

5; Also see 125

Aire Services; €4

SP

Cobbled car park with 5 large bays; Restaurants and hospital adj. Town centre with bell foundry open to public, 1 min. Inspected 2012.

VILLEDIEU LES POELES 2

125 D4 N48°50.243' W001°13.415' 50800

Directions: Parc de la Commanderie, Rue Taillemache. Signed in town centre. Turn off D924 opp church up small side street to car park and Aire, signed.

Sanitation:

Parking:

10

None; See 124

SP

Surrounded by water with weir situated in a wooded dell. Town centre with bell foundry open to public, 1 min. Inspected 2012.

AGON COUTAINVILLE — 126 — D4 — N49°03.190' W001°35.482' — 50230

Directions: Rue du Vieux Coutainville. Turn off D651, sp 'Agon-Coutainville', and follow sp 'Agon' and 'Hippodrome'. Turn onto D361, sp 'Aire d'Acceuil' and 'Hippodrome'. Aire on left 100m past campsite. Insert CC to open Flot Bleu Park barrier.

Sanitation:

Parking:

40; €6.10/24hrs inc 2amp elec; CC

Flot Bleu Océane

Former campsite converted to Aire. Insert CC to exit. Town with numerous commerce 5 mins. Inspected 2012.

COUDEVILLE PLAGE — 127 — D4 — N48°53.215' W001°33.982' — 50290

Directions: D351/Avenue de la Mer. Turn off D971 onto D351, sp 'Cordeville s Mer-Plage'. Follow road for 2.5km. Aire on left before beach.

Sanitation:

Parking:

12; €5.50/night; Pay at Service Point; Max 24hrs

Urba Flux; CC

Lovely sandy beach; Couple of restaurants; Small shop. Inspected 2012.

GRANVILLE — 128 — D4 — N48°50.093' W001°36.597' — 50400

Directions: Rue du Roc, at Pointe du Roc. Follow sp 'Pointe du Roc', 'Aquarium' and signed. Once reach WW2 emplacements follow signs on one way system. Aire at top of town.

Sanitation:

Parking:

20; €5/7pm-10am; CC Max 24hrs; Pay at machine

Aire Services; €2

World War II gun emplacement 300m. Inspected 2012.

ST PAIR SUR MER — 129 — D4 — N48°49.028' W001°34.184' — 50380

Directions: Ave Léon Jozeau Marigné, off D911. Turn off D911 at the roundabout to the north of the town, sp 'Aire de Service'. Aire by tennis club car park.

Sanitation:

Parking:

21; €5/24hrs; Max 48hrs; Pay at machine

Raclet; €2

Walking distance from town and beach; Skateboarding. Market Thurs. Inspected 2012.

JULLOUVILLE — 130 — D4 — N48°46.668' W001°34.050' — 50610

Directions: Ave du Docteur Lemonnier. Turn off D911, main route, sp 'Camping D Lemonnier'. Service Point immediately on right adj to height restricted car park.

Sanitation:

Parking:

None

Aire Services Tall

Service Point only. Inspected 2012.

NORMANDY

HAVE YOU VISITED AN AIRE? **GPS co-ordinates in this guide are protected by copyright law**

Take at least 5 digital photos showing
• Signs
• Service Point
• Parking
• Overview
• Amenities

Visit www.all-the-aires.co.uk/submissions.shtml to upload your updates and photos.

Sanitation:

Aire Details:

Submit updates
- Amendments
- New Aires
- Not changed

CAROLLES — 132 — D4 — N48°44.992' W001°33.417' — 50740

Directions: Rue des Jaunets. From one-way system in town follow sp 'Camping'. Turn right in front of church and follow sp 'Camping' to the campsite located beside the Mairie. The Service Point is outside Camping La Gueriniere Municipal campsite.

Sanitation:

Parking:

None; €8 to stay in campsite

Custom; €2

Service Point outside campsite. Poss to stay at campsite. Village with local commerce 1 min. Inspected 2012.

CAROLLES PLAGE — 133 — D4 — N48°45.566' W001°34.224' — 50740

Directions: D61. Turn off D911 onto D61, sp 'Carolles-Plage'. Aire on left at roundabout, signed.

Sanitation:

Parking:

12; €5 8am-5pm; €7/24hrs; Purchase ticket from adj restaurant; Grass parking

Aire Services; €3 (3x€1)

Small seaside resort with 3 restaurants adj. Sandy beach 1 min. Inspected 2012.

LA LUCERNE D'OUTREMER — 134 — D4 — N48°47.075' W001°25.636' — 50320

Directions: D35/D109. Aire signed at centre of village, opp village shop/Tabac off D35/D109. Access is difficult due to two difficult turns. May be best to reverse into parking area from road.

Sanitation:

Parking:

6; Max 48hrs; Max 8m

Custom; 2 16amp Continental elec points

SP

Old Aire with difficult access and 1 local shop in village. Inspected 2012.

AVRANCHES — 135 — D4 — N48°41.189' W001°22.058' — 50300

Photo: Peter Evans

Directions: Jardin des Plantes, off D7. Follow D7 through town and turn off, sp 'Camping-Car'. Follow road 50m into car park, signed.

Sanitation:

Parking:

20

Aire Services; €2

Town 2 mins uphill, worth a visit. Views across countryside. Inspected 2012.

DUCEY — 136 — D4 — N48°37.493' W001°17.658' — 50220

Directions: D78, opp ZI du Domaine. Exit Ducey to north along river on D78, sp 'St Quentin'. Aire adj to D78 in 400m on left opposite large commercial building, signed.

Sanitation:

Parking:

20

Raclet; €2

Commercial area, lorries likely as truck stop for dairy. Always likely to have space. Inspected 2012.

ST JEAN LE THOMAS — 137 — D4 — N48°43.511' W001°31.405' — 50530

Directions: Rue St Michel. Turn off D911 onto VC, sp 'Camping Municipal' and signed. At roundabout turn right, signed. Turn left next to Ecole du Mer, signed.

Sanitation:

Parking:

17; €7.50/night; CC; Pay at Service Point

Aire Service; CC; €2

Sea glimpses from some bays. Campsite adj. Beach cafés 2 mins. Village with local shops 4 mins. Inspected 2012.

LE MONT ST MICHEL 1 — 138 — D4 — N48°36.503' W001°30.483' — 50170

Directions: D976. Parking at Le Mont St Michel visitor car park. Follow signs to separate motorhome parking area. Take ticket from barrier in entrance, pay as exit.

Sanitation:

Parking:

75; €12.50/12hrs €25/24hrs

None

Parking is at the main visitor parking on the mainland. All previous parking has been removed. Inspected 2012.

LE MONT ST MICHEL 2 - MOIDREY — 139 — D4 — N48°34.783' W001°30.897' — 50170

Directions: Aire de Moidrey. Turn off D976 as exit Beauvoir towards Pontorson, sp 'Village des Gites' and signed. Aire on left in 150m, signed. Electronic entrance barrier.

Sanitation:

Parking:

74; €8/24hrs; CC

Aire Services; CC; €3

Foot/cycle path along river to Le Mont St Michel. WiFi available. Inspected 2012.

LE MONT ST MICHEL 3 - BEAUVOIR — 140 — D4 — N48°35.654' W001°30.739' — 50170

Directions: D976. From Le Mont St Michel drive towards Pontorson. The Aire is adj to D976 as exit Beauvoir, opp L'Hermitage hotel and restaurant.

Sanitation:

Parking:

100; €12.50

Aire Services

Under construction at time of inspection. Foot/cycle path along river to Le Mont St Michel. Inspected 2012.

LE MONT ST MICHEL 4 - LA BIDONNIERE | 141 | D4 | N48°36.240' W001°28.635' | 50170

Directions: Route de la Rive Ardevon. Turn off D275 at La Rive 4km before Le Mont St Michel, signed. Follow road to Aire on right, signed.

Sanitation:

Parking:

20; €10/24hrs inc service

Custom; Elec 4amp €3.50/24hrs; CEE plug

SP

Restaurant and regional products shop adj; View of Mont St Michel which is 4km away. Inspected 2012.

ST HILAIRE DU HARCOUET | 142 | D4 | N48°34.554' W001°05.509' | 50600

Directions: D334. Turn off D977, sp 'Domfront'. Then follow sp 'Plan d'Eau' and 'Piscine'. Parking to right of large church, just off main square, signed.

Sanitation:

Parking:

5

Raclet; €2

SP

Excellent facility for town. Walks around lake; D177 Fougères-St-Hilaire nice road to drive. Inspected 2012.

MORTAIN | 143 | D4 | N48°38.923' W000°56.697' | 50140

Directions: Place du Château, D133. Signed in town. Turn off D977 onto D133, sp 'Romagny' and 'Camping'. Aire 100m down hill in large car park with château.

Sanitation:

Parking:

6

Euro Relais Junior

SP

2 mins to town; Walking trails to waterfall 'Petite Cascade'. Inspected 2012.

PONTORSON | 144 | D4 | N48°33.495' W001°30.464' | 50170

Directions: D976, at Carrefour supermarket. Service Point to rear of fuel station. Parking to rear of supermarket parking, signed.

Sanitation:

Parking:

20

Euro Relais Junior; Token (ER)

SP

Supermarket adj; Laundrette adj. Inspected 2012.

ST MARS D'EGRENNE | 145 | D4 | N48°33.668' W000°43.758' | 61350

Directions: Off D976. Turn off D976 alongside Mairie, opp church and D217, sp 'Passais'. Aire on left in 200m.

Sanitation:

Parking:

6; 9m bays

Raclet; 2 unmetered CEE elec points; No drive over drain

SP

Surrounded by houses; Village with baker 1 min. Inspected 2012.

ST FRAIMBAULT

146 D4 N48°29.275' W000°41.733' 61350

Directions: Off D24. Enter village on D24 from Ceaucé. The Aire is signed on left in pay car park (€1), adj to the cemetery.

Sanitation:

Parking:

10; Hedged bays; €1

SOS; Water €1; Elec €4 Apr-Sept, €5 Oct-Mar

SP

Pleasant spot in a well maintained village. Inspected 2012.

CEAUCE

147 E4 N48°29.898' W000°37.516' 61330

Directions: Off D962. Head north out of town on D962, sp 'Domfront'. Turn off in 200m at roundabout, sp 'Camping'. In 200m turn left, signed. The Service Point is on the end of the building with parking beyond.

Sanitation:

Parking:

5

Custom; €5

SP

Village with local commerce 2 mins. Lake and sports facility adj. Inspected 2012.

COUTERNE

148 E4 N48°30.738' W000°24.877' 61410

Directions: Rue Alexis Barre, off D916. Turn off D976, sp 'Euro Relais'. Take next right and Aire on right opp La Poste and behind church, sp 'Euro Relais'.

Sanitation:

Parking:

2

Custom; Building in progress at time of inspection, future unknown.

SP

In town centre with shops and cafés; Limited parking. Inspected 2012.

DOMFRONT

149 E4 N48°35.335' W000°39.044' 61700

Directions: Rue du Champ Passais. Turn off D976, sp 'Camping'. Service Point at campsite entrance.

Sanitation:

Parking:

None

Euro Relais Junior; Token (2/1); €3

SP

Poss to stay in adj municipal campsite at campsite rates. Inspected 2012.

BAGNOLES DE L'ORNE

150 E4 N48°33.024' W000°24.116' 61410

Directions: D916, at Super U. Exit Bagnoles de L'Orne on D916 towards Couterne. Service Point at Super U supermarket next to laverie (laundry) and car wash. The Service Point outside the campsite has been removed.

Sanitation:

Parking:

5

Euro Relais Mini; Token (ER)

SP

Supermarket. Self service laundrette. Inspected 2012.

LA FERTE MACE 151 E4 N48°35.418' W000°21.291' 61600

Directions: Ruelle des Fournelles, off D916. Car park opp church adj to D16, signed.

Sanitation:

Parking:

5; Very sloping

Custom

SP

Town adj. Inspected 2012.

LA FERRIERE AUX ETANGS 152 E4 N48°39.573' W000°31.033' 61450

Directions: Rue de l'Etang. From D18 turn onto D21, sp 'Domfront'. Turn left at end of lake, sp 'Camping'. Turn left again, sp 'Camping'. Service Point immediately on left, outside basic municipal campsite.

Sanitation:

Parking:

5; When campsite closed

Bollard; €2

SP

Views of lake; Campsite adj; Swimming. Inspected 2012.

FLERS 153 E4 N48°44.610' W000°33.783' 61100

Directions: D264. Turn off D18 onto D264 at traffic lights, sp 'Laval'. The Service Point is to the rear of the fuel station at the Intermarché supermarket.

Sanitation:

Parking:

Poss

Euro Relais Mini; €2; No drive over drain

SP

Supermarket adj. Inspected 2012.

TINCHEBRAY 154 D4 N48°45.780' W000°44.266' 61800

Directions: D911/Rue André Breton. Follow sp 'Sourdeval' in town. On D911 as exit town west towards Soudeval, signed.

Sanitation:

Parking:

3

Raclet; 1 CEE unmetered elec socket

SP

Town 2 mins. Inspected 2012.

SOURDEVAL 155 D4 N48°43.556' W000°55.388' 50150

Directions: Parc Saint-Lys, Rue Jean-Baptiste Janin. Turn off D977 at the roundabout in town onto D911, sp 'Brécey' and signed. Take 1st exit at next roundabout and turn right, sp 'Pique Nique'. Aire on right opp cemetery, signed.

Sanitation:

Parking:

5

Euro Relais Junior; 2 unmetered CEE elec points

SP

Local commerce 2 mins; Far enough from D977 to be quiet. Inspected 2012.

VIRE | 156 | D4 | N48°50.458' W000°53.350' | 14500

Directions: Place du Champ de Foire, on north edge of town. Easiest approach from north on D577. Turn left bottom of hill before the town centre, sp 'Champ de Foire' and signed. Follow road up hill. Service Point adj to bus parking. Large, unrestricted parking on several terraces.

50

Custom

Large town with numerous shops adj. Market Sunday. Inspected 2012.

CONDE SUR NOIREAU | 157 | E4 | N48°51.061' W000°33.231' | 14110

Directions: Rue des Prés Guillets, in central square. At roundabout junction of D512 and D562 turn onto D512, sp 'Vire'. Turn 2nd right onto Rue des Prés Guilet, sp 'Mairie'. Go past stop sign and Aire on left behind Mairie, signed.

5; None 6am-2pm Wednesday - market

Aire Services; Token (3/3)

Town 2 mins with local commerce. Skateboard park; Market in car park 6am-2pm Wednesday. Inspected 2012.

PONT D'OUILLY | 158 | E4 | N48°52.675' W000°24.767' | 14690

Directions: Rue de la Libération/D167. Turn off D511 onto D167 at river bridge on the east side of river, sp 'La Suisse Normande' and signed. The Aire is 600m on the left at village boundary, signed. Enter through CC-operated Flot Bleu Park barrier.

35; €10/24hrs €14/48hrs inc 4amp elec continental plug; Closed Dec-Jan

Flot Bleu Euro; CC

20 bays with river views; Village with local commerce 2 mins. Inspected 2012.

THURY HARCOURT | 159 | E3/4 | N48°59.211' W000°28.459' | 14220

Directions: Chemin du Pont Benoît, off D6 outside campsite. Follow sp 'Camping du Traspy' in town. Aire outside campsite, behind restaurant. GPS co-ordinates 500m from Aire on entry road to avoid GPS confusion.

4; €8/24hrs inc elec and shower

Raclet; €2.50

Swimming lake adj; Views of lake from Aire. Campsite adj. Inspected 2012.

BRETTEVILLE SUR LAIZE | 160 | E3 | N49°02.625' W000°19.648' | 14680

Directions: Rue de la Criquetière/D23. Exit town to southwest on D23, sp 'Barbery'. Pass the church and the Service Point is 50m on right against the building Atelier Communal, signed.

None

Custom

Parking at Stade du Manoir. Inspected 2012.

GRAINVILLE LANGANNERIE

161 E4 N49°00.844' W000°16.071' 14190

Directions: Rue de Lapford. Turn off main route through village, sp 'CampingCar'. Aire 50m on left, signed.

Sanitation:

Parking:

5

Aire Services; CC

Village adj. Just off N158. Also parking at Musée de la Mine adj to D237 at St Germain le Vasson: N49°00.002' W000°19.152'. Inspected 2012.

SOUMONT ST QUENTIN

162 E4 N48°58.725' W000°15.046' 14420

Directions: Rue de Plateau. In Village turn onto D658, sp 'Aisy'. Turn left in 100m, sp 'Filmasport'. Drive towards water tower and Aire is in front of tower, signed through gates.

Sanitation:

Parking:

10; €5.50/night; Grass parking

Custom; 6amp CEE elec sockets

Commercial Aire surrounded by industrial units. Some road noise. Inspected 2012.

FALAISE

163 E4 N48°53.786' W000°11.426' 14700

Directions: D658, behind Carrefour supermarket. The Service Point is located in the fuel station at rear of Carrefour supermarket. Difficult access due to curbs.

Sanitation:

Parking:

Poss

Euro Relais Junior; Token (ER); €1

Supermarket adj; Town with interesting fortifications/castle 5 mins. Inspected 2012.

VIMOUTIERS

164 E4 N48°55.907' E000°11.762' 61120

Photo: Carol and Duncan Weaver

Directions: D916. On west side of Vimoutiers on D916 from Argentan towards Lisieux on left-hand side. Adj to campsite.

Sanitation:

Parking:

6

Aire Services; 2 CEE elec points (1 button push = 30 mins elec)

Adj to noisy D916; Supermarket 1 min; Town centre 4 mins. Park opp. Inspected 2012.

PUTANGES PONT ECREPIN

165 E4 N48°45.652' W000°14.745' 61210

Directions: Chemin du Frich. Service Point outside campsite. Follow sp 'Camping' through town.

Sanitation:

Parking:

None

Urba Flux Tall; Token; €2.50

Service Point only. Camping €9/night. All town parking prohibits motorhomes 8pm-8am. Inspected 2012.

SEES | 166 | F4 | N48°36.391' E000°11.089' | 61500

Directions: D3/Rue d'Argentré. Enter town on D3 from east. Aire at roundabout on right at Intermarché. Service Point next to car wash on left.

Sanitation:

Parking:

Poss

Euro Relais Mini; €1/50L

Intermarché adj; Netto opp. Inspected 2012.

HAVE YOU VISITED AN AIRE? GPS co-ordinates in this guide are protected by copyright law

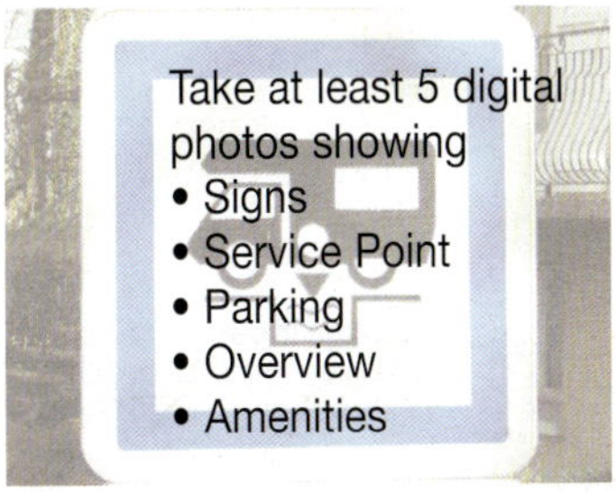
Take at least 5 digital photos showing
• Signs
• Service Point
• Parking
• Overview
• Amenities

Visit www.all-the-aires.co.uk/submissions.shtml to upload your updates and photos.

Sanitation:

Aire Details:

Submit updates
- Amendments
- New Aires
- Not changed

SOLIGNY LA TRAPPE | 168 | F4 | N48°37.011' E000°32.645' | 61380

Directions: D32. Turn off D32, main route, sp 'Walking and cycling' and signed. Aire outside cattle market. The Aire will be busy and noisy Tue morning due to the cattle market. Park Residentual du Perche is a holiday village with no designated motorhome parking.

Sanitation:

Parking:

10

Raclet; Token (ER); €2

Adj to cattle market; Village 3 mins. Walking and cycling trail to abbey and local forest. Inspected 2012.

NOTRE DAME DE COURSON | 169 | E4 | N48°59.443'E000°15.540' | 14140

Directions: D4. Exit village on D4, sp 'Livarot'. Aire on right as exit village, signed.

Sanitation:

Parking:

5; Large marked bays

Flot Bleu Pacific; €2; 6 unmetered Cont elec points in grass

Pleasant Aire surrounded by green space, shallow river adj. 1 min from village. Inspected 2012.

BRETONCELLES | 170 | F4 | N48°26.147' E000°53.196' | 61110

Directions: Off D918. 500m north of village, sp 'Complexe Sportif' and signed. Unhook chain to enter.

Sanitation:

Parking:

6

Euro Relais Junior; €2

Small pleasant Aire; Village with local commerce 2 mins. Stream, sports facilities and outdoor pool adj. Inspected 2012.

GACE — 171 — E4 — N48°47.730' E000°17.767' — 61230

Directions: Place de Château, Rue du Marché aux Bestiaux. From south on D438 turn onto D722c into Gacé, following sp 'Centre Ville'. Turn right, sp 'Mairie', 'Château', and signed. Aire in centre of town. Sp 'Tourist Office' from all directions.

Sanitation:

Parking:

Parking in town sq 5pm-10am only

Euro Relais Junior; Token (ER)

SP

Town centre, château and shops adj. Inspected 2012.

ARGENTAN — 172 — E4 — N48°44.408' W000°01.041' — 61200

Directions: Rue Charlotte Corday. Follow sp 'Camping Municipal' through town. Aire in car park adj to campsite, signed.

Sanitation:

Parking:

4

Euro Relais Junior; Token (ER); €2.20

SP

Large town with historic buildings 4 mins. Lake and park adj. Inspected 2012.

LE SAP — 173 — E4 — N48°53.722' E000°19.823' — 61470

Photo: Peter Marriot

Directions: D12, on left as exit village west towards Vimoutiers. Parking and Service Point alongside entry road to factory/commercial building, beside Sapeurs Pompiers (fire station) and overlooking pond.

Sanitation:

Parking:

5

Aire Services; 2 CEE elec points (1 button push = 30 mins elec)

SP

Pond; Village 5 mins with shops. Football pitch opp. Factory noise. Inspected 2012.

LA MADELEINE BOUVET — 174 — F4 — N48°28.255' E000°54.120' — 61110

Directions: Rue des Sources. Adj to D36 and D920 as you enter the village from Bretoncelles. Adj to lake and church.

Sanitation:

Parking:

10

Euro Relais Junior; Token (ER); €2

SP

Lake views. Pleasant. Village 1 min with bar/tabac. Inspected 2012.

RUGLES * — 175 — F4 — N48°49.370' E000°42.619' — 27250

Directions: Rue Notre Dame. Turn off D830 at traffic lighted crossroads, sp 'Village Retraite'. Then turn left, sp 'La Poste'. Follow road beside La Poste, signed. Aire 100m on left, signed. Further parking and 4 unmetered electric points in next car park on left.

Sanitation:

Parking:

10

Aire Services; 2 unmetered elec point

SP

Very pleasant area adj to riverside park and watermill. Village 2 mins with local commerce. Inspected 2012.

GISAY LA COUDRE | 176 | F4 | N48°56.954' E000°37.984' | 27330

Directions: Off D159. From D833 in La Barre-en-Ouche follow sp 'Gisay la Coudre'. Aire adj to D159 before village, signed.

Sanitation:

Parking:

5

Raclet; Token (ER)

Rural; Quiet; Adj to small fishing pond, no swimming. Inspected 2012.

CHANDAI | 177 | F4 | N48°45.249' E000°44.252' | 61300

Directions: Rue de l'Ancienne Poste. Turn off D926 at church, signed. Follow signs to left through narrow pinch point and Aire is on left, signed. To avoid pinch point drive towards L'Aigle on D926 past church and turn 1st right into Rue de l'Ancienne Post.

Sanitation:

Parking:

5

Custom

Aire relocated 50m from previous location to a peaceful location. Inspected 2012.

IRAI | 178 | F4 | N48°40.149' E000°41.842' | 61190

Directions: D601. Exit village on D601, Sp ' Salle Polyvalente'. The Service Point is on the left, opp the Church, signed. Parking is 200m on D258 at the school next to the Mairie. N48°40.281' E000°41.898'

Sanitation:

Parking:

7; max 48hrs

Euro Relais Mini

Village with bar/tabac 1 min. Near Foret de Perche with walking and cycling. Inspected 2012.

BROGLIE | 179 | F4 | N49°00.346' E000°31.802' | 27270

Directions: D49. From north turn off D438 at roundabout, sp 'Broglie'. In centre turn onto D49, sp 'La Barre-en-Ouche' and signed. Aire adj to D49 as exit village, sp 'Voie Vert' and signed.

Sanitation:

Parking:

8; €5; Payment collected

Euro Relais Junior; Token (ER); €2.50

Voie Vert cycle/walking path to Brogle adj. Riverside park adj. Town centre 1min. Inspected 2012.

L'OUDON | 180 | E4 | N48°58.148' E000°04.320' | 14170

Info/Photo: Mel & Chris Hughes

Directions: D39. At the village exit towards St Pierre sur Dives. Entrance looks like a private drive and signed only on way into village. Also sp Site Naturel at Le Billot.

Sanitation:

Parking:

4

Euro Relais Junior; €2.50; Token

Pleasant rural location with panoramic views. Local commerce 150m. Woodland walks adj. Visited 2012.

Coucy-le-Château, *Photo: Janet and John Watts*

NORTHERN FRANCE

Le Crotoy 2

BRAY DUNES | 1 | G1 | N51°03.780' E002°31.324' | 59123

Directions: Rue Pierre Decock. Driving towards Belgium on the D601 turn left and cross canal, sp 'Bray Dunes'. Service Point 100m on right at fuel station of Carrefour supermarket.

Sanitation:

Parking:

Poss

Euro Relais Junior; Token from laundrette; €2

Supermarket adj. Laundrette adj. Inspected 2012.

BERGUES | 2 | G1 | N50°57.941' E002°26.145' | 59380

Directions: Rue Joseph Dezitter. Turn off D916, sp 'P Camping Cars'. Then turn immediately right, sp 'Stade S Andrias' and 'P Reserve Camping Car'. Follow road to parking area, signed.

Sanitation:

Parking:

20; Max 48hrs

None

Fortified town 2 mins; Playing fields adj. Inspected 2012.

HONDSCHOOTE | 3 | G1 | N50°58.588' E002°34.836' | 59122

Directions: Impasse Spinnewyn. On D110 from Bergues turn right as enter town, sp 'Moulin de la Victoire'. Service Point on right just past turning to windmill. Parking at windmill.

Sanitation:

Parking:

10; At windmill

Euro Relais Junior; Token (ER); €2

Sports park adj; Windmill adj. Town 2 mins; Pleasant. Tokens from house between Service Point and windmill. Inspected 2012.

CASSEL | 4 | G1 | N50°47.596' E002°29.314' | 59670

Directions: Route d'Oxelaëre/C301. From D933 turn off just after Bavinchove onto C301, sp 'Oxelaëre'. Drive past Oxelaëre towards Cassel. The Aire is on your left at the sports ground before entering Cassel.

Sanitation:

Parking:

5

Custom; Token; €2

Views over fields but roadside location. Nice town 15 mins. Inspected 2012.

DUNKERQUE - ST MALO LES BAINS | 5 | G1 | N51°03.189' E002°24.864' | 59240

Directions: Avenue de la Mer. In Malo les Bains follow sp to 'Camping La Licorne' then to 'Parc du Vert' and finally 'P de la Licorne'. Designated parking to left before height barrier, signed. Aire 500m from camping La Licorne, from campsite head west and turn right and right again into P de la Licorne.

Sanitation:

Parking:

20

Inside campsite

Parking adj to large tidal sandy beach, no view. Walk through sand dunes or promenade along beach. Service Point advertised is inside campsite. Inspected 2012.

GRAVELINES 1

6 G1 N50°59.310' E002°07.363' 59820

Directions: Rue du Port. Exit A16 at Junction 51 and turn left. Go straight on at traffic lights and at stop junction. After bridge over lock turn left, sp 'Pt Fort Philippe'. At the roundabout follow sp 'Pt Fort Philippe'. Turn left, sp 'Port de Plaisance', and the parking is on the right, signed.

Sanitation:

Parking:

20; €6/24hrs Apr-Sept; €3 Oct-Mar

None; See 7

Overlooking boats. Star fort adj. Inspected 2012.

GRAVELINES 2

7 G1 N50°59.611' E002°07.910' 59820

Directions: Rue de la Gendarmerie. From Gravelines 1 turn left, signed. Turn left again, sp 'Pt Port Philip'. Turn right, sp 'Les Huttes'. At the roundabout turn left, sp 'Sportica'. Turn 1st right in 100m and the Service Point is 100m on right, signed.

Sanitation:

Parking:

None; See 6

Aire Services; CC; €2

Service Point only. Inspected 2012.

GRAND FORT PHILIPPE

8 G1 N51°00.069' E002°06.526' 59153

Directions: Blvd Carnot. From A16 exit at Junction 51, and follow sp 'Gravelines'. Turn left at traffic lights onto D940, sp 'Gd Fort Philippe'. Follow sp 'Gd Fort Philippe'. Turn immediately right in front of Super U, sp 'Port Plage'.Go straight over roundabout sp 'Camping'. The Aire is on the right, adj to water, signed.

Sanitation:

Parking:

8; Max 24hrs; Park in marked bays

Aire Services; CC; €2

Parking overlooking tidal river, with pleasure boats. Local commerce adj; 15 mins promenade to end of sea defence. Inspected 2012.

OYE PLAGE

9 G1 N50°58.619' E002°02.384' 62215

Directions: D219. Turn off D940 onto D219, sp 'Calais'. Aire on right in 200m.

Sanitation:

Parking:

5

Custom; On right side of building

Small town with local shops and two small supermarkets. Beach 2km. Inspected 2012.

CALAIS 1

10 G1 N50°57.958' E001°50.624' 62100

Directions: Avenue Raymond Poincaré, Gaston Berthe. From ferry port follow sp 'Calais Centre Ville'. Then follow sp 'Plage'. Veer to right when approaching Calais centre. Then follow sp 'P Camping Car'. Always keep ferry terminals on right. You are literally driving around the port. Aire on right just past campsite, adj to beach.

Sanitation:

Parking:

50; €7/24hrs; Pay at campsite

Raclet

Views of harbour/ferries. Sandy beach 2 mins. Restaurant/shops adj. Toilets open June-Sept. Can be noisy. Inspected 2012.

CALAIS 2 — 11 — G1 — N50°57.645' E001°50.781' — 62100

Directions: Rue du Paradis. Exit A16 at Junction 43 and follow D940 towards Sangatte. Go straight over roundabouts, sp 'Sangatte' and 'Parking'. Turn right, sp 'Parking', then follow sp 'Camping-Car'. Signed at entrance. 700m from Calais 1 and campsite.

Sanitation:

Parking:

50; €7 April-Oct; Free Nov-Mar; Pay at Campsite

None; See Calais 1

Overlooking marina. Local commerce adj. 700m from beach. Inspected 2012.

CALAIS (CITE EUROPE) — 12 — G1 — N50°55.980' E001°48.666' — 62231

Directions: Blvd du Kent. From A16/E402 exit at Junction 43, sp 'Cite de Europe Est'. Follow sp 'Cite de Europe'. Aire in large car park across from entrance to Cite de Europe, signed on Boulevard du Kent.

Sanitation:

Parking:

50

None

Cite de Europe shopping centre adj. Due to proximity to Channel tunnel, use additional locks and set alarm. Inspected 2012.

WISSANT — 13 — G1 — N50°53.210' E001°40.224' — 62179

Directions: D940. Aire adj to D940 as exit Wissant towards Calais, signed.

Sanitation:

Parking:

22

Custom

Village with local commerce. Sandy beach 5 mins. 20 mins south of Calais, ideal before ferry crossing. Inspected 2012.

ESCALLES — 14 — G1 — N50°54.939' E001°43.288' — 62179

Directions: D243. Adj to D243 as exit Escalles towards Peuplingues and A16, signed.

Sanitation:

Parking:

22; No parking 11pm-6am

None

Footpath from parking to coast and village. Other motorhome symbols refer to Les Erables which is a campsite charging €9/night 500m from Aire. Inspected 2012.

TARDINGHEN — 15 — G1 — N50°51.771' E001°38.955' — 62179

Directions: D249. From D940 in Tardinghen turn onto D249 in village, sp 'Audembert' and 'Ferme de l'Horloge'. Farm on left in 1.5km. Grass and hard standing parking behind barn.

Sanitation:

Parking:

20; €5/night

Custom; €3; Elec €3/24hrs

CL style Aire on farm. Local brewery 100m, Brasserie 2 Caps open to public. Sign at farm entrance details other farm parking, all €5/night. Inspected 2012.

COQUELLES

16 G1 N50°56.557' E001°48.638' 62100

Directions: Ave R Salengro. On D243 at Auchan supermarket between Calais and Coquelles. Service Point between the motorhome fuel pump and truck fuel to the left of the main fuel station, sp 'Camping-Cars'.

Sanitation:

Parking:

Poss

Euro Relais Mini; Token (ER)

Supermarket adj. Inspected 2012.

BOULOGNE SUR MER

17 G1 N50°44.645' E001°35.842' 62200

Directions: Parking Moulin Wibert. Exit A16 Junction 32, sp 'Wimereux Sud' and 'Nausicaa'. At roundabout take D96, sp 'Nausicaa'. Drive to sea and turn left onto D940, sp 'Nausicaa'. Aire 300m on right, signed. Narrow, one-way access road; difficult with large motorhomes when busy.

Sanitation:

Parking:

20; €5.20/night; 10 bays on incline

Aire Services; €3

Clifftop location with some sea/harbour views. The slope will make levelling difficult. Sandy beach and Nausicaa Aquarium 5 mins. Inspected 2012.

ST MARTIN BOULOGNE

18 G1 N50°43.982' E001°40.119' 62280

Directions: N42. Exit A16 at Junction 31 and follow sp 'Centre Commercial' and 'l'Inquetrie'. Then follow sp 'Centre Commercial'. The Service Point is at Auchan fuel station, follow sp 'Camping-Car' behind fuel station.

Sanitation:

Parking:

Poss

Raclet; Token (ER)

In large commercial out of town shopping area. No designated motorhome parking. Inspected 2012.

LE PORTEL

19 G1 N50°42.688' E001°34.534' 62480

Directions: Rue des Champs. Approach from Outreau on D119. Turn left at roundabout and follow road around town centre, signed. Turn left before 3.5t weight restriction. Drive past old Aire and turn right, signed. Aire through automated barrier.

Sanitation:

Parking:

25; €4 May-Sept; €3 Oct-Apr; Pay at machine; CC

Urba Flux Tall; €2; 12 elec points; €2/4hrs

On cliff top, no views. Sports facilities adj. Local commerce 3 mins. Market on Friday. Inspected 2012.

EQUIHEN PLAGE

20 G1 N50°40.787' E001°34.117' 62224

Directions: Rue du Beurre Fondu. Turn off D119 onto D236E. At roundabout turn into the main street. Take 1st right, turning down road by Café L'Océan, signed. In 200m turn right and Aire on left, signed.

Sanitation:

Parking:

10; €5; Collected 9am

Custom; Token; €3; 1 token provides 12hrs elec

On cliff overlooking sea. Adj to small sewerage works, noisy at times. Town 5 mins. Inspected 2012.

LE TOUQUET PARIS PLAGE 2

21 G2 N50°32.155' E001°35.563' 62520

Photo: Malcolm Webb

Directions: Avenue Jean Ruet, at Centre Nautique du Touquet. Follow sp 'Hippotel' and 'Parking International de la Canche'. At Hippotel follow sp 'Office du Tourisme'. Drive past first Aire and follow road turning right in 400m when road bends to the left, signed.

Sanitation:

Parking:

50; €9.50/24hrs; Pay at machine

Aire Services; €2

SP

Adj to boat yard/marina. Adj to beach. Very well maintained expensive beach resort. Inspected 2012.

LE TOUQUET PARIS PLAGE 1

22 G2 N50°31.585' E001°35.907' 62520

Directions: Boulevard de la Canche, at Parc International de la Canche. Follow sp 'Hippotel' and 'Parking International de la Canche'. At Hippotel follow sp 'Office du Tourisme'. Aire 200m on right. Marked by horse on Michelin map.

Sanitation:

Parking:

100; €9.50/24hrs; Grass parking; Pay at machine

Aire Services; €2

SP

Walks to sea; Motorhomes banned during horse events. Town 5 mins. Surface can be bumpy. Inspected 2012.

CUCQ TRÉPIED STELLA PLAGE

23 G2 N50°28.491' E001°34.646' 62155

Directions: Cours de Champs-Elysées. Drive through town to sea front. At sea front turn left. Designated parking on left in front of large sand dune, signed.

Sanitation:

Parking:

20

None

SP

Change to: Adj large sand dune. Town 4 mins. Merlimont has unrestricted day parking N50°27.611' E001°34.820'. Cycle/walking path to Le Touquet. Inspected 2012.

MONTREUIL SUR MER

24 G2 N50°27.567' E001°45.577' 62170

Directions: Approach and drive into Montreuil sur Mer on D138 from Campagne les Hesdin. At roundabout turn right, sp 'Montreuil Centre'. Turn 1st right in 200m into Ave des Gerennes, sp 'Aire de Camping-Car'. Aire in 50m on left.

Sanitation:

Parking:

10; Max 48hrs

Aire Services; €2

SP

Boules court adj. Town centre with local commerce 4 mins. Inspected 2012.

EMBRY

25 G2 N50°29.717' E001°57.953' 62990

Directions: D108. Exit village to north towards Maninghem. Turn off D108 onto C1, sp 'St Wandrille'. Turn immediately left, signed. Sp 'Camping Car de l'Embryenne' through village. Steep approach, risk of grounding.

Sanitation:

Parking:

5; €6; Collected

Flot Bleu Pacific; Token; €2.50; Flot Bleu Elec; €2.50/4hrs

SP

Very pleasant Commercial Aire located in countryside with rural views. Immaculately kept with showers and BBQ. Inspected 2012.

BERCK (BELLEVUE) 26 G2 N50°25.415' E001°34.057' 62600

Directions: Rue du Docteur Calot, Aire Terminus at Bellevue suburb north of Berck. From D317 turn right onto Blvd de Anglais and follow road to sea. At seafront turn left and the Aire is on left, signed.

Sanitation:

Parking:

40; €5.50; Pay at machine

Custom

Sand dunes and beach adj. Aire is a sun trap with no shade. Inspected 2012.

BERCK SUR MER 27 G2 N50°23.798' E001°33.823' 62600

Directions: Chemin aux Raisins. Turn off D940 at D940/D303 roundabout with McDonalds, sp 'Berck Plage'. Turn left at roundabout with ALDI onto Chemin Aux Raisins, sp 'Aire de Camping Car'. Aire at end of road adj to beach, signed.

Sanitation:

Parking:

75; €6.50/night; Pay at machine

Custom

1 min from large, sandy, duned beach. Shops 10mins. Inspected 2012.

GPS Co-ordinates for SatNav

The GPS Co-ordinates published in this guide were taken onsite by our inspectors. We consider them a valuable and unique asset and at the time of publishing have decided not to publish them as electronic files for use on navigation devices. You have permission to type in the co-ordinates of an Aire you intend to visit but not to store or share them. For the security of our copyright:

- **Do not compile them into lists**
- **Do not publish, share or reproduce them anywhere in any format**

FORT MAHON PLAGE 29 G2 N50°20.320' E001°33.345' 80790

Directions: Rue de la Bistouille, off D32. Follow D32, main route through town, towards sea. Aire on left behind car park and in front of sand dune. Well signed.

Sanitation:

Parking:

50; €8 Apr-Oct; €5 rest of year; Pay at machine

Custom

In town centre; Backs onto sand dunes; Beach 2 mins. Very pleasant. Sheltered, total suntrap. Inspected 2012.

QUEND PLAGE LES PINS 30 G2 N50°19.412' E001°33.326' 80120

Directions: D332/Route de la Plage. Located adj to D332 as exit Quend Plage les Pins towards Fort Mohan Plage, signed.

Sanitation:

Parking:

30; €7/24hrs; Pay at machine

Aire Services; €2

Pleasant, shaded parking adj to cycle/walking route. Village and beach 3 mins. Inspected 2012.

LE HOURDEL | 31 | G2 | N50°12.861' E001°33.170' | 80410

Photo: Mel and Chris Hughes

Directions: D102. Turn off D940 at roundabout onto D3, sp 'Pointe le Hourdel'. At roundabout turn off D3 onto D102, sp 'Pointe le Hourdel'. At entrance of village, turn left, then follow road to car park at end.

Sanitation:

Parking:

20

None

SP

This is an isolated car park adj to beach which is obscured by sand dunes. Village 500m bans motorhomes. Inspected 2012.

LE CROTOY 1 | 32 | G2 | N50°13.713' E001°36.738' | 80550

Directions: Chemin du Marais. From D940 turn onto D4 at roundabout, sp 'La Plage' and 'St Quentin en T'. In 800m turn left at roundabout onto D104, sp 'Crotoy Centre'. Then turn immediately right and right again. Aire on left, signed.

Sanitation:

Parking:

30; €5/24hrs; Pay at machine

Aire Services; €2

SP

On beach; Sand dunes adj. Town 10 mins. Pleasant but a little isolated. Beach popular with kite surfers. Inspected 2012.

LE CROTOY 2 | 33 | G2 | N50°13.094' E001°37.992' | 80550

Directions: Le Port, Ave des Ecluses. From D940 at roundabout turn onto D104, sp 'Le Crotoy'. In town turn left, sp 'Le Port'. At end of road turn left again and Aire is in car park.

Sanitation:

Parking:

70; €5/24hrs; Pay at machine

Aire Services; €2

SP

Views over port. Town 2 mins; Restaurants; Walks around seafront/harbour. Pleasant spot. Inspected 2012.

HAVE YOU VISITED AN AIRE? | GPS co-ordinates in this guide are protected by copyright law

Take at least 5 digital photos showing
• Signs
• Service Point
• Parking
• Overview
• Amenities

Visit www.all-the-aires.co.uk/submissions.shtml to upload your updates and photos.

Sanitation:

Aire Details:

Submit updates
- Amendments
- New Aires
- Not changed

ST VALERY SUR SOMME | 35 | G2 | N50°10.934' E001°37.743' | 80230

Directions: Rue de la Croix l'Abbé. Turn off D940 onto D2, sp 'P des Corderies'. Turn right before D3 junction, signed 'Aire de Camping Cars' on small brown sign. Aire 500m on left, signed. Barriered entrance. Upon departure pay and exit within 10 mins.

Sanitation:

Parking:

100; €9/24hrs; Pay at machine

Custom; inc

SP

Commercial Aire. 15 mins downhill walk to St Valery and the coast. Inspected 2012.

CAYEUX SUR MER

36 F2 N50°12.181' E001°31.576' 80410

Directions: Rue Faidherbe la Mollière. At La Mollière Aval turn off D3, sp 'Camping les Galets'. Follow road and the Aire is on left opp Camping les Galets, signed.

Sanitation:

Parking:

60; €5/24hrs; Pay at campsite opp

Euro Relais Junior; €3

Adj to sand dunes. Difficult acess to sea due to terrain. Town 10 mins. Tokens from campsite reception. Inspected 2012.

AULT ONIVAL

37 F2 N50°06.227' E001°27.079' 80460

Directions: Rue Léon Blum, at Centre Medico. From St Valery turn off D940 at roundabout onto D463, sp 'Onival'. Follow road through town. Turn left, sp 'P' and signed. 3.5t weight restriction on Aire.

Sanitation:

Parking:

9

Euro Relais Junior; Token (ER); €2

Sea 3 mins downhill. Town 2 mins; Pleasant uncommercialised seaside town. Inspected 2012.

MERS LES BAINS

38 F2 N50°03.673' E001°24.110' 80350

Directions: D1015. Turn off D1015 at Le Mutant supermarket, signed. Aire 50m on left, signed. Entrance barrier under construction at time of inspection. The Aire has been relocated from town centre.

Sanitation:

Parking:

40; €5/night

Aire Services; €2

Deep gravel in places. Supermarket adj. Auchan supermarket and retail area 200m. Town 5 mins. Inspected 2012.

NUNCQ HAUTECOTE

39 G2 N50°18.335' E002°17.589' 62270

Directions: D916/ Domaine de la Pommeraie. Adj to D916 in the village, signed.

Sanitation:

Parking:

3; €5/night; €2/2hrs

Euro Relais Junior; €2; Elec CEE plug €5/night

Manicured, immaculately kept Commercial Aire adj to a B&B and a restaurant. Inspected 2012.

AUXI LE CHATEAU

40 G2 N50°13.844' E002°06.991' 62390

Directions: Rue des Gobelets. From south approach on D933. Turn right, sp 'P de l'Authie'. Turn left in 20m into car park. Aire has 3.5t weight restriction.

Sanitation:

Parking:

10; Max 7m

Urba Flux

Aire located in quiet car park adj to stream. Local commerce 2 mins. Inspected 2012.

DOULLENS

41 G2 N50°09.238' E002°20.535' 80600

Directions: From south follow N25 into town. Turn left onto Rue du Pont á l'Avoine, signed, and the Aire is on the left, signed.

Sanitation:

Parking:

4; 6m bays plus overhang

Custom; Lift grid for WC emptying

SP

Citadel 5 mins; Town 2 mins. Inspected 2012.

CONTY

42 G3 N49°44.595' E002°09.347' 80160

Directions: Rue du Marais. Enter Conty from east and follow sp 'Fleury'. Turn off at roundabout, sp 'Etangs' and signed. Aire on right just past children's play area, signed.

Sanitation:

Parking:

40; Grass parking

Custom; Token; €2

SP

Village 2 mins. On old railway line converted into walk called 'La Coulee Vert'. Fishing ponds 3 mins. Inspected 2012.

BEAUVAIS 1

43 G3 N49°25.943' E002°04.298' 60000

Directions: Rue Lucien Lainé. Aire located to west of town in car park off roundabout with Hyper U. Follow sp 'P St Quentin' through town.

Sanitation:

E

Parking:

6; Max 72hrs; Park lengthways

None; See 44 or 45

SP

Very convenient parking for town. Hyper U opp. Inspected 2011.

BEAUVAIS 2

44 G3 N49°25.455' E002°04.810' 60000

Directions: Rue Aldebert Bellier. Follow sp 'Camping Municipal', then 'Aire Camping-Car' through town. Turn off D139 at traffic lights, sp 'Sapeurs Pompiers' and signed. Follow road uphill and turn right, signed. Turn left up steep slope, signed. Aire on right past campsite, signed.

Sanitation:

Parking:

14; Max 48hrs; Open May-Sept; Grass parking

Aire Services

SP

In residential area. Adj park overlooks cathedral and has steps down to town. Inspected 2012.

BEAUVAIS 3

45 G3 N49°24.549' E002°06.992' 60000

Directions: Avenue Descartes. Approach from south on D1001. Turn right at traffic lights, sp 'Clermont', into retail park. Turn right at next roundabout and Service Point is on left in Auchan fuel station; 3.6m height barrier.

Sanitation:

E

Parking:

None; See 43 and 44

Flot Bleu Fontaine; Token

SP

Service Point only. Inspected 2012.

SERIFONTAINE

46 G3 N49°21.331' E001°46.857' 60590

Directions: Route de Chamignolles. In the village turn off D915 onto Rue de Cocagne, signed. Follow road uphill, sp 'Aire d'Accueil Camping Car'. Aire on right at top of village. Narrow access due to parked cars.

Sanitation:

Parking:

25; €7.50/night; €10 Jul-Aug

Custom

Commercial Aire also used as motorhome storage in winter. Phone for access if no one around. Inspected 2012.

SOUPPES SUR LOING

47 H5 N48°10.858' E002°43.388' 77460

Directions: D207. Turn off D697 at traffic lights onto D207, sp 'Camping-Cars'. Go straight on across river bridges, signed. After crossing canal bridge turn immediately right, signed. Aire 100m on right, signed.

Sanitation:

Parking:

€5/24hrs inc elec; Max 72hrs

Custom; Water and CEE elec only

Adj to canal with views. Village 3 mins over canal bridge. Noise from trains and adj factory. Inspected 2012.

BRAY SUR SEINE

48 H4 N48°24.934' E003°14.440' 77480

Directions: Quai de l'Ile. Turn off D412 at south side of river just before bridge, sp 'Aire Camping Car' and 'P 200 spaces'. Turn towards large industrial building then turn right under bridge into car park. Service Point on left in large car park adj to river Seine, signed. Parking 100m past Service Point in P Tapas.

Sanitation:

Parking:

20; 5m bay + 2m overhang

Custom

No river view from parking. Pleasant park adj. Pleasant spot. Busy on Friday - market day. Inspected 2012.

PROVINS

49 H4 N48°33.708' E003°16.785' 77160

Directions: Chemin de la Belle Fille. From D231/D619 roundabout turn into Provins, sp 'Centre' and 'Cité Médiévale'. Turn next left, sp 'Camping-Cars'. The Aire is at the far end of the car park, signed.

Sanitation:

Parking:

20; €4

Urba Flux Tall; CC

Adj to very imposing medieval hilltop town, 200m. Town closed to traffic Mar-Nov. TO adj. Inspected 2012.

DISNEYLAND - PARIS 1

50 H4 N48°52.355' E002°47.838' 77700

Directions: At Esso garage outside Hotel Santa Fé, just off Ave Robert Schuman. From A4 exit Junction 14, sp 'Disneyland'. Turn onto D344, sp 'Magny le Hongre' and 'Montry'. At roundabout turn left onto Ave Robert Schuman, sp 'Hôtels Disney' and 'Police'.

Sanitation:

Parking:

6; Must ask permission at cash desk

Flot Bleu Standard Plus; Token; €4

In Disneyland Paris. LPG avail. Tokens avail from garage. Parking at discretion of manager. Inspected 2012.

DISNEYLAND PARIS 2

51 H4 N48°52.560' E002°47.789' 77700

Directions: Blvd du Parc. Turn off D344 onto Ave Robert Schuman and follow sp 'Parc Disneyland'. Aire in motorhome section of main car park.

Sanitation:

Parking:

50; €30 (free to annual pass holders)

Showers and WC closed 7pm-8am

Car park gets mechanically swept at about 3am. Inspected 2012.

ST CYR SUR MORIN

52 H4 N48°54.381' E003°11.088' 77750

Directions: D31/Ave Daniel Simon. From D407 turn off onto D68 towards St Ouen sur Morin. In village turn right onto D31, sp 'St Cyr'. Aire between Mairie and church.

Sanitation:

Parking:

5

Custom; By bridge

Pretty village adj; Basket ball; Table tennis; Local commerce 1 min. Inspected 2012.

SEPT-SORTS

53 H4 N48°56.724' E003°06.696' 77260

Directions: D603. Located in retail park just off D603 between Sept-Sorts and La Ferte s/s Jouarre. Service Point in fuel station.

Sanitation:

Parking:

Poss

Euro Relais Junior; Token (ER)

Supermarket adj; McDonalds adj; Chinese buffet restaurant opp. Inspected 2012.

CHATEAU THIERRY 1

54 H3 N49°02.195' E003°22.966' 02400

Directions: Ave d'Essômes. Turn off ring road at D969 roundabout, sp 'Centre Ville', 'Piscine' and 'Aire d'Aquile Camping-Car'. Turn right at next roundabout by McDonalds, signed. Aire on left after McDonalds, enter through barrier.

Sanitation:

Parking:

13; €6/24hrs; CC

Urba Flux Tall; Elec €1/12hrs; Toilet and shower block

River adj but fenced off. 2 bays with river views. Swimming pool adj; McDonalds adj. Inspected 2012.

CHATEAU THIERRY 2

55 H3 N49°02.073' E003°23.508' 02400

Directions: Rue de la Plaine. At Intermarché off outer ring road between D969 and D1/D15 junctions. South of river in retail park at fuel station, just past truck fuel, adj to road and gas bottles.

Sanitation:

Parking:

Poss; See entry **54**

Flot Bleu Standard Plus; €3

Supermarket and other retail park shops. Parking possible but undesirable. Inspected 2012.

CHAMANT

56 G3 N49°13.268' E002°35.585' 60300

Directions: D1330. Turn off D1330, sp 'Centre Commercial Villevert'. Service Point just before Total fuel station adj to D1330.

Sanitation:

Parking:

None

Euro Relais Junior; Token (ER); €5

SP

Barriered exit. LPG at Total fuel station. All supermarket parking has 2.7m height barrier. Inspected 2012.

SOISSONS

57 H3 N49°22.994' E003°19.804' 02200

Directions: Rue Ernest Ringuier. Enter on D1 from north. Turn right at junc by Esso Express fuel station, follow sp 'Centre Ville' and 'Camping'. Cross river bridge and turn left, sp 'Centre Ville'. Aire on left at 'Halte Fluviale'. Access to Service Point difficult for large vehicles.

Sanitation:

Parking:

4

Aire Services; €0;50/1hr; No drive over drain

SP

At boat moorings adj to river near town centre with numerous commerce. Renovated in 2012. Inspected 2012.

BEAUTOR

58 H3 N49°39.650' E003°20.970' 02800

Directions: Rue du Port. Turn off D338/D55 roundabout opp ALDI, sp 'Base de Loisirs'. Turn left in 50m, signed. Aire on left, signed.

Sanitation:

Parking:

3

Euro Relais Junior; €2; Closed Dec-Apr

SP

Adj to canal but no view. ALDI 1 min. Inspected 2012.

ROYE

59 H3 N49°41.861' E002°47.552' 80700

Directions: Place de la Republique. Turn off main route through at rear of church, sp 'Aire Camping-Car'. Turn left into car park. Service Point beside toilets and recycling bins.

Sanitation:

Parking:

10

Aire Services; €2

SP

In car park near fire station. Town centre with local commerce 2 mins. Inspected 2012.

NOYON

60 H3 N49°34.641' E002°59.720' 60400

Directions: Ave Jean Bouin. Exit D145/D932 roundabout with monument, sp 'Gare SNCF' and 'Aire de Service Camping-Car'. Turn left, sp 'Piscine' and 'Aire de Service Camping-Car'. Service Point immediately on left, signed.

Sanitation:

Parking:

Poss; Local parking available

Flot Bleu Euro; CC; €2

SP

Service Point only adj to numerous sports facilities. No designated parking provided but local parking available. Inspected 2012.

ANOR

61 | I2 | N49°59.448' E004°05.891' | 59186

Directions: Service Point: Rue Georges Clemenceau, off D156. Adj to D156, outside La Poste and opp Carrefour supermarket. Parking: Adj to D963 as exit towards Trélon, signed: N49°59.525' E004°05.767'.

Sanitation:

Parking:

4

Flot Bleu Océane; Token; €3.50

SP

Supermarket adj. Park adj. Village 2 mins uphill. Inspected 2012.

EPPE SAUVAGE

62 | I2 | N50°07.174' E004°08.354' | 59132

Directions: Off D133D, near Lac du Val Joly. Follow D133 towards Eppe Sauvage. Turn onto D133D, sp 'Val Joly' and 'Coeur de Station'. Turn off, sp 'Coeur de Station'. The Aire is located in Parking 2.

Sanitation:

Parking:

20

Flot Bleu Euro; CC; €2

SP

Adj to large leisure lake; Main facilities 500m further down road. www.valjoly.com. Inspected 2012.

BELLICOURT

63 | H2 | N49°57.079' E003°14.131' | 02420

Directions: D1044/Aire de Riqueval. Approach the village from south on D1044. After boat take 1st turning on left. Follow this lane to the rear of TO, signed.

Sanitation:

Parking:

2; Very sloping

Urba Flux; Token; €4/12 mins

SP

Aire above 5km Napoleonic canal tunnel, walk through adj woods for views. American WW1 memorial north on D1044. Inspected 2012.

PERONNE

64 | H2 | N49°56.044' E002°56.455' | 80200

Directions: Rue Georges Clemenceau, outside camping municipal. Turn off D1017 main route, sp 'Camping'. The Service Point is located directly outside the campsite.

Sanitation:

Parking:

None

Urba Flux Tall: CC

SP

Service Point only. Unrestricted parking locally. Inspected 2012.

CATILLON SUR SAMBRE

65 | H2 | N50°04.560' E003°38.780' | 59360

Directions: N43, on east edge of town adj to canal just off N43. If full use large overflow parking area: N50°04.617' E003°38.652'. On opp side of canal and opp side of road turn down Rue de la Gare, signed.

Sanitation:

Parking:

4; €5; Max 72hrs

Custom; 4 unmetered elec points

SP

Edge of town; Overlooking canal. Overflow car park takes 25 and can accommodate large motorhomes. Inspected 2012.

LE CATEAU CAMBRESIS | 66 | H2 | N50°06.117' E003°33.292' | 59360

Directions: N43/Ave du Marechal Leclerc. From town centre exit on N43, sp 'Charleville-M'. The Aire is adj to main route, 150m from LIDL.

Sanitation:

Parking:

5; Max 48hrs

Raclet Maxi; 4 unmetered CEE elec points

Town 7 mins down hill with plenty of commerce. Inspected 2012.

BAVAY | 67 | I2 | N50°17.984' E003°47.766' | 59570

Directions: Chemin de Ronde. From D24/D2649 roundabout turn off, sp 'Maubeuge'. Turn 1st right and Aire on right in 200m.

Sanitation:

Parking:

20; Max 72hrs

Custom; Hosepipe useful

At sports facilities, but these fenced off. Park adj; Village centre 5 mins. Inspected 2012.

ST QUENTIN | 68 | H2 | N49°51.441' E003°15.153' | 02100

Directions: D1029. At fuel station of Auchan supermarket. Service Point at far side of 24/24 pumps.

Sanitation:

Parking:

Poss

Euro Relais Junior; Token (ER)

Busy retail park and hypermarket adj. Inspected 2012.

BERTRY | 69 | H2 | N50°05.455' E003°26.904' | 59980

Directions: Rue Victor Hugo. From south turn off D932 at Maurois onto D115, sp 'Bertry'. Follow D115 into Bertry and turn right immediately after crossing railway line, signed. Follow road parallel to railway line and Aire is on right near Bertry train station.

Sanitation:

Parking:

4

Custom; 4 unmetered CEE elec points

Pleasant Aire adj to park and by a very small train station. Inspected 2012.

BANTEUX | 70 | H2 | N50°03.741' E003°12.060' | 59266

Directions: Rue du Port. Turn off D644 onto D103, sp 'Banteux'. In 400m turn right onto D103A, sp 'Banteux'. Follow road over canal bridge and to the right past the church, then turn right into Rue du Port, signed. Follow road to canal, then turn left, signed. Aire on right before building.

Sanitation:

Parking:

4; €4 inc elec; Pay Mairie; Open Mar-Oct

Custom; 4 unmetered Cont elec sockets; Open Mar-Oct

Canal view obstructed by trees. Inspected 2012.

CRESPIN

71 H2 N50°25.175' E003°39.753' 59154

Directions: Rue du Vivier. Turn off D954 near the church, signed. Aire 200m on right, signed. Tokens from supermarket.

Sanitation:

Parking:

3; 8m max

Urba Flux Tall; Token; €2

Quiet location. LIDL and other shops along main route. Inspected 2012.

MARCOING

72 H2 N50°07.273' E003°10.918' 59159

Directions: Rue des Masnières. Exit town on D15, sp 'Cambrai'. Cross canal and turn right, sp 'Masnieres'. Turn immediately left, signed, and Aire 150m uphill.

Sanitation:

Parking:

6

Custom; 4 unmetered CEE elec points

SP

Aire is located between the railway track and the canal but there is no view of either. Local shops 4 mins. Inspected 2012.

BELLAING

73 H2 N50°21.909' E003°26.047' 59135

Directions: D13, at the E'Leclerc supermarket. Service Point to left of fuel station. Fuel station and supermarket have 3.2m height barrier.

Sanitation:

Parking:

None

Euro Relais Tall; Token (ER)

Supermarket and car wash adj. Inspected 2012.

ARRAS

74 H2 N50°17.688' E002°47.310' 62000

Directions: Rue des Rosati. From central Arras follow sp 'St Laurent Blagney' then 'Parc des Expositions'. The Aire is adj to the exhibition hall parking, signed.

Sanitation:

Parking:

10

Euro Relais Junior; €2

Supermarket 2 mins, Arras centre 7 mins. Historic tunnels under town hall worth a visit. Inspected 2012.

BAPAUME

75 H2 N50°06.079' E002°51.023' 62450

Directions: Rue Flandres Dunkerque 1940. From south enter town on D917. Turn left before church by memorial. The Service Point is on the right before the church and the parking is on the left, signed.

Sanitation:

Parking:

2; Roadside bays

Aire Services; Token (3/3)

Town with numerous commerce 2 mins. Inspected 2012.

NOEUX LES MINES

76 G2 N50°29.182' E002°40.208' 62290

Directions: Rue de l'Égalité. Turn off D937 onto D65 at roundabout with Esso garage, sp 'Dechetterie'. Turn left at traffic lights, sp 'Dechetterie'. Aire on right at recycling centre. Barriered when recycling not open.

Sanitation:

Parking:

None

Aire Services; Token (3/3); €4; Open Mar-Oct

Only use if desperate and in office hours. Parking allowed at Ruitz. Inspected 2012.

ST VENANT

77 G1 N50°37.543' E002°32.900' 62350

Directions: Off Rue du 8 Mai 1945, adj to canal. Turn off D916 to St Venant. Take 1st right off church square and follow road. Turn right at T junction and then follow road to left. Service Point by boat moorings.

Sanitation:

Parking:

2; Max 2hrs; On Service Point

Urba Flux

Unrestricted parking locally but no designated parking. Inspected 2012.

ARQUES

78 G1 N50°44.731' E002°18.276' 62510

Directions: Rue Michelet, off D210 near lake. Located behind Camping Beauséjour. Take D210 north out of town, sp 'Clairmarais' and 'Camping'. Follow sp 'Camping' through residential streets to campsite. Drive behind reception to parking.

Sanitation:

Parking:

30; €3/24hrs; Open Mar-Oct; Barriered when closed

Euro Relais Junior; Token (ER)

Pay at campsite reception No views of lake; English speaking vet in town. Inspected 2012.

LUMBRES

79 G1 N50°42.854' E002°06.614' 62380

Directions: Off N42, at Centre Commercial. Exit N42, sp 'Lumbres'. Turn left under road bridge and left again at roundabout, sp 'Centre Commercial'. The Service Point is accessed via the truck fuel pump and is at the fuel station kiosk.

Sanitation:

Parking:

None

Raclet; 1 unmetered elec point

Large E'Leclerc supermarket adj. Inspected 2012.

RICHEBOURG

80 H1 N50°34.826' E002°44.792' 62136

Directions: Rue de la Briqueterie. From D171 turn off onto D166, sp 'Richebourg-Centre' and signed. Follow D166 past church then turn right, sp 'Complexe Sportif' and signed. Follow road to left and Aire is outside Salle Omnisports on left, signed.

Sanitation:

Parking:

6; Max 48hrs

Aire Services; €2

Aire in rural location with excellent info board of local history. Convenience store 5 mins. Indian cemetery and memorial on D171/D947 roundabout. Inspected 2012.

WATTEN

81 F2 N50°49.880' E002°12.506' 59143

Directions: Rue Paul Mortier. Turn off D300 onto D207, sp 'Watten'. Turn left at end of road onto D213, sp 'Cassel' and 'Centre Ville'. Before bridge turn left, signed. Aire 150m on left, signed.

Sanitation:

Parking:

8

Aire Services; Token (3/3); €2

SP

Adj to canal with partial views. Town centre with local shops 2 mins. Inspected 2012.

COUCY LE CHÂTEAUE

T

82 H3 N49°31.199' E003°18.805' 02380

Directions: Chemin du Val Serain. Turn off D1 onto D934 at roundabout sp 'Coucy le Chateau'. Turn right onto D937 sp 'Jumencourt' follow road to right, signed, and turn right sp 'Stade' and signed. Aire on right in 50m. Village centre has 3.3m height, 2.5m width and 7.5ton weight restrictions.

Sanitation:

Parking:

5; €5/24hrs; Pay at machine; Pin code for toilet, elec, and SP

Urba Flux Tall; CEE 16amp elec; Service only €1/10 mins

SP

Aire located in quiet location with views of castle. Historic village with castle ruins 7 mins uphill. Convenience store 3 mins. Inspected 2012.

LAON

83 H3 N49°33.779' E003°37.786' 02000

Info/Photo: Brenda and Maurice Cope

Directions: Promenade de la Couloire. From the south of the city follow the D967 and sp 'Cite Medievale'. The parking is on the left adjacent to the road under the city wall on Promenade de la Citadelle.

Sanitation:

Parking:

6

None

SP

10 mins to cathedral and historic centre. Adj to road but quiet at night. Visited 2012.

BRUYERES ET MONTBERAULT

84 H3 N49°31.515' E003°39.640' 02860

Info/Photo: Brenda and Maurice Cope

Directions: Avenue de Verdun. From Laon follow the D4 into town and turn right on the D252 Avenue de Verdun sp 'Vorges'. The Parking area is on the left in 200m, signed.

Sanitation:

Parking:

4

None

SP

This small landscaped Aire has four asphalt bays. The village is 8km south-east of historic Laon, so easy to reach on public transport. Local commerce 4 mins. Visited 2012.

CHAVIGNON

85 H3 N49°28.753' E003°32.058' 02000

Info/Photo: Patricia Houghton

Directions: D23, 16 Rue Léon Paquin. Exit N2 Soissons/Laon onto D23, sp Chavignon stay on the D32 and follow signs to the museum sp 'Les Ateliers de L'Abeille'. The Aire is 200m from the N2 flyover. Enter through barrier.

Sanitation:

Parking:

5; €6/24hrs; Token

Custom

SP

Commercial Aire adj to a bee museum. Entry Token can be obtained from museum shop 0900-1200, 1400-1830 Mon, Wed, Thurs, Fri, Sat. Other Token outlets in village. Road noise from N2. Visited 2012.

Precigne

PAYS DE LOIRE

Le Poire sur Vie

LANDIVY
1 D4 N48°28.583' W001°01.622' 53190

Directions: Lotissement des Terriers. Exit the village on D122 to the east. Turn right, sp 'Aire de Camping Car', past the Gendarmerie onto Rue des Combattants. Follow signs to Stade des Terriers.

Sanitation:

Parking:

5

Custom; 1 unmetered elec point

Adj to sports facilities and surrounded by new housing development; No satellite dish impediment. Inspected 2010.

JUVIGNE
2 D5 N48°13.668' W001°02.239' 53380

Directions: D29. Adj to D29 to the south of the village at the bottom of the hill, signed.

Sanitation:

Parking:

10; Max 24hrs

Custom

Adj to village pond; Community facilities. Inspected 2010.

LA BACONNIERE
3 D5 N48°11.010' W000°53.496' 53240

Directions: D123. In car park at rear of the church.

Sanitation:

Parking:

4; Behind Mairie opp

Euro Relais Junior

Directly adj to church; Village with local commerce adj; Inspected 2010.

CHANGE
4 D5 N48°06.028' W000°47.150' 53810

Directions: Rue du Port. From Laval follow road around church and over river bridge. Then turn left at roundabout off D561, sp 'Plan d'Eau' and signed. Follow road to end, signed.

Sanitation:

Parking:

10

Raclet

Lakeside, near to canal towpath. Can be busy at weekends and bank holidays. Inspected 2010.

LAVAL
5 D5 N48°04.564' W000°46.273' 53000

Directions: Turn off N162 at the Changé roundabout onto D104, sp 'Laval Centre'. Follow sp 'Centre Ville' and the Aire is in the car park on the left after the traffic lights, signed.

Sanitation:

Parking:

3; 6m bays

Euro Relais Junior

Nice large town, 2 mins to centre. Car park not suitable for 6m+ motorhomes. 3 bays to rear of car park. Inspected 2010.

HAVE YOU VISITED AN AIRE? **GPS co-ordinates in this guide are protected by copyright law**

Take at least 5 digital photos showing
- Signs
- Service Point
- Parking
- Overview
- Amenities

Visit www.all-the-aires.co.uk/submissions.shtml to upload your updates and photos.

Sanitation:

Aire Details:

Submit updates
- Amendments
- New Aires
- Not changed

CHAILLAND

7 D5 N48°13.297' W000°51.945' 53420

Directions: D165. Exit D31 onto D165 following sp 'Chailland'. Drive through Chailland and the Aire is at the far end of town, adj to D165 outside the Cocci Market, signed.

Sanitation:

Parking:

10

Custom

Supermarket adj. Challand is a "small city of character" with an emphasis on small. Local commerce is 2 mins downhill. Inspected 2012.

GORRON

8 D4 N48°24.438' W000°48.583' 53120

Directions: Route de Brécé. From south turn into town at large roundabout junction of D5 and D107, sp 'Centre Ville'. From town follow sp 'Mayenne' and 'Complexe Sportif'. Signed from main road.

Sanitation:

Parking:

7

Custom; 2 unmetered elec points

Views over sports ground and river. 5 mins to town. Inspected 2010.

ST GEORGES BUTTAVENT

9 D4 N48°18.594' W000°41.680' 53100

Directions: N12. In car park of Vivéco mini market at the D5/N12 traffic light junction.

Sanitation:

Parking:

Small parking area; Night halt only

Euro Relais; Token; €2

Small mini market adj; On busy road junction. Inspected 2010.

ST JEAN SUR MAYENNE

10 D5 N48°07.670' W000°45.134' 53240

Directions: Rue Maurice Courcelle. Approach from east on D131. Cross river and turn left at roundabout onto D162, signed. Turn left, signed, and Aire on left, signed.

Sanitation:

Parking:

16; €6.20 + €0.80pp/night; Open Apr-Nov

Custom; Inc unmetered elec and showers

Former campsite turned Aire. Water adj but no view from parking. Nice green, open space with BBQ area adj to water. Voie Verte cycle/walk along river. Inspected 2012.

ST LOUP DE GAST — 11 — E4 — N48°23.229' W000°35.126' — 53300

Directions: Zone Artisanale. Follow D258 towards Montreuil-Poulay. Turn left, sp 'Chantrigny', past velo rail on village outskirts. Turn 1st left, sp 'Zone Artisanale'. Aire at end of road between light industrial buildings.

Sanitation:

Parking:

8; Hard standing and grass parking

Custom

Located on the edge of the village the Aire is in a small industrial estate but may feel isolated at night. Velo Rail, 2 mins, opens in summer. Village centre 4 mins. Inspected 2012.

MAYENNE — 12 — E4 — N48°17.976' W000°37.232' — 53100

Directions: Quai Carnot. Sp 'Euro Relais' in town centre. Situated beside river directly underneath road viaduct.

Sanitation:

Parking:

5; Max 48hrs

Euro Relais Junior; Token (ER)

River view from parking; Isolated spot on dead end road likely to be popular with kids. Other parking opportunities in town. Inspected 2010.

LASSAY LES CHATEAUX — 13 — E4 — N48°26.262' W000°29.890' — 53110

Directions: Approach from the west on D33 from Ambrieres-les-Vallées. At the 1st roundabout turn into the town, sp 'Château XV'. When the château is on the left, turn right into a narrow car park entrance, signed.

Sanitation:

Parking:

5

Euro Relais Junior; Token (ER); €2

Large château and gardens adj; Footpath to village centre and small park adj. Inspected 2010.

JAVRON LES CHAPELLES — 14 — E4 — N48°25.161' W000°20.187' — 53250

Directions: Place Georges Morin. Turn off N12, sp 'Les Chapelles', 'Salle Polyvalente' and signed, onto 3.5t weight restricted road. Follow sp 'Salle Polyvalente' to car park and the Service Point is on left adj to road.

Sanitation:

Parking:

6

Euro Relais Junior; Token; €2

Access to Service Point can be made difficult by parked cars. Plenty of unrestricted parking. Inspected 2010.

PRE EN PAIL — 15 — E4 — N48°27.847' W000°11.499' — 53140

Directions: N12, at Super U as exit town towards Alençon. Service Point by gas bottles.

Sanitation:

Parking:

Poss

Euro Relais Mini; Token (ER); €2

Supermarket adj; Village with commerce 500m uphill. Inspected 2010.

ST PIERRE DES NIDS | 16 | E4 | N48°24.134' W000°05.323' | 53370

Directions: D121. Exit village on D121 towards 'Alençon'. Aire adj to D121 at the roundabout by the Plan d'Eau, signed.

Sanitation:

Parking:

8

Euro Relais Junior

SP

By pond with picnic tables; Village with restaurants 600m uphill. Inspected 2010.

VILLAINES LA JUHEL/AVERTON | 17 | E4 | N48°20.846' W000°14.659' | 53700

Directions: Exit Villaines la Juhel on D121, sp 'Gesvres'. Follow D121 for 2km then turn right, sp 'Site des Perles'. Follow road and Aire is in the car park at the end.

Sanitation:

E

Parking:

10

Euro Relais Junior

SP

Carp fishing and leisure lake 50m, but no view due to trees. Walking and cycling routes, and BMX track. Will be isolated if alone. Inspected 2012.

MONTSURS | 18 | E5 | N48°08.112' W000°33.467' | 53150

Directions: D32. Turn off D24, main route through, onto D32, sp 'St Cenere'. Aire 200m on right and far end of car park, signed.

Sanitation:

Parking:

10; Parking behind Service Point

Custom

SP

Sports facilities adj. Town with local commerce 2 mins.

DEUX EVAILLES | 19 | E5 | N48°12.152' W000°31.190' | 53150

Directions: Off D129. Exit the village on D129 towards Jublains. The Aire is at the leisure lake to the north of Deux Evailles, sp 'Site de la Fenderie'.

Sanitation:

Parking:

10; Grass and Gravel

Raclet; Token (2/1)

SP

Particularly attractive fishing lake adj; No lake views from Aire. Significant Roman ruins nearby. Inspected 2012.

EVRON | 20 | E5 | N48°09.034' W000°24.794' | 53600

Directions: D20/Blvd du Maréchal Juin. Adj to D20 in lay-by outside municipal campsite. Follow sp 'Camping' in town.

Sanitation:

E

Parking:

None

Raclet; Token (2/1)

SP

Outside municipal campsite by leisure facilities. Inspected 2010.

ST PAUL LE GAULTIER

21 E4 N48°19.206' W000°06.474' 72130

Directions: D105. From D15 turn onto D105, sp 'Plan d'Eau' and signed. Aire outside small municipal campsite adj to fishing lake.

Sanitation:

Parking:

Banned 10pm-6am

Custom

Pleasant; Adj to small, inexpensive municipal campsite. Inspected 2010.

ST LEONARD DES BOIS

22 E5 N48°21.198' W000°04.848' 72130

Directions: D112. Adj to D112 in lay-by on left as exit village towards St Pierre des Nids. The village is narrow in places.

Sanitation:

Parking:

4

Custom

SP

Natural spring water point adj; Main road adj; Pretty village 2 mins. Inspected 2010.

FRESNAY SUR SARTHE

23 E5 N48°16.903' E000°01.794' 72130

Directions: Rue de la Gare, at the old train station. On D310 as enter town from Mamers turn left past Le Mutant shop onto Ave de la Gare, sp 'P Le Mutant' and signed. Aire on left, signed.

Sanitation:

Parking:

10

Custom

Nice town 5 mins with commerce store; Mini market adj; Circus school adj. Inspected 2010.

ST REMY DU VAL

24 E4 N48°20.912' E000°15.397' 72600

Directions: Car park of Maison de la Ruralité. Turn in village by side of square, sp 'Musée de la Ruralité' and signed. Aire adj to green building marked Maison de la Ruralité, signed.

Sanitation:

Parking:

6; 6m bays

Water only; In public WC

Rural museum open in summer, entrance €1.60. Small village with local commerce 2 mins. Inspected 2010.

MAMERS 1

25 E4 N48°21.324' E000°22.308' 72600

Directions: Rue de la Piscine. From D311/D3 roundabout follow sp 'Base de Loisirs', then 'Aire Camping Cars'. Aire next to campsite. Motorhome campsite fenced with security gate; access code from adj campsite or TO.

Sanitation:

Parking:

8; €5; Pay/access at campsite

Custom; 16amp elec point on each bay

SP

Tennis courts adj. Park and lake 2 mins. Inspected 2010.

MAMERS 2 | 26 | E4 | N48°21.060' E000°23.188' | 72600

Directions: D311. At the Super U fuel station, off the D311 roundabout. At Super U fuel station.

Sanitation:

Parking:

4; 6m bays

Raclet; Token (2/1); €2

Supermarket adj. Inspected 2010.

BALLON | 27 | E5 | N48°10.511' E000°14.294' | 72290

Directions: D6. Exit town centre on D6, sp 'St Mars'. Service Point on right opp Intermarché supermarket, signed.

Sanitation:

Parking:

2; 8m bays

Euro Relais Junior; Token (ER)

Service Point with limited parking opp supermarket. Local commerce 2 mins. Inspected 2012.

SILLE LE GUILLAUME | 28 | E5 | N48°10.901' W000°07.867' | 72140

Directions: Off D310, at train station. Follow sp 'Gare SNCF' from D310. Drive to right of train station, signed.

Sanitation:

Parking:

20

Raclet; Token (2/1)

Train station adj; Town 3 mins. Service Point taped up and marked 'closed 7/7/10'. Inspected 2010.

MONTBIZOT | 29 | E5 | N48°08.643' E000°11.013' | 72380

Directions: D47. Enter Montbizon on D47 from south. Turn right at village entrance opp stone cross. Aire is immediately on right, signed.

Sanitation:

Parking:

10

Euro Relais Junior; Token; €2

Parking on grass or concrete; Tokens from adj campsite or Mairie. Inspected 2010.

COULANS SUR GEE | 30 | E5 | N48°01.294' E000°00.911' | 72550

Directions: D357. From east turn off D357, sp 'Coulans sur Gée'. Aire is immediately on right by tennis courts.

Sanitation:

Parking:

6

Custom; Water and toilet waste in building

Old Aire; Much of the parking has been bollarded off and the electric points have been disconnected. Inspected 2010.

LE MANS

31 E5 N48°00.147' E000°11.357' 72000

Directions: Enter Le Mans from north on D300, then D147n through Coulaines, following sp 'Le Mans', then 'Centre Ville'. Once the road is alongside the river turn right across 2nd bridge, sp 'Palais de Congress'. Turn immediately left, sp 'Palais de Congress'. Follow this road along the river and the Aire is on left, signed.

Sanitation:

Parking:

7; Max 24hrs

Euro Relais Mini

Adj to river and small marina but views obstructed by shrubbery. Inspected 2010.

ARNAGE

32 E5 N47°55.825' E000°11.062' 72230

Directions: Rue du Port, off D147s. Turn off the D147s, main route, sp 'Complex Sportif'. Follow road to end and Aire is signed. Town is currently rearranging road layout.

Sanitation:

Parking:

2; 6m bays

Urba Flux; CC; No drive over drain

2 small bays overlooking river outside height barriered car park. Town 2 mins. Inspected 2010.

LA SUZE SUR SARTHE

33 E5 N47°53.333' E000°01.850' 72210

Directions: Off D289, parking along the river Sarthe. Signed by river bridge on D289. Some parking along river edge with 4 elec points, and other parking behind with 6 elec points.

Sanitation:

Parking:

20; €3/24hrs; Pay at machine

Euro Relais Maxi; 10 unmetered elec points but long cable needed

Village with local commerce 2 mins. Inspected 2010.

LAIGNE EN BELIN

34 E5 N47°52.695' E000°13.627' 72220

Directions: D139/Route de Laigné. Just off roundabout junction of D144 and D139 in car park in front of the church.

Sanitation:

Parking:

5

Custom

In heart of village. 10km from Le Mans race circuit. Local commerce. Inspected 2010.

MEZERAY

35 E5 N47°49.385' W000°00.885' 72270

Directions: D133. Exit village on D133, sp 'Cerans' and signed. Aire on left, signed.

Sanitation:

Parking:

20

Euro Relais Box; €2

Aire on outskirts of village in uninspiring car park. Always likely to have space. Inspected 2012.

ECOMMOY | 36 | E5 | N47°50.021' E000°16.776' | 72220

Directions: Rue de la Charité. Turn off D338 onto Rue de la Charité following sp 'Camping'. Aire outside campsite.

Sanitation:

Parking:

Roadside

Urba Flux; CC; €2

Campsite open May-Sept; Some roadside parking. Self service laundry at Super U. Inspected 2012.

ST MARS D'OUTILLE | 37 | E5 | N47°52.219' E000°19.991' | 72220

Directions: D32. Located in car park adj to D32 as you exit village towards Le Grand-Lucé, near La Poste.

Sanitation:

Parking:

5; Max 48hrs

Custom

Village 2 mins. WC used for toilet disposal. Inspected 2010.

ST CALAIS | 38 | F5 | N47°55.425' E000°44.657' | 72120

Directions: D357/Blvd du Docteur Gigon. From Le Mans follow D357 through town, turning left and then right. Aire in car park across from swimming pool, sp 'Piscine' through town and signed at car park.

Sanitation:

Parking:

10

Euro Relais Junior

By sports facilities; Basketball; Play park; Swimming pool adj. Town 2 mins through park. Inspected 2010.

MAYET | 39 | E5 | N47°45.672' E000°16.444' | 72360

Directions: Ave de la Liberté. As enter village from north on D30 turn right, signed. Turn right onto Avenue de la Liberté, sp 'Pontvallain'. Aire on right.

Sanitation:

Parking:

5

Euro Relais Junior; Token (ER)

Village 2 mins; Noisy church bells. Inspected 2010.

LUCHE PRINGE | 40 | E5 | N47°42.313' E000°04.184' | 72800

Info/Photo: John Watts

Directions: Rue des Prunus. Between D54 and D13. Exit town on D13 to west. Turn right, signed and Aire on left opp fire station, Sapeurs Pompiers, signed.

Sanitation:

Parking:

20

Aire Services; €2

Aire situated in a residential development 5 mins from town centre with local commerce. Visited 2012.

VAAS

41 E5 N47°40.025' E000°18.668' 72500

Directions: Rue du Port Liberge. Follow D305 through village and turn off onto 3.5t weight restricted road, sp 'Stade' and 'Camping'. Aire is opp campsite, signed.

Sanitation:

Parking:

10; Park at furthest point from campsite

Euro Relais Junior; 1 unmetered elec point, not working at time of inspection

SP

Parking adj to Espace Culturel and sports ground so the parking may occasionally be busy. Campsite open May-Sept. Inspected 2012.

LE LUDE

42 E5 N47°38.856' E000°09.207' 72800

Directions: D307. In car park adj to D307 main route, signed. Motorhomes are banned from narrow town centre, be careful when following GPS.

Sanitation:

Parking:

10

Euro Relais Junior; 1 unmetered elec point

SP

Impressive château and gardens in town; Adj to main truck route and truck parking. Inspected 2010.

CLEFS

43 E5 N47°37.471' W000°04.615' 49150

Directions: D938. Adj to D938, sp 'Aire de Repos' on bypass around Clefs, at roundabout.

Sanitation:

Parking:

5

Custom

SP

Lay-by adj to main road. Inspected 2010.

LA FLECHE

44 E5 N47°41.866' W000°04.732' 72200

Directions: D323. Enter from Durtal on D323. Aire in car park on right adj to river, opp Carrefour mini market and Hôtel le Relais du Loir, signed. Aire occupied by market Thursday morning.

Sanitation:

Parking:

10

Custom; Very basic tap and drain

SP

Parking adj to river overlooking château; Many restaurants. Inspected 2010.

HAVE YOU VISITED AN AIRE?

GPS co-ordinates in this guide are protected by copyright law

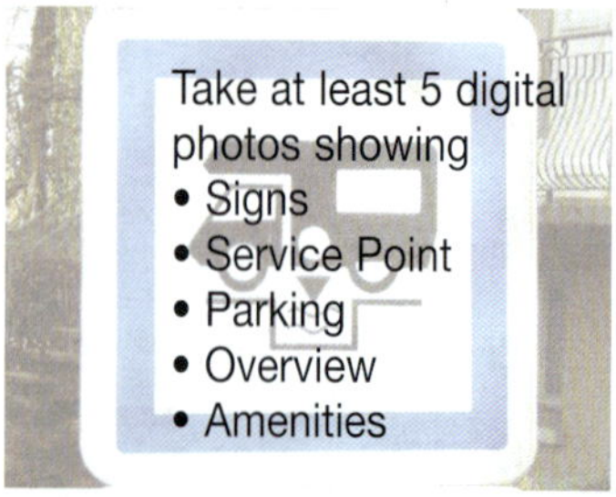
Take at least 5 digital photos showing
• Signs
• Service Point
• Parking
• Overview
• Amenities

Visit www.all-the-aires.co.uk/submissions.shtml to upload your updates and photos.

Sanitation:

Aire Details:

Submit updates

- Amendments
- New Aires
- Not changed

DURTAL

46 E5 N47°40.281' W000°14.435' 49430

Directions: D323, Place de la Poste. Adj to D323 as exit town from La Flèche in car park adj to La Poste, signed.

Sanitation:

Parking:

5

Raclet; €2

SP

Pretty town along Loire river with château. Sloping car park, but always likely to have space. Inspected 2010.

PRECIGNE

47 E5 N47°46.127' W000°19.614' 72300

Directions: Rue de la Piscine. Exit town on D24 towards Sable, sp 'Aire de Jeux'. At cemetery turn left onto D18bis, sp 'Pince' and 'Aire de Jeux'. Follow road straight on and over roundabout, then turn left just after swimming pool on right, signed.

Sanitation:

Parking:

8; Max 24hrs; Grass parking

Euro Relais Junior; Token (ER)

SP

Aire adj to campsite, part of which has been used to create Aire. Low trees may impede access. Sports facilities opp. Inspected 2012.

SABLE SUR SARTHE

48 E5 N47°49.891' W000°19.904' 72300

Directions: Allée du Québec, outside Camping de l'Hippodrome. From D309 turn left as enter town, sp 'Camping Municipal'. Follow sp 'Camping Municipal' to Service Point.

Sanitation:

Parking:

Poss when campsite closed

Flot Bleu Océane; €1

SP

Service Point only. Campsite open Apr-Sept. See 50. Inspected 2010.

GREZ EN BOUERE

49 E5 N47°52.371' W000°31.373' 53290

Directions: Rue de la Mairie. Turn off D28, main road in village, sp 'Mairie' and signed. Service Point behind Mairie.

Sanitation:

Parking:

50

Euro Relais Junior

SP

Large village car park. Village 2 mins. Inspected 2010.

BOUERE

50 E5 N47°51.811' W000°28.582' 53290

Directions: Rue des Sencies. Turn off D28 to Bouère, signed. Go through village on D14 heading south towards St Denis d'Anjou. Aire is past church on left, at bottom of small hill.

Sanitation:

Parking:

11

Euro Relais; €2

SP

Park and lake behind Aire. Village with local commerce and lovely church. Inspected 2010.

MESLAY DU MAINE

51 E5 N47°56.958' W000°33.321' 53170

Directions: Rue de la Gare. Enter town on D152 from north, sp 'Salle des Sports'. Turn left at roundabout after junction with D21 and Aire in 150m, in car park, signed.

Sanitation:

Parking:

5

Custom

In small car park, may be blocked by parked cars. Inspected 2010.

VAIGES

52 E5 N48°02.512' W000°28.981' 53480

Directions: D57/Rue Robert Gletron. Exit village on D57 towards Laval. The Aire is on left in picnic area before roundabout. Go around roundabout to access.

Sanitation:

Parking:

5

Euro Relais Junior; Token (2/1)

Views over village pond; Village 3 mins; Sink. Inspected 2010.

ST DENIS DU MAINE

53 E5 N47°57.942' W000°31.837' 53170

Directions: At lake, off D152. Follow sp 'Base de Loisirs La Chesnaie'. The Service Point is outside the campsite and parking is 300m further around the lake: N47°57.855' W000°32.068'.

Sanitation:

Parking:

10; Max 1 night; Grass parking

Custom

Large pleasant leisure lake; Swimming beach; Fishing permits available. Inspected 2010.

VILLIERS CHARLEMAGNE

54 D5 N47°55.234' W000°40.919' 53170

Directions: Rue des Sports. Follow sp 'Village Vacances et Pêche'. At lake outside holiday village.

Sanitation:

Parking:

10; Free 1st night, then €7.70/night

Euro Relais Junior; 3 unmetered elec points

On edge of carp and coarse fishing lake – tickets available €8.50/day for 3 lines. No view of lake from Aire. Inspected 2010.

COSSE LE VIVIEN

55 D5 N47°56.625' W000°54.768' 53230

Directions: D771. Just off D771 one-way system, signed on left. Parking outside Salle des Fêtes on right.

Sanitation:

Parking:

Poss

Removed; See below

Service Point is still signed but has been removed. It will be replaced in 2013 in a new location, poss outside Salle des Fêtes. Please update Vicarious Books once it has been relocated. Inspected 2012.

LE LION D'ANGERS 1 | 56 | D5 | N47°37.839' W000°42.734' | 49220

Directions: Route Château Gontier. Exit town towards Laval. Cross river bridge and turn 1st left. Service Point outside campsite, signed.

Sanitation:

Parking:

None

Custom; Tap in bushes to left of drain when facing road.

Service Point only. Inspected 2012.

LE LION D'ANGERS 2 | 57 | D5 | N47°36.820' W000°42.452' | 49220

Directions: D775. Turn off D775 to south of town into the Super U supermarket. Service Point at the fuel station of the Super U.

Sanitation:

Parking:

Poss

Aire Services; €2

Supermarket adj. Inspected 2012.

CHATEAU GONTIER | 58 | D5 | N47°49.485' W000°42.102' | 53200

Directions: Quai du Docteur Lefevre. Turn off N162 at roundabout near river onto D22, sp 'Office de Tourisme' and 'Centre Hospitalier'. At roundabout turn right, sp 'Centre Hospitalier' and cross river bridge. Turn right at roundabout immediately after crossing bridge, sp 'Centre Hospitalier'. Parking at end of road on right.

Sanitation:

Parking:

40; 5pm-10am only

At campsite: N47°50.350' W000°42.084'

Walk along river into town 5 mins. Park opp side 10-30 Aug during festival. Inspected 2012.

DAON | 59 | D5 | N47°45.024' W000°38.477' | 53200

Directions: Rue Creuse. Turn off D22 onto D213, sp 'Menil' and signed. Turn immediately right onto C4, 'Formusson' and signed. Turn 1st left into Rue Creuse and Aire 100m on right, signed.

Sanitation:

Parking:

20

Custom

Near lake but no views. Voie Verte cycle/walking route to Château-Gontier. Local commerce 2 mins. Inspected 2012.

CHENILLE CHANGE | 60 | E5 | N47°41.960' W000°40.023' | 49220

Directions: D78. Signed off D78 main road, by cemetery.

Sanitation:

Parking:

10; €2.50 inc token

Custom; Token; €2.50

On terrace overlooking campsite by river; Small pleasant village 1 min; Bus stop adj; Token from adj cafe. Inspected 2010.

CHATEAUNEUF SUR SARTHE — 61 — E5 — N47°40.657' W000°29.227' — 49330

Directions: D89. By bridge as enter town on D89 from south, signed. Contact Mairie to notify of your arrival.

Sanitation:

Parking:

15; Bays and riverside parking

Custom; In disrepair

SP

Riverside parking; Facilities falling into disrepair. Inspected 2010.

TIERCE — 62 — E5 — N47°36.894' W000°27.462' — 49125

Directions: D74/Route de Seiches Loir. Adj to D74 as enter village from Seiches-sur-le-Loir, immediately on right, signed. Near sports ground.

Sanitation:

Parking:

None

Custom

SP

Service Point only. Inspected 2010.

VILLEVEQUE * — 63 — E5 — N47°33.725' W000°25.313' — 49140

Directions: Rue du Port. In parking area adj to river by D113 road bridge to Soucelles. Follow sp 'Le Port' in town.

Sanitation:

Parking:

8

Custom; Token (2/1); €1

SP

River adj; Village with restaurant adj; Swimming beach; Car park does flood, closed if flooded. Inspected 2010.

BRIOLLAY — 64 — E5 — N47°34.051' W000°30.434' — 49125

Directions: Just off Grande Rue. From D52 follow sp 'Camping'. Take 1st turning on right as enter village from north. Turn right again, then left. Signed.

Sanitation:

Parking:

10

Aire Services; Token (3/3)

SP

Prone to flooding. Village 2 mins. Service Point and parking away from river. Inspected 2010.

FENEU — 65 — E5 — N47°34.229' W000°35.617' — 49460

Directions: Service Point is on D768, opp church. Overnight parking at Port Albert in riverside car park. Follow sp 'Port Albert' towards Grez-Neuville: N47°33.968' W000°36.583'.

Sanitation:

Parking:

10

Custom; Difficult

SP

Lovely riverside parking. Service Point is difficult to use. Inspected 2010.

MONTREUIL JUIGNE

66 D5 N47°32.500' W000°36.912' 49460

Directions: D103. Turn off D768 by river bridge, sp 'La Meignanne'. Aire on right in car park.

Sanitation:

Parking:

8

Flot Bleu Océane

No river views; Village 2 mins. 2 large motorhome/truck bays in car park. Inspected 2010.

GREZ NEUVILLE

67 D5 N47°36.072' W000°41.105' 49220

Directions: Off D291/Rue du Port. On outskirts of village by river bridge, sp 'Bibliothèque' (library) and signed. Parking between trees, signed.

Sanitation:

Parking:

8; Grass parking

Custom; Water and toilet disposal

View of river. Grassy area - campsite style layout. Village 2 mins. Inspected 2010.

ANGERS

68 D6 N47°27.972' W000°33.944' 49000

Directions: Blvd Olivier Couffon. 200m from castle along road parallel to D323. Due to one way system must drive around block to get to entrance of Aire; virtually impossible to find without GPS.

Sanitation:

Parking:

None

Euro Relais Junior

Service Point only. Inspected 2010.

STE GEMMES SUR LOIRE

69 D6 N47°25.415' W000°33.092' 49130

Directions: Rue de l'Authion. In Ste Gemmes sur Loire follow sp 'La Loire L'Authion' and 'Camping'. The Aire is adj to the park before the river.

Sanitation:

Parking:

None

Flot Bleu Fontaine; No drive over drain

All parking is height barriered. Inspected 2010.

LE FRESNE SUR LOIRE

70 D6 N47°23.910' W000°56.024' 49123

Directions: Rue de la Bastille. Turn off D723 onto D22, sp 'Le Fresne sur Loire' and 'Camping'. Follow D22 to right before river, sp 'Camping'. Service Point outside Camping de Bastille.

Sanitation:

Parking:

None

Custom

Service Point only; Difficult access. All local parking bans motorhomes and roads very narrow. There is no reason to come here. Inspected 2010.

CHAMPTOCE SUR LOIRE | 71 | D6 | N47°24.687' W000°52.164' | 49123

Directions: Rue de la Hutte. Turn off D723 alongside the church, sp 'Complexe Sportif'. Then turn right at church, sp 'Complexe Sportif'. Follow road to Aire at end.

Sanitation:

Parking:

10

Custom

Adj to sports facilities; Always likely to have space. Village 2 mins. Inspected 2010.

ST GEORGES SUR LOIRE | 72 | D6 | N47°24.372' W000°45.767' | 49170

Directions: Rue de la Villette. Enter town on D961 from south. Turn left past pond, sp 'Aire de Stationnement'. Turn right at mini roundabout, signed. Aire on right in 150m, signed.

Sanitation:

Parking:

10

Custom

Town 3 mins. Pond with picnic tables and green space 2 mins. Inspected 2010.

CHALONNES SUR LOIRE | 73 | E6 | N47°20.965' W000°44.879' | 49290

Directions: D751. Exit the town on D751 towards Rochefort sur Loire. Turn right at the far side of the lake, sp 'La Gare'. The Aire is in 100m. The Service Point is in the 3.5t weight restricted car park above the lake, whilst parking is by the lake down a steep gravel slope.

Sanitation:

Parking:

5

Custom

Restful Aire alongside lake in park. Inspected 2010.

LA POSSONNIERE | 74 | D6 | N47°22.316' W000°41.091' | 49170

Directions: Boulevard du Port. Service Point outside Camping Municipal du Port. From D111, main route, turn towards river, signed. Pass under 3.3m railway bridge and Service Point is on right.

Sanitation:

Parking:

10; €7/night Jul-Aug; Elec €2

Custom; Outside campsite

Campsite. Village 2 mins; River adj. Inspected 2010.

ST AUBIN DE LUIGNE | 75 | D6 | N47°19.679' W000°40.246' | 49190

Directions: D125. From village centre take D125, sp 'Mairie' and 'Camping'. In 100m turn left, sp 'Camping' and signed. Service Point in far right corner, signed.

Sanitation:

Parking:

Poss; Oct-April

Custom

Must stay in adj campsite when open, May-Sept. Village is set in a beautiful vine covered valley. Local commerce 1 min. Inspected 2012.

CHARCE ST ELLIER SUR AUBANCE

76 E6 N47°21.360' W000°24.674' 49320

Directions: Place de l'Eglise. Just off D423, opp church in village. Service Point is outside the toilets.

Sanitation: E WC F

Parking: P F

5

Custom

SP

Pretty village; Very pleasant spot surrounded by green space. Inspected 2010.

LA DAGUENIERE

77 E6 N47°25.327' W000°26.338' 49800

Directions: Rue du Stade, adj to sports facilities. From D952 follow signs. Turn by church and follow road past cemetery to sports facilities. See **79** for other parking.

Sanitation: E WC F

Parking: P F

10

Custom

SP

At sports ground; Large asphalt parking area; Village commerce 2 mins. Inspected 2010.

CHAVAGNES

78 E6 N47°16.207' W000°27.256' 49380

Directions: Rue de l'Eglise. Turn off in village towards church, sp 'Mairie'. Aire at base of church, signed.

Sanitation: E WC F

Parking: P F

5; Behind church

Custom

SP

In village centre. Picnic area and limited sports facilities adj. Ideal stop if you like to park alone. Inspected 2012.

PORT MAYLARD LA DAGUENIERE

79 E6 N47°25.071' W000°26.257' 49800

Directions: Turn off D952 towards river almost opp church, sp 'Port Maylard'. Small sign.

Sanitation: E WC F

Parking: P F

10; Grass parking

None; See **77**

SP

River views; Boating; Swimming; Fishing; BBQ point. Inspected 2010.

ST SATURNIN SUR LOIRE

80 E6 N47°23.557' W000°25.965' 49320

Directions: D751/Route de Saumur, at the Aire de Repos. Adj to D751 in village behind bus stop.

Sanitation: E WC F

Parking: P F

2

Custom

SP

Parking may extend into green space in summer. Inspected 2010.

BLAISON GOHIER | 81 | E6 | N47°23.951' W000°22.504' | 49320

Directions: D132/Rue Thibault de Blaison. Adj to D132, main route through narrow village.

Sanitation:

Parking:

10

Euro Relais Mini

Small village 2 mins; Park adj. Inspected 2010.

BOUCHEMAINE | 82 | D6 | N47°25.127' W000°36.696' | 49080

Directions: D111/Rue Chevrière. At village turn at roundabout by river bridge, sp 'La Possonnière' and 'Camping'. Aire 100m on left, visible from river bridge.

Sanitation:

Parking:

35; €8/night May-Sept; CC

Custom; €2.55 inc elec

Commercial Aire; Free outside peak season; Views across river Loire; Pleasant; Bus stop adj. Laundry and showers in season. Inspected 2010.

ST REMY LA VARENNE | 83 | E6 | N47°23.891' W000°18.964' | 49250

Directions: Off D132, behind the church. Between the church and the sports field, signed.

Sanitation:

Parking:

5

Euro Relais Mini

Sports field adj; Walk to river Loire; Village adj. Inspected 2010.

MAZE | 84 | E6 | N47°27.045' W000°16.938' | 49630

Directions: Off D55. From D347 turn onto D55 at roundabout towards St Mathurin sur Loire. Turn right off D55 in 600m, sp 'Aire de la Loire'. Service Point outside small, well kept municipal campsite. Parking 75m past campsite.

Sanitation:

Parking:

4

Custom; Outside campsite

Pleasant area with river views; Fishing with disabled fishing swim. Inspected 2010.

LE VIEIL BAUGE | 85 | E6 | N47°31.879' W000°07.171' | 49150

Directions: Corner of Impasse de la Fontaine and Rue de la Croix De Mission, off D61. From Baugé enter Le Vieil-Baugé and turn left past the church, sp 'P 50m'. Follow road past 3.5t weight restricted car park to Service Point. There is further unrestricted parking past the Service Point, opp pond.

Sanitation:

Parking:

10

Custom; Water inside toilet

Pretty village famous for the crooked church spire 2 mins. Pond adj. Inspected 2010.

CHENEHUTTE LES TUFFEAUX 86 E6 N47°18.471' W000°09.153' 49350

Directions: D751/Rue des Bateliers. Aire adj to main road, signed. Do not park outside of marked bays.

Sanitation: E WC F

Parking: P F

4

Removed

SP

Views over Loire river. Pleasant drive on D751. Inspected 2010.

BAUGE 1 87 E5/6 N47°32.352' W000°05.781' 49150

Directions: Chemin du Pont des Fées. On D766 towards Noyant turn left at roundabout onto Chemin du Pont des Fées and Aire outside municipal campsite. Well signed and sp 'Camping' from all directions in town. Do not go through middle of town.

Sanitation: E WC F

Parking: P F

10; Max 48hrs

Urba Flux; CC; €3

SP

Marked bays; Campsite adj; No twin axles; Interesting town. Inspected 2010.

BAUGE 2 88 E5/6 N47°32.743' W000°06.611' 49150

Directions: D766. Located north of town just off the D938/D766 roundabout in the fuel station of the Super U supermarket. Service Point behind car wash.

Sanitation: E WC F

Parking: P F

Poss

Aire Services; €2

SP

Supermarket adj. Inspected 2012.

LE GUEDENIAU 89 E6 N47°29.630' W000°02.687' 49150

Directions: D58. Just off D58 at the Plan d'Eau. To the south of the village down small lane, signed.

Sanitation: E WC F

Parking: P F

10

Custom

SP

Pond with green space and picnic tables adj. Village with bar 2 mins. Inspected 2010.

MOULIHERNE 90 E6 N47°27.934' E000°00.877' 49390

Directions: D79. Exit the village on D79, sp 'Longué-Jumelles'. The Aire is in the car park on the right as exit village. Village centre is narrow in places.

Sanitation: E WC F

Parking: P F

10

Raclet

SP

Restaurants adj; Village centre 1 min. Inspected 2010.

LONGUE JUMELLES 1

91 E6 N47°22.834' W000°06.893' 49160

Directions: Blvd Victor Hugo. Follow the very clear signs from D347 through town. Service Point to right. Parking to left: N47°22.857' W000°06.746'.

Sanitation:

Parking:

7

Custom

SP

Pleasant park with access to pretty town adj. Inspected 2010.

LONGUE JUMELLES 2

92 E6 N47°22.314' W000°05.881' 49160

Directions: At Super U adj to D347, at car wash. Off roundabout junction of D347 and D79.

Sanitation:

Parking:

None; See **91**

Euro Relais Mini; Token (2/1); No drive over drain

SP

Parking has 3m height barriers. See **91** for parking in town. Inspected 2010.

ST CLEMENT DES LEVEES

93 E6 N47°19.860' W000°10.813' 49350

Directions: Follow D952 towards Saumur and turn left after church, signed. Turn right in 200m, signed. Service Point is on left, signed.

Sanitation:

Parking:

5

Euro Relais Mini; Token (2/1)

SP

Service Point and parking in unkempt industrial/agricultural area. Inspected 2010.

TURQUANT

94 E6 N47°13.430' E000°01.754' 49730

Directions: Rue des Ducs d'Anjou. Turn off D947 into village. Take the 1st turning on right before entering village, opp stone wall with featured turret.

Sanitation:

Parking:

5

Custom; Token; €2

SP

Basketball; Table tennis; BBQ; Pretty troglodyte village in wine region. Inspected 2010.

CUNAULT

95 E6 N47°19.610' W000°11.679' 49350

Directions: D751. Adj to D751 between Tréves-Cunault and Cunault. Steep entrance and access road.

Sanitation:

Parking:

30; Grass parking

Euro Relais Maxi; CC; 4 elec points; €3/100L water or 6hrs elec

SP

Adj to river Loire but views of flood plain gravel. Looks like former campsite. Inspected 2010.

RABLAY SUR LAYON — 96 — E6 — N47°17.865' W000°34.656' — 49750

Directions: D54. Approach Rablay-sur-Layon on D54 from Beaulieu-sur-Layon. Turn right immediately after crossing river bridge, signed. Service Point immediately on left.

Sanitation:

Parking:

10; Grass parking

Custom

Riverside park adj but no river view from parking. This is a pleasant place to spend a few quiet days at what appears to be a former Aire Naturelle campsite. Inspected 2012.

GENNES — 97 — E6 — N47°20.511' W000°13.900' — 49350

Directions: D751/Ave des Cadets de Saumur. Turn off D751 in village, sp 'Camping'. Service Point to right by toilets.

Sanitation:

Parking:

2

Custom

Very unlevel; Unrestricted parking; Campsite adj. 86 has better parking. Inspected 2010.

SAUMUR — 98 — E6 — N47°14.476' W000°01.366' — 49400

Photo: Colin Salter

Directions: D947. Off D949 between Saumur and Parnay, signed.

Sanitation:

Parking:

50; Apr-Nov

Urba Flux

Former campsite close to river Loire. 20 mins cycle to Saumur along riverside. Inspected 2010.

VILLEBERNIER — 99 — E6 — N47°15.182' W000°02.167' — 49400

Directions: D952. Approach Villebernier from Saumur on D952. At village entrance turn right towards river, signed. Follow road to river edge and Aire is on right, signed.

Sanitation:

Parking:

20; €3/night plus tax; Open April-Oct; Grass parking

Custom; Token

Adj to river Loire, but no view. Former municipal campsite trying to appeal exclusively to motorhomes, but management appears a little confused. Inspected 2012.

PARNAY — 100 — E6 — N47°13.882' E000°00.665' — 49730

Directions: D947. Adj to D947 in Parnay, next to the river. New road layout makes entrance difficult. As better Aires have been developed on this road this Aire will probably close.

Sanitation:

Parking:

5

Euro Relais Junior; Token

On main road. Village with restaurant adj. Evidence of troglodyte caves. 94 is a better night stop, 2 mins drive. Inspected 2010.

FONTEVRAUD L'ABBAYE

101 E6 N47°11.065' E000°02.963' 49590

Directions: Approach on D947 from Montsoreau. Turn left at the 1st roundabout, signed. Turn right at the 2nd roundabout, signed. The Aire is in P1 which is the 1st car park on the left.

Sanitation:

Parking:

3

Custom

SP

Very sloping small car park; Acceptable if visiting abbey and tourist village, 5 mins. Inspected 2010.

LE COUDRAY MACOUARD

102 E6 N47°11.288' W000°07.053' 49260

Directions: D163/Route de Bron. Turn off D347 into village. Exit village at roundabout on Rte de Bron. Aire on left, signed.

Sanitation:

Parking:

10

Custom

SP

Peaceful oak glade with red squirrels. Interesting weather vane shop in village, 2 mins. Inspected 2010.

MONTREUIL BELLAY

103 E6 N47°07.956' W000°09.483' 49260

Directions: From D347/D938/D360 roundabout take D360, sp 'Montreuil-Bellay' and 'Les Nobis'. Turn left off D360, sp 'Les Nobis' and 'Auberge des Isles'. Follow this road and the Aire is on the left past the campsite. Aproaching from any other way involves two narrow, impassable arches.

Sanitation:

Parking:

Restricted; 7pm-10am 15 Jun-15 Sept

Urba Flux; Token

SP

River location with view of town castle. 2 mins to historic town. C15 ramparts to wander round. Inspected 2010.

LE PUY NOTRE DAME

104 E6 N47°07.434' W000°13.935' 49260

Directions: Rue du Parc. From Montreuil-Bellay take D77 to Le Puy-Notre-Dame. On entering the village turn left onto D178, signed. Take the next right, signed. Service Point opp cemetery. Do not drive through town, very narrow!

Sanitation:

Parking:

3

Custom

SP

Church and town centre 2 mins. Plenty of wine tasting opportunities; Possibility to discover troglodyte caves. Inspected 2010.

CONCOURSON SUR LAYON

105 E6 N47°10.439' W000°20.589' 49700

Directions: D960. Located on D960 at picnic area, near exit towards Vihiers. Parking on river edge for small motorhomes. Asphalt parking on roadside for large motorhomes.

Sanitation:

Parking:

10

Urba Flux; Token; €2; Toilet waste disposal in WC

SP

River adj; Table tennis; Village 2 mins; Inspected 2010.

SAULGE L'HOPITAL

106 E6 N47°17.915' W000°23.011' 49320

Directions: D761. Exit off D761 on new bypass following sp 'Saulge l'Hopital'. In the village turn off the main route through, sp 'Salle de la Perrine' and signed. The Service Point is to the rear of the 7.5t weight restricted parking area.

Sanitation:

Parking:

10

Custom

Green space adj; Village 2 mins. Inspected 2010.

AUBIGNE SUR LAYON

107 E6 N47°12.698' W000°27.830' 49540

Directions: Rue du 19 Mars 1962. Turn off D748 onto D84, sp 'Valanjou' and 'Chemille'. Take the next right and the Aire is in the village on the right, signed.

Sanitation:

Parking:

5

Custom

Worth a wander- lots of architecture to see with info panels in English. Wine tasting. Inspected 2010.

MARTIGNE BRIAND

108 E6 N47°14.129' W000°25.740' 49540

Directions: Jardin des Vieux Pressoirs, off D748. On exiting village towards Angers, Aire located on left at junction of D748 and D70. Signed through town.

Sanitation:

Parking:

5

Custom

2 mins to town; Adj to main road. Abbey in town. Market on Saturday. Wine caves and vines 2 mins. Inspected 2010.

BRISSAC QUINCE 1

109 E6 N47°21.289' W000°26.770' 49320

Directions: Rue des Jardins. Turn by stone cross opp large château, signed. Aire 100m on right in far car park. Steep junction at exit. Don't confuse for other Rue des Jardins located on northeastern edge of village.

Sanitation:

Parking:

10; €4/24hrs; 7m bays; Custodian will call

Custom

Impressive château and gardens; Town 2 mins uphill with many restaurants and tourist facilities; River walk adj. Inspected 2010.

BRISSAC QUINCE 2

110 E6 N47°21.663' W000°26.104' 49320

Directions: From château follow D55 through town, sp 'Camping de l'Etang'. Turn right and follow road to left. Follow D55 for 1km and turn right, sp 'Camping de l'Etang'. Aire on left in 300m, signed. Pay at campsite reception.

Sanitation:

Parking:

6; 15/5-15/8 €13.50; €8 inc elec rest of year; Max 48hrs

Custom

Commercial Aire. Use of facilities of surrounding campsite in season. Inspected 2010.

ROCHEFORT SUR LOIRE — 111 — D6 — N47°21.648' W000°39.343' — 49190

Directions: D106. Adj to D106 as cross river towards Béhuard, sp 'Aire de Repos'. Service Point behind building on left, access to grass parking past Service Point.

Sanitation:

Parking:

10; Grass parking

Aire Services; 1 unmetered elec point; No drive over drain

Village 2 mins across bridge. River adj, no views; Inspected 2010.

CHANZEAUX — 112 — D6 — N47°15.333' W000°38.307' — 49750

Directions: D121/Rue du Bel Air. Exit village following sp 'Valanjou' and 'Aire du Poizeaux'. Aire adj to D121, signed.

Sanitation:

Parking:

10

Raclet; Token (2/1)

Overlooking countryside and fishing ponds; Pleasant; Ideal for fishermen, €5/day; BBQ point. Inspected 2010.

VALANJOU ★ — 113 — D6 — N47°12.996' W000°36.199' — 49670

Directions: D84. Signed off D84 on west side of village as exit towards Chemillé, sp 'Camping Cars' and 'Pique-nique'. Aire has narrow entrance.

Sanitation:

Parking:

5

Custom; 1 unmetered Cont elec socket

River views; River walk to village with ruined abbey 2 mins; Exercise trail through park; Lovely spot. Inspected 2010.

VIHIERS — 114 — E6 — N47°08.605' W000°32.145' — 49310

Directions: Rue du Champ de Foire des Champs. Follow sp 'Centre Ville' through town and Aire located off the main town square behind the large church. Signed on entrance to village.

Sanitation:

Parking:

5

Custom

Adj to large pleasant town with nice town square lined with commerce 2 mins. Inspected 2010.

LA POITEVINIERE — 115 — D6 — N47°13.650' W000°53.750' — 49510

Directions: D15. Just off D15, sp 'Aire de Fontaine'. To the right of the church at the Plan d'Eau.

Sanitation:

Parking:

5

Raclet; Token (2/1); 2 unmetered elec points

Quiet spot adj to village pond. Local commerce 1 min. Free token from local shops. Inspected 2010.

HAVE YOU VISITED AN AIRE? **GPS co-ordinates in this guide are protected by copyright law**

Take at least 5 digital photos showing
- Signs
- Service Point
- Parking
- Overview
- Amenities

Visit www.all-the-aires.co.uk/submissions.shtml to upload your updates and photos.

Sanitation:

Aire Details:

Submit updates
- Amendments
- New Aires
- Not changed

ANCENIS — 117 — D6 — N47°22.023' W001°10.446' — 44150

Directions: D14. Turn off D723, sp 'Lire'. Adj to river on Route to Liré. Aire on opp side to river by roundabout Barriere St Pierre, signed on right.

Sanitation:

Parking:

2; Max 24hrs; 6m bays

Urba Flux; Token; €1

Can see river Loire across road. Town centre 5 mins. Inspected 2010.

LIRE — 118 — D6 — N47°20.470' W001°10.043' — 49530

Directions: Rue de la Turmelière. Turn off D751 at traffic lights, sp 'Centre Ville' and signed. Follow road up hill and turn right at top opp Cocci Mini Market, signed, onto road to La Turmelière. Aire on right, signed.

Sanitation:

Parking:

6

Custom; 2 unmetered elec points

Mini supermarket and local commerce opp. Inspected 2010.

CHAMPTOCEAUX — 119 — D6 — N47°20.284' W001°15.925' — 49270

Directions: Place de Niederheimbach, behind church. Access down one way street off D751 from Liré, signed. Turn into church and follow car park around.

Sanitation:

Parking:

5; Max 48hrs

Custom; €3

Pay at TO; Gardens; Local commerce; Swimming pool adj. Inspected 2010.

LE CELLIER — 120 — D6 — N47°19.186' W001°20.884' — 44850

Directions: Rue de Bel-Air, behind the church to the right in the village, sp 'Parc de la Mothe' and signed on tiny sign.

Sanitation:

Parking:

5

Custom

Water tap hidden behind post. There is no reason to come here as both parking and Service Point are inadequate. Inspected 2010.

LA PIERRE PERCEE

121 D6 N47°17.068' W001°22.837' 44450

Directions: D751, adj to road in riverside parking area, sp 'Le Port Miniature'.

Sanitation:

Parking:

7

None

Parking area overlooking Loire river by small marina. Very pleasant. Inspected 2010.

LA BOISSIERE DU DORE

122 D6 N47°13.882' W001°13.142' 44430

Directions: Adj to D763, sp 'Aire de Camping Car' as exit towards Vallet.

Sanitation:

Parking:

2; Max 24hrs

Urba Flux; Token; €1

Very sloping parking area. Small grassy park adj. Close to D763. Fine as night halt. Inspected 2010.

GESTE

123 D6 N47°10.963' W001°06.658' 49600

Directions: Rue des Lilas. From church take D223, sp 'Montrevault'. At roundabout turn left into car park, signed. Aire at far end of car park.

Sanitation:

Parking:

4

Custom

Small town commerce 2 mins. There is a pleasant lunch spot at a windmill on D223 towards Tilliers: N47°09.156' W001°09.743'. Inspected 2012.

ST MACAIRE EN MAUGES

124 D6 N47°06.867' W000°59.439' 49450

Directions: D91/Avenue de l'Europe. By the fuel station of the Super U to the south of the town towards St André de la Marche.

Sanitation:

Parking:

Poss; 2

Aire Services

Supermarket adj; Vet adj. Inspected 2010.

LA SEGUINIERE

125 D6 N47°03.591' W000°59.439' 49280

Directions: D753/Ave de Nantes. Adj to D753 at picnic area in village. Signed.

Sanitation:

Parking:

5

Raclet; €2

Adj to busy main road; Village adj; Green space and picnic tables to rear. Inspected 2010.

MORTAGNE SUR SEVRE

126 D6 N46°59.644' W000°56.668' 85290

Directions: Ave de la Gare. From Cholet on D160 take 1st exit to Mortagne-sur-Sèvre. Follow road to village and turn left onto Avenue de la Gare, signed. Service Point in 200m, adj to TO, signed.

Sanitation:

Parking:

10

Custom

Parking on corner as turn into Ave de la Gare; TO adj; Town 5 mins. Inspected 2010.

CLISSON

127 D6 N47°05.747' W001°16.944' 44190

Directions: D763. Approach town from north on D763. Turn right at the roundabout after LIDL and McDonalds. Service Point on left outside Camping du Moulin.

Sanitation:

E

Parking:

Poss, when campsite closed

SOS; 1 unmetered CEE elec point

Service Point only, but it would be possible to park overnight when the campsite is closed from mid-Oct to mid-April. Inspected 2012.

MOUZILLON

128 D6 N47°08.380' W001°16.884' 44330

Directions: D763, at rear of church. Adj to D763 on south edge of village in car park which backs onto the church, signed.

Sanitation:

WC

Parking:

5; Max 24hrs

Urba Flux; Token

Large car park with truck parking; Church bells quiet at night; Wine producing village adj. Inspected 2012.

LE PALLET

129 D6 N47°08.105' W001°19.819' 44330

Directions: D149. Adj to D149 on left as enter village from Clisson, sp 'Musée du Vignoble' and signed. Entrance marked by 2 barrels.

Sanitation:

Parking:

5

Urba Flux; Token

At wine museum with disabled access, entrance €4.50. Open Jun-Sept 10am-6pm; Apr-Nov 2-6pm; Closed Sat. www.vignoble-nantais.eu. Inspected 2010.

BOUSSAY

130 D6 N47°02.539' W001°11.190' 44190

Directions: Allée de la Vergne. From D149 turn into Boussay on D60. Follow road and turn left between Hôtel de Ville and pharmacy. Service Point in corner of car park.

Sanitation:

E

Parking:

5

Raclet; Token (2/1)

SP

Village centre with local commerce 2 mins. Inspected 2010.

TREIZE SEPTIERS 131 D6 N46°59.057' W001°13.487' 85600

Directions: D753. Turn off D753 at roundabout on east edge of town, signed. Aire on left in 50m, signed.

Sanitation:

Parking:

None

Custom

Service Point only. Inspected 2012.

CHAMBRETAUD 132 D6 N46°55.375' W000°58.318' 85500

Directions: Rue Notre Dame, off D27 roundabout at Aire de Diamants. Lay-by services adj to D27 at roundabout northwest of Chambretaud.

Sanitation:

Parking:

5

Custom; €2

View of countryside; 3 mins from village. Inspected 2010.

GRAND PARC DU PUY DU FOU 133 D6 N46°53.680' W000°55.526' 85590

Directions: Grand Parc du Puy du Fou. From D27 follow sp 'Puy du Fou', then sp 'Camping Cars'. Aire in parking area G.

Sanitation:

Parking:

100; €5/night; Apr-Sept; Pay at machine

Euro Relais Junior; Token; €2

Open Apr-Sept; Adults €25. Re-enactment theme park, inc Vikings, Romans, and dramatic stage shows. www.puydufou.com. Inspected 2010.

ST MICHEL MONT MERCURE 134 D6 N46°49.961' W000°52.919' 85700

Directions: Rue de l'Orbrie. From D752 turn towards the church at the cemetery. Turn left at the bottom of the church steps and follow road. Aire is on the right to the rear of the church, signed. 3.5m width restriction at entrance.

Sanitation:

Parking:

20

Custom; €2

Very pleasant parking area with 360° views and interesting church adj. Village with local commerce 2 mins down hill. Inspected 2010.

LE BOUPERE 135 D6 N46°48.126' W000°55.891' 85510

Directions: Exit village on D79 towards St Mars la Réothe. The Aire is on the left at Stade Henri Goussaud sports ground. The Service Point is to the rear of the car park.

Sanitation:

Parking:

5

Custom

At the sports facilities on edge of town; Village 2 mins walk. Inspected 2010.

CHAVAGNES EN PAILLERS

136 D6 N46°53.476' W001°15.000' 85250

Directions: Rue de la Petite Maine. Enter town on D6 from Belleville sur Vie. Turn right between Crédit Mutuel and 8 à Huit. Aire behind retail area, signed.

Sanitation: E WC F

Parking: P F

3

Aire Services; Token (3/3); €2

SP

Rural views; Field and river adj with access. Village 2 mins. Very sloping. Inspected 2010.

MESNARD LA BAROTIERE

137 D6 N46°51.174' W001°07.081' 85500

Directions: Enter village on D11 and follow sp 'Etang de la Tricherie'. Service Point near entrance to campsite.

Sanitation: E WC F

Parking: P F

5

Custom; Token from fishing kiosk; €3 by CC

SP

Activity lake; Bar/crêperie; High ropes course; Carp fishing tickets available. Inspected 2010.

VENDRENNES

138 D6 N46°49.619' W001°07.294' 85250

Directions: D160. Signed off D160 as enter village from Les Herbiers, opp bakery. Turn down roadway banning caravans and other vehicles.

Sanitation: E WC F

Parking: P F

6

Custom; Token

SP

Pleasant; Away from main road; Surrounded by green space. Inspected 2010.

CHANTONNAY

139 D7 N46°41.246' W001°02.469' 85110

Directions: Rue Arc en Ciel. Enter on D949bis from La Châtaigneraie. At roundabout turn right to stay on D949bis, sp 'Pouzauges' and signed. Turn left at next junction, signed, then turn left again, signed. The Service Point is on the left.

Sanitation: E WC F

Parking: P F

2

Raclet; Token (ER)

SP

Some unrestricted parking but primarily a Service Point. Inspected 2010.

POUZAUGES 1

140 D6 N46°46.500' W000°50.681' 85700

Directions: Super U. From D43/D752 roundabout turn off, sp 'Pouzauges'. Super U off next roundabout. Service Point in the Super U fuel station hidden by gas bottles.

Sanitation: E WC F

Parking: P F

Poss

Raclet; €2; No drive over drain

SP

Supermarket. Inspected 2010.

POUZAUGES 2 | 141 | D6 | N46°46.576' W000°49.701' | 85700

Directions: Rue du Pré de Foire/D49. Located in car park just off the D203/D960b roundabout, opp turning to Montournais.

Sanitation:

Parking:

5

Custom

In car park on edge of town. Inspected 2010.

LA MEILLERAIE TILLAY | 142 | D7 | N46°44.329' W000°50.723' | 85700

Directions: Rue des Ombrages. Drive through village on D13. Turn down Rue des Monts, sp 'La Tallud Ste G' and signed. Take 2nd left and Aire on right, signed.

Sanitation:

Parking:

10

Custom

Very pleasant village 2 mins; Large green space with picnic tables and kids play area adj. Inspected 2010.

LA CHATAIGNERAIE | 143 | D7 | N46°38.832' W000°44.699' | 85120

Directions: D938, at Super U. Aire on right side of supermarket. Accessible when entering or exiting town on D938.

Sanitation:

Parking:

4

Euro Relais Junior; Token; €2

Supermarket adj; Town 5 mins; Service Point closed Nov-Mar. Inspected 2010.

ST PIERRE DU CHEMIN | 144 | D7 | N46°41.836' W000°41.905' | 85120

Info/Photo: Paul & Ann Taylor

Directions: D938ter. From the centre of the village take the D938ter sp Cerizay. The Aire is 100m on the left signed.

Sanitation:

Parking:

10

Custom

The Aire is adj to a nature park with a walk alongside a stream, around ponds and open air performance space. Local commerce 1 min. Visited 2011.

FOUSSAIS PAYRE | 145 | D7 | N46°31.800' W000°40.898' | 85240

Directions: D31. Turn off D49 alongside the church onto D31, sp 'Payré-sur-Vendée'. Turn left, signed. Aire to rear of large, tree-lined car park.

Sanitation:

Parking:

10

Custom

In centre of pretty village with local commerce. Forest de Mervent-Vouvant 10km. Inspected 2010.

VOUVANT 146 D7 N46°34.462' W000°46.498' 85120

Directions: From north on D938ter follow sp 'Vouvant' onto D31. On entering village on D31 the Aire is the 1st parking area on left, signed.

Sanitation:

Parking:

20; €5

Custom

Views; On edge of Forest de Mervent Vouvant; Adj village is pretty with restaurants and a castle. Inspected 2010.

MERVENT 147 D7 N46°31.413' W000°45.854' 85200

Directions: Chemin du Chêne Tord, off D99. At the large crucifix on D99 turn up road, sp 'Cemetery' and signed. The Aire is opp the cemetery.

Sanitation:

Parking:

30

Raclet; Token (2/1)

Views; Full sunshine all day; Located in the Forest de Mervent Vouvant with footpaths, cycle routes, boating, and fishing. Inspected 2010.

FONTENAY LE COMTE 148 D7 N46°27.711' W000°48.338' 85200

Directions: D948bis/Ave du Général Charles de Gaulle. On D949 from west, turn onto D948bis at large roundabout. Follow D948bis to the Aire on your right in large parking area by river bridge, opp Gendarmerie.

Sanitation:

Parking:

22; €5/24hrs; CC

Urba Flux; €2

5 mins to large town. On busy main road. Inspected 2012.

MAILLEZAIS 149 D7 N46°22.243' W000°44.469' 85420

Directions: Rue de l'Ecole. From centre of village take D15 south towards Maillé. Aire in far end of car park 50m from church, signed.

Sanitation:

Parking:

20

Raclet; €2

Village adj with local commerce and abbey. Inspected 2010.

CHAILLE LES MARAIS 150 D7 N46°23.560' W001°01.254' 85450

Directions: D25/Rue du 8 Mai 1945. Adj to D25 to the south of the village outside the sports facilities. Follow sp 'Complex Sportif'. Limited roadside parking. Sports facility parking may be height barriered.

Sanitation:

Parking:

2

Euro Relais Mini; Token; €3

No parking Wed evening/Thurs morning due to market. Local commerce adj; Inspected 2010.

BENET — 151 — D7 — N46°22.167' W000°35.716' — 85490

Directions: D25. At parking just off D25, main route, beside the Intermarché supermarket. Car park can be busy with cars during the day.

Sanitation:

Parking:

20

Custom; By toilet

Intermarché supermarket adj; Local commerce; Tap in toilet. Inspected 2010.

MAILLE — 152 — D7 — N46°20.384' W000°47.747' — 85420

Directions: Place du Port. Turn off D25, sp 'Camping'. Follow road behind church, across bridge and then turn right. Service Point is to rear of large parking area on left before campsite.

Sanitation:

Parking:

€8; Banned 8pm-8am in town

Custom; April-Sept

Service Point outside campsite. Inspected 2012.

MOUTIERS SUR LE LAY — 153 — D7 — N46°33.227' W001°09.290' — 85320

Directions: Turn off D19, sp 'Aire Naturelle de Camping', 'Salle Omnisports' and 'Camping-Car'. The Aire is on grassy area to left, signed.

Sanitation:

Parking:

5; Honesty box

Custom; Waist height toilet disposal

Washing sinks and mini toilet block; Village 2 mins. Inspected 2010.

ST MICHEL EN L'HERM — 154 — D7 — N46°21.104' W001°14.898' — 85580

Directions: D746, main route through village, near centre.

Sanitation:

Parking:

7

Custom; €2

By small square; Pleasant. 2 mins to main square, commerce. Inspected 2010.

L'AIGUILLON SUR MER — 155 — D7 — N46°19.894' W001°18.481' — 85460

Directions: Off D746, between two lakes. Follow sp 'L'Aiguillon sur Mer' then 'Centre Ville' through town. Aire is signed by marina, water slide, and TO along seafront. Sp 'Ecole de Voile' (sailing school).

Sanitation:

Parking:

20; €5/night

Custom; €2

Skateboard park; Sailing school; Riverfront location; Town and TO 2 mins. Inspected 2010.

LA TRANCHE SUR MER 1 — 156 — D7 — N46°20.964' W001°26.886' — 85360

Directions: Behind Salle Omnisports. Just off D105/Rue des Sables, main route, signed from road.

Sanitation:

Parking:

12; Pay Jul-Aug €7/24hrs €12/48hrs; Max 48hrs

Aire Services; CC; €3

SP

10 mins from sea. There are better places to stay along this coast, try 159. Inspected 2010.

LA TRANCHE SUR MER 2 — 157 — D7 — N46°21.024' W001°26.208' — 85360

Directions: Avenue du Général De Gaulle, off D105bis. As enter town from east Aire is past Super U towards La Phare outside Stade de L'Atlantique.

Sanitation:

Parking:

10; €7/night; €12/48hrs; Pay Jul-Aug; Policeman will call; Max 48hrs

None; See 156

SP

Uninspiring roadside car park. Inspected 2010.

ST VINCENT SUR JARD — 158 — D7 — N46°24.623' W001°32.478' — 85520

Directions: Chemin des Roulettes. Turn off D21, sp 'Maison de Clemenceau', 'Tennis' and signed. Follow sp 'Maison de Clemenceau'. The Aire is on the right just past the tennis courts. Not suitable for 8m+ motorhomes when busy due to bay sizes.

Sanitation:

Parking:

18; €5/night

Aire Services; CC; €2

SP

Beach access over sand dune opp. Inspected 2010.

JARD SUR MER — 159 — D7 — N46°24.632' W001°35.589' — 85520

Directions: Rue des Goffineaux. Follow sp 'Port de Plaisance' and 'Aire Camping Car' from main road, well signed.

Sanitation:

Parking:

20; €6/24hrs €10/48hrs; Max 48hrs; Pay at machine

Custom; €2

SP

Adj to sea; Arrive early for sea view as only 6 sea view bays; Access to rocky beach. Inspected 2010.

TALMONT ST HILAIRE 1 — 160 — C7 — N46°28.106' W001°37.675' — 85440

Directions: D949. At the Super U on the west side of the town. In car park with 3.2m height barrier.

Sanitation:

Parking:

Poss

Raclet; €2

SP

Supermarket adj. Inspected 2010.

TALMONT ST HILAIRE 2 | 161 | C7 | N46°28.052' W001°37.031' | 85440

Directions: Rue des Gâtines. From D949 turn off at traffic lights in centre of village, sp 'La Roche s Yon' and 'Hotel de Ville'. Take 2nd right and turn left immediately, signed, into a narrow, one-way road. Wide motorhomes should inspect on foot before proceeding. Cross the next junction and Aire is on right.

Sanitation:

Parking:

20; €5/24hrs; Max 48hrs

Custom; CC; €3

There are footbridges over a stream to the lakeside and children's play area and into the village. Castle 2 mins walk. Inspected 2010.

BOURGENAY/QUERRY PIGEON | 162 | C7 | N46°26.459' W001°39.810' | 85440

Directions: Avenue de la Plage. From north take D4a to Bourgenay/Querry Pigeon. At the roundabout turn left towards Plage de Veillon. The Aire is on the left. Motorhomes are banned overnight from the parking at Plage de Veillon.

Sanitation:

Parking:

20; €5/24hrs

Aire Services; CC; €3

Large sand and stone beach 10 mins walk. Inspected 2010.

STE FOY | 163 | C7 | N46°32.792' W001°40.334' | 85150

Photo: Rita Renninghoff

Directions: Allée De La Mairie. Turn off the D80/D109 at the roundabout by the Church, sp 'Salle Polyvalente'. At the Mairie turn right and follow road to left. Aire on left, signed.

Sanitation:

Parking:

3

Custom: Unmetered CEE elec

Local commerce 1 min. Visited 2012.

CHATEAU D'OLONNE | 164 | C7 | N46°29.471' W001°44.494' | 85180

Photo: David Harris

Directions: Rue des Plesses. Approach from Talmont St Hilaire. Turn off D2949 to right, sp 'Château d'Olonne-Centre' and signed. At roundabout turn left, signed. Go straight over next roundabout to Aire, signed.

Sanitation:

Parking:

16; €6/night

Urba Flux Tall; €2/6 mins; CC

An uninspiring Aire in a semi industrial area lacking all seaside charm. Inspected 2012.

LES SABLES D'OLONNE | 165 | C7 | N46°29.787' W001°46.494' | 85100

Directions: Rue Printanière. Turn off main route through, sp 'Salle d'Amitie'. Follow road to right and Aire on left through barriers, signed.

Sanitation:

Parking:

40; €9/night inc elec and service; CC

Custom; 28 CEE elec points

Vinci managed barriered car park. 1st hour free. Motorhomes only allowed to park at official places at this town. Inspected 2012.

OLONNE SUR MER

166 C7 N46°32.551' W001°46.336' 85340

Directions: At Super U adj on D32 north of the town. Service Point by Lavage (car wash).

Sanitation:

Parking:

Poss

Euro Relais Mini; Token (ER); €2

Supermarket adj; Toilet in supermarket. Inspected 2010.

ST GILLES CROIX DE VIE

167 C7 N46°42.187' W001°56.823' 85800

Directions: Rue Rabalette. Turn off D38bis ring road, sp 'Centre Ville', 'Les Ports', and signed. Follow signs through town.

Sanitation:

Parking:

50; €5/24hrs; Free Nov-Mar; Max 48hrs

Custom; Token (2/2); €2.50

Sports facilities adj; Pond to walk around; Town 7 mins walk. Inspected 2010.

BRETIGNOLLES SUR MER

168 C7 N46°37.592' W001°51.341' 85470

Directions: On D38, at Super U fuel station.

Sanitation:

Parking:

Poss

Euro Relais Mini; €2

Supermarket; Town 2 mins. Inspected 2010.

COEX

169 C7 N46°41.813' W001°45.898' 85220

Directions: D40. Exit D6 bypass onto D40, sp 'Coex'. Follow D40 towards village and Aire in car park on left before entering village, signed.

Sanitation:

Parking:

4; Max 48hrs

Aire Services; Token (3/3)

Located in a bus and car park 2 mins from the village centre. Small town commerce. Inspected 2012.

AIZENAY

170 C6 N46°44.056' W001°35.412' 85190

Directions: Rue de la Roche. Approach from south on D948 and turn off at the roundabout, near McDonalds, sp 'Aizenay'. At next roundabout turn right, signed. Turn left, sp 'Tennis' and signed. Service Point on right, signed.

Sanitation:

Parking:

None

Custom; Pay at campsite (reception turns water on)

Service Point only. Inspected 2012.

LE POIRE SUR VIE — 171 — D6 — N46°46.099' W001°30.669' — 85170

Directions: D6. From central square by church take D6, sp 'Aizenay'. In 150m turn left, signed. Follow road for 50m and Aire on right, signed.

Sanitation:

Parking:

6; Max 7 days

Custom; 6 unmetered 16amp CEE elec points - 4 working

Aire located behind church adj to park. Village centre with local commerce 2 mins uphill. Bells chime all night. Inspected 2012.

BELLEVILLE SUR VIE 1 — 172 — D6 — N46°46.586' W001°25.633' — 85170

Directions: D937, at Super U. Adj to D937 as exit town towards La Roche-sur-Yon. Well sp through town.

Sanitation:

Parking:

Poss; See 173

Aire Services; Token

Supermarket adj. Inspected 2010.

BELLEVILLE SUR VIE 2 — 173 — D6 — N46°46.882' W001°25.737' — 85170

Directions: D101 by church. Turn onto D101 from D937 and turn left after 50m by La Poste. Follow sp 'Salle des Fêtes'. Aire at Salle des Fêtes.

Sanitation:

Parking:

15

None; See 172

Town 2 mins with numerous commerce. Green space and sports facilities adj. Inspected 2010.

LA ROCHE SUR YON — 174 — D7 — N46°40.098' W001°25.096' — 85000

Directions: Blvd d'Italie/N2160. Signed on N2160. From D760 follow sp 'La Roche Centre', 'Acti-Sud', and 'Centre Ville'. Turn left at the 3rd set of traffic lights, signed. Aire on left, signed.

Sanitation:

Parking:

15; Max 36hrs

Aire Services; 2 unmetered elec points; Not working June 2012

Town centre 15 mins; €35 fine if exceed 36hrs. Inspected 2010.

LES ESSARTS — 175 — D7 — N46°46.420' W001°14.082' — 85140

Directions: Rue de la Piscine. From D160 turn onto D7/Rue George Clemenceau into village. Cross over roundabout and turn left onto Rue de la Piscine. Aire on right, outside campsite.

Sanitation:

Parking:

2; 9m bays

Aire Services; Token (3/3)

Campsite adj; Swimming pool adj; Village 3 mins. Inspected 2010.

VIEILLEVIGNE — 176 — D6 — N46°58.285' W001°25.699' — 44116

Directions: D753. Approach town on D753 from east. Turn left at town entrance, signed. Service Point on left and parking at rear.

Sanitation:

Parking:

7; Reinforced grass parking

Euro Relais Mini; Toilet emptying at rear

Located adj to noisy main route but set back from the road. 3 local walks signed. Town with small town commerce 3 mins. Inspected 2012.

CORCOUE SUR LOGNE — 177 — D6 — N46°57.735' W001°34.840' — 44650

Directions: D72. Follow D178 through village towards Legé. Turn onto D72, sp 'Touvois'. Aire on left across bridge, signed. Service Point 100m further along by La Poste, signed.

Sanitation:

Parking:

4; Hedged bays

Custom; Empty toilet in special toilet

River and parkland adj; Pleasant. Walk up rocky grotto. Inspected 2010.

ST PHILBERT DE BOUAINE — 178 — D6 — N46°59.315' W001°30.966' — 85660

Directions: On right-hand side of northbound D937 in roadside lay-by.

Sanitation:

Parking:

4

Euro Relais Mini

Good views of open countryside; Village 300m; Main road adj. Inspected 2010.

LA LIMOUZINIERE — 179 — D6 — N46°59.617' W001°35.983' — 44310

Directions: Rue de Bonne Fontaine off D63/Rue Charles De Gaulle. Follow sp 'Aire de Camping-Cars' as exit village towards 'Paulx'.

Sanitation:

Parking:

6; Max 48hrs; 9m bays

Custom

Local commerce and garage nearby. Handy for Pilote Motorhome factory. Inspected 2010.

ST PHILBERT DE GRAND LIEU — 180 — C6 — N47°02.703' W001°38.504' — 44310

Directions: Chemin de la Plage, off D65. From D117 exit onto D65 at Super U roundabout towards village centre. At next roundabout, turn right onto Chemin de la Plage, signed. Aire is 100m on left.

Sanitation:

Parking:

5

Custom

Town centre 2 mins with ancient abbey; River fishing permit from tackle shop. Very pleasant. Inspected 2010.

LA HAIE FOUASSIERE

181 D6 N47°08.999' W001°24.016' 44690

Directions: Allée des Sources. Exit N249 at Junction 2b and follow sp 'La Haie Fouassiere'. At roundabout with flying saucer turn right onto D74, sp 'Le Port'. Follow D74 through and out of town, sp 'Maisdon'. After bend, just before river bridge, turn right, sp 'Le Port'. Aire immediately on left, signed.

Sanitation:

Parking:

3; Very sloping

Aire Services; Token (3/3)

Aire adj to riverside park with partial river view, river 2 mins. The bays are sloping and there is road noise. Inspected 2012.

LES SORINIERES

182 D6 N47°08.894' W001°31.316' 44840

Directions: Rue de l'Oasis. From Vetou approach on D115. After crossing motorway turn right, sp 'Complexe Sportif'. At roundabout go right, then follow road. Aire on left, 2nd turning after Gendarmerie, signed.

Sanitation:

Parking:

4

Euro Relais Box; 1 unmetered CEE elec socket, not working at time of inspection

Aire adj to main road. Located in a southern suburb 10km from Nantes centre. Picnic area adj. Inspected 2012.

LA MARNE

183 C6 N46°59.843' W001°44.206' 44270

Info/Photo: Michael van Kleeff

Directions: D87. Turn off the D117 onto the D87, sp 'La Marne'. Aire in in the car park of the Vival convenience store, just off D87 the large roundabout before entering La Marne, signed.

Sanitation:

Parking:

Poss

Custom; Donation

Convenience store adj. Visited 2012.

CHALLANS

184 C6 N46°51.021' W001°52.486' 85300

Directions: Boulevard Viaud Grand Marais. Enter Challans from the east on D753. At the roundabout by the Esso fuel station turn right, sp 'Parking Viaud Grand Marais' and signed. Aire is 200m on right before next roundabout, signed.

Sanitation:

Parking:

15

Custom

2 mins to boulangerie; 5 mins to town centre. Inspected 2010.

ST HILAIRE DE RIEZ 1 - Base des Vallées

185 C6 N46°43.879' W001°54.713' 85270

Directions: Chemin des Vallées. Turn off D754, sp 'Plan d'Eau des Vallées'. Follow road along causeway, then turn left opp campsite into Aire, signed.

Sanitation:

Parking:

10

Urba Flux Tall; €2.60; CC

Aire adj to interesting wetlands and large sailing lake but no view. Small arms shooting range adj. Beginners scramble bike/mountain bike course adj. Inspected 2012.

ST HILAIRE DE RIEZ 2 - Des Becs | 186 | C6 | N46°45.609' W002°01.588' | 85270

Directions: Avenue des Becs. Turn off D38 at roundabout, sp 'Les Becs'. Follow road and turn right at roundabout onto D123, sp 'St Jean des Monts' and signed. Follow road and Aire is on left, signed. Entry through Urba Flux bollard.

Sanitation:

Parking:

20; €5/night; Max 3 nights; CC; Pay at Urba Flux bollard

Urba Flux Tall; €2.60; CC; Inside barrier

Located in a kiss-me-quick beach resort with plenty of entertainment, but deserted and closed out of peak season. Inspected 2012.

ST HILAIRE DE RIEZ 3 - Champ Gaillard | 187 | C6 | N46°46.176' W002°02.021' | 85160

Directions: Avenue des Becs. Follow road past ST HILAIRE DE RIEZ 2 - Des Becs A on left and go right when the road forks, signed. Aire on left, signed.

Sanitation:

Parking:

28; Room for more

None

Located amongst sand dunes away from the beach resorts and may feel isolated if alone. Sandy beach 5 mins. Inspected 2012.

ST HILAIRE DE RIEZ 4 - Preneau Plage | 188 | C6 | N46°43.673' W001°59.424' | 85270

Directions: Preneau-Plage. Turn off D38 at roundabout, sp 'Les Becs'. Follow road and turn left at roundabout onto D123, sp 'St Hilaire de Riez'. Follow road and turn right at roundabout, sp 'Sion sur l'Océan'. Turn right, signed, and Aire on left at end of road, signed.

Sanitation:

Parking:

48; €5/night; CC; Pay at machine

None

Adj to the beach behind a sand dune but close enough to fall asleep listening to breaking waves. Commerce 10 mins. Parking free 10am-7pm. Inspected 2012.

MACHECOUL | 189 | C6 | N46°59.542' W001°48.832' | 44270

Directions: D117/Rue de Nantes. Le Jardin de Europe alongside D117 as enter the town from the east, signed.

Sanitation:

Parking:

10; Max 24hrs

None

Village adj; Park adj; In beautiful plane tree ave. Inspected 2010.

BEAUVOIR SUR MER | 190 | C6 | N46°55.018' W002°02.789' | 85230

Directions: D758. Signed off D758, main road through town. Truck parking also in car park.

Sanitation:

Parking:

20; €5/night; Max 48hrs; 8m bays

Urba Flux Tall; CC; €2

2 mins to town; Salt marshes surround town; €2.50 for 15 mins elec! Inspected 2010.

LA BARRE DE MONTS — 191 — C6 — N46°53.105' W002°07.137' — 85550

Directions: Chemin du Querruy, off D22 and D38. Aire is behind Mairie, which is beside the church. Signed from road.

Sanitation:

Parking:

8

Euro Relais Junior; Token

Work taking place at time of inspection, may close; Sandy beach and sailing school at Fromentine – 10 mins. Inspected 2010.

ST JEAN DE MONTS 1 — 192 — C6 — N46°47.937' W002°04.375' — 85160

Info/Photo: Florie B.

Directions: 38 Rue de Notre Dame de Monts. Aire Le Repos Des Tortues. In St Jean de Monts, follow sp to 'Notre Dame de Monts' and 'Noirmoutier', onto the D38. After roundabout with D51 the Aire is on the right signed. Entrance through Flot Bleu Park barrier.

Sanitation:

Parking:

49; €8-€12/24hrs inc elec; CC

Flot Bleu Pacific; Elec 4amps

Walk through sand dunes to beach 25 mins. Local commerce 12 mins. For €3 you can access shower block and aquatic complex at Bois Joly campsite 50m. Visited 2012.

ST JEAN DE MONTS 2 — 193 — C6 — N46°47.587' W002°04.757' — 85160

Directions: Rue de la Parée Jésus. On D38 from west take 3rd roundabout onto Blvd Maraîchins, sp 'La Parée Jésus'. At next roundabout turn right, then take next right and the Aire is on right.

Sanitation:

Parking:

28; €5; Apr-Sept; Max 48hrs; 7m bays

Flot Bleu Pacific; Token; €2

In wooded recreational area; Pay at Tennis courts, need reg and pitch number. 5 mins to large sandy beach; Inspected 2010.

ST JEAN DE MONTS 3 — 194 — C6 — N46°47.720' W002°02.780' — 85160

Directions: D753. At Super U towards Challans, turn off at D753/D38b roundabout. Parking in Intermarché opp: N46°47.790' W002°02.944'.

Sanitation:

Parking:

13; In Intermarché opp

Raclet; Token (ER)

Supermarket; Retail park. Inspected 2010.

NOTRE DAME DE MONTS 1 — 195 — C6 — N46°50.089' W002°08.533' — 85690

Directions: Rue de la Clairière/D38a. Small but frequent signs on D38a through town. Also sp 'Jardin du Vent', 'Camping Car Clairière' or 'Camping Car'.

Sanitation:

Parking:

20; €5/24hrs; Mar-Nov; 7m bays; Pay at machine; Max 48hrs

Custom

2 mins from beach; Nice wooded area adj. Inspected 2010.

NOTRE DAME DE MONTS 2 | 196 | C6 | N46°49.865' W002°07.790' | 85690

Directions: On D38, main road through town opp TO, sp 'P Général de Gaulle'.

Sanitation:

Parking:

10; €5/24hrs; Mar-Nov; Pay at machine

Custom; Difficult; Lift grate

SP

2 mins from town. WiFi €1/day plus card charges. Inspected 2010.

LA GUERINIERE | 197 | C6 | N46°57.960' W002°12.893' | 85680

Directions: D38. The Aire is adj to D38 near Camping le Caravan'île. Turn off roundabout into village, sp 'Camping 'île'. Turn immediately left and follow road past Camping Caravan'île and Aire is on right, signed.

Sanitation:

E WC F

Parking:

P F

20; €7/night Apr-Sept; €4.50/night Oct-Mar; Pay at machine; Max 48hrs;

Flot Blue Fontaine

SP

Uninspiring parking area. Inspected 2010.

L'EPINE | 198 | C6 | N46°58.8139' W002°15.846' | 85740

Directions: Rue des Ormeaux. Just northeast of L'Epine turn off D38bis or D95 at roundabout, sp 'Aire Camping Car'. Entrance via barrier. Aire adj to roundabout.

Sanitation:

E WC F

Parking:

P F

36; €7/24hrs; €13/48hrs; €19/72hrs; Max 72hrs

Aire Services; Unmetered elec included

SP

Inspected 2010.

L'HERBAUDIERE | 199 | C6 | N47°01.198' W002°18.062' | 85330

Directions: Chemin du Corps de Garde. Drive north on D5 from Noirmoutier en L'Île to L'Herbaudière. Aire on left behind Mairie, signed.

Sanitation:

E WC F

Parking:

P F

18; €7/9pm-9am; Pay at meter

Raclet Maxi; €2

SP

Adj to beach, some sea views through breaks in hedge; Pleasant seaside village adj; Nicest Aire on the island. Inspected 2010.

NOIRMOUTIER EN L'ILE | 200 | C6 | N47°00.066' W002°15.169' | 85330

Directions: Place Florent Caillaud/Rue de la Prée au Duc. Follow D948 towards L'Herbaudière, signed. Aire can be seen from road on left, signed.

Sanitation:

E WC F

Parking:

P F

200; €7/9pm-9am; Pay at machine

Raclet; €2

SP

On edge of seaside town; 5 mins to commerce; Salt producing area. Inspected 2010.

BOURGNEUF EN RETZ

201 C6 N47°02.476' W001°57.384' 44580

Directions: At TO on D758, entrance opp Citröen Garage. Just off roundabout junction of D13 and D758. Follow sp 'Maison de Tourisme'. Next to Bibliothèque Municipale.

Sanitation:

Parking:

10

Custom

Town 2 mins; Sports facilities adj; Main road adj. Inspected 2010.

ST HILAIRE DE CHALEONS

202 C6 N47°06.239' W001°51.974' 44680

Directions: Allée du Presbytère, off D61. The Service Point is outside the campsite hidden by bushes. Unrestricted car park adj.

Sanitation:

Parking:

2; Max 1 night

Euro Relais Junior

Grotto and religious figures adj; Village centre 2 mins. Inspected 2010.

ROUANS

203 C6 N47°11.599' W001°51.266' 44640

Directions: D66. Turn off D723 onto D66, sp 'Rouans'. Cross river and turn right, signed. Aire adj to river, signed.

Sanitation:

Parking:

7; €3/night

Custom

Aire adj to a pleasant Aire Naturelle campsite overlooking river. Both Aire and Campsite €3 pay at Mairie. Truck parking also adj. Inspected 2012.

ARTHON EN RETZ

204 C6 N47°06.917' W001°57.020' 44320

Directions: D5. Turn of D751 onto D5 towards Arthon-en-Retz. The Aire is at the Super U, adj to D5.

Sanitation:

Parking:

Poss

Euro Relais Junior; Token (ER); €2

Supermarket adj. Inspected 2010.

ST VIAUD

205 C6 N47°15.560' W002°00.896' 44320

Directions: From Paimboeuf exit D723 onto D86 to St Viaud. Turn right when enter St Viaud, signed. Turn immediately right again, signed. Aire is located on the far side of the tennis courts.

Sanitation:

Parking:

10; 15/11-30/3

Custom; 2 elec points powered 12.30-1.30 and 7.30-9pm; Closed Nov-Mar

SP

At the leisure facilities; Lake with rowing boats; Football pitches and other sports facilities. Inspected 2010.

LA BERNERIE EN RETZ

206 C6 N47°04.699' W002°02.030' 44760

Directions: Salle des Fêtes, Rue Jeanne d'Arc. On D97 coast road through town follow sp 'P37 spaces' and signed.

Sanitation:

Parking:

37; €6/night Jul-Aug; €4/night Sept-Mar; Pay at machine

Aire Services; Token

SP

In town centre with tourist shops and cafés; 100m from beach. Inspected 2010.

PORNIC

207 C6 N47°07.212' W002°05.511' 44210

Directions: Aquacentre. Approach from south on D213. Exit D213 onto D86, sp 'Pornic Centre'. Turn right, sp 'Pornic Sud' and signed. Turn left, sp 'Centre Sportif' and signed. In 50m turn left into Centre Sportif. Aire by Aquacentre, signed.

Sanitation:

Parking:

7; 6m bays

Flot Bleu Euro; CC

SP

Undesirable Aire adj to noisy main road in a busy sports centre but is likely to feel very isolated at night. Motorhome parking is used as cut through by sports centre patrons. Inspected 2012.

LE PLAINE SUR MER 1

208 C6 N47°07.789' W002°11.443' 44770

Directions: Chemin de Leverite. At the D751/D313 roundabout take the D313 towards Pointe de Gildas. At the next roundabout come back towards previous roundabout and the Aire is down the 2nd road on the right, signed.

Sanitation:

Parking:

30; €3; Apr-Oct

None; See 209

SP

Rural car park; Beach 15 mins down hill. Inspected 2010.

LA PLAINE SUR MER 2

209 C6 N47°08.413' W002°11.438' 44770

Directions: On D96 from Tharon-Plage pass Intermarché supermarket and the Service Point is opp football ground. The parking is up adj side street travelling back towards Tharon-Plage, signed.

Sanitation:

Parking:

5; Max 24hrs

Raclet Mini

SP

2 mins from town and Intermarché; Green space and sports facilities adj. Inspected 2010.

ST MICHEL CHEF CHEF

210 C6 N47°10.949' W002°08.844' 44730

Directions: Rue du Chevecier. As you drive into centre on D78, main route, the Aire is on the left, opp Mairie.

Sanitation:

Parking:

26; €5/24hrs; Pay at machine

Raclet; Token (ER); €2.90

SP

Beachside parking banned. 2 mins from village commerce. Inspected 2010.

LE POULIGUEN

211 C6 N47°16.320' W002°25.972' 44510

Directions: Ave de l'Océan. Turn off D245/D45 roundabout onto D45, sp 'Camping'. At roundabout turn left, sp 'Coubertin Stades'. Turn left at next roundabout, sp 'Camping du Clein'. Aire on right, signed. Entrance through CC operated barrier.

Sanitation:

Parking:

26; €5.20/24hrs Oct-Feb, €7.20/24hrs Mar-Sept, €10.20/24hrs July-Aug; CC

Aire Services; €3.30/24hrs 6amp elec

Automated motorhome-only section of Camping Le Clein. Inspected 2012.

PREFAILLES

212 C6 N47°08.055' W002°12.704' 44770

Directions: D313/C52. From La Plaine sur Mer turn off D313 at turning to Prefailles, sp 'Prefailles – Centre' and signed. Aire on left.

Sanitation:

Parking:

3; €3/24hrs May-Sept

Euro Relais Mini; Token; €2.50

Tokens available from TO. Inspected 2010.

POINTE DE ST GILDAS

213 C6 N47°08.220' W002°14.328' 44770

Directions: Chemin des Pinettes, off D313/Rue des Fossettes. Follow D313 towards Pointe de St Gildas. Turn into Aire on right before sea, signed.

Sanitation:

Parking:

30; €3/24hrs; Max 48hrs

None; See 212

Sea views; Footpath to beach; Town 4 mins; Always popular. Inspected 2010.

ST MARC

214 C6 N47°14.218' W002°18.032' 44600

Directions: Route de l'Océan. Follow the coast road from St Marc towards Ste Marguerite. The Aire is located adj to the road on the left, signed.

Sanitation:

Parking:

15

Raclet; Token (ER)

View of the sea from the cliff top over road. Sandy beach 150m down hill. Inspected 2010.

LA BAULE

215 C6 N47°16.917' W002°25.508' 44500

Directions: Stade Moreau-Defarges. Turn off D213 onto D192 and follow sp 'La Baule-Centre'. Continue on D192, sp 'La Boule - Ouest'. Enter La Boule Escoublac and turn right at the roundabout, sp 'Stade'. Turn right at roundabout, sp 'Stade Moreau Defarges'. Service Point and parking 50m on right, signed.

Sanitation:

Parking:

14; 8.5m bays

Aire Services; €3; CC

Designated parking overlooking a pleasure boat marina. Parallel parking may be required when busy and there are limited bays marked for large motorhomes. Inspected 2012.

HAVE YOU VISITED AN AIRE? GPS co-ordinates in this guide are protected by copyright law

Take at least 5 digital photos showing
• Signs
• Service Point
• Parking
• Overview
• Amenities

Visit www.all-the-aires.co.uk/submissions.shtml to upload your updates and photos.

Sanitation:

Aire Details:

Submit updates
• Amendments
• New Aires
• Not changed

LE POULIGUEN 217 C6 N47°16.415' W002°26.394' 44510

Directions: D45/Blvd de l'Atlantique. Adj to D45, signed.

Sanitation:

Parking:

None

Raclet; €2

Service Point only. Inspected 2010.

BATZ SUR MER 218 C6 N47°16.055' W002°27.239' 44740

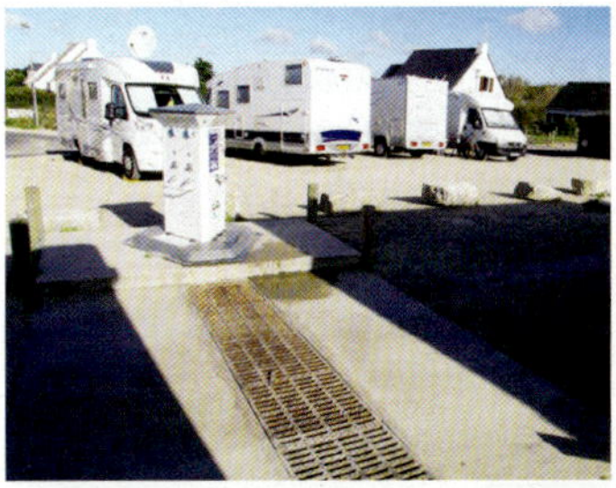

Directions: Rue de Kerjacot, adj to D45 opp the beach to the east of Batz-sur-Mer. Follow D45 along coast and turn into Rue de Ker Jacot, opp beach parking.

Sanitation:

Parking:

7; Max 7m

Euro Relais Junior; €2

Views across road and dunes to sea. Sandy beach opp. Pleasant, busy Aire. Inspected 2010.

LE CROISIC 1 219 C6 N47°17.398' W002°30.328' 44490

Directions: Rue des Courlis, Gare SNCF. From D245 turn right by train station, then right at roundabout and next left, sp 'Borne de Service'.

Sanitation:

Parking:

15; €5/9pm-9am; Max 48hrs; Pay at Service Point

Urba Flux Tall; CC; inc

By train station; Working area; Coach parking onsite. 2 mins to salt farm. Inspected 2010.

LE CROISIC 2 220 C6 N47°17.937' W002°31.301' 44490

Directions: Chemin du Lingorze. From Le Croisic 1 go straight on. In town follow road to right, sp 'Salle des Fêtes', along 3.5t harbour side road. Follow sp 'Océarium' straight on along harbour. At large roundabout turn left, sp 'Océarium'. Pass Océarium to Aire on left, signed.

Sanitation:

Parking:

9; €5.30/8pm-9am; CC; Pay at machine; Max 48hrs

Urba Flux Tall; €2.20/10 mins; CC; Closed Oct-Mar

Harbour and pleasant town centre 4 mins. Town is 3.5t weight restricted. Inspected 2012.

LE CROISIC 3 | 221 | C6 | N47°17.365' W002°32.229' | 44490

Directions: From Le Croisic 2 follow road around coast. Aire on left, signed. Only suitable for motorhomes less than 7m.

Sanitation:

Parking:

9; €5.30/8pm-9am; CC; Pay at machine; Max 48hrs; Max 7m

None

Tiny Aire overlooking low cliffs directly out to Atlantic. Isolated location when the adj holiday homes are vacant. Inspected 2012.

LA TURBALLE 1 | 222 | C6 | N47°19.867' W002°29.947' | 44420

Directions: Blvd de la Grande Falaise. Exit D92 onto Blvd de la Grande Falaise, sp 'Camping Municipal' and Aire on left, signed. Road has 3.5t weight restriction.

Sanitation:

Parking:

10; €2.90/24hrs; Max 5 days

Flot Bleu Fontaine

Beach 5 mins; Crazy Golf adj; Town 10 mins. Salt marsh (still producing salt) adj. Inspected 2010.

LA TURBALLE 2 | 223 | C6 | N47°21.817' W002°31.556' | 44420

Directions: D99. From La Turballe head towards Piriac-sur-Mer. The Aire is on the left hand side along D99, signed.

Sanitation:

Parking:

20; €2.90/24hrs; Max 5 days

Flot Bleu Fontaine

Adj to main road. Sandy beach 2 mins, accessible from car park across road. Inspected 2010.

LA TURBALLE 3 | 224 | C6 | N47°20.931' W002°30.473' | 44420

Directions: Rue Alphonse Daudet, in back streets of town. Follow signs through town.

Sanitation:

Parking:

20; €2.90/24hrs; Max 5 days

Flot Bleu Fontaine

Town 2 mins; Beach 5 mins. Inspected 2010.

PIRIAC SUR MER 1 | 225 | C6 | N47°22.709' W002°32.516' | 44420

Directions: Parking de la Tranchée, Rue de la Tranchée. Off D99 coast road, sp 'Aire Camping Cars', 'Le Port' and signed.

Sanitation:

Parking:

10; €5

Flot Bleu Fontaine

Sunny spot, not as good as Piriac sur Mer 2. Inspected 2010.

PIRIAC SUR MER 2 (PARKING DE LERAT) | 226 | C6 | N47°22.078' W002°31.966' | 44420

Directions: Route du Mesquène. Turn off D99 in Lerat, sp 'Aire Camping Cars'. The Service Point is 100m on right, signed. There are several seperate parking areas.

Sanitation:

Parking:

20; €5

Flot Bleu Fontaine

Sandy beach and harbour across road; Commerce 3 mins. One of the most pleasant stops on this section of coast. Inspected 2010.

PIRIAC SUR MER 3 | 227 | C6 | N47°23.774' W002°30.784' | 44420

Directions: D52/Ave Général de Gaulle, Parking Brambel. Adj to D52 on coast road north of Piriac sur Mer, signed.

Sanitation:

Parking:

15; €5/night

Flot Bleu Fontaine

Sea views over road. As this has the best sea views of all the local Aires it is always busy. Sandy beach adj. Inspected 2010.

MESQUER | 228 | C6 | N47°23.768' W002°28.074' | 44420

Directions: Route de Kerlagadec/D52. Aire adj to D52 in roadside lay-by in eastbound lane shortly after junction with D252.

Sanitation:

Parking:

2

Raclet; Token; €2

In roadside lay-by. Other local Aires are better. Inspected 2010.

GUERANDE | 229 | C6 | N47°20.028' W002°25.237' | 44350

Directions: D51, just off main bypass roundabout junction of D99e/D51, sp 'Guérande' and 'Centre Ville'. Turn onto D51/Ave de la Briére and follow road to right, sp 'Parking - Salle des Sports'.

Sanitation:

Parking:

10

Aire Services; €6; CC

Out of town Aire next to busy main road. Inspected 2010.

ST LYPHARD | 230 | C6 | N47°23.818' W002°18.098' | 44410

Directions: D47. Turn off D47, sp 'Camping Les Brières de Bourg' and signed. Turn into entrance to campsite and the Service Point is left of campsite, signed.

Sanitation:

Parking:

None

Custom; Token; €2

Service Point only. Inspected 2010.

ASSERAC 1

231 C6 N47°25.883' W002°26.749' 44410

Directions: Le Creneau. From Assérac on D82 follow sp 'Pen Be'. Turn left onto D282, signed, then turn right, signed. Service Point is on left.

Sanitation:

Parking:

None; See 232

Euro Relais; €2

Service Point only; Surrounding parking is private and a high fee is charged for use. Inspected 2010.

ASSERAC 2

232 C6 N47°25.613' W002°23.492' 44410

Directions: Off D33/Rue de la Mairie. Parking by Mairie, signed.

Sanitation:

Parking:

5

None; See 231

Small village with local commerce. Undesignated parking in village car park. Inspected 2010.

MISSILLAC

233 C6 N47°28.660' W002°10.766' 44780

Directions: D2, near junction with N165/E60. Aire on D2 towards village at TO, adj to water tower.

Sanitation:

Parking:

6

Custom; €1

In roadside lay-by. Village with château 5 mins. Inspected 2010.

GUENROUET

234 C6 N47°31.313' W001°56.971' 44530

Directions: D2. From Guenrouet turn off D2 between Guenrouet and St Clair, before crossing river. Aire outside Camping Saint Clair.

Sanitation:

Parking:

None

Bollard; €2

Old Service Point outside campsite. Motorhomes are banned from local river parking. Inspected 2010.

MONTOIR DE BRETAGNE

235 C6 N47°19.562' W002°08.886' 44550

Directions: Rue Jean Jaures. Follow D50 through town. Service Point adj to car wash at Super U. Parking: N47°19.676' W002°08.986'. Exit Super U between fuel station and supermarket. Turn left onto D50 opp Hôtel de Ville. Turn right and right again, sp 'Hôtel de Ville' and signed. Aire behind Hôtel de Ville, signed.

Sanitation:

Parking:

12 marked bays, 12 unmetered CEE elec points

Raclet; At Super U

Town centre location with small town commerce and supermarket. Distant road noise. Inspected 2012.

DONGES

236 C6 N47°19.185' W002°04.818' 44480

Directions: Rue du Stade/D4. On main road opp Stade Municipal to the west side of the village towards St Nazaire, signed. Entrance to the left of height barrier.

Sanitation:

Parking:

6; Max 48hrs

Euro Relais Junior; Token (ER)

Skateboard park; Football pitches. Oil refinery town. Inspected 2010.

ST ETIENNE DE MONTLUC

237 C6 N47°16.200' W001°46.504' 44360

Directions: D17. Turn off D17 to the south of the town into the Super U car park. The Service Point is at the far side of the Super U fuel station.

Sanitation:

Parking:

Poss

Euro Relais Junior

Parking has 3.2m height restriction; Supermarket adj. Inspected 2010.

SUCE SUR ERDRE

238 D6 N47°20.365' W001°31.501' 44240

Directions: Enter from south on D37. Cross river bridge and turn right towards Tourist Office. Service Point opp Tourist Office adj to river.

Sanitation:

Parking:

None

Euro Relais Junior; €2

Service Point only. Maybe obstructed by parked cars. Inspected 2012.

FAY DE BRETAGNE

239 C6 N47°24.880' W001°47.240' 44130

Directions: Espace Madeline. Exit village on D16 towards Heric. Service Point on right at village boundary, signed. Parking: N47°24.800' W001°47.201'. Turn 1st right after Service Point, signed, and parking is on left, signed.

Sanitation:

Parking:

10; Max 48hrs

Custom

Parking adj to village ponds with walking/exercise route. Designated parking does not have a lake view but is away from the noisy D16 truck route. Local commerce 2 mins. Inspected 2012.

PRINQUIAU

240 C6 N47°22.011' W002°00.722' 44260

Directions: Rue de Champoul. In village by church take D100, sp 'Campbon'. Turn left when the road forks, sp 'La Maziere'. Aire 100m on right, signed.

Sanitation:

Parking:

10; Max 48hrs

Custom

Aire adj to cemetery. Sign advises no motorhome parking in cemetery parking. Village with local commerce 3 mins. Inspected 2012.

SAVENAY — 241 — C6 — N47°22.458' W001°56.278' — 44260

Directions: D3. Located near D3 north of Savenay, sp 'Centre Commercial' and 'Parc commercial La Collerage'. In the fuel station of the Hyper U.

Sanitation:

Parking:

Poss

Aire Services; €2

SP

Very large hyper market with numerous other shops. Inspected 2010.

NOZAY 1 — 242 — D5 — N47°34.499' W001°37.491' — 44170

Directions: D121/Route de Rennes. Turn off N137 to Nozay and then onto D121, sp 'Nozay'. The Aire is on the left just after the lake, sp 'Étangs de Loisirs' and signed.

Sanitation:

E

Parking:

20; €5 inc unmetered elec points

Custom; 10 elec points

SP

Aire adj to lake with partial views; Super U and local commerce in pleasant town approx 1.6km. Inspected 2010.

NOZAY 2 — 243 — D5 — N47°34.262' W001°37.768' — 44170

Directions: Blvd du Petit Versailles. Exit Nozay 1 to the right then turn 2nd left into Blvd de Petit Versailles. Service Point at the Super U supermarket.

Sanitation:

Parking:

Poss

Euro Relais Junior; €2

SP

Supermarket adj. Inspected 2012.

JANS — 244 — D5 — N47°37.332' W001°36.717' — 44170

Directions: Off D39. Just off one-way street around church and behind Mairie, signed.

Sanitation:

Parking:

5

Custom

SP

Pleasant, village. Inspected 2010.

HAVE YOU VISITED AN AIRE?

GPS co-ordinates in this guide are protected by copyright law

Take at least 5 digital photos showing
• Signs
• Service Point
• Parking
• Overview
• Amenities

Visit www.all-the-aires.co.uk/submissions.shtml to upload your updates and photos.

Sanitation:

E

Aire Details:

Submit updates

- Amendments
- New Aires
- Not changed

NORT SUR ERDRE * — 246 — D6 — N47°26.247' W001°29.701' — 44390

Directions: Place du Bassin, just off D164. From roundabout with war memorial follow sp 'Plan d'Eau' and signed. Turn off road in 200m at bend, signed. Drive past marina and the Service Point is on the left and parking is on the right, signed.

Sanitation:

Parking:

20; Max 24hrs

Urba Flux; €2

River views, marina adj. This Aire will be popular in summer. Skateboarding; Basketball; Showers at harbour office. Inspected 2010.

LA MEILLERAYE DE BRETAGNE — 247 — D5 — N47°33.413' W001°24.042' — 44520

Directions: Camping Municipal Parc des Lavandières, off Chemin de la Vieille Cure. Follow sp 'Camping' through village. Turn by pharmacy. Access to the campsite is available all year but services turned off when campsite closed.

Sanitation:

Parking:

20; 3 hardstanding; Pitch €1.70 + €1.70pp

Custom; Elec €1.70

Shower; Service Point in bay adj to lake access. Small Aire Natural campsite; Village commerce 1 min. Inspected 2010.

MESANGER — 248 — D6 — N47°25.911' W001°13.775' — 44522

Directions: D25. Exit village on D25, sp 'La Roche Blanche'. Service Point on left in fuel station of Super U Express supermarket, signed.

Sanitation:

Parking:

Poss

Aire Services; €2

Supermarket adj. Inspected 2012.

RIAILLE — 249 — D5 — N47°30.847 W001°17.272' — 44440

Photo: Charlie and Angie Anderson

Directions: Rue de la Benâte, Aire de la Benâte. Turn off D33 onto D14, sp 'Teille' and signed. Take next left, signed. Aire on right-hand side, signed.

Sanitation:

Parking:

5; Max 48hrs

Custom

Well laid out, spacious Aire. Town commerce 3 mins. Inspected 2010.

ST AIGNAN SUR ROE — 250 — D5 — N47°51.794' W001°04.104' — 53390

Directions: From St Aignan sur Roë follow sp 'La Rincerie' for 7km to Etang de la Guiardiere. The Service Point and parking are at the main entrance, but the best parking is at: N47°52.052' W001°03.665'.

Sanitation:

Parking:

100; In 3 places; Max 48hrs

Aire Services; €2

At large leisure lake; 5km circular walk around lake. Parking on far side is fishermen's paradise. Inspected 2010.

PAYS DE LOIRE

CHATEAUBRIANT 1 — 251 D5 N47°42.378' W001°23.092' 44110

Directions: Intermarché fuel station. From west exit D771 at roundabout adj to McDonalds, sp 'ZI la Ville en Bois'. Follow road through retail area to Intermarché supermarket. Service Point adj to fuel station.

Sanitation:

Parking:

Poss

Euro Relais Mini; Token (2/1); €2

Supermarket adj. Self-service laundry adj. Inspected 2012.

CHATEAUBRIANT 2 — 252 D5 N47°42.188' W001°22.660' 44110

Directions: Rue de Tugny. Approach on D178 from south and turn right, sp 'Camping Municipal'. The Service Point is in the car park of the campsite and sports facility on left.

Sanitation:

Parking:

5; When campsite closed

Bollard; 1 unmetered elec point

Outside campsite. Inspected 2010.

POUANCE — 253 D5 N47°45.134' W001°10.786' 49420

Directions: Rue de l'Hippodrome. Exit town on D6 and turn left, sp 'Senonnes'. If you get to roundabout with gendarmerie you have gone too far. Follow road across bridge, past church and the Aire is on the left, signed.

Sanitation:

Parking:

4; €2.50 inc elec

Custom; 4 elec points

Overlooking large lake with parkland adj. Inspected 2010.

ANGRIE — 254 D5 N47°34.343' W000°58.486' 49440

Directions: Rue du Vieux Bourg. From the church follow D770 towards Vern d'Anjou. Turn left in 20m at the crucifix. The Aire is in the wooded area 50m on left.

Sanitation:

Parking:

5

Custom

Picnic area under trees with banks ideal for bike jumps. Sports facilities adj. Inspected 2010.

COMBREE - BEL AIR — 255 D5 N47°42.781' W000°59.925' 49520

Directions: Rue de Bretagne. Exit Combrée on D281, sp 'Bel Air de Combrée'. Follow D281 across D775 into Bel Air de Combrée. Aire on left in picnic area, signed.

Sanitation:

Parking:

2

Custom

Aire at small picnic area adj to main route through. 4 car parking bays under trees adj to toilets. Woods for walking/cycling adj. Inspected 2012.

SEGRE 1 * | 256 | D5 | N47°41.062' W000°52.406' | 49500

Directions: Rue Emile Zola. Exit town on D71 towards Châteaubriant. Turn right, sp 'No Entry except Parking', down an 18% hill. The Aire is on the left in the car park before no entry signs.

Sanitation:

Parking:

20

Custom

Town 2 mins along river. Cobbled streets and hidden restaurants. Idyllic spot. Skate park; Weir. Inspected 2010.

SEGRE 2 | 257 | D5 | N47°41.160' W000°51.999' | 49500

Directions: Rue du Port. Turn off D775 at roundabout on east side of Segre, sp 'Aire de l'Europe'. Go straight on at next roundabout, then turn right in 300m, sp 'Centre Culturel' and signed. Service Point at bottom of hill on right, signed.

Sanitation:

Parking:

10

Urba Flux

Adj to river but no views. Cultural centre and cinema adj. Pretty riverside town 4 mins through car park. Inspected 2012.

SEGRE 3 - Aire de l'Europe | 258 | D5 | N47°41.101' W000°51.437' | 49500

Directions: Aire de l'Europe. Turn off D775 at roundabout on east side of Segre, sp 'Aire de l'Europe'. Turn right at next roundabout, then immediately right, sp 'Aire de l'Europe'. Service Point on left, signed.

Sanitation:

Parking:

4

Custom; Lift grid to empty toilet

Roadside lay-by/picnic spot adj to very noisy main route. Inspected 2012.

AMPOIGNE | 259 | D5 | N47°48.652' W000°49.491' | 53200

Directions: Place de la Liberty. Service Point at public toilets adj to D114 in centre of village, outside Mairie. Parking: N47°48.774' W000°49.386'. Exit village on D114, sp 'Laigne', and the parking is by the pond on the left.

Sanitation:

Parking:

5

Custom; No drive over drain

The Service Point is in the centre of the village and the parking is on the outskirts of village overlooking a small lake. Inspected 2012.

ST MARS LA JAILLE | 260 | D5 | N47°31.381' W001°10.975' | 44540

Directions: Rue Neuve. Approach from south on D878. Go straight over roundabout, sp 'Pannece'. At next roundabout turn right, sp 'Plan d'Eau' and signed. Aire on right, signed.

Sanitation:

Parking:

7; Max 48hrs

Point Belle Eau

Pleasant Aire adj to recreation area and lake. Voie Verte cycle/walking route to Nantes. Local commerce 2 mins. Inspected 2012.

Montmorillon

POITOU

Mouthiers sur Boeme

MAULEON

1 D6 N46°55.070' W000°45.133' 79700

Directions: Rue de la Bachelette. Follow sp 'Niort' south out of town on D744. Turn right up lane after exiting town, sp 'Complexe Sportif' and signed. Follow lane into housing estate until reach sports fields. Aire signed on left.

Sanitation:

Parking:

5, Max 48hrs

Custom

Swimming pool with waterslide adj. Sports field adj. Town 20 mins. Inspected 2010.

ST AMAND SUR SEVRE 1

2 D6 N46°52.154' W000°47.998' 79700

Directions: Rue Fontaine, off D154. Located directly on C56.

Sanitation:

Parking:

5; Max 48hrs; Reinforced grass parking

Custom

Village 2 mins. Riverside 2 mins. Inspected 2010.

ST AMAND SUR SEVRE 2

3 D6 N46°53.033' W000°49.546' 79700

Directions: C2. Sp 'Bar Moulin de Chaligny' from road. Located on C2, between St Amand-s-Sèvre and Treize-Vents. 2.5km from D34 junction.

Sanitation:

Parking:

10; €5/night; Grass parking

Custom; €3; Unmetered elec available

Private Aire at bar/restaurant surrounded by fields located at beautiful riverside spot; Inspected 2010.

BRESSUIRE

4 E6 N46°50.221' W000°29.660' 79300

Directions: Place de la Libération, off D748. Service Point opp Parking St Jaques, a large parking area well signed in town just off D748.

Sanitation:

Parking:

30; Max 24hrs

Custom; Water tap by urinal

130 shops in town, some local commerce adj; Parking St Jacques unrestricted. Inspected 2010.

ST MAURICE LA FOUGEREUSE

5 E6 N47°01.974' W000°30.509' 79150

Directions: Espace de la rivière Juliot. Turn off D748 in La Fougereuse onto D161, sp 'St Maurice'. In St Maurice turn right into car park, opp D33 junction, sp 'Espace de la rivière Juliot.

Sanitation:

Parking:

4

Custom; 2 unmetered CEE elec points in toilet

Aire adj to pleasant village pond and park. Local commerce 2 mins. Inspected 2012.

BOISME

6 | E6 | N46°46.655' W000°26.007' | 79300

Directions: Rue des Essarts. From north on D139. In Boisme turn left onto D135, sp 'Chiche' and signed. Follow road around lake and Aire is in the car park at the far end of the lake, signed.

Sanitation:

Parking:

5

Custom

Aire adj to pleasant lake and park. Walk around lake to local commerce in village centre, 5 mins. Inspected 2012.

LA CHAPELLE ST LAURENT

7 | E6 | N46°44.871' W000°28.544' | 79430

Directions: D748. Turn off D748 at La Poste, sp 'Vallée Verte' and signed. Aire 100m on right, signed.

Sanitation:

Parking:

10

Custom

Located just far enough away from the D748 and overlooking a landscaped park. Voie Verte cycle/walking route 2 mins, goes 11km to Bressuire and 23km to Parthenay. Inspected 2012.

CLESSE

8 | E7 | N46°43.082' W000°24.257' | 79350

Directions: Route de Laubrecais. At roundabout by church turn onto D19, sp 'Parthenay' and signed. Turn left onto D177, sp 'Chiche' and signed. Service Point 100m on left, signed. Parking is possible in village centre.

Sanitation:

Parking:

5

Custom

The Service Point is at the municipal storage buildings but has no parking. It is possible to park in any of the village car parks but the car park on at the D19/D139 is suggested. Inspected 2012.

L'ABSIE

9 | D7 | N46°37.987' W000°34.642' | 79240

Directions: Rue des Halles, adj to D949bis. From D949bis turn onto D179 at mini roundabout, sp 'La Chapelle St Etienne' and signed. Aire on right in village square below truck parking.

Sanitation:

Parking:

10

Custom; 4 unmetered elec points

In central village square with local commerce; Main road 100m. Inspected 2010.

VERNOUX EN GATINE *

10 | E7 | N46°38.196' W000°30.882' | 79240

Photo: motorhomeandaway.co.uk

Directions: D143. From D949bis in village turn onto D143, sp 'Neuvy-Bouin'. Turn left before church, signed. Entrance to Aire beside mausoleum, signed.

Sanitation:

Parking:

6; Grass parking; 7m max

Custom; 6 unmetered elec points

Grass parking not suitable when wet; Pleasant; Bells. Inspected 2010.

LA FORET SUR SEVRE

11 D7 N46°46.510' W000°38.842' 79380

Directions: Rue de Beauchêne. Turn off D744 at roundabout into town, signed. Turn right in 100m, signed. Aire 200m on left, signed. Entrance has passable bollards. If barrier closed the padlock code is available for free from local shops. Not accessible on Sunday.

Sanitation:

Parking:

30

Custom

Very pleasant space; Like a campsite, but free. Covered seating area and fishable river. Inspected 2010.

PARTHENAY

12 E7 N46°38.437' W000°15.982' 79200

Directions: Rue de Boisseau. As enter Parthenay on D949bis turn left, sp 'Base de Loisirs de Parthenay'. Aire on right, signed. Coded barrier at exit.

Sanitation:

Parking:

10; €6-8/24hrs; Open Apr-Oct

Custom

Pay at campsite reception for exit code. Overlooking lake; Pleasant; Disabled fishing swim. Inspected 2010.

VASLES

13 E7 N46°34.402' W000°01.394' 79340

Directions: Rue de la Cité. From D59 follow sp 'Parking' and 'Espace Mouton Village', both with sheep heads. Aire at large parking area near stadium, between D59 and D121.

Sanitation:

Parking:

20

Custom

At Sheep Village with lots of items celebraiting sheep; Entry to park €9 in high season. www.moutonvillage.fr Inspected 2010.

MENIGOUTE

14 E7 N46°29.887' W000°03.450' 79340

Directions: Rue des Vignes. From the village centre take D21, sp 'La Pagerie'. Turn immediately right into Rue des Vignes. Drive past SPA supermarket and Aire is on left.

Sanitation:

Parking:

7

Custom

In centre of small town adj to open access sports field. SPA supermarket adj. Inspected 2012.

AYRON

15 E7 N46°39.382' E000°05.286' 86190

Directions: Off N149/E62, outside campsite at Etang de Fleix. Take N149/E62 east out of town. Pass barn and in 650m turn off N149, sp 'Camping' and 'Le VIP Peche'. Service Point outside the campsite, parking on right before campsite, signed.

Sanitation:

Parking:

30; €3/8pm-8am; Pay at bar

Flot Bleu Pacific; €4

Fishing lake and bait shop 2 mins; No view of lake from parking and no swimming in lake. Inspected 2010.

ST LOUP LAMAIRE

16 E7 N46°47.128' W000°09.850' 79600

Directions: From the west follow D46. Cross the river and after passing under the railway bridge turn off D46 onto D121, sp 'Clemille' and signed. The Aire is on the left in 100m.

Sanitation:

Parking:

30; Grass parking

Custom

Large grass parking on outskirts of pretty village with local commerce. Near river, but no views. Inspected 2010.

AIRVAULT

17 E6 N46°49.506' W000°08.578' 79600

Directions: Rue de la Gare. Approach from south on D46 and at the roundabout take D725E, sp 'St Varent'. Turn right across railway track onto D27, sp 'Airvault' and signed. At the next roundabout go almost right around and enter car park on left, signed. Aire at far end. Do not drive through village centre is narrow, 3.5t weight and 2.2m height restricted in places.

Sanitation:

Parking:

5

Custom; Self cleaning toilet

Located just off the edge of town in a quiet car park. Market Saturday. Inspected 2012.

ST VARENT

18 E6 N46°53.857' W000°14.490' 79330

Directions: D28. Turn off D28 beside Collage F Villon, signed. The Aire is outside the municipal campsite.

Sanitation:

Parking:

10; Max 48hrs

Custom

Supermarket 150m; Parking next to sports field/centre. Inspected 2010.

THOUARS

19 E6 N46°58.579' W000°12.702' 79100

Directions: Place Ferdinand Buisson, outside old city wall. Turn off D938 at roundabout, sp 'Centre Ville'. Follow sp 'Centre Ville'. After passing the cemetery follow sp 'Autre Directions', then 'P Cemetery'. Aire 200m on left, signed.

Sanitation:

Parking:

8; 7m narrow bays

Campsite bollard

Pleasant location against town ramparts; Town 3 mins uphill; Motorhomes restricted to small part of car park. Inspected 2010.

ST MARTIN DE SANZAY

20 E6 N47°05.529' W000°12.082' 79290

Directions: La Zona de Loisirs La Ballastière, at Etang la Ballastière. Head north from St Martin de Sanzay on D158, following sp 'Etang la Ballastière' and signed. The Aire is at the leisure lake. Barrier entry; Access via card from local shops, €20 deposit.

Sanitation:

Parking:

50; €5; Grass parking

Custom; Token; inc

Leisure lake adj but no views; Holiday place in summer, looks abandonded in winter. Inspected 2010.

OIRON

21 E6 N46°56.875' W000°04.954' 79100

Directions: Salle Polyvalente, in village centre. Follow D64/D145 south, sp 'Salle Polyvalente' and signed. Parking is in Salle Polyvalente car park. Service Point is behind a building.

Sanitation:

Parking:

10

Custom; Token

Pretty village with local commerce 2 mins; Château de Oiron in village, entry €7 www.oiron.fr. Inspected 2012.

LOUDUN

22 E6 N47°01.108' E000°05.313' 86200

Directions: Avenue de Ouagadougou. Enter Loudun from north on D147 and follow sp 'Z.I. Nord', then 'Ave de Ouagadougou'. Follow this road for 650m and the Service Point is at the car wash on the right.

Sanitation:

Parking:

4

Flot Bleu Standard Plus (Yellow); €2

In urban industrial estate at car wash; 1 car wash suitable for motorhomes. Inspected 2010.

CHALAIS

23 E6 N46°57.510' E000°06.279' 86200

Directions: D347. Turn off D347, sp 'Aire de Repos de la Briande'. Aire at rear, signed. Be aware, two private Aires signed at Mirebeau, €5/night: N46°46.842' E000°11.638'. Agressais is a France Passion site. Inspected 2012.

Sanitation:

Parking:

8

Custom; 4 CEE 10amp unmetered elec points

This landscaped Aire with hedged bays is to rear of a roadside lay-by just off the noisy D347 main route. Café and local products for sale. Inspected 2012.

POITIERS - FUTUROSCOPE

24 E7 N46°39.813' E000°22.094' 86360

Directions: Avenue du Futuroscope, at Futuroscope off D20d. Aire adj to roundabout junction of D910 and D20d. Aire on right after automated barrier off smaller D20d roundabout.

Sanitation:

Parking:

100; €6/24hrs; 1st hr parking free

Euro Relais Maxi; €4

Futuroscope adj. www.futuroscope.com Inspected 2010.

LA ROCHE POSAY

25 F7 N46°47.630' E000°47.874' 86270

Directions: D725. Adj to D725 as you approach the town from Coussay les Bois. The Aire is at the Super U, adj to the large roundabout junction of D725 and D725b. Adj to fuel station, signed.

Sanitation:

Parking:

Poss

Aire Services; 1 unmetered elec point

Supermarket adj. Inspected 2010.

CHAUVIGNY — T — 26 — F7 — N46°34.386' E000°38.812' — 86300

Directions: Rue Porte Chevreau. Turn off D951/D749 roundabout, sp 'Camping'. Turn left onto D2, sp 'Camping' and signed. Follow road up hill, then turn left, signed. Go straight on at stop junction, then turn left, signed. Aire 50m on left beside cemetery, signed.

Sanitation:

Parking:

10

Toilets only

Adj to medieval city with narrow streets to wander around. Campsite: N46°34.255' E000°39.206' has Service Point inside and charges motorhomes €6/night. Inspected 2012.

VICQ SUR GARTEMPE — 27 — F7 — N46° 43.447' E000°51.719' — 86260

Photo/Info: John Cox

Directions: D5. Exit village on D5, sp 'La Roche Posay'. Aire is 300m on the left, signed.

Sanitation:

Parking:

10

Custom

Large parking area by boules courts. Could have road noise. Village with local commerce 2 mins. Visited 2012.

POITIERS — 28 — E7 — N46°36.102' E000°20.318' — 86000

Directions: Rue des Mille Bosses. As approach from north turn off N147 onto D910. Follow sp 'Camping du Porteau'. The Service Point is outside the campsite near river.

Sanitation:

Parking:

None

Flot Bleu Euro; CC

Service Point only; Campsite adj. Inspected 2010.

VIVONNE — 29 — E7 — N46°25.553' E000°15.773' — 86370

Directions: Avenue de la Plage. Turn off D4 at TO opp turning to campsite, sp 'Office de Tourisme'. Campsite signs show Aire but don't follow.

Sanitation:

Parking:

3

Aire Services; €2

Pretty town with swimming pool and commerce. Lots of green open spaces. Inspected 2010.

CHATEAU LARCHER — 30 — E7 — N46°24.869' E000°18.938' — 86160

Photo: Sid Thomas

Directions: Off D88. Turn off D88, sp 'Camping' and 'Stade'. Aire at sports ground. Gate has digital lock.

Sanitation:

Parking:

10; €3/24hrs inc elec; Open Mar-Oct

Custom; €3

At sports ground. River adj. Nice walk through sports ground to castle and village. Pleasant spot. Inspected 2010.

FLEURE — 31 — E7 — N46°28.708' E000°31.406' — 86340

Directions: D2, northeast of village. Parking at the church. Aire signed from N147.

Sanitation:

Parking:

5

None

Church adj; Village 2 mins. Inspected 2010.

NIEUIL L'ESPOIR — 32 — E7 — N46°29.113' E000°27.268' — 86340

Directions: D1/Allée du Champ de Foire. On D1 as enter village from north, sp 'Camping Car'. Signed from N147.

Sanitation:

Parking:

10; Reinforced grass parking

Euro Relais Junior; Token

Very pleasant spot. Town 2 mins. Inspected 2010.

GENCAY — 33 — E7 — N46°22.384' E000°24.373' — 86160

Directions: Rue de Civray. Follow D741 towards Civray through town. Turn left just before D1 turning to Brion. Service Point to left, in car park under trees.

Sanitation:

Parking:

10; Under/between trees

Aire Services; Token; Toilets and water at water tower

Aire located in large car park at foot of water tower. Low trees. Road noise from D741. Local commerce 2 mins. Inspected 2012.

LHOMMAIZE — 34 — F7 — N46°26.101' E000°35.811' — 86410

Directions: Adj to junction of N147/E62 and D8. From N147 turn onto D8 in village towards Verrières. Aire on right behind Mairie, sp 'Aire de Repos'.

Sanitation:

Parking:

2

Custom; 2 unmetered elec points

River adj. Town quite pleasant. Sheltered from road. Inspected 2010.

LUSSAC LES CHATEAUX — 35 — F7 — N46°24.165' E000°43.534' — 86320

Directions: Place de l'Amitie, D11/Rue du Quai. In main town centre parking, sp 'Aire de Repos' off N147/E62.

Sanitation:

Parking:

1; 5m bay

Custom

In town centre with local commerce; Very limited designated parking. Inspected 2010.

MONTMORILLON 1 — 36 — F7 — N46°25.129' E000°51.285' — 86500

Directions: D727/Route to Lussac-les-Châteaux, at E'Leclerc. At the Centre Commercial by the lavage (car wash).

Sanitation:

Parking:

10

Euro Relais Junior; 1 unmetered elec point

Supermarket adj; Likely to be quieter than Moulismes 38. Inspected 2010.

MONTMORILLON 2 — 37 — F7 — N46°25.389' E000°52.069' — 86500

Directions: Rue Léon Dardant. Approach on D54 from south. At traffic lights turn left onto D727, sp 'Chauvigny'. Cross river bridge and turn right at traffic lights. Turn right again, then left, then right, signed. Some of these turns are narrow due to parked cars, large motorhome owners advised to inspect before attempting.

Sanitation:

Parking:

10

Urba Flux Tall; CC

Parking adj to river, but no view. Town with numerous commerce 3 mins. Inspected 2012.

MOULISMES — 38 — F7 — N46°19.985' E000°48.578' — 86500

Directions: N147/E62, at north end of town, sp 'Aire de Repos'. Not the truck stop in town.

Sanitation:

Parking:

80

Custom; Token (ER); €3

Very popular overnight motorhome stop. N147 is a very busy, noisy truck route but parking poss 200m away. Inspected 2010.

ROMAGNE — 39 — E7 — N46°16.123' E000°18.247' — 86700

Directions: Espace Detente. From church take D25, sp 'Brux'. Then turn left on D27, sp 'Civray' and signed. Go straight on, sp 'St Romain' and signed. Aire on right at the sports facilities, signed.

Sanitation:

Parking:

6; Max 72hrs

Custom; 6 unmetered 5amp elec points

Landscaped Aire at sports facilities. Pleasant well maintained area located 2 mins from village centre with local commerce. Inspected 2012.

LATHUS ST REMY — 40 — F7 — N46°19.974' E000°57.431' — 86390

Photo/Info: Vera Ward

Directions: D10. Exit village centre on the D10, sp 'St Remy'. Aire outside campsite opp l'etang de la Trie, signed.

Sanitation:

Parking:

8

Euro Relais Junior; 1 unmetered electric point, long lead needed

Very pleasant spot opp lake. Aire is outside Camping Municipal which was closed at time of visit July 2012. Signed walks in local area. Local commerce includes convenience store. Visited 2012.

COUHE 41 E7 N46°17.907' E000°10.705' 86700

Directions: Rue de Bel-Air/D26. Turn off D2 onto D26/Rue de Bel-Air at covered market. Drive through parking area and take 2nd turning on left into larger parking area. Service Point on left by toilet.

Sanitation:

Parking:

5; In designated bays

Custom

Views; Town commerce and lovely covered market 2 mins; Very convenient to N10. Inspected 2010.

PAMPROUX 42 E7 N46°23.770' W000°03.506' 79800

Directions: D329/Rue de la Cueille. Turn off D5 or D5e to west of village centre, sp 'D329' and 'Fomperron'.

Sanitation:

E

Parking:

3; 12m bays

Flot Bleu Océane; €2

Pleasant village centre with good selection of local commerce 2 mins; Rural views. Inspected 2010.

LA MOTHE ST HERAY 43 E7 N46°21.589' W000°07.083' 79800

Directions: D5/Rue du Pont l'Abbe. At junction between D737/D5 as enter village. Signed on building.

Sanitation:

Parking:

3

Flot Bleu Fontaine; €1

Village 4 mins; Adj to busy main road; Washing sinks. Inspected 2010.

ROUILLE 44 E7 N46°25.247' E000°02.247' 86480

Directions: D611. Turn off D611 in town centre into 3.5t weight restricted car park opp church, signed. Service Point on right before Sapeurs Pompiers (fire station).

Sanitation:

Parking:

7

Custom

Large parking area adj to very noisy road. Local commerce adj. Inspected 2012.

LA CRECHE 45 E7 N46°21.621' W000°18.389' 79260

Directions: D7/D182 roundabout, at Stade Georges André Groussard. Sp 'Aire de Repos' and 'Camping Car' from N11 and in town. Aire on north edge of town, sp 'D7 Cherveux'.

Sanitation:

Parking:

10

Flot Bleu Fontaine

At sports park with stream, 3 mins to town centre. Inspected 2010.

MAGNE

46 E7 N46°18.963' W000°33.404' 79460

Directions: D9, at the Super U. Turn off D1 onto D9 into Magné. Aire just off large roundabout to west of town, adj to fuel station but accessible from other side.

Sanitation:

Parking:

Poss

Euro Relais Junior; €1.50

Supermarket adj. Inspected 2010.

NIORT

47 E7 N46°19.763' W000°27.870' 79000

Directions: Rue de Bessac, on northwest side of town centre. Enter town from west on D148/D648 following sp 'Centre Ville'. Travel south towards centre and turn left at 4th roundabout onto Blvd Main. Turn right at next roundabout and turn close left onto Rue de Bessac which is one-way. Aire in car park on right.

Sanitation:

Parking:

15; €7.50/24hrs inc unmetered elec; Max 7 days; Must park in designated bays only

Euro Relais Junior

Nice stop; River adj and can walk directly into town over bridges from Aire. Adria dealer on D948. Inspected 2010.

COULON

48 D7 N46°19.244' W000°35.464' 79510

Photo: John M McMahon

Directions: D123. Enter town on D1, go across river and turn left at crossroads. Aire adj to D123 as exit village to west in large, open field, signed.

Sanitation:

Parking:

30; €6; Apr Oct; Collected by Mairie; Grass parking

Custom; In adj car park

In area known as 'Green Venice'. 2 mins from village centre. Inspected 2010.

MOUGON

49 E7 N46°17.574' W000°17.700' 79370

Directions: Rue René Gaillard. Turn off D948 in village centre, sp 'Melle' by greenhouses. The Service Point is in the fuel station of the SPAR supermarket.

Sanitation:

Parking:

None

Custom

In commercial area in front of Spar supermarket and car wash area. Inspected 2010.

MONTIGNE

50 E7 N46°12.752' W000°14.337' 79370

Photo/Info: John Watts

Directions: D103. Exit the village on the D103 towards Perigne. Aire on right, signed. Steep access into the Aire from road and may be difficult for larger motorhomes.

Sanitation:

Parking:

10; Grass parking

Custom

This Aire is in a pleasant spot amongst mature trees making it feel like a picnic area. Service point consists of a tap and drain but usable. Visited 2011.

CELLES SUR BELLE

51 E7 N46°15.754' W000°12.494' 79370

Directions: Rue des Halles. Follow D948, main road, then turn off, signed. Drive down cobbled streets past church and TO. Turn left at bottom of hill opp impressive gates.

Sanitation:

Parking:

20

Custom; Water opp disposal

SP

TO and town 2 mins. Abbey adj with gardens and buildings. Goats cheese made locally. Motorbike museum at abbey. Inspected 2010.

HAVE YOU VISITED AN AIRE?

GPS co-ordinates in this guide are protected by copyright law

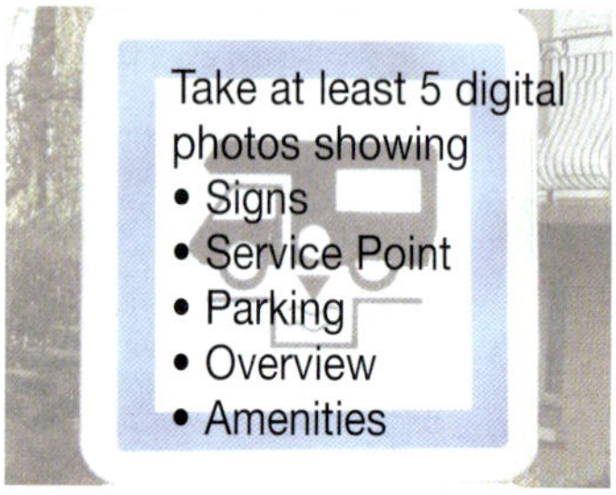
Take at least 5 digital photos showing
• Signs
• Service Point
• Parking
• Overview
• Amenities

Visit www.all-the-aires.co.uk/submissions.shtml to upload your updates and photos.

Sanitation:

Aire Details:

Submit updates

- Amendments
- New Aires
- Not changed

MELLE

53 E7 N46°13.907' W000°08.643' 79500

Directions: Rue de la Croix Casselin, outside municipal campsite. Turn off D737 and follow sp 'Camping'. Service Point outside campsite. Parking available in town, follow sp 'Parking du Jardin': N46°13.361'W000°08.394'.

Sanitation:

Parking:

In town

Custom

SP

Service Point only. Campsite adj. Inspected 2010.

CHEY

54 E7 N46°18.246' W000°02.980' 79120

Directions: From D950, main route, turn off near church by boulangerie, signed. Aire behind boulangerie, signed.

Sanitation:

Parking:

3

Custom

SP

Village with local commerce 1 min. Inspected 2010.

LEZAY

55 E7 N46°15.884' W000°00.685' 79120

Directions: Place du Marché, Rue de Gâte-Bourse. Aire in rear of car park behind TO and beside large cattle market in town centre. Follow sp 'Office de Tourisme'.

Sanitation:

Parking:

20

Custom

SP

Large indoor market; Town centre and TO adj. Inspected 2010.

ROM

56 E7 N46°17.463' E000°06.850' 79120

Directions: D14, adj to river by bridge. Signed.

Sanitation:

Parking:

10

Custom; By building at far end

River adj; Basketball court; Poss bar/restaurant in summer. Inspected 2010.

CHAUNAY

57 E7 N46°12.356' E000°09.823' 86510

Directions: D25/Grande Rue. At rear of large parking area in village centre, signed.

Sanitation:

Parking:

5

Urba Flux; 7 unmetered elec points

Local commerce adj. Lots of space in car park. Inspected 2010.

SAUZE VAUSSAIS

58 E7 N46°08.123' E000°06.399' 79190

Directions: Place des Halles in main town square. Follow sp 'Office de Tourisme'. Aire in back corner by Sapeurs Pompiers (Fire Station).

Sanitation:

Parking:

10

Flot Bleu Océane; Token for elec only

In town square. TO adj. Inspected 2010.

CHEF BOUTONNE

59 E7 N46°06.607' W000°04.626' 79110

Directions: Chemin du Parc. From D737, main route, follow sp 'Melle'. Turn off opp cemetery, sp 'Aire Naturelle' and signed.

Sanitation:

Parking:

10; Grass parking

Custom

Water is turned off Nov-Mar. Town 5 mins. Parking on grass, some parts slope but plenty of flat areas too. Inspected 2010.

LONDIGNY

60 E7 N46°05.010' E000°08.102' 16700

Directions: Place de l'Eglise. From D26 turn into Londigny, then turn left, sp 'Place de l'Eglise'. The Aire is at the church.

Sanitation:

Parking:

5; Max 48hrs

Custom; Mar-Oct; 1 unmetered elec point

Rural; No facilities in village. Private château 500m. Bells 3 times/day. Trees obstruct some parking. Inspected 2010.

ST MARTIN L'ARS

61 F7 N46°13.189' E000°31.804' 86350

Photo/Info: Kevin Holley

Directions: D741. Aire at D741/D28 crossroads opp D28, signed.

Sanitation:

Parking:

3
Euro Relais Junior; €2

Local commerce 1 min. Lake 1 min. Chateau within walking distance. Visited 2012.

CHARROUX

62 E7 N46°08.573' E000°24.411' 86250

Directions: D148/Route de Limoges. From east on D148 at roundabout do not follow ring road to right but take 3rd exit towards village centre on old D148. Aire on left in 1.2km, signed. 200m before tower.

Sanitation:

Parking:

15
Aire Services; Token (3/3); €2

Interesting abbey ruins 220m. Plenty of local commerce. Tokens available from shops. Inspected 2010.

VERTEUIL SUR CHARENTE

63 E8 N45°58.788' E000°14.122' 16510

Directions: Rue de la Fontaine, off D26. Follow sp 'Aire de Détente' through town; narrow access through town.

Sanitation:

Parking:

10; Max 48hrs
Custom; 4 elec points €2/24hrs; See Mairie

Pretty village with château, park, and river 1 min; Pleasant spot. Local commerce 2 mins. Inspected 2010.

CONFOLENS 2

64 F8 N46°01.104' E000°40.519' 16500

Directions: D952/Avenue de Saint-Germain. From south on D948 turn right in Confolens onto D51/D952 and follow one way system, sp 'Camping'. Travel north, parallel to river, sp 'Saint-Germain'. Aire is on left in 350m, adj to Camping Municipal des Ribières.

Sanitation:

Parking:

20; €5; May-Sept
Custom; inc

Walkable to town. LIDL and Super U on outskirts. Inspected 2010.

ST LAURENT DE CERIS

65 F8 N45°56.446' E000°28.984' 16450

Directions: In village centre. Service Point opp Champ de Foire and next to children's play area. The Service Point is difficult to access. The Champ de Foire parking is across the road and has 4 unmetered CEE elec points.

Sanitation:

Parking:

7; Parking adj to Service Point impractical, park opp
Custom; Diff access; 7 unmetered CEE elec points

Local commerce and convenience store 1 min. Inspected 2012.

CHIRAC

66 F8 N45°54.837' E000°39.440' 16150

Directions: D59. Exit Chirac on D59 towards Chabanais. Turn left before river bridge into parking area. Aire at far corner of parking area.

Sanitation:

Parking:

3

Custom; Only water and 4 unmetered CEE elec points.

Small, unsigned parking area on edge of village. Shallow river adj but no view. Inspected 2012.

HAVE YOU VISITED AN AIRE?

GPS co-ordinates in this guide are protected by copyright law

Take at least 5 digital photos showing
• Signs
• Service Point
• Parking
• Overview
• Amenities

Visit www.all-the-aires.co.uk/submissions.shtml to upload your updates and photos.

Sanitation:

Aire Details:

Submit updates

- Amendments
- New Aires
- Not changed

CHABANAIS

68 F8 N45°52.833' E000°44.200' 16150

Directions: N141/E603, at Super U. From west on N141/E603 pass through Chabanais and Super U is at roundabout 1.7km east of town. Service Point and designated spaces are at rear of car wash, adj to main road.

Sanitation:

Parking:

2

Euro Relais Mini; Token (ER); €2

Supermarket and fuel station. Washing facilities for large vehicles adj. Inspected 2010.

ROUMAZIERES LOUBERT

69 E8 N45°52.962' E000°34.351' 16270

Directions: Aire de Repos, adj to N141/E603. Aire on N141/E603 west of village on northbound side but accessible from both directions, sp 'Aire de Détente' and signed.

Sanitation:

Parking:

10

Euro Relais Junior

Adj to main road; Very noisy. Village shops and restaurants 5 mins. Inspected 2010.

CHASSENON

70 F8 N45°51.025' E000°46.352' 16150

Directions: D29. Off D29 as exit the village to east, sp 'Autocars' and 'Picnic Site'.

Sanitation:

Parking:

3

Custom; Water point in toilet

Village 5 mins. Unusually quiet and rural spot with picnic area. Parc Archelogique adj for ancient Roman town Cassinomagus. Inspected 2010.

ST QUENTIN SUR CHARENTE/PRESSIGNAC 71 F8 N45°49.633' E000°41.287' 16150

Directions: At 'Barrage de Lavaud', D214. From St Quentin sur Charente take D161, sp 'Pressignac'. Turn right onto D214, sp 'Barrage de Lavaud' and 'Les Versennes'. Aire in car park at end of road, adj to dam.

Sanitation:

Parking:

10; Max 72hrs

Custom; 4 unmetered elec points; Open Apr-Oct

SP

Reservoir/lake adj. No view of lake from Aire. Boats without propellers only. Inspected 2010.

LESIGNAC DURAND 72 F8 N45°48.700' E000°38.283' 16310

Directions: Rue du Presbytere, off D52 and D162. From east on D13 turn right in Massignac onto D52 and follow sp 'Lesignac Durand'. Aire in 4km in village centre, at rear of church and next to Mairie. Signed from D162, but also accessible from D52.

Sanitation:

Parking:

6; Max 72hrs

Custom; Open Apr-Oct; 6 unmetered elec points

SP

Restaurants, fuel station. Near to leisure/activity lakes. Inspected 2010.

MASSIGNAC 73 F8 N45°46.786' E000°39.304' 16310

Directions: D163. In Massignac village centre turn off D13 onto D163 at TO. Turn right immediately between Mairie and church. Aire in small car park behind Mairie and alongside church. Further parking in picnic area at rear of church: N45°46.805' E000°39.340'.

Sanitation:

Parking:

5

Custom; 2 unmetered elec points

SP

Local commerce 1 min. Inspected 2010.

CHASSENEUIL SUR BONNIEURE 74 F8 N45°49.493' E000°27.100' 16260

Directions: Rue du 8 Mai 1945, off D27. In the central village square, entrance just before Intermarché.

Sanitation:

Parking:

4

Euro Relais Junior; €2

SP

Village adj; Intermarché adj; Local commerce; Market day Wed. Inspected 2010.

CELLEFROUIN 75 E8 N45°53.655' E000°23.179' 16260

Directions: Off D739, to west of village. As enter village from Mansle on D739 turn off, sp 'Aire de Loisirs' and 'Pique-nique'. Drive past tennis court and Service Point at toilet block in far corner of car park.

Sanitation:

Parking:

30

Custom

SP

Tap and WC disposal behind toilet block. Nice rural area. Local commerce in village, 2 mins. Inspected 2010.

MANSLE — 76 — E8 — N45°52.674' E000°10.894' — 16230

STATIONNEMENT
RESERVE

Directions: Rue de Watlington. As enter Mansle from north on D18 turn left, sp 'Camping le Champion'. Service Point outside campsite.

Sanitation:

Parking:

2; In low season only

Raclet; €2

Town 5 mins; Restaurant La Marmite adj. Inspected 2010.

HAVE YOU VISITED AN AIRE? — GPS co-ordinates in this guide are protected by copyright law

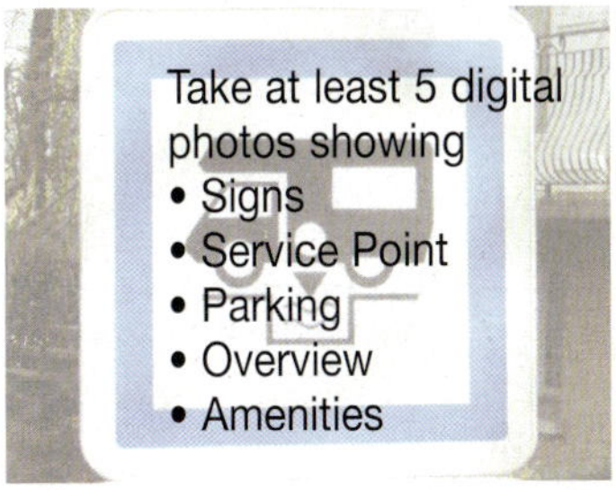
Take at least 5 digital photos showing
• Signs
• Service Point
• Parking
• Overview
• Amenities

Visit www.all-the-aires.co.uk/submissions.shtml to upload your updates and photos.

Sanitation:

Aire Details:

Submit updates

- Amendments
- New Aires
- Not changed

AIGRE — 78 — E8 — N45°53.603' E000°00.329' — 16140

Directions: Rue des Charrières. From west on D739 turn off, sp 'Aire de Repos' and 'Camping Car'. Aire on right.

Sanitation:

Parking:

5; €5 inc elec; May-Oct

Bollard

Pleasant Aire in small parkland setting. €5 includes shower, toilets, all services and elec. Inspected 2010.

ROUILLAC — 79 — E8 — N45°46.592' W000°03.678' — 16170

Directions: Rue de Genac. From southeast on D939 as enter town take 3rd exit at roundabout towards Super U supermarket. Aire on left opp Super U fuel station and overlooking large open grassy area.

Sanitation:

Parking:

7

Euro Relais; Token (ER)

Supermarket opp; Village 5 mins. Lots of open, green space adj. Inspected 2010.

HIERSAC — 80 — E8 — N45°39.978' W000°00.022' — 16290

Directions: D14. Exit village on D14 towards Châteauneuf sur Charente. Aire on left just before village boundary.

Sanitation:

Parking:

3

Urba Flux Tall; €2/20 mins; CC

Aire located on the edge of the village. Local commerce inc convenience store on N141 4 mins. Inspected 2012.

SERS — 81 — E8 — N45°35.788' E000°19.298' — 16410

Directions: Rue du Champ de Foire. Turn off D25 onto Rue du Champ de Foire at either end of village, signed. Easiest entrance is from east. Aire just off central square, signed. Fencing and bushes look like they restrict entrance but it is over 3m wide.

Sanitation:

Parking:

7; Grass parking; Max 48hrs

Euro Relais Junior; Token (ER); €3

SP

Aire adj to sports facilities just off central square. Local commerce 1 min. Inspected 2012.

TOUVRE — 82 — E8 — N45°39.657' E000°15.489' — 16600

Directions: Route du Pontil. Follow D57 to south. After crossing railway line turn 1st right onto D408, sp 'Soyaux'. Aire 20m on right, signed.

Sanitation:

Parking:

7

Aire Services

SP

Landscaped Aire adj to a railway line. Bus stop adj. Inspected 2012.

CHATAIN BESSON — 83 — E8 — N45°40.983' E000°33.579' — 16220

Directions: D699. Clearly signed off D699 in Chatain Besson, opp La Poste and Salle Municipale.

Sanitation:

Parking:

10

Euro Relais Mini

SP

In village. Toilets avail at rear of Salle Municipale across road with picnic area. Inspected 2010.

LA ROCHEFOUCAULD — 84 — E8 — N45°45.053' E000°23.275' — 16110

Directions: Route de Limoges. Exit town towards N141, sp 'Taponnat'. Aire 400m on left outside E'Leclerc supermarket, signed. There are two E'Leclerc supermarkets in town, the other bans motorhomes.

Sanitation:

Parking:

7

Euro Relais Box; €2

SP

Designated parking against noisy main route. All other parking has 2.5m height restriction. Supermarket adj. Inspected 2012.

NERSAC — 85 — E8 — N45°37.555' E000°03.004' — 16440

Directions: Rue de la Foucaudie, by lovely turreted building in village centre. From D699, main route, follow signs though village. Aire is next to police station.

Sanitation:

Parking:

7; Max 48hrs

Custom; 4 unmetered elec points

SP

Lovely Aire in very nice village, well worth a look around. Inspected 2010.

LA COURONNE

86 E8 N45°36.378' E000°06.019' 16400

Directions: D32/Rue de la Libération. At the Champ de Foire parking adj to main route through. Narrow in town and parking area.

Sanitation:

Parking:

5; No parking Wed am - market

Custom

Village centre shops inc boulangerie, laundry and Spar adj. Inspected 2010.

ROULLET ST ESTEPHE

87 E8 N45°34.785' E000°02.704' 16440

Directions: Off D210. Take Exit 7 from N10 for Roullet Centre. At roundabout turn onto D210. Turn off to Aire, opp YPO Camping Cars.

Sanitation:

Parking:

20

Custom

River, park, town 5 mins. Recently resurfaced. Inspected 2010.

VOEUIL ET GIGET

88 E8 N45°35.092' E000°09.292' 16400

Directions: Rue de la Mairie. Turn off D674 as exit village by covered water feature. Aire 20m on right, behind church.

Sanitation:

Parking:

3

Flot Bleu Océane; €2

In village; Restaurant adj. Pretty church and stream adj. Inspected 2010.

VILLEBOIS LAVALETTE

89 E8 N45°28.900' E000°16.583' 16320

Directions: Place du Champ de Foire, off D16. From west on D16 go straight over roundabout into town. Take next right and another immediate right and Aire on left.

Sanitation:

Parking:

2

Urba Flux Tall; €2

Pleasant spot. Impressive château in town. WiFi at TO at end of car park. Toilets underground in road below car park. Inspected 2010.

MOUTHIERS SUR BOEME

90 E8 N45°33.254' E000°07.493' 16440

Directions: Chemin de la Chauveterie. Turn off D12 at the roundabout to the north of the village into Place du Champ du Foire, signed. Follow road to right and the Aire is in front of the church, signed.

Sanitation:

Parking:

5

Custom

Pleasant Aire overlooking church. Square with convenience store, local commerce and small market on Thursday morning adj. Inspected 2012.

ST SEVERIN — 91 — E8 — N45°18.750' E000°15.300' — 16390

Directions: Rue de la Pavancelle, off D709 in the centre of the village. Near the Mairie (town hall), opp the SPAR supermarket.

Sanitation:

Parking:

3

Custom; Unmetered elec

SP

Aire set between D709 and Rue de la Pavacelle in well kept village. Inspected 2010.

MONTMOREAU ST CYBARD — 92 — E8 — N45°23.948' E000°07.963' — 16190

Directions: Rue de la Tude, off D674. From south on D674 turn right at mini roundabout into Rue de la Tude opp La Poste, signed.

Sanitation:

Parking:

8

Flot Bleu Pacific; €2; 8 elec points

SP

Open, slightly sloping square. Grassy area between parking and river Tude. Château in town. Inspected 2010.

AUBETERRE SUR DRONNE — 93 — E9 — N45°16.162' E000°10.606' — 16390

Directions: D2/Route de Riberac, at Base de Loisirs. Adj to D2 to east of town after crossing river. Parking near Service Point in summer. Riverside parking allowed in winter.

Sanitation:

Parking:

5

Flot Bleu Océane; €2

SP

Outside municipal campsite beside river; Kayak hire; Quiet; Shop 300m; Short walk into beautiful old village. Inspected 2012.

SIREUIL — 94 — E8 — N45°37.034' E000°00.411' — 16440

Directions: Chemin du Ponton. Turn off D7 north of village, sp 'Lavoir Ancien' and signed. At T-junction turn right and parking is immediately on right adj to river.

Sanitation:

Parking:

3; Grass parking

None

SP

Idyllic riverside parking isolated from the village. BBQ and picnic area onsite. Village centre 2 mins. Inspected 2012.

HAVE YOU VISITED AN AIRE?

GPS co-ordinates in this guide are protected by copyright law

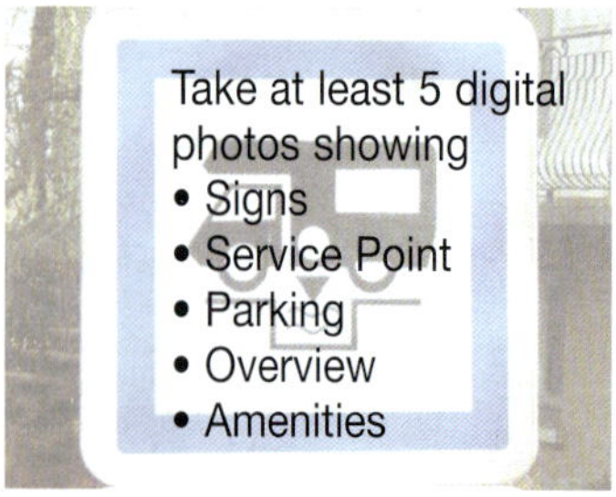
Take at least 5 digital photos showing
• Signs
• Service Point
• Parking
• Overview
• Amenities

Visit www.all-the-aires.co.uk/submissions.shtml to upload your updates and photos.

Sanitation:

Aire Details:

Submit updates

- Amendments
- New Aires
- Not changed

CHATEAUNEUF SUR CHARENTE — 96 — E8 — N45°35.924' W000°03.403' — 16120

Directions: Rue due Prieure. Turn off D699 opp D84 turning, sp 'Centre Ville' and 'Hôpital'. Turn right, sp 'Hôpital', then left. Follow road to right past church, sp 'P Centre Ville Prieure'. Turn left, sp 'P Centre Ville Prieure'. Aire in car park on left, signed. Access through town diff due to narrow streets.

Sanitation:

Parking:

4

Urba Flux Tall; €2/20 mins; CC

This is a good town centre Aire in a car park that is unlikely to be full of local cars. Small town commerce 2 mins. Cognac producer 1 min. Inspected 2012.

BROSSAC — 97 — E8 — N45°19.974' W000°02.738' — 16480

Directions: Turn off D731 onto D7, Rue de la Gare. Turn sharp right into Rue du Château d'Eau. Aire adj to stadium.

Sanitation:

Parking:

4

Flot Bleu Euro; CC; €5

Pleasant, quiet spot by stadium; Lots of green space; Each bay has own drain; Toilet at stadium 100m. Inspected 2010.

MONTGUYON — 98 — E9 — N45°13.075' W000°10.990' — 17270

Directions: Rue de Vassiac. From northwest on D730 take 2nd exit at roundabout. Go straight across next roundabout and follow main road around right-hand bend. Turn left onto D158/Rue de Vassiac. As D158 bends left go straight ahead into Rue de Vassiac. Aire on right in 400m at stadium.

Sanitation:

Parking:

10

Custom

At stadium with comprehensive sports facilities. Town 5 mins. Inspected 2010.

CLERAC — 99 — E9 — N45°10.754' W000°13.693' — 17270

Directions: D261e1/Route des Vignes. Turn off D158 in the centre of the village onto the D261e towards Cercoux. The Aire is adj to the pond, next to the boulangerie.

Sanitation:

Parking:

5

Euro Relais Junior; 1 unmetered elec point

Lovely Aire on edge of village overlooking pond and countryside. Inspected 2010.

MONTLIEU LA GARDE — 100 — E8 — N45°14.919' W000°15.071' — 17210

Directions: Les Coupries, off D910. Exit N10/E606 onto D730, sp 'Montlieu la Garde'. Turn left onto D910/D13 and follow signs through village to Aire. Well signed. Pay with CC on entry to lower chain barrier.

Sanitation:

Parking:

10; €8

Custom; CC/Token; €1; inc elec

Automated Aire/municipal campsite on edge of village. Min of 1 night required to use Service Point. Showers avail by token, €1. Inspected 2010.

LEOVILLE

101 E8 N45°22.752' W000°20.112' 17500

Photo: Joy and Bob Podesta

Directions: Off D253e3. From D142 in village turn onto D253e3, sp 'Aire de Loisirs'. Turn right in 150m. Aire on right at end of road.

Sanitation:

Parking:

6

Euro Relais Mini; Token (ER)

SP

Pleasant parkland area with lake and footpath to village. Tokens avail from boulangerie facing church. Inspected 2010.

BAIGNES STE RADEGONDE

102 E8 N45°23.045' W000°13.776' 16360

Directions: D131. From N10/E606 take D2, sp 'Baignes'. In town turn right onto D14. Turn right onto D131 opp Intermarché supermarket. Aire on right next to dechetterie. Well signed from N10.

Sanitation: E F

Parking: P F

10+

Custom; 2 unmetered elec points

SP

Basic tarmac area with Service Point next to 'Voie Verte' cycle track. Town with commerce 400m. Inspected 2010.

JONZAC

103 E8 N45°26.849' W000°25.959' 17500

Directions: Place du 8 Mai 1945. From D142/D28/D134 roundabout take D28, sp 'Cognac'. Turn left, sp 'P Mai 1945' and signed. Service Point 100m on left.

Sanitation: E WC

Parking: P F

2

Euro Relais Junior; Token (2/1)

SP

Town 5 mins. Additional unrestricted parking available. Inspected 2010.

ARCHIAC

104 E8 N45°31.205' W000°18.277' 17520

Directions: Rue du Pâtis, off D699. Aire at foot of water tower behind La Poste in village centre.

Sanitation: WC F

Parking: F

5

Euro Relais Mini

SP

Village adj. Service Point in rear right-hand corner of car park by toilets. Small market Sat am. Inspected 2010.

CRITEUIL LA MAGDELEINE

105 E8 N45°32.279' W000°12.906' 16300

Directions: Off D151. From west on D699 turn right onto D151, sp 'Criteuil'. At right-hand bend continue straight onto C2 into village. Aire on right in village centre by school and behind Mairie, signed.

Sanitation: E WC F

Parking: F

2

Euro Relais Junior; 1 unmetered elec point

SP

No amenities in village; No real parking. Inspected 2010.

LIGNIERES SONNEVILLE

106 E8 N45°33.413' W000°10.957' 16130

Directions: Off D90. From D699 turn onto D90 in town. Follow D90 south for 300m then turn left and Aire on left in 100m.

Sanitation:

Parking:

20

Custom

Large, gravel parking area adj to football pitch and ancient restored barn. In grounds of 17th century moated château now housing Mairie; Pretty historic village. Inspected 2010.

BOURG CHARENTE 1

107 E8 N45°40.427' W000°13.461' 16200

Directions: Rue du Port. From Cognac (west) on N141/E603 turn left onto D158 sp' Bourg Charente'. At sharp right hand bend go straight ahead into Rue du Port. Aire in car park opp Restaurant 'La Ribaudiere'

Sanitation:

Parking:

6; Nov-Apr

None; See 108

Pleasant riverside spot with tap and toilet adj. Inspected 2010.

BOURG CHARENTE 2

108 E8 N45°40.344' W000°13.677' 16200

Directions: Off D158, adj to river. Turn left off D158 before river, sp 'Camping'. Service Point outside campsite. Difficult access; 6m max.

Sanitation:

Parking:

None; See 107

Euro Relais Junior

Service Point difficult to access, recommend larger vans park at 107 and walk to access (900m). Inspected 2010.

JARNAC

109 E8 N45°40.598' W000°10.390' 16200

Directions: Aire de Loisirs de l'Ile Madame, on Quai l'Ile Madame off D736. From N141/E603 turn onto Ave Carnot/D736, sp 'Camping'. Turn right immediately before river bridge. Aire outside Camping l'Ile Madame in riverside car park, Aire de Picnic. Signed on entry to town.

Sanitation:

Parking:

Day; Banned 8pm-8am

Euro Relais Junior; Drive over drain 18cm high!

Beautiful spot. Interesting town. Commerce 2 mins. Swimming, restaurant, and pizza adj. Inspected 2010.

SEGONZAC

110 E8 N45°36.869' W000°13.255' 16130

Directions: Place du Jardin Public, adj to Rue Henri Gourry. From D763 turn onto Rue Gourry and follow to end. Aire on right. Signed from all directions.

Sanitation:

Parking:

4 (each with elec); Max 4 days

Custom; 4 unmetered elec points

Village 5 mins; Sign showing local cognac producers. Inspected 2010.

GENTE

111 E8 N45°37.732' W000°18.921' 16130

Directions: Off D148. From Cognac (north) on D731 turn left onto D148, sp 'Gente'. After 1.2km fork right into Lieu-Dit La Vallade. Aire on right in 400m by sports field and boules pitches.

Sanitation:

Parking:

5; Max 2 nights

Custom; 6 unmetered elec points

Well maintained Aire and surroundings on edge of village; Skate park adj; WCs at boules pavilion. Inspected 2010.

COGNAC

112 E8 N45°41.910' W000°19.962' 16100

Photo: Carol and Duncan Weaver

Directions: Place de la Levade. Enter town on D48. Follow sp 'Centre Ville'. At roundabout turn off, sp 'Centre Ville'. In 50m turn, sp 'Parking Gratuit' and 'Aire de Camping Car'. Follow road to end and turn towards river. Aire by river just past tanker depot, adj to river bridge.

Sanitation:

Parking:

6

Raclet; €2

View across river. Town 2 mins. Cognac producers in town. Inspected 2010.

CHERVES RICHEMONT

113 E8 N45°44.410' W000°21.350' 16370

Directions: Allée des Coquelicots, off D85. From Cognac (south) on D731 at roundabout in village turn right onto D85. Aire on left in 500m next to bar/restaurant, signed.

Sanitation:

Parking:

5

Aire Services

Good sized bays overlooking garden of restaurant. Residential area of village. Inspected 2010.

MATHA

114 E8 N45°51.937' W000°19.321' 17160

Directions: Boulevard Bossais. From west on D939 turn off at roundabout, sp 'Matha' and 'DID Centre d'Exploitation'. At 2nd roundabout turn right and Aire is on right in 200m, adj to pond.

Sanitation:

Parking:

5

Custom; 5 unmetered elec points

Gatehouse of old château and pond adj. Toilets locked at time of inspection. Additional grass parking. Inspected 2010.

AULNAY

115 E8 N46°01.344' W000°20.716' 17470

Directions: D129/Rue de Salles. Exit town to north on D129, sp 'Chef-Boutonne'. Aire 200m on right, signed.

Sanitation:

Parking:

15

Custom

Town 3 mins; Market Thursday. Inspected 2010.

LOULAY

116 E7 N46°02.858' W000°30.688' 17330

Directions: Rue des Tilleuls, off D150. From St Jean D'Angely take D150 north. At Loulay turn right into Place du Général de Gaulle. Drive around the outside of the car park/square, following sp 'P Poids Lourds' and signed. Turn left into Rue des Tilleuls (one-way and heads back to main road). Aire on left at rear of La Poste and Mairie.

Sanitation: E WC F

Parking: P F

3

Custom

SP

Small roadside Aire in one way street; Attractive small town square (up steps behind Aire) with market on Fridays. Inspected 2010.

ST JEAN D'ANGELY 2

117 E8 N45°56.722' W000°32.249' 17400

Photo: Keith Seymour

Directions: Avenue de Marennes/D18. From east cross river and turn off D18 before junction with D218, sp 'Base de Plein Aire' and signed. 3 designated bays in car park at Base Nautique.

Sanitation: E WC F

Parking: P F

3; Max 2 Nights

Custom

SP

Lots of green space; Mini golf, skate park, table tennis, sandpit, football pitch, outdoor swimming pool, river adj; No views. Inspected 2010.

BURIE

118 E8 N45°46.317' W000°25.467' 17770

Directions: D131. Adj to D131 as exit village towards St Bris des Bois. Signed from D731.

Sanitation: E WC F

Parking: P F

5; Grass parking

Custom

SP

Mostly grass parking with gravel access roadway. Village centre 2 mins. Inspected 2010.

ST CESAIRE

119 E8 N45°45.231' W000°30.444' 17770

Photo: Rodney Martin

Directions: Rue de Lilas. From D134, main road, turn up small lane opp church, sp 'Cimitière' and signed. Aire 30m on left.

Sanitation: E WC F

Parking: P F

5

Custom

SP

Small village 2 mins. Inspected 2010.

SAINTES

120 D8 N45°45.300' W000°37.711' 17100

Directions: Rue de Courbiac, off D128. From town centre head northeast following sp 'Camping au Fil de l'Eau'. Aire is adj to campsite on west bank of river.

Sanitation: E WC F

Parking: P F

10; Max 24hrs

Aire Services; CC; €5

SP

Adj to indoor swimming pool; Showers avail in campsite, €2; Riverside path to town 20 mins. Inspected 2010.

PONS 1

121 D8 N45°36.051' W000°32.195' 17800

Directions: Exit Pons to north on D137, sp 'Saintes'. After 1.2km turn right. At end of road turn right onto D234. After 300m turn left onto D234e5, sp 'Château Renaud', 'Bougneau', 'Aire de Château Renaud', and signed. Aire on right in 500m.

Sanitation:

Parking:

3; Max 24hrs

None; See 122

Parking adj to country lane. Pretty woodland area with river. Feels remote. Inspected 2010.

PONS 2

122 D8 N45°34.667' W000°33.315' 17800

Directions: Ave du Poitou. On D137 turn off, sp 'Camping'. Follow sp and Aire outside municipal campsite.

Sanitation:

Parking:

5

Raclet; Token (2/1); €6

Sports facilities opp; Campsite adj. Inspected 2010.

ST GENIS DE SAINTONGE

123 D8 N45°28.785' W000°34.108' 17240

Directions: Avenue Alcide Beauvais, off D137. Turn onto D2 by Gendarmerie at D2/D137 roundabout, sp 'Jonzac'. Turn immediately left, signed. Aire 100m on right.

Sanitation:

Parking:

6; Max 48hrs

Custom; 4 16amp elec points

Pleasant parking area in village centre; Hot water at sink in toilet. Inspected 2010.

ST THOMAS DE CONAC

124 D8 N45°23.279' W000°41.401' 17150

Directions: D145. Signed off D145, adj to village boules court. 100m from church.

Sanitation:

Parking:

5; Max 72hrs

Custom

Small Aire with views over horse paddocks and countryside. Inspected 2010.

ST DIZANT DU GUA

125 D8 N45°25.840' W000°42.343' 17240

Directions: D145. As you exit the village towards Conac.

Sanitation:

Parking:

5

Euro Relais Junior; €2

Mini market adj; Small river adj. Village 5 mins. Cycle lanes around vines. Inspected 2010.

MORTAGNE SUR GIRONDE 126 D8 N45°28.550' W000°47.681' 17120

Directions: Quai des Pêcheurs, at Le Port. From town follow sp 'Le Port'. Aire on south side of river marina. Popular Aire, recommended to arrive early.

Sanitation: E

Parking: P

40; €7.20 inc elec; Collected in morning

Custom; inc; 400m from parking

SP

River marina with restaurants. Very pleasant spot. Service Point opp parking. Inspected 2010.

COZES 127 D8 N45°35.177' W000°49.999' 17120

Directions: Ave de la Gare. Enter town from north on D17. Turn right after crossing railway track, sp 'Talmont'. Turn right in 50m, signed. Aire at far end of car park.

Sanitation: E WC F

Parking: P F

3

Custom

SP

Adj to sports facilities and velo rail. Hire a velo cart in summer and pedal along the disused railway. Inspected 2012.

ST SEURIN D'UZET 128 D8 N45°30.061' W000°50.097' 17120

Directions: Place du Creac, off D145 next to river. Signed from D145, main road. Aire on opp side of marina to church.

Sanitation: E

Parking: P

5; €6.50 inc elec

Custom; Token; €1

SP

Overlooking boats in village centre. Grass area adj with benches. Inspected 2010.

SAUJON 129 D8 N45°40.513' W000°55.905' 17600

Directions: Route des Ecluses. Exit N150 onto D1, sp 'Saujon-Le Lande' and follow sp 'Port de Riberou'. Turn right, sp 'Port de Riberou'. Aire on left, signed. 5.5t weight restriction on parking.

Sanitation: E

Parking: P

20; €4/24hrs, €10/72hrs; CC; Max 6 days

Euro Relais Maxi; €4; CC

SP

Adj to former campsite and fairly busy main road. Adj to pond and river with footpath to town, 3 mins. Inspected 2012.

MESCHERS SUR GIRONDE 130 D8 N45°33.377' W000°56.695' 17132

Directions: Routes des Salines. From south on D145 turn left on entry to Meschers sur Gironde, sp 'Le Port' into Route des Salines. Aire and Service Point at end of road next to 'Capitainerie'. Additional parking on left of road prior to Service Point

Sanitation: E F

Parking: P

30; €6

Custom; 4 unmetered elec points

SP

Near working port with restaurants/bars on quay. WiFi at Capitainerie. Inspected 2010.

SOUBISE 131 D8 N45°55.703' W001°00.401' 17780

Directions: Rue Colbert. Exit D733 onto D238e1 sp 'Soubise'. Continue into centre of village. At first roundabout take 1st exit D238e1. At next roundabout continue straight on D238e1. At sharp left hand bend turn right into Rue du Docteur Savigny, sp 'Zone Portuare' and signed. Aire at end of road slightly to right.

Sanitation:

Parking:

23; €6.50 inc elec; Pay at machine

Custom; inc

SP

Lovely Aire at port, no views; Adj restaurant overlooks harbour; Heated showers and toilets avail at rear of Capitainerie. Inspected 2010.

ST GEORGES DE DIDONNE 132 D8 N45°36.261' W000°59.974' 17110

Directions: Rue du Docteur Maudet/Rue du Stade, opp stadium. From south on D25e travel north towards Royan. Go straight across large roundabout. At next roundabout turn right and follow road until opp stadium. Aire on right.

Sanitation:

Parking:

8; Max 1.5hrs

Custom

5 mins to beach and town centre. Opp sports facilities. Pleasant seaside town with large sandy beach. Inspected 2010.

PONT L'ABBE D'ARNOULT 133 D8 N45°49.700' W000°52.348' 17250

Directions: Rue de la Cité. From church follow D18, sp 'Saintes'. Turn right into Rue de la Cité, signed. Service Point on corner, parking opp.

Sanitation:

Parking:

5

Custom

SP

Aire in a residential location. Local commerce, decorative church and historic covered market 2 mins. Inspected 2012.

ST PORCHAIRE 134 D8 N45°49.243' W000°46.946' 17250

Directions: Place du Champ de Foire. From Saintes follow D137 north. Turn off D137 onto D237, sp 'St Porchaire'. After 1.7km in village centre turn right into Place du Champ de Foire. Turn right again and Aire is at end of car park.

Sanitation:

Parking:

6

Custom

Pleasant Aire adj to grassy area in village centre. Inspected 2010.

ST SAVINIEN 135 D8 N45°52.682' W000°41.068' 17350

Directions: D18, Route de St. Savinien. From St. Jean D'Angely take D18 west sp 'St. Savinien'. Continue through St. Savinien and cross river onto island following sp 'Ile aux Loisirs'. Service Point 200m on left outside camp site.

Sanitation:

Parking:

None

Custom

Service Point outside 'Ile Aux Loisirs' campsite. Available even when campsite closed. Inspected 2010.

ECHILLAIS 136 D8 N45°53.847' W000°57.335' 17620

Directions: From south on D733 turn right onto D238, sp 'Echillais'. At cross roads go straight on. Aire in car park on right in 350m.

Sanitation:

Parking:

10; €4; Collected in morning

Custom; inc

Village and TO 2 mins. Map at water tap. Pleasant landscaped Aire with flowering shrubs and hedges. Inspected 2010.

ST AGNANT 137 D8 N45°51.987' W000°57.885' 17620

Directions: Place de Verdun, off D123. Enter town on D123/Ave Charles de Gaulle. Aire in car park with memorial, sp 'Place de Verdun' and 'Médi@thèque'. Signed from traffic light crossroads.

Sanitation:

Parking:

10

None

Village 2 mins; There is no Service Point. Inspected 2010.

TONNAY CHARENTE 138 D8 N45°56.371' W000°52.897' 17430

Directions: Quai Auriol Roy-Bry. To avoid town approach from east on D739. At the roundabout turn onto D137, sp 'Saintes'. Turn right onto D124, sp 'Tonnay-Charente'. Follow road under 4m bridge and Aire on left, signed.

Sanitation:

Parking:

16; Max 7 days

Custom

Aire outside municipal campsite, adj to river but no view. Small town 4 mins. Distant road noise. Inspected 2012.

NIEULLE SUR SEUDRE 139 D8 N45°45.153' W001°00.131' 17600

Directions: Place de la Mairie, off D241. From Marennes take D728 southeast. Fork right onto D131. Then turn right onto D118, sp 'Nieulle sur Seudre'. At end of road turn right onto D241 and Aire on right in centre of village outside school.

Sanitation:

Parking:

3

Euro Relais Junior; Token (2/1); €4

Small square outside school, La Poste, and Mairie. Take care using services as corner of building overhangs Service Point. Inspected 2010.

LE GUA 140 D8 N45°43.538' W000°56.684' 17600

Directions: Place 19 Mars 1962. Enter village on D1 from south. At roundabout turn left. Aire 50m on left.

Sanitation:

Parking:

2; Depending on parked cars

Raclet; Token (2/1)

Small parking area just off the central square. Local commerce 1 min. Market Sunday. Inspected 2012.

ST JUST LUZAC — 141 — D8 — N45°47.950' W001°02.900' — 17320

Directions: Avenue des Vignes, off D728 at ZI Fief de Luzac. From Marennes take D728 southeast. In St Just Luzac at roundabout junction with D18 and D241e1 turn right onto D241e1 towards Luzac. Take 1st right into Rue des Vignes. Aire in 80m in small industrial estate.

Sanitation: E

Parking: F

2

Euro Relais Junior; Token (2/1); €4

SP

In industrial estate. Not picturesque. Boulangerie adj. Inspected 2010.

LA TREMBLADE — 142 — D8 — N45°45.986' W001°08.343' — 17390

Directions: Rue de la Resinerie. Enter town on D14 from south. Take 1st right after crossing canal. Aire on left in 200m.

Sanitation: E WC F

Parking: P F

50; €5/24hrs; Mar-Nov

Custom

SP

Train des Mouettes (steam train) runs from Aire May-Sept. Market 100m, Sat am. Inspected 2010.

LES MATHES — 143 — D8 — N45°42.848' W001°08.864' — 17570

Directions: Rue de la Garenne. Exit La Palmyre on D141e1 sp 'Les Mathes'. At roundabout take 1st exit into village. At next roundabout take 1st exit into Avenue Pierre Sibard. Turn next left into Rue de la Garenne. Aire on right adj to 'Espace Multi-Loisirs' (large purple building).

Sanitation: E WC F

Parking: P F

40; €8; Sept-Jun only; Max 7 Days; 10m bays

Custom; Token (ER); €4

SP

Some shade. Poss free Dec and Jan. Inspected 2010.

LA PALMYRE 1 — 144 — D8 — N45°41.483' W001°11.352' — 17570

Directions: Avenue de L'Atlantique. Turn off D25 at large roundabout, sp 'Le Port'. Then turn onto Blvd de Bonne Anse, sp 'Tennis'. At end of road turn right into Avenue de L'Atlantique. Aire on left. Barriered entry, pay by CC. Service Point outside barrier.

Sanitation: E WC F

Parking: P F

83; €8/24hrs; 10m bays; Max 7 days

Euro Relais Junior (ER); €2

SP

Town 5 mins. Sand dunes and wooded area adj. Change machine gives tokens or €1 coins. Inspected 2010.

LA PALMYRE 2 — 145 — D8 — N45°40.982' W001°10.818' — 17570

Directions: Blvd de la Plage. From southeast on D25 follow signs for La Palmyre Zoo. At 1st roundabout by zoo continue straight across. At large roundabout by TO take 5th exit into Avenue de l'Océan. At end of road turn right. Aire on left, adj to marina.

Sanitation: E WC F

Parking: P F

56; €8; Open Sept-Jun; Max 7 days; 10m bays

None; See 144

SP

Beautiful coastal location. Motorhomes banned July and Aug. Town 700m on cycle path. Beach 1 min. Inspected 2010.

MARENNES 1

146 D8 N45°49.399' W001°06.127' 17320

Directions: Rue Ovide Beillard, at E'Leclerc supermarket. From D728 ring road turn south onto D3 into town. Turn left into Rue Robert Etchebarne. E'Leclerc fuel station directly ahead. Access Service Point by driving past fuel station and turning between wall and bottled gas lockers. Service Point by car wash.

Sanitation:

Parking:

5

Euro Relais Mini; Token (ER); €3

In town; Supermarket adj. Inspected 2010.

MARENNES 2

147 D8 N45°49.561' W001°05.819' 17320

Directions: Rue Jean Moulin. From D728 turn onto D3 into town. Turn left onto Rue Jean Moulin and Aire on right across from ZA les Grossines, opp Intermarché supermarket.

Sanitation:

Parking:

20

Euro Relais Junior; Token (2/1)

Large, open gravel parking area in residential area. Adj to supermarket. Inspected 2010.

ST TROJAN LES BAINS 1

148 D8 N45°50.624' W001°12.533' 17370

Directions: Place de la Liberté. From north on D126 enter town and go straight across 1st roundabout. Turn 2nd right into Place de la Liberté. Aire on right next to car park.

Sanitation:

Parking:

20

None; See 149

Town and sea 2 mins. TO at roundabout 50m. Inspected 2010.

ST TROJAN LES BAINS 2

149 D8 N45°49.626' W001°13.052' 17370

Directions: Avenue des Bris. From D126 turn onto Ave des Bris at roundabout. Follow for 1.9km and Aire at ZI les Bris on right.

Sanitation:

Parking:

None; See 148

Euro Relais Junior; Token

Service Point out of service at time of inspection. Inspected 2010.

LE GRAND VILLAGE PLAGE (ILE D'OLERON)

150 D8 N45°51.714' W001°14.436' 17370

Directions: Allée des Pins. Follow D26 to Grand Village. Turn right at roundabout onto D126, sp 'La Cotiniere'. Turn left at next roundabout, sp 'Plage'. Turn 1st right, then left in front of Camping les Pins to Aire, signed.

Sanitation:

Parking:

9; €6/24hrs

Urba Flux Small; €4; CC

Landscaped Aire under shady pine trees. Bays are unlevel and some are impractical, but there is additional parking that is practical. Inspected 2012.

LE CHATEAU D'OLERON 2 — 151 — D8 — N45°53.791' W001°12.125' — 17480

Directions: Blvd Phillippe Daste. Follow D734 sp 'Chateau D'Oleron'. At roundabout in Chateau D'Oleron take D240 Boulevard Philippe Daste. Aire on left in 1.2km facing sea. Pay with CC upon entry.

Sanitation:

Parking:

100; €8/night inc elec

Euro Relais Junior; inc

Former campsite. Seafront adj. Showers avail. Inspected 2010.

DOLUS D'OLERON — 152 — D8 — N45°54.701' W001°15.261' — 17550

Directions: From south on D734, at 2nd roundabout in Dolus D'Oleron turn right onto D126, sp 'Boyardville'. In 700m turn right into Route du Stade. Service Point on left by tennis courts. Parking 50m at rear of tennis club, signed.

Sanitation:

Parking:

30; €5/24hrs; €30/7days

Euro Relais Tall; CC or Token (ER); €4

Approx 14 hardstanding for winter use, but mostly grass parking. Pay for both services and parking by CC on Service Point. Inspected 2010.

LA COTINIERE (ILE D'OLERON) — 153 — D8 — N45°55.425' W001°20.576' — 17310

Directions: Ave des Pins. In St Pierre turn off D734 at traffic lights onto D274, sp 'La Cotiniere'. Follow sp 'La Cotiniere' to end of rd. Turn left, sp 'La Cotiniere', and Aire is 50m on left before Camping Municipal Fauche-Prere. It is poss to drive through town but narrow with 3.5t restrictions in places.

Sanitation:

Parking:

5; Pay in season

Raclet; €2; Token

Small parking area under trees next to municipal campsite. Beach 100m through campsite. Inspected 2012.

LA BREE LES BAINS — 154 — D7 — N46°00.508' W001°21.437' — 17840

Directions: D273, at ZA de la Brée les Bains. Turn off D734 into La Brée les Bains on D273. Aire in industrial area on right before you enter town.

Sanitation:

Parking:

14

Euro Relais Junior; €4.50

Adj to recycling point and caravan sales/storage. Tokens from TO 1km. Inspected 2010.

LA MORELIERE — 155 — D7 — N46°02.651' W001°23.924' — 17650

Directions: D734. North of St Denis at end of D734.

Sanitation:

Parking:

None; See 156

Flot Bleu Euro; Token or CC; €5

Service Point only. Inspected 2010.

ST DENIS D'OLERON 156 D7 N46°01.659' W001°22.993' 17650

Directions: Route des Huttes. From the south approach St Denis d'Oléran on D734. Turn left onto Route des Huttes. Follow signs and Aire is 300m on right.

Sanitation:

Parking:

160; €8 inc 5amp elec and showers; Max 4 nights; Grass parking

Custom

SP

Former campsite with old amenities block. Laundry. Some shade. 1 mile from town and seafront. Inspected 2010.

BOYARDVILLE 157 D8 N45°58.140' W001°14.268' 17190

Directions: Avenue de la Plage. From D126 turn left before river bridge, sp 'Centre Ville' and 'Camping Cars'. Follow road around marina, following signs, past large car park to Aire. Well signed.

Sanitation:

Parking:

None

Euro Relais Junior; Token; Poss removed

SP

Report suggests this Service Point has closed. Inspected 2010.

CHATELAILLON PLAGE 1 158 D7 N46°03.735' W001°05.509' 17340

Directions: Chemin Vert, at Cercle de Voile in harbour. From D137/E602 turn onto D109 towards beach in Loin-du-Bruit. At 2nd roundabout turn right onto D202/l'Hippodrome. After 1.5km take 2nd exit at roundabout onto Rue Georges Michaud. After 450m turn left and immediately right. Aire on right in 180m.

Sanitation:

Parking:

7; Max 48hrs

Aire Services

SP

Adj to small harbour (no views) and swimming pool. Town 800m- 1km. Inspected 2010.

CHATELAILLON PLAGE 2 159 D7 N46°04.351' W001°05.162' 17340

Directions: Rue des Tennis. From D137/E602 turn onto D109 west towards beach in Loin-du-Bruit. Cross over two roundabouts, then turn left at next roundabout onto Rue Bir Hakeim-Foch. Turn 2nd right onto Rue des Tennis and Aire on left.

Sanitation:

Parking:

7; Max 48hrs

None; See 158

SP

Shady parking between trees at tennis courts. More space and more pleasant than harbour. Better for larger units. Inspected 2010.

CHATELAILLON PLAGE 3 160 D7 N46°04.635' W001°05.253' 17340

Directions: Allée du Stade, off D202. From D137/E602 turn onto D109 west towards beach in Loin-du-Bruit. Cross over two roundabouts, then turn sharp right at next roundabout. Aire in gravel parking area between TO and stadium.

Sanitation:

Parking:

15; Max 48hrs

None; See 158

SP

TO and stadium adj. Beach 500m. Inspected 2010.

CHATELAILLON PLAGE 4 — 161 — D7 — N46°04.611' W001°05.317' — 17340

Directions: D202/Ave de Strasbourg. From D137/E602 turn onto D109 west towards beach in Loin-du-Bruit. Cross over three roundabouts, D109 becomes D202, and Aire on right by TO.

Sanitation:

Parking:

5; Max 48hrs

None; See 158

Adj to TO; Opp Gendarmerie. Inspected 2010.

BOURCEFRANC LE CHAPUS 1 — 162 — D8 — N45°50.755' W001°08.948' — 17560

Directions: Rue du President Kennedy, off D728. From south on D728, main route, turn onto Rue du President Kennedy at 2nd roundabout and Aire on right in 200m.

Sanitation:

Parking:

10; Max 24hrs

None; See 163

Large parking area in town centre. Boules club and pharmacy adj. Inspected 2010.

BOURCEFRANC LE CHAPUS 2 — 163 — D8 — N45°49.867' W001°09.048' — 17320

Directions: Barre à L'Anglais. From Marennes take D728, sp 'Bourcefranc'. At roundabout continue straight across on D26e1, sp 'Île d'Oleron'. At traffic lights turn left onto Route Touristique and follow road along coast. Service Point on left outside Camping La Giroflee in 1.5km. Parking on right adj to beach in a further 850m: N45°49.564' W001°08.582'.

Sanitation:

Parking:

30; €5.50/night

Euro Relais Junior; Token (ER)

Overlooking sea and island. Service Point on sand, some parts deep. Tokens avail from TO. Inspected 2010.

PORT DES BARQUES — 164 — D8 — N45°56.800' W001°05.400' — 17730

Directions: Avenue des Sports and Route des Anses, off D125. From town follow D125 west along the coast towards Île Madame. Turn left into Route des Anses and the Aire is 500m on left. Entry barrier requiring CC payment. Service Point outside barrier.

Sanitation:

Parking:

30; €6/night; CC; Mar-Nov

Aire Services; CC; €2

Uninspiring car park but good for Île Madame across causeway.

FOURAS 1 — 165 — D8 — N45°58.894' W001°05.210' — 17450

Photo: Janet and John Watts

Directions: Avenue Philippe Jannet, adj to beach. Signed from main road. Follow main road towards coast then follow Avenue Philippe Jannet southeast along coast to Aire.

Sanitation:

Parking:

None

Custom; Token; €1

Beach opp; Sea views and views of regional fishing huts. Town 5 mins; Main road adj. Tokens avail from TO and campsite. Inspected 2010.

FOURAS 2 — 166 D8 N45°59.528' W001°05.202' 17450

Directions: D937c/Avenue du Cadoret. Outside Camping Le Cadoret, just off roundabout. Signed from main road. 3.5t weight restriction on Aire.

Sanitation:

Parking:

6; €7

Custom; Token; €1

Next to campsite and mini golf. 5 mins to town. Inspected 2010.

HIERS BROUAGE — 167 D8 N45°51.166' W001°04.636' 17320

Directions: D3. Exit Hiers Brouage north on D3. Service Point on right of road on bend by boat, set in small roadside municipal garden.

Sanitation:

Parking:

None

Raclet; Token (ER); €4

Marsh area. Tokens available from Mairie. Service Point out of service at time of inspection. Inspected 2010.

ROCHEFORT 1 — 168 D8 N45°55.687' W000°57.289' 17300

Directions: Ave de la Charente. From south cross bridge and turn right onto D911, sp 'Rochefort'. At roundabout turn left onto D911, sp 'Rochefort'. At next 2 roundabouts turn right, sp 'Camping Municipal'. Turn left, sp 'Camping Municipal'. Drive past campsite and Aire is on left, signed.

Sanitation:

Parking:

30; €6/24hrs; Pay at machine

Custom

Aire in residential area near municipal campsite. Town centre with numerous commerce 7 mins. Inspected 2012.

ROCHEFORT 2 — 169 D8 N45°56.648' W000°57.443' 17300

Directions: Quai Le Moyne De Sérigny, off D911/Ave William Ponty. Aire by swing bridge for marina, signed.

Sanitation:

Parking:

No overnight parking

Custom

Marina adj. Service Point only. Inspected 2010.

MURON — 170 D8 N46°02.176' W000°49.660' 17430

Photo: Dr WTR Pryce

Directions: Place du Champ de Foire. Exit D911, sp 'Muron'. The Aire is clearly signed in the village.

Sanitation:

Parking:

5

Custom

Small village centre 1 min; Motorhome weather vane at Aire. Inspected 2010.

ST GERMAIN DE MARENCENNES | 171 | D7 | N46°04.632' W000°47.247' | 17700

Directions: Place St André. From north on D911 turn right onto Rue de Trois Ponts and follow into St Germain de Marencennes. Aire on left before village centre.

Sanitation:

Parking:

6

Custom

Village 1 min. Inspected 2010.

ANGOULINS SUR MER 1 | 172 | D7 | N46°06.377' W001°08.151' | 17690

Directions: Place de la Platère. Drive through Angoulins towards the sea and beach. After crossing the train tracks go straight across roundabout. Follow the road past 173 on left, then to right. The Aire is along this road near the boat club.

Sanitation:

Parking:

17

None; See 173

Sea and beach adj but no views; Isolated spot. Inspected 2010.

ANGOULINS SUR MER 2 | 173 | D7 | N46°06.357' W001°06.995' | 17690

Directions: Chemin des Marais, in Salle Polyvalente by tennis courts. Follow D111e1, main route, through town west towards the coast following sp 'Tennis Club'. After crossing train tracks the Service Point is on the left.

Sanitation:

Parking:

None; See 172

Euro Relais Mini

Service Point only. Inspected 2010.

AIGREFEUILLE D'AUNIS | 174 | D7 | N46°07.447' W000°54.869' | 17290

Directions: Lac de Frace. Exit village on D113, sp 'Virson'. Exit village and turn right, sp 'Lac de Frace' and signed. Follow road to Service Point on right and parking 50m on left.

Sanitation:

Parking:

20; Max 24hrs

Urba Flux Tall; 1 unmetered elec point not working

By leisure/fishing lake but no views from parking. Walk around lake. May feel isolated at night. Night fishing prohibited. Inspected 2012.

ANGOULINS / AYTRE | 175 | D7 | N46°06.778' W001°07.381' | 17690

Directions: Route de la Plage. Exit Angoulins along the coast towards Aytré. Turn left onto Route de la Plage and cross the railway track. Take next left at Camping de la Plage. Drive through parking area to Aire.

Sanitation:

Parking:

30

Custom

Enclosed bay of sand and stone adj, but no view. Isolated. Huge out of town shopping area at Angoulins. Inspected 2010.

LA ROCHELLE 1

176 D7 N46°09.959' W001°09.255' 17000

Directions: Esplanades des Parcs, Parc Charruyer. Turn off N237 onto D104 into town. Stay on main road, going straight across all junctions and roundabouts. After 3rd roundabout the car park is signed on right.

Sanitation:

Parking:

24; 7m bays; Must park within lines of designated bays or face €35 fine

Custom

10 mins walk or cycle to interesting town centre through park. Town parking bans motorhomes. Inspected 2010.

LA ROCHELLE 2

177 D7 N46°09.134' W001°08.390' 17000

Photo: Dr Pryce

Directions: Rue des Jars, on south side of railway station. Accessible from D937 ring road. Sp 'P+R Vieux Port' through town. Aire closed Sunday; able to exit.

Sanitation:

Parking:

50; €10.50/24hrs

Custom

Frequent bus links to town centre, except Sundays, inc in price. Closed Sunday. No access 8pm-7am. Inspected 2010.

LA ROCHELLE 3

178 D7 N46°09.060' W001°09.491' 17000

Directions: Avenue Michel Crépeau. In small lay-by on main road at Marina des Minimes, opposite campsite. Follow sp 'Port du Plaisance - Les Minimes' and 'Camping'.

Sanitation:

Parking:

None; See 176 or 177

Custom

Service Point only; All local parking bans motorhomes. Inspected 2010.

ST CLEMENT DES BALEINES

179 D7 N46°13.662' W001°32.787' 17590

Directions: Rue de la Fôret. From south on D735 ignore 1st left into town. Take next left and follow signs for campsite; also signed but difficult to see. When opp La Côte Sauvage campsite turn right and Aire on left.

Sanitation:

Parking:

40; €7/24hrs; CC; Max 48hrs

Euro Relais Junior; Token; €2

Large open space; Sun trap. Inspected 2010.

LES PORTES EN RE

180 D7 N46°13.756' W001°29.001' 17880

Directions: Route du Fier/D101. Follow D101 through Les Portes-en-Ré. Road reaches coast and turns sharply to south becoming Route du Fier/D101. Continue to follow until you reach Aire near the sea at end of road.

Sanitation:

Parking:

7; €10/24hrs; Pay at machine; 10m bays

SOS; Token; €3.50; Water free at time of inspection in Nov

Parking 20m from beach, no view. Inspected 2010.

ST MARTIN DE RE

181 D7 N46°11.955' W001°21.905' 17410

Directions: Rue du Rempart. Due to narrow streets turn off D735 at roundabout on west side, signed. Follow sp 'Aire Camping-Car' past municipal campsite and Aire on left through barrier, signed.

Sanitation:

Parking:

17; €12; CC; Max 72hrs; 8m bays

Custom; Inside barrier

SP

Fortified town with interesting ramparts; Easy walk to town with picturesque port; Cycling all around island. Inspected 2010.

RIVEDOUX PLAGE - Ile de Re

182 D7 N46°09.571' W001°16.285' 17940

Directions: D735. From bridge on D735 drive 1km and Aire adj to D735 at entrance to municipal campsite Le Platin, signed.

Sanitation:

Parking:

17; €5 Nov-Mar €10 Summer; 9m bays

SOS; Token

8 bays with sea views; Cheapest and best located winter Aire on island. Inspected 2010.

MARANS 1

183 D7 N46°18.759' W000°59.895' 17230

Directions: Quai du 11 Novembre, at Le Port. Turn off D105, sp 'Z.I. Du Port'. Follow sp 'Z.I. Du Port' and the Service Point is against a building. Motorhomes are banned from car park nearest to town. Exit same way enter to avoid narrow streets.

Sanitation:

Parking:

5; None; See **184**

Custom

Adj to river with sailing boats, restaurants, etc. Town 5 mins. Inspected 2010.

MARANS 2

184 D7 N46°18.773' W000°59.529' 17230

Directions: N137. At the Super U supermarket adj to the N137 as exit town to the north. The Service Point is located at the edge of the car park opp the car wash, not in the fuel station.

Sanitation:

Parking:

Poss

Euro Relais Mini; €2

Supermarket adj. Inspected 2010.

ST JEAN DE LIVERSAY

185 D7 N46°16.200' W000°52.349' 17170

Directions: Rue St-Jean. In village turn off D109, sp 'St Cyr du Doret'. Service Point immediately on right. It is difficult to turn around to return to D109. From Service Point turn right past church, into 3.5t restricted road. Follow road past Mairie and parking is on right: N46°16.217' W000°52.540'.

Sanitation:

Parking:

5

Flot Bleu Océane; Token

Over engineering makes it difficult to exit Service Point. Parking adj to sports facilities. Local commerce 1 min. Inspected 2012.

TAUGON 186 D7 N46°18.363' W000°50.156' 17170

Directions: D109. Adj to D109 in front of cemetery as exit village towards St Jean de Liversay.

Sanitation:

Parking:

Poss

Flot Bleu Océane; €2

SP

Service Point only. There is limited parking adj. Inspected 2012.

LA LAIGNE 187 D7 N46°12.782' W000°45.226' 17170

Directions: D114. Adj to D114 as exit village towards Noirt on right, signed.

Sanitation:

Parking:

5

Flot Bleu Océane; €2

SP

Service Point in popular truck parking area. Inspected 2012.

LA RONDE 188 D7 N46°18.306' W000°48.294' 17170

Directions: D116/Rue du Port. Follow D116 north from village and Aire is 500m on left at the Aire de Repos, signed.

Sanitation:

Parking:

10; Grass parking

Flot Bleu Océane; €2

SP

Grass area adj to dyke. Located in area known as 'Green Venice'. Inspected 2010.

ARCAIS 189 D7 N46°17.786' W000°41.249' 79210

Photo: Janet and John Watts

Directions: D102. Just off D102 in car park, signed. Located on the east edge of the village. Entrance via barrier.

Sanitation:

Parking:

40; €6/night Apr-Oct; Grass parking

Custom

SP

In 'Green Venice', a popular tourist destination. Inspected 2010.

MAUZE SUR LE MIGNON 190 D7 N46°11.990' W000°40.857' 79210

Directions: Rue du Port, off Rte de Saint-Hilaire/D101. Aire across river from D101 on edge of town, sp 'Camping'. Outside campsite, but in different area.

Sanitation:

Parking:

10

Flot Bleu Pacific; Token; €3

SP

Nice pond water feature adj; Village with local commerce 5 mins; Campsite adj. Inspected 2010.

COULONGES SUR L'AUTIZE — 191 — D7 — N46°28.812' W000°35.629' — 79160

Directions: D744. Aire adj to D744, sp 'Aire de Repos' and signed. Large motorhomes may struggle to turn around, assess before entering.

Sanitation:

Parking:

2; Limited additional parking

Custom; 4 unmetered CEE elec points

Adj to busy and noisy main road. Small park adj. Town centre with small town commerce 4 mins. Inspected 2012.

ESNANDES — 192 — D7 — N46°15.167' W001°07.200' — 17137

Directions: Rue de l'Ocean. Turn off D105 onto Rue de l'Ocean. The service point is in 400m on the right outside camping Les Misottes.

Sanitation:

Parking:

None

Raclet; €1.50

Service point only. Inspected 2010.

HAVE YOU VISITED AN AIRE?

GPS co-ordinates in this guide are protected by copyright law

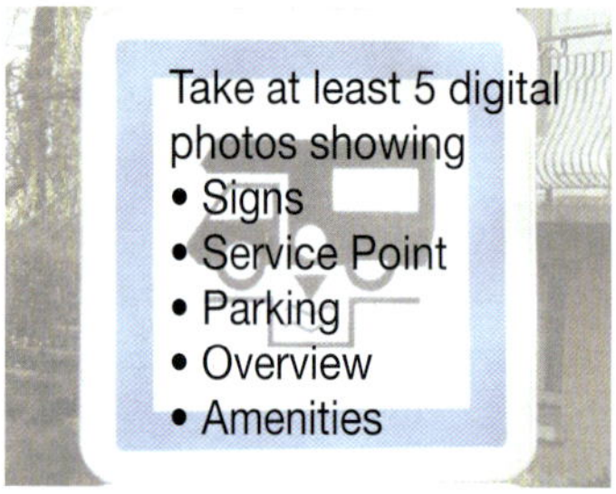
Take at least 5 digital photos showing
• Signs
• Service Point
• Parking
• Overview
• Amenities

Visit www.all-the-aires.co.uk/submissions.shtml to upload your updates and photos.

Sanitation:

Aire Details:

Submit updates

- Amendments
- New Aires
- Not changed

Romagne

Les Deux Alpes *Photo: Heidi Hardwick*

RHONE-ALPS

Saillans, *Photo Jean and Ken Fowler*

ST MARTIN D'ESTREAUX | 1 | I7 | N46°12.434' E003°47.888' | 42620

Directions: D52, at Place des Gouttes. From south on N7 take 3rd exit at roundabout, sp 'St Martin D'Estréaux'. Follow road through town and turn right onto D52, sp 'Aire Camping Cars', then turn left onto Place des Gouttes. Aire on right 150m.

Sanitation:

Parking:

4; Max 48hrs

Custom

Convenient stop when travelling north/south on N7. Inspected 2010.

LE CROZET | 2 | I7 | N46°10.164' E003°51.448' | 42310

Directions: D35. Exit N7 at Junction 59, sp 'La Pacaudière'. Follow road to La Pacaudière and turn right onto D35, sp 'Le Crozet'. Follow road under 3.8m arched railway bridge up towards village. Turn sharp left, signed. Aire on left, signed.

Sanitation:

Parking:

2; Max 72hrs

Custom; €2; Elec €2/4hrs

Small Aire with 2 spaces. Need to reverse out into a quiet road. 600m walk from medieval village. Inspected 2010.

ST RIRAND | 3 | I7 | N46°04.503' E003°51.015' | 42370

Directions: Le Moulin, off D41 opp church. From Renaison take D9 then turn left onto D41, sp 'St Rirand'. At start of village turn left into Lieu-Dit Le Moulin opp church. Aire 100m on left.

Sanitation:

Parking:

3

Custom

Small Aire in lovely, quiet, rural setting on edge of village adj to children's play equipment. Covered picnic benches on decking 'islands'. Inspected 2010.

AMBIERLE | 4 | I7 | N46°06.395' E003°53.623' | 42820

Directions: Rue du 19 Mars 1962. Follow signs from D52 in Ambierle centre by château. When road ends go straight across and follow road. Imperative to follow correct route; 7m vehicles only! Parking at new sports complex, near cemetery.

Sanitation:

Parking:

5

Custom

Views. Interesting church/château complex in centre. Inspected 2010.

ST GERMAIN LESPINASSE | 5 | I7 | N46°06.317' E003°57.737' | 42640

Directions: D18/Route de Vivans. From south on N7 turn left onto D4, sp 'St Germain Lespinasse'. In town turn right onto D18. Aire in car park on left just beyond village centre.

Sanitation:

Parking:

3

Custom

Small parking area with some shade and lovely views across open countryside. Interesting old village. Market Thurs. Inspected 2010.

RENAISON

6 | I7 | N46°02.863' E003°55.276' | 42370

Directions: Chemin Rural de la Bernarde, off D8. Turn left off D47 onto D8. D8 turns left again and heads south, follow for 400m then turn right onto Chemin Rural de la Bernarde. Aire at stadium. Well signed.

Sanitation:

Parking:

5

Custom

Pleasant Aire by small river and weir at edge of town. Shady and quiet, some parking on grass available. Inspected 2010.

ST ANDRE D'APCHON

7 | I7 | N46°02.040' E003°55.625' | 42370

Directions: La Prébande/Rue du 11 Novembre 1918. Between church and cemetery, turn off D8 at roundabout into St André d'Apchon and follow signs through town. Narrow access through village.

Sanitation:

Parking:

2

Custom

Really just a Service Point; Village 2 mins; Additional parking adj. Inspected 2010.

ARCON

8 | I8 | N46°00.574' E003°53.292' | 42370

Directions: D51. From St André d'Apchon follow D51 to Arcon. Aire on right between double bend just after village.

Sanitation:

Parking:

6

Custom

Small but well laid out Aire with space for 3 motorhomes next to Service Point and 3 more on terrace above. Inspected 2010.

LES NOES

9 | I8 | N46°02.459' E003°51.105' | 42370

Directions: D47. From Renaison on D9 turn left onto D47. Follow road to Les Noës and Aire on left at start of village, approx 7.8km.

Sanitation:

Parking:

10

Custom

Walks from Aire and also lots of walking at lakes 5km east. Inspected 2010.

VILLEREST *

10 | I8 | N45°59.189' E004°02.578' | 42300

Directions: D18. Exit D53, sp 'Lac de Villerest'. Travel 3.7km to roundabout in village centre. Turn right, sp 'Plan d'Eau'. Follow for approx 1km and Aire is on right overlooking lake. Pay at adj mini golf.

Sanitation:

Parking:

20; €5 inc service; Free Oct-Apr; Max 72hrs

Flot Bleu Pacific; Token; €4

Tap next to Flot Bleu, drive over gulley and proper toilet emptying place in the toilet block. Flot Bleu only in use in low season (Oct-Apr) €4 (2 x €2 tokens). Inspected 2010.

ST JUST EN CHEVALET

11 I8 N45°54.852' E003°50.840' 42430

Directions: D495/D53/D1/Rue de Vichy. From Roanne on D53 turn left in centre of village and Service Point on left next to toilets just prior to D53/D1 turning right.

Sanitation:

Parking:

Poss; In village car park

Urba Flux; Elec €2

Service Point only. Inspected 2010.

CHAMPOLY

12 I8 N45°51.454' E003°50.063' 42430

Directions: At church in village centre. Approach roads may be narrow. Accessible from A72/E70 to D24 or on D44.

Sanitation:

Parking:

3

Euro Relais Junior; €2; reports suggest this may have been removed

In the centre of the village. Inspected 2010.

ROANNE

13 I7 N46°02.267' E004°04.969' 42300

Directions: Allée de l'Amiral Merveilleux Du Vignaux. Enter on D482 and follow through town. Turn left just past Point P builders merchant, where road meets canal, sp 'Capitainerie'. Cross canal on bridge, sp 'Capitainerie'. Follow road to right and Aire is 200m past the Capitainerie alongside canal.

Sanitation:

Parking:

10; €6/night inc token; Max 72hrs

Flot Bleu Euro; CC; €2.10; Elec 1 token/12hrs

Lovely outlook over canal basin and boats. Nicely laid out Aire with plenty of space and grass between the large level bays. Inspected 2010.

ST HAON LE CHATEL

14 I7 N46°03.830' E003°54.777' 42370

Directions: D39/La Judée. From south on D8 turn left onto D39. Continue through village and Aire on right at end of village, signed.

Sanitation:

Parking:

3

Custom

Small, newly created Aire with 3 level bays and Service Point on edge of village. Inspected 2010.

POUILLY SOUS CHARLIEU

15 I7 N46°08.589' E004°06.515' 42720

Directions: Rue de la République. From D4 turn onto D482, sp 'Roanne'. Aire 200m on left opp mini Casino market, sp 'Espace Loisirs'. Just before D35 junction.

Sanitation:

Parking:

10; No parking Sundays 6am-1pm market day

Aire Services

Town 2 mins with commerce. Info board shows other motorhome parking places without services. Inspected 2010.

COURS LA VILLE | 16 | I7 | N46°06.243' E004°19.400' | 69470

Directions: Chemin de la Rivière. From south on D8 turn left at town square opp sp 'Information'. Follow road downhill and Aire is ahead, signed. Large vehicles travel 600m past square and turn left down Rue de la Rampe. Follow downhill and Aire on right.

Sanitation:

Parking:

10; Grass parking

Custom

SP

Quieter parking adj to 'Salle Omnisports'; Stream adj; Factory adj. Inspected 2010.

BELMONT DE LA LOIRE | 17 | I7 | N46°09.928' E004°20.772' | 42670

Directions: Place de l'Eglise, at the church. Signed from village roundabout by church. Follow D4 and turn left at roundabout, then immediately left again. Service Point against church.

Sanitation:

WC

Parking:

5

Custom

SP

Small village with aged Service Point and limited parking. Looks better than it is! Inspected 2010.

AMPLEPUIS | 18 | I8 | N45°58.217' E004°19.850' | 69550

Directions: Rue Paul de la Goutte. From south on D8, exit at D8/D10 roundabout onto D8e, sp 'Thizy'. Turn 1st right after 250m, sp 'Aire Camping Car'. Aire on right, by bus stop, in 120m at Rue Paul de la Goutte, signed. 7.5t weight restriction on Aire.

Sanitation:

Parking:

10; Max 48hrs

Custom

SP

Parking at 'Salle des Sports Daniel Pierrefeu'. Water below ground under large red flaps, may be turned off in winter. Risk of grounding at entrance. Inspected 2010.

JOUX | 19 | I8 | N45°53.302' E004°22.553' | 69170

Directions: At 'Salle des Fêtes' on D79. From east on N7 turn left onto D79, sp 'Joux'. Aire on left in 1.3km at start of village, sp 'Salle des Fêtes'.

Sanitation:

Parking:

10

Custom

SP

Service Point at bottom of very sloping car park with loose gravel; Adj to village hall. Better level parking at lakeside: N45°53.439' E004°22.953'. Inspected 2010.

LES SAUVAGES | 20 | I8 | N45°55.238' E004°22.627' | 69170

Directions: 'Les Pres de Sienne', off D121. From Tarare (southeast) on D8 turn left onto D121, sp 'Les Sauvages' and signed. Follow road for 600m through village and turn right at end of village sign by small memorial, sp 'Stade'.

Sanitation:

WC

Parking:

20

Custom; donation box

SP

Choice of 3 parking areas: 1 adj to stadium and Service Point with some shade and 2 across road with good views adj to self-service weighbridge. Inspected 2010.

VIOLAY

21 | I8 | N45°51.153' E004°21.306' | 42780

Directions: Place Giroud. Turn off D1 opp D49 turning to Villecheneve, signed. Turn left into car park, the Aire is located at the far end.

Sanitation:

Parking:

3

Custom; 3 Cont elec points not working.

Adj to panoramic view but obstructed by conifers. Local commerce 1 min, adj to D1. Inspected 2012.

PONTCHARRA SUR TURDINE

22 | I8 | N45°52.452' E004°29.491' | 69490

Directions: Place Albert Schweitzer. From east on N7 take 1st exit onto D31 at roundabout as enter village. After 1.4km pass Casino supermarket and turn left onto D27. Take 1st left into Rue de Verdun then left again and Aire in small car park in front of La Poste.

Sanitation:

Parking:

4

Custom

Seating area; Dog toilet adj; Town 2 mins. Inspected 2010.

ST FORGEUX

23 | I8 | N45°51.458' E004°28.601' | 69490

Directions: From east on N7 take 1st exit onto D31 at roundabout at start of Pontcharra sur Turdine. After 1.4km turn left onto D27. After 2.3km turn sharp left (tight turn) onto D632/Rue du Moulin. Continue downhill and Aire on left in 300m.

Sanitation:

Parking:

10

Custom; 2 unmetered elec points

Aire in rural setting on edge of pretty, well kept village. View of village on hillside across field. Inspected 2010.

L'ARBRESLE

24 | I8 | N45°49.373' E004°36.338' | 69210

Directions: Place des 3 Communes. Exit town on D389, sp 'Clermont FD'. At roundabout turn right into retail park, sp 'Eveux'. At next roundabout turn right and the Service Point is off the next roundabout, adj to recycling bins.

Sanitation:

Parking:

None

Custom

Service Point only. Adj retail park has numerous shops inc Super U with self-service laundry. Inspected 2012.

BELLEVILLE

25 | J7 | N46°06.392' E004°45.253' | 69220

Directions: Rue du Vivier. Exit A6/E15 at Junction 30, sp 'Belleville'. At roundabout take 1st exit onto D37d. At next roundabout take 2nd exit onto D337, signed. At 3rd roundabout take 2nd exit, Ave de Salzkotten, then immediately left into Rue du Vivier. Aire at end of road.

Sanitation:

Parking:

6; Max 48hrs; 11m bays

Custom

Handy stop for travelling north/south. Under trees; Located between A6/E15 toll motorway and D306/N6 primary route. Inspected 2010.

TREVOUX | 26 | J8 | N45°56.400' E004°46.050' | 01600

Directions: Chemin du Camping. From D933 exit roundabout by river, sp 'Camping'. Aire on left outside municipal campsite. Service Point visible from road.

Sanitation:

Parking:

10

Euro Relais Junior; Token (ER); €2.50; From campsite Apr-Sept

Easy access; Shaded parking. Municipal campsite adj. 100m from river Saône. Inspected 2010.

BEAUJEU | 27 | J7 | N46°09.747' E004°34.420' | 69430

Info/Photo: Carol Weaver

Directions: Rue du Stade. Turn off the D37 at village boundary towards Les Depots, sp 'Le Stade' and signed. Service Point and parking at the sports facilities.

Sanitation:

Parking:

5

Euro Relais Mini; Token (ER)

Small village with local commerce 4mins. Woodland walks adj. Visited 2012.

PONT DU VAUX (ST BENIGNE) | 28 | J7 | N46°26.218' E004°57.183' | 01190

Photo: Geoff Myatt

Directions: D2, Rue de l'Hôpital. From Pont De Vaux take D2 to St Trivier-de-Courtes. After approx 1.5km turn right at the roundabout. The Aire is at the ATAC supermarket on the right adj to D2. Service Point next to fuel station.

Sanitation:

Parking:

By request

Euro Relais Junior; Token (ER); €2

Overnight parking on request. Motorhome parking not designated but large car park. Toilets during store hours. Inspected 2010.

ST TRIVIER DE COURTES | 29 | J7 | N46°27.540' E005°04.838' | 01560

Directions: Petit Tour. From south D975 exit D2/Rue des Carrons and turn left into Petit Tour at roundabout. Or from north on D2 take 3rd exit at roundabout onto Petit Tour. Sp 'Aire de Repos' in town. Water point outside fire station off D2.

Sanitation:

Parking:

3

Custom

Village adj. Limited services and parking. Old Aire unlikely to be developed. Inspected 2010.

ST ANDRE SUR VIEUX JONC | 30 | J7 | N46°09.173' E005°09.116' | 01960

Directions: From Bourg en Bresse head south on D1083. At roundabout turn right onto D117, then 1st left onto D67a, sp 'St Andre-s-Vieux-Jonc'. After 4km turn left into Chemin du Suc. At roundabout take 2nd exit into Chemin du Stade. Aire on left in 200m. Well signed.

Sanitation:

Parking:

3

Custom

Pleasant, quiet, garden setting with open views to fields beyond football pitches. Inspected 2010.

HAVE YOU VISITED AN AIRE? **GPS co-ordinates in this guide are protected by copyright law**

Take at least 5 digital photos showing
• Signs
• Service Point
• Parking
• Overview
• Amenities

Visit www.all-the-aires.co.uk/submissions.shtml to upload your updates and photos.

Sanitation:

Aire Details:

Submit updates
- Amendments
- New Aires
- Not changed

SANDRANS

32 J7 N46°03.707' E004°58.347' 01400

Directions: D27. From south on D2 turn left onto D27 by the church in Sandrans, signed. Follow road for 700m and turn left, sp 'Camping-Pêche'.

Sanitation:

Parking:

None

Raclet; Token (2/1)

SP

Adj to fishing lake and campsite. Campsite has reopened €9/night. Inspected 2010.

GPS Co-ordinates for SatNav

The GPS Co-ordinates published in this guide were taken onsite by our inspectors. We consider them a valuable and unique asset and at the time of publishing have decided not to publish them as electronic files for use on navigation devices. You have permission to type in the co-ordinates of an Aire you intend to visit but not to store or share them. For the security of our copyright:

- **Do not compile them into lists**
- **Do not publish, share or reproduce them anywhere in any format**

PANISSIERES

34 I8 N45°47.292' E004°20.634' 42360

Directions: Allée des Acacias. From north on D60 turn left, sp 'Ferme Seigne'. Follow road then turn left again, sp 'Ferme Seigne'. Turn right, sp 'Relais Camping-Car'. Aire on right adj to building, signed.

Sanitation:

Parking:

7; €6.20/night inc elec

Custom; 7 10amp continental elec points.

SP

There is an additional €3.20pp charge to use the toilet block with showers and laundry. Local commerce 2 mins. Inspected 2012.

BIBOST

35 I8 N45°47.699' E004°33.085' 69690

Directions: D91. Turn off D389 onto D91, sp 'Bibost'. As enter village take 1st turning on left down slope to sports facilities, signed.

Sanitation:

Parking:

5

Urba Flux, customised

SP

Pleasant stop on outskirts of village. Several bar/restaurants in village, 4 mins. Inspected 2012.

CHAMBOST LONGESSAIGNE — 36 — I8 — N45°46.354' E004°21.990' — 69770

Directions: D101. Exit village on D101, sp 'Panissieres'. Turn left, signed, 400m before 3.5m height restriction. Aire on left, signed.

Sanitation:

Parking:

2

Custom

Aire located on edge of village adj to recycling point. Local commerce 3 mins. Inspected 2012.

CHAUSSAN — 37 — I8 — N45°38.037' E004°38.279' — 69440

Directions: D34. In Mornant turn onto D34, sp 'Chaussan'. In Chaussan turn left at roundabout, signed.

Parking:

None

Custom; Tap on side of building; Dysfunctional

Service Point only, limited use and access! Inspected 2012.

ST SYMPHORIEN SUR COISE — 38 — I8 — N45°38.026' E004°27.532' — 69590

Directions: D4. Follow sp 'Lyon' to navigate one-way system onto D4 northbound. Aire in car park adj to D4, signed.

Sanitation:

Parking:

5; Popular local residence parking

Custom; Token (See nearest toilet); Free from Tabac/Mairie

D4 is a busy and noisy road. Town centre with local commerce 3 mins. Inspected 2012.

ST MARTIN EN HAUT — 39 — I8 — N45°38.535' E004°32.111' — 69850

Directions: Exit St Martin en Haut on D311 to St Symphorien-sur-Coise. Turn off D311, sp 'Village Vacanes l'Oree du Bois' and signed. Follow road down hill, across stream and up other side then turn 1st left. Aire on left, signed.

Sanitation:

Parking:

5; Grass and gravel parking

Custom

In a remote, rural location adj to vacation village with café and fishing lake. Voi Verte cycle route/walks adj. Inspected 2012.

FONTANES — 40 — I8 — N45°32.808' E004°26.408' — 42140

Directions: Hameau de Chantemerle. Approach Fontanes from south on D3. Turn left as enter village down a steep slope, signed. Follow road and Aire is on right, signed.

Sanitation:

Parking:

3

Custom

Aire adj to sports facilities in a quiet rural village. History info panel and walking panel adj. Local shop selling regional produce 2 mins uphill. Inspected 2012.

MORNANT

41 J8 N45°36.935' E004°40.254' 69440

Directions: Rue Boiron. Adj to D30 outside municipal campsite, signed.

Sanitation:

Parking:

None

Euro Relais Junior; 2 unmetered CEE elec points

Service Point only. Inspected 2012.

ST PRIEST EN JAREZ

42 I8 N45°28.721' E004°21.522' 42270

Directions: N82. Exit A72 at Junction 10 and turn right, sp 'St Priest en Jez'. Aire adj to N82 at the fuel station of the Casino supermarket, signed.

Sanitation:

Parking:

Poss

Flot Bleu Euro; €2; CC

Supermarket adj. Inspected 2012.

ST JEAN BONNEFONDS

43 I8 N45°27.243' E004°26.821' 42650

Directions: Off D32. From village centre follow D32, sp 'St Chamond'. Turn left as exit village into car park, signed. This is a steep and sharp turn that is unsuitable for vehicles that are underpowered or have low overhangs. Service Point at far side of car park, signed.

Sanitation:

Parking:

Poss, but extremely unlevel

Euro Relais Mini; Token (ER)

The parking angle is about 8 per cent so this is really just a Service Point which is difficult to access. Inspected 2012.

ST VICTOR SUR LOIRE

44 I8 N45°26.900' E004°15.387' 42230

Directions: Lieu-Dit St Victor sur Loire. From St Etienne head west on D32 to St Victor sur Loire. Follow sp 'P Base Nautique'. At marina follow one way loop right round, ignore old Flot Bleu by toilets and continue uphill then turn sharp right at island. Aire on right overlooking lake.

Sanitation:

Parking:

9

Flot Bleu Pacific; Free; Flot Bleu Electric (avail from Mairie); 1 token 4hrs elec

SP

Moved to better position, higher and level. Inspected 2010.

LE BESSAT

45 I8 N45°22.117' E004°31.668' 42660

Directions: Croix de Chaubouret. Turn off D8 at Croix de Chaubouret onto D2, sp 'La Villa'. Aire on left in 50m, signed.

Sanitation:

Parking:

6; Other undesignated parking

Flot Bleu Pacific; €2.50; Token; Flot Bleu Electric; 4 CEE elec points; 1 Token/4hrs

Alt 1201. Ski centre opp. In national park with walking trails. In a sheltered spot without views. Inspected 2012.

PLANFOY | 46 | I8 | N45°22.467' E004°26.945' | 42660

Directions: D1082. From Planfoy head south for 1.5km on D1082, look for a small sign on your left and turn off, sp 'Le Vignolet', 'Stade' and signed. The Aire is in 200m on the left.

Sanitation:

Parking:

10

Flot Bleu Pacific; Token; €2; Elec 1 token/6hrs; 4 sockets

Next to sports ground, walk to lake and village. Inspected 2010.

BOULIEU LES ANNONAY | 47 | J8 | N45°16.139' E004°40.188' | 07100

Directions: Chemin du Lavoir. Turn off D820 opp D342 turning to St Clair into Rue du Musard. Take 1st left past 1914-18 war memorial, then turn right and right again, signed. Follow road round bend and turn right. At end of road turn left into Aire.

Sanitation:

Parking:

6; Other undesignated parking

Custom; Donation

Adj to park. Charming medieval centre 2 mins with local shops and restaurants. Inspected 2012.

LES ROCHES DE CONDRIEU | 48 | J8 | N45°27.239' E004°46.094' | 38370

Directions: D4. Cross bridge from Condrieu and drive straight on. The Aire is in the 1st car park on left, signed.

Sanitation:

Parking:

20

Custom

2 mins from Rhône river with port and local commerce. Inspected 2010.

VIENNE | 49 | J8 | N45°32.320' E004°52.352' | 38200

Directions: N7. Heading south from Lyon on A7 exit at Junction 9, sp ' Vienne'. Follow dual carriageway along river Rhône. Turn left at traffic lights, sp 'St Symphorien'. Go under bridge and turn left at roundabout onto N7, sp ' St Symphorien' and signed. After two sets of traffic lights turn right into car park, signed. Take 3rd row on left to Aire.

Sanitation:

Parking:

6

Custom

Town commerce and bank adj, but Vienne centre 10 mins walk. Market in car park Fri 12-8pm. River Rhône access restricted by road. Inspected 2012.

ST GEORGES D'ESPERANCHE | 50 | J8 | N45°33.348' E005°04.504' | 38790

Directions: Chemin des Picarnus. From D75, exit roundabout onto D53c, sp 'St Georges d'Espéranche Centre' and signed. Go straight over two roundabouts, following road until it ends. Then follow signs through car park to Aire. Narrow access and 3.5t weight restriction on Aire.

Sanitation:

Parking:

10

Custom

Town with shops and restaurants 5 mins. Pleasant stop. Inspected 2010.

ST JEAN DE BOURNAY

51 J8 N45°30.060' E005°08.300' 38440

Directions: Parking 'Place du Marché' at Place François Mitterrand. From roundabout on D518 follow truck route into town on Rte de Villeneuve. Turn right onto Rue du Dr Paillard and then left on Place du Marché. Aire on right.

Sanitation:

Parking:

50; No parking on Mondays from 5am-2:30pm - market

Custom

Small town commerce 2 mins. Inspected 2010.

EYZIN PINET

52 J8 N45°28.481' E004°59.984' 38780

Directions: Rue du Stade. Turn off D502 onto D38, sp 'Eyzin-Pinet'. Follow D38 into village and the Aire is on the left, signed. Follow road to rear of car park.

Sanitation:

Parking:

8; Max 48hrs

Custom

Pleasant, well located Aire adj to green space but only 1 min from village centre with local commerce. Inspected 2012.

GPS Co-ordinates for SatNav

The GPS Co-ordinates published in this guide were taken onsite by our inspectors. We consider them a valuable and unique asset and at the time of publishing have decided not to publish them as electronic files for use on navigation devices. You have permission to type in the co-ordinates of an Aire you intend to visit but not to store or share them. For the security of our copyright:

- **Do not compile them into lists**
- **Do not publish, share or reproduce them anywhere in any format**

ST SORLIN EN VALLOIRE

54 J8 N45°17.417' E004°57.250' 26210

Directions: D483, at Super U supermarket. From east on D1 take 1st exit onto D483 at roundabout on edge of St Sorlin en Valloire and supermarket is 250m on left.

Sanitation:

Parking:

Poss

Euro Relais Mini

Service Point beyond fuel station, adj to car wash. Toilets in supermarket. Inspected 2010.

HAUTERIVES

55 I8 N45°15.296' E005°01.738' 26390

Directions: Off D187. From south on D538 turn right onto D187 opp Ecomarché, sp 'Aire de Camping Car 500m'. Turn left at right-hand bend, sp 'Aire de Camping Car 200m'. Follow road to gravel parking area. Service Point on left by boules club.

Sanitation:

Parking:

10

Custom; €2

Large gravel parking area. Only 13km from Lafuma Factory Shop in Anneyron; Outdoor equipment specialists. Open 7 days a week. Inspected 2010.

ST DESIRAT — 56 — J8 — N45°15.515' E004°47.546' — 07340

Directions: D291. From D82 turn, sp 'St Désirat'. At roundabout turn right, sp 'Musée'. Aire 500m on right in visitor parking.

Sanitation:

Parking:

10; Max 1 night

Custom; 4 unmetered Cont elec points

At wine distillery and museum. Restaurant. Pleasant rural spot. Inspected 2010.

BEAUSEMBLANT — 57 — J8 — N45°13.085' E004°49.980' — 26240

Directions: D122/Rue du 11 Nov 1918. Turn off D122 opp boulangerie in town, sp 'Aire de Camping Car'. Well signed.

Sanitation:

Parking:

6; Max 48hrs

Custom

Local commerce 2 mins. Inspected 2010.

ARDOIX — 58 — J9 — N45°11.322' E004°44.217' — 07290

Directions: D506. From Sarras follow sp 'Ardoix' onto D506. As enter village turn left at the roundabout, signed. Aire on left, signed.

Sanitation:

Parking:

4; Large motorhomes must reverse for overhang

Euro Relais Junior; Token (ER)

Rural views from parking area on edge of village. Local commerce 2 mins. Inspected 2012.

ST ROMAIN D'AY — 59 — J9 — N45°09.856' E004°39.810' — 07290

Directions: D6. Turn off D6 at east edge of village, sp 'Notre Dame d' Ay', 'Halle Marche' and signed. Aire immediately on left.

Sanitation:

Parking:

4 designated bays; Max 7m

Flot Bleu Pacific; Token; Flot Bleu Electric; 1 Token/4hrs

Covered community space adj. Local commerce 2 mins. Inspected 2012.

HAVE YOU VISITED AN AIRE?

GPS co-ordinates in this guide are protected by copyright law

Take at least 5 digital photos showing
• Signs
• Service Point
• Parking
• Overview
• Amenities

Visit www.all-the-aires.co.uk/submissions.shtml to upload your updates and photos.

Sanitation:

Aire Details:

Submit updates

- Amendments
- New Aires
- Not changed

LALOUVESC

61 I9 N45°07.277' E004°32.036' 07520

Info/Photo: Carol Weaver

Directions: D532. Turn off D532 in centre onto one-way system around central car park, sp 'Station Service'. Service Point next to fuel station. Parking: N45°07.176' E004°32.035' From Service Point turn left on D532. Take the next right next to Mairie, sp 'P'. Turn 1st left and designated parking is on the right, signed.

Sanitation:

Parking:

3

Euro Relais Junior; Token (ER); May-Sept

Local commerce 2 mins. Market Tursdays mornings, 0600-1300hrs, in central car park. Visited 2011.

ST FELICIEN

62 I9 N45°05.078' E004°37.718' 07410

Directions: Off D234. From south on D234 turn off opp Sapeurs Pompiers (fire station), signed. The Aire is 100m on right.

Sanitation:

Parking:

6

Euro Relais Junior; €2

Village 5 mins walk. Inspected 2010.

ARLEBOSC

63 J9 N45°02.204' E004°39.145' 07410

Info/Photo: Carol Weaver

Directions: Place du Marche, off D578. From north on D578 turn right at start of village into Place du Marche, sp 'Place du Marche', 'Poste', 'Mairie', and signed. Service Point at old weighbridge. Signed.

Sanitation:

Parking:

6

Custom

Aire in centre of pretty, old village. Visited 2012.

COLOMBIER LE VIEUX

64 J9 N45°03.967' E004°41.641' 07410

Directions: D234. From east on D234 turn right just before church and Service Point is located immediately behind the church. Signed.

Sanitation:

Parking:

3

Custom

Some parking on small gravel area and some on grass adj to Service Point. Inspected 2010.

GERVANS

65 J9 N45°06.546' E004°49.831' 26600

Directions: Rue de l'Ecole. From N7 turn off, sp 'Gervans village' and signed. Follow signs through village; narrow access.

Sanitation:

Parking:

5; Max 24hrs

Custom; donation

Views across Rhône Valley, grape vines on hills. Skateboard park; Basketball courts. Ideal if Tournon **66** full. Inspected 2010.

TOURNON SUR RHONE

66 J9 N45°04.403' E004°49.291' 07300

Directions: At Parking Labeaume off D86/Avenue de Lyon. From south on D86 continue through town and turn right at roundabout into Chemin de Labeaume. Pass bus parking and Aire on left at rear of car park. In front of 'Point P' builders merchants.

Sanitation:

Parking:

25; Max 24hrs

Euro Relais Junior

SP

Aire in corner of car park north of town adj to derelict industrial building. Inspected 2010.

ST DONAT SUR L'HERBASSE

67 J9 N45°07.122' E004°58.301' 26260

AMPING
CAR

Directions: D67. Adj to D67 west of town at the Super U. At supermarket follow signs through car park to car wash on far left of premises and the Service Point is on the left of the car wash.

Sanitation:

Parking:

Poss

Raclet; €2

SP

Super U adj. Numerous other shops adj. Service Point in poor condition at time of inspection. Inspected 2010.

HAVE YOU VISITED AN AIRE?

GPS co-ordinates in this guide are protected by copyright law

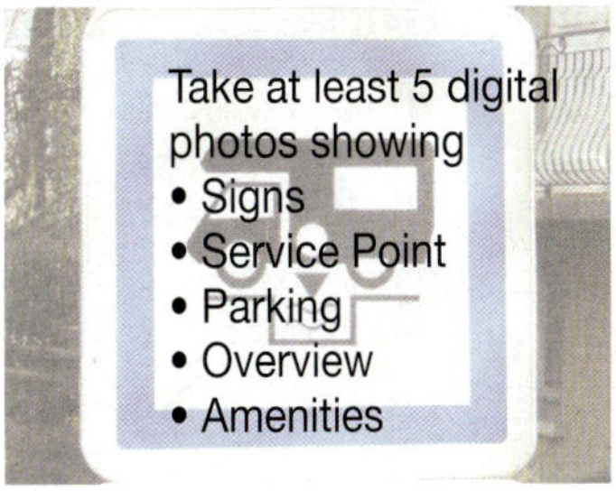
Take at least 5 digital photos showing
• Signs
• Service Point
• Parking
• Overview
• Amenities

Visit www.all-the-aires.co.uk/submissions.shtml to upload your updates and photos.

Sanitation:

Aire Details:

Submit updates

- Amendments
- New Aires
- Not changed

ST AGREVE

69 J9 N45°00.618' E004°23.599' 07320

Info/Photo: Carol Weaver

Directions: D120. Drive through town centre on D120. Aire in car park on left as exit centre to west, signed.

Sanitation:

Parking:

10; Max 48hrs

Aire Services; Token 3/3 €2.50

SP

Aire in large car park. Local commerce 3 mins. Visited 2011.

COLUMBIER LE JEUNE

70 J9 N45°00.676' E004°42.088' 07270

Directions: D209. Service Point located in village square/parking just off D209. Parking at tennis court: N45°00.677' E004°41.958' also adj to D209 as exit village towards Le Crestet.

Sanitation:

Parking:

3

Euro Relais Mini

SP

Rural village with local commerce inc convenience store. Inspected 2012.

LAMASTRE

71 I9 N44°59.221' E004°34.760' 07270

Photo: Barry Crawshaw

Directions: Place Pradon. From Tournon sur Rhône on D534 enter town and at sharp left-hand bend turn right/straight ahead onto D236/Ave Boissy D'Anglas. After 250m turn 1st right into Place Pradon. Service Point is 140m on right.

Sanitation:

Parking:

10; Not available Monday night/Tuesday due to large market

Raclet; Token

SP

250m from town centre; Riverside park adj. Inspected 2010.

ST ROMAIN DE LERPS

72 J9 N44°58.785' E004°47.771' 07130

Directions: D287. Adj to D287 at village boundary by rock terraced parking, signed.

Sanitation:

Parking:

4; Park adj to rd as terraced parking has narrow exit

Euro Relais Junior; Token (2/1)

SP

Rural village with historic building. Parking poss but no designated bays. Inspected 2012.

VERNOUX EN VIVARAIS

73 J9 N44°54.149' E004°38.977' 07240

Directions: D14. Exit the town on D14 travelling north. The Service Point is adj to D14 outside Camping Bois de Prat, signed.

Sanitation:

Parking:

8; Max 48hrs; Grass parking

Euro Relais Junior; Token (ER); €2

SP

Parking is on grass bays separated by hedges just before the campsite barrier. Inspected 2010.

LE CHEYLARD

74 I9 N44°54.722' E004°26.451' 07160

Directions: D120, at Super U. From Le Cheylard, take D120 east towards Beauvene. At roundabout turn left to Super U. Service Point in own bay at rear of fuel station and adj to Vulco tyres.

Sanitation:

Parking:

None

Euro Relais Junior

SP

No parking as 2.2m height barrier and 2t weight restriction in car park. Inspected 2010.

PORTES LES VALENCE

75 J9 N44°50.993' E004°52.153' 26800

Directions: D7, at Intermarché. Just off D7 as enter town from south, signed.

Sanitation:

Parking:

Poss

Custom

SP

Service Point in 24hr fuel station. Parking at supermarket 150m. Inspected 2010.

GRANE

76 | J9 | N44°45.338' E004°52.061' | 26400

Directions: Domaine Distaise. On D104 from Loriol sur Drôme head towards Crest/Grane and the private Aire is 3km on left, signed.

Sanitation:

Parking:

2; €2/24hrs; Free 1st night for France Passion

None; Water €1

SP

Private Aire. Swimming pool €1pp, English speaking owner, bread, fruit, meals, rural fruit farm and gites. Inspected 2010.

LA VOULTE SUR RHONE

77 | J9 | N44°48.447' E004°47.550' | 07800

Photo: Peter and Sue Coward

Directions: D86, ZI Quai Jean Jaurés. At Intermarché supermarket adj to the river.

Sanitation:

E

Parking:

F

Poss

Euro Relais Junior; Token

SP

Service Point at rear of supermarket car park. Inspected 2010.

PRIVAS

78 | J9 | N44°44.245' E004°36.068' | 07000

Info/Photo: T & M Valentine

Directions: Chemin du Tram. Exit town on D2, sp 'Les Olloeres' and signed. Turn right immediately before bridge, signed. Aire 200m on right in lower terrace of car park, signed. C28 beyond car park is a narrow road for 1.5km.

Sanitation:

F

Parking:

F

10

Urba Flux

SP

There is a pleasant valley view from the Aire. Steps to town commerce 100m. Top terrace of car park is reserved for residents only. Visited 2011.

ST DIDIER SOUS AUBENAS

79 | I9 | N44°36.683' E004°24.550' | 07200

Directions: N102, at Casino supermarket. From south on N102 Casino supermarket is on left-hand side of road in commercial area just before the roundabout north of town. Flot Bleu to right of fuel station, behind the gas bottles at edge of car park.

Sanitation:

E

Parking:

F

Poss; but noisy

Flot Bleu Pacific; Token; €2

SP

Mr Bricolage and a motor factors adj. Inspected 2010.

MEYRAS

80 | I9 | N44°40.768' E004°16.113' | 07380

Directions: Chemin des Diligences, off D26/Rue de la Dame de Ventadour. From N102 turn onto D26, sp 'Meyras'. Travel 1.6km into village and turn left into Chemin des Diligences. Aire on right at stadium. Signed from N102.

Sanitation:

E

Parking:

20; €4 Apr-Nov; Free Dec-Mar; Max 48hrs

Aire Services; €3

SP

Village 2 mins. Some areas have shade from small trees. Tokens from Mairie and TO. Service Point free in winter. Inspected 2010.

THUEYTS | 81 | I9 | N44°40.350' E004°13.137' | 07330

Directions: Turn off N102 in town, sp 'Stade-Tennis'. Follow road to end. Aire at sports facilities.

Sanitation:

Parking:

10; Max 24hrs

Aire Services; €2

Village 2 mins with local commerce. Exercise circuit adj. Inspected 2010.

LE LAC D'ISSARLES | 82 | I9 | N44°49.183' E004°03.700' | 07470

Photo: Rita Renninghoff

Directions: Off D116. Turn off N102 at La Fayette onto D110. At Coucouron take D16, sp 'Le Lac d'Issarlès'. After 12km take 1st exit at roundabout onto D116. After 850m turn right and Aire on left on 2nd bend.

Sanitation:

Parking:

10; €8

Custom; Numerous unmetered elec points

Local commerce nearby. Lake 500m away, no views. Showers. Inspected 2010.

COUCOURON | 83 | I9 | N44°48.073' E003°58.237' | 07470

Directions: Off D16, outside municipal campsite at entrance to village. From N102 take D16. At roundabout turn left and almost immediately right and Service Point is on the left after the football pitch.

Sanitation:

Parking:

None

Custom; Summer only

Service Point only. Inspected 2010.

LARGENTIERE | 84 | I9 | N44°32.312' E004°17.515' | 07110

Directions: D5. Turn off D104 at roundabout onto D5, sp 'Montreal' and 'Largentière'. Follow D5 and turn left into car park adj to Carrefour Contact supermarket, 200m after 3.9m height restricted bridge. Follow road to right and Service Point on left, signed.

Sanitation:

Parking:

5; Level parking adj to Service Point

Aire Services; €3; CC

Adj to supermarket but in separate municipal car park. Inspected 2012.

VINEZAC | 85 | I9 | N44°32.363' E004°19.496' | 07110

Directions: Car park, off D423. Turn off D104 onto D423, sp 'Vinezac'. After 1.8km turn left in village, sp 'Mairie' and 'Stade'. Follow road to left, then right to car park adj to Mairie. Service Point down slope and sharp right into Place du 19 Mars 1962.

Sanitation:

Parking:

5

Euro Relais Junior; €2

Care needed at Service Point as there is an unbarriered kerb on either side. Inspected 2010.

BANNE

86 I10 N44°21.917' E004°09.417' 07460

Directions: Parking at church. Travel 1.6km north on D901 from Les Avelas. Turn left uphill on unmarked, hard surface road. Follow road for 1.4km. Turn left at church, not clearly signed. Narrow access road and very narrow through village. Max length 8m.

Sanitation:

Parking:

5

Euro Relais Junior; Token (2/1); €3

Good children's playground adj. Inspected 2010.

LES BORRELS (CASTELJAU)

87 I10 N44°23.974' E004°12.808' 07460

Directions: D285. Turn off D104 onto D252, sp 'Casteljau'. Follow road for 1.5km, then turn right onto D285, sp 'Casteljau -Les Borrels'. Go straight on then follow road to right. Pass through a 10m length/2.8m width restricted section of road and the Aire is opp the church.

Sanitation:

Parking:

10

Euro Relais Junior; Token (2/1)

Aire in centre of quiet, remote village only 20 mins drive from Gorges de l'Ardeche. Inspected 2012.

ST ALBAN AURIOLLES

88 I10 N44°25.628' E004°18.059' 07120

Directions: Rue Marius Perbost, off D208. From D104 turn onto D208 on southern edge of Maison-Neuve village. After 7.3km, in St Alban Auriolles, turn left into Rue Marius Perbost, signed. Aire on left in 60m at rear of 'Foyer Rural'.

Sanitation:

Parking:

20

Euro Relais Junior; Token (ER)

100m walk to village with TO. Interesting walks. Aire overlooking village. Scenic drive north through gorge on D4 (3.1m height through tunnel). Inspected 2010.

VALLON PONT D'ARC

89 I10 N44°24.303' E004°23.841' 07150

Directions: Chemin du Chastelas, off D390. From south on D290 at roundabout take 1st exit onto D390. After 750m turn right into Chemin du Chastelas, signed. Aire on right in 80m.

Sanitation:

Parking:

30; €7

Custom

Short steep walk up into a very pleasant town with small bars and restaurants. Inspected 2010.

GPS Co-ordinates for SatNav

The GPS Co-ordinates published in this guide were taken onsite by our inspectors. We consider them a valuable and unique asset and at the time of publishing have decided not to publish them as electronic files for use on navigation devices. You have permission to type in the co-ordinates of an Aire you intend to visit but not to store or share them. For the security of our copyright:

- **Do not compile them into lists**
- **Do not publish, share or reproduce them anywhere in any format**

ST REMEZE

91 | I10 | N44°23.739' E004°30.375' | 07700

Directions: Les Chais du Vivarais, D362. Entering St Remeze on D4, in village turn onto D362. Aire on left leaving village at Cave Co-operative.

Sanitation:

Parking:

6; Open Mar-Nov; Max 48hrs

Custom

Village Co-operative cave, no purchase necessary. 5 mins walk to attractive small town. Inspected 2010.

HAVE YOU VISITED AN AIRE? **GPS co-ordinates in this guide are protected by copyright law**

Take at least 5 digital photos showing
• Signs
• Service Point
• Parking
• Overview
• Amenities

Visit www.all-the-aires.co.uk/submissions.shtml to upload your updates and photos.

Sanitation:

Aire Details:

Submit updates
- Amendments
- New Aires
- Not changed

ORGNAC L'AVEN

93 | I10 | N44°18.247' E004°25.964' | 07150

Info/Photo: Carol Weaver

Directions: D217. Adj to D217 100m beyond centre of village on right hand side when heading south, well signed.

Sanitation:

Parking:

5

Custom

Aire located in a small village adj to a boules court and childrens play area. Local commerce 100m. Visited 2011.

ST JUST

94 | I10 | N44°18.097' E004°36.350' | 07700

Directions: Domaine la Favette/D290. From Pont St Esprit on D86 head north and at roundabout at edge of St Just take 2nd exit onto D290. Aire on right in 700m.

Sanitation:

Parking:

6; €5 inc bottle of wine

Flot Bleu; €2

Commercial Aire adj to farm/wine shop. Fruit in season and wine €1.25/litre in bulk, can fill your own bottles. Inspected 2010.

DONZERE

95 | I10 | N44°26.452' E004°43.132' | 26290

Directions: At roundabout as enter town on D541/N7. Motorway service feel.

Sanitation:

Parking:

Not recommended

Custom; No drive over drain

Convenient stop to visit village centre, 1km. Inspected 2010.

BOURG ST ANDEOL

96 | I10 | N44°22.527' E004°38.620' | 07700

Directions: Enter town on D4. Turn left off D4 when signed into Ave de la Gare. Drive past LIDL and Aire signed in town car park, adj to railway station, at corner of Chemin de la Barriere and Rue Jacques Merletti.

Sanitation:

Parking:

20

Aire Services; 2 unmetered elec points

Unpicturesque car park by railway line but scenic Gorges de l'Ardeche only 10km southwest of Aire. Inspected 2010.

LARNAS

97 | I10 | N44°26.929' E004°35.874' | 07220

Directions: D262. Take D262 from St Montan to Larnas. The Aire is behind the Mairie on the right just before exiting the village.

Sanitation:

Parking:

5

Euro Relais Junior

Bit of a mess as plant and materials stored around perimeter. Inspected 2010.

ALBA LA ROMAINE

98 | I9 | N44°33.205' E004°35.836' | 07400

Directions: Turn off N102 onto D263a, sp 'Alba la Romaine'. After 600m go straight over roundabout and follow D263 into town. Turn right at TO into Rue du Barry. Aire in 140m to right/straight ahead.

Sanitation:

Parking:

5

Euro Relais Junior; Token (2/1)

Pleasant location on the edge of the village. Inspected 2010.

AUBIGNAS *

99 | J9 | N44°35.236' E004°37.899' | 07400

Photo: Mary and Rees Pryce

Directions: D363. From N102 turn onto D363, sp 'Aubignas'. After 550m turn left to stay on D363. After another 800m turn left again. Stay on D363 following sp 'Aubignas' and 'Village' a further 1.3km. Then take sharp left and Aire 100m, signed.

Sanitation:

Parking:

10; €2 donation

Raclet

Hillside village. Aire has panoramic views. Very quiet and peaceful. Village 2 mins. Can be windy. Inspected 2010.

LES CROTTES/ST THOME

100 | J9 | N44°30.045' E004°38.052' | 07220

Directions: D107. Adj to D107 just before entrance to Les Crottes from Viviers. Signed.

Sanitation:

Parking:

None

Raclet

Service Point only at this small village. Inspected 2010.

VIVIERS

101 J9 N44°28.802' E004°41.537' 07220

Directions: Turn off D86 at roundabout onto D86i, sp 'Donzere'. Turn right past the TO into grass parking area or continue down road and turn left, sp 'Port de Plaisance'. Follow road then turn right, sp 'Parking du Creux': N44°29.027' E004°41.447'.

Sanitation:

Parking:

Poss in two locations; New Aire under consultation

None

Old Aire has been closed and Service Point removed. It is poss to park in the two locations described but this will change once new Aire is built. Inspected 2012.

VILLENEUVE DE BERG

102 J9 N44°34.310' E004°30.703' 07170

Info/Photo: Carol Weaver

Directions: N102. Turn off the D102 at the D902/N102 roundabout into the Intermarché supermarket. Service Point at the back of the fuel station.

Sanitation:

Parking:

Poss

Euro Relais Mini; Token (ER)

Supermarket adj. Visited 2012.

LE TEIL

103 J9 N44°33.079' E004°41.370' 07400

Directions: Allée Paul Avon. On N102 towards Montélimar turn right just before bridge over Rhône towards Le Teil centre. Aire 170m on left in what looks like the car park for 'Des Allées' restaurant. Aire behind and to left of restaurant.

Sanitation:

Parking:

6

Custom

2 hardstanding and 4 grass bays. Slightly scruffy looking area. Nicer Aire Aubignas **99**. Inspected 2010.

MONTELIMAR

104 J9 N44°33.907' E004°45.407' 26200

Directions: Chemin du Bois de Laud. In town follow sp 'Valance', then 'Aire de Camping-Car'. Follow signs past E'Leclerc supermarket, fuel station and up hill. Turn right, sp 'Aire Camping-Car'. Aire down slope. Access through credit card operated bollards.

Sanitation:

Parking:

12; €4.20/24hrs inc service; CC; Max 48hrs; Grass parking

Urba Flux Tall; Entry code on receipt

Commercial Aire. Supermarket 2 mins. Walled city and town centre with small town commerce 5 mins. Inspected 2012.

CLANSAYES

105 J10 N44°22.161' E004°47.807' 26130

Directions: Aire de Toronne. From St Paul-Trois-Châteaux on D133 turn onto D571, sp 'Clansayes'. Aire on right, signed.

Sanitation:

Parking:

40; €10-€13; Elec €4

Custom; inc

Commercial Aire in a nice peaceful spot. Swimming pool; Showers; BBQ. Rural views. Inspected 2010.

ST PAUL TROIS CHATEAUX

106 J10 N44°20.845' E004°46.209' 26130

Directions: 'Parking Chausy', Lieu-Dit le Courreau. From east on D59 at 2nd roundabout in town take 1st exit into Ave Paul Faure, sp 'Parking Chausy 120 spaces'. Turn 1st left then left again into car park. Well signed.

Sanitation:

Parking:

20

Custom

Car park adj to TO, Police Municipal and alongside an open grass park. Historic town centre 150m. Inspected 2010.

ROCHEGUDE

107 J10 N44°14.828' E004°49.819' 26790

Directions: D817. Take D117, D11 or D817 into village and turn onto D817 in village centre, sp 'Lagarde-Pareol'. Aire immediately on right.

Sanitation:

Parking:

5

Euro Relais Mini

Small roadside Service Point and parking area under trees. Inspected 2010.

SUZE LA ROUSSE

108 J10 N44°17.385' E004°50.887' 26790

Directions: Impasse de la Zone Artisanale. Exit town on D94, sp 'Nyons'. As exit village turn left onto D251, sp 'Bouchet'. In 200m turn right, signed. Service Point immediately on right.

Sanitation:

Parking:

None

Custom

Service Point only. Inspected 2012.

PIERRELATTE

109 J10 N44°22.588' E004°42.194' 26700

Directions: Rue Antoine de St Exupery. Turn off D458 at roundabout onto D358, sp 'Pierrelatte'. Follow road to roundabout above train track and take the 2nd exit onto D13, sp 'Mairie'. Turn right, and right again and the Service Point is on the right.

Sanitation:

Parking:

Poss on road, car park height barriered

Euro Relais Junior; Token (ER)

Service Point only. Inspected 2012.

GRIGNAN

110 J10 N44°25.198' E004°53.624' 26230

Directions: D541. Exit town on D541 towards Donzere. In 1.5km turn left into the Intermarché supermarket. The Aire is behind the supermarket, signed.

Sanitation:

Parking:

10

Euro Relais Junior; Token (ER); No drive over drain

Adj to supermarket with self-service laundry. Grignan town is pleasant but bans motorhomes from parking. Inspected 2012.

MONTBRISON

111 J10 N44°26.187' E005°01.052' 26770

Directions: D24, near junction with D538. From south on D538 turn left in village onto D24, signed. Aire on right. Service Point is 1.7km away. Follow D538 southeast from Aire for 1km. Turn right, sp 'Stade': N44°25.671' E005°01.465'.

Sanitation:

Parking:

6; At the Mairie

Euro Relais Mini; Token (2/1); €2; 4 unmetered elec points at Mairie

Pleasant village. Aire has a tap by the play equipment. Inspected 2010.

MIRABEL AUX BARONNIES

112 J10 N44°18.767' E005°05.983' 26110

Directions: Chemin de Grottes. From D538 on northern edge of village, turn into Allée des Soupirs. After 200m turn left and Aire is immediately ahead, signed.

Sanitation:

Parking:

6; Max 48hrs; Donation

Custom

Small Aire. Inspected 2010.

NYONS

113 J10 N44°21.489' E005°08.315' 26110

Directions: Promenade de la Digue. From north on D538 turn off in town just prior to river bridge, signed. Aire 200m on right. 3.5t weight restriction on D94/D538 river bridge (on approach from south).

Sanitation:

Parking:

15; €9/24hrs; Max 48hrs

Flot Bleu Pacific

Outdoor swimming pool adj, river across road. Inspected 2010.

MONTBRUN LES BAINS

114 J10 N44°10.458' E005°26.460' 26570

Info/Photo: Carol Weaver

Directions: D542. At Express U on D542. Service Point to the right of the store entrance.

Sanitation:

Parking:

Poss

Flot Bleu Pacific; €2

Supermarket adj. Visited 2012.

ST RESTITUT

115 J10 N44°19.877' E004°47.455' 26130

Directions: D859. Turn off D59 at roundabout onto D859, sp 'St Restitut'. After passing village boundry sign on left, fork right, sp 'Centre Ville', then immediately left into car park, signed. Aire at far end of car park.

Sanitation:

Parking:

5

Custom

Aire adj to hilltop village. Large caves open to public, follow sp 'Caves Cathèdrale . Local commerce 1 min. Inspected 2012.

MARSANNE

116 J9 N44°38.762' E004°52.317' 26740

Directions: D57. Exit village centre on D57, sp 'Mirmande'. Aire 150m on left, signed.

Sanitation:

Parking:

5

Custom

Located on the edge of the village opp a school and adj to Aire Naturalle campsite. There is a play area and exercise trail behind the Aire and a ruined fortification beyond. Local commerce 1min. Inspected 2012.

DIEULEFIT

117 J9 N44°31.215' E005°03.364' 26220

Directions: D540. Approach on D540 from Le Poet-Laval. Turn right into the Super U car park and Service Point is in the far left corner by self-service laundry, signed.

Sanitation:

Parking:

Poss; Behind supermarket

Euro Relais Mini; €2; Token (ER)

Supermarket and self-service laundry adj. D538 has lavender/honey/wine producers/sellers offering motorhome parking. Inspected 2012.

PUY ST MARTIN

118 J9 N44°37.624' E004°58.507' 26450

Directions: Impasse de Fleurs. Turn off D6 in village onto D107, sp 'Manas', 'Mairie' and signed. Turn left at crossroads into Rue de Lavoir, signed. Turn right, signed, then left into Aire.

Sanitation:

Parking:

20; Donation; Max 48hrs; Grass parking

Custom

Former municipal campsite turned motorhome Aire. Village with local commerce and supermarket 1 min. Inspected 2012.

CHAROLS

119 J9 N44°35.498' E004°57.259' 26450

Directions: Place Carrovolis. Approach from Cleon d'Andran on D9. Turn left onto D128 at roundabout. In 10m turn right into the adj car park. The Aire is at the far end of the car park.

Sanitation:

Parking:

10

Custom; Elec points not working

Pleasant village Aire with plenty of space. Convenience store adj. village with local commerce 1 min. Inspected 2012.

SAILLANS

120 J9 N44°41.729' E005°11.633' 26340

Directions: Montmartel. From village centre take D493 sp 'Gite Rural and Gendarmerie'. Cross bridge and fork left sp, 'Gite Rural and Gendarmerie'. Turn right before Gendarmerie sp 'Gite Rural' and signed. Aire 20m in car park behind Centre Secours Pompiers shed, signed.

Sanitation:

Parking:

10

Euro Relais Mini; Token ER

Parking adj to river, no views. Local commerce 5 mins. Visited 2012.

CREST 1

121 J9 N44°43.554' E005°01.241' 26400

Directions: D538. From west on D104 turn left at traffic lights onto D538, sp 'Centre Ville'. After 600m take 1st exit at roundabout into car park. Long motorhome spaces along right-hand edge of car park, adj to boules club. Service Point across car park. Car park has 3.5t weight restriction.

Sanitation:

Parking:

25

Aire Services; €5; CC

Historic town on river Drôme with steep cobbled lanes. Laundry 400m in Rue Général Berlier. WiFi. Inspected 2010.

CREST 2

122 J9 N44°44.297' E005°00.285' 26400

Directions: D538. At fuel station of Casino supermarket just off D538/D93 roundabout, signed.

Sanitation:

Parking:

Poss

Flot Bleu Euro; €2/20mins; CC

Supermarket adj. Inspected 2012.

CHICHILIANNE

123 J9 N44°48.741' E005°34.534' 38930

Info/Photo: Colin Robinson

Directions: D7B. Turn off the D7 onto the D7B, sp 'Chichilianne'. Aire 600m on right adj to D7B.

Sanitation:

Parking:

10; Grass parking

Aire Services; Token

Remote village Aire with mountain views. D7 goes over Col de Menee altitude 1457m. Visited 2012.

DIE 1

124 J9 N44°45.033' E005°21.983' 26150

Directions: Lieu-Dit Largner. From south on D93, at roundabout take 2nd exit onto D238. After 1km turn left at traffic lights, sp 'Camping Municipal' and signed. Follow signs to 'Camping Municipal de Justin'. Service Point outside campsite.

Sanitation:

Parking:

None

Flot Bleu Océane; Token; €3; Open May-Sept only.

Handy Service Point when Die 125 in town is busy or on market days. Inspected 2010.

DIE 2

125 J9 N44°45.060' E005°22.391' 26150

Directions: Car park 'Aire de Meyrosse' on D238. From south on D93 take 2nd exit at roundabout onto D238. After 600m turn right into car park. Aire straight ahead. Service Point adj to toilet block in main car park.

Sanitation:

Parking:

20; €5/24hrs

Custom

Busy on market days, Wed and Sat mornings. Historic town with shops and restaurants. Inspected 2010.

VASSIEUX EN VERCORS

126 J9 N44°53.857' E005°22.210' 26420

Photo Carol Weaver

Directions: D76. From Die follow D518 for 21km over very scenic Col de Rousset (winding road with hairpins but wide enough). Fork left onto D76 and follow road for 8km. Aire on right in very large, open area just after village.

Sanitation:

Parking:

30

Custom

SP

Alt 1100m. On plateau with excellent views of mountains. Memorial de Resistance 800m. Nice village with shops, restaurants, etc. Inspected 2010.

ST JEAN EN ROYANS

127 J9 N45°01.200' E005°17.425' 26190

Directions: Rue de la Gare. Approach from north on D76. Go straight over roundabout, signed. In 300m turn right, signed. In 150m turn left, signed.

Sanitation:

Parking:

6

Custom

SP

This is a quiet, tranquil location away from the main roads just 1 min from commerce. Supermarket 2mins downhill. Inspected 2012.

ST MARCELLIN

128 J9 N45°09.316' E005°19.160' 38160

Directions: Blvd Riondel. Enter town on D1092 from east. At roundabout turn onto D518, sp 'St Verand' and 'Roybon'. Go straight on at traffic lights, sp 'St Verand' and 'Roybon'. In 100m turn right, sp 'P Champ de Mars' (N45°09.282' E005°19.073'). Service Point around square, right turn then 150m on right, signed.

Sanitation:

Parking:

5; Popular town parking adj

Custom

SP

Adj to shaded central square (market Sat 5am-2pm) that has a Germanic maypole. Bars, restaurants and shops, inc LIDL surround the square. Roybon, 15 mins drive, has miniature statue of liberty. Inspected 2012.

ST ANTOINE L'ABBAYE

129 J8 N45°10.387' E005°13.070' 38160

Info/Photo: Jean & Ken Fowler

Directions: D27. In centre of village turn off D27 into large gravel car park to Aire.

Sanitation:

Parking:

12

Urba Flux Tall; €2

SP

Lovely anchient town adj. Several walks around area - TO has leaflet. Visited 2011

ST ETIENNE DE ST GEOIRS

130 J8 N45°21.219' E005°20.097' 38590

Directions: Chemin de la Pierre. Exit St Etienne de St Geoirs towards 'La Cote St Andre' and airport 'Grenoble st Geoirs' on D154D. Go straight over the roundabout in the retail park, then turn immediately right, sp 'Super U Essence'. The Service Point is on the left before the fuel station, signed.

Sanitation:

Parking:

Poss

Flot Bleu Standard Plus; €2

SP

Supermarket adj. McDonalds adj. Inspected 2012.

ST HUGUES DE CHARTREUSE SKI 131 K8 N45°19.029' E005°48.207' 38380

Directions: D57b, at Parking du Cret des Egaux. From St Pierre de Chartreuse take D512 south. After approx 1.5km turn left onto D57b. Follow road for 2km and Aire is on left just before right-hand bend and small 'drag' ski lift.

Sanitation:

Parking:

4

None

Alt 950m. Small rural car park with lovely 360° views. Inspected 2010.

ST PIERRE DE CHARTREUSE SKI 132 K8 N45°20.578' E005°48.743' 38380

Info/Photo: Carol Weaver

Directions: P du Couzon. Turn off the D512 by the church. Take the 1st left turn past the church and the Aire is on the right, sp 'P du Couzon' and signed.

Sanitation:

Parking:

50

Euro Relais Mini; Token

This Aire was previously located at P Le Bourg. Local commerce 2 mins. Additional parking at base of Telesiege Combe de l'Ours chairlift. Turn right off D512 heading north, N45°21.467' E005°49.967'. Visited 2012.

VIRIEU SUR BOURBRE 133 J8 N45°28.898' E005°28.669' 38730

Directions: Rue du May. Turn off D73 in village centre onto D17, sp 'Le Pin' and signed. Aire on left as exit village opp boundary sign, signed.

Sanitation:

Parking:

4

Custom

Parking in shady dell adj to water-wheel and grassy, terraced picnic area. Lake de Paladru further up D17. Village centre 2 mins. Market on Friday afternoon. Inspected 2012.

LE PONT DE BEAUVOISIN 134 J8 N45°31.726' E005°41.438' 73330

Directions: D1006, at the Super U. From Les Echelles the Super U is located on D1006 before it meets D82 and D921e.

Sanitation:

Parking:

Poss

Flot Bleu Euro; CC; €2

Supermarket adj; Self-service laundry adj. Inspected 2010.

LA BATIE MONTGASCON 135 J8 N45°34.704' E005°31.709' 38110

Directions: Rue des Tisserands. From La Tour du Pin on D1516 turn right onto D145, sp ' St Andre le Gaz. Service Point on right adj Musée du Tisserand, signed. Large level parking in centre: N45°34.853' E005°31.707'. From Service Point turn left, then right onto D1515. Turn left onto D91, sp 'Faverges', and the car park is on left.

Sanitation:

Parking:

10; Max 48hrs

Custom; Donation

Service Point adj to textile museum. Can also park at stadium: N45°34.511' E005°31.845' (quiet/5mins from centre) and cemetery: N45°34.723' E005°31.858' (quiet/unlevel). Inspected 2012.

CHAMBERY

136 K8 N45°33.772' E005°55.982' 73000

Directions: Espace Sportif Delphine et Jonathan. Exit N201 at Junction 18 towards Chambery on D1006. Go under bridge and fork left, sp 'Lyon' and 'Valence'. Go straight over roundabout, sp 'Parkings'. Turn left at next roundabout into sports centre and Aire is at end.

Sanitation:

Parking:

10

Custom

Town 10 mins. Small car park adj to sports centre. Inspected 2010.

CHALLES LES EAUX

137 K8 N45°32.900' E005°59.262' 73190

Directions: 'Parking Colombier' in Rue Claudius Perrotin. From south on D1006 turn right at traffic lights in town onto D9/Avenue Dr Louis Domenget, sp 'Casino'. As D9 bends left, go straight towards casino. Follow road to right. Aire in small car park straight ahead.

Sanitation:

Parking:

5

Custom

Shady parking in small gravel car park in residential area of town. Adj to attractive gardens and park. Inspected 2010.

LA FECLAZ

138 K8 N45°38.515' E005°59.016' 73230

Directions: D206a. From D912 turn onto D913, sp 'La Féclaz'. In 2.8km at entrance to village turn left, sp 'P Camping Cars'. Follow road and parking on right, signed.

Sanitation:

Parking:

40; Pay at TO

Raclet; Token (ER)

Button ski lift 100m; Small ski/walking resort; Cross country skiing; Ski passes €200 per week. Inspected 2010.

LE BOURGET DU LAC

139 K8 N45°39.195' E005°51.772' 73370

Directions: Outside Camping International L'lle aux Cygnes. From south on D1504 turn right onto D14. After 300m turn right into Boulevard Ernest Coudurier. Follow road round right-hand bend and Aire at end of road outside campsite.

Sanitation:

Parking:

20; €6; Max 7 days

Custom; Open Mar-Oct

Lake nearby but no views. Use of toilets, showers, laundry, private beach. 20 hardstanding pitches plus 10 on grass. Low season free but no services. Inspected 2010.

CHANAZ

140 K8 N45°48.683' E005°47.343' 73310

Info/Photo: Harry Ridsdale

Directions: Chemin de Cavettaz. Turn off D291, sp 'Camping'. Follow sp 'Camping' and the Service Point is just outside campsite entrance.

Sanitation:

Parking:

Poss; when campsite closed

Aire Services; Token 3/3

Lots of gravel parking adj but no official motorhome parking. Canoe hire and marina close by. Very pretty, tourist village by canal. Visited 2010.

SERRIERES EN CHAUTAGNE 141 K8 N45°52.843' E005°50.591' 73310

Directions: Off D991. From Mairie's office, parking beyond Service Point to left of lake.

Sanitation:

Parking:

6; Max 72hrs

Flot Bleu Fontaine

SP

Village with local commerce. Adj to small swimming lake. Inspected 2010.

ANNECY 142 K8 N45°53.437' E006°08.341' 74000

Directions: Chemin de Colmyr, off D1508/Rue des Marquisats. 1km south of Annecy on D1508. Behind car park and Park and Ride at traffic lights. Need to arrive early, busy at peak times. 3.5t weight restriction on access road.

Sanitation:

Parking:

10; Max 24hrs

Custom

SP

Opp side of road to lake, cycle track and foot path. Lovely resort town. Inspected 2010.

ANNECY LE VIEUX 143 K8 N45°54.433' E006°09.117' 74940

Directions: Rue Centrale. From D909/Avenue du Petit Port, on northern shore of lake, turn into Rue Centrale. Service Point 300m on left.

Sanitation:

Parking:

None

Custom

SP

Service Point only but could be useful as access to services can be difficult when Annecy 142 is full. Inspected 2010.

LA BALME DE SILLINGY 144 K7 N45°58.290' E006°01.888' 74330

Directions: D1508. Just off D1508 at edge of village by lake.

Sanitation:

Parking:

14; €5/24hrs; Open Apr-Nov; Max 48hrs

Custom

SP

By lake; café. Inspected 2010.

PONCIN 145 J7 N46°05.222' E005°24.269' 01450

Directions: Place 19 Mars 1962. From N1084 turn onto D91, sp 'Poncin Centre' and signed. After 220m turn left into Ave du Parc and follow for another 220m. Turn left into Rue de la Verchere and the Aire is 130m on the right.

Sanitation:

Parking:

20

Custom

SP

At sports facilities: basketball, football. Village 5 mins. Adj to cemetery. Inspected 2010.

NANTUA * | 146 | J7 | N46º09.260' E005º35.827' | 01130

Directions: D74. At lake turn off, sp 'Aire de Pique-nique', 'Monument aux Déportés', and signed. Follow road around lake, signed.

Sanitation:

Parking:

10; €5 + €0.40pp

Custom

Amazing lake/mountain views. Lake swimming. Town 5 mins, lots of shops. Aire renovated April 2012. Visited 2012.

BELLEYDOUX | 147 | K7 | N46°15.331' E005°46.793' | 01130

Photo: Carol Weaver

Directions: D13/D33. Adj to the D13/D33 in the village. Adj to recycling area, signed.

Sanitation:

Parking:

3

Flot Bleu Pacific; Token; €2

Small village. Inspected 2010.

BELLEGARDE SUR VALSERINE | 148 | K7 | N46°06.420' E005°49.900' | 01200

Info/Photo: Janet & John Watts

Directions: Place des Frères Zanarelli. Exit town on the D1206, sp 'Geneve' and 'Gex'. Cross river and turn right at traffic lights, by side of Gendarmerie, sp 'Borne Camping Car'. Aire is on the right in the car park at the end of the road.

Sanitation:

Parking:

2

Aire Services; €3; CC

Aire alongside river. Small town commerce 4 mins. Visited 2011.

ST GENIS POUILLY | 149 | K7 | N46°15.816' E006°01.814' | 01630

Directions: D984c. Turn off the D984c/D35a roundabout north of town. The Service Point is in the Intermarché supermarket car park, at rear of supermarket building opp Intersport.

Sanitation:

Parking:

Poss

Raclet; Token; €2

Service Point at supermarket. Inspected 2010.

MIJOUX SKI | 150 | K7 | N46°22.155' E006°00.133' | 01410

Info/Photo: Janet & John Watts

Directions: D50. Exit Mijoux on the D50, sp 'Le Tabagnoz' and signed. Aire 450m on the left in the woods, signed.

Sanitation:

Parking:

10

Aire Services; Token; €3.50

Rural location, with woodland views. May feel isolated. Chair lift 500m in village centre with local commerce. Visited 2011.

LOISIN

151 K7 N46°16.117' E006°19.002' 74140

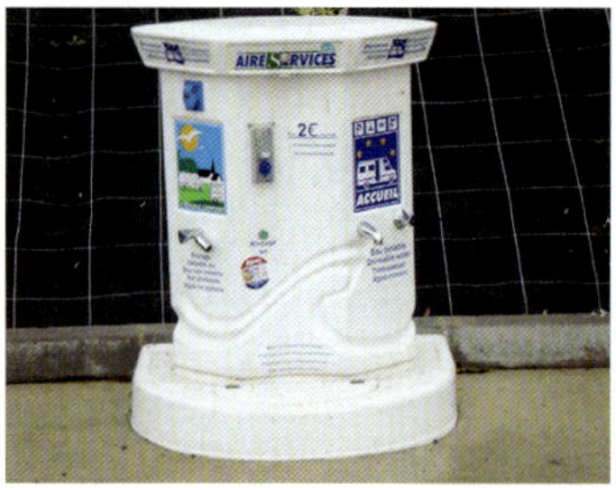

Directions: Turn off the D1206/D35 roundabout sp 'Centre Commercial'. The Service Point is in the Super U fuel station.

Sanitation:

Parking:

Poss

Aire Services; Token; €2

Supermarket adj. Visited 2012.

LE PRAZ DE LYS * SKI

152 K7 N46°08.656' E006°35.577' 74440

Photo: Andy and Sue Glasgow

Directions: D308. From Les Gets take D902 south and turn right onto D307/D328/D308, sp 'Le Praz de Lys'. After 6.6km Aire on left prior to bridge.

Sanitation:

Parking:

64; €10; Free spring/autumn

Flot Bleu Pacific; €2

Nice ski area, good Nordic ski. Inspected 2010.

SOMMAND SKI

153 K7 N46°09.681' E006°33.293' 74440

Directions: D308. From Taninges take D907 west. At roundabout in Mieussy turn right onto D308. Follow road for 10km. After small lake on right, take right-hand fork into large parking area at base of ski lifts. Flot Bleu 500m, turn left after lake, at: N46°09.539' E006°32.959'.

Sanitation:

Parking:

50

Flot Bleu Pacific; €2

Alt 1413m. Fishing lake adj. Scenic location with lots of summer walking and good Nordic ski area. Inspected 2010.

CHATEL SKI

154 L7 N46°15.447' E006°49.773' 74390

Directions: Rte des Freinets, off D228a. From northwest on D22 turn right into D228a in Châtel centre, sp 'Telecabine du Linga' and 'Pres la Joux'. Follow road for 1.8km then turn right, sp 'Camping L'Oustalet'. Aire on right in 300m, opp Camping L'Oustalet.

Sanitation:

Parking:

12; €6/night

Flot Bleu Pacific; €6

Rural ski resort/summer walking. Access to Portes de Soleil ski area and ski to Switzerland. Elec €2/hr. Inspected 2010.

AIX LES BAINS

155 K7 N45°42.309' E005°53.281' 73100

Info/Photo: Mike Crampton/Carol Weaver

Directions: Avenue du Grand Port/ D991. Follow sp 'Port du Luc'. The Aire is on the right 200m from the port. The nearest service point is at Camping du Sierroz in 700m following the lake south. Servicing costs €5.

Sanitation:

Parking:

16; Max 48 hrs

None

Popular Aire 200m from the lake, no views. Insufficient space for demand. Nice walking beside lake. Plenty of cafes and bars nearby. Visited 2012.

LES GETS — SKI — 156 — K7 — N46°08.993' E006°39.495' — 74260

Directions: D902/Route de Taninges. Situated on D902 at the entrance to the village if approached from Cluses. Aire at bottom of lift at parking 'Perrieres'. Flot Bleu 100m, turn left, then 1st right: N46°08.996' E006°39.411'.

Sanitation:

Parking:

30; €14/night; Max 7 days

Flot Bleu Euro; CC; €4.50

Superb Aire next to a ski lift, at bottom of ski slope. 800m from village. Pleasant in summer, popular in winter (early arrival essential) Appears free in summer. Inspected 2010.

SAMOENS 1 — SKI — 157 — L7 — N46°04.338' E006°42.159' — 74340

Photo: Andy and Sue Glasgow

Directions: D254. Exit Samoën southwest on the D4 and travel 800m towards Morillon. Pass Camping Le Giffre and cross the river bridge onto D254 and continue for 1.8km to Vercland. The Aire and Service Point are at the bottom of Vercland ski lift.

Sanitation:

Parking:

Poss

Flot Bleu Pacific; €5

Remote Aire with only a bar/restaurant and chairlift. All other facilities are 3km along D4 in village. See Samoëns 2 158. Inspected 2009.

SAMOENS 2 — 158 — L7 — N46°04.626' E006°43.154' — 74340

Directions: D4, outside Camping le Giffre. Leave Samoëns and head south on D4. Flot Bleu on right in 700m in roundabout lay-by, opp campsite.

Sanitation:

Parking:

None

Flot Bleu Euro; CC; €5

Flot Bleu not working at time of inspection but notice states service available at same price in campsite opp. Inspected 2010.

LA ROCHE SUR FORON — 159 — K7 — N46°03.846' E006°18.780' — 74800

Directions: Parking du Canada. Located at Parking du Canada 200m from town centre, signed. Not suitable for large motorhomes and has very steep, narrow access.

Sanitation:

Parking:

20

Euro Relais Junior

Pleasant town with 13th century quarter. Inspected 2010.

ST PIERRE EN FAUCIGNY — 160 — K7 — N46°03.555' E006°22.506' — 74800

Directions: D208/Avenue de la Gare. Exit A40 at Junction 16 and take D1203 towards Bonneville. Turn right onto D12/Avenue des Digues just before river. Follow road for 1.5km. Turn right onto D208/Ave de la Gare and Aire on left in station car park.

Sanitation:

Parking:

4; Max 48hrs

Custom; 2 unmetered elec points

Some train noise, but trains are electric and don't run at night. Shade from trees in afternoon. Inspected 2010.

LE REPOSOIR

161 K7 N46°00.600' E006°32.180' 74950

Photo: Carol Weaver

Directions: D204. From roundabout on D1205 at Cluses take D4, sp 'Le Reposoir'. Follow road for 11km. Turn left onto D204 in Le Reposoir between church and Mairie. Small sign on map adj to church. Aire on right in approx 150m.

Sanitation: WC

Parking: P F

5

Custom; Toilets at Mairie 100m

Alt 980m. 1151 Monatere Charteuse du Reposir nearby. Inspected 2010.

LE CHINAILLON SKI

162 K7 N45°58.529' E006°27.638' 74450

Directions: Lieu-Dit Le Chinaillon, off D4. From La Clusaz take D909 north to St Jean de Sixt. At roundabout turn right onto D12/D4, sp 'Le Grand Bornand'. Follow road for 10km. At Le Chinaillon take 1st right and follow road past ski lifts to Aire on right.

Sanitation: F

Parking: P F

10; Max 48hrs

Custom

Alt 1296m. Service Point signed at Chalet ski lift ticket window, 200m downhill. Inspected 2010.

LE GRAND BORNAND SKI

163 K7 N45°56.485' E006°26.178' 74450

Photo: Heidi Hardwick

Directions: Chemin Du Terret a La Broderie. Drive through town towards Col de les Annes, turn first right over the stream, sp 'L'Envers de Villeneuve'. Aire is on left in 100m, sp 'La Possey' and signed.

Sanitation:

Parking: P F

None

10; Max 48hrs

Motorhome parking area 10 minutes walk from pleasant ski resort with local commerce. Ski bus in season. Visited 2012.

LES CARROZ D'ARACHES SKI

164 K7 N46°01.517' E006°38.632' 74300

Directions: Impasse des Sablets. From Cluses take D1205 south and turn onto D6, sp 'Les Carroz D'Arâches'. Follow D6 then D106 for 10km. In village centre turn left into Route du Battieu. Follow road round right-hand bend, then left into Impasse des Sablets. Aire opp ski lift.

Sanitation: E WC F

Parking:

10; Open 1/5-14/12

Bollard; 5 unmetered elec points; No drive over drain

For skiing see Flaine **165** Village centre 500m. In winter used as ski bus parking. Inspected 2010.

FLAINE SKI

165 L7 N46°00.274' E006°41.345' 74300

Directions: From Cluses on D1205 take D6 then D106 to Flaine. Road full of hairpin bends into Flaine. Aire in car park P1.

Sanitation: WC

Parking:

30; €4/24hrs; Pay at machine

None; Do not empty cassette in toilet

Alt 1600m. At entrance to car park there is ticket office, toilet and sandwich room with sink and tap. Inspected 2010.

SIXT FER A CHEVAL

166 L7 N46°03.399' E006°46.783' 74740

Directions: D907. From Samoëns on D907 follow sp 'Sixt Fer à Cheval' and 'Cirque du Fer à Cheval'. Pass through village from east and Aire on right next to river just after end of village sign.

Sanitation:

Parking:

30

Euro Relais Junior; Elec only by Token (ER) €4/12hrs; 4 elec points

Pleasant scenic valley setting adj to river. Cirque du Fer à Cheval 5.5km further up road. Inspected 2010.

CHAMONIX MONT BLANC SKI

167 L7 N45°54.951' E006°52.171' 74400

Directions: Parking Grepon, off D1506. Turn off D1506 at roundabout, sp 'P+R Grepon' and 'Aiguille du Midi'. Aire in parking for the Gondola to Aiguille du Midi. Barriered entry, pay prior to exit.

Sanitation:

Parking:

100; €12.50/24hrs; Or by hr; CC or cash

Custom; inc

Free bus to town centre under cable car to Aiguille du Midi. Inspected 2010.

LE TOUR SKI

168 L7 N46°00.235' E006°56.758' 74400

Directions: Place du Tour. From Chamonix follow D1506 north for 9km. After Argentière turn right into Route de Montroc, sp 'Le Tour'. Follow road through to Le Tour for 2.3km. Large sloping car park at end of road on both sides of river.

Sanitation:

Parking:

Tolerated

None

Snack bar; Ski pass office. Lovely setting with fine views of Mont Blanc and under Le Tour glacier. Inspected 2010.

PLAINE JOUX

169 L8 N45°57.033' E006°44.353' 74480

Directions: D43/Route de Plaine-Joux. From Chamonix exit N205 at Junction 22 at Le Fayet and follow D43 north 16km through Plateau-D'Assy to Plaine-Joux. Aire on both sides of road in large parking area before restaurants and paragliding centre.

Sanitation:

Parking:

20; €9/night

Flot Bleu Pacific; Token; €2; 8 unmetered elec points; €1

Alt 1360m. 2 areas with fantastic views of Mont Blanc. 12 pitches on opp side of road without elec. Inspected 2010.

LES HOUCHES (CHAMONIX) SKI

170 L8 N45°54.942' E006°46.017' 74130

Photo: Andy and Sue Glasgow

Directions: Aire de la Fontaine, N205. From N205 exit, sp 'Aire de la Fontaine'. Accessible and signed from both directions.

Sanitation:

Parking:

Poss

Custom

Alt 866m. Handy Service Point when enter/leave Chamonix region. Inspected 2010.

ST GERVAIS LES BAINS SKI 171 L8 N45°53.250' E006°42.783' 74170

Directions: D909. Signed behind Patinoire (skating rink) in town centre.

Sanitation:

Parking:

15

Raclet; Token; €2

All motorhomes parked at base of ski gondola, 200m away. Noisy location. Inspected 2010.

THONES 172 K8 N45°52.858' E006°19.275' 74230

Photo: Heidi Hardwick

Directions: Chemin de Paradis. From Annecy on D909, at first roundabout in Thones turn right onto D12, sp 'Office du Tourisme'. Turn 1st right, sp 'Office du Tourisme'. Follow road across river/storm drain bridge and turn right. The parking area is 200m on left, signed

Sanitation:

Parking:

7; Max 48hrs

None

Small town nestled amongst the hills. The designated motorhome parking between trees. Local commerce and LIDL 5 mins. Visited 2012.

UGINE 173 K8 N45°44.791' E006°25.034' 73400

Directions: D1508. From west on D1508 turn right into service road immediately after 1st roundabout, signed. Parking in bays on right, Service Point adj to TO.

Sanitation:

Parking:

17

Flot Bleu Euro; CC; €2

Toilets and TO in old railway station building adj. Cycle path to Annecy and Albertville. Inspected 2010.

LES SAISIES 1 SKI 174 K8 N45°45.749' E006°32.024' 73620

Photo: Andy and Sue Glasgow

Directions: From Albertville follow D925, sp 'Beaufort' and 'Les Saisies', for 16km. Turn left onto D218b, sp 'Les Saisies'. Follow road for 15.5km, passing through Les Saisies. At 4th roundabout turn right into Aire. Signed. Ski info: www.aed-montagne.com.

Sanitation:

Parking:

100; €7.50/24hrs; Pay at machine

Flot Bleu Pacific, €2

Alt 1650m. Mountain Aire in popular family ski resort with Olympic Nordic ski course. Inspected 2010.

LES SAISIES 2 175 K8 N45°44.817' E006°32.123' 73620

Directions: D123. From Les Saisies follow D123 up hill, sp 'Quartier de la Fôret'. Service Point on left at bend in road, opp 'Camping Caravaneige Le Grand Tetras'. Signed from Les Saisies. Advise approach from Les Saisies, not Villard sur Doron.

Sanitation:

Parking:

None

Flot Bleu Standard Plus; €2

Service Point only in lay-by on forest road. Inspected 2010.

FAVERGES

176 K8 N45°44.969' E006°17.159' 74210

Directions: D2508/Route de Annecy. From Annecy take D1508 south for 23km. At roundabout take 2nd exit, sp 'Faverges'. Aire on right in 1.3km, just prior to Carrefour supermarket, sp 'Parking Stade'.

Sanitation:

Parking:

15

Custom

Adj to stadium and supermarket with laundry. Pleasant Aire with nice views. Inspected 2010.

ALBERTVILLE

177 K8 N45°40.443' E006°23.828' 73200

Photo: Charlie and Angie Anderson

Directions: D105. From N90 turn onto D1212. After 1.5km turn right onto D925, sp 'Venthon'. Cross river and continue up hill on D105 to Venthon. Aire in car park on right opp cemetery on outskirts of town. Well signed to Flot Bleu from main road.

Sanitation:

Parking:

6; Max 24hrs

Flot Bleu Pacific

Town 5 mins. Conflans is a medieval town worth a visit, 5 mins further up road. Inspected 2010.

BEAUFORT

178 K8 N45°43.192' E006°34.026' 73270

Directions: D925/Avenue des Sports. From Albertville follow D925, sp 'Beaufort', for 18km. The Aire is at the start of the village on the left in the car park for cross country skiing, next to the fire station.

Sanitation:

Parking:

7

Flot Bleu Fontaine

In pleasant tree clad valley. 700m walk to centre of pretty alpine village with amenities. Lots of walking and cycling from village. Inspected 2010.

LA ROSIERE SKI

179 L8 N45°37.482' E006°51.369' 73700

Photo: Andy and Sue Glasgow

Directions: D1090. Follow D1090 north out of Bourg St Maurice. Aire signed on left just before village behind Sapeurs Pompiers (fire station).

Ski info: www.larosiere.net

Sanitation:

Parking:

20; Max 15 days

Flot Bleu Pacific; Token; €10

Alt 1850m. Nice family resort with sunny south facing slopes, link to Italian resort La Thuile. Inspected 2010.

BOURG ST MAURICE

180 L8 N45°36.210' E006°45.960' 73700

Directions: Lieu-Dit La Regence, off D220. From south on N90 turn right onto D220, sp 'Hauteville Gondon' and 'Gendarmerie'. Follow road for 1km and turn left just before river bridge. Aire immediately on left.

Sanitation:

Parking:

20; €6/night; Max 48hrs

None

Aire adj to river (no views) with international Kayak course. Showers (€1.50) and toilets at kayak centre. Inspected 2010.

LES ARCS — SKI — 181 — L8 — N45°35.795' E006°47.520' — 73700

Photo: Andy and Sue Glasgow

Directions: D120, Arc 1600. From Bourg St Maurice on D1090 turn onto D119, sp 'Les Arcs'. Follow road for 13.5km. Then at roundabout take 2nd exit onto D120, sp 'Arc 1600'. Aire on left in 500m.

Sanitation:

Parking:

10; Tolerated

None

Views of Mont Blanc; Free ski bus to slopes. Popular campsite 'Le Versoyen' at Bourg St Maurice. Inspected 2010.

LA PLAGNE — SKI — 182 — L8 — N45°30.392' E006°41.205' — 73210

Photo: Andy and Sue Glasgow

Directions: D221 up from Aime to La Plagne. Past Service Point on left (N45°30.543'E006°40.824'), at roundabout follow D233, sp 'La Plagne - Villages'. Pass top station of small triple gondola and fork sharp left under high bar.

Sanitation:

Parking:

40

Flot Bleu Pacific; 3 x €0.50

Nice ski Aire - next to slopes, ticket office 100m. Ideal for intermediates with links to Les Arcs. Inspected 2010.

LE PRAZ COURCHEVEL — SKI — 183 — K8 — N45°25.831' E006°37.485' — 73120

Directions: D91a. Pass through village of Le Praz on D91a towards Courchevel. Aire on left in parking Jean Blanc just after bend leaving village. Flot Bleu near entrance. Extensive parking amongst cars.

Sanitation:

Parking:

20

Flot Bleu Pacific; €3

Large level car park, 250m to village. Fine views, ski down to main lifts in village with excellent links to Courchevel/Meribel. Inspected 2010.

COURCHEVEL LA TANIA — SKI — 184 — K8 — N45°25.895' E006°36.030' — 73120

Directions: D98. From Moûtiers take D915, then D91a. At Le Praz turn right onto D98 and pass the ski jump. Follow D98 for 1.8km. Aire on left, signed. Service Point 400m further up D98 on right in bus stop/lay-by: N45°25.932' E006°35.736'.

Sanitation:

Parking:

6

Flot Bleu Pacific; 400m up hill

100m to village. Service Point is very old and at time of visit appeared to have been out of use for a long time. Inspected 2010.

LES MENUIRES * — SKI — 185 — K8 — N45°19.542' E006°32.026' — 73440

Directions: Can approach from north or south on D117/D117a. Turn off roundabout, sp 'Val Thorens' and 'Aire de Camping Cars' (D117/D117a), and travel 1.3km to Aire. Signed and located under Tortollet chair lift. Barrier entranced system.

Sanitation:

Parking:

74; €10/24hrs

Flot Bleu Pacific; Token; €2; Elec €2/4hrs

Good popular Aire, busy in holidays. Main choice for 3 valleys and the easily reached resort of Val Thorens. Ticket office and free lift to village nearby. Inspected 2010.

LANSLEBOURG MONT CENIS 186 L8 N45°17.066' E006°52.290' 73480

Directions: D1006. From west on D1006 the Service Point is in a lay-by on right as you enter village at 'Lanslebourg' town sign.

Sanitation:

Parking:

None

Euro Relais Junior; €2

Service Point at attractive alpine village. Inspected 2010.

VALLOIRE SKI 187 L8 N45°10.135' E006°25.761' 73450

Directions: Route des Villards/Rue de la Bonne Eau. From south on D902 turn left onto Rue de la Bonne Eau, sp 'Camping'. Follow road downhill alongside river. At end of road Service Point is ahead, slightly to left, outside Camping Sainte Thecle.

Sanitation:

Parking:

None

Custom

Alt 1385m. Campsite has free snow mini train to slopes. Excellent skiing with 150km of pistes. Inspected 2010.

ST JEAN DE MAURIENNE 188 K8 N45°16.766' E006°20.826' 73300

Directions: Place du Champ de Foire. From south on D1006 turn left onto D77. Turn right at roundabout on D77. After 700m turn right into Rue Jean Jaurés. Go straight over roundabout and Aire in 1st car park on left. Service Point in lower car park.

Sanitation:

Parking:

10; Max 48hrs

Flot Bleu Pacific; €4; 2 x €2 coins

Pleasant mountain town with all facilities. Casino supermarket 200m. Inspected 2010.

VAUJANY SKI 189 K9 N45°09.410' E006°04.803' 38114

Directions: Off D43a. From D526 turn onto D43a. After 2km turn left to stay on D43a. After another 2km turn right, sp 'Espace Loisirs' and signed, and follow road to Aire. Building works at Aire March 2012.

Sanitation:

Parking:

15

Euro Relais Mini; Token; Elec €5

Alt 1250. In large ski area with plenty of ski lifts adj. View of large waterfall opp. Inspected 2010.

ALPE D'HUEZ SKI 190 K9 N45°05.204' E006°04.750' 38750

Directions: East of ski station. From D1091 turn onto D211 and follow road to ski station. At the top follow signs towards the airfield, tennis and Aire. Signed.

Sanitation:

Parking:

75; €10.40/day; CC; Pay at machine

Raclet; inc

Ski resort at 1860m alt with good views. 2 good sized Service Points. Tennis courts and golf course adj. Inspected 2010.

LA LECHERE

191 K8 N45°31.180' E006°29.057' 73260

Directions: Parking 3, 'Village 92', Thermal Spa Complex. From south exit N90 at Junction 37, sp 'La Léchère'. Turn left at T-Junction onto D93a. Follow road under N90, cross railway and turn left into Lieu-Dit Château Feuillet. At roundabout take 2nd exit into car park of Thermal Baths.

Sanitation:

Parking:

19; 48hrs free; 49hrs-21 days €1.50/day

Flot Bleu Fontaine

Parking at thermal spa, restaurant, cafe, bar onsite. Riverside walks. Inspected 2010.

AIGUEBELLE

192 K8 N45°32.586' E006°18.374' 73220

Directions: Rue des Écoles. From south on D1006 turn right at traffic lights in centre of village into Rue Carret, sp 'Parking V. L. @ 50m'. At end of road turn right and the Aire is immediately on left.

Sanitation:

Parking:

10

Custom

Aire in small car park with some grass parking. Can be busy with lorries, especially market day Tues when best to arrive after 2pm. Railway noise at night. Inspected 2010.

BOURGNEUF

193 K8 N45°33.165' E006°12.653' 73390

Directions: D925. From south on D925 turn right at roundabout with D204 into village. Take 1st turning left off D925, sp 'Restaurant Pizzeria' and signed. Follow red, surfaced road in front of pizzeria and parking is in large open area behind boulangerie.

Sanitation:

Parking:

10

Flot Bleu Océane; Elec €2/20mins

Parking on edge of village with lovely views of mountains across fields. Boulangerie adj. Inspected 2010.

SUSVILLE

194 K9 N44°55.487' E005°46.965' 38350

Directions: N85. Service Point at the Casino supermarket fuel station adj to the N85.

Sanitation:

Parking:

Poss

Flot Bleu Euro; €2 CC

Supermarket adj. Visited 2012.

LE BOURG D'OISANS

195 K9 N45°03.418' E006°02.077' 38520

Directions: D1091B. Service Point at the Casino supermarket fuel station adj to the D1091B.

Sanitation:

Parking:

Poss

Flot Bleu Euro; €2 CC

Supermarket adj. Visited 2012.

St Pierre de Chartreuse, *Photo: Carol Weaver*

LES DEUX ALPS | SKI | 197 | K9 | N45°01.401' E006°07.326' | 38860

Info/Photo: Heidi Hardwick

Directions: D213. From valley bottom on D213, the Aire is on left just before entering town, sp bus parking.

Sanitation:

Parking:

40; €7/24 hours -inc elec and water; Max 7 days

Urba Flux Tall

15 mins uphill small town with commerce. Ice skating rink, ski lifts and glacial skiing open all year. Free shuttle bus in summer. Les Deux Alps is very popular with skiers, snowboarders and mountain bikers.

AILLON LE JEUNE | 198 | K8 | N45°36.547' E006°06.266' | 73340

Info/Photo: Carol Weaver

Directions: D32B. Turn off D206 in Aillon le Jeune by the Mairie and church onto D32A, sp 'Aillon le Jueune – Station'. Follow road for 2km, then go straight over roundabout. Aire 500m on right behind Intersport Shop.

Sanitation:

Parking:

5

Custom

Rural. Lovely countryside. Visited 2012.

BELLEY | 199 | K8 | N45°45.345' E005°40.691' | 01300

Info/Photo: Brenda & Maurice Cope/Carol Weaver

Directions: Rue de la Poisatte. Follow sp 'St Germain les Paroisses' through village onto D41. Aire is on right by sports facilities, signed.

Sanitation:

Parking:

8

Urba Flux; €2 (2 x €1 coin)

Local commerce 8 mins. Lake 2km. Visited 2012.

ST HILAIRE DU TOUVET | 200 | K8 | N45°18.152' E005°52.821' | 38660

Info/Photo: Carol Weaver

Directions: Chemin du Bec Margain. Turn off D30 in village by sports facilities, sp 'Terrain du Foot'. Aire adj to tennis courts.

Sanitation:

Parking:

2

Custom

Alt 1017m. Village adj with local commerce and convenience store. Visited 2012.

Rhone - St Rambert d'Albon

Atlantic - Ste Colombe en Bruilhois

MOTORWAYS

Motorway Aires. Do not park overnight at motorway service stations and rest areas!

French motorway service and rest areas often allocate parking with car and caravan signs. The parking areas may look nice, however motorhomes, caravans, trucks and vans are frequently broken into at motorway rest areas. Often the occupants are asleep during the burglary; surely a situation you would not want to be in. The following motorway service areas all have a motorhome/coach Service Point. We have observed that they are often broken, full of rubbish or obstructed by parked trucks. Vicarious Books recommends that you never park overnight at motorway services and rest areas and maintain vigilance at all times when using them.

KEY: BS = Service station accessible from both sides of motorway.

Service station accessible when traveling N north, NE northeast, NW northwest, S south, etc.

Town	Map ref.	Grid ref.	GPS	Aire name and location
ATLANTIC				
SAUGON S	A	D9	N45°11.330' W000°29.550'	Aire de Saugon. A10/E5 between Junction 38 and 39a, southbound towards Bordeaux.
SAUGON N	A	D9	N45°11.364' W000°29.392'	Aire de Saugon. A10/E5 between Junction 38 and 39a, northbound towards Niort.
BORDEAUX N	B	E9	N44°38.853' W000°26.160'	Aire des Landes. A62/E72 between Junction 1.1 and 2 , northbound towards Bordeaux.
BORDEAUX SE	B	E9	N44°38.659' W000°26.279'	Aire des Landes. A62/E72 between Junction 1.1 and 2, southeast towards Toulouse.
AGEN BS	C	E10	N44°11.978' E000°30.367'	Aire d'Agen Porte D'Aquitane. A62/E72, Junction 6 and 7. Accessable both sides.
LESPERON N	D	D10	N43°56.260' W001°05.400'	Aire du Souquet. N10/E70 between Junction 12 and 13. Accessable both sides.
BAYONNE NE	E	C11	N43°25.390' W001°35.963'	Aire de Bidart. A63/E80 between Junction 3 and 4, northeast towards Bayonne.
BAYONNE SW	E	C11	N43°25.306' W001°35.813'	Aire de Bidart. A63/E80 between Junction 3 and 4, southwest towards Spain.
PAU SE	F	D11	N43°25.262' W000°35.911'	Aire de Lacq-Audejos. A64/E80 between Junction 8 and 9, southeast towards Pau.
BRITTANY				
RENNES NW	A	C5	N48°09.992' W001°52.017'	Aire d'Armor et d'Argoat. N12/E50 between D21 and D68, northwest towards Saint Brieuc.
RENNES E	A	C5	N48°09.994' W001°52.457'	Aire d'Armor et d'Argoat. N12/E50 between D21 and D68, eastbound towards Rennes.

Town	Map ref.	Grid ref.	GPS	Aire name and location
BURGUNDY				
DIJON S	A	J6	N47°13.102' E005°00.175'	Aire de Gevrey-Chambertin. A31/E17, 15km southbound from Dijon just after A311/A21 merge.
AUXONNE S	B	J6	N47°10.762' E005°19.931'	Aire de Pont Chene d'Argent. A39/E31 between Junction 5 and 6, southbound towards Lyon.
CENTRE				
JARDIN DES ARBRES BS	A	H5	N47°51.081' E002°41.022'	Aire du Jardin des Arbres. A77 at Junction 18.1. Accessible both sides.
CHATEAUROUX S	B	G7	N46°42.954' E001°35.674'	Aire des Mille Etangs. A20/E9 between Junction 14 and 15, southbound towards Limoges.
CHATEAUROUX N	B	G7	N46°43.445' E001°36.260'	Aire du Val de l'Indre. A20/E9 between Junction 14 and 15, northbound towards Châteauroux.
CHAMPAGNE				
REIMS S	A	I3	N49°10.537' E004°09.778'	Aire de L'Esperance. A4/E17 after Junction 27, southbound towards Troys.
REIMS N	A	I3	N49°10.519' E004°09.910'	Aire de La Vasle. A4/E17 before Junction 27, northbound towards Reims.
SOMMESOUS BS	B	I4	N48°43.843' E004°13.633'	Aire de Sommesous. A26/E17 at Junction 20. Accessible both sides. Halfway Rheims and Troyes.
EASTERN FRANCE				
SELESTAT BS	A	L4	N48°14.000' E007°24.369'	Aire du Haut Koenigsbourg. A35/E25 between Junctions 17 and 18 accessible both sides.
ECOT NE	B	K5	N47°26.506' E006°43.835'	Aire d'Ecot. A36/E60 between Junction 6 and 6.1, northeast towards Mulhouse.
BESANCON NE	C	K6	N 47°19.558' E006°07.253'	Aire de Besançon Marchaux. A36/E60 between Junction 4 and 4.1, northeast towards Mulhouse.
BESANCON SW	C	K6	N47°19.794' E006°07.842'	Aire de Besançon Champoux. A36/E60 between Junction 4 and 4.1, southwest towards Besançon.
LUNEVILLE W	D	K4	N48°35.458' E006°25.482'	Aire de Vitrimont. N333 between Junction 7 on A33 and Luneville exit on N333.
LIMOUSIN/AUVERGNE				
ST SULPICE LES FEUILLES S	A	F7	N46°18.765' E001°25.052'	Aire de Boismandé. A20/E9 between Junction 21 and 22, southbound towards Limoges.
ST SULPICE LES FEUILLES N	A	F7	N46°18.833' E001°25.223'	Aire de Boismandé. A20/E9 between Junction 21 and 22, northbound towards Châteauroux.
LORLANGES BS	B	H8	N45°20.122' E003°16.338'	Aire de La Fayette. A75/E11 at Junction 21, accessible both sides.
ST FLOUR BS	C	H9	N45°01.910' E003°08.095'	Aire de Service du Cantal. D909 off A75/E11 exit at Junction 29 to St Flour, accessible both sides.
MEDITERRANEAN				
LA LOZERE BS	A	H9	N44°52.177' E003°14.947'	Aire de la Lozere. A75/E11 exit at Junction 32, accessible both sides.
AUMONT AUBRAC BS	B	H9	N44°44.418' E003°17.358'	Aire de l'Aubrac. A75/E11 exit at Junction 35, SP at Simply supermarket.
LE CAYLAR BS	C	H10	N43°51.896' E003°18.714'	Aire du Caylar. A75/E11 exit at Junction 49, accessible both sides.
CAPENDU E	D	G11	N43°10.590' E002°32.584'	Aire des Corbières. A61/E80 between Junction 24 and 25, eastbound towards Narbonne.

Town	Map ref.	Grid ref.	GPS	Aire name and location
CAPENDU W	D	G11	N43°10.736' E002°32.541'	Aire des Corbières. A61/E80 between Junction 24 and 25. westbound towards Carcassonne.
BANYULS DELS ASPRES BS	E	H12	N42°34.797' E002°50.785'	Aire du Village Catalan. A9/E15 between Junction 42 and 43. Second Service Point N42°34.767' E002°50.767'
CAVES N	F	H12	N42°56.993' E002°58.346'	Aire de La Palme. A9/E15 between Junction 39 and 40, northbound towards Narbonne.
CAVES S	F	H12	N42°57.047' E002°58.109'	Aire de La Palme. A9/E15 between Junction 39 and 40, southbound towards Perpignan.
NARBONNE NE	G	H11	N43°12.926' E003°05.633'	Aire de Narbonne-Vinassan. A9/E80 between Junction 36 and 37, northeast towards Béziers.
NARBONNE S	G	H11	N43°12.866' E003°05.328'	Aire de Narbonne-Vinassan. A9/E80 between Junction 36 and 37, southbound towards Narbonne.
BEZIERS NE	H	H11	N43°21.530' E003°20.795'	Aire de Béziers-Montblanc. A9/E80 between Junction 34 and 35, northeast towards Montpellier.
BEZIERS S	H	H11	N43°21.609' E003°20.577'	Aire de Béziers-Montblanc. A9/E80 between Junction 34 and 35, southbound towards Béziers.
NIMES SW	I	I10	N43°52.512' E004°26.888'	Aire de Nimes-Marguerittes. A9/E15 between Junction 23 and 24, southwest towards Nimes.
LANCON PROVENCE SW	J	J11	N43°35.325' E005°11.543'	Aire de Lancon de Provence. A7/E80/E714 between Junction 27 and 28, southbound towards Marseille/Nice.
LANCON PROVENCE N	J	J11	N43°35.405' E005°11.510'	Aire de Lancon de Provence. A7/E80/E714 between Junction 27 and 28, northbound towards Lyon.
ROUSSET E	K	K11	N43°28.305' E005°38.637'	Aire de Rousset. A8/E80 between Junction 32 and 33, eastbound towards Aix en Provence.
ROUSSET W	K	K11	N43°28.079' E005°39.375'	Aire de l'Arc. A8/E80 between Junction 32 and 33, westbound towards Brignoles.
AIRE DE CAMBARETTE BS	L	K11	N43°25.322' E005°59.480'	Aire de Cambarette. A8/E80 between Junction 34 and 35. In middle, accessible both sides.
VIDAUBAN E	M	K11	N43°24.872' E006°27.256'	Aire de Vidauban Sud. A8/E80 between Junction 35 and 36, eastbound towards Italy.
MIDI-PYRENEES				
SEVERAC LE CHATEAU BS	A	H10	N44°19.839' E003°04.930'	Aire de l'Aveyron. A75/E11. N88 Junction 42, accessible both sides.
MONTANS NE	B	G10	N43°51.786' E001°53.844'	Aire des Issarts. A68 between Junction 8 and 9, northeast towards Albi.
MONTANS SW	B	G10	N43°51.120' E001°52.831'	Aire de Sanbatan. A68 between Junction 8 and 9, southwest towards Toulouse.
CAPENS W	C	G11	N43°20.262' E001°14.742'	Aire du Volvestre. A64/E80 between Junction 27 and 28, westbound towards Bayonne.
AVIGNONET-LAURAGAIS BS	D	G11	N43°21.311' E001°48.271'	Aire de Port-Lauragais. A61/E80 between Junction 20 and 21, accessible both sides.
NORMANDY				
BOLLEVILLE BS	A	F3	N49°36.850' E000°32.846'	Aire de Bolleville. A29/E44 between Junction 7 and 8, accessible both sides.
ALENCON BS	B	E4	N48°27.407' E000°07.577'	Aire de la Dentelle d'Alencon. A28/E402 at Junction 18, accessible both sides.

Town	Map ref.	Grid ref.	GPS	Aire name and location
NORTHERN FRANCE				
SAILLY FLIBEAUCOURT BS	A	G2	N50°10.053' E001°45.353'	Aire de la Baie de Somme. A16/E402 between Junction 23 and 24, accessible both sides.
PAYS DE LOIRE				
LES HERBIERS BS	A	D6	N46°54.241' W001°02.847'	Aire des Herbiers. A87 Exit at Junction 29, accessible both sides.
POITOU				
VILLIERS EN PLAINE E	A	E7	N46°25.734' W000°30.328'	Aire de la Chateaudrie. A83 between Junction 9 and 10, eastbound towards Poitiers.
VILLIERS EN PLAINE W	A	E7	N46°25.828' W000°30.241'	Aire de la Canepetière. A83 between Junction 9 and 10, westbound towards Nantes.
NIORT S	B	E7	N46°17.777' W000°22.770'	Aire du Poitou-Charentes. A10/E5 between Junction 32 and 33, southbound towards Bordeaux.
BEDENAC S	C	E9	N45°10.397' W000°19.956'	Aire de Bedenac. N10/E606 between D145 and D250 junctions, southbound towards Bordeaux.
PAMPROUX N	D	E7	N46°27.275' W000°01.036'	Aire de Rouill Pamproux. A10/E5 between Junction 30 and 31, northbound towards Angoulême.
PAMPROUX S	D	E7	N46°27.066' W000°00.956'	Aire de Rouill Pamproux. A10/E5 between Junction 30 and 31, southbound towards Bordeaux.
RHONE-ALPS				
DRACE S	A	J7	N46°08.649' E004°46.068'	Aire de Drace. A6/E15 between Junction 29 and 30, southbound towards Lyon.
L'ISLE D'ABEAU E	B	J8	N45°36.721' E005°12.552'	Aire de l'Isle d'Abeau. A43/E70 between Junction 6 and 7, eastbound towards Chambry.
L'ISLE D'ABEAU NE	B	J8	N45°36.818' E005°12.729'	Aire de l'Isle d'Abeau. A43/E70 between Junction 6 and 7, northeast towards Lyon.
CHATEAUNEUF E	C	K8	N45°32.829' E006°09.376'	Aire du Val Gelon. A43/E70 at Junction 23, eastbound towards Italy.
CHATEAUNEUF W	C	K8	N45°32.898' E006°09.332'	Aire de l'Arclusaz. A43/E70 at Junction 23, westbound towards Chambery.
ST RAMBERT D'ALBON S	D	J9	N45°16.490' E004°49.576'	Aire de St Rambert d'Albon. A7/E15 between Junction 12 and 13, southbound towards Marseille.
ST RAMBERT D'ALBON N	D	J9	N45°16.563' E004°49.754'	Aire de St Rambert d'Albon. A7/E15 between Junction 12 and 13, northbound towards Lyon.
PONT DE L'ISERE N	E	J9	N45°01.237' E004°52.615'	Aire de Latitude 45. A7/E15 between Junction 13 and 14, northbound towards Lyon.
LA BAUME D'HOSTUN SW	F	J9	N45°04.500' E005°12.551'	Aire Porte de la Drome. A49/E713 between Junction 8 and 9, southwest towards Valence.
LA BAUME D'HOSTUN NE	F	J9	N45°04.291' E005°12.730'	Aire de Royans-Vercors. A49/E713 between Junction 8 and 9, northeast towards Grenoble.
SAULCE SUR RHONE N	G	J9	N44°43.178' E004°47.276'	Aire de Saulce. A7/E15 between Junction 16 and 17, northbound towards Lyon.
MONTELIMAR S	H	J9	N44°30.980' E004°46.757'	Aire de Montélimar. A7/E15 Between Junction 17 and 18, southbound towards Marseille.
MONTELIMAR N	H	J9	N44°30.779' E004°46.834'	Aire de Montélimar. A7/E15 Between Junction 17 and 18, northbound towards Lyon.

CLOSED AIRES

Champagne - Geraudot CLOSED Sept 2012.

Poitou - Merignac CLOSED 2010.

This list of closed Aires is provided to prevent unnecessary journeys. The Aires have been confirmed closed by inspectors on location. Closed Aires that have no alternative Aire are marked with a X on the mapping. Closed Aires are listed in each region, alphabetically by town name. The map reference number from the edition in which they were published is also provided. Alternative Aires, when available, are listed in the final column.

Town	GPS	Year closed	Alternatives
ATLANTIC			
BERGERAC 54 3rd Ed	N44°50.760' E000°29.275'	2010	
BRANTOME 78 3rd Ed	N45°21.416' E000°39.167'	2010	203, 204
CAVIGNAC 93 3rd Ed	N45°05.964' W000°23.279'	2010	196
MUSSIDAN 60 3rd Ed	N45°02.508' E000°21.137'	2010	
PERIGUEUX 74 3rd Ed	N45°10.882' E000°43.357'	2010	114
BRITTANY			
ERDEVEN 24 3rd Ed	N47°38.472' W003°09.487'	2010	206
ETEL 27 3rd Ed	N47°39.316' W003°12.383'	2010	26, 28
HILLION 129 3rd Ed	N48°30.876' W002°40.027'	2010	51
KERGROES 66 3rd Ed	N47°48.143' W003°41.523'	2010	
LOCQUIREC 112 3rd Ed	N48°41.189' W003°40.579'	2010	
MATIGNON 137 3rd Ed	N48°35.977' W002°17.204'	2010	
MOELAN SUR MER 60 3rd Ed	N47°49.286' W003°37.044'	2010	
PLOUEZEC 124 3rd Ed	N48°44.845' W002°59.104'	2010	
PLOUGUERNEAU 99 3rd Ed	N48°36.346' W004°30.273'	2010	126
ROSCOFF 104 3rd Ed	N48°43.526' W003°58.224'	2010	116, 117
ST AUBIN D'AUBIGNE 4 3rd Ed	N48°15.676' W001°36.387'	2010	
ST CAST LE GUILDO 136 3rd Ed	N48°38.595' W002°14.767'	2010	42-44
ST MELOIR DES ONDES 148 3rd Ed	N48°38.081' W001°54.149'	2010	
ST MICHEL EN GREVE 165 3rd Ed	N48°41.100' W003°33.890'	2010	
BURGUNDY			
BUXY 49 3rd Ed	None	2010	
COULANGES LES NEVERS 7 3rd Ed	N47°00.594' E003°10.546'	2012	
CLUNY 45 3rd Ed	N46°26.258' E004°38.984'	2012	
LAIGNES 55 3rd Ed	N47°50.898' E004°21.678'	2012	
POUILLY EN AUXOIS 72 3rd Ed	N47°15.761' E004°33.172'	2012	

Town	GPS	Year closed	Alternatives
CENTRE			
BLERE 103 3rd Ed	N47°19.677' E000°59.812'	2012	
BLOIS 31 3rd Ed	N47°35.372' E001°20.507'	2010	103
BOURGUEIL 36 3rd Ed	N47°16.374' E000°10.063'	2010	
MONT PRES CHAMBORD 92 3rd Ed	N47°33.497' E001°27.826'	2012	
MONTRESOR 33 3rd Ed	N47°09.176' E001°11.751'	2010	44
STE MAURE DE TOURAINE 61 3rd Ed	N47°06.517' E000°36.864'	2010	53, 54
SULLY SUR LOIRE 41 3rd Ed	N47°46.286' E002°21.729'	2012	144
TROGUES 63 3rd Ed	N47°05.950' E000°30.256'	2012	
CHAMPAGNE			
GERAUDOT 20 3rd Ed	N48°18.132' E004°20.086'	2012	28
EASTERN FRANCE			
XONRUPT LONGEMER 70 3rd Ed	N48°04.717' E006°56.431'	2010	
LIMOUSIN & AUVERGNE			
AYDAT 35 3rd Ed	N45°39.630' E002°58.628'	2010	81
MEDITERRANEAN			
ARGELES SUR MER 62 3rd Ed	N42°34.627' E003°02.125'	2010	
BORMES LES MIMOSAS 130 3rd Ed	N43°09.317' E006°20.800'	2010	
CARNON PLAGE 94 3rd Ed	N43°33.198' E004°00.590'	2010	100
DRAGUIGNAN 53 3rd Ed	N43°31.974' E006°26.976'	2010	
FONTCOUVERTE 131 2nd & 3rd Ed	None	2008	
FONTIES D'AUDE 37 3rd Ed	N43°11.154' E002°27.154'	2012	
FREJUS 140 3rd Ed	N43°25.238' E006°44.550'	2010	196
FREJUS 141 3rd Ed	N43°25.458' E006°44.264'	2010	196
LA MOTTE 48 3rd Ed	N43°29.457' E006°32.081'	2010	192
LA REDORTE 95 3rd Ed	N43°14.912' E002°39.520'	2010	
LE LAVANDOU 4 3rd Ed	N43°07.458' E006°21.456'	2010	
MARSEILLAN PLAGE 39 3rd Ed	N43°18.999' E003°32.715'	2010	
PELVOUX 200 3rd Ed	N44°52.133' E006°29.100'	2010	
PONT DU FOSSE 5 3rd Ed	N44°40.075' E006°13.870'	2010	225
PUICHERIC 17 3rd Ed	N43°13.628' E002°37.618'	2010	
SETE BEACH 2 3rd Ed	N43°22.964' E003°38.458'	2010	67
ST GILLES 110 3rd Ed	N43°40.337' E004°26.020'	2010	
TREBES 98 3rd Ed	N43°12.539' E002°26.798'	2010	
MIDI-PYRENEES			
CASTELSARRASIN 41 3rd Ed	N44°02.279' E001°06.835'	2012	187
CASTRES 87 3rd Ed	N43°37.225' E002°15.203'	2012	100
CUQ LES VIELMUR 62 3rd Ed	N43°38.464' E002°05.846'	2010	
GOURDON 92 3rd Ed	N44°44.948' E001°22.535'	2010	6
LISLE SURE TARN 77 3rd Ed	N43°51.708' E001°49.122'	2012	
MARCIAC 164 3rd Ed	N43°31.571' E000°09.759'	2010	
NORMANDY			
AUMALE 25 3rd Ed	N49°45.976' E001°44.730'	2010	
BAGNOLES DE L'ORNE 14 3rd Ed	N48°32.876' W000°25.204'	2012	150
BENOUVILLE 103 3rd Ed	N49°14.988' W000°16.838'	2010	
BOURGTHEROULDE INFREVILLE 42 3rd Ed	N49°17.829' E000°52.446'	2012	

CLOSED AIRES

Town	GPS	Year closed	Alternatives
FECAMP 24 3rd Ed	N49°45.809' E000°21.903'	2012	27
LE HAVRE 17 3rd Ed	N49°29.536' E000°05.765'	2010	30
LE MONT ST MICHEL 71 3rd Ed	N48°37.711' W001°30.466'	2012	138-141
LE MONT ST MICHEL 114 3rd Ed	N48°36.832' W001°30.440'	2012	138-141
NORTHERN FRANCE			
AMIENS 18 3rd Ed	N49°53.907' E002°17.606'	2010	
ATTICHY 27 3rd Ed	N49°24.342' E003°03.199'	2010	
AUDRESSELLES 42 3rd Ed	N50°49.184' E001°35.820'	2010	
CAUDRY 24 3rd Ed	N50°07.549' E003°25.398'	2010	
GRAVELINES 23 3rd Ed	N50°58.966' E002°08.487'	2010	6, 7
LE TOUQUET PARIS PLAGE 9 3rd Ed	N50°30.943' E001°37.077'	2010	21, 22
LILLE - VILLENEUVE D'ASCQ 21 3rd Ed	N50°38.644' E003°08.438'	2010	
PAYS DE LOIRE			
GUERANDE 13 3rd Ed	N47°19.526' W002°25.849'	2010	229
L'EPINE 20 3rd Ed	N46°59.174' W002°17.626'	2010	198
OLONNE SURE MER 32 3rd Ed	N46°33.199' W001°48.610'	2010	166
PAIMBOEUF 138 3rd Ed	N47°17.380' W002°01.728'	2012	
PAIMBOEUF 206 3rd Ed	N47°17.056' W002°00.997'	2012	
ST BREVIN L'OCEAN 103 3rd Ed	N47°13.936' W002°10.786'	2010	
ST GILLES CROIX DE VIE 00 2nd & 3rd Ed	N46°42.041' W001°56.315'	2008	167
ST MAIXENT SUR VIE 161 3rd Ed	N46°44.493' W001°49.300'	2010	
POITOU			
AVAILLES LIMOUZINE 61 3rd Ed	N46°07.385' E000°39.626'	2010	
CONFOLENS 79 3rd Ed	N46°00.768' E000°40.047'	2010	64
DISSAY 44 3rd Ed	N46°42.750' E000°24.810'	2010	
LA PALMYRE 69 3rd Ed	N45°41.432' W001°10.610'	2010	144
LE CHATEAU D'OLERON 111 3rd Ed	N45°53.303' W001°12.298'	2010	151
LES MATHES 42 3rd Ed	N45°43.063' W001°08.870'	2010	143
MERIGNAC 64 3rd Ed	N45°41.687' W000°05.141'	2010	
PORT DES BARQUES 136 3rd Ed	N45°56.950' W001°05.733'	2010	164
PORT LES MINIMES 62 3rd Ed	N46°08.533' W001°10.277'	2010	
ROCHEFORT 39 3rd Ed	N45°56.597' W000°57.518'	2010	169
RONCE LES BAINS 92 3rd Ed	N45°47.582' W001°09.010'	2010	
SECONDIGNY 32 3rd Ed	N46°36.274' W000°24.979'	2010	
ST JEAN D'ANGELY 59 3rd Ed	N45°56.960' W000°32.178'	2010	117
ST YRIEIX 26 3rd Ed	N45°41.160' E000°08.857'	2010	
RHONE-ALPS			
AIGUEBLANCHE 50 3rd Ed	N45°30.169'E006°30.068'	2010	
AIX LES BAINS 95 3rd Ed	N45°42.180' E005°53.186'	2010	155
CHATILLON EN DIOIS 81 3rd Ed	N44°40.952' E005°26.873'	2010	
DONZERE (MARKET) 2 3rd Ed	N44°26.600'E004°42.598'	2010	
MORZINE 106 3rd Ed	N46°10.456' E006°42.623'	2010	
ST CIRGUES EN MONTAGNE 77 3rd Ed	N44°45.351' E004°05.706'	2010	
ST PAUL DE VARAX 71 3rd Ed	none	2010	
ST PIERRE DE CHARTREUSE 87 3rd Ed	N45°20.477' E005°49.059'	2010	132
TOURNON SUR RHONE 28 3rd Ed	N45°04.230' E004°49.716'	2010	66
VILLARS LES DOMBES 43 3rd Ed	N45°59.572' E005°01.548'	2012	

LPG - GPL cup adaptor.

LPG - GPL cup hand gun.

666 LPG fuel stations are listed here. Coordinates were taken onsite at 259 and the remainder have been remotely generated. TOTAL kindly gave us permission to publish the addresses on their trade distribution list. In November 2012 TOTAL were supplying LPG to 500 of the 1700 fuel stations across France that sell GPL as it is named in France. LPG is available at most motorway service stations and the cup shaped connector is standard across France.

TOWN	GPS	DIRECTIONS
ATLANTIC		
AGEN	N44°10.708' E000°38.004'	Geant supermarket. From south take D17 into southern suburbs.
AIRE D'AGEN PORTE D'AQUITAINE	N44°11.963' E000°30.501'	Total. A62, Toll road, between junctions 6 and 7 accessable both sides. Good access for large motorhomes.
AIRE SUR L'ADOUR	N43°43.342' W000°15.874'	Total. D824, Route de Bordeaux. 2km north of town. Good access for large motorhomes.
ARCACHON	N44°39.141' W001°08.819'	Avia. D650, Boulevard Mestrezat. 200m from Aire. Good access for large motorhomes.
BAYONNE	N43°30.290' W001°26.721'	E'Leclerc supermarket. D817, at roundabout Junction with D107. Northeast of town. Access not ideal for motorhomes over 8m.
BAYONNE	N43°29.543' W001°27.541'	Total. Avenue du Marechal Juin. In industrial area bordering northern bank of L'Adour river. Good access for large motorhomes.
BERGERAC	N44°50.100' E000°26.867'	E'Leclerc supermarket. D936. At roundabout west of town.
BERGERAC	N44°49.950' E000°29.800'	Total . N21, Route D'Agen. South of town. Good access for large motorhomes. Pump not under main canopy.
BIDART	N43°25.306' W001°35.813'	Total. Aire de Bidart. A63/E80 between Junction 3 and 4, southwest towards Spain.
BIDART	N43°25.390' W001°35.963'	Total. Aire de Bidart. A63/E80 between Junction 3 and 4, northeast towards Bayonne.
BIGANOS	N44°38.183' W000°57.583'	Auchan supermarket. D3e13. South of town in commercial area. LPG pump under 2.95m high canopy. Diesel pump outside alongside of access road, signed for HGV's and motorhomes.
BILLIÈRE	N43°18.349' W000°24.186'	Total. 90 Route de Bayonne. Off D834 roundabout northwest of town.
BISCARROSSE	N44°23.417' W001°09.650'	Super U supermarket. D652, Avenue Marechal Lyautey, in town centre. Good access for large motorhomes. Pump not under main canopy.
BIZANOS	N43°18.214' W000°19.374'	Total Access. N117/D817 northeast of town.
BORDEAUX	N44° 52.971' W000°33.796'	Auchan. CC du Lac. North of Bordeaux.
BORDEAUX (GRADIGNAN)	N44°47.133' W000°35.733'	Avia . A630/E05/E70 motorway (known as Rocade de Bordeaux), south of Bordeaux. Eastbound carriageway between junctions 16 and 17. Good access for large motorhomes. LPG pump on far right of forecourt under canopy.
BORDEAUX (MERIGNAC)	N44°51.033' W000°40.067'	Total.A630/E05/E70 motorway (known as Rocade de Bordeaux), west of Bordeaux. Southbound carriageway between junctions 9 and 10. Good access for large motorhomes. LPG pump on far right of forecourt and not under canopy.

LPG - GPL

TOWN	GPS	DIRECTIONS
BOULAZAC	N45°11.138' E000°46.488'	Carrefour. At roundabout Junction of N221 and D5. Southeast of Perigueux. Follow Carrefour signs. Good access for large motorhomes. LPG pump is on far right of forecourt.
CASTELJALOUX	N44°19.167' E000°05.600'	Intermarche supermarket Adj to D933N, northeast of town centre. Access to pump ok as its not under the canopy. May need to reverse off pump as canopy is in front and only 2.85m high. Plenty of manoeuvring space.
CESTAS	N44°44.544' W000°42.435'	Total. Aire de Bordeaux. A63 eastbound.
DAX	N43°43.032' W001°03.072'	Total fuel station. D129, 28 Route Georges Chaulet, north of town.
DAX	N43°44.467' W001°01.000'	Total fuel station. Off D824. Open 7-9 Mon to Sat.
EYSINES	N44°53.545' W000°40.058'	Total access. Off D1215 roundabout, 388 Avenue du Médoc west of town.
FUMEL	N44°29.500' E000°58.183'	Intermarche supermarket. Avenue de Ladhuie, off D710 at roundabout south of river Lot. Good access for large motorhomes. Pump not under main canopy.
GUJAN MESTRAS	N44°37.001' W001°04.447'	Super U. Avenue de Césarée, just off A660 south of town.
LA TESTE	N44°38.793' W001°09.437'	Fuel station. Off D1250 roundabout, Route Lagrua north of town.
LACQ-AUDEJOS	N43°25.300' W000°35.900'	Agip. Aire de Lacq-Audejos, service station on A64/E80 toll motorway between junctions 8 and 9, eastbound towards Pau. Good access for large motorhomes.
LANGON	N44°33.126' W000°15.893'	Total. On D116/D8 roundabout, 8 Route de Villandraut, west of Langon.
LANGON	N44°32.509' W000°15.298'	E'Leclerc. Off D22 roundabout 1km southwest of centre.
LESPARRE MEDOC	N45°18.083' W000°56.043'	Total. D1215, Route de Bordeaux, south of town.
LIBOURNE	N44°53.864' W000°12.524'	Total. D670, Avenue du Général Leclerc, southeast of town.
LORMONT	N44°52.416' W000°30.407'	Total. Rocade Est de Bordeaux. N230, southeast of town.
MARMANDE	N44°30.316' E000°09.032'	Total fuel station. D813, 84 Route Jean Jaurès , northwest of Marmande.
MARMANDE	N44°29.333' E000°10.817'	Carrefour fuel station at supermarket. Off D813, southeast of town centre. Good access for large motorhomes.
MARSAC SUR L'ISLE	N45°11.650' E000°39.583'	Auchan supermarket fuel station. At Centre Commercial off D710e, west of Perigueux. Good access for large motorhomes.
MERIGNAC	N44°49.659' W000°40.264'	Elf. At roundabout on D106, Avenue de la Somme, southwest of town.
MÉRIGNAC	N44°50.516' W000°39.866'	Total. 127 Avenue de l'Yser, southwest of town centre.
MÉRIGNAC	N44°49.659' W000°40.265'	Total Access. D106, Avenue de la Somme, southwest of town.
MIMIZAN	N44°12.433' W001°14.550'	Esso fuel station. D626, Avenue de la Plage. From Mimizan Plage garage is on right just after Junction with D87 and D67. Good access for large motorhomes. LPG pump not under canopy (4.3m).
MONT DE MARSAN	N43°53.137' W000°29.700'	Total access. D30, 394 Avenue Georges Clemenceau, south of town.
MONTPON-MENESTEROL	N45°00.367' E000°08.550'	Intermarche supermarket fuel station. D6089, Avenue Georges Pompidou. At roundabout junction with D9, west of town. Good access for large motorhomes. Pump not under main canopy.
MUSSIDAN	N45°02.467' E000°21.100'	Super U supermarket. D6089, at roundabout north of town. Good access for large motorhomes.
OLORON SAINTE MARIE	N43°11.432' W000°37.041'	Total. D936, Avenue Charles Mourieu, at roundabout west of town.
ORTHEZ	N43°29.114' W000°45.923'	Total. D817, 10 Avenue Francis Jammes east of town centre.
ORTHEZ	N43°29.367' W000°47.800'	E'Leclerc supermarket fuel station. D817, Route de Bayonne. West of town. Good access for large motorhomes.
PAU	N43°18.417' W000°22.583'	Avia fuel station. D834, Avenue Jean Mermoz in Pau centre. Good access for large motorhomes.
PAU	N43°19.118' W000°22.722'	Total fuel station. D834, Avenue Jean Mermoz in Pau centre. Just north of roundabout adj to Lidl. Good access for large motorhomes.
PAU (LE LUY)	N43°21.600' W000°23.017'	Intermarche supermarket. D716, Route D'Uzein. Just off roundabout Junction with D834, north of Pau. Good access for large motorhomes.
PAU (LONS)	N43°19.767' W000°22.850'	Geant Casino supermarket. Avenue du Perlic, off D834, Avenue Didier Daurat. Good access for large motorhomes.
PERIGUEUX	N45°11.849' E000°42.019'	Total. D939, 138 Route Pierre Sémard northwest of Périgueux.
PERIGUEUX	N45°11.638' E000°39.610'	Auchan. D710/D939 at Marsac-sur-Isle.

TOWN	GPS	DIRECTIONS
PERIGUEUX	N45°11.417' E000°44.150'	Total fuel. D6021, Avenue Michel Grandou. Northeast of towncentre. North of the river. Not very good access as forecourt crowded with cars for sale.
PESSAC	N44°46.865' W000°38.980'	Total. Off A63 Junction 26a, Avenue de Haut Lévèque southwest of town.
PONT DU CASSE	N44°13.606' E000°40.317'	Total. D656 southwest of town.
SARLAT LA CANEDA	N44°52.697' E001°13.015'	Avia. D704 near roundabout Junction of D704 with D57, just south of town centre. Adj to railway bridge.
SAUGNAC ET MURET	N44°21.719' W000°51.072'	Total. Aire de Muret N10/E5 southbound as you leave Saugnac et Muret.
ST ANDRE DE CUBZAC	N44°58.724' W000°25.881'	Total. A10 between Junction 40a and 41 southbound towards Bordeaux.
ST ASTIER	N45°08.702' E000°31.424'	E'Leclerc. Off D3.
ST LAURENT SUR MANOIRE	N45°09.021' E000°47.919'	Total. Aire du Manoire. A89 off Junction 16 accessible both sides.
ST MICHEL DE RIEUFRET	N44°38.659' W000°26.279'	Total. Aire des Landes. A62/E72 between Junction 1.1 and 2, southeast towards Toulouse.
ST PIERRE-DU-MONT	N43°52.586' W000°30.370'	Total. Route de Saint-Sever southeast of town.
ST SEVER	N43°46.400' W000°34.033'	Intermarche supermarket. D924, Route de Tartas. North of town at St. Sever (Pere). Good access for large motorhomes. LPG pump is behind the pay kiosk, beyond the gas bottles. Plenty of turning space.
ST VINCENT DE PAUL	N43° 44.451'W001°01.047'	Total. D824 off roundabout west of town.
ST VINCENT DE TYROSSE	N43°40.000' W001°17.183'	E'Leclerc supermarket. D810, to east of town towards Dax. Good access for large motorhomes.
STE COLOMBE EN BRUILHOIS	N44°11.978' E000°30.367'	Total. Aire d'Agen Route D'Aquitane. A62/E72, Junction 6 and 7. Accessible both sides.
STE FOY LA GRANDE (PINEUILH)	N44°50.483' E000°14.633'	E'Leclerc supermarket. D936e2, Route de Bergerac, in commercial area east of town. Good access for large motorhomes. Space to turn and reverse in if needed.
TERRASSON LAVILLEDIEU	N45°07.708' E001°19.043'	Total. D6809 as exit town to east.
TONNEINS	N44°24.012' E000°17.906'	E'Leclerc. Off D813 north of town.
TRELISSAC	N45°11.421' E000°44.142'	Total. D6021, 54 Route de Limoges , west towards Perigueux
TRESSES-MELAC	N44°50.416' W000°29.626'	Elf. On D936, Avenue de Branne. Exit N230/E05/E70 (known as 'Rocade de Bordeaux') at Junction 24 onto D936 sp 'Bergerac'. Elf garage just after 1st roundabout. Good access for large motorhomes. LPG pump away from main canopy with space to turn round if needed.
VILLENEUVE SUR LOT	N44°24.252' E000°41.341'	Total. D911, Route de Bordeaux, west of town. Good access for large motorhomes.
BRITTANY		
BAIN DE BRETAGNE	N47°48.075' W001°41.429'	Total. Aire de Pomméniac. N137/E3 southbound from Bain de Bretagne.
BREST	N48°24.782' W004°29.383'	Total Access. D205, Blvd de l'Europe 1.5km north of Brest.
CANCALE	N48°40.735' W001°51.911'	Super U. D355, 0.5km to west of town.
CESSON SEVIGNE	N48°06.763' W001°35.350'	Carrefour. N136/E50,Exit at Junction 2 for Centre Commercial.
COETMIEUX	N48°28.620' W002°35.448'	Elf. N12/E50 1km south of town.
HILLION	N48°28.751' W002°37.528'	Avia. N12/E401 towards Lamballe.
LAMBALLE	N48°27.691' W002°30.844'	E'Leclerc. N12/D14, exit N12/E401 at Lamballe Gare and head north.
LORIENT	N47°44.124' W003° 22.316'	Total. 2 Route Benoit Frachon, off D465 south of centre.
LORIENT	N47°43.990' W003°23.051'	Géant. D29, southwest of town.
MALESTROIT	N47°48.566' W002°23.583'	Casino. D776, west of town.
MONDEVERT	N48°05.377' W001°05.883'	Total. Aire de Mondevert. N157/E50 north of town.
NOSTANG	N47°46.719 W003°11.732'	Total. Aire de Boule Sapin. N165/E60 north of town.
PLANCOET	N48°31.485' W002°14.357'	Hyper U. Off D768, west side of town.
PLEHEDEL	N48°42.357' W003° 01.295'	Total. D7, 2 Route de l'Avenir, northwest of town.
PLOERMEL	N47°55.154' W002° 21.808'	Total. Aire sud Malville. N24, southwest of town.

TOWN	GPS	DIRECTIONS
PLOUGOUMELEN	N47°39.928' W002°54.290'	Total. N165/E60 north of town, southbound towards Vannes.
PLURIEN	N48°37.134' W002°25.348'	Total. D786, west of town towards La Ville Ory.
PONT L'ABBE	N47°51.849' W004°14.152'	E'Leclerc. Same directions as Aire.
PONTIVY	N48°03.429' W002°57.754'	Total. D768A, 22 Route Albert de Mun, south of town.
QUIMPER	N48°00.011' W004°05.366'	Total. 57 Route de Brest, southeast of town.
QUIMPER	N47°58.768' W004°05.418'	Total Access. D783A, 27 Boulevard des Flandres Dunkerque, south of town.
QUIMPERLE	N47°52.792' W003°33.272'	Carrefour. D6, 119 Route de Couëdic north of town.
RENNES	N48°07.484' W001°42.067'	Total. 15 Av Charles Tillon, northwest of centre.
RENNES	N48°05.048' W001°40.560'	Elf. CC Alma - Route du Bosphore, south of centre.
RENNES	N48°06.430' W001°43.540'	Total. N24, 202 Route de Lorient, west of centre.
RENNES	N48°07.672' W001°38.990'	Total Access. 254 Route de Fougères, northeast of centre.
ST BRICE EN COGLES	N48°24.965' W001°23.148'	Super U. D155, as exit town towards Antrain.
ST BRIEUC	N48°29.877' W002°44.753'	Total Access. D700, Route Guillaume Apollinaire, southeast of town.
ST GILLES	N48°10.086' W001° 52.612'	Total. Aire du Pays de Rennes, west of St Gilles.
ST JOUAN DE L'ISLE	N48°16.355' W002°10.507'	Total. N12/E50 southwest of town. Fuel station on either side.
ST RENAN	N48°25.710' W004°36.811'	Super U. Allée du Chemin De Fer, between lake and D67.
ST SERVAN SUR MER	N48°37.733' W002°00.328'	Total Access. D137 southeast as leaving town towards Rennes.
ST YVI	N47°57.572' W003°57.481'	Total. N165/E60, southwest of town.
TREMUSON	N48°31.491' W002°53.418'	Total. N12/E50, between St Briac and Guingamp.
VERN SUR SEICHE	N48°03.268' W001°36.629'	Total Access. D163 heading north out of town.
BURGUNDY		
AIRE DE PONT CHENE D'ARGENT	N47°11.017' E005°19.900'	A39, southbound between Junctions 5 and 6.
AUTUN 1	N46°57.388' E004°17.198'	Avia. D981, south of town.
AUTUN 2	N46°57.303' E004°19.043'	Avia. Opp Aire.
AUXERRE	N47°48.307' E003°34.967'	Total. D84 as head into town from north.
BEAUNE	N47°01.029' E004°50.158'	BP. Opp Aire.
BROGNON	N47°25.442' E005°10.197'	Total. Aire de Dijon Brognon. A31/E17 north of town.
COMBLANCHIEN	N47°05.755' E004°54.736'	Avia. D974, 0.5km southwest of town.
COSNE COURS SUR LOIRE	N47°25.071' E002°55.658'	Total. D955A, 103 Route du Gal Leclerc heading north out of town.
DIGOIN	N46°28.986' E003°58.511'	Total. D979.
DIJON	N47°21.817' E005°02.815'	Total. D974, 170 Route de Langres 3 km from centre heading north out of town.
DIJON	N47°16.807' E005°01.144'	E'Leclerc supermarket. D122 towards Dole, 2.8m height barrier.
MACON	N46°17.106' E004°48.462'	Total Access. N6, 97 Route de Lyon, 2km southwest of centre.
MARSANNAY LA COTE	N47°16.826' E005°00.472'	Total. D974, 5 Route de Beaune, 1.5km northeast of Marsannay la Côte.
MERCEUIL	N46°57.934' E004°50.243'	Total. Aire de Beaune Tailly. A6 southbound 1.5km north of Merceuil.
MERCEUIL	N46°57.579' E004°50.185'	Total. Aire de Merceuil. A6 northbound 1.5km north of Merceuil.
PARAY LE MONIAL	N46°28.033' E004°06.794'	E'Leclerc hypermarket. N70/N79.
PRECY SUR VRIN	N47°58.406' E003°12.000'	Total. Aire de la Couline. A6 northbound 3km west of Precy sur Vrin.
ST ALBAIN	N46°25.057' E004°51.892'	Total. Aire de Mâcon la Salle. A6 northbound 1km southwest of St Albain.
ST DENIS LES SENS	N48°13.009' E003°16.620'	E'Leclerc. Off D173A 2km south of St Denis.
TALANT	N47°20.433' E005°00.309'	Total Access. Route de Troyes 0.5km north of centre.
VARENNES VAUZELLES	N47°00.498' E003°09.151'	Total. D907, 16 Boulevard Camille Dagonneau 4km south of Varennes Vauzelles.
VENOY	N47°47.278' E003°40.305'	Total. Aire du Venoy. A6 southbound 3km southeast of Venoy.
CENTRE		
AMBOISE	N47°24.232' E001°01.080'	E'Leclerc supermarket. D31 /D61 roundabout east side of town.
BLOIS	N47°36.249' E001°18.887'	Total. 107 Avenue Vendôme. Drive into town on the D957, 1km on left.

TOWN	GPS	DIRECTIONS
BLOIS (ST GERVAIS LA FORET)	N47°34.192' E001°22.312'	Auchan supermarket. From D765/D956/D9230 roundabout take the D174 north and take the first exit. South of Blois at Zone d'Activition.
BOSC MAUCOMBLE	N49°40.704' E001°20.370'	A28/E44, southbound between Junction 10 and 11.
BOSC MESNIL	N49°40.520' E001°20.100'	A28/E44, northbound between Junction 10 and 11.
BOURGES	N47°05.639' E002°23.441'	Total. 10 Avenue des Prés le Roi. Enter town on D2076, cross railway and turn left. Total 400m on left.
BOURGUEIL	N47°16.459' E000°10.035'	Super U supermarket. D749, as enter town from south.
BROU	N48°14.449' E001°05.099'	Total. A11/E50 Aire de Brou-Frazé. Between Junction 3 and 4 halfway between Chartres and Le Mans.
BROU	N48°14.374' E001°04.868'	Esso. A11/E50 Aire de Brou-Dampierre. Between Junction 3 and 4 halfway between Le Mans and Chartres.
CHARTRES	N48°26.974' E001°30.364'	Elf. D910. Drive straight into town on D910. 2km west of A10/E50 Junction 2.
CHARTRES	N48°26.200' E001°31.236'	Total. Avenue François Arago. Enter town on D939. Go over A11/E50 and turn left at roundabout onto D910. Take service road to Total 200m on right.
CHARTRES	N48°28.019' E001°34.743'	Total. A11/E50 Aire de Chartres-Bois Paris 2km eastbound from Chartres.
CHARTRES	N48°28.075' E001°34.672'	Esso. A11/E50 Aire de Chartres-Gasville 2km westbound towards Chartres.
CHATEAU LA VALLIERE	N47°32.511' E000°20.030'	Super U supermarket. D959, southeast edge of town.
CHATEAUDUN	N48°05.335' E001°20.103'	Intermarche. N10/D3955/D31 roundabout, north edge of town. 2.9m height restriction.
CHATEAUROUX	N46°47.577' E001°42.976'	Total Access. D920/Route Montaigne, southern outskirts of town.
CHATEAUROUX	N46°49.244' E001°40.139'	E'Leclerc hypermarket. D943 northwest of town. 3km from Junction 13 A20/E9
CHATEAUROUX N	N46°43.357' E001°36.191'	Shell. A20/E9 Aire du Val de l'Indre. Between Junction 14 and 15, northbound towards Châteauroux.
CHATEAUROUX S	N46°42.984' E001°35.737'	Total. A20/E9 Aire des Mille Etangs. Between Junction 14 and 15, southbound towards Limoges.
DREUX	N48°44.582' E001°23.382'	Total. N154. 126 Avenue du Général Leclerc, exit N12 at N154 eastern Junction, go under motorway and Total 300m.
FEURS	N45°44.572' E004°12.460'	Total. D1089 Route de Clermont, 200m east from river bridge. 2km from A72/E70 Junction 6.
FLEURY LES AUBRAIS	N47°56.131' E001°53.730'	Total. D2020/Avenue André Dessaux. 3.5km north of town centre. Good access large motorhomes
GIEN	N47°41.268' E002°37.243'	Auchan supermarket. Quai Lestrade, adj to river. From south on D941 cross river and turn left. Supermarket 600m on right.
GIEN	N47°41.823' E002°36.557'	Opel garage. D952/Route d'Orléans , northwest of town.
LA CHATRE	N46°34.934' E002°00.087'	Super U supermarket. D943, east suburbs of town.
LES SALLES E	N45°51.279' E003°48.568'	Shell. A89/E70 Aire du Haut-Forez. Eastbound between Junction 4 and 5.
LES SALLES W	N45°51.366' E003°48.860'	Total. A89/E70 Aire du Haut-Forez. westbound between Junction 4 and 5.
MEUNG SUR LOIRE	N47°49.202' E001°40.916'	Super U supermarket. D2152/ D2 roundabout south edge of town.
MONNAIE	N47°28.387' E000°46.492'	Total. A10/E60 Aire de Tours - Val de Loire, north bound. 2km northeast for A28/E505 Junction.
MONNAIE	N47°28.557' E000°46.658'	Total. A10/E60 Aire de Tours - La Longue Vue. south bound 2km from A28/E505 Junction.
NEUVY EN BEAUCE N	N48°16.201' E001°51.283'	Shell. A10/E5 Aire Val de Neuvy. Northbound between Junction 11 and 12.
NEUVY EN BEAUCE S	N48°16.549' E001°51.375'	Total. A10/E5 Aire de Francheville. Southbound between Junction 11 and 12.
NOGENT LE ROTROU	N48°19.824' E000°49.850'	E'Leclerc. D922 400m from the D923/D918 roundabout northeastern edge of town.
ORLEANS	N47°54.147' E001°53.587'	Total Access. D2020/Boulevard Jean Jaurès. Town centre 200m from river.
ORLEANS	N47°54.391' E002°03.486'	Shell. D2060 east of Orleans, at Aire de Bateux.

TOWN	GPS	DIRECTIONS
ORLEANS GIDY N	N47°58.498' E001°51.572'	BP. A10 Aire de Orléans - Gidy. 4km northbound from Orleans suburbs.
ORLEANS GIDY S	N47°58.727' E001°51.482'	Total. A10 Aire de Orléans - Saran. Southbound 4km north of Orleans suburbs.
ORLEANS OLIVET	N47°50.424' E001°54.851'	Total. D2020/Avenue de Sologne. Southern suburbs 400m from D2271/D920 Junction.
RICHELIEU	N47°01.255' E000°20.019'	Intermarche supermarket. D757 north of town, signed from Au Dir.
ROUEN	N49°24.248' E001°06.672'	Total. D18e, south of town near junction with D94.
ST ETIENNE	N45°27.910' E004°22.670'	Total. 11 Avenue de Verdun. 100m from Junction 10 A72/E70.
ST ETIENNE	N45°26.527' E004°24.562'	Elf. N488, 100 Route de la Montat. On right as drive into St Étienne
SULLY SUR LOIREST PERE SUR LOIRE	N47°46.818' E002°22.507'	Super U. D948, as enter town from north.
TOURS	N47°24.844' E000°42.197'	Total. Boulevard du Maréchal Juin. Exit A10/E5 at Junction 21 and cross river on bridge 500m west of A10. 1.5km north of bridge.
TOURS - SAINT PIERRE DES CORPS	N47°22.831' E000°43.803'	Total. Avenue Jacques Duclos. Drive into town on D140 from west.
TOURS - SAINT PIERRE DES CORPS	N47°23.799' E000°43.012'	Total. 74/76 Levée de la Loire. Exit A10/E5 at Junction 21 and drive east along river for 600m.
VELLES - VAL DE L'INDRE	N46°43.385' E001°36.205'	A20/E9, northbound between Junction 14 and 15.
VERT EN DROUAIS	N48°44.885' E001°16.196'	Total Access. N12. Direction Dreux, 5km west.
VIERZON	N47°14.372' E002°05.521'	Carrefour supermarket. D926 northeast side of town.
VIERZON	N47°13.627' E002°03.232'	Total. N76/Route Léo Mérigot. Exit A20/E9 at Junction 6 and drive into town on N76.
VILLARS	N45°28.557' E004°20.661'	Auchan. Adj to D201 400m south from A72/E70 Junction 10.
VINEUIL	N47°34.363' E001°22.181'	Elf. Le haut des Sablons. D174 heading north 2km from river bridge.
CHAMPAGNE		
CHALONS EN CHAMPAGNE	N48°56.121' E004°24.089'	Elf. N44, Route de Vitry le François 1km southeast of St Memmie.
CHARLEVILLE MEZIERES	N49°44.410' E004°43.492'	Total. D8051A Route de Francheville 2km south of centre.
CHAUMONT	N48°07.041' E005°08.436'	Elf. D619, 8/10 Avenue Carnot 0.5km north of centre.
EPERNAY	N49°01.533' E003°56.734'	E'Leclerc supermarket. D951/Route Jules Lobet, southwest of Epernay.
EPERNAY	N49°02.781' E003°57.380'	Total. Boulevard de la Motte, by Gare d'Epernay S.N.C.F.
FRESNOY LE CHATEAU	N48°12.672' E004°14.465'	Total. Aire de Troyes. A5 1km east of Fresnoy le Chateau.
LANGRES	N47°52.210' E005°19.679'	Total. N19, Fbg de la Collinière 0.5km north of centre.
RECY	N48°59.465' E004°20.536'	Total Access. Off N44/D1 rounabout 2km east of Recy.
REIMS	N49°15.880' E004°03.554'	Total Access. N51, 252 Bis Avenue Jean Jaurés 2km east of centre.
REIMS	N49°14.310' E004°02.707'	Total Access. N51, 2 Route Albert Thomas 2km south of centre.
REIMS	N49°15.544' E004°03.387'	Total. N51, 55 Boulevard du Dauphinot 2km east of centre.
REIMS	N49°15.276' E004°01.026'	Total Access. 12 Avenue Brébant, 1km west of centre adj to river Vesle.
SAULCES MONCLIN	N49°35.610' E004°30.194'	Total. Aire des Ardennes. Off A34 Junction 14 2km north of town.
SEDAN	N49°41.906' E004°55.483'	E'Leclerc. D8043A, 14 Avenue Pasteur 1km west of centre.
SEDAN	N49°41.942' E004°55.591'	Total. D8043A, 6 Avenue de la Marne 1km west of centre.
ST BRICE COURCELLES	N49°16.881' E004°00.164'	E'Leclerc. Off D944, La Croix Maurencienne 2km northeast of town.
ST DIZIER	N48°37.644' E004°58.419'	E'Leclerc. Off N4, Route des Loyes 2km southeast of town.
ST DIZIER	N48°38.536' E004°54.165'	Shell. N4, accessible from both sides.
STE SAVINE	N48°17.522' E004°02.264'	Total Access. D661, 82 Avenue du General Leclerc 4.5km west of town.
EASTERN FRANCE		
AIRE DE VITRIMONT (LUNEVILLE) N333	N48°35.458' E006°25.482'	Esso. N333 west of Luneville sp 'Aire de Vitrimont'.
ANOULD	N48°11.268' E006°57.255'	Total. D415, 104 Route de Colmar 0.5km northeast of town.
BATZENHEIM	N47°50.127' E007°23.686'	Total. Aire de Battenheim. A35 2km northeast of town.

TOWN	GPS	DIRECTIONS
BELFORT	N47°38.320' E006°52.679'	Total. D419, Avenue d'Altkich 1km east of centre.
BESANCON MARCHAUX	N47°19.656' E006°07.721'	A36 and D486, southwest of Champoux outside Marchaux.
BEURE	N47°12.435' E005°59.943'	Agip. N83, south of Besançon.
BURNHAUPT LE BAS	N47°43.044' E007°08.330'	Total. Aire de la Porte d'Alsace. A36 westbound 1km west of town.
CHAMPAGNOLE	N46°44.889' E005°54.435'	Super U. D5, at roundabout on northern edge of Champagnole.
COLMAR	N48°05.386' E007°21.611'	Total. D201, 10 Route des Cigognes 1km north of centre.
CONTREXEVILLE	N48°11.286' E005°53.616'	Total. Off D164, Avenue de la Division Leclerc as exit town to north.
ECOT	N47°26.433' E006°43.657'	Avia. A36, at Aire d'Écot accessible from both sides.
FERGERSHEIM	N48°29.607' E007°40.661'	Total. D1083, Route de Strasbourg 0.5km north of town.
FORBACH	N49°11.416' E006°54.503'	Total. N3, 19 Route Nationale 1km northeast of town.
GEISPOLSHEIM	N48°31.290' E007°41.739'	E'Leclerc. Off D84/D222 roundabout, Route du Fort (Rt de Strasbourg) 3km east of town.
GERARDMER	N48°04.526' E006°53.051'	Elf. 68, Boulevard Kelsch, 1 km northeast of town.
HAUCONCOURT	N49°12.864' E006°10.206'	E'Leclerc. Off A31 Junction 35, 1.5km west of town.
HAUT KOENIGSBOURG	N48°14.000' E007°24.369'	E'Leclerc supermarket. A35/E25, southwest of Sélestat. Narrow entrance.
HUTTENHEIM	N48°21.759' E007°34.467'	Total Access. D1083, Route de Lyon 2.5km northwest of town.
KESKASTEL	N48°58.287' E007°04.156'	Total. Aire de Kerkastel Est. A4 northbound, 2km east of town.
LE THILLOT	N47°52.917' E006°45.648'	Total. N66.
LES ROUSSES	N46°28.636' E006°03.890'	Avia. N5, south of Les Rousses.
LONGEVILLE	N49°07.972' E006°39.642'	Total. Aire de Longeville sud. A4 2km north of town.
LUNEVILLE	N48°35.955' E006°29.677'	E'Leclerc supermarket. Route de la Tannerie, off D914 on northern bank of river La Vezouze, north of Lunéville centre.
MARCHAUX	N47°19.560' E006°07.276'	Total. Aire de Besançon Marchaux. A36 eastbound 1km northwest of town.
METZ	N49°06.066' E006°09.785'	Total. D5, 51/59 Avenue du 20 ème Corps 2km southwest of centre.
MOLSHEIM	N48°31.776' E007°29.862'	Total. D2422, Route de la Commanderie 1km south of town.
NANCY	N48°41.003' E006°11.822'	Auchan supermarket. 127 Boulevard Lobau 1km southeast of centre.
NOIDANS LES VESOUL	N47°37.361' E006°08.312'	Total. Off D457, Route des Faines 1km north of town.
OBERNAI	N48°27.583' E007°29.686'	Total. D426, 8 Route Maréchal Juin 0.5km east of town.
PAGNY SUR MEUSE	N48°41.120' E005°43.532'	Total Access. Off D36/D636 roundabout adj to N4.
PONT A MOUSSON 1	N48°54.038' E006°03.911'	Total. D120, just south of N57 bridge over river La Moselle.
PONT A MOUSSON 2	N48°51.372' E006°05.309'	Total. Aire de l'Obrion, A31 between Pont à Mousson and Millery.
PONTARLIER	N46°54.565' E006°20.047'	Total. Off D72/E23 roundabout, Route de la Fee Verte 1km northwest of town.
REMIREMONT	N48°00.194' E006°36.859'	Cora. D466, exit town sp 'Rupt-Sur-Moselle'.
ROUFFACH	N47°56.671' E007°17.287'	Total. D83, Route de Belfort 1km southwest of town.
SCHILTIGHEIM	N48°36.230' E007°45.484'	Total. Avenue Pierre Mendès France 0.5km east of centre.
ST AVOLD	N49°07.120' E006°42.566'	Total. D633, Avenue du Général Patton 1km north of centre.
ST CLAUDE	N46°22.762' E005°50.333'	Total. D436/Route de Lyon, west of St Claude.
ST LOUIS	N47°35.602' E007°33.333'	Total. Off D105/D66 roundabout, 122 Route de Mulhouse 0.5km northwest of centre.
STE MARIE AUX MINES	N48°15.268' E007°12.402'	Total. N59, Route Nationale 50 1.5km northeast of town.
STRASBOURG	N48°35.726' E007°42.570'	Total. D41, 142 Route Oberhausbergen 2km northwest of centre.
THIONVILLE	N49°21.140' E006°09.598'	Total. Rond Point Merlin 0.5km southwest of centre.
VANDOEUVRE LES NANCY	N48°39.295' E006°11.150'	Total Access. D570, Le Dernier Sou 0.5km southeast of town.
VERDUN	N49°08.554' E005°24.543'	Cora supermarket. D903, southeast of Verdun.
LIMOUSIN & AUVERGNE		
BELLERIVE SUR ALLIER	N46°07.059' E003°24.670'	Total. D2209, 22 Avenue de la République east of town centre.

TOWN	GPS	DIRECTIONS
BRIVE LA GAILLARDE	N45°09.885' E001°30.649'	Total. D1089, 90 Avenue Ribot 1km northwest of centre.
CLERMONT-FERRAND	N45°47.326' E003°06.520'	Total. 120, Avenue de la République 1km northeast of centre.
CLERMONT-FERRAND	N45°47.350' E003°07.070'	Total. D2009, 24 Boulevard Amboise Bruguière 1.5km northeast of centre.
CLERMONT-FERRAND	N45°48.839' E003°06.545'	Auchan. D2009 from north of town.
GUERET	N46°10.621' E001°53.899'	Intermarché. N145/E62 roundabout at Junction 47.
LAGUENNE	N45°14.740' E001°46.407'	Auchan supermarket. D1120, north of town.
LE PUY EN VALEY	N45°02.827' E003°53.583'	Total. N88, at Impasse Boulevard de Cluny on east side of ring road.
LIMOGES	N45°50.945' E001°14.815'	Elf. 91 Boulevard de Vigenal 1km north of centre.
MALEMORT SUR CORREZE	N45°10.129' E001°33.640'	Géant Casino supermarket. D1089, west of town.
MAURIAC	N45°12.945' E002°20.331'	Carrefour. D681, Marsalou Route d'Aurillac 0.25km southeast of town.
MAURIAC	N45°12.865' E002°20.801'	Carrefour. D922 southbound.
MAURS	N44°42.538' E002°11.763'	Total. N122, Route de Bagnac southwest of town.
MONLUCON	N46°20.288' E002°34.041'	Auchan. 3.5m height restriction.
MONTMARAULT	N46°19.413' E002° 57.855'	Heep. D2371 as enter from Le Montet.
PARSAC	N46°11.865' E002°11.130'	Total. Aire de Service de Parsac. N145 1.5km east of town.
RIOM	N45°52.707' E003°06.992'	Carrefour supermarket. D6, at Riom Sud Centre Commercial.
ST JUNIEN	N45°53.839' E000°55.215'	Carrefour supermarket. Off D941, Avenue Nelson Mandela 1km northeast of centre.
ST POURCAIN SUR SIOULE	N46°17.687' E003°17.695'	Total. D2009, Route de Gannat 1km south of town.
THIERS	N45°50.546' E003°30.879'	Local fuel station. D2089, Avenue du General de Gaulle 1.5km southwest of town.
USSEL	N45°32.592' E002°17.843'	E'Leclerc. D157, near large roundabout junction with D1089.
VALENCE	N44°56.572' E004°51.571'	Avia. D533 in retail area near St Peray.
VICHY BELLERIVE SUR ALLIER	N46°07.055' E003°24.683'	Total. N209/D2209, at large roundabout between D984 and D1093.
YZEURE (MOULINS)	N46°33.273' E003°20.191'	Total. D707, 28 Route de Lyon 1km south of centre.
MEDITERRANEAN		
AIMARGUES	N43°41.752' E004°12.051'	Elf. D6313, Quartier la Guarrigue 0.5km north of town.
AIX EN PROVENCE	N43°31.704' E005°25.957'	Total. D64, 16 Route de Galice 0.5km west of centre.
AIX EN PROVENCE	N43°30.957' E005°27.980'	Total Access. Avenue Henri Mauriat near A8 Junction 31, 1km southeast of centre.
APT	N43°52.990' E005°22.870'	Total. D900, Avenue de Lançon 1km northwest of centre.
ARLES	N43°40.212' E004°37.282'	Total. D35, Route de Port Saint Louis 1km southwest of town.
ARLES	N43°39.109' E004°40.148'	Total. N113/E810 2.5km southeast of Arles.
AUBAGNE	N43°17.557' E005°35.606'	Auchan supermarket. Les Paluds 1km west of centre.
AVIGNON	N43°55.928' E004°46.980'	Elf. Boulevard Charles de Gaulle 1.5km southwest of centre.
BEZIERS	N43°19.896' E003°14.875'	Total Access. 1 Avenue de la Devèze 1.5km southeast of centre.
BEZIERS	N43°21.260' E003°13.756'	Elf. Avenue du Docteur Jean Marie Fabre 1km northeast of town.
BRIANCON	N44°54.234' E006°37.739'	Total Access. Avenue du Dauphiné 0.5km northwest of town.
CANNES	N43°33.309' E007°00.339'	Total. 57 Boulevard du Riou 0.5km northwest of town.
CANNES LA BOCCA	N43°33.056' E006°57.461'	E'Leclerc. Parc d'activités des Tourrades, off D6007 roundabout 1km west of town.
CARCASSONNE	N43°12.431' E002°20.140'	Total. D118, Route de Limoux 0.5km west of town.
CAVAILLON	N43°49.854' E005°03.270'	Total. D973/264 Avenue de Cheval Blanc, as exit Cavaillon towards Pertuis.
CHATEAU ARNOUX ST AUBAN	N44°05.172' E006°00.494'	Total. D4096, Le Bélvédère 0.5km south of town.
CHATEAUREDON	N44°01.015' E006°12.733'	Local fuel station. N85, L'Hubac et Saint Jean north as exit town.
COGOLIN	N43°15.823' E006°34.653'	Total. Carrefour de la Foux 2km northeast of town.

TOWN	GPS	DIRECTIONS
DIGNE LES BAINS	N44°05.379' E006°14.229'	Intermarche. D19 towards Thermes.
FOS SUR MER	N43°25.664' E004°57.947'	Elf. N568, Route de Port de Bouc 1km southeast of town.
FOS SUR MER	N43°28.274' E004°54.490'	Elf. N568, Z.I - Secteur 83 2.5km northwest of town.
FREJUS	N43°26.121' E006°43.489'	Total. Avenue de Verdun 0.5km northwest of town.
FUVEAU	N43°27.948' E005°36.384'	Total. D6, Saint Charles - Route de Trets
GAP	N44°32.479' E006°03.471'	Total. N85, Avenue de Provence 1.5km southwest of town.
HYERES	N43°07.456' E006°08.914'	Intermarche. 98 Avenue de Lattre de Tassigny 1km east of town.
LE LUC	N43°22.883' E006°18.250'	E'Leclerc. D97, southwest of town at supermarket. Good access for large motorhomes.
LE PONTET	N43°58.619' E004°51.469'	Total. D907, Route de Lyon 1km north as exit town.
LES PENNES-MIRABEAU	N43°24.558' E005°19.264'	Elf. Off D368, Route de Martigues 0.5km east of town.
LODEVE	N43°43.516' E003°19.380'	Avia. Near Junction 53 on A75, south of town. Good access for large motorhomes.
MANOSQUE	N43°49.347' E005°47.262'	Shell. D4096 south west of town.
MANOSQUE 1	N43°50.267' E005°48.300'	E'Leclerc . D4096, just northeast of town. Good access for large motorhomes.
MANOSQUE 2	N43°51.017' E005°49.417'	Auchan supermarket. D4096, northeast of town.
MARIGNANE	N43°26.587' E005°13.439'	Total. Aéroport Marseilles Provence 1.5km north of town.
MARSEILLE	N43°17.165' E005°25.649'	Total. D2, 359 Boulevard Mireille Lauze 2.5km east of Marseille.
MARSEILLE	N43°20.969' E005°20.558'	Elf. D5, 450 Chemin du Littoral 3.5km north of Marseille.
MARSEILLE	N43°19.433' E005°27.199'	Elf. D4, Avenue F. Mistral 4km northeast of Marseille.
MARSEILLE	N43°19.659' E005°21.958'	Total. 99 Route de Lyon 2km north of Marseille.
MARVEJOLS	N44°33.791' E003°17.520'	Total. D809, 38 Avenue Theophile Roussel 1km north of town.
MAUGIO	N43°37.085' E003°59.312'	Total. D24, Route de Montpellier 1km west of town.
MONTPELLIER	N43°38.095' E003°49.375'	Total. 70 Avenue de l'Europe 3km northwest of Montpellier.
MONTPELLIER	N43°35.712' E003°50.889'	Total Access. Avenue de Vanières, 1.5km southwest of Montpellier.
NARBONNE	N43°10.468' E002°59.552'	Total. Off D6009, southwest of Narbonne. 200m from service point at Casino supermarket. Good access for large motorhomes.
NICE	N43°39.818' E007°12.108'	Total. Aéroport de Nice Côte d'Azur 3km southwest of Nice.
NICE	N43°40.179' E007°12.994'	Total. Square Kichner - Boulevard René Cassin 2.5km southwest of Nice.
NICE	N43°42.412' E007°17.544'	Total. 10 Boulevard de l'Armée des Alpes 1.5km northeast of Nice.
NIMES	N43°48.609' E004°19.744'	Total. N113, 2075 Route de Montpellier 2km southwest of Nimes.
NIMES	N43°49.304' E004°19.761'	Elf. N106, Boulevard Pasteur Marc Boegner 1.5km southwest of Nimes.
PERPIGNAN	N42°40.673' E002°53.451'	Total. Route D'Espagne 1km south of town.
PERPIGNAN	N42°40.125' E002°53.000'	Auchan. D900, southwest of Perpignan. Good access for large motorhomes.
PERTUIS	N43°40.844' E005°30.028'	Carrefour. D956 south of town.
PORT DE BOUC	N43°25.233' E004°58.667'	Agip. N568, northwest of town. Good access for large motorhomes.
QUISSAC	N43°54.850' E003°59.717'	Vulco. D999/Avenue de l'Aigoual, south of Sauve, north of Quissac. Narrow for large motorhomes.
RODEZ	N44°22.170' E002°35.412'	Total. D988, Route de l'Espalion 1.5km northeast of town.
ROQUEFORT LES CORBIERES	N42°59.367' E002°58.339'	Total. D6009, Route Nationale 9 1km east of town adj to A9.
RUOMS	N44°26.563' E004°20.936'	Super U. D579.
SALON DE PROVENCE	N43°37.961' E005°05.890'	Total. 666 Boulevard du Roy René south of town centre.
SALON DE PROVENCE	N43°37.150' E005°05.766'	Total. D538/Avenue de la Patrouille de France. Good access for large motorhomes.
SARRIANS	N44°04.867' E004°59.000'	Intermarché. At roundabout junction of D950 and D221, southeast of Sarrians. Tight for large motorhomes.
ST MAXIMIN LA ST BAUME	N43°26.836' E005°51.739'	Total. Chemin de Tourves south of town centre.
TOULON	N43°07.027' E005°56.454'	Total. 322 Avenue Edouard le Bellegou 0.5km southeast of Toulon.

LPG - GPL

TOWN	GPS	DIRECTIONS
TOULON	N43°07.387' E005°56.279'	Total. N97, 160 Avenue Georges Clemenceau 0.5km east of centre.
VAISON LA ROMAINE	N44°14.525' E005°04.831'	Total. 72 Avenue Victor Hugo east of centre.
VENCE	N43°42.908' E007°07.022'	Total. D236, 891 Route de St Paul 0.5km south of town.
VITROLLES	N43°25.252' E005°16.113'	Total. ZAC de l'Anjoly adj to A7 2.5km south of Vitrolles.
MIDI-PYRENEES		
ALBI	N43°55.167' E002°07.900'	Total. Avenue François Verdier, off N88, southwest of town centre. Good access for large motorhomes.
ALBI	N43°55.100' E002°06.450'	E'Leclerc supermarket. New shopping centre on north side of N88. Access from junction adj to airport. Good access for large motorhomes.
AUCH	N43°39.883' E000°35.500'	E'Leclerc supermarket. Off junction of N21 and N124, north of Auch.
AUSSILLON-MAZAMET	N43°30.535' E002°21.680'	Elan. N112, Boulevard du Thore 1km north of Aussillon.
BAGNERES DE BIGORRE	N43°04.850' E000°08.350'	Total. D935, north of town. Good access for large motorhomes. Single-sided pump, filler needs to be on right.
BALMA	N43°36.580' E001°29.570'	Total Access. D50, Avenue de Toulouse 0.5km northwest of town.
BALMA	N43°35.369' E001°30.837'	Total. D826, Route de Castres 1km southeast of town.
BESSIERES	N43°47.882' E001°36.743'	Super U. D630.
BLAGNAC	N43°38.282' E001°23.416'	Total Access. D2, 120 Route de Grenade 0.5km northwest of centre.
BLAGNAC	N43°38.480' E001°22.483'	Elf. D902, Rocade de Blagnac 1km northwest of town.
BLAYE LES MINES	N44°01.617' E002°09.333'	Super U. On D73 east of Blaye-les-Mines between Carmaux and Le Garric. Good access for large motorhomes.
CAHORS	N44°25.467' E001°26.433'	Total. D820/Route de Toulouse, south of Cahors. Good access for large motorhomes.
CASTELSARRASIN	N44°02.584' E001°06.294'	Total. D813 to west.
CASTELSARRASIN	N44°03.850' E001°05.833'	E'Leclerc supermarket. D813/Route de Moissac, north of town. Exit Junction 9 of A62, sp 'Moissac'. Good access for large motorhomes.
CASTRES	N43°35.309' E002°11.123'	Auchan. N126.
CASTRES	N44°01.631' E002°09.324'	Super U. D73/D988.
CASTRES	N43°37.033' E002°14.650'	Avia. D89/Avenue de Roquecourbe, north of town. Good access for large motorhomes.
CAZAUBON	N43°56.050' W000°03.800'	Elan. D626/Boulevard des Pyrénées, east of town. Good access for large motorhomes.
CAZERES	N43°12.650' E001°05.050'	Carrefour supermarket. Off D6, just north of town centre. Good access for large motorhomes.
CONDOM	N43°57.083' E000°22.267'	Total. D930, south of town centre. Good access for large motorhomes.
ESTANCARBON	N43°06.764' E000°47.271'	Total. D817, RN 117 0.5km north of town.
FIGEAC	N44°36.667' E002°01.667'	Esso. D840/Avenue du Général de Gaulle. At roundabout junction with D19 and D2. Good access for large motorhomes.
FOIX	N42°56.883' E001°37.550'	Total. D117/Route d'Espagne, south of Foix in the direction of Montgaillard. Exit Junction 11, both directions. Good access for large motorhomes.
FONBEAUZARD	N43°40.672' E001°25.403'	Total. D4, 114 Route de Fronton 1km west of town.
GOURDON	N44°43.243' E001°22.103'	Elan. D673/Route du Fumel, southwest of town next to LIDL. Good access for large motorhomes. After filling drive right around building to exit.
LALOUBERE	N43°12.617' E000°04.517'	Géant Casino supermarket. Route de l'Allée, off D935/Route du Marechal Foch, just south of Tarbes and south of E80/A64 motorway. Good access for large motorhomes.
LANDORTHE	N43°06.750' E000°47.283'	Total. D817, east of St Gaudens. Good access for large motorhomes.
LAVAUR	N43°41.762' E001°48.968'	Agip. D87 towards Castres.
LAVELANET	N42°55.455' E001°50.275'	Super U supermarket. Off D117 roundabout, Rye des Pyrénées 1km southwest of town.
LECTOURE	N43°54.983' E000°37.683'	Elan. N21, south of town. Good access for large motorhomes.
LOMBEZ	N43°28.233' E000°55.367'	Intermarché supermarket. Turn off D626 to east of Lombez, signed. Good access for large motorhomes.

TOWN	GPS	DIRECTIONS
LOURDES	N43°06.591' W000°02.282'	E'Leclerc supermarket. N21/Avenue François Abadie Alexandre Marqui, north of town centre. On southbound side of dual carriageway from Tarbes. Good access for large motorhomes. Single-sided pump, filler needs to be on right.
LOURDES	N43°05.835' W000°02.295'	Total. D97/Boulevard du Lapacca, at junction with Route Capdangelle. Good access for large motorhomes. Double-sided pump.
MOISSAC	N44°06.598' E001°06.162'	Total. D927, 56 Avenue du Chasselas 1km northeast of town.
MONTAUBAN	N44°00.267' E001°20.478'	Total. N2020, 350 Route de Toulouse 0.5km southwest of town.
OLEMPS LA MOULINE	N44°19.517' E002°33.467'	Super U. Off D888, just south of Rodez. Good access for large motorhomes.
PAVIE	N43°37.000' E000°34.517'	Total. N21, southwest of Auch. Good access for large motorhomes.
PORTET SUR GARONNE	N43°31.492' E001°24.021'	Total Access. D120, 43 Route d'Espagne, head south out of town.
PORTET SUR GARONNE	N43°31.475' E001°23.941'	Elf. D120, 106 Route d'Espagne head south out of town.
POUZAC	N43°04.857' E000°08.365'	Total. D935, 77 Avenue de la Mongie southeast of town.
REVEL	N43°27.823' E002°00.417'	Elan. D622 on left as exit town towards Castres.
RIEUMES	N43°24.817' E001°06.950'	Carrefour supermarket. D28/Avenue du Casteras Route de Samatan, as exit town towards Samatan. Motorhomes over 8m may need to reverse off pump.
SEBAZAC CONCOURES	N44°23.633' E002°36.167'	E'Leclerc supermarket. Off D988 at Centre Commercial, north of Rodez.
SEVERAC LE CHATEAU	N44°19.817' E003°04.850'	Total. L'Aveyron services, A75 Junction 42. Also accessible from N88. Good access for large motorhomes.
ST AFFRIQUE	N43°57.483' E002°52.217'	Super U. Route Chantefriboule, off D999 on western side of town toward Vabres L'Abbaye.
ST ALBAN	N43°41.015' E001°25.232'	Elf. D4, 16 Route de Fronton 0.5km southeast of town.
TARBES	N43°14.374' E000°03.632'	Total. On D935A/D935B roundabout, Avenue du Maréchal Joffre 1km northwest of centre.
TOULOUSE	N43°39.480' E001°25.175'	Total. D820, 353 Avenue des Etats Unis 3.5km north of Toulouse.
TOULOUSE	N43°35.292' E001°25.411'	Total. 7, Boulevard Déodat de Séverac southwest of centre across river.
TOULOUSE	N43°37.894' E001°28.966'	Auchan. Off D112/D64D roundabout, Chemin de Gabardie 1.5km northeast of centre.
TOULOUSE	N43°34.856' E001°23.735'	Total Access. 22 Route Saint Simon 2km west of centre.
VENERQUE	N43°25.700' E001°26.733'	Intermarché supermarket. D19 at roundabout junction with D35, south of town. Good access for large motorhomes.
VIC EN BIGORRE	N43°23.086' E000°03.062'	Intermarche. D6 towards Pau.
VILLEFRANCHE DE ROUERGUE	N44°21.550' E001°59.182'	Elan. D911, just before roundabout junction with D1 and D926, west of town. Good access for large motorhomes.
NORMANDY		
ALENCON	N48°26.609' E000°05.951'	Elf. D438/126 Avenue de Basingstoke, 1.5km northeast of town.
ALENCON	N48°27.407' E000°07.577'	Aire de La Dentelle d'Alencon. Exit 18 of A28. Suitable for large motorhomes.
AMFREVILLE LA CAMPAGNE	N49°12.448' E000°56.112'	Total. D840/Route de La Republique, exit D66.
ANGERVILLE LA CAMPAGNE	N48°59.735' E001°09.343'	Total. D6154/4 Route d'Orleans, north of town.
ARGENCES	N49°07.139' W000°10.473'	Intermarche supermarket. D80, off D613/D80 roundabout.
ARGENTAN	N48°45.116' W000°00.816'	E'Leclerc supermarket. D916, north of town.
BAYEUX	N49°17.030' W000°43.513'	Total. D613/Route de Cherbourg, 2km northwest of town.
BIHOREL	N49°27.437' E001°06.491'	Shell. D928/184 Route de Neufchatel.
BRETTEVILLE SUR ODON	N49°09.863' W000°25.260'	Elf. Route de Bretagne, off A84.
CAEN	N49°11.355' W000°20.867'	Total. D515/75 Boulevard Georges Clemenceau, 3km northeast of town.
CAEN	N49°10.378' W000°23.376'	Total. Boulevard Yves Guillou, 3km southwest of town.
CAEN	N49°11.984' W000°21.609'	Elf. D7/Avenue de la Cote de Nacre, 4km northeast of town.

LPG - GPL

TOWN	GPS	DIRECTIONS
CARENTAN	N49°18.534' W001°15.253'	Total. D974/Route de Cherbourg, 1.5km northwest of town.
CARSIX	N49°09.306' E000°40.296'	Total. D613/La Haute Sente, 3.5km north of town.
CHERBOURG	N49°38.063' W001°36.747'	Elf. D901/Avenue Amiral Lomonnier, in centre.
CHERBOURG (TOURLAVILLE)	N49°38.092' W001°35.455'	E'Leclerc supermarket. D901.
CONDE SUR NOIREAU	N48°51.301' W000°32.516'	Total. D562/Route Saint Jacques, 1km northeast of town.
COURSEULLES SUR MER	N49°19.335' W000°27.164'	Carrefour supermarket. D79.
COUTANCES	N49°04.076' W001°25.864'	E'Leclerc supermarket. D971 adj to to ring road.
FALAIS	N48°54.419' W000°12.466'	E'Leclerc supermarket.D157 north of town, 658/D6 roundabout, 3m height barrier.
FALAISE	N48°54.404' W000°12.442'	Super U. D6/D511 roundabout, north of town near Junction 10 of A88.
FECAMP	N49°45.072' E000°24.136'	Total. D28/209 Route Gustave Couturier, 2km southeast of town.
FLERS	N48°44.471' W000°33.714'	E'Leclerc supermarket. D264.
GOUVETS	N48°54.479' W001°06.242'	Shell. A84, at La Vallee de la Vire, southwest of town.
HARFLEUR	N49°30.637' E000°11.969'	Total. D925/1 Route Frederic Chopin, off D6015.
HEROUVILLE ST CLAIR	N49°12.067' W000°20.642'	Total. 1 Route Guyon de Guercheville, west of town.
HONFLEUR	N49°24.774' E000°15.043'	Elf. D580/Cours Jean de Vienne, 2km southeast of town.
HONFLEUR	N49°24.774' E000°15.035'	Elf. D580 as enter Honfleur on right.
IFS	N49°08.448' W000°20.199'	E'Leclerc supermarket. N158/190 Route de Rocquencourt, off D235 roundabout, 2km east of town.
IGOVILLE	N49°19.099' E001°09.402'	Super U. N15/D6015, at D6015/D79 roundabout.
LA FERTE MACE	N48°34.495' W000°22.217'	E'Leclerc supermarket. D916 towards Bagnoles de L'orne.
LA GLACIERE	N49°36.022' W001°35.930'	Auchan fuel station. D352/N13.
LE GRAND QUEVILLY	N49°24.111' E001°03.891'	Total. D938/Avenue des Canadiens, 3.5km southeast of town.
LE HAVRE	N49°29.929' E000°09.537'	Total. N15/E05, towards car ferry.
LE HAVRE	N49°29.934' E000°09.546'	Total. D6015/Boulevard de Leningrad. Road to ferry.
LES PIEUX	N49°31.006' W001°47.913'	Intermarche supermarket. D23/D4 roundabout.
LISIEUX	N49°08.283' E000°10.320'	Esso. D613/D613a, at roundabout.
LOUVIERS	N49°12.603' E001°10.171'	Total. D133/4 Place Jean Jaures, off D6155 roundabout.
MALBROUCK	N49°09.310' E000°40.294'	Total. P613 by D613/D438.
PONTORSON	N48°33.528' W001°30.541'	Carrefour supermarket.
QUERQUEVILLE	N49°39.633' W001°41.163'	E'Leclerc supermarket. Off D901/Route Claire at roundabout, 2km southeast of town.
ROTS	N49°12.001' W000°27.552'	Cora supermarket. Off N13/E46 junction with D83c.
SOTTEVILLE LES ROUEN	N49°24.232' E001°06.646'	Total. Off E402/Boulevard Industriel, 3km southeast of town.
ST LO	N49°06.074' W001°04.958'	Intermarché supermarket. Off D86, 3km southeast of town.
ST LO	N49°06.146' W001°06.878'	Total. D999 by N174 junction.
ST LO	N49°05.968' W001°04.933'	Intermarche supermarket, opp McDonalds.
ST OVENDU TILLEUL	N49°17.594' E000°57.283'	Total. D313 towards Elbeuf as exit village.
ST VALERY EN CAUX	N49°51.488' E000°41.573'	E'Leclerc supermarket. D79/D925b, at roundabout.
TOURGEVILLE	N49°21.660' E000°03.662'	Avia. D513, exit Deauville towards Villers-S-Mer.
VALOGNES	N49°30.440' W001°27.941'	Total. D974/1 Boulevard de Verdun, in centre of town.
VERNEUIL SUR AVRE	N48°43.934' E000°55.233'	Intermarche supermarket. N12, south of town.
VIRE	N48°51.227' W000°52.795'	Total. D577/Route de Caen, 2km northeast of town.
NORTHERN FRANCE		
ALBERT	N50°00.472' E002°39.938'	Total. D4929/164 Avenue du General Faidherbe, 1.5km northeast of town.
ARRAS	N50°17.437' E002°47.049'	Total. Off D260/Route des Rosati, 1km east of centre.
AVRAINVILLE	N48°33.761' E002°13.681'	Elf. N20, 2km west of town.
BALLAINVILLIERS	N48°40.652' E002°16.953'	Total. N20 southbound, 4km northwest of town.

TOWN	GPS	DIRECTIONS
BEAUTOR	N49°39.583' E003°20.741'	ALDI supermarket. Towards Tergnier on R at E'Leclerc . 3m 30 height restriction.
BEAUVAIS	N49°26.015' E002°05.563'	BP. D1001/Route de Clermont. 1km from centre.
BEAUVAIS	N49°26.535' E002°05.577'	Intermarche supermarket. D1001/Avenue du 8 Mai 1945. 2km northeast of town.
BEAUVAIS	N49°24.550' E002°06.991'	Auchan supermarket. D1001, in industrial park.
BOIS-D'ARCY	N48°47.923' E002°00.221'	Total. Off N12, exit town D127.
BRIE COMTE ROBERT	N48°41.846' E002°36.393'	Total. D319/7 Avenue de General L'Eclerc. 2km northwest of town.
BRIIS SOUS FORGES	N48°38.227' E002°08.902'	Shell. Off A10 southbound at Aire de Limours, northeast of town.
BRUAY LA BUISSIERE	N50°28.646' E002°32.066'	Total. D941/Route de la Republique. Exit D7 onto D941 from centre, southwest of town.
BUGNICOURT	N50°17.423' E003°09.113'	Total. D643/Route Nationale, before D643 roundabout.
BUSSY ST GEORGES	N48°49.810' E002°44.855'	Total. Off A4 at Aire de Bussy St Georges. Between Junctions 12 and 13, 5km southeast of town.
CALAIS	N50°57.346' E001°54.517'	Total. Off N216 roundabout, 5km east of town.
CALAIS	N50°56.759' E001°50.225'	Shell. At D940 roundabout, 4km west of centre.
CARVIN	N50°28.864' E002°56.191'	Total. D165, at D917/D919 roundabout, southwest of town.
CAUDRY	N50°06.768' E003°24.968'	Esso. Boulevard du 19 Mars 1945 (ring road). Also at Intermarché 200m further.
CHAMANT (SENLIS)	N49°13.268' E002°35.585'	Total. D1330 southbound, 2km northwest of town.
CHAMBLY	N49°11.305' E002°14.098'	Elf. Off D1001/Route Nationale 1, southbound. Exit town on D923.
CHATEAU THIERRY	N49°02.075' E003°23°493'	Intermarche supermarket. N3, south of town.
CHAUMONTEL	N49°07.678' E002°25.843'	Total. D316/Route de Paris towards Luzarches.
CHELLES	N48°52.712' E002°36.663'	Total. D934/119 Route du Gendarme Castermant. 2km east of town.
CLAYE SOUILLY	N48°57.152' E002°39.965'	Total. D212/Chemin de Compas. 5km northwest of town.
COMPIEGNE	N49°23.190' E002°47.094'	Total. Off D200, after Carrefour Robert Schumann roundabout. 6km southwest of town.
COQUELLES	N50°56.556' E001°48.594'	Auchan supermarket. D243 towards Calais.
CORBEIL-ESSONNE	N48°36.663' E002°27.151'	Total. D446/46 Avenue du 8 Mai 1945. 3km west of town.
COURBEVOIE	N48°54.093' E002°15.591'	Total. D908/72 Boulevard de Verdun, in town centre.
CRÉTEIL	N48°47.050' E002°26.841'	BP. D86/Route de Choisy, 3km southwest of town.
CUCQ - LE TOUQUET	N50°30.568' E001°37.656'	Total. D939/Avenue General de Gaulle. 4km north of town.
DAMMARIE LES LYS	N48°31.151' E002°39.267'	Elf. Off D606/Avenue General L'Eclerc. 2.5km northeast of centre.
DRAVEIL	N48°41.194' E002°24.171'	Elf. D931/108 Avenue du General de Gaulle, in centre.
DUNKERQUE	N51°01.462' E002°21.647'	Total. D202DV/Avenue de La Villette, at D202DV roundabout.
EPINAY SUR SEINE	N48°56.885' E002°20.561'	Total. D24/53 Route de Saint Leu, exit N14 onto D24, 3km southeast of town.
EPONE	N48°57.678' E001°48.715'	Elf. D130/Route de Gargenville. Exit D113, north of town.
ESCAUDOEUVRE	N50°11.073' E003°15.262'	Auchan supermarket. Off D630/Route Jean Jures. Exit town on D630, 1km from centre.
ESSIGNY LE GRAND	N49°47.152' E003°20.030'	Total, Off A26. Exit D1 onto A26 at Aire D'Urvillers, northeast of town.
ETAMPES	N48°26.935' E002°10.292'	Total. D207/94 Boulevard Saint Michel, 2km northeast of town.
ETAPLES	N50°31.526' E001°37.681'	ATAC. D940 towards Boulogne. Different exit, 3.3m height restriction.
ETAPLES	N50°30.564' E001°37.673'	Total. D9/N39, between Etaples and Le Touquet Paris Plage.
EVRY	N48°37.424' E002°26.491'	Total. D93/Boulevard des Coquibus, 1km south of town.
FEUQUIERES EN VIMEU	N50°04.033' E001°36.422'	Total. D48, at D48/D29 roundabout.
FORGES	N48°25.608' E002°55.611'	Total. Off A5 at Aire de Jonchets Grande Paroisse. Between junctions 16 and 17, 4km northwest of town.
GENICOURT	N49°04.914' E002°04.168'	Total. Off D915/Route de Paris a Dieppe.
GISORS	N49°16.620' E001°45.748'	Intermarche supermarket. D14/D150 roundabout to west of town.
GONESSE	N48°58.823' E002°26.874'	Elf. D370/Route Nungesser et Coli, 1km southwest of town.
GRANDE SYNTHE	N51°00.288' E002°17.150'	Auchan supermarket. Off D131, at roundabout 2nd exit.

TOWN	GPS	DIRECTIONS
GRAVELINES	N50°59.776' E002°08.968'	Total. D6001/40 Route Nationale, 2km northeast of town.
HALLENNES LEZ HAUBOURDIN	N50°36.158' E002°56.586'	Total. N41, southbound. 3km southwest from town.
HARLY ST QUENTIN	N49°50.537' E003°19.40'	E'Leclerc supermarket. Off N2029, at roundabout.
HEM	N50°39.888' E003°10.950'	Total Access. D6D/Avenue Charles de Gaulle. 1km from centre.
IVRY SUR SEINE	N48°48.349' E002°22.570'	Total. D5/160-180 Boulevard de Stalingrad, 1km southwest of town.
LA COURNEUVE	N48°56.027' E002°23.440'	Shell. Off A1 at Aire de la Corneuve Est. Between Junctions 4 and 5, 1km northwest of town.
LE CATEAU CAMBRESIS	N50°05.630' E003°32.196'	Intermarche supermarket. D12/D21, as exit town to south.
LENS	N50°25.438' E002°49.204'	Total. D55/Route d'Arras, heading towards town centre.
LES ESSARTS LE ROI	N48°43.050' E001°52.962'	Elf. N10 northbound, 2km northwest of town.
LES ULIS	N48°40.659' E002°11.871'	Total. D118/1-4 Avenue de l'Oceanie, 3km east of town.
LIEVIN	N50°25.027' E002°46.082'	Total. D58E2/Route du Marechal de Lattre de Tassigny, in centre of town.
LILLE	N50°37.787' E003°02.138'	Total. D933/Route de Turrenne. West of town.
LILLE	N50°36.184' E003°03.345'	Total. D549/Route du Faubourg d'Arras. 2km south of town.
LOUVECIENNES	N48°52.513' E002°07.087'	Total. D113/9 Ter Quai Conti, adj to river. 5km northeast of town.
MADELEINE	N50°39.049' E003°03.811'	Total. Off D749/Boulevard Robert Schumann. Exit D617 onto D749.
MANTES LA JOLIE	N48°58.944' E001°41.855'	Total. D928/48 Boulevard Roger Salengro. 1.5km southwest of town.
MASSY	N48°44.382' E002°18.108'	Shell. D920/190 Avenue du General L'Eclerc, northeast of town.
MEAUX	N48°56.960' E002°52.797'	Elf. Off D360/30-34 Route Francois Tessan. 3km south of town.
MELUN	N48°32.469' E002°40.516'	Total. N5/5 Route de Montereau. 2km east of town.
MERS LES BAINS	N50°03.682' E001°24.403'	Auchan supermarket. D940/D1015, in industrial area.
MONS EN BAROEUL	N50°38.851' E003°05.887'	Shell. Off D356 northbound. Exit D14 from town onto D356. 2km northwest of town.
MONTIGNY LES CORMEILLES	N48°59.825' E002°11.330'	Elf. D14/Boulevard Victor Bordier, 1.5km north of town.
MONTRY	N48°53.048' E002°50.574'	Total. D934 near Disneyland.
MORAINVILLIERS	N48°56.610' E001°57.018'	Total. Off A13 southbound at Aire de Morainvilliers Sud, northeast of town.
MORET SUR LOING	N48°21.857' E002°51.172'	Elf. Avenue de Sens, off D606, 6km southeast of town.
NANTERRE	N48°53.271' E002°11.237'	Total. D991/84-90 Avenue Lenine, 3km west of town.
NANTERRE	N48°55.153' E002°13.372'	Total. D992/Boullevard du Havre, 5km northeast of town.
NEMOURS	N48°16.013' E002°42.481'	Total. D403/10 Avenue du General de Gaulle.
NOISIEL	N48°50.420' E002°37.272'	Total. 4/6 Avenue Pierre Mendes France. 2.5km to centre.
ORGEVAL	N48°55.827' E001°58.527'	Shell. D113/Route des 40 Sous, 2km northeast of town, exit D45.
ORGEVAL	N48°56.412' E001°57.300'	Total. Off A13 northbound at Aire de Morainvilliers Nord, northeast of town.
ORLY	N48°44.774' E002°22.982'	Total. D153/106 Avenue de la Vicatoire. Exit D264, 1.5km west of town.
OZOIR LA FÉRRIERE	N48°46.014' E002°39.046'	Elf. N4/Route Nationale. 2km northwest of town.
PARIS	N48°50.075' E002°15.942'	Total. D7/Quai d'Issy les Moulineaux. Adj to river, 9km west of town.
PARIS	N48°51.230' E002°24.915'	Total. D38. Off Place de la Porte de Montreuil roundabout, towards Montreuil.
PARIS	N48°49.898' E002°21.547'	Elf. Boulevard Vincent Auriol, towards river.
PARIS	N48°52.796' E002°22.232'	Total. 152 Boulevard de la Villette, 4km northeast of town.
PARIS	N48°49.026' E002°21.594'	Total. D7/Avenue de la Porte d'Italie. 5km south of town.
PARIS	N48°54.036' E002°22.551'	Total. N301/Boulevard Peripherique, 7km northeast of town.
PARIS (DISNEYLAND)	N48°52.355' E002°47.838'	Esso. At Disneyland Paris Resort, off main ring road.
PECQUENCOURT	N50°22.840 E003°13.235'	Total. D225/Route d'Estiennes d'Orves. Northeast of town, at D25 roundabout.
PETITE FORET	N50°22.040' E003°29.025'	Total. Off A23 northbound. 4km east of town.
PHALEMPIN	N50°31.731' E003°02.752'	Aire Phalempin, A1/E17 towards Lille.
PIERREFITTE SUR SEINE	N48°58.399' E002°21.957'	Total. Off N1/185 Boulevard Mermoz, in town centre.

TOWN	GPS	DIRECTIONS
PLESSIS BELLEVILLE	N49°05.926' E002°45.154'	Total. D84/5 Route de Paris, after D84/D100 roundabout.
PONTAULT COMBAULT	N48°47.581' E002°37.128'	Total. N104 Junction 15, 1km southeast of centre.
QUIEVRAIN	N50°24.229' E003°40.558'	Shell. N51/D630, just over Belgian border (Belgium)
QUINCY SOUS SENART	N48°40.627' E002°31.586'	Total. D33/61 Route de Brunoy, 1km northwest of town.
RANG DU FLIERS	N50°24.868' E001°36.551'	Intermarche supermarket. D940/D317, at Centre Commercial.
RESSONS SUR MATZ	N49°31.357' E002°43.322'	Total. A1 northbound, Junction 11 at Aire de Ressons.
ROCQUENCOURT	N48°50.174' E002°05.741'	Total. D307/11 Route de Maule. 1.5km west of town.
ROSNY SOUS BOIS	N48°52.662' E002°28.920'	Total. N302/12 Boulevard Gabriel Peri, 1.5km northwest of town.
ROUBAIX	N50°41.851' E003°09.945'	Total. Off D775/Avenue des Nations Unies towards Tourcoing.
SACLAY	N48°44.143' E002°10.441'	Total. N118/Route de Paris, 2km west of town.
SAGY	N49°03.838' E001°58.984'	Total. D14/Lieu dit La Marlière, 5km northeast of town.
SECLIN	N50°32.795' E003°02.978'	Elf. D549 southbound, after D549/D925 roundabout, east of town.
SECLIN	N50°31.972' E003°02.797'	Total. Off A1, southbound at Aire de Phalempin. Southeast of town.
SEDAN	N49°41.960' E004°55.621'	Total. Avenue de la Marne/D764 as enter town.
SENLIS	N49°12.648' E002°35.566'	Total. D1017/Avenue du Marechal Foch. Exit town on D1017 towards Le Poiteau.
SOISSONS	N49°22.218' E003°20.351'	Elf. N31/Route de Villeneuve. 1km to town centre, southeast.
ST FARGEAU	N48°32.623' E002°30.868'	Total. D607, southwest of town near Pringy.
ST FARGEAU PONTHIERRY	N48°32.595' E002°30.904'	Total. Off D607, 2.5 km northwest of town.
ST GERMAIN ARPAJON	N48°36.561' E002°15.134'	Total Access. N20, 1km north of town.
ST GERMAIN SUR MORIN	N48°53.046' E002°50.574'	Total. D934 main route through town.
ST MARTIN BOULOGNE	N50°43.988' E001°40.112'	Auchan supermarket. N42, at Centre Commerical.
ST OUEN L'AUMONE	N49°02.892' E002°07.993'	Total. N184, 3km northeast of town.
ST QUENTIN	N49°51.451' E003°15.133'	Auchan supermarket. N29/E44, at Centre Commercial adj to large roundabout.
ST SOUPPLETS	N48°54.313' E002°38.470'	Total. N330/Route de Meaux, 1km southwest of town.
ST VALERY SUR SOMME	N50°10.520' E001°38.270'	Carrefour supermarket. D940/D48, at roundabout.
ST-CLOUD	N48°51.310' E002°13.361'	Total. D7/65 Quai Marcel Dassault. Adj to river, 3km northeast of town.
STEENVOORDE	N50°49.520' E002°35.166'	Total. A25 northbound, Aire de St Laurent, between Junctions 13 and 14.
TRAPPES	N48°46.897' E002°01.299'	Total. Off N10, 2km northeast of town.
VELIZY	N48°46.867' E002°10.432'	Total. Off A86 at Aire de Velizy Ouest, Junction 31.
VÉMARS	N49°04.473' E002°33.080'	Total. Off A1 southbound at Aire de Vemars Ouest. Between Junctions 6 and 7, northwest of town.
VERSAILLES	N48°47.580' E002°08.640'	Total. 71 Route des Chantiers, 1.5km southeast of town.
VILLABÉ	N48°35.616' E002°26.644'	Total. Off A6 northbound at Aire de Villabe, northwest of town.
VILLENEUVE-SOUS-DAMMARTIN	N49°02.001' E002°38.181'	Total. D401/Route de Paris, in centre.
VILLEPINTE	N48°57.240' E002°32.036'	Elf. D115/Boulevard Robert Ballenger, 1km southwest of town.
VILLEVAUDÉ	N48°54.342' E002°38.450'	Total. A104 southbound, at Aire de Villevaude. Southwest of town.
VIRY CHATILLON	N48°39.065' E002°22.139'	Total. D445/Route de Fleury, 3km northeast of town.
VIRY-NOUREUIL	N49°38.574' E003°15.630'	Auchan supermarket. D338 just off D1032 towards Tergnier.
PAYS DE LOIRE		
AIZENAY	N46°43.985' W001°35.586'	Super U. Off D948, 2km southeast of town.
ANGERS	N47°27.888' W000°38.134'	Elf. D523, 8km southwest of town.
ANGERS	N47°27.220' W000°33.277'	Elf. D312/Route de l'Etanduère, 4km southeast of town.

LPG - GPL

TOWN	GPS	DIRECTIONS
AZE CHATEAU GONTIER	N47°50.192' W000°41.351'	Total. N162/Avenue Rene Cassin, towards La Sargerie.
BEAUCOUZE	N47°27.965' W000°37.804'	Total. D523, southeast of town.
BELLVILLE SUR VIE	N46°46.579' W001°25.615'	Super U. D937, as enter from south.
BRETIGNOLLES SUR MER	N46°37.592' W001°51.341'	Super U. D38, as exit town to south.
CHALLANS	N46°51.190' W001°53.751'	E'Leclerc supermarket. Off D2948, 2km northwest of town.
CHANTONNAY	N46°40.864' W001°02.921'	Super U. D949, to south of town.
CHATEAU GONTIER	N47°49.877' W000°41.163'	E'Leclerc supermarket. N162, near roundabout junction with D28 east of town.
CHATEAUBRIANT	N47°42.361' W001°23.521'	E'Leclerc supermarket. Off D771, 3km southwest of town.
CHOLET	N47°04.320 W000°51.420'	Elf. D13/Boulevard de Touraine, 3km northeast of town.
CRAON	N47°50.559' W000°58.253'	Super U. D771, southwest of town.
DOUE LA FONTAINE	N47°11.377' W000°17.447'	Super U. D69/Boulevard du Dr Lionet, south west of town.
ECOMMOY	N47°50.233' E000°15.655'	Super U. D338, northwest of Écommoy
FONTENAY LE COMTE	N46°27.079' W000°48.376'	Super U. D938ter, southwest of town.
GORRON	N48°24.330' W000°48.395'	Super U. D5/Route de Rennes, southeast of town.
LA CHATAIGNERAIE	N46°38.790' W000°44.661'	Super U. D938ter, as exit town to south.
LA ROCHE SUR YON	N46°41.526' W001°25.781'	Esso. D937/Route de Nantes, northbound. 2km north of town.
LA ROCHE SUR YON	N46°40.361' W001°24.286'	E'Leclerc supermarket. D760/N2160, northeast of town.
LAVAL	N48°03.511' W000°46.130'	Elf. D57/Boulevard des Trappistines, south of town.
LAVAL	N48°04.184' W000°47.603'	Total. D57/Route de Rennes, west of town.
LE MANS	N48°01.374' E000°10.970'	Elf. D338/Av du Rhin et Danube. 2km northwest of town.
LE MANS	N47°59.769' E000°11.206'	Total. Boulevard Demorieux. 2km southwest of town.
LE MANS	N47°56.886' E000°11.678'	Total. D323 northbound. 6km south of town.
LE MANS	N47°58.823' E000°13.219'	Elf. D304/Avenue du Docteur Jean Mac. 4km northeast of town.
LES SABLES D'OLONNE	N46°31.071' W001°46.545'	Total. D32. 5km northeast of town.
LONGUE JUMELLES	N47°22.281' W000°05.945'	Super U. D347/ La Metairie, at roundabout.
LUCON	N46°28.031' W001°06.647'	Total. At D137/D949 roundabout.
MONTAIGU	N46°58.766' W001°17.947'	Intermarche supermarket. Off D753 from east.
MORTAGNE SUR SEVRE	N46°59.417' W000°56.765'	Total. N149, as exit town to southeast.
OLONNE SUR MER	N46°31.077' W001°46.547'	Total. D32, as exit town to south.
PORNIC	N47°06.685' W002°04.217'	Intermarche supermarket. D751, 3km east of town.
SARGE LES LE MANS	N48°03.331 E000°15.345'	Carrefour. A11, northeast of town.
SEGRE	N47°41.807' W000°52.297'	Super U. D775, near large roundabout junction with D923.
ST ETIENNE DE MONTLUC	N47°16.208' W001°46.507'	Super U. D17, as exit town to south towards Couëron.
ST GILLES CROIX DE VIE	N46°42.022' W001°55.781'	Total. D38B. 2km northeast of town.
ST JEAN DE MONTS	N46°47.720' W002°02.780'	Super U. Sp off roundabout junction of D753 and D38b.
ST NAZAIRE	N47°18.672' W002°12.072'	Shell. N171 towards Nantes, 8km north of town.
ST NAZAIRETRIGNAC	N47°18.124' W002°12.697'	Auchan supermarket. N471, at Centre Commercial near junction with D213.
ST NICOLAS DE REDON	N47°38.752' W002°04.594'	E'Leclerc supermarket. D164, towards Redon.
ST PHILBERT DE GRAND LIEU	N47°02.843' W001°38.427'	Super U. D65/D117 junction to north of town.
VALLET	N47°10.147' W001°15.987'	Super U. D763, as enter Vallet from north.
POITOU		
CHASSENEUIL-DU-POITOU	N46°37.875' E000°21.421'	Total. D910/Route de Paris, From N147/E62 Junction drive 1km north on the D910 to the Total on the right.

TOWN	GPS	DIRECTIONS
GÉMOZAC	N45°34.549' W000°40.658'	Super U supermarket. D6, off D732/D6 roundabout north side of village.
LA ROCHELLE	N46°09.405' W001°07.185'	Total. D108, ring road. 500m north from N137/E602 Junction heading towards town centre.
MONTMORILLON	N46°25.135' E000°51.270'	E'Leclerc supermarket. D727 west side of town towards Lussac Les Châteaux.
NAINTRE 1	N46°45.234' E000°29.042'	Q8. D910 northbound in southern outskirts of village.
NAINTRE 2	N46°45.406' E000°29.083'	Intermarché supermarket. D23, near large roundabout junction with D910.
NEUVILLE DE POITOU	N46°41.079' E000°15.277'	Total. Exit town east on D62 towards Janunay Clan. Total on left.
NEUVILLE DE POITOU	N46°41.082' E000°15.289'	Total. D62, 500m east of town centre.
NIORT	N46°18.994' W000°28.369'	Total. D811/D611,. On left, 800m from centre when heading into town centre. Good access for large motorhomes.
NIORT CHAURAY	N46°20.428' W000°23.708'	Elf. D611/Route de Paris. Southeast suburbs of Niort of Chauray. Southeast bound side.
NIORT VOUILLE	N46°17.835' W000°22.297'	Total. Aire du Poitou-Charentes. A10/E5 between Junction 32 and 33, northbound towards Poitiers.
PAMPROUX	N46°27.177' W000°01.043'	Total. A10/E5 Aire de Rouillé-Pamproux. Direction Poitiers. Halfway between Niort and Poitiers.
PAMPROUX	N46°27.089' W000°01.107'	Shell. A10/E5 Aire de Rouillé-Pamproux. Direction Noirt. Halfway between Niort and Poitiers.
POITIERS	N46°36.252' E000°19.944'	Total. D910/Rocade Ouest. Exit N147/E62 onto D910 around town for 2.3km.
PUILBOREAU	N46°10.601' W001°06.219'	Total. N11/E601 Aire de Puilboreau, between N137 and D9 Junctions eastbound towards Niort.
ROYAN	N45°37.907' W000°59.524'	E'Leclerc supermarket. Route Augustin Fresnel 600m northeast from N150/D25 Junction.
RUFFEC	N46°01.260' E000°11.386'	E'Leclerc supermarket. D736, Route D'Aigre. Southwest of town centre towards ring road. Good access for large motorhomes. LPG far right hand side.
SAINT HILAIRE	N45°27.641' W000°08.649'	Total, Centre Routier. Exit N10 at D24 Junction. Service station signed off roundabout.
SAINTES	N45°42.183' W000°37.466'	Total. D137/Route de Bordeaux, 2km south of Saintes. Good access for large motorhomes.
SAINTES	N45°45.384' W000°39.100'	Carrefour supermarket. D128/Boulevard de Vladimir, northwest of town. Exit A10/E5 at Junction 35 follow sp 'Centre Hospitalier' then camping signs.
SAINTES	N45°45.363' W000°39.100'	Carrefour supermarket. At roundabout off D128, Boulevard de Vladimir. Northwest of town centre. (Exit A10/E05 at Junction 35). Good access for large motorhomes.
ST GENIS DE SAINTONGE	N45°29.371' W000°33.951'	Total. D137/Avenue de Saintes, northern outskirts of town. Good access for large motorhomes.
ST JEAN D'ANGELY	N45°56.667' W000°30.333'	E'Leclerc supermarket. Centre Commercial, D218. Off D939 east side of town. Good access for large motorhomes.
ST MAIXENT L'ECOLE	N46°24.438 W000°13.537'	E'Leclerc supermarket. D8, 200m from large roundabout junction with D611/D8 southwest side of town.
TONNAY CHARENTE	N45°57.010' W000°55.599'	Total. D137, Avenue D'Aunis. Exit A837/E602 at Junction 32 and take D137 3km to east. Good access for large motorhomes.
VILLEGATS	N45°00.045' E000°12.040'	Shell. Aire de Service de L'Eglantier on N10, northbound carriageway. 2.5km south of Ruffec.
RHONE-ALPS		
ALBERTVILLE	N45°39.664' E006°22.991'	Total. N90. Heading northeast towards Albertville exit N90, at Junction 29 Grignon. Fuel station adj to N90.
ALBY SUR CHÉRAN	N45°49.128' E006°00.261'	Total. D1201/Route d'Aix les Bains. Exit A41/E712 at Junction 15 sp Rumilly. Fork right onto D3. turn left onto D1201 towards Annecy. Total 200m on right.
ANNECY	N45°54.558' E006°07.063'	Total. D1501/Boulevard de la Rocade. Exit A41 Junction 16 onto D3508 then take D1501 2km north to Total on right.

TOWN	GPS	DIRECTIONS
BRON	N45°44.340' E004°54.298'	Total Access. D683 northbound between A43 and D29 junctions.
CALUIRE	N45°48.287' E004°51.556'	Auchan. Chemin Jean Petit/D48E, off D1.
CHAMBÉRY	N45°35.598' E005°53.804'	Total Access, previously Elf. N201/Route Eugene Ducretet exit at Junction 14. Exact location unconfirmed.
CLUSES	N46°03.687' E006°33.776'	Total. D1205/Avenue de la Republique. Exit A40/E25 at Junction 18 direction Sallanches. Take D304 sp ,Clauses' then follow signs to 'Centre Nautique' and 'Stade'. Total at Stade.
COMMUNAY	N45°35.458' E004°49.686'	TOTAL. A46 Aire de Communay-Nord, 2km east of A7 Junction.
COMMUNAY	N45°35.356' E004°49.529'	Total. A46 Aire de Communay-Sud, 2km east of A7 Junction.
DARDILLY	N45°48.477' E004°46.161'	Total. A6 Aire de Paisy, northbound, between junctions 34 and 33.2, 2km before Péage.
DARDILLY	N45°49.23' E004°45.969'	Auchan. Exit A6 at Junction 33.1. Supermarket adj to slip road, station has own slip road.
DRACÉ	N46°08.612' E004°46.056'	Total. Aire de Dracé A6/E15 between Junctions 29 and 30 southbound towards Villefranche sur Saône.
FEYZIN	N45° 40.486' E004°50.908'	Elf. D312, 200m south of A7 Junction for D312 Z.I. LES ILES. Good access for large motorhomes.
LA BATHIE	N45°36.733' E006°27.008'	Elan. N90 Aire de Langon. Southbound, at Junction 34 accessible from both sides.
LA BATHIE	N45°36.700' E006°27.000'	Elan. Aire de Langon, N90 Junction 34. Accessible from both directions. Good for large motorhomes.
LA MOTTE SERVOLEX	N45°36.628' E005°53.194'	Total access. N201. Heading southbound towards Chambery take exit Z.I. les Landiers nord just before Junction 14, A41.
LA RAVOIRE	N45°34.119' E005°57.777'	Total. D1006 Avenue de Chambéry towards Chambéry airport at La Ravoire. Good access for large motorhomes.
LA RAVOIRE	N45°34.120' E005°57.774'	Total. D1006, north of La Ravoire towards Saint Alban Leysse. Good access for large motorhomes.
LES HOUCHES	N45°53.901' E006°48.725'	Total. N205/Route Blanche, at Junction 28 direction Sallanches.
LORIOL SUR DROME	N44°45.640' E004°50.282'	Intermarché. N7 northeast of town at roundabout N7/D104a.
LYON	N45°44.099' E004°50.361'	Total. Avenue Tony Garnier. Exit D383 at Junction 16 and head north. Turn right in 1km and drive 1km to Total on left.
MACON	N46°17.107' E004°48.470'	Total. N6/Route de Lyon, 200m from McDonalds roundabout, south of town. Good access for large motorhomes.
MONTELIMAR	N44°33.317' E004°44.250'	Casino supermarket. D540, southwest of town centre (650m from N7).
PIERRE BÉNITE	N45°41.834' E004°49.492'	Total. D15/Boulevard de L'Europe. 400m north of A450 Junction 5 sp Irigny. south of town. Good access for large motorhomes.
SAINT GÉNIS LAVAL	N45°40.728 E004°47.529'	Auchan. Adj to A450, exit at Junction 6 or 6b, at Auchan Centre Commercial.
SAINT PRIÈST	N45° 42.425' E004°59.210'	Total Access. D306/Route de Grenoble. 1.5km east of N346 Junction 10. northeast of town. Good access for large motorhomes.
SALLANCHES	N45°56.686' E006°37.798'	Total Access, previously Elf. D1205/Avenue de Geneve. Exit A40/E25 at Junction 20. Take D1205 south for 2km toTotal on left.
SEREZIN DU RHÔNE	N45°37.787' E004°49.077'	Total. A7 Aire de Sérézin du Saône. 4km north of the A47 Junction, northbound.
SOLAIZE	N45°39.138 E004°50.208'	Elf. A7 Aire de Solaiz, southbound 7km from the A46 junction.
ST JEAN DE BOURNAY	N45°29.933' E005°08.250'	Intermarché. Off D518, between D41F and D502 roundabouts. Good access for large motorhomes.
ST RAMBERT	N45°16.542' E004°49.752'	BP. A7/E15 northbound between Junctions 13 and 12. Aire de Saint Rambert d'Albon D'ALBON. Good access for large motorhomes.
ST VALLIER	N45°11.700' E004°48.855'	Total. N7, 2km north of town centre. Good access for large motorhomes.

A

INDEX

C

INDEX

D

INDEX

INDEX

INDEX

W

Y

USER UPDATES

The French Aires situation is constantly changing and customer feedback has proven vital in keeping the guide up to date. Photographs are essential because they provide the supporting evidence we need to confirm that your submissions are accurate. The truth is that Submissions without photos are like reading a book in the dark. Filling in a submission form onsite is best practice because you are unlikely to remember everything, however it is essential that you record GPS coordinates onsite. The best way to keep an accurate record is with your digital camera by following this photographic checklist.

Take photos of the:

- Parking area from several angles
- Surrounding area from several angles
- Service Point showing all working parts/sides
- Close-up of the payment slot to identify token or payment type.
- Close-up of the electricity points and trip-switches to identify plug type and amperage
- Designation signs and information boards, including close-ups of text.
- Also take GPS coordinates onsite

Please name photos by the town name, region, and the person's name to be credited if they are published.

You can submit your text and digital photos online at www.All-the-Aires.co.uk/submissions.shtml.
We cannot process printed photos, but they are still useful as record shots.
If you have lots of submissions and photos burn them to disk and post them to:

Vicarious Books
62 Tontine Street
Folkestone
CT20 1JP

Considerable thanks goes to the Aire Heads who have provided photographs and information about the Aires they have visited. Some of the Aire Heads are listed below:

Andy Comber, Alan Hoida, Andy & Tracey Holmes, Andy & Sue Glasgow, Michael van Kleeff, Barrie Avis, Barry Norris, Bob Podesta, Ann Beck, Carol Weaver, Clive Mott-Gotobed, Colin Salter, David Harris, D Cox, Dot Palastanga, John Dunn, Liam Madden, Rita Renninghoff, Graham Hay, Chris Hamson & Margaret Chmielewski, Heidi Hardwick, Ian Cooper, Janet & John Watts, J Leach, Jean & Ken Fowler, John Cox, John & Margaret McMahon, John & Janet Thay, Jytte Jakobsen, Kevin Holley, Malcolm Webb, Brenda & Maurice Cope, Martin & Gail Boizot, Mel & Chris Hughes, Mike Crampton, Mary Preston, Donna Garner, G Myatt, Paul & Lynda Kennedy, Peter Chapman, Peter Slade, Florie B, Pat & Phil Wilde, Patricia Houghton, Keith Seymour, Roy & Karen Geddes, Rich & Dot Owen, Richard Edwards, Colin Robinson, Rod & Liz Sleigh, Sally Dingle, Paul & Ann Taylor, Linda Denning, T & M Valentine, Alan & Pam Wallace, Doug & Jean King, Vera Ward, Violette Coombs, Barry & Muriel Crawshaw, Harry ridsdale, Brian Bagnall, Barry Mills, Chris & Di Ruoff, Diane Anderson, Dorothy Hunt, Mel & Sally Harrison, Ian Tasker, Ian Jackson, John Hancox, Jan Denton, John Eaton, Kartone Spring, Karen Evans, Keith Halliday, A I Gill, Margaret Dean, Peter & Margarite Brown, Malcolm Watts, Paul, Julia and Alice Mullarkey, Robin Culverhouse, Brian Craig, G Holley.

AIRE/LPG SUBMISSION FORM

Please use this form to update Aires information in this guide. If the Aire is already listed, complete only the sections where changes apply. Please write in capital letters and circle appropriate symbols.

Town/Village:

Region:

Road name/number:

Date Visited:

Surroundings:

Coastal	Rural	Farm	Tourism
Residential	Village	Park	Warning
Urban	Riverside or lakeside	Day parking	

Please circle 1 or more symbols as appropriate

Page Number: Postcode – if known:

Number of Spaces:

Time limit: Cost:

Parking symbols:

Overnight parking possible	Hard surface	Large motorhomes
Designated motorhome parking	Sloping	Free of charge
	Illuminated	Open all year
	Noisy	

Please circle 1 or more symbols as appropriate

Service Point type: Cost:

Payment/Token type:

Sanitation symbols:

Water	Electric hook up	Free of charge
Grey water disposal	Toilets	Open all year
Toilet disposal	Disabled toilet	

Please circle 1 or more symbols as appropriate

Leisure Information Symbols:

Shaded parking	Children's play area	Marked cycle route
Green space suitable for dogs/children	Boules	Fishing
	Tennis	Boating (unmotorised)
Picnic tables/benches	Walking - path or trail	Washing machine

Please circle 1 or more symbols as appropriate

Please turn over

AIRE/LPG SUBMISSION FORM

Directions - Brief, specific directions to Aire/LPG:

GPS Coordinates:

Information - Brief description of location and amenities:

Name and email or address - so information can be credited:

Your feedback is vital to keep this guide up to date. Fill in this form whilst you are at the Aire. Please name photos with the town name, region, and the name you want credited if they are published. Please submit your text and digital photos online at **www.All-the-Aires.co.uk/submissions.shtml** or post your completed forms and CDs of photos to **Vicarious Books, 62 Tontine Street, Folkestone, CT20 1JP.** You can print off more forms at **www.All-the-Aires.co.uk**

Please include at least five photos showing the parking area in different directions and close-ups of any signs. Photograph the service point showing working parts, and the token slot, so that we may identify the token type, don't forget the grey drain. Submissions without photos are like reading a book in the dark. We cannot process printed photos, but they are still useful as record shots.

Thank you very much for your time.

By supplying details and photographs you are giving unrestricted publication and reproduction rights to Vicarious Books Ltd.

AIRE/LPG SUBMISSION FORM

Please use this form to update Aires information in this guide. If the Aire is already listed, complete only the sections where changes apply. Please write in capital letters and circle appropriate symbols.

Town/Village: ....

Region: ....

Road name/number: ....

Date Visited: ....

Surroundings:

	Coastal		Rural		Farm	T	Tourism
	Residential		Village		Park	!	Warning
	Urban		Riverside or lakeside		Day parking		

Please circle 1 or more symbols as appropriate

Page Number: .... Postcode – if known: ....

Number of Spaces: ....

Time limit: .... Cost: ....

Parking symbols:

	Overnight parking possible		Hard surface		Large motorhomes
P	Designated motorhome parking		Sloping	F	Free of charge
			Illuminated		Open all year
			Noisy		

Please circle 1 or more symbols as appropriate

Service Point type: .... Cost: ....

Payment/Token type: ....

Sanitation symbols:

	Water	E	Electric hook up	F	Free of charge
	Grey water disposal	WC	Toilets		Open all year
	Toilet disposal		Disabled toilet		

Please circle 1 or more symbols as appropriate

Leisure Information Symbols:

SP	Shaded parking		Children's play area		Marked cycle route
	Green space suitable for dogs/children		Boules		Fishing
			Tennis		Boating (unmotorised)
	Picnic tables/benches		Walking - path or trail		Washing machine

Please circle 1 or more symbols as appropriate

Please turn over

AIRE/LPG SUBMISSION FORM

Directions - Brief, specific directions to Aire/LPG:

GPS Coordinates:

Information - Brief description of location and amenities:

Name and email or address - so information can be credited:

Your feedback is vital to keep this guide up to date. Fill in this form whilst you are at the Aire. Please name photos with the town name, region, and the name you want credited if they are published. Please submit your text and digital photos online at **www.All-the-Aires.co.uk/submissions.shtml** or post your completed forms and CDs of photos to **Vicarious Books, 62 Tontine Street, Folkestone, CT20 1JP.** You can print off more forms at **www.All-the-Aires.co.uk**

Please include at least five photos showing the parking area in different directions and close-ups of any signs. Photograph the service point showing working parts, and the token slot, so that we may identify the token type, don't forget the grey drain. Submissions without photos are like reading a book in the dark. We cannot process printed photos, but they are still useful as record shots.

Thank you very much for your time.

AIRE/LPG SUBMISSION FORM

Please use this form to update Aires information in this guide. If the Aire is already listed, complete only the sections where changes apply. Please write in capital letters and circle appropriate symbols.

Town/Village: ....

Region: ....

Road name/number: ....

Date Visited: ....

Surroundings:

	Coastal		Rural		Farm	T	Tourism
	Residential		Village		Park	!	Warning
	Urban		Riverside or lakeside		Day parking		

Please circle 1 or more symbols as appropriate

Page Number: .... Postcode – if known: ....

Number of Spaces: ....

Time limit: .... Cost: ....

Parking symbols:

	Overnight parking possible		Hard surface		Large motorhomes
P	Designated motorhome parking		Sloping	F	Free of charge
			Illuminated		Open all year
			Noisy		

Please circle 1 or more symbols as appropriate

Service Point type: .... Cost: ....

Payment/Token type: ....

Sanitation symbols:

	Water	E	Electric hook up	F	Free of charge
	Grey water disposal	WC	Toilets		Open all year
	Toilet disposal		Disabled toilet		

Please circle 1 or more symbols as appropriate

Leisure Information Symbols:

SP	Shaded parking		Children's play area		Marked cycle route
	Green space suitable for dogs/children		Boules		Fishing
			Tennis		Boating (unmotorised)
	Picnic tables/benches		Walking - path or trail		Washing machine

Please circle 1 or more symbols as appropriate

Please turn over

AIRE/LPG SUBMISSION FORM

Directions - Brief, specific directions to Aire/LPG:

GPS Coordinates:

Information - Brief description of location and amenities:

Name and email or address - so information can be credited:

Your feedback is vital to keep this guide up to date. Fill in this form whilst you are at the Aire. Please name photos with the town name, region, and the name you want credited if they are published. Please submit your text and digital photos online at **www.All-the-Aires.co.uk/submissions.shtml** or post your completed forms and CDs of photos to **Vicarious Books, 62 Tontine Street, Folkestone, CT20 1JP.** You can print off more forms at **www.All-the-Aires.co.uk**

Please include at least five photos showing the parking area in different directions and close-ups of any signs. Photograph the service point showing working parts, and the token slot, so that we may identify the token type, don't forget the grey drain. Submissions without photos are like reading a book in the dark. We cannot process printed photos, but they are still useful as record shots.

Thank you very much for your time.